Analytical Perspectives

Budget of the U.S. Government

Fiscal Year 2025

Office of Management and Budget

Lanham • Boulder • New York • London

Published by Bernan Press
An imprint of The Rowman & Littlefield Publishing Group, Inc.
4501 Forbes Boulevard, Suite 200, Lanham, Maryland 20706
www.rowman.com

86-90 Paul Street, London EC2A 4NE

The Rowman & Littlefield Publishing Group, Inc., does not claim copyright on U.S. government information.

ISBN: 979-8-89205-053-1

⊗™ The paper used in this publication meets the minimum requirements of American National Standard for Information Sciences—Permanence of Paper for Printed Library Materials, ANSI/NISO Z39.48-1992.

TABLE OF CONTENTS

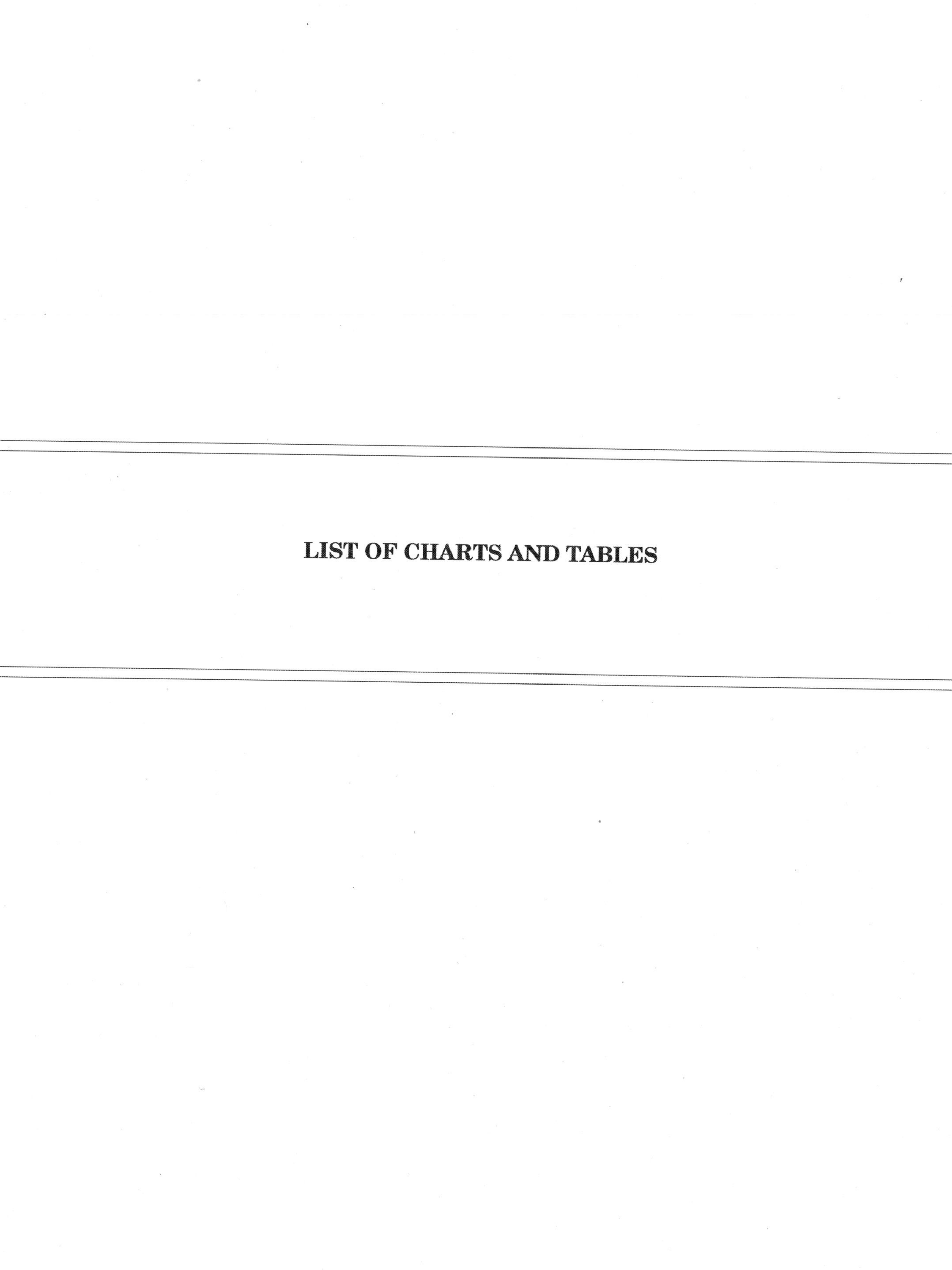

LIST OF CHARTS AND TABLES

LIST OF CHARTS AND TABLES

LIST OF CHARTS

LIST OF TABLES

 *Available on the internet at *http://www.whitehouse.gov/omb/analytical-perspectives/*

*Available on the internet at *http://www.whitehouse.gov/omb/analytical-perspectives/*

Page

 *Available on the internet at *http://www.whitehouse.gov/omb/analytical-perspectives/*

*Available on the internet at *http://www.whitehouse.gov/omb/analytical-perspectives/*

INTRODUCTION

1. INTRODUCTION

The *Analytical Perspectives* volume presents analyses that highlight specific subject areas or provide other significant data that contextualize the President's 2025 Budget and assist the public, policymakers, the media, and researchers in better understanding the Budget. This volume complements the main *Budget* volume, which presents the President's Budget policies and priorities, and the Budget *Appendix* volume, which provides appropriations language, schedules for budget expenditure accounts, and schedules for selected receipt accounts.

Presidential budgets have included separate analytical presentations of this kind for many years. The 1947 Budget and subsequent budgets included a separate section entitled *Special Analyses and Tables* that covered four, and later more, topics. For the 1952 Budget, the section was expanded to 10 analyses, including many subjects still covered today, such as receipts, investment, credit programs, and aid to State and local governments. With the 1967 Budget, this material became a separate volume entitled *Special Analyses*, and included 13 chapters. The material has remained a separate volume since then, with the exception of the Budgets for 1991–1994, when all of the budget material was included in one volume. Beginning with the 1995 Budget, the volume has been named *Analytical Perspectives*.

The *Analytical Perspectives* volume, and some supplemental materials, are available online. Tables included online are shown in the List of Tables in the front of this volume with an asterisk.

Overview of the Chapters

Economic Analyses

Economic Assumptions. This chapter reviews recent economic developments; presents the Administration's assessment of the economic situation and outlook; compares the economic assumptions on which the 2025 Budget is based with the assumptions for last year's Budget and those of other forecasters; provides sensitivity estimates for the effects on the Budget of changes in specified economic assumptions; and reviews past errors in economic projections.

Long-Term Budget Outlook. This chapter assesses the long-term budget outlook under current policies and under the Budget's proposals. It focuses on 25-year projections of Federal deficits and debt to illustrate the long-term impact of the Administration's proposed policies. It also discusses the uncertainties of the long-term budget projections and discusses the actuarial status of the Social Security and Medicare programs.

Special Analyses and Presentations

Budget Process. This chapter describes the Administration's approach and proposals related to budget enforcement, such as sequestration and Pay-As-You-Go procedures, and budget presentation, such as adjustments to the baseline to improve comparisons of the cost of policy. It discusses suggested reforms in budgeting, including for large Federal capital projects.

Federal Investment. This chapter discusses federally financed spending that yields long-term benefits. It presents information on annual spending on physical capital, research and development, and education and training.

Research and Development. This chapter presents a crosscutting review of research and development funding in the Budget.

Credit and Insurance. This chapter provides crosscutting analyses of the roles, risks, and performance of Federal credit and insurance programs and Government-sponsored enterprises (GSEs). The chapter covers the major categories of Federal credit (housing, education, small business and farming, energy and infrastructure, and international) and insurance programs (deposit insurance, pension guarantees, disaster insurance, and insurance against terrorism-related risks). Five additional tables address transactions including direct loans, guaranteed loans, and GSEs. These tables are available online.

Aid to State and Local Governments. This chapter presents crosscutting information on Federal grants to State and local governments. The chapter also includes a table showing historical grant spending and a table displaying budget authority and outlays for grants in the Budget. Tables showing State-by-State spending for major grant programs are available online.

Social Indicators. This chapter presents a selection of statistics that offers a numerical picture of the United States and illustrates how this picture has changed over time. Included are economic, demographic and civic, socioeconomic, health, security and safety, and environmental and energy statistics.

Leveraging Federal Statistics to Strengthen Evidence-Based Decision-Making. This chapter discusses the role of the Federal statistical system in generating data that the public, businesses, and governments need to make informed decisions. The chapter describes how operating as a seamless Federal statistical system, with enhanced statistical capacity and infrastructure, will improve its ability to meet growing demands while addressing new and emerging challenges. The chapter highlights 2025 Budget proposals for Office of Management and Budget (OMB)-recognized statistical agencies and units, and achievements of Statistical Officials. The chapter also presents examples of increasing collaboration and innovative developments across the system, as well as advancements in the development of Government-wide statistical standards and guidance and implementation of the Foundations for Evidence-Based Policymaking Act of 2018.

Analysis of Federal Climate Financial Risk Exposure. This chapter discusses the financial risks that the Federal Government faces due to realized and projected climate change impacts. It summarizes recent Federal agency analyses and provides a demonstration of the various approaches currently being employed to assess climate risk to agency programs, facilities, and services.

Management Priorities

Delivering a High-Performance Government. This chapter reviews the Administration's Performance Framework approach to organizational performance management and organizational health. Actions by the Administration and investments supported by the Budget to advance "the Framework" are detailed, including a section summarizing insights and themes from the work by agencies to implement frameworks and routines for measuring, monitoring, and assessing organizational health and organizational performance in the context of evolving agency work environments.

Building and Using Evidence to Improve Government Effectiveness. This chapter discusses the Administration's commitment to evidence-based policymaking through its efforts to build and promote a culture of evidence and evaluation across the Federal Government. It highlights Government-wide progress, Administration accomplishments, and new initiatives to advance an evidence-based Government. The chapter provides examples of programmatic agency investments that are supported by evidence of effectiveness, and details investments in the Budget to enhance evaluation capacity at agencies. This chapter also describes future directions for the Federal evidence agenda.

Strengthening the Federal Workforce. This chapter presents summary data on Federal employment, compensation, and personnel priorities, and discusses the Administration's strategic approach to rebuilding and investing in the Federal workforce.

Information Technology and Cybersecurity Funding. This chapter addresses Federal information technology (IT) and cybersecurity, highlighting initiatives and proposed funding levels to deliver critical citizen services, keep sensitive data and systems secure, and further the vision of modern Government. The Administration will invest in modern, secure technologies and services to drive enhanced efficiency and effectiveness. This will include undertaking complex Government-wide modernization efforts, driving improved delivery of citizen-facing services, and improving the overall management of the Federal IT portfolio. The Administration will also continue its efforts to further build the Federal IT workforce and seek to reduce the Federal Government's cybersecurity risk in order to better serve and protect the American public.

Technical Budget Analyses

Budget Concepts. This chapter includes a basic description of the budget process, concepts, laws, and terminology, and includes a glossary of budget terms.

Coverage of the Budget. This chapter describes activities that are included in Budget receipts and outlays (and are therefore classified as "budgetary") as well as those activities that are not included in the Budget (and are therefore classified as "non-budgetary"). The chapter also defines the terms "on-budget" and "off-budget" and includes illustrative examples.

Governmental Receipts. This chapter presents information on estimates of Governmental receipts, which consist of taxes and other compulsory collections. It includes descriptions of tax-related legislation enacted in the last year and describes proposals affecting receipts in the 2025 Budget.

Offsetting Collections and Offsetting Receipts. This chapter presents information on collections that offset outlays, including collections from transactions with the public and intragovernmental transactions. In addition, this chapter presents information on "user fees," which are charges associated with market-oriented activities and regulatory fees. Detailed tables of offsetting receipts and offsetting collections in the Budget are available online.

Tax Expenditures. This chapter describes and presents estimates of tax expenditures, which are defined as revenue losses from special exemptions, credits, or other preferences in the tax code.

Federal Borrowing and Debt. This chapter analyzes Federal borrowing and debt and explains the budget estimates. It includes sections on special topics such as trends in debt, debt held by the public net of financial assets and liabilities, investment by Government accounts, and the statutory debt limit.

Current Services Estimates. This chapter discusses the conceptual basis of the Budget's current services, or "baseline," estimates, which are generally consistent with the baseline rules in the Balanced Budget and Emergency Deficit Control Act of 1985, as amended (BBEDCA). The chapter presents estimates of receipts, outlays, and the deficit under this baseline. Supplemental tables addressing factors that affect the baseline and providing details of baseline budget authority and outlays are available online.

Trust Funds and Federal Funds. This chapter provides summary information about the two fund groups in the Budget—trust funds and Federal funds. In addition, it provides detailed information about income, outgo, and balances for the major trust funds and certain Federal fund programs.

Comparison of Actual to Estimated Totals. This chapter compares the actual receipts, outlays, and deficit for 2023 with the estimates for that year published in the 2023 Budget.

Supplemental Materials

The following supplemental materials are part of the *Analytical Perspectives* volume online:

Detailed Functional Table

Detailed Functional Table. Table 25–1, "Budget Authority and Outlays by Function, Category, and Program," displays budget authority and outlays for major Federal program categories, organized by budget function (such as healthcare, transportation, or national defense), category, and program.

Federal Budget by Agency and Account

Federal Budget by Agency and Account. Table 26–1, "Federal Budget by Agency and Account," displays budget authority and outlays for each account, organized by agency, bureau, fund type, and account.

Federal Drug Control Funding

Federal Drug Control Funding. The Federal Drug Control Funding crosscut displays enacted and proposed drug control funding for Federal Departments and Agencies to implement the President's National Drug Control Strategy.

Calfed Bay-Delta Program Federal Budget Crosscut

Calfed Bay-Delta Program Crosscut. The Calfed Bay-Delta Program interagency budget crosscut report provides an estimate of Federal funding by each of the participating Federal agencies with authority and programmatic responsibility for implementing this program, fulfilling the reporting requirements of section 106(c) of Public Law 108–361.

Columbia River Basin Federal Budget Crosscut

Columbia River Basin Federal Budget Crosscut. The Columbia River interagency budget crosscut report includes an estimate of Federal funding by each of the participating Federal agencies to carry out restoration activities within the Columbia River Basin, fulfilling the reporting requirements of section 123 of the Clean Water Act (33 U.S.C. 1275).

Lead Pipe Federal Budget Crosscut

Lead Pipe Federal Budget Crosscut. The lead pipe interagency budget crosscut report provides an estimate of Federal funding by agency that can be used for investments in lead pipe replacement and related activities, fulfilling the commitment made in the Biden-Harris Lead Pipe and Paint Action Plan.

Long Range Budget Projections for the FY 2025 Budget

Long Range Budget Projections for the FY 2025 Budget. The long range projections contain 25-year estimates of deficits and debt as a percent of GDP under current policies, the Budget's proposals, and alternative assumptions.

ECONOMIC ANALYSES

2. ECONOMIC ASSUMPTIONS

This chapter presents the economic assumptions that underlie the Administration's 2025 Budget.[1] It provides an overview of the recent performance of the American economy, presents the Administration's projections for key macroeconomic variables, compares them with other prominent forecasts, and discusses the inherent uncertainty of multiyear forecasts.

The chapter proceeds as follows. The first section provides an overview of the recent performance of the U.S. economy based on a broad array of key economic indicators. The second section presents a detailed exposition of the Administration's economic assumptions underlying the 2025 Budget and how key macroeconomic variables are expected to evolve over the 11-year window from 2024 through 2034. The third section compares the forecast of the Administration with those of the Congressional Budget Office (CBO), the Federal Open Market Committee of the Federal Reserve (FOMC), and the consensus from the Blue Chip Economic Indicators panel of professional forecasters available at the time the Administration's forecast was being finalized. The fourth section discusses the sensitivity of the Administration's projections of Federal receipts and outlays to alternative paths of macroeconomic variables. The fifth section considers the errors in past Administration forecasts, comparing them with the errors in forecasts produced by the CBO and the Blue Chip Economic Indicators panel of professional forecasters. The sixth section uses information on past accuracy of Administration forecasts to provide context for the uncertainty associated with the Administration's current forecast of the budget balance.

Recent Economic Performance

The Administration has made significant progress on the President's top economic priority—achieving stable, steady economic growth and a robust labor market while lowering inflation. Inflation has fallen substantially, the economy is growing and adding jobs, and the unemployment rate has remained low for the longest stretch in half a century. A robust labor market alongside lower inflation has led to real wages increases and real average hourly earnings above pre-pandemic levels. The state of the economy in 2023 shows that the President's plan to build an economy from the bottom up and middle out is working.

The Labor Market

Employment—The labor market was strong in 2023. The unemployment rate averaged 3.6 percent over the year, and has remained at or below 4.0 percent in every month since the start of 2022. That reflects significant progress from the COVID-19 recession; the unemployment rate averaged 8.1 percent during 2020 and 5.4 percent in 2021. Other indicators of labor market health also showed signs of strength in 2023, with several measures remaining near multidecade lows, including the long-term unemployment rate, the number of marginally attached and discouraged workers as shares of the labor force, and the share of the labor force working part-time for economic reasons (e.g., those unable to find full-time employment). Notably, sustained labor market strength in 2023 occurred simultaneously with a sharp reduction in inflation.

Following robust growth over 2022, job gains continued at a steady clip through 2023. The economy added an average of 255,000 jobs per month in 2023, roughly twice the number needed to accommodate population growth. Total employment at the end of the year was roughly 5.0 million above its pre-pandemic peak. Additionally, by the end of 2023 the prime-age labor force participation rate exceeded its pre-pandemic level by 0.2 percentage point.

Inflation—Price growth slowed considerably over 2023. For example, inflation measured by the Consumer Price Index for all Urban Consumers (CPI-U) was 3.4 percent over the year ending in December 2023 (on a non-seasonally adjusted basis), compared with a 6.5 percent increase over the preceding 12 months. Core CPI-U inflation, which excludes food and energy prices, was 3.9 percent over the year ending in December 2023, down from a 5.5 percent increase over the preceding 12 months. While overall and core CPI-U 12-month inflation remain elevated relative to the Federal Reserve's target,[2] the marked slowdown in inflation over 2023 was broad based. 12-month price growth slowed across each major component of the CPI-U from December 2022 to December 2023. One of the factors supporting slower inflation in 2023 was improvements in the supply side of the economy, including global supply chains (see Chart 2-1), which facilitated domestic and international trade and eased price pressures. Labor supply gains helped bring the labor market into better balance as well.

Wages—Wage growth over 2023 was robust across a variety of measures. Over the year ending in December 2023, average hourly earnings (AHE) rose 4.3 percent across all private-sector workers, and 4.6 percent across private-sector workers in production and nonsupervisory positions. Similarly, over the year ending in 2023:Q4, wages and salaries increased 4.3 percent across both all private-sector workers as well as the subset of private-sector workers who are not in an incentive-paid

[1] Economic performance, unless otherwise specified, is discussed in terms of calendar years (January-December). Budget figures are discussed in terms of fiscal years (October-September).

[2] The Federal Reserve's inflation target is 2 percent annual growth as measured by the Personal Consumption Expenditures price index. The rate of CPI-U annual inflation consistent with this target is approximately 2.3 percent.

Chart 2-1. Supply Chains Pressure Index

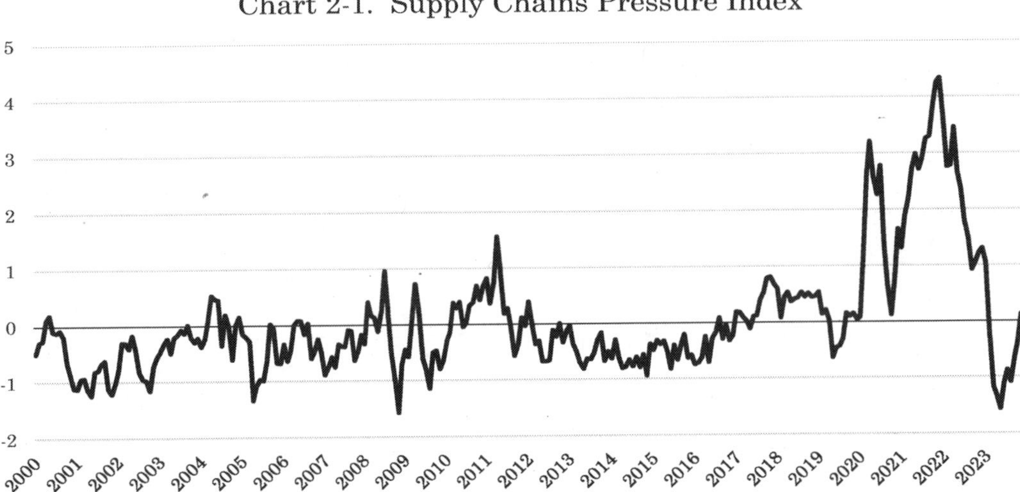

Source: Federal Reserve Bank of New York Global Supply Chain Pressure Index

position, according to the Employment Compensation Index (ECI)—ECI is a measure of worker compensation that accounts for changes in the composition of the workforce. Wage growth in 2023 outpaced consumer price inflation. For example, over the year ending in December 2023, real AHE rose 1.0 percent across all private-sector workers and 1.4 percent for private-sector workers in production and nonsupervisory positions. Wages and salaries as measured by the ECI also increased in real terms over the year, rising 0.9 percent across all private-sector workers and 1.0 percent for private-sector workers who are not in an incentive-paid position. Looking ahead, sustaining the labor market's solid performance while continuing to bring inflation down for American workers remains an important economic priority for the Administration.

Gross Domestic Product[3]

Overview—Real GDP, which adjusts for inflation, rose 3.1 percent over 2023 (fourth-quarter-over-fourth-quarter), the highest among America's peer nations. The COVID-19 recession and its recovery have significantly shaped GDP dynamics in recent years: real GDP fell 1.1 percent over 2020, reflecting the COVID-19 recession and initial recovery, grew 5.4 percent over 2021, and increased 0.7 percent over 2022. GDP growth in 2023 was broad-based, with positive contributions from all major components of GDP, including consumption, non-residential business investment, net exports, and government expenditures.

Consumption—Household consumption of goods and services accounts for roughly two-thirds of U.S. GDP. Real personal consumption expenditures (PCE) increased by 2.7 percent during the four quarters of 2023. The consumption of durable goods increased 5.7 percent over 2023, while the consumption of nondurable goods rose 2.1 percent and the consumption of services increased 2.3 percent.

Nonresidential Fixed Investment—Real nonresidential fixed investment rose 4.2 percent in 2023 (fourth-quarter-over-fourth-quarter). Over the past three years, real nonresidential fixed investment fell 3.7 percent in 2020, rose 4.9 percent in 2021, and rose 5.6 percent in 2022. Investment in structures was the primary contributor to 2023 business investment growth, rising 16.0 percent over the year, driven by growth in manufacturing structures investment. That reflects a rebound for structures investment, which fell an average of 7.9 percent annually over 2020 and 2021 and rose a modest 0.8 percent in 2022. Equipment investment fell 0.8 percent during 2023, while intellectual property investment increased 2.9 percent.

The Government Sector—Real government expenditures on consumption and investment increased 4.5 percent in the four quarters ending 2023:Q4, which reflects a 3.9 percent increase in Federal spending and a 4.9 percent increase in State and local government spending. Within the Federal spending category, nondefense spending increased 4.7 percent and defense spending increased 3.2 percent.

Trade—Real exports of goods and services increased 2.1 percent in the four quarters ending 2023:Q4, reflecting increases of 1.5 percent in goods and 3.2 percent in services. Real imports were unchanged over the same period, reflecting an increase of 0.5 percent in goods and a 2.1 percent decline in services.

Economic Projections

The Administration's economic assumptions for the 2024-2034 budget window informs the 2025 Budget and assumes implementation of the Administration's policy proposals. The Administration's projections are reported in Table 2-1 and summarized below. The Administration finalized the economic assumptions in early November 2023, and this forecast is broadly in line with the prevail-

[3] The data reported here on GDP and its underlying components reflect "second" estimates from the Bureau of Economic Analysis. These estimates are subject to revision.

Table 2–1. ECONOMIC ASSUMPTIONS[1]

(Calendar Years, Dollar Amounts in Billions)

	Actual 2022	Projections											
		2023	2024	2025	2026	2027	2028	2029	2030	2031	2032	2033	2034
Gross Domestic Product (GDP)													
Levels, Dollar Amounts in Billions:													
Current Dollars	25,744	27,347	28,507	29,640	30,863	32,139	33,466	34,870	36,368	37,947	39,594	41,313	43,110
Real, Chained (2017) Dollars	21,822	22,347	22,728	23,136	23,600	24,072	24,553	25,059	25,601	26,164	26,739	27,328	27,929
Chained Price Index (2017=100), Annual Average	118	122	125	128	131	134	136	139	142	145	148	151	154
Percent Change, Fourth-Quarter-over-Fourth-Quarter:													
Current Dollars	7.1	5.6	3.6	4.1	4.1	4.1	4.1	4.2	4.3	4.3	4.3	4.3	4.4
Real, Chained (2017) Dollars	0.7	2.6	1.3	2.0	2.0	2.0	2.0	2.1	2.2	2.2	2.2	2.2	2.2
Chained Price Index (2017=100)	6.4	3.0	2.3	2.1	2.1	2.1	2.1	2.1	2.1	2.1	2.1	2.1	2.1
Incomes, Billions of Current Dollars													
Domestic Corporate Profits	2,736	2,795	2,659	2,438	2,472	2,693	2,944	3,151	3,353	3,582	3,835	4,083	4,343
Employee Compensation	13,439	14,267	14,978	15,644	16,360	17,100	17,859	18,637	19,453	20,307	21,203	22,137	23,115
Wages and Salaries	11,116	11,823	12,402	12,967	13,557	14,168	14,792	15,435	16,109	16,818	17,555	18,325	19,148
Nonwage Personal Income	6,101	6,452	6,813	7,196	7,533	7,877	8,300	8,638	9,007	9,384	9,780	10,246	10,679
Consumer Price Index (All Urban)[2]**:**													
Level (1982–1984=100), Annual Average	293.0	305.0	314.0	321.0	328.0	336.0	344.0	352.0	360.0	368.0	376.0	385.0	394.0
Percent Change, Fourth-Quarter-over-Fourth-Quarter	7.1	3.4	2.5	2.3	2.3	2.3	2.3	2.3	2.3	2.3	2.3	2.3	2.3
Unemployment Rate, Civilian, Percent													
Annual Average	3.6	3.6	4.0	4.0	3.9	3.9	3.8	3.8	3.8	3.8	3.8	3.8	3.8
Q4 Level	3.6	3.8	4.1	4.0	3.9	3.8	3.8	3.8	3.8	3.8	3.8	3.8	3.8
Interest Rates, Percent													
91-Day Treasury Bills	2.0	5.1	5.1	4.0	3.3	3.1	2.9	2.8	2.8	2.7	2.7	2.7	2.7
10-Year Treasury Notes	3.0	4.1	4.4	4.0	3.9	3.8	3.8	3.7	3.7	3.7	3.7	3.7	3.7

[1] Based on information available as of November 2023.

[2] Seasonally Adjusted

ing consensus at that time. Since early November, data for 2023 have come in better than expected for a range of indicators. The labor market remained strong, with the unemployment rate edging down from 3.8 percent in October to 3.7 percent in December. Economic growth was also strong, with real GDP increasing 3.2 percent annualized during the fourth quarter of 2023. Furthermore, broad price pressures continued to ease, with three-month annualized CPI-U inflation slowing from 3.9 percent in October to 1.9 percent in December. Had these data been available when the Administration's forecast was finalized, the forecast would likely feature a lower unemployment rate path and higher GDP growth, just as many other more frequently produced external forecasts have shown in updates since early November.

Real GDP—The Administration's economic assumptions project real GDP growth of 2.6 percent over the four quarters of 2023; subsequently released data show that actual real GDP growth over that period was 3.1 percent. Real GDP growth is expected to be 1.3 percent in 2024, and to average 2.0 percent between 2025-2029, and 2.2 percent during 2030-2034.

Unemployment—The Administration's economic assumptions project a 3.6 percent unemployment rate on average over 2023, in line with published data. The unemployment rate is projected to rise modestly in 2024, before declining over the forecast horizon to a long-run rate of 3.8 percent by 2028.

Interest Rates—After rising over the past couple years, interest rates are expected to broadly hold steady through 2024. The 91-day Treasury bill rate is expected to average 5.1 percent over 2023 and 2024, before falling to a terminal rate of 2.7 percent in 2031. The 10-year rate is projected to average 4.1 percent over 2023, edge up to 4.4 percent over 2024, and then fall to a terminal rate of 3.7 percent in 2029. For 2023, the economic assumption's forecast for the 91-day rate is consistent with subsequently released data, while the 10-year rate forecast is slightly higher than in the data (4.0 percent).

Inflation—The Administration's forecast anticipates further declines in inflation rates over the next two years, following the elevated pace during 2021 and 2022. Specifically, the assumptions anticipate that, after growing 7.1 percent on a fourth-quarter-over-fourth-quarter basis in 2022, inflation as measured by the CPI-U would be 3.4 percent in 2023, compared with the 3.2 percent reported. The assumptions forecast CPI-U inflation of 2.5 percent in 2024, and 2.3 percent in 2025 and in subsequent years.

Changes in Economic Assumptions from Last Year's Budget—Table 2-2 compares the Administration's forecast for the 2025 Budget with that from the 2024 Budget and Mid-Session Review. Compared with the

Table 2–2. COMPARISON OF ECONOMIC ASSUMPTIONS IN THE 2024 AND 2025 BUDGETS

	2023	2024	2025	2026	2027	2028	2029	2030	2031	2032	2033
(fourth-quarter-over-fourth-quarter percent change)											
Real GDP:											
2024 Budget Assumptions	0.4	2.1	2.4	2.0	2.0	2.0	2.1	2.2	2.2	2.2	2.2
2024 MSR Assumptions	0.4	1.8	2.4	2.0	2.0	2.0	2.1	2.2	2.2	2.2	2.2
2025 Budget Assumptions	2.6	1.3	2.0	2.0	2.0	2.0	2.1	2.2	2.2	2.2	2.2
GDP Price Index:											
2024 Budget Assumptions	2.8	2.1	2.1	2.1	2.1	2.1	2.1	2.1	2.1	2.1	2.1
2024 MSR Assumptions	3.2	2.3	2.1	2.1	2.1	2.1	2.1	2.1	2.1	2.1	2.1
2025 Budget Assumptions	3.0	2.3	2.1	2.1	2.1	2.1	2.1	2.1	2.1	2.1	2.1
Consumer Price Index (All-Urban):											
2024 Budget Assumptions	3.0	2.3	2.3	2.3	2.3	2.3	2.3	2.3	2.3	2.3	2.3
2024 MSR Assumptions	3.3	2.5	2.3	2.3	2.3	2.3	2.3	2.3	2.3	2.3	2.3
2025 Budget Assumptions	3.4	2.5	2.3	2.3	2.3	2.3	2.3	2.3	2.3	2.3	2.3
(calendar year average)											
Civilian Unemployment Rate:											
2024 Budget Assumptions	4.3	4.6	4.4	4.3	4.2	4.1	4.0	3.9	3.8	3.8	3.8
2024 MSR Assumptions	3.8	4.4	4.2	4.1	4.1	4.1	4.0	3.9	3.8	3.8	3.8
2025 Budget Assumptions	3.6	4.0	4.0	3.9	3.9	3.8	3.8	3.8	3.8	3.8	3.8
91-Day Treasury Bill Rate:											
2024 Budget Assumptions	4.9	3.8	3.0	2.5	2.3	2.2	2.3	2.4	2.4	2.5	2.5
2024 MSR Assumptions	5.0	4.1	3.2	2.7	2.4	2.3	2.3	2.3	2.4	2.5	2.5
2025 Budget Assumptions	5.1	5.1	4.0	3.3	3.1	2.9	2.8	2.8	2.7	2.7	2.7
10-Year Treasury Note Rate:											
2024 Budget Assumptions	3.8	3.6	3.5	3.4	3.4	3.4	3.4	3.4	3.4	3.4	3.4
2024 MSR Assumptions	3.7	3.7	3.5	3.4	3.3	3.3	3.4	3.4	3.4	3.4	3.4
2025 Budget Assumptions	4.1	4.4	4.0	3.9	3.8	3.8	3.7	3.7	3.7	3.7	3.7

2024 Budget forecast, the Administration's interest rate forecasts towards the end of the Budget window are now higher. The upward revisions are consistent with changes across market-based measures and external forecasts. Interest rates aside, the Administration's expectations over the outyears of the forecast are little changed from the 2024 Budget forecast. Revisions to the near-term largely reflect the more current economic data available at the time the current assumptions were finalized.

Comparison with Other Forecasts

This section compares the Administration's forecast with the then-available forecasts from CBO, the FOMC, and the Blue Chip panel of professional forecasters.

There are important methodological differences across these forecasts. Aside from the inherent uncertainty of forecasting economic variables, different projections make different assumptions about which policies of the Administration are enacted. The Administration's forecast assumes implementation of the Administration's proposed policies—such as expanding access to affordable, high-quality early childcare and learning, improving college affordability, and modernizing our immigration system. In contrast, the CBO forecast assumes no changes to current law. It is unclear to what extent Blue Chip panelists incorporate policy implementation expectations into their respective outlooks. The Blue Chip panel comprises a large number of private-sector forecasters, who have different expectations about the enactment of the Administration's proposed policies and different views about how those policies might affect economic growth.

A second key difference is that the various forecasts were published on different dates. For example, while the forecast published by the Administration is based on data available as of early November 2023, the Blue Chip forecasts are drawn from a survey administered in early October. In addition, the Federal Reserve's FOMC projections were released in mid-September and the CBO forecast was published in July 2023.

Real GDP—The Administration forecasts an average real GDP growth rate of 2.0 percent (fourth-quarter-over-fourth-quarter) during the 11 years from 2024 to 2034, modestly higher than the 1.8 percent average of both Blue Chip and the median FOMC participant over the same window and the 1.9 percent average of CBO over 2024-2033. Over the near term, the Administration forecasts an average growth rate of 1.7 percent during 2024-2025, which is above the 1.3 percent average for Blue Chip, below the 2.0 percent average from CBO, and in line with the median FOMC participant's forecast.

Unemployment—The Administration, Blue Chip consensus, CBO, and the median FOMC participant all

Table 2–3. COMPARISON OF ECONOMIC ASSUMPTIONS [1]

	2023	2024	2025	2026	2027	2028	2029	2030	2031	2032	2033	2034
(fourth-quarter-over-fourth-quarter percent change)												
Real GDP:												
2025 Budget (November 2023)	2.6	1.3	2.0	2.0	2.0	2.0	2.1	2.2	2.2	2.2	2.2	2.2
Blue Chip [2] (October 2023)	2.1	0.9	1.7	2.1	1.9	1.9	1.8	1.8	1.8	1.8	1.8	1.8
CBO [3] (July 2023)	0.9	1.5	2.4	2.4	2.1	1.9	1.9	1.8	1.8	1.8	1.7	....
Federal Reserve [4] (September 2023)	2.1	1.5	1.8	1.8	1.8	1.8	1.8	1.8	1.8	1.8	1.8	1.8
Consumer Price Index (CPI-U):												
2025 Budget (November 2023)	3.4	2.5	2.3	2.3	2.3	2.3	2.3	2.3	2.3	2.3	2.3	2.3
Blue Chip [2] (October 2023)	3.3	2.4	2.3	2.2	2.2	2.2	2.1	2.2	2.2	2.2	2.2	2.2
CBO [3] (July 2023)	3.3	2.7	2.2	2.0	2.1	2.2	2.3	2.3	2.3	2.3	2.3	....
Federal Reserve [4,5] (September 2023)	3.3	2.5	2.2	2.0	2.0	2.0	2.0	2.0	2.0	2.0	2.0	2.0
(calendar year average)												
Unemployment Rate:												
2025 Budget (November 2023)	3.6	4.0	4.0	3.9	3.9	3.8	3.8	3.8	3.8	3.8	3.8	3.8
Blue Chip [2] (October 2023)	3.7	4.2	4.2	4.0	4.0	4.0	4.0	4.0	4.0	4.0	4.0	4.0
CBO [3] (July 2023)	3.7	4.5	4.6	4.6	4.5	4.5	4.5	4.5	4.5	4.5	4.5	....
Federal Reserve [4,6] (September 2023)	3.8	4.1	4.1	4.0	4.0	4.0	4.0	4.0	4.0	4.0	4.0	4.0
91-Day Treasury Bills (discount basis):												
2025 Budget (November 2023)	5.1	5.1	4.0	3.3	3.1	2.9	2.8	2.8	2.7	2.7	2.7	2.7
Blue Chip [2] (October 2023)	5.3	4.8	3.4	2.8	2.7	2.7	2.6	2.7	2.7	2.7	2.7	2.7
CBO [3] (July 2023)	5.1	4.7	3.6	2.2	2.2	2.3	2.3	2.3	2.3	2.3	2.3	....
10-Year Treasury Notes:												
2025 Budget (November 2023)	4.1	4.4	4.0	3.9	3.8	3.8	3.7	3.7	3.7	3.7	3.7	3.7
Blue Chip [2] (October 2023)	4.0	4.0	3.6	3.5	3.5	3.5	3.5	3.5	3.5	3.5	3.5	3.5
CBO [3] (July 2023)	3.8	4.0	3.7	3.8	3.8	3.8	3.8	3.8	3.8	3.8	3.8	....

Sources: Administration; CBO, The Budget and Economic Outlook: 2023 to 2033, February 2023; CBO, An Update to the Economic Outlook: 2023 to 2025, July 2023; October 2023 Blue Chip Economic Indicators, Aspen Publishers, Inc.; Federal Reserve Open Market Committee, September 22, 2023

[1] Calendar Year

[2] GDP & CPI growth rates are year-over-year after 2024. Values for 2030-2034 are 5 year averages.

[3] Values for 2023–2025 are from July 2023 report; values for 2026-2033 are from February 2023 report.

[3] Median of FOMC Participants' Projections

[4] PCE Inflation

[5] Average rate during 4th quarter.

forecast that the average unemployment rate during 2024 will be slightly elevated compared with 2023. Across 2024 and 2025, the Administration forecasts that the unemployment rate will average 4.0 percent, compared with CBO, Blue Chip, and median FOMC participant averages of 4.6, 4.2, and 4.1 percent during that window, respectively. Over the long run, the Administration projects a terminal unemployment rate of 3.8 percent, compared with 4.0 percent for both Blue Chip and the median FOMC participant, and 4.5 percent for CBO.

Interest Rates—The Administration's 91-day interest rate forecast is qualitatively consistent with the Blue Chip consensus forecast over the forecast horizon, though modestly higher in magnitude during most years. The Administration expects the annual average short-term interest rate will start to fall in 2025, whereas CBO and Blue Chip forecast declines will begin during 2024. The Administration and Blue Chip forecast the 91-day Treasury rate will stabilize at 2.7 percent by the end of the Budget window, while CBO forecasts a 2.3 percent rate. A similar overall pattern holds for the 10-year Treasury rate, and the Administration projects a 3.7 percent terminal rate, compared with 3.5 percent by Blue Chip and 3.8 percent by CBO.

Inflation—The Administration's forecast for CPI-U inflation (on a fourth-quarter-over-fourth-quarter basis) is broadly consistent with outside forecasts throughout the budget window. The Administration, Blue Chip consensus, CBO, and the median FOMC participant all project that inflation will continue to moderate through 2025. The Administration's projection for the long-term CPI-U inflation rate of 2.3 percent equals CBO's long-term projection, is 0.1 percentage point higher than Blue Chip's long-term projection, and is approximately consistent with the FOMC's 2.0 percent target for PCE inflation

Sensitivity of the Budget to Economic Assumptions

Federal spending and tax collections are heavily influenced by developments in the economy. Income tax receipts are a function of growth in incomes for households and firms. Spending on social assistance programs may rise when the economy enters a downturn, while in-

Table 2–4. SENSITIVITY OF THE BUDGET TO ECONOMIC ASSUMPTIONS

(Fiscal Years; In Billions of Dollars)

Budget Effect	2024	2025	2026	2027	2028	2029	2030	2031	2032	2033	2034	Total of Budget Effects: 2024–2034
Real Growth and Employment:												
Budgetary effects of 1 percentage point lower real GDP growth:												
(1) For calendar year 2024 only, with real GDP recovery in 2025–2034:[1]												
Receipts	-20.4	-32.1	-16.4	-2.6	*	*	*	*	*	*	*	-71.1
Outlays	14.2	30.0	15.8	4.3	3.9	3.7	3.6	3.5	3.5	3.6	3.6	89.7
Increase in deficit (+)	34.6	62.1	32.2	7.0	3.8	3.6	3.5	3.4	3.4	3.5	3.6	160.7
(2) For calendar year 2024 only, with no subsequent recovery:												
Receipts	-20.4	-42.6	-49.8	-52.1	-54.0	-56.1	-58.3	-60.6	-63.0	-65.5	-68.2	-590.7
Outlays	14.2	36.3	41.2	45.4	50.1	54.9	59.7	64.5	69.9	75.6	81.5	593.2
Increase in deficit (+)	34.6	78.9	90.9	97.4	104.2	111.0	118.0	125.2	132.8	141.1	149.7	1,183.9
(3) Sustained during 2024–2034, with no change in unemployment:												
Receipts	-20.5	-63.5	-115.6	-171.8	-230.9	-294.0	-361.5	-433.5	-509.9	-592.0	-679.6	-3,472.7
Outlays	0.4	1.7	3.9	7.2	11.2	15.8	20.8	26.4	32.9	39.6	46.6	206.5
Increase in deficit (+)	20.8	65.2	119.5	179.0	242.1	309.9	382.3	459.9	542.7	631.6	726.2	3,679.3
Inflation and Interest Rates:												
Budgetary effects of 1 percentage point higher rate of:												
(4) Inflation and interest rates during calendar year 2024 only:												
Receipts	21.6	42.2	44.4	44.6	46.2	47.9	49.8	51.8	53.8	55.9	58.2	516.3
Outlays	69.4	100.1	74.4	74.5	74.7	73.5	72.1	73.4	73.3	78.3	78.4	841.9
Increase in deficit (+)	47.8	57.9	30.0	30.0	28.5	25.5	22.3	21.6	19.5	22.4	20.2	325.6
(5) Inflation and interest rates, sustained during 2024–2034:												
Receipts	21.6	65.0	113.7	165.2	219.8	278.9	342.9	412.4	486.8	568.0	655.7	3,329.8
Outlays	69.7	178.5	265.3	355.7	452.4	541.8	646.4	753.4	868.1	1,008.8	1,121.3	6,261.5
Increase in deficit (+)	48.1	113.6	151.6	190.5	232.7	263.0	303.4	341.1	381.3	440.8	465.6	2,931.7
(6) Interest rates only, sustained during 2024–2034:												
Receipts	1.6	3.9	5.0	5.4	5.8	6.1	6.4	6.6	6.9	7.2	7.5	62.4
Outlays	51.8	128.8	179.0	225.3	269.7	313.7	352.8	392.7	432.6	473.5	514.1	3,333.9
Increase in deficit (+)	50.1	125.0	174.0	219.8	263.9	307.6	346.4	386.1	425.7	466.3	506.6	3,271.5
(7) Inflation only, sustained during 2024–2034:												
Receipts	19.9	61.0	108.6	159.5	213.7	272.4	336.1	405.2	479.4	560.1	647.5	3,263.5
Outlays	18.0	50.0	87.0	131.4	184.2	230.0	296.0	363.6	439.0	539.2	611.7	2,949.8
Decrease in deficit (–)	-1.9	-11.1	-21.6	-28.1	-29.5	-42.5	-40.2	-41.6	-40.4	-20.9	-35.8	-313.7
Interest Cost of Higher Federal Borrowing:												
(8) Outlay effect of $100 billion increase in borrowing in 2024	2.8	4.8	4.0	3.8	3.7	3.7	3.7	3.8	3.9	4.0	4.1	42.2

* $500 million or less.

[1] The unemployment rate is assumed to be 0.5 percentage point higher per one percent shortfall in the level of real GDP.

creases in nominal spending on Social Security and other programs are dependent on consumer price inflation. A robust set of projections for macroeconomic variables assists in budget planning, but unexpected developments in the economy have ripple effects for Federal spending and receipts. This section seeks to provide an understanding of the magnitude of the effects that unforeseen changes in the economy can have on the budget.

To make these assessments, the Administration relies on a set of heuristics that can predict how certain spending and receipt categories will react to a change in a given subset of macroeconomic variables, holding nearly everything else constant. These sensitivity analyses provide a sense of the broad changes one would expect after a given development, but do not attempt to anticipate how policy makers would react and potentially change course in such an event. For example, if the economy were to suffer an unexpected recession, tax receipts would decline and spending on programs such as unemployment insurance would rise. However, policy makers might enact policies to stimulate the economy, leading to secondary and tertiary changes that are difficult to predict. Another

Table 2–5. FORECAST ERRORS, 2002-PRESENT

REAL GDP ERRORS			
2-Year Average Annual Real GDP Growth	Administration	CBO	Blue Chip
Mean Error	1.2	0.5	0.7
Mean Absolute Error	1.3	0.8	0.8
Root Mean Square Error	1.6	1.2	1.2
6-Year Average Annual Real GDP Growth			
Mean Error	1.4	1.2	1.0
Mean Absolute Error	1.4	1.2	1.0
Root Mean Square Error	1.5	1.3	1.2
INFLATION ERRORS			
2-Year Average Annual Change in the Consumer Price Index	Administration	CBO	Blue Chip
Mean Error	-0.3	-0.3	-0.0
Mean Absolute Error	0.7	0.8	0.7
Root Mean Square Error	1.0	1.0	0.9
6-Year Average Annual Change in the Consumer Price Index			
Mean Error	0.2	0.1	0.3
Mean Absolute Error	0.3	0.3	0.4
Root Mean Square Error	0.4	0.4	0.5
INTEREST RATE ERRORS			
2-Year Average 91-Day Treasury Bill Rate	Administration	CBO	Blue Chip
Mean Error	0.6	0.5	0.7
Mean Absolute Error	0.8	0.7	0.8
Root Mean Square Error	1.1	1.1	1.2
6-Year Average 91-Day Treasury Bill Rate			
Mean Error	2.0	2.1	2.2
Mean Absolute Error	2.0	2.1	2.2
Root Mean Square Error	2.2	2.3	2.4

caveat is that it is often unrealistic to suppose that one macroeconomic variable might change while others would remain constant. Most macroeconomic variables interact with each other in complex and subtle ways. Be mindful of these considerations when examining Table 2-4.

For real GDP growth and employment:

- The first panel in the table illustrates the effect on the deficit resulting from a one percentage point reduction in real GDP growth, relative to the Administration's forecast, in 2024 that is followed by a subsequent recovery in 2025 and 2026. The unemployment rate is assumed to be half a percentage point higher in 2024 before returning to the baseline level in 2025 and 2026.
- The next panel in the table reports the effect of a reduction of one percentage point in real GDP growth in 2024 that is not subsequently made up by faster growth in 2025 and 2026. Consistent with this output path, the rate of unemployment is assumed to rise by half a percentage point relative to that assumed in the Administration's forecasts.
- The third panel in the table shows the impact of a GDP growth rate that is permanently reduced by one percentage point, while the unemployment rate is not affected. This is the sort of situation that would arise if, for example, the economy was to experience a permanent decline in productivity growth.

For inflation and interest rates:

- The fourth panel in Table 2-4 shows the effect on the budget in the case of a one percentage point higher rate of inflation and a one percentage point higher nominal interest rate in 2024. Both inflation and interest rates return to their assumed levels in 2025. This would result in a permanently higher price level and nominal GDP level over the course of the forecast horizon.
- The fifth panel in the table illustrates the effects on the budget deficit of a one percentage point higher inflation rate and interest rate than projected in every year of the forecast.
- The sixth panel reports the effect on the deficit resulting from an increase in interest rates in every year of the forecast, with no accompanying increase in inflation.
- The seventh panel in the table reports the effect on the budget deficit of a one percentage point higher

Table 2–6. DIFFERENCES BETWEEN ESTIMATED AND ACTUAL SURPLUSES OR DEFICITS FOR FIVE-YEAR BUDGET ESTIMATES SINCE 1985

	Current Year Estimate	Budget Year Estimate	Estimate for Budget Year Plus: One Year (BY + 1)	Two Years (BY + 2)	Three Years (BY + 3)	Four Years (BY + 4)
Mean Error	-0.4	0.8	1.6	-2.2	-2.6	-2.9
Mean Absolute Error	1.4	1.9	2.5	3.1	3.6	3.9
Root Mean Squared Error	2.3	2.9	3.6	4.2	4.6	4.7

inflation rate than projected in every year of the forecast window, while the interest rate remains as forecast.

- The table also shows the effect on the budget deficit if the Federal Government were to borrow an additional $100 billion in 2024, while all of the other projections remain constant.
- These simple approximations that inform the sensitivity analysis are symmetric. This means that the effect of, for example, a one percentage point higher rate of growth over the forecast horizon would be of the same magnitude as a one percentage point reduction in growth, though with the opposite sign.

Forecast Errors for Growth, Inflation, and Interest Rates

This section evaluates the historical accuracy of past Administration forecasts for real GDP growth, inflation, and short-term interest rates from 2002 to the present day, and compares this accuracy with that of forecasts produced by the CBO and Blue Chip panel. For this exercise, forecasts produced by all three entities are compared with realized values of these variables. As with any forecast, the Administration's projections are inherently uncertain because they are based on underlying assumptions about future social, political, and global conditions. It is impossible to foresee every eventuality over a one-year horizon, much less over ten or more years.

The results of this exercise are reported in Table 2-5 and contain three different measures of accuracy. The first is the average forecast error. A forecast with an average error of zero is unbiased, in the sense that realized values of the variables have not been systematically above or below the forecasted value. The second is the average absolute value of the forecast error, which offers a sense of the magnitude of errors. Thus, even if a forecast's errors are unbiased, the forecast can still be very inaccurate with very large positive and negative errors cancelling one another out. The table also reports the square root of the mean of squared forecast error (RMSE). This metric applies a harsher penalty to forecasts with larger errors. The table reports these measures of accuracy at both the 2-year and the 6-year horizons, thus evaluating the relative success of different forecasts in the short and medium run.

Past Administration forecasts have 2-year real GDP growth and average annual interest rates that were higher than realized, on average, by 1.2 percentage points and 0.6 percentage points, respectively. This is partly due to the assumption that Administration policy proposals contained in the Budget will be enacted, which may not come to pass. The 2-year average forecast error for inflation is smaller, -0.3 percentage points, and similar to other forecasts' errors.

Uncertainty and the Deficit Projections

This section assesses the accuracy of past budget forecasts for the deficit or surplus, measured at different time horizons. The results of this exercise are reported in Table 2-6, where the average error, the average absolute error, and the RMSE are reported.

In Table 2-6, a negative number signifies that the Federal Government budget ran a larger surplus or a smaller deficit than was expected, while a positive number in the table indicates a smaller surplus or a larger deficit. In the current year in which the budget is published, the Administration has tended to understate the surplus (or, equivalently, overstate the deficit by an average of 0.4 percent of GDP. For the budget year, however, the historical pattern has been for the budget to understate the deficit by an average of 0.8 percent of GDP.[4] One possible reason for this is that past Administrations' policy proposals have not all been implemented. The forecast errors tend to grow with the time horizon, which is not surprising given that there is much greater uncertainty in the medium run about both the macroeconomic situation and the specific details of policy enactments.

Chart 2-2 uses the historical forecast errors summarized in Table 2-6 to construct a probabilistic range of outcomes for the deficit over the budget window. These probabilistic ranges are derived from the RMSE of previous forecast errors and assume these errors are normally distributed. This exercise is repeated at every forecast horizon from the current year through fours year after the budget year. The middle line represents the Administration's expected deficit as a percent of GDP and the 50th percentile outcome. The highest line reports the 95th percentile of the distribution of outcomes over 2024 to 2029, meaning that there is a 95 percent probability that the actual deficit in those years will be below that line. Similarly, there is a 95 percent probability that the deficit will be above the lowest line in the chart.

[4] Additionally, the CBO's deficit forecasts have on average been smaller than what materialized.

Chart 2-2. Range of Uncertainty for the Budget Deficit

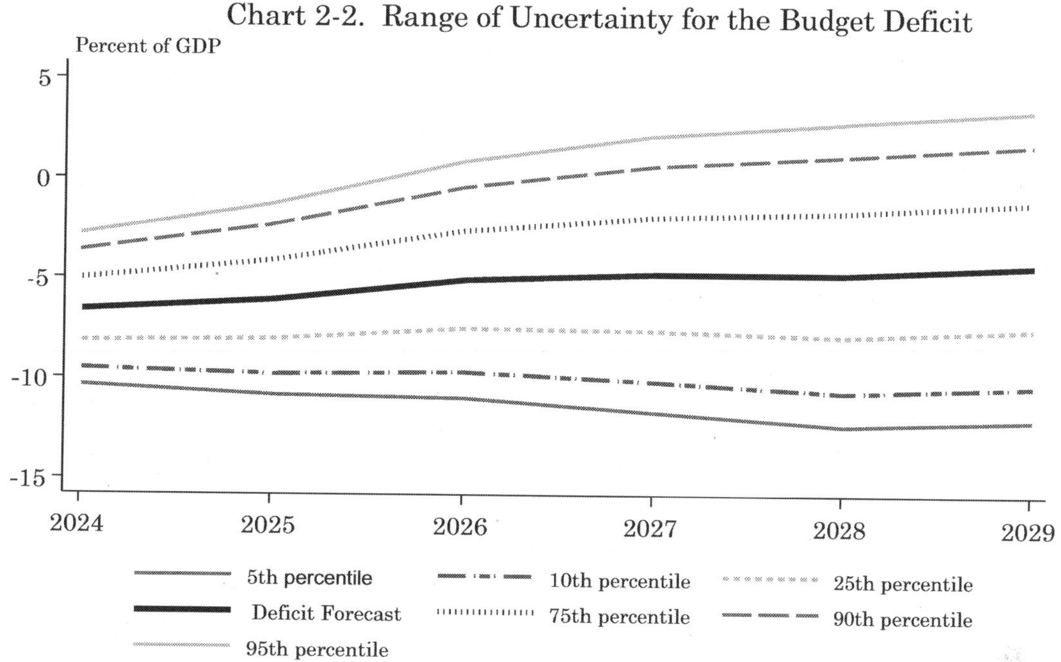

3. LONG-TERM BUDGET OUTLOOK

The horizon for most of the analysis in this Budget is ten years. This ten-year horizon reflects a balance between the importance of considering both the current and future implications of budget decisions made today and a practical limit on the construction of detailed budget projections for years in the future.

Nonetheless, it can be informative to look further into the future, despite the uncertainty surrounding the assumptions needed for such estimates. This chapter begins by discussing the fiscal outlook under current law over the next 25 years. The second section discusses the fiscal impact of the Administration's policies, finding they will cut deficits and debt compared with the baseline. In the third section, alternative assumptions about the evolution of key variables and uncertainties in the projections are discussed, including the macroeconomic risks of climate change. The fourth section discusses the actuarial projections for Social Security and Medicare. The *technical note* to this chapter provides further detail on data sources, assumptions, and other methods for estimation.

Long-Run Projections under Continuation of Current Policies

The baseline long-term projections assume that current policy continues for Social Security, Medicare, Medicaid, other mandatory programs, and revenues.[1] Projections for all mandatory programs and revenues maintain consistency with other Federal Agency projections. From 2034-2049, total mandatory spending grows by 0.6 percentage point as a share of gross domestic product (GDP), while revenues increase by 0.5 percentage point. The Budget provides a specific path for discretionary spending over the next ten years. Thereafter, the baseline long-run projections assume that real per-person discretionary funding remains constant, implying an average growth rate of 2.8 percent per year. The technical note

[1] The long-run baseline projections are consistent with the Budget's baseline concept, which is explained in more detail in the "Current Services Estimates" chapter of this volume. The projections assume full payment of scheduled Social Security and Medicare benefits without regard to the projected depletion of the trust funds for these programs. Additional baseline assumptions beyond the ten-year window are detailed in the technical note to this chapter.

Chart 3-1. Comparison of Annual Deficit

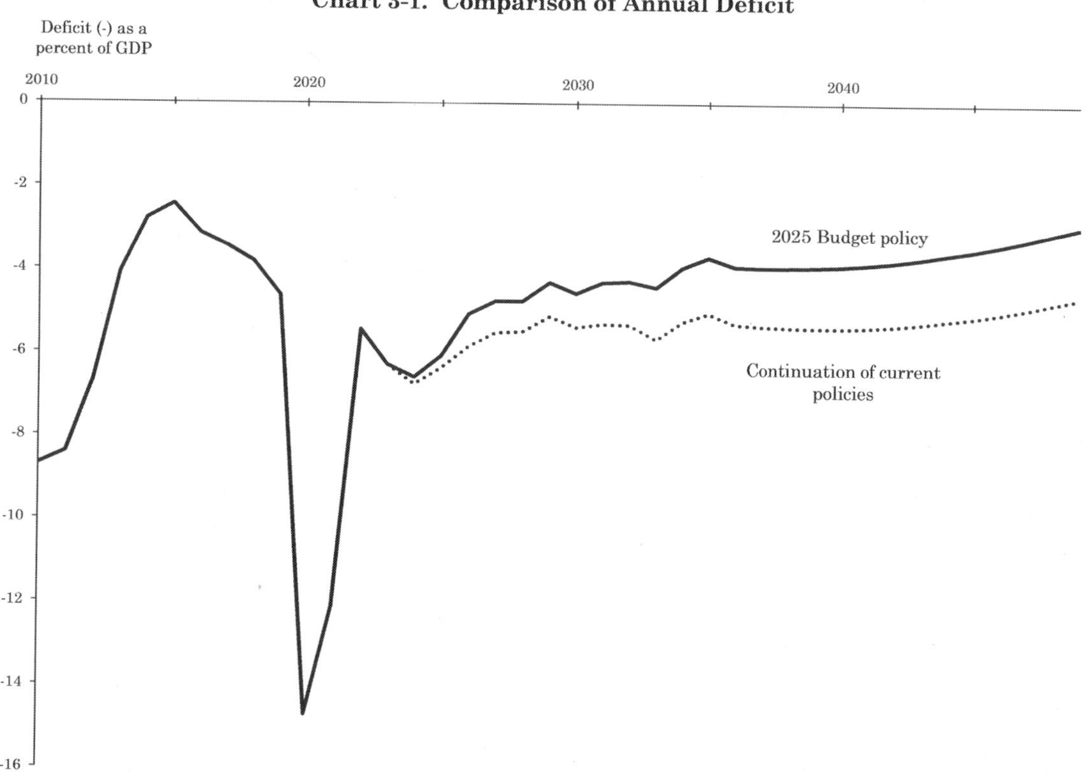

Chart 3-2. Comparison of Publicly Held Debt

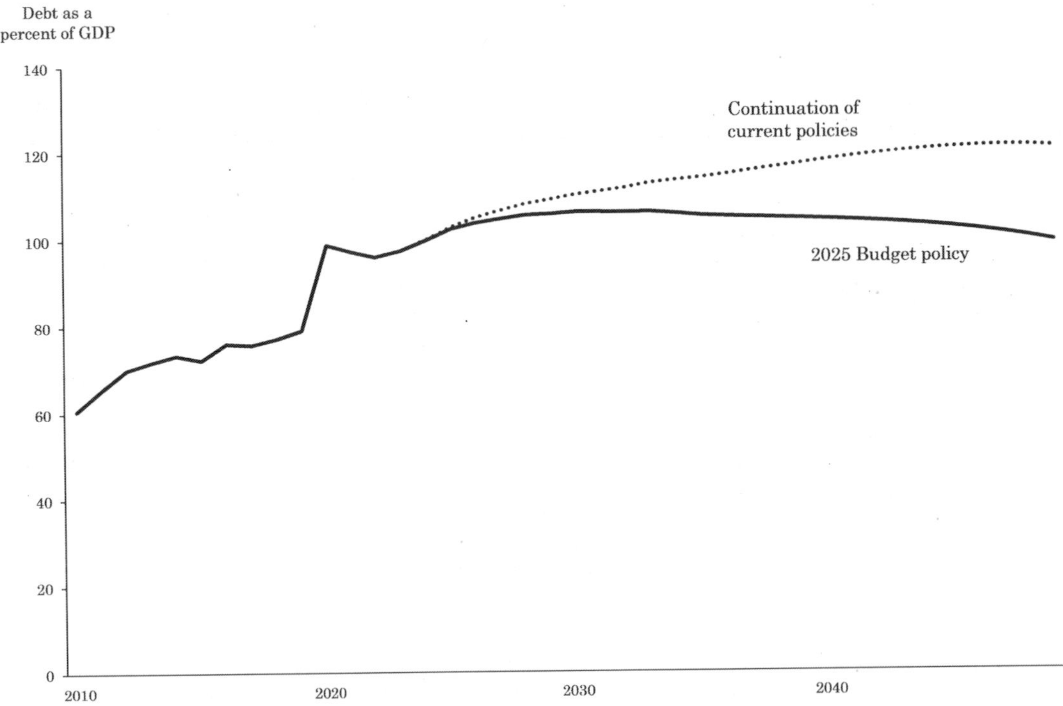

provides additional detail on the methodology behind these projections.

Under the baseline, the deficit is projected to average 5.5 percent of annual GDP through the ten-year window. (See Table S-2 of the main *Budget* volume.) Debt is projected to rise to 113.3 percent of GDP in 2034 under current policies. Beyond the ten-year horizon, Chart 3-1 shows that deficits under the baseline projections fall from 5.2 percent of GDP in 2034 to 4.6 percent of GDP by the end of the 25-year window. Chart 3-2 shows that debt under the baseline projections continues to rise as a share of GDP, with increases slowing in the 2040s and debt as a share of GDP peaking in 2048. From 2034 to 2040, debt is projected to increase from 113.3 to 117.8 percent of GDP under the baseline projections, an increase of 0.8 percentage point per year. In contrast, from 2040 to 2048, debt is projected to increase from 117.8 to 120.9 percent of GDP under the baseline projections, an increase of 0.4 percentage point per year. At the end of the 25-year window, debt as a share of GDP in the baseline projections begins to decline. Real net interest rises from 1.4 to 1.5 percent of GDP between 2034 and 2047 under the baseline projections, and subsequently starts to decline.

Debt as a share of GDP grows more slowly over time in part because of the projected slowdown in population aging from 2024 forward. Consistent with the demographic assumptions in the 2023 Social Security Trustees' report (see Chart 3-3 below), the elderly (aged 65 or older) share of the U.S. population is projected to rise from 16.8 percent in 2022 to 21.2 percent in 2038 as more baby boomers retire. This aging of the baby-boom cohorts into retirement reduces the rate of labor force growth and therefore the rate of economic growth. However, by the late 2030s, the elderly share of the U.S. population is projected to plateau. As a result, the demographic drag on economic growth from the aging of the U.S. population is projected to subside from 2030 forward, which, all else equal, reduces the growth in debt as a share of GDP.

Impact of 2025 Budget Policies on the Long-Term Fiscal Outlook

The 2025 Budget proposes major investments to grow the economy from the middle out and the bottom up, to reduce everyday costs for Americans, and to invest in working families and improve health outcomes. These investments are coupled with major reforms to both corporate and individual taxation. Because the Budget's reforms to the tax system and reforms to reduce spending—for example, on subsidies to pharmaceutical companies—far exceed the proposed investments, the Budget substantially improves the long-term fiscal outlook.

The Budget's policies lower annual deficits compared with the baseline projections in every year, beginning immediately. To assess the long-run impact, this chapter develops 25-year projections for the impact of the Administration's policies on the Budget, as described in the technical note. The resulting projections show that the revenue increases in the President's Budget more than offset net spending increases in every year, while generating additional savings over the long run. In total,

Chart 3-3. Elderly (Age 65+) Share of the U.S. Population

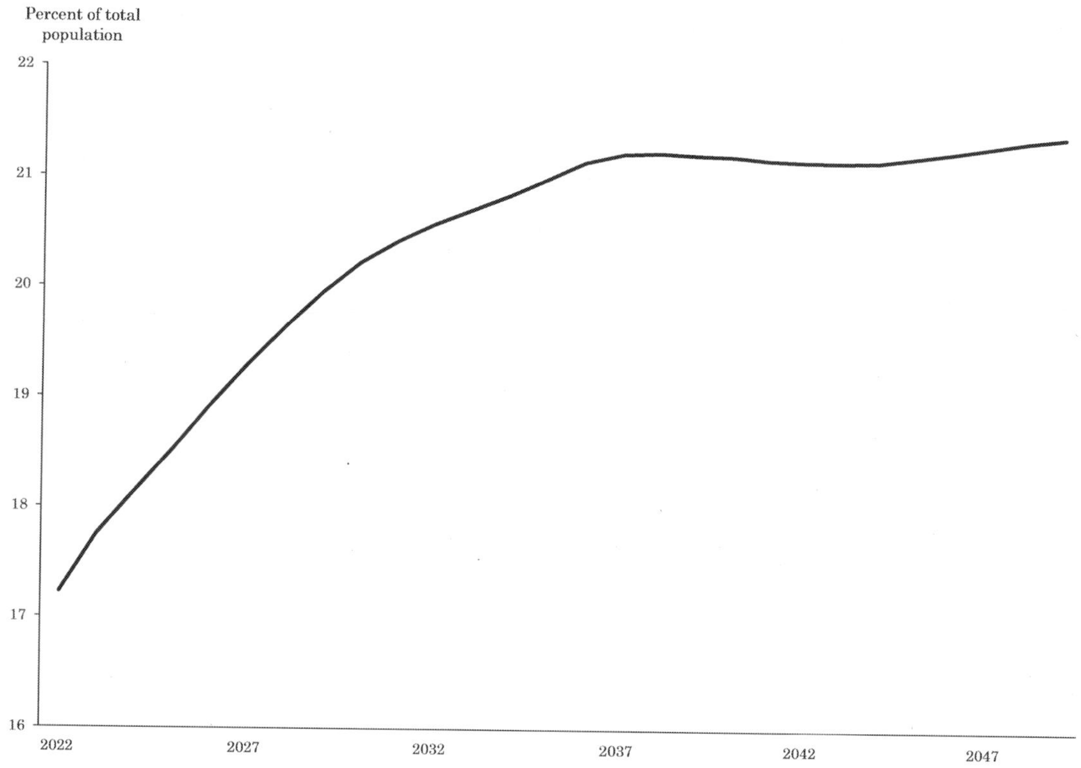

Percent of total population

all Budget proposals are projected to reduce deficits by roughly $8 trillion in the second decade and improve the fiscal outlook over the long run.

Charts 3-1 and 3-2 illustrate the improvement in deficits and debt. The Budget improves the fiscal outlook over the short and long term, with lower deficits throughout the 25-year window. Similarly, the Budget's policies significantly flatten the projected debt increase compared with the baseline. Debt as a percent of GDP starts to decline in the second half of the budget window, and declines an additional 6.7 percentage points from 2034 to 2049. Debt as a percent of GDP is projected to reach 98.9 percent in 2049 under the Budget's policies, bringing it below its level in 2024. Budget proposals would result in further improvement in the fiscal outlook after 25 years.

Table 3–1. 25-YEAR DEBT PROJECTIONS UNDER ALTERNATIVE BUDGET SCENARIOS
(Percent of GDP)

2025 Budget Policy	98.9
Real Economic Growth:	
Lower climate damages to real GDP	100.0
Intermediate climate damages to real GDP	100.7
Higher climate damages to real GDP	101.4
Health:	
Excess cost growth 0.5 ppt higher	105.6
Excess cost growth 0.5 ppt lower	94.7
Discretionary Spending:	
Grow with GDP	105.3
Grow with inflation only	96.6

Uncertainty and Alternative Assumptions

Future budget outcomes depend on a host of unknowns: changing economic conditions, unforeseen international developments, unexpected demographic shifts, and unpredictable technological advances. The longer budget projections are extended, the more the uncertainties increase. These uncertainties make even short-run budget forecasting quite difficult. For example, the Budget's projection of the deficit in five years is 4.3 percent of GDP, but a distribution of probable outcomes ranges from a deficit of 10.3 percent of GDP to a surplus of 1.7 percent of GDP, at the 10th and 90th percentiles, respectively.[2]

This section considers some specific sources of uncertainty in the projections above, which are summarized in Table 3-1.

Climate Risk.—Real economic growth is highly uncertain. Going forward, real GDP growth is projected to be below its longer-run historical average of 2.5 percent per year, as the slowdown in population growth and the increase in the population over age 65 reduce labor supply growth. In these projections, real GDP growth averages 2.1 percent per year for the period following the end of the ten-year budget window.

Over the long run, the path of real GDP is subject to significant downside risk from climate change. Absent

[2] These estimates are presented in Chart 2-2 in the "Economic Assumptions" chapter of this volume.

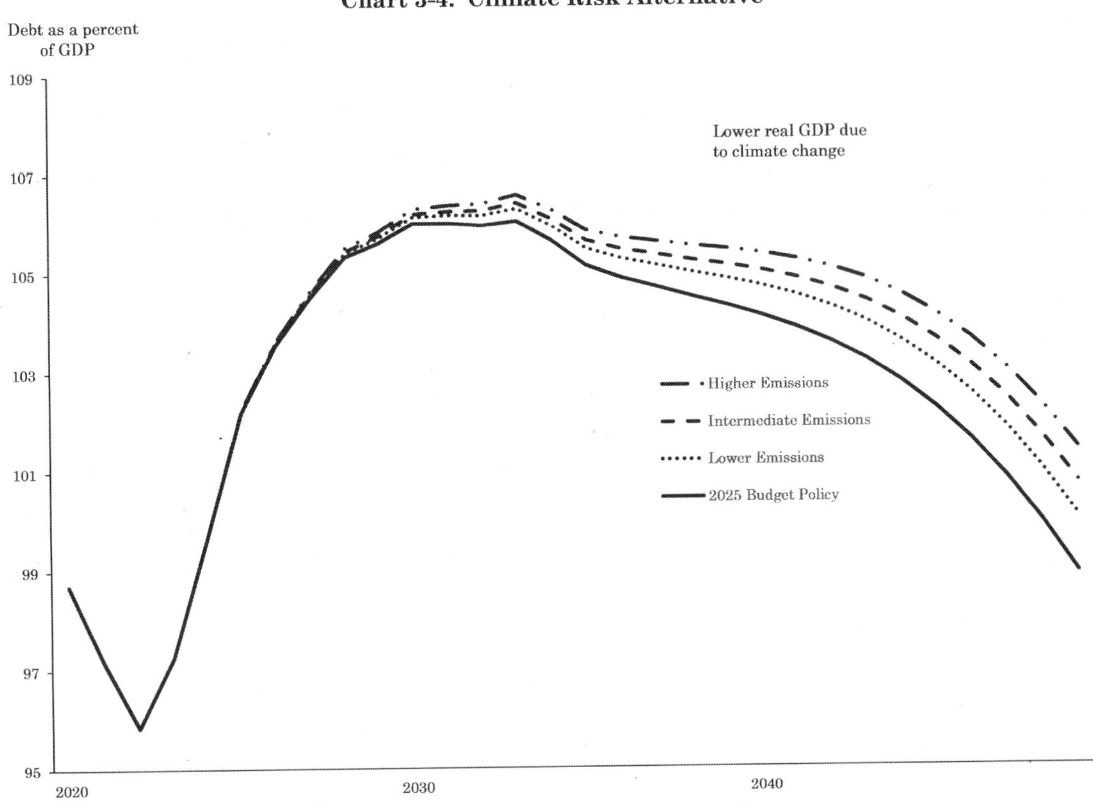

further action to slow the rate of greenhouse gas (GHG) emissions, global temperatures remain on pace to increase over two degrees Celsius from their pre-industrial average by the end of this century. Warming on this scale may have profound impacts on the American economy and the Federal fiscal outlook.

Climate change leads to physical changes that can impact the economy through a variety of pathways. Acute physical risks from an increased rate and severity of natural disasters can harm the productivity of American farms, factories, offices, and infrastructure. Chronic risks like sea level rise and warmer temperatures have the potential to do the same. The combined effects of climate change are projected to lead to lower economic output in the United States.

The severity of future climate change and U.S. vulnerability to this change will reflect past and current actions, future domestic policy and economic decisions, as well as policy choices and economic decisions made abroad. While the United States has pledged to reach net-zero GHG emissions by 2050, a primary source of uncertainty regarding physical climate risks to the United States are the GHG emission mitigation choices of other countries. To illustrate the implications of this uncertainty, this chapter analyzes the Federal budget impacts of three potential scenarios for GHG emission reductions.[3] All scenarios are consistent with the U.S. emissions reduction commitments. Under the "lower emissions" scenario, other countries also eliminate net GHG emissions by 2050. Under the "intermediate emissions" scenario, other countries maintain their current policies. Under the "higher emissions" scenario, other countries weaken their current GHG reduction policies.

As Chart 3-4 shows, even under the lower emissions scenario, climate change's consequences to the macroeconomy weaken the fiscal outlook. Debt to GDP under the lower emissions scenario is projected to reach 100.0 percent by 2049, compared with 98.9 percent in the policy baseline. Debt to GDP is projected to be even higher under the intermediate and higher emissions scenarios, reaching 100.7 percent and 101.4 percent, respectively,

[3] Specifically, these are the Shared Socioeconomic Pathways scenarios 1-2.6, 2-4.5, and 3-7.0, which were developed by an international community of climate modeling experts. In contrast to the Budget policy path, each of these alternate climate scenarios accounts for the estimated effects of future emissions on future changes in temperatures, which, in turn, affect future GDP projections. The damage from these scenarios on GDP only capture the impacts associated with rising temperatures, and do not explicitly account for changes in the severity or intensity of extreme weather events. The estimates are generated using a composite of recent, peer-reviewed models. For more detail, please see the 2023 CEA-OMB white paper on "Methodologies and Considerations for Integrating the Physical and Transition Risks of Climate Change into Macro-Economic Forecasting for the President's Budget."

Chart 3-5. Alternative Health Care Costs

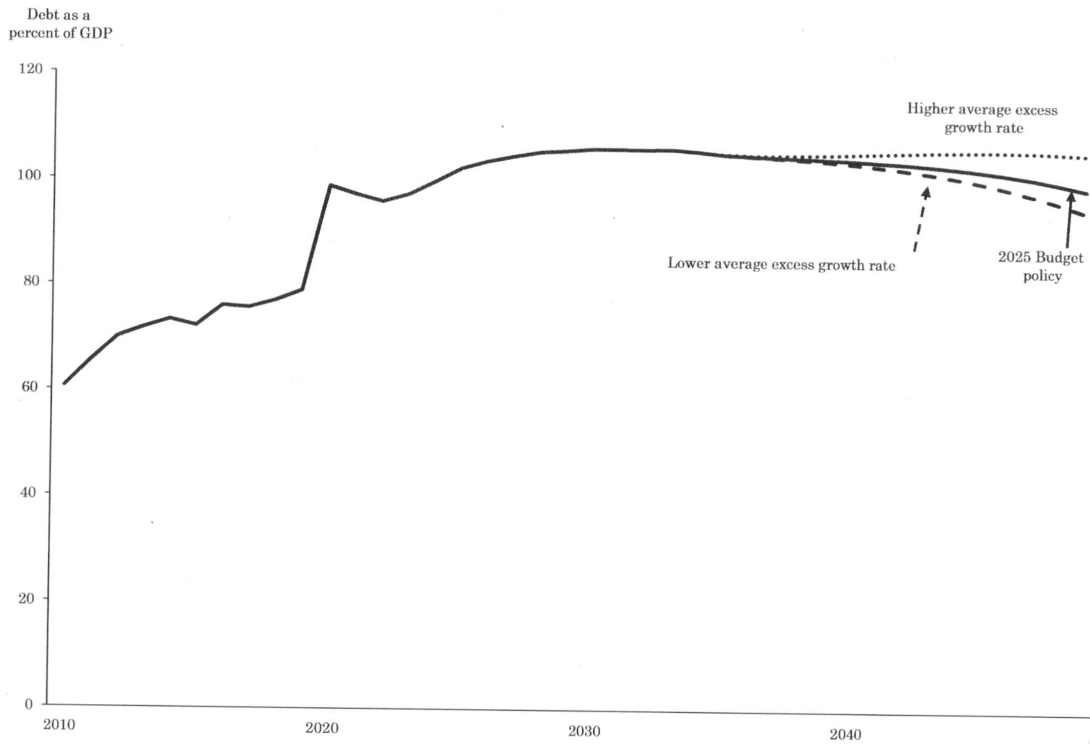

by 2049. Beyond the 25-year window considered here, the macroeconomic outlooks under these emissions scenarios diverge further over time. As a consequence, the higher emissions scenario, in particular, would lead to even further deteriorations in the longer-term fiscal outlook. This underscores both the macroeconomic and the fiscal risks posed by climate change, as well as the benefits of reducing future emissions. This is one of many reasons why there is an urgent need for continued action on climate change and why the 2025 President's Budget proposes significant investments to reduce the Federal Government's long-term fiscal exposure to climate-related financial risks and to reduce future risks for all Americans.[4]

Future Pandemics.—A future pandemic could also have a large impact on both the economy and the Federal balance sheet. While these impacts are not quantified here, during the COVID-19 pandemic, the U.S. Government provided around $4.6 trillion to support the American taxpayer, including expanded unemployment benefits, small business cash infusions, payments to families to cover child-related expenses, and checks to over 170 million Americans. In spite of these well-targeted investments, the lost economic output due to the pandemic could have been as high as $1.5 trillion as of the end of 2021. Globally, the estimated direct effect of a pandemic-induced economic slowdowns ranges from between 0.5 to 2.0 percent of global GDP. While harder to calculate, there were also increased indirect costs due to increased mortality and lost human capital.

To address these risks, the Budget includes transformative investments in pandemic preparedness. These investments are intended to reduce harm to lives and livelihoods. But they also could lead to better long-term economic and fiscal outcomes than if these investments were not made.

Healthcare Cost Growth.—Another significant source of uncertainty is healthcare cost growth. As noted above, the baseline projections follow the Medicare Trustees in assuming that, on average, Medicare per-beneficiary costs annually grow about 1.2 percentage points faster than GDP per capita ("excess cost growth") over the next 25 years, starting at high excess growth rates that steadily approach zero. A primary input to these projections is overall national health expenditures, the sum of all private and government health expenditures. In the past, especially prior to 1990, national health expenditures grew even more rapidly than the economy. For example, throughout the 1980s, national health per-beneficiary costs grew 3.1 percentage points faster than GDP per capita. However, on average since 2010, per-enrollee healthcare costs have grown roughly in line with GDP, with particularly slow growth in Federal health expenditures for Medicare and Medicaid.

Chart 3-5 shows the debt ratio in 25 years under different healthcare cost growth trajectories, reflecting the variability of recent trends in healthcare cost growth. If

[4] For more information, please see the "Analysis of Federal Climate Financial Risk Exposure" chapter of this volume.

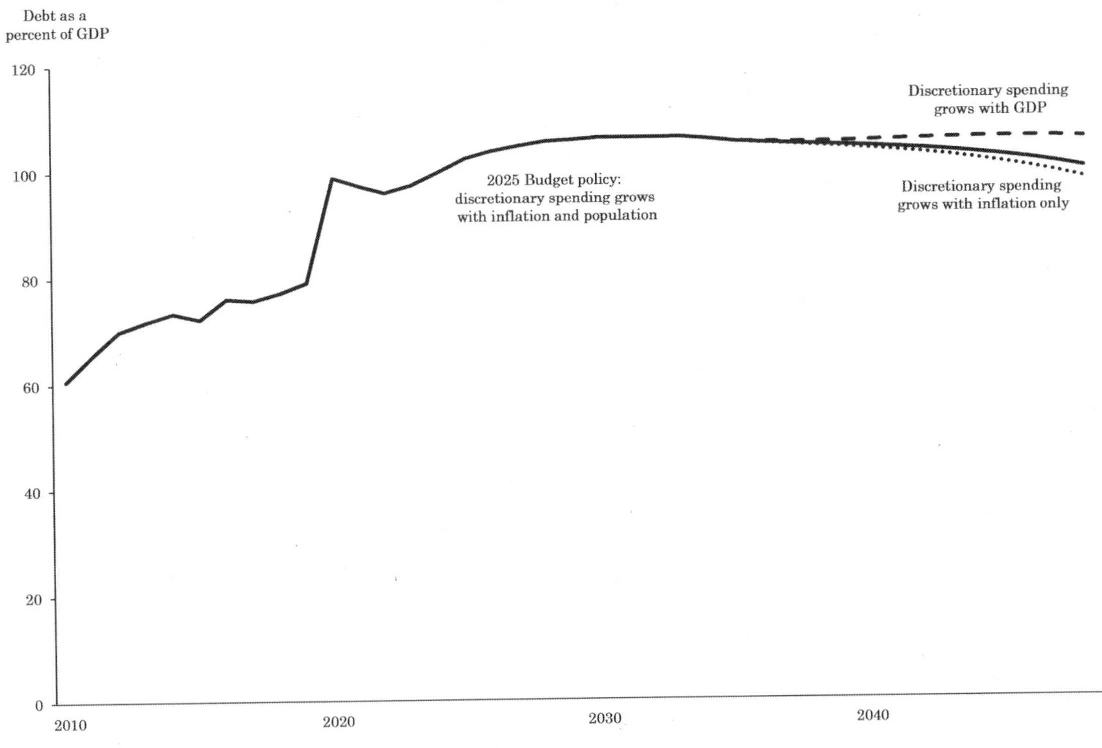

excess healthcare cost growth was 0.5 percentage point faster than the Medicare Trustees' projections, the debt ratio in 25 years would increase from 98.9 percent of GDP under the base case Budget policy to 105.6 percent of GDP, with larger deviations every year thereafter. In contrast, if excess healthcare cost growth was 0.5 percentage point slower than the Medicare Trustees' projections, the debt-to-GDP ratio would fall to 94.7 percent of GDP by the end of the 25-year period. This slower trajectory more closely aligns with recent trends.

Tax Policy.—Policy choices will also have a large impact on long-term budget deficits and debt, as evident from the discussion of the 2025 Budget proposals. Small permanent changes can have significant long-term impacts. In the base case policy projections, revenues gradually increase with rising real income, since real bracket creep—the change in average tax rates as taxpayers' incomes rise faster than tax bracket thresholds—increases individual income taxes as a share of GDP. If receipts remain a constant percent of GDP after the budget window, the debt ratio would be expected to increase compared with the base case.

Discretionary Growth Rates.—The base case policy projections for discretionary programs assume that after 2034, discretionary spending grows with inflation and population (see Chart 3-6). Alternative assumptions could include growing discretionary spending with GDP or with inflation only. At the end of the 25-year horizon, the debt ratio ranges from 96.6 percent of GDP in the inflation-only case to 105.3 percent of GDP in the GDP case, with the base case falling in the middle.

Interest Rates.—A final major source of uncertainty is interest rates. A rise in real interest rates would increase the burden of debt, forcing the Federal Government to raise additional revenue, reduce spending, or increase borrowing in order to pay off old debt. Over the last two decades, interest rate projections have been, on average, too high. Chart 3-7 shows the path of actual ten-year Treasury rates from 2000 to 2023, along with previous Administration forecasts for the ten-year Treasury rate. Chart 3-8 shows the equivalent chart for CBO forecasts. Table 2-5 of the "Economic Assumptions" chapter of this volume shows the average forecast errors in economic projections from past Federal budgets, CBO, and the Blue Chip panel of professional forecasters. On average, all three groups of forecasters have been about 0.6 percentage point too high in projecting the three-month Treasury rate two years into the future and about 2.1 percentage points too high projecting the same rate six years out.

The Administration's forecast for interest rates over the next decade show the ten-year Treasury note rate stabilizing to 3.7 percent in 2034. Beyond 2034, this chapter's projections assume interest rates stay constant at the 2034 level. If the actual interest rate path were lower, this would result in a lower debt-to-GDP ratio over the long run. Alternatively, as CBO projects, interest rates could continue to rise after the ten-year budget window, which would result in a higher debt-to-GDP ratio over the long run. While rates have risen recently, the Blue

Chart 3-7. Historical Values and Budget Projections for 10-Year Treasury Rates

Vintages of Budget projections for 10-year Treasury rates

Historical 10-year Treasury rates

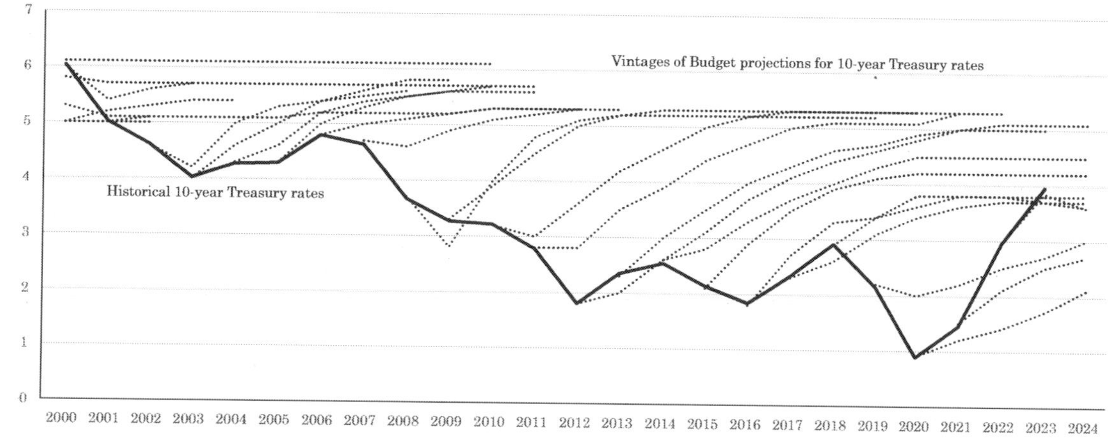

Chip panel of professional forecasters, as of October 2023, has a consensus forecast for the 2034 ten-year Treasury note rate of 3.5 percent, lower than the Administration's forecast.[5]

Actuarial Projections for Social Security and Medicare

While the Administration's long-run projections focus on the unified budget outlook, Social Security Old-Age and Survivors Insurance (OASI) and Disability Insurance (DI) and Medicare Hospital Insurance (HI) benefits are paid out of trust funds financed almost entirely by dedicated payroll tax revenues. Projected trust fund revenues plus current trust fund asset reserves fall short of the levels necessary to finance projected benefits scheduled in current law over the next 75 years.

[5] Long range projections of the Blue Chip panel are collected twice a year. As of the time of this writing, the October 2023 survey is the most current one available.

The Social Security and Medicare Trustees' reports feature the actuarial balance of the trust funds as a summary measure of their financial status. For each trust fund, the actuarial balance is calculated as the magnitude of change in receipts or program benefits (expressed as a percentage of taxable payroll) that would be needed to preserve a small positive balance in the trust fund at the end of a specified time period. The estimates cover periods ranging in length from 25 to 75 years.

Table 3-2 shows the projected income rate, cost rate, and annual balance for the Medicare HI and Social Security combined OASI and DI trust funds at selected dates under the Trustees' intermediate assumptions in the 2023 reports. There is a continued imbalance in the long-run projections of the HI program due to revenues that do not match costs over time. According to the 2023 Trustees' report, the HI trust fund reserves are projected to become depleted in 2031; in that year, dedicated revenues would be expected to be able to cover 89 percent of scheduled payments. The President's Budget includes

Table 3–2. INTERMEDIATE ACTUARIAL PROJECTIONS FOR OASDI AND HI, 2023 TRUSTEES' REPORTS

	2022	2023	2032	2040	2090
			Percent of Payroll		
Medicare Hospital Insurance (HI):					
Income Rate	3.4	3.4	3.7	3.8	4.4
Cost Rate	3.3	3.4	4.2	4.7	4.8
Annual Balance	0.1	0.0	–0.5	–0.9	–0.4
Projection Interval:			25 years	50 years	75 years
Actuarial Balance			–0.7	–0.7	–0.6
			Percent of Payroll		
Old Age Survivors and Disability Insurance (OASDI):					
Income Rate	12.7	13.3	13.2	13.3	13.4
Cost Rate	13.7	14.5	16.1	16.8	17.9
Annual Balance	–1.0	–1.2	–2.9	–3.5	–4.5
Projection Interval:			25 years	50 years	75 years
Actuarial Balance			–2.5	–3.2	–3.6

Chart 3-8. Historical Values and CBO Projections for 10-Year Treasury Rates

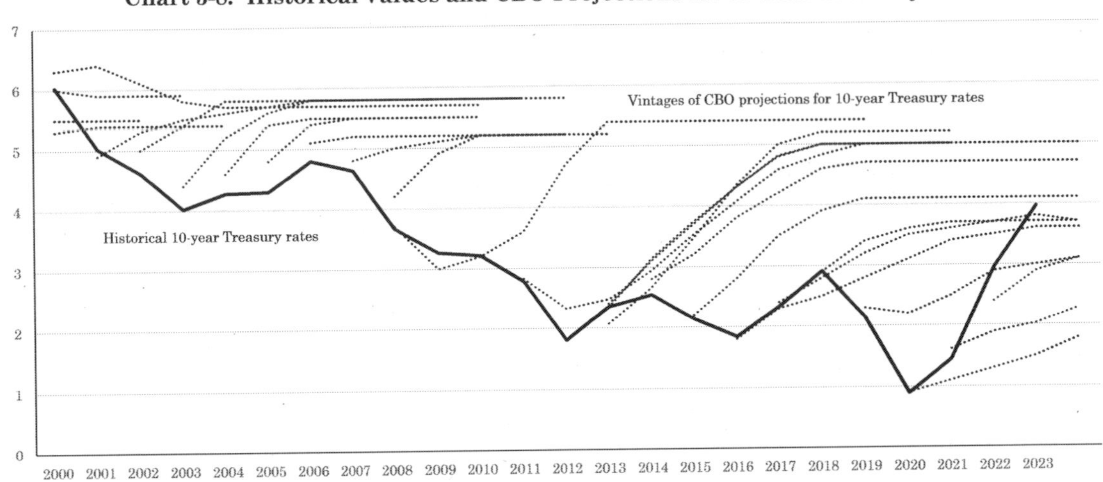

proposals that will extend the solvency of the Medicare trust fund indefinitely.

The 2023 Social Security Trustees' report projects that under current law, there is a long-term mismatch between program revenue and costs. Social Security is currently drawing on its trust fund reserves to cover the revenue shortfall. Over time, as the ratio of workers to retirees falls, costs are projected to rise further while revenues excluding interest are projected to rise less rapidly. In the process, the Social Security combined OASI and DI trust fund reserves, which were built up since 1983, would be drawn down and eventually become depleted in 2034, based on the projections in the 2023 report. At that point, the dedicated revenues could pay for 80 percent of program scheduled benefits for the rest of 2034, declining to 74 percent for 2097.

The long-term budget projections in this chapter assume that benefits would continue to be paid in full despite the projected depletion of the trust fund reserves through a hypothetical change in law that would provide general revenue transfers as needed.

TECHNICAL NOTE: SOURCES OF DATA AND METHODS OF ESTIMATING

The long-run budget projections are based on actuarial projections for Social Security and Medicare as well as demographic and economic assumptions. A simplified model of the Federal budget, developed at OMB, is used to compute the budgetary implications of these assumptions after the ten-year budget window.

Demographic and Economic Assumptions.—For the years 2024-2034, the assumptions are drawn from the Administration's economic projections used for the 2025 Budget. The economic assumptions are extended beyond this interval by holding the inflation rate, interest rates, and the unemployment rate constant at the levels assumed in the final year (2034) of the Budget forecast. Population growth and labor force growth are extended using the intermediate assumptions from the 2023 Social Security Trustees' report. The projected rate of growth for real GDP is built up from the labor force assumptions and an assumed rate of productivity growth. Productivity growth, measured as real GDP per hour, is assumed to equal its terminal annual rate of growth in the Budget's economic assumptions: 1.7 percent per year.

The CPI inflation rate is held constant at 2.3 percent per year, the unemployment rate is held constant at 3.8 percent, the yield to maturity on ten-year Treasury notes is held constant at 3.7 percent, and the 91-day Treasury bill rate is held constant at 2.7 percent. Consistent with the demographic assumptions in the Trustees' report, U.S. population growth slows slightly from an average of about 0.5 percent per year during the budget window to about three-quarters of that rate by the end of the 25-year projection period. Real GDP growth is projected to be less than its historical average of around 2.5 percent per year, because the slowdown in population growth and the increase in the population over age 65 reduce labor supply growth. In these projections, real GDP growth averages 2.1 percent per year for the period following the end of the ten-year budget window. The economic and demographic projections described above are set exogenously and do not change in response to changes in the budget outlook across the alternate scenarios presented in this chapter.

Baseline Projections.—For the period through 2034, receipts and outlays in the baseline and policy projections follow the 2025 Budget's baseline and policy estimates respectively. Outside the budget window, discretionary spending grows at the rate of inflation and population growth. Long-run Social Security spending is projected by the Social Security actuaries using this chapter's long-run economic and demographic assumptions. Medicare benefits follow a projection of beneficiary growth and excess healthcare cost growth from the 2023 Medicare Trustees' report current law baseline. Excess cost growth for private health insurance is assumed to grow at a rate that averages the excess cost growth assumed in the Medicare actuarial assumptions and provided in their Illustrative Alternative. In these projections, private health insurance excess cost growth averages 0.9 percent after 2034. Medicaid outlays are based on the economic and demographic projections in the model, which assume average excess cost growth of approximately 0.7 percentage point above growth in GDP per capita after 2034. Other entitlement programs are projected based on rules of thumb linking program spending to elements of the economic and demographic projections such as the poverty rate. Individual income tax revenues are projected using a microsimulation model that incorporates real bracket creep. Corporate tax and other receipts are projected to grow with GDP.

SPECIAL ANALYSES AND PRESENTATIONS

4. BUDGET PROCESS

This chapter addresses several broad categories of budget process—the budget enforcement framework and related proposals, presentation, and reforms issues. First, the chapter provides a recent history on budget enforcement and discusses related proposals. The proposals and discussions include: an explanation of the discretionary levels in the 2025 Budget; adjustments to base discretionary levels including program integrity initiatives, funding requests for disaster relief and wildfire suppression; limits on advance appropriations; the proposals and explanations supporting veterans medical care and the Cost of War Toxic Exposures Fund; a discussion of the system under the Statutory Pay-As-You-Go Act of 2010 (PAYGO) of scoring legislation affecting receipts and mandatory spending; and an extension of the spending reductions required by Section 251A of the Balanced Budget and Emergency Deficit Reduction Act (BBEDCA).

Second, this chapter describes adjustments and proposals in budget presentation. The Budget Presentation section begins with a discussion about adjustments to the BBEDCA baseline which provide for a more accurate reflection of the Administration's 2025 policy choices. It then discusses two proposed reclassifications--Contract Support Costs (CSCs) and Payments for Tribal Leases accounts in the Department of the Interior's Bureau of Indian Affairs and the Department of Health and Human Services' (HHS's) Indian Health Service (IHS), and the Survey and Certification program at the Centers for Medicare and Medicaid Services at HHS, both beginning in 2026; the Pell Grant program; a discussion of the budgetary presentation of the proposal to extend the United States' participation in the International Monetary Fund, a discussion of how BBEDCA Section 251A sequestration is shown in the Budget; and the budgetary treatment of the housing Government-sponsored enterprises and the United States Postal Service.

Third, this chapter describes reform proposals to improve budgeting with respect to individual programs as well as across Government. These proposals include: changes to capital budgeting for large civilian Federal capital projects; protections for the rental payments made to the Federal Buildings Fund by Federal agencies; reclassifying funding for the Indian Health Service at HHS; and a discussion related to the timing of the release of the President's Budget.

I. BUDGET ENFORCEMENT FRAMEWORK AND PROPOSALS

History of Recent Budget Enforcement

The Federal Government uses statutory budget enforcement mechanisms to control revenues, spending, and deficits. The Statutory Pay-As-You-Go Act of 2010, enacted on February 12, 2010, reestablished a statutory procedure to enforce a rule of deficit neutrality on new revenue and mandatory spending legislation. Most recently, the Fiscal Responsibility Act of 2023 (FRA; Public Law 118-5), enacted on June 3, 2023, amended BBEDCA by reinstating limits ("caps") on the amount of discretionary budget authority that could be provided through the annual appropriations process for fiscal years 2024 and 2025. Prior to the FRA, the Budget Control Act of 2011 (BCA; Public Law 112-25), enacted on August 2, 2011, included caps for the years 2012 through 2021. Similar enforcement mechanisms were established by the Budget Enforcement Act of 1990 and were extended in 1993 and 1997, but expired at the end of 2002. The BCA also created a Joint Select Committee on Deficit Reduction that was instructed to develop a bill to reduce the Federal deficit by at least $1.5 trillion over a 10-year period, and imposed automatic spending cuts to achieve $1.2 trillion of deficit reduction over nine years after the Joint Committee process failed to achieve its deficit reduction goal.

The original enforcement mechanisms established by the BCA—the caps on spending in annual appropriations and instructions to calculate reductions to achieve the $1.2 trillion deficit reduction goal—expired at the end of fiscal year 2021, although the sequestration of mandatory spending has been extended through 2031 for most programs and the first month of 2033 for Medicare. Prior to the expiration of the BCA, the discretionary limits were revised upward a number of times, with changes usually occurring in the form of two-year budget agreements: the 2014 and 2015 limits were revised by the Bipartisan Budget Act of 2013 (BBA of 2013; Public Law 113-67); the 2016 and 2017 limits were revised by the Bipartisan Budget Act of 2015 (BBA of 2015; Public Law 114-74); the 2018 and 2019 limits were revised by the Bipartisan Budget Act of 2018 (BBA of 2018; Public Law 115-123); the 2020 and 2021 limits were revised by the Bipartisan Budget Act of 2019 (BBA of 2019; Public Law 116-37); and most recently, limits were reinstated for 2024 and 2025 by the FRA.

The threat of sequestration if the limits were breached, and the ability to adjust the limits for certain types of spending, proved sufficient to ensure compliance with these statutorily adjusted discretionary spending caps. When limits are in place, BBEDCA has required OMB to adjust them each year for: changes in concepts and definitions; appropriations designated by the Congress and the President as emergency requirements; and appropriations designated by the Congress and the President for Overseas Contingency Operations/Global War on

Terrorism (OCO/GWOT). BBEDCA also specifies cap adjustments (which are limited to fixed amounts) for: appropriations for continuing disability reviews and redeterminations by the Social Security Administration and specified program integrity and anti-fraud activities; the healthcare fraud and abuse control program at HHS; appropriations designated by the Congress as being for disaster relief; appropriations for reemployment services and eligibility assessments; appropriations for wildfire suppression at the Department of Agriculture and the Department of the Interior; and, for 2020 only, appropriations provided for the 2020 Census at the Department of Commerce.

Separate from the above adjustments, the FRA specified that certain previously-enacted discretionary funding that continues under current law would not be counted for purposes of budget enforcement under the discretionary limits. This includes emergency-designated funding enacted in the Bipartisan Safer Communities Act (Public Law 117-159), the Infrastructure Investment and Jobs Act (Public Law 117-58), and section 443(b) of division G of the Consolidated Appropriations Act, 2023 (Public Law 117-328). Because this funding was enacted during a period of time when statutory limits were not in place, the FRA addressed spending on these programs by directing it be treated as not being within the BBEDCA limits, including those established for 2024 and 2025 by the FRA, or as any adjustments allowed under BBEDCA. This funding is reflected in the 2025 Budget at the enacted levels, but is not counted under the statutory limits. In addition, section 101 of the Water Resources Development Act of 2020 (division AA of Public Law 116-260) exempts from budget enforcement appropriations from the Harbor Maintenance Trust Fund and appropriations designated in statute for carrying out section 2106(c) of Public Law 113-121, which includes amounts for environmental remediation at ports. Finally, the 21st Century Cures Act (Public Law 114-255) directed that funds appropriated for certain activities cannot be counted for purposes of budget enforcement so long as the appropriations were specifically provided for the authorized purposes. As a result of these statutory exemptions, each of these amounts are displayed outside of the discretionary totals in Budget tables and OMB reports.

The FRA also created alternative interim discretionary spending limits which are applicable if any discretionary appropriation account is under a short-term continuing-resolution (CR) as of January 1, 2024, for fiscal year 2024, and January 1, 2025, for fiscal year 2025. In both cases, the defense and non-defense spending levels adjust to the interim limits, which are only in place until passage of all full-year appropriations bills. Budget enforcement, through the sequestration of the amounts exceeding the interim limits, if any, would go into effect on April 30 of the respective year if passage of all full-year appropriations bills has not occurred. These interim limits are meant to encourage passage of all full-year appropriations bills in a timely manner.

Discretionary Spending Levels

The 2025 Budget builds on the success of the Administration's previous Budgets by requesting funding levels that are sufficient to protect veterans, provide for a robust national defense, and continue to build the Nation's human and physical capital through non-defense discretionary spending. The Administration intends to continue working with the Congress on reinvesting in research, education, public health, and other core functions of Government. The Budget reflects discretionary funding levels that adhere to the discretionary spending limits enacted in the FRA for 2025 while allowing for adjustments to those levels above base activities, for activities including program integrity, disaster relief, and wildfire suppression and emergency requirements. In addition, the Budget highlights veterans' healthcare by carving out the Department of Veterans Affairs (VA) medical care program starting in 2026 to ensure the Nation meets its commitments to veterans while also providing the Congress with the appropriate tools for oversight, independent of other discretionary spending.

For base defense programs, the 2025 Budget proposes a level of $895.2 billion, in line with the discretionary spending limit enacted in the FRA. The amounts in the 2025 Budget are in line with the National Security and National Defense strategies and the Department of Defense Future Years Defense Program, which includes a five-year appropriations plan and estimated expenditures necessary to support the programs, projects, and activities of the Department of Defense. After 2029, the Budget reflects outyear growth rates consistent with prior President's Budgets.

For non-defense, the 2025 Budget requests appropriations at $710.7 billion, consistent with the discretionary spending limit enacted in the FRA. The Budget also includes $23.2 billion in funding for base activities that is designated as emergency requirements. This "shifted base" funding concept was included in 2023 appropriations and was also part of a broader FRA agreement to provide additional resources for non-defense activities above the FRA cap. Non-defense receives current services growth in all years after 2025, with limited exceptions as described below.

The 2025 Budget requests $112.6 billion for the Veterans Affairs (VA) medical care programs in 2025, and again proposes, beginning in 2026, for this program to be budgeted as its own category of spending separate from the rest of discretionary spending. The VA medical care program is budgeted for $131.4 billion in 2026 and grows at the current services level subsequently. The program and approach are discussed in more detail below.

The discretionary policy levels are reflected in Table S–7 of the main *Budget* volume. The proposed adjustments to the base appropriations levels and the approach to VA medical care and the Cost of War Toxic Exposures Fund and are described below.

ADJUSTMENTS TO BASE DISCRETIONARY FUNDING LEVELS

Program Integrity Funding

There is compelling evidence that investments in administrative resources can significantly decrease the rate of improper payments and recoup many times their initial investment for certain programs. In such programs, using adjustments to base discretionary funding for program integrity activities allows for the expansion of oversight and enforcement activities in the largest benefit programs including Social Security, Unemployment Insurance, Medicare and Medicaid. In such cases, where return on investment using discretionary dollars is proven, adjustments to base discretionary funding are a useful budgeting tool. Formerly, when statutory spending limits on the discretionary budget were in place under the BCA, the law allowed the limits to be adjusted upward to account for additional discretionary funding that supported savings in these mandatory programs. The FRA continues these adjustments for 2024 and 2025. Such adjustments are needed because budget scoring rules do not allow the mandatory savings from these initiatives to be credited for budget enforcement purposes.

The Administration continues to support making discretionary investments in program integrity activities and keeps the same structure in place in the FRA by supporting base levels sufficient to receive an adjustment under the new limits. The outyears continue to assume the base and adjustment funding amounts extend through 2034 at the rate of inflation assumed in the 2025 Budget for the amounts dedicated to Medicare savings. Funding for the Unemployment Insurance program adopts the outyear levels adopted in the BBA of 2018 through 2027, then allows the amounts to grow with inflation through the Budget window. For Social Security the requested funding stream in the outyears reflects a full complement of program integrity activities described below.

The Budget shows the mandatory program savings derived from 10 years of discretionary program integrity funding separately in an adjustment to the baseline projections for spending in Social Security, Unemployment Insurance, Medicare, and Medicaid. This separation allows the Administration to clearly show the effects of the savings from these proposed discretionary program integrity amounts that receive special budgetary treatment, while recognizing the savings in these mandatory programs has been a historical and consistent part of program operations.

The following sections explain the benefits and budget presentation of the proposed level of adjustments to base discretionary funding for program integrity activities.

Social Security Administration (SSA) Dedicated Program Integrity Activities.—SSA takes seriously its responsibilities to ensure eligible individuals receive the benefits to which they are entitled, and to safeguard the integrity of benefit programs to better serve recipients. The Budget's proposed discretionary amount of $1,903 million ($273 million in base funding and $1,630 million in cap adjustment funding) is consistent with the adjustment amount specified in BBEDCA, as amended by the FRA. This level will allow SSA to conduct 575,000 full medical continuing disability reviews (CDRs) and approximately 2.5 million Supplemental Security Income (SSI) non-medical redeterminations of eligibility. SSA conducts medical CDRs, which are periodic reevaluations to determine whether disabled Old-Age, Survivors, and Disability Insurance (OASDI) or SSI beneficiaries continue to meet SSA's standards for disability. Redeterminations are periodic reviews of non-medical eligibility factors, such as income and resources, for the means-tested SSI program and can result in a revision of the individual's benefit level. Program integrity funds also support the anti-fraud cooperative disability investigation (CDI) units and special attorneys for fraud prosecutions. To support these important anti-fraud activities, the Budget provides for SSA to transfer $19.6 million to the SSA Office of Inspector General to fund CDI unit activities.

The Budget includes a discretionary cap adjustment for 2025 at the FRA level, and assumes continued funding of these activities through the remainder of the budget window. As a result of the discretionary funding requested in 2025, as well as the fully-funded base and continued funding of adjustment amounts in 2026 through 2034, the OASDI, SSI, Medicare and Medicaid programs would recoup approximately $82 billion in gross Federal savings, including approximately $60 billion from access to adjustments, with additional savings after the 10-year period, according to estimates from SSA's Office of the Chief Actuary and the Centers for Medicare and Medicaid Services' Office of the Actuary. Access to increased adjustment amounts and SSA's commitment to fund the fully-loaded costs of performing the requested CDR and redetermination volumes would produce net deficit savings of approximately $41 billion in the 10-year window, and provide additional savings in the outyears. These costs and savings are reflected in Table 4-1.

SSA is required by law to conduct medical CDRs for all beneficiaries who are receiving disability benefits under the OASDI program, as well as all children under age 18 who are receiving SSI. Per the agency's regulations to create uniformity across programs, SSA conducts medical CDRS for disabled adult SSI recipients. SSI redeterminations are also required by law. SSA uses predictive models to prioritize the completion of redeterminations based on the likelihood of change in non-medical factors. The frequency of CDRs and redeterminations relies on the availability of funds to support these activities. The mandatory savings from the base funding in every year and the 2024 discretionary cap adjustment funding authorized in the FRA are included in the baseline, as the baseline assumes the continued funding of program integrity activities. The Budget shows the savings that would result from the increase in CDRs and redeterminations made possible by the discretionary cap adjustment funding requested in 2025, and continued through 2034 as an adjustment to the baseline. These amounts fully support the dedicated program integrity workloads. With access to the proposed funding, SSA is on track to regain curren-

Table 4–1. PROGRAM INTEGRITY DISCRETIONARY ADJUSTMENTS AND MANDATORY SAVINGS

(Budget authority and outlays in millions of dollars)

	2025	2026	2027	2029	2029	2030	2031	2032	2033	2034	10-year Total
Social Security Administration (SSA) Program Integrity:											
Discretionary Budget Authority (non add) [1]	*1,630*	*1,749*	*1,777*	*1,747*	*1,851*	*1,930*	*1,956*	*1,993*	*2,052*	*2,104*	*18,789*
Discretionary Outlays [1]	1,630	1,746	1,776	1,748	1,848	1,928	1,955	1,992	2,051	2,102	18,776
Mandatory Savings [2]	–15	–2,216	–3,678	–5,023	–5,450	–6,734	–7,711	–8,635	–9,964	–10,375	–59,801
Net Savings	1,615	–470	–1,902	–3,275	–3,602	–4,806	–5,756	–6,643	–7,913	–8,273	–41,025
Health Care Fraud and Abuse Control Program:											
Discretionary Budget Authority (non add) [1]	*630*	*649*	*668*	*688*	*709*	*730*	*752*	*775*	*798*	*822*	*7,221*
Discretionary Outlays [1]	442	602	622	640	659	679	700	721	742	765	6,572
Mandatory Savings [2,3]	–1,215	–1,287	–1,362	–1,441	–1,485	–1,529	–1,575	–1,623	–1,671	–1,722	–14,910
Net Savings	–773	–685	–740	–801	–826	–850	–875	–902	–929	–957	–8,338
Unemployment Insurance (UI) Program Integrity:											
Discretionary Budget Authority (non add) [1]	*271*	*608*	*633*	*648*	*662*	*678*	*693*	*709*	*726*	*742*	*6,370*
Discretionary Outlays [1]	270	592	631	648	661	677	692	709	725	741	6,346
Mandatory Savings [2]	–388	–741	–768	–779	–789	–810	–826	–845	–861	–883	–7,690
Net Savings	–118	–149	–137	–131	–128	–133	–134	–136	–136	–142	–1,344

[1] The discretionary costs are equal to the outlays associated with the budget authority levels proposed for adjustments to the non-defense discretionary levels in the 2025 Budget. For SSA, the costs for 2025 through 2034 reflect the costs to complete the anticipated dedicated program integrity workloads for SSA; for HCFAC the costs for each of 2025 through 2034 are equal to the outlays associated with the budget authority levels inflated from the 2025 level for HCFAC, using the 2025 Budget assumptions. The UI discretionary costs for 2025 through 2027 are equal to outlays from the budget authority amounts authorized for congressional enforcement, while the outlays from the remaining years are from the budget authority inflated off of the 2027 level.

[2] The mandatory savings from the discretionary adjustment funding are included as proposals in the Budget and displayed as savings in the Social Security, Medicare, Medicaid, and UI programs. For SSA, adjustment savings amounts are based on SSA's Office of the Chief Actuary's and the Centers for Medicare and Medicaid Services' Office of the Actuary's estimates of savings. For UI, amounts are based on the Department of Labor's Division of Fiscal and Actuarial Services' estimates of savings.

[3] These savings are based on estimates from the HHS Office of the Actuary for return on investment (ROI) from program integrity activities.

cy in its CDR workload in 2026 and prevent new backlogs from forming throughout the budget window.

Current estimates indicate that CDRs conducted in 2025 will yield a return on investment (ROI) of about $9 on average in net Federal program savings over 10 years per $1 budgeted for dedicated program integrity funding, including OASDI, SSI, Medicare and Medicaid program effects. Similarly, SSA estimates indicate that non-medical redeterminations conducted in 2025 will yield a ROI of about $3 on average of net Federal program savings over 10 years per $1 budgeted for dedicated program integrity funding, including SSI and Medicaid program effects. The Budget assumes the full cost of performing CDRs to ensure that sufficient resources are available. The savings from one year of program integrity activities are realized over multiple years, as some reviews find that beneficiaries are no longer eligible to receive OASDI or SSI benefits.

The savings resulting from redeterminations will be different for the base funding and the allocation adjustment funding levels in 2025 through 2034 because redeterminations of eligibility can uncover both underpayment and overpayment errors. SSI recipients are more likely to initiate a redetermination of eligibility if they believe there are underpayments, and these recipient-initiated redeterminations are included in the base program amounts provided annually. The estimated savings per dollar budgeted for CDRs and non-medical redeterminations in the baseline reflects an interaction with the Affordable Care Act's expansion of Medicaid to additional low-income adults, as a result of which some SSI recipients, who would otherwise lose Medicaid coverage due to a medical CDR or non-medical redetermination, would continue to be covered.

Health Care Fraud and Abuse Control Program (HCFAC).—The Budget proposes base and adjustment funding levels over the next 10 years growing at the rate of inflation in the Budget. The discretionary base funding of $311 million and adjustment of $630 million for HCFAC activities in 2025 includes funding to invest in additional Medicare medical review; strengthen program integrity in Medicare Part C and Part D; support Medicaid systems; and measure improper payments in the Health Insurance Marketplaces. The funding is to be allocated among the Centers for Medicare & Medicaid Services (CMS), the HHS Office of Inspector General, and the Department of Justice.

Over 2025 through 2034, as reflected in Table 4-1, this $7.2 billion investment in HCFAC adjustment funding will generate approximately $14.9 billion in savings to Medicare and Medicaid. This results in net deficit reduction of $8.3 billion over the 10-year period, reflecting prevention and recoupment of improper payments made to providers, as well as recoveries related to civil and criminal penalties. For HCFAC program integrity efforts, CMS actuaries conservatively estimate at least $2 is saved or averted for every additional $1 spent.

Reemployment Services and Eligibility Assessments (RESEA).—The BBA of 2018 established a new adjustment to discretionary base funding for program integrity efforts targeted at Unemployment Insurance through 2027. The RESEA adjustment is permitted up to a maximum amount specified in the law if the underlying appropriations bill first funds a base level of $117 million for Unemployment Insurance program integrity activities. The Budget proposes cap adjustment levels at the same amount enacted in the FRA with outyears at the levels enacted in the BBA, as amended. Program integrity funding in 2028 through 2034 continues to rise by the rate of inflation estimated in the Budget. Table 4-1 shows the mandatory savings of $7.7 billion over 10 years, which includes an estimated $165 million reduction in State unemployment taxes. When netted against the discretionary costs for the cap adjustment funding, the 10-year net savings for the program is $1.3 billion.

Internal Revenue Service, Significant Returns on Investment from Extending Inflation Reduction Act Funding.—The 2025 Budget continues the Administration's commitment to ensuring that IRS tax administration is fair, equitable, and remains focused on the core function of collecting taxes in a democracy by maintaining base discretionary funding while also proposing to maintain and extend the mandatory funding provided by the Inflation Reduction Act of 2022 (IRA, Public Law 117-169). The IRA supplemented base IRS funding by providing significant increases that are allowing the IRS to dramatically improve customer service, modernize decades-old computer systems, and improve enforcement with respect to complex partnerships, large corporations, and high-income individuals.

The estimates of enforcement revenue generated by IRA funding, which are included in the revenue estimates in the 2025 Budget, are based on traditional modeling of revenues directly resulting from increased enforcement staffing. This approach ignores many activities that will influence revenue, including enhancing services to improve voluntary compliance, modernizing technology, and adopting analytic advances that can dramatically improve productivity. The current approach also ignores the deterrence effect of compliance activities on taxpayers' behavior. The Budget reflects $498 billion in enforcement revenue associated with IRA-funded initiatives, assuming enactment of proposed mandatory funding to continue those initiatives through 2034.

A comprehensive analytical approach that emphasizes efficiency gains, information technology and analytical advancements, service, and compliance through deterrence as key revenue drivers would more fully capture the revenue impact of IRS activities. This approach would potentially yield an additional $353 billion in revenue from existing and proposed funding over the 10-year budget window, as documented by the IRS in its recent white paper: Return on Investment: Re-Examining Revenue Estimates for IRS Funding (*www.irs.gov/pub/irs-pdf/p5901.pdf*). The scorekeeping guidelines and concepts governing the budget process that are used by the Executive and Legislative Branch require that such effects be direct and well-documented in order to be recorded as part of the Administration's baseline estimates of tax revenues. The estimation methodology for enforcement revenue will evolve over time as additional data are collected and studied.

Disaster Relief Funding

The 2025 Budget maintains the same methodology for determining the funding ceiling for disaster relief used in previous budgets and adopted in the FRA. For the 2025 Budget, OMB estimates the total adjustment available for disaster funding for 2025 at $23.2 billion. This ceiling estimate is based on three components: a 10-year average of disaster relief funding provided in prior years that excludes the highest and lowest years ($13.6); 5 percent of Robert T. Stafford Disaster Relief and Emergency Assistance Act (Stafford Act) amounts designated as emergency requirements since 2012 ($9.3 billion); and carryover from the previous year ($0.3 billion). For the 10-year average, an enacted level of $20.1 billion is assumed for 2024, which is the level provided in the Continuing Appropriations Act, 2024 (division A of Public Law 118-15; the "2024 CR"). Although the final enacted level may be $0.3 billion higher in compliance with the disaster ceiling for 2024 when 2024 is completed, the formula must assume the current-law level at this time. In addition, the estimate of emergency requirements for Stafford Act activities is updated based on applicable amounts provided for 2024 in the 2024 CR. For 2025, the Administration is requesting $22.7 billion in funding for the Federal Emergency Management Agency's (FEMA) Disaster Relief Program, of which approximately $1 billion will go towards Building Resilient Infrastructure and Communities (BRIC), and nearly $0.5 billion for the Small Business Administration's Disaster Loans Program. The request covers the costs of Presidentially-declared major disasters, including identified costs for previously declared catastrophic events and the estimated annual cost of non-catastrophic events expected to be obligated in 2025.

Consistent with past practice, the 2025 request level does not seek to pre-fund anticipated needs in other programs that may arise out of disasters that have yet to occur. After 2025, the Administration does not have adequate information about known or future requirements necessary to estimate the total amount that will be requested in future years. Accordingly, the Budget does not explicitly request any disaster relief funding in any year after the budget year and includes a placeholder in each of the outyears that is equal to the 10-year average ($13.6 billion) of disaster relief currently estimated under the formula for the 2025 ceiling. This funding level does not reflect a specific request but a placeholder amount that, along with other outyear appropriations levels, will be decided on an annual basis as part of the normal budget development process.

Wildfire Suppression Operations at the Departments of Agriculture and the Interior

Wildfires naturally occur on public lands throughout the United States. The cost of fighting wildfires has increased due to landscape conditions resulting from drought, pest and disease damage, overgrown forests, expanding residential and commercial development near the borders of public lands, and program management decisions. In the past, when these costs exceeded the funds appropriated, the Federal Government covered the shortfall through transfers from other land management programs. For example, in 2018, Forest Service wildfire suppression spending of $2.6 billion required transfers of $720 million from other non-fire programs. Historically, these transfers had been repaid in subsequent appropriations; however, such "fire borrowing" impedes the missions of land management agencies to reduce the risk of catastrophic fire and restore and maintain healthy functioning ecosystems.

To create funding certainty in times of wildfire disasters, the Consolidated Appropriations Act of 2018 enacted a new cap adjustment to BBEDCA, which began in 2020. This adjustment has been used since that time, and the Administration proposes continuing this adjustment in the Budget. The adjustment is permitted so long as a base level of funding for wildfire suppression operations is funded in the underlying appropriations bill. The base level is defined as being equal to average cost over 10 years for wildfire suppression operations that was requested in the President's 2015 Budget. These amounts have been determined to be $1,011 million for the Department of Agriculture's Forest Service and $384 million for the Department of the Interior (DOI). The 2025 Budget requests these base amounts for wildfire suppression and proposes the full $2,750 million adjustment specified in BBEDCA, as amended, for 2025, with $2,390 million included for Forest Service and $360 million included for DOI. Providing the full level will ensure that adequate resources are available to fight wildland fires, protect communities, and safeguard human life during the most severe wildland fire seasons.

For the years after 2025, the Administration does not have sufficient information about future wildfire suppression needs and, therefore, includes a placeholder in the 2025 Budget for wildfire suppression in each of the outyears that is equal to the current 2025 request. Actual funding levels, up to but not exceeding the authorized funding adjustments, will be decided on an annual basis as part of the normal budget process.

Limit on Discretionary Advance Appropriations

An advance appropriation first becomes available for obligation one or more fiscal years beyond the year for which the appropriations act is passed. Budget authority is recorded in the year the funds become available for obligation, not in the year the appropriation is enacted.

There are legitimate policy reasons to use advance appropriations to fund programs. For example, some education grants are forward funded (available beginning July 1 of the fiscal year) to provide certainty of funding for an entire school year, since school years straddle Federal fiscal years. This funding is recorded in the budget year because the funding is first legally available in that fiscal year. However, $22.6 billion of this education funding is advance appropriated (available beginning three months later, on October 1) rather than forward funded. Prior Congresses increased advance appropriations and decreased the amounts of forward funding as a gimmick to free up room in the budget year without affecting the total amount available for a coming school year. This approach works because the advance appropriation is not recorded in the budget year but rather the following fiscal year. However, it works only in the year in which funds switch from forward funding to advance appropriations; that is, it works only in years in which the amounts of advance appropriations for such "straddle" programs are increased.

To curtail this approach, which allows over-budget funding in the budget year and exerts pressure for increased funding in future years, congressional budget resolutions since 2001 have set limits on the amount of discretionary advance appropriations and the accounts which can receive them. By freezing the amount that had been advance appropriated to these accounts at the level provided in the most recent appropriations bill, additional room within discretionary spending limits cannot be created by shifting additional funds to future fiscal years.

The 2025 Budget requests $28,768 million in advance appropriations for 2026, consistent with limits established in recent congressional budget resolutions, and freezes them at this level in subsequent years. Outside of these limits, the Administration's Budget would request discretionary advance appropriations for veterans medical care, as is required by the Veterans Health Care Budget Reform and Transparency Act (Public Law 111-81). The Department of Veterans Affairs has included detailed information in its Congressional Budget Justifications about the overall 2026 veterans medical care funding request.

For a detailed table of accounts that have received discretionary and mandatory advance appropriations since 2023 or for which the Budget requests advance appropriations for 2026 and beyond, please refer to the Advance Appropriations chapter in the *Appendix*.

Veterans Affairs (VA) Category and the Cost of War Toxic Exposures Fund

Starting in 2026, the Budget separates VA medical care as a third category within the discretionary budget based on a recognition that VA medical care has grown much more rapidly than other discretionary spending over time, largely due to systemwide growth in healthcare costs. Additionally, the enactment of the Sergeant First Class Heath Robinson Honoring our Promise to Address Comprehensive Toxics Act of 2022, or the Honoring our PACT Act of 2022, (Public Law 117-168; "PACT Act") created the Cost of War Toxic Exposures Fund (TEF) to ensure that there is sufficient funding available to cover costs associated with providing healthcare and benefits to veterans exposed to environmental hazards, without shortchanging other elements of veteran care and services.

Veterans Affairs Medical Care Program, Third Category. The 2025 Budget adheres to the discretionary limits enacted in the FRA for 2025, which include $112.6 billion in advance appropriations provided for discretionary medical care services in the 2024 Budget. Starting in 2026, the Budget provides $131.4 billion for discretionary medical care services and proposes such spending be treated as a third category of discretionary spending, alongside the Defense Category and the Non-Defense Category. The Administration's proposal to create a third category of discretionary spending will allow the Congress to consider the funding needs for veterans' healthcare holistically, taking into account both discretionary and mandatory funding streams. Setting a separate budget allocation for VA medical care accomplishes two important goals. First, it helps ensure adequate funding for veterans' healthcare without adversely impacting other critical programs, whether inside or outside of VA. Second, it also ensures that other critical priorities--both defense and non-defense--will not adversely impact veterans' healthcare.

Cost of War Toxic Exposures Fund. The PACT Act authorized the TEF to fund the incremental costs above 2021 for healthcare associated with environmental hazards and for any expenses incident to the delivery of healthcare and benefits associated with exposure to environmental hazards, as well as medical research relating to exposure to environmental hazards. Consistent with the law, the Administration limited the TEF request to those increases only and excluded costs not associated with exposure to environmental hazards.[1] The PACT Act directs the TEF appropriations to be mandatory funding requiring an annual appropriation, similar to the Medicaid and Supplemental Nutrition Assistance programs. The FRA appropriated funding for the TEF in 2024, along with $24.5 billion in 2025. Since the TEF will require annual appropriations starting in 2026, the 2025 Budget includes an advance appropriation for TEF of $22.8 billion in 2026 for medical care to align with the advance discretionary request for 2026 medical care. Overall, the mandatory baseline reflects the estimates of TEF funding for the next 10 years, consistent with the baseline rules for mandatory funding.

Statutory PAYGO

The Statutory Pay-As-You-Go Act of 2010 (PAYGO Act; Public Law 111-139) requires that new legislation changing mandatory spending or revenue must be enacted on a "pay-as-you-go" (PAYGO) basis; that is, that the cumulative effects of such legislation must not increase projected on-budget deficits. PAYGO is a permanent requirement, and it does not impose a cap on spending or a floor on revenues. Instead, PAYGO requires that legislation reducing revenues must be fully offset by cuts in mandatory programs or by revenue increases, and that any bills increasing mandatory spending must be fully offset by revenue increases or cuts in mandatory spending.

This requirement of deficit neutrality is not enforced on a bill-by-bill basis, but is based on two scorecards maintained by OMB that tally the cumulative budgetary effects of PAYGO legislation as averaged over rolling 5- and 10-year periods, starting with the budget year. Any impacts of PAYGO legislation on the current year deficit are counted as budget year impacts when placed on the scorecard. PAYGO is enforced by sequestration. Within 14 business days after a congressional session ends, OMB issues an annual PAYGO report. If either the 5- or 10-year scorecard shows net costs in the budget year column, the President is required to issue a sequestration order implementing across-the-board cuts to nonexempt mandatory programs by an amount sufficient to offset those net costs. The list of exempt programs and special sequestration rules for certain programs are contained in sections 255 and 256 of BBEDCA.

The PAYGO effects of legislation may be directed in legislation by reference to statements inserted into the *Congressional Record* by the chair of the House and Senate Budget Committees. Any such estimates are determined by the Budget Committees and are informed by, but not required to match, the cost estimates prepared by the Congressional Budget Office (CBO). If this procedure is not followed, then the PAYGO effects of the legislation are determined by OMB. Provisions of mandatory spending or receipts legislation that are designated in that legislation as an emergency requirement are not scored as PAYGO budgetary effects.

The PAYGO rules apply to the outlays resulting from outyear changes in mandatory programs made in appropriations acts and to all revenue changes made in appropriations acts. However, outyear changes to mandatory programs made in appropriations acts as part of provisions that have zero net outlay effects over the sum of the current year and the next five fiscal years are not considered under the PAYGO rules.

The PAYGO rules do not apply to increases in mandatory spending or decreases in receipts that result automatically under existing law. For example, mandatory spending for benefit programs, such as unemployment insurance, rises when the number of beneficiaries rises, and many benefit payments are automatically increased for inflation under existing laws.

Changes to off-budget programs (Social Security and the Postal Service) do not have budgetary effects for the purposes of PAYGO and are not counted, though they may have a real effect on the deficit. Provisions designated by the Congress in law as emergencies appear on the scorecards, but the effects are subtracted before computing the scorecard totals.

In addition to the exemptions in the PAYGO Act itself, the Congress has enacted laws affecting revenues or direct spending with a provision directing that the budgetary effects of all or part of the law be held off of the PAYGO

[1] VA developed methodologies for its programs with costs incident to the delivery of veterans' healthcare and benefits that underpins the TEF allocations. Current methodologies are available here: https://department.va.gov/financial-policy-documents/financial-document/chapter-12-toxic-exposures-fund/?redirect=1

scorecards. In the most recently completed congressional session, two laws were enacted with such a provision.

As was the case during an earlier PAYGO enforcement regime in the 1990s, PAYGO sequestration has not been required since the PAYGO Act reinstated the statutory PAYGO requirement. For the first session of the 118th Congress, the most recently completed session, enacted legislation placed savings of $1.2 billion in each year of the 5-year scorecard and $0.9 billion in each year of the 10-year scorecard. These savings combined with the balances on the scorecards from previous sessions of Congress to total costs of $442 billion on the 5-year scorecard and $242 billion on the 10-year scorecard. However, the budget year balance on each of the PAYGO scorecards was set to zero in 2024 because the Consolidated Appropriations Act, 2023 (Public Law 117-328) shifted the debits on both scorecards from fiscal year 2024 to fiscal year 2025. Consequently, no PAYGO sequestration was required in 2024.[2]

BBEDCA Section 251A Reductions

In August 2011, as part of the BCA, bipartisan majorities in both the House and Senate voted to establish the Joint Select Committee on Deficit Reduction to recommend legislation to achieve at least $1.5 trillion of deficit reduction over the period of fiscal years 2012 through 2021. The failure of the Congress to enact such comprehensive deficit reduction legislation to achieve the $1.5 trillion goal triggered a sequestration of discretionary and mandatory spending in 2013, led to reductions in the discretionary caps for 2014 through 2021, and forced additional sequestrations of mandatory spending in each of fiscal years 2014 through 2021.

[2] OMB's annual PAYGO report is available on OMB's website at https://www.whitehouse.gov/omb/paygo/.

Although the original provisions of the BCA ended in 2021, sequestration of mandatory resources has been extended in a series of laws for each year through 2031 for most programs and the first month of 2033 for Medicare. This sequestration is now called the BBEDCA 251A sequestration, after the Balanced Budget and Emergency Deficit Control Act, as amended (BBEDCA), which is the law where mandatory sequestration continues to be extended. The Budget proposes to continue mandatory sequestration through 2034, which generates $90 billion in deficit reduction.

Section 251A of BBEDCA requires that non-exempt mandatory defense spending be reduced by 8.3 percent each year through 2031, mandatory non-defense spending be reduced by 5.7 percent each year through 2031 (and by 2 percent for a small subset of programs), and Medicare spending be reduced by 2 percent each year through the first month of 2033. These reductions to mandatory programs are triggered annually by the transmittal of the President's Budget for each year and take effect on the first day of the fiscal year. Because the percentage reduction is known in advance, the Budget presents these reductions in the baseline at the account level.

The 2025 Budget shows the net effect of these mandatory sequestration reductions by accounting for reductions in 2025, and each outyear, that remain in the sequestered account and are anticipated to become newly available for obligation in the year after sequestration, in accordance with section 256(k)(6) of BBEDCA. The budget authority and outlays from these "pop-up" resources are included in the baseline and policy estimates and amount to a cost of $2.5 billion in 2025. Additionally, the Budget annually accounts for lost savings that results from the sequestration of certain interfund payments, which produces no net deficit reduction. Such amount is $2 billion in 2025.

II. BUDGET PRESENTATION

Adjustments to BBEDCA Baseline

In order to provide a more realistic outlook for the deficit under current legislation and policies, the Budget proposals are presented relative to a baseline that makes adjustments to the statutory baseline defined in BBEDCA. Section 257 of BBEDCA provides the rules for constructing the baseline used by the Executive and Legislative Branches for scoring and other legal purposes. The adjustments made by the Administration are not intended to replace the BBEDCA baseline for these purposes, but rather are intended to make the baseline a more useful benchmark for assessing the deficit outlook and the impact of Budget proposals. The Administration's adjusted baseline makes three adjustments, each described below.

First, the Budget inserts spending adjustments to bring the 2024 discretionary spending amounts in line with the topline appropriations agreement announced by Congressional leadership in January. These adjustments assume that appropriations will be enacted in line with the original FRA spending caps in 2024 and 2025, certain savings will be included to achieve those caps, and cap adjustments will be enacted at authorized levels in BBEDCA. In addition, these adjustments also assumed that "shifted base" funding will continue to be used as a concept in final 2024 and 2025 appropriations bills.

Second, the Budget removes the outyear effects of emergency spending, excluding the aforementioned "shifted base" amounts. Because emergency funding varies significantly from year to year, removing this funding provides a more consistent discretionary baseline for policy comparison. Eliminating this spending in an adjustment to the baseline, which is consistent with the historical practice of not projecting specific emergency needs in the Budget, also avoids the unintended suggestion of savings in policy when compared to the BBEDCA baseline.

The last adjustment relates to the mandatory savings associated with discretionary program integrity amounts. The adjusted baseline captures the savings generated in these mandatory entitlement programs from continuing these initiatives over 10 years at the levels requested by the Administration in the 2025 Budget. This presentation acknowledges the historical tendency to fully-fund these discretionary program integrity initatives and therefore provides a more accurate representation of expected mandatory outlays for these programs. Each of the dedicated discretionary funding adjustments for program integrity are described above under Adjustments to Base Discretionary Levels, Program Integrity.

These adjustments to baseline are detailed in this Volume in Chapter 22, "Current Services Estimates."

Reclassification of Contract Support Costs and Payments for Tribal Leases at HHS's Indian Health Service and the Department of the Interior's Bureau of Indian Affairs

The 2025 Budget proposes to reclassify as mandatory, beginning in FY 2026, Contract Support Costs (CSCs) and Payments for Tribal Leases, programs that historically have been funded as discretionary in HHS's Indian Health Service (IHS) and the Department of the Interior's Bureau of Indian Affairs. Specifically, the Budget proposes that the CSCs and Payments for Tribal Leases accounts will continue to be funded through the annual appropriations process but will be reclassified as mandatory funding beginning in 2026. For CSCs and Payments for Tribal Leases, the Budget requests $1.9 billion in discretionary resources for 2025 for both BIA and IHS and the reclassification totals $17.8 billion from 2026 to 2034. This shift is shown in the discretionary funding tables in the Budget by reducing the base discretionary in the amount of the projected 2026 Budget need, inflated into the 10-year window. Separately, the Administration is proposing broader changes to the funding of IHS starting in 2026 as described in the third section of this Chapter (Budget Reform proposals).

Reclassification of Nursing Home Related Survey and Certification Program at the Centers for Medicare and Medicaid Services at HHS

The Budget also proposes, beginning in 2026, to shift funding for nursing home surveys from discretionary to mandatory. The Budget requests $435 million in mandatory resources in 2026 to cover 100 percent of statutorily-mandated nursing home surveys, adjusted annually for inflation. The increase in mandatory funding is partially offset by reductions in discretionary spending equal to the projected 2026 need inflated into the 10-year window. This reclassification provides stable resources to the program, which will guard against negligent care and ensure that Americans receive high quality, safe services within these facilities.

Pell Grants

The Pell Grant program includes features that make it unlike other discretionary programs, including that Pell Grants are awarded to all applicants who meet income and other eligibility criteria. This section provides some background on the unique nature of the Pell Grant program and explains how the Budget accommodates changes in discretionary costs.

Under current law, the Pell program has several notable features:

- The Pell Grant program acts like an entitlement program, such as the Supplemental Nutrition Assistance Program or Supplemental Security Income, in which anyone who meets specific eligibility requirements and applies for the program receives a benefit. Specifically, Pell Grant costs in a given year are determined by the maximum award set in statute, the number of eligible applicants, and the award for which those applicants are eligible based on their needs and costs of attendance. The maximum Pell award for the academic year 2024-2025 (based on the fiscal year 2024 annualized CR) is $7,395, of which $6,335 was established in discretionary appropriations and the remaining $1,060 in mandatory funding is provided automatically by the College Cost Reduction and Access Act as amended (CCRAA).

- The cost of each Pell Grant is funded by discretionary budget authority provided in annual appropriations acts, along with mandatory budget authority provided not only by the CCRAA but also the Health Care and Education Reconciliation Act of 2010. There is no programmatic difference between the mandatory and discretionary funding.

- If valid applicants are more numerous than expected, or if these applicants are eligible for higher awards than anticipated, the Pell Grant program will cost more than projected at the time of the appropriation. If the costs during one academic year are higher than provided for in that year's appropriation, the Department of Education funds the extra costs with the subsequent year's appropriation.[3]

- To prevent deliberate underfunding of Pell costs, in 2006 the congressional and Executive Branch scorekeepers agreed to a special scorekeeping rule for Pell. Under this rule, the annual appropriations bill is charged with the full Congressional Budget Office estimated cost of the Pell Grant program for the

[3] This ability to "borrow" from a subsequent appropriation is unique to the Pell program. It comes about for two reasons. First, like many education programs, Pell is "forward-funded"—the budget authority enacted in the fall of one year is intended for the subsequent academic year, which begins in the following July. Second, even though the amount of funding is predicated on the expected cost of Pell during one academic year, the money is made legally available for the full 24-month period covering the current fiscal year and the subsequent fiscal year. This means that, if the funding for an academic year proves inadequate, the following year's appropriation will legally be available to cover the funding shortage for the first academic year. The 2025 Budget appropriations request, for instance, will support the 2025-2026 academic year beginning in July 2024 but will become available in October 2024 and can therefore help cover any shortages that may arise in funding for the 2024-2025 academic year.

Table 4–2. DISCRETIONARY PELL FUNDING NEEDS
(Budget authority in millions of dollars)

Discretionary Pell Funding Needs (Baseline)

	2025	2026	2027	2028	2029	2030	2031	2032	2033	2034
Estimated Program Cost for $6,335 Disc. Maximum Award	30,075	30,136	30,553	31,816	32,150	32,484	32,841	33,116	33,483	33,674
Baseline Discretionary Appropriation - 2023 Enacted	22,475	22,475	22,475	22,475	22,475	22,475	22,475	22,475	22,475	22,475
Surplus/Funding Gap from Prior Year	5,130	–1,299	–7,790	–14,698	–22,868	–31,373	–40,211	–49,407	–58,877	–68,715
Mandatory Budget Authority Available	1,170	1,170	1,170	1,170	1,170	1,170	1,170	1,170	1,170	1,170
Baseline Discretionary Surplus/Funding Gap (–)	–1,299	–7,790	–14,698	–22,868	–31,373	–40,211	–49,407	–58,877	–68,715	–78,744

Effect of 2025 Budget Policies on Discretionary Pell Funding Needs

	2025	2026	2027	2028	2029	2030	2031	2032	2033	2034
Increase Discretionary Maximum Award by $100 to $6,435	–521	–525	–529	–557	–561	–570	–578	–584	–594	–604
Increase Mandatory Add-On to Double Grant by 2029	19	37	53	34	43	48	53	58	62	67
Mandatory Funding Shift [1]	–15	–14	–14	–16	–18	–17	–16	–18	–18	–17
Increase Discretionary Appropriation by $2.1 billion	2,101	2,101	2,101	2,101	2,101	2,101	2,101	2,101	2,101	2,101
Annual Effect of 2025 Budget Policies	1,584	1,599	1,611	1,562	1,565	1,562	1,560	1,557	1,551	1,547
Cumulative Effect of 2025 Budget Policies	1,584	3,183	4,794	6,356	7,921	9,483	11,043	12,600	14,151	15,698
2025 Budget Discretionary Surplus/Funding Gap (–)	285	–4,607	–9,904	–16,512	–23,452	–30,728	–38,364	–46,277	–54,564	–63,046

[1] Some budget authority, provided in previous legislation and classified as mandatory but used to meet discretionary Pell grant program funding needs, will be reallocated to support new mandatory costs associated with the discretionary award increase.

budget year, plus or minus any cumulative shortfalls or surpluses from prior years.

Given the nature of the program, it is reasonable to consider Pell Grants an individual entitlement for purposes of budget analysis and enforcement. The discretionary portion of the award funded in annual appropriations acts counts against appropriations allocations established annually under §302 of the Congressional Budget Act.

The total cost of Pell Grants can fluctuate from year to year, even with no change in the maximum Pell Grant award, because of changes in enrollment, college costs, and student and family resources. The Budget includes historical trends in applications for the Free Application for Federal Student Aid (FAFSA) to project Pell-eligible applicants. Current enrollment levels of Pell-receiving students help determine the likelihood that eligible applicants become future recipients, which the Budget projects to increase by about one percent annually, on average, over the course of the ten-year budget window In general, the demand for and costs of the program are countercyclical to the economy; more people go to school during periods of higher unemployment, but return to the workforce as the economy improves. During the COVID pandemic, however, enrollment continued its decline since the end of the Great Recession. In the 2023-2024 school year, however, enrollment in undergraduate education grew for first time since the beginning of pandemic, up 2% over the prior school year. Community college experienced even more growth with an increase of 4% over 2022-2023. In addition, growth of Pell-eligible students is greater than that of the overall undergraduate enrollment leading to nearly half a million more Pell recipients in 2023-2024 than in 2022-2023. Given the increases in enrollment, higher discretionary maximum awards over the past few years, and eligibility changes due to implementation of the FAFSA Simplification Act, costs of the Pell program have increased by nearly 15% over the past year. Assuming no changes in current policy, the 2025 Budget baseline projects a shortfall of nearly $1.3 billion in 2025 (see Table 4-2). These estimates have changed from year to year, which illustrates difficulty in forecasting Pell program costs.

The 2025 Budget, coupled with the past two years of Pell award increases, reflects a significant step toward the President's goal of doubling the Pell Grant. The Budget would increase the discretionary maximum award by $100 for a total discretionary award of $6,435. The Budget would also increase the mandatory add-on by $650 for students at public and non-profit institutions, for a total maximum award of $8,145. The total maximum award for students at proprietary institutions would be $7,495. The increase to the grant would increase future discretionary Pell program costs by $5.1 billion over 10 years, shown in Table 4-2 by combining the 10-years of increases in the discretionary maximum award and 10-years of increases in the mandatory add-on, under the Effects of 2025 Budget Policies. The Budget provides $24.6 billion in discretionary budget authority in 2025 to support this increase, $2.1 billion more than 2023. The Budget projects that the Pell program will have sufficient discretionary funds to meet program costs in 2025.

International Monetary Fund (IMF), Quota Subscription Increase and the New Arrangements to Borrow

As part of a broader set of reforms at the IMF, the Administration supports a proposal to increase the U.S. Quota Subscription to the IMF, rollback a portion of the U.S. commitment to the New Arrangements to Borrow (NAB), and extend U.S. participation in the NAB. Because U.S. participation in the Quota constitutes an exchange of monetary assets, the Administration does not score it as budget authority or outlays, and it is not included in the total funding requested by the Administration. Budget authority is the authority to enter into obligations that are liquidated by outlays. U.S. transactions with the IMF do not result in outlays. The Administration's position follows the recommendation made by the 1967 President's Commission on Budget Concepts that "Subscriptions, drawings, and other transactions reflecting net changes in the U.S. position with the International Monetary Fund should be excluded from budget receipts and expenditures." There is little basis for treating IMF quota subscriptions or NAB increases differently from other financial asset exchanges, such as deposits of cash in Treasury's accounts at the Federal Reserve Bank or purchases of gold, which are not recorded as either budget authority or outlays.

Fannie Mae and Freddie Mac

The Budget continues to present Fannie Mae and Freddie Mac, the housing Government-sponsored enterprises (GSEs) currently in Federal conservatorship, as non-Federal entities. However, Treasury equity investments in the GSEs are recorded as budgetary outlays, and the dividends on those investments are recorded as offsetting receipts. In addition, the budget estimates reflect collections from the 10-basis point increase in GSE guarantee fees that was enacted under the Temporary Payroll Tax Cut Continuation Act of 2011 (Public Law 112-78) and extended by the IIJA. The Budget also reflects collections from a 4.2 basis point set-aside on each dollar of unpaid principal balance of new business purchases authorized under the Housing and Economic Recovery Act of 2008 (Public Law 111-289) to be remitted to several Federal affordable housing programs. The GSEs are discussed in more detail in Chapter 7, "Credit and Insurance."

Postal Service Treatment

The Postal Service is designated in statute as an off-budget independent establishment of the Executive Branch. This designation and budgetary treatment was most recently mandated in 1989. To reflect the Postal Service's practice since 2012 of using defaults to on-budget accounts to continue operations, despite losses, the Administration's baseline reflects probable defaults in the on-budget account showing no payment for Civil Service Retirement and Disability. This treatment allows for a clearer presentation of the Postal Service's likely actions. See the discussion of the Postal Service in the 2025 Budget Appendix for further explanation of this presentation and updates for the recently enacted Postal Reform Act.

Under current scoring rules, savings from any proposals for reform of the Postal Service would affect the unified deficit but would not directly affect the PAYGO scorecard. Any savings to on-budget accounts through lower projected defaults in future legislation affect both the PAYGO scorecard and the unified deficit.

III. BUDGET REFORM PROPOSALS

Federal Capital Revolving Fund

The structure of the Federal budget and budget enforcement requirements can create hurdles to funding large-dollar capital investments that are handled differently at the State and local government levels. Expenditures for capital investment are combined with operating expenses in the Federal unified budget. Both kinds of expenditures must compete for limited funding within the discretionary funding levels. Large-dollar Federal capital investments can be squeezed out in this competition, forcing agency managers to turn to operating leases to meet long-term Federal requirements. These alternatives are more expensive than ownership over the long-term because: (1) Treasury can always borrow at lower interest rates; and (2) to avoid triggering scorekeeping and recording requirements for capital leases, agencies sign shorter-term consecutive leases of the same space. For example, the cost of two consecutive 15-year leases for a building can far exceed its fair market value, with the Government paying close to 180 percent of the value of the building. Alternative financing proposals typically run up against scorekeeping and recording rules that appropriately measure cost based on the full amount of the Government's obligations under the contract, which further constrains the ability of agency managers to meet large capital needs.

In contrast, State and local governments separate capital investment from operating expenses. They are able to evaluate, rank, and finance proposed capital investments in separate capital budgets, which avoids direct competition between proposed capital acquisitions and operating expenses. If capital purchases are financed by borrowing, the associated debt service is an item in the operating budget. This separation of capital spending from operating expenses works well at the State and local government levels because of conditions that do not exist at the Federal level. State and local governments are required to balance their operating budgets, and their ability to borrow to finance capital spending is subject to the discipline of private credit markets that impose higher interest rates for riskier investments. In addition, State and local governments tend to own capital that they finance. In contrast, the Federal Government does not face a balanced budget requirement, and Treasury debt has historically been considered the safest investment regardless of the condition of the Federal balance sheet. Also, the bulk of Federal funding for capital is in the form of grants to lower levels of Government or to private entities, and it is difficult to see how non-federally owned investment can be included in a capital budget.

To deal with the drawbacks of the current Federal approach, the Budget proposes: (1) to create a Federal Capital Revolving Fund (FCRF) to fund large-dollar,

Chart 4-1. Scoring of $3.5 billion GSA Construction Project using the Federal Capital Revolving Fund*

(Budget authority in millions of dollars)

Federal Capital Revolving Fund	Year 1	Years 2-15
Mandatory:		
Transfer to purchasing agency to buy building	3,500	
Purchasing agency repayments	-233	-3,267

Purchasing Agency	Year 1	Years 2-15
Mandatory:		
Collection of transfer from Federal Capital Revolving Fund	-3,500	
Payment to buy building	3,500	
Discretionary:		
Repayments to Federal Capital Revolving Fund	233	3,267

Total Government-wide Budget Impact	Year 1	Years 2-15	Total
Mandatory:			
Purchase building	3,500		3,500
Collections from purchasing agency	-233	-3,267	-3,500
Discretionary:			
Purchasing agency repayments	233	3,267	3,500
Total Government-wide	3,500	---	3,500

*The 2025 Budget proposes one project, the FBI Headquarters Campus in Greenbelt, MD, estimated project balance of $3.5 billion.

federally owned, civilian real property capital projects; and (2) provide specific budget enforcement rules for the FCRF that would allow it to function, in effect, like State and local government capital budgets. This proposal incorporates principles that are central to the success of capital budgeting at the State and local level—a limit on total funding for capital investment, annual decisions on the allocation of funding for capital projects, and spreading the acquisition cost over 15 years in the discretionary operating budgets of agencies that purchase the assets. The 2025 Budget proposes that that FCRF would be capitalized initially by a $10 billion mandatory appropriation, and scored with anticipated outlays over the 10-year window for the purposes of pay-as-you-go budget enforcement rules. Balances in the FCRF would be available for transfer to purchasing agencies to fund large-dollar capital acquisitions only to the extent projects are designated in advance in appropriations Acts and the agency receives a discretionary appropriation for the first of a maximum of 15 required annual repayments. If these two conditions are met, the FCRF would transfer funds to the purchasing agency to cover the full cost to acquire the capital asset. Annual discretionary repayments by purchasing agencies would replenish the FCRF and would become available to fund additional capital projects. Total annual capital purchases would be limited to the lower of $5 billion or the balance in the FCRF, including annual repayments.

The Budget uses the FCRF concept to fund construction of a suburban FBI Headquarters campus with an estimated project balance of $3.5 billion when taking into account available GSA balances previously appropriated for this project. A project of this size and scope, if funded through the traditional discretionary appropriations process would account for potentially all GSA capital funding for consecutive fiscal years. In accordance with the principles and design of the FCRF, the 2025 budget requests appropriations language in the General Services Administration's (GSA) Federal Buildings Fund account, designating that the project to be funded out of the FCRF, which is also housed within GSA, along with 1/15 of the full purchase price, or $233 million for the first-year repayment back to the FCRF. The FCRF account is displayed funding the FBI project with additional unspecified projects being funded in future years, along with returns to the account from the annual project repayments.

The flow of funds for the FBI project is illustrated in Chart 4–1. Current budget enforcement rules would require the entire $3.5 billion building cost to be scored as discretionary budget authority in the first year, which would negate the benefit of the FCRF and leave agencies and policy makers facing the same trade-off constraints. As shown in Chart 4-1, under this proposal, transfers from the FCRF to agencies to fund capital projects, $3.5 billion in the case of the proposed project in 2025, and the actual execution by GSA would be scored as direct spending (shown as mandatory in Chart 4-1), while agencies would use discretionary appropriations to fund the annual repayments to the FCRF, or $233 million for the first-year repayment. The proposal allocates the costs between direct spending and discretionary spending—the up-front cost of capital investment would already be reflected in the baseline as direct spending once the FCRF is enacted with $10 billion in mandatory capital. This scoring approves a total capital investment upfront, keeping individual large projects from competing with annual operating expenses in the annual appropriations process. On the discretionary side of the budget the budgetary trade off would be locking into the incremental annual cost of repaying the FCRF over 15-years. Knowing that future discretionary appropriations will have to be used to repay the FCRF provides an incentive for agencies, OMB, and the Congress to select projects with the highest mission criticality and returns. In future years, OMB would review agencies' proposed projects for inclusion in the President's Budget, as shown with the GSA request, and the Appropriations Committees would make final allocations by authorizing projects in annual appropriations Acts and providing the first year of repayment. This approach would allow for a more effective capital planning process for the Government's largest civilian real property projects, and is similar to capital budgets used by State and local governments.

Protecting Funding for the Federal Buildings Fund

Since 2011, the Congress has under-funded the General Services Administration (GSA) Federal Building Fund (FBF), the primary source of maintenance, repair, and construction for GSA's federally owned building inventory. Over the last 15 years $12.9 billion in agency rental payments, intended to maintain and construct GSA facilities, were not appropriated. By enacting an FBF appropriations level below the estimated annual rent collections, the Congress creates an offset that allows the Appropriations Committee to fund other priorities. When that occurs, actual collections remain in the Fund as unavailable.

At the same time, the GSA inventory of federally owned buildings is seeing an increase in deferred maintenance while experiencing cost increases year over year for unfunded projects. This year, the Budget again proposes a reform to ensure that all agency rental payments can be used for construction and maintenance and repair, as intended, rather than merely sitting unavailable for use in the Fund. The Budget proposes directed scoring, to take effect starting in fiscal year 2026, that would not credit, or score, any savings from limiting the spending in the FBF. FBF revenues would be utilized for the intended purposes of maintaining and operating the GSA owned and leased buildings portfolio. In this way, the Congress will have every incentive to set new obligational authority (NOA) at the level of the estimated collections from across Federal agencies.

The FBF has hit a tipping point with a growing backlog of deferred maintenance and an increasing number of missed opportunities to consolidate from leases into more cost effective federally-owned space – particularly given the unique opportunity to re-shape the Federal footprint and optimize building utilization. Meanwhile, Government-wide, agencies continue to pay rent to the GSA FBF, but do not receive the commercially equivalent space and services that they pay for in accordance with the GSA statute that governs rent-setting, particularly in terms of capital reinvestment. Table 4-3, Federal Buildings Fund 2010 to 2024, shows 15 years of budget estimates of GSA rental collections (President's Budget Revenue Estimate) against the NOA enacted in the final appropriations process. The chart tells the story of years of rental payments being withheld from spending, thus creating an offset that allowed a reprioritization of spending away from the original purpose of the collections. Since 2011, the negative enacted net budget authority for the FBF for all years except one shows the annual appropriations process has gained $12.9 billion at the expense of the GSA Federal building inventory.

The Budget prioritizes FBF spending of collections, and provides the GSA with additional funding above the anticipated level of rental collections to make progress on the backlog of repairs and fund critical construction priorities. The Administration looks forward to working with the Congress to assure that the rental payments made to the FBF are prioritized for investment occupied by the agencies that paid them.

Table 4–3. FEDERAL BUILDINGS FUND 2010–2024
(In thousands of dollars)

	President's Budget Revenue Estimate	Enacted New Obligational Authority	Net Budget Authority[1]
2010	8,222,539	8,443,585	287,406
2011	8,870,933	7,597,540	–1,202,123
2012	9,302,761	8,017,967	–1,205,174
2013	9,777,590	8,024,967	–1,665,003
2014	9,950,560	9,370,042	–580,518
2015	9,917,667	9,238,310	–679,357
2016	9,807,722	10,196,124	388,402
2017	10,178,339	8,845,147	–1,333,192
2018	9,950,519	9,073,938	–876,581
2019	10,131,673	9,285,082	–846,591
2020	10,203,596	8,856,530	–1,347,066
2021	10,388,375	9,065,489	–1,322,886
2022	10,636,648	9,342,205	–1,294,443
2023	10,488,857	10,013,150	–475,707
2024[2]	10,728,410	10,013,150	–715,260
Total			**–12,868,093**

[1] Net Budget Authority includes redemption of debt and does not include rescission of prior year funding, transfers, supplemental, or emergency appropriations.
[2] Annualized CR amount.

Funding for the Indian Health Service in HHS

Building on the enactment of an advance appropriation for 2024 received in the Consolidated Appropriations Act, 2023 (Public Law 117-328), the 2025 Budget requests $8.0 billion in discretionary funding for 2025 for HHS's Indian Health Service (IHS). This includes increases for clinical services, preventative health, facilities construction, contract support costs, and leases. Starting in 2026, the Budget moves all of IHS out of the annual appropriations process and reclassifies funds as mandatory. Overall, the Budget proposes to increase amounts for IHS annually for total funding of $288.9 billion with a net cost of $208.5 billion from 2026 to 2034. This proposal is presented as a part of the Administration's commitment to provide stable funding for tribal healthcare needs.

Submission Date of the President's Budget

According to the Congressional Budget and Impoundment Control Act of 1974 (Public Law 93-344), the President is required to submit a Budget for the following fiscal year no later than the first Monday in February. That date assumed a "regular order" budget formulation process, where annual appropriations bills are enacted before the start of the fiscal year, on October 1. In effect, the Congressional Budget Act envisioned a process in which the Executive Branch developed its budget request for the following year only after funding levels for the current year were established.

In practice, however, the Congress rarely enacts all appropriations before the start of the next fiscal year. In fact, the Congress regularly enacts short-term Continuing Resolutions (CRs) for most or all appropriations bills to bridge the gap prior to the final passage of the annual bills, and fiscal year 2024 is no exception. At the time of preparing the Budget, the Congress had not completed action on any of the fiscal year 2024 appropriations bills. The 2025 Budget can no longer await final passage, and therefore does not reflect final 2024 appropriations.

Late congressional action on appropriations bills makes it difficult for an administration to account for current year funding and policy in the next year's President's Budget. As a result, administrations are frequently faced with a choice between preparing a Budget using assumptions as a placeholder for the prior fiscal year, knowing that level would not align with final appropriations action, or delaying the release of the Budget in order to reflect enacted appropriations and new program authorizations. Even without completion of the 2024 appropriations, the 2025 Budget provides a robust agenda of the President's programs and policies for the American people.

It is to the benefit of both policymakers and the public to better align the release of the President's Budget with the actual enactment of annual appropriations, as was intended by the Congressional Budget Act. The benefits of doing so include:

- Ensuring that the Congress and the public have the most recent information on the trajectory of Government spending;
- Giving administrations sufficient time to make well-informed decisions relative to the most recently enacted funding bills; and,
- Providing the Congress with the most useful and actionable information regarding Administration priorities as the annual budget process begins.

For these reasons, the Administration will continue to prioritize providing to the Congress and the public useful and actionable information that incorporates the most recent funding levels and policy decisions, whenever possible, balancing the enormous benefits to the public and the Congress of providing the President's agenda in a timely manner. The Administration looks forward to working with the Congress to ensure that the annual budget and appropriations processes better align to the vision laid out in the Congressional Budget Act.

5. FEDERAL INVESTMENT

Federal investment is the portion of Federal spending of taxpayer money intended to yield long-term benefits for the economy and the Nation. This spending promises greater benefits than if that money had been allocated in the private sector. It promotes improved efficiency within Federal agencies, as well as growth in the national economy by increasing the overall stock of capital. Investment spending can take the form of direct Federal spending or grants to State, local, tribal, and territorial governments.[1] It can be designated for physical capital—a tangible asset or the improvement of that asset—that increases production over a period of years or increases value to the Government. It can also be used for research and development, education, or training, all of which are intangible, but can still increase income in the future or provide other long-term benefits.

Most presentations in the *Analytical Perspectives* volume combine investment spending with spending intended for current use. In contrast, this chapter focuses solely on Federal and federally financed investment, providing a comprehensive picture of Federal spending for physical capital, research and development, and education and training. Because the analysis in this chapter excludes spending for non-investment activities, it gives only a partial picture of Federal support for specific national needs, such as defense.

Total Federal investment spending was $536.1 billion in 2023. It is expected to increase by 69.4 percent in 2024 to $907.9 billion. The Budget proposes a 5.9 percent decrease from 2024, for a total of $854.1 billion in 2025.

[1] For more information on Federal grants to State and local governments see the "Aid to State and Local Governments" chapter of this volume.

DESCRIPTION OF FEDERAL INVESTMENT

The Budget uses a relatively broad definition of investment. It defines Federal investment as encompassing spending for research, development, education, and training as well as physical assets such as land, structures, infrastructure, and major equipment. It also includes spending regardless of the ultimate ownership of the resulting asset or the purpose it serves. For the purposes of this definition, however, Federal investment does not include "social investment," meaning investments in healthcare or social services programs where it is difficult to separate out the degree to which the spending provides current versus future benefits. The distinction between investment spending and current outlays is a matter of judgment, but the definition used for the purposes of this analysis has remained consistent over time and is useful for historical comparisons.[2]

Investment in physical assets can be for the construction or improvement of buildings, structures, and infrastructure, including the development or acquisition of major equipment. The broader research and development category includes spending on the facilities in which these activities occur and major equipment for the conduct of research and development, as well as spending for basic and applied research, and experimental development.[3] Investment in education and training includes vocational rehabilitation, programs for veterans, funding for school systems and higher education, and agricultural extension services. This category excludes training for military personnel or other individuals in Government service.

The Budget further classifies investments as either grants to State, local, tribal, and territorial governments (e.g., for highways or education) or "direct Federal programs." The "direct Federal" category consists primarily of spending for assets owned by the Federal Government, such as weapons systems and buildings, but also includes grants to private organizations and individuals for investment, such as capital grants to Amtrak, Pell Grants, and higher education loans to individuals. For grants made to State, local, tribal, and territorial governments, it is the recipient jurisdiction, not the Federal Government, that ultimately determines whether the money is used to finance investment or for current use. This analysis classifies outlays based on the category in which the recipient jurisdiction is expected to spend a majority of the money. General purpose fiscal assistance is classified as current spending, although in practice, some may be spent by recipient jurisdictions on investment.

Additionally, in this analysis, Federal investment includes credit programs that are for investment purposes. When direct loans and loan guarantees are used to fund investment, the subsidy value is included as investment. The subsidies are classified according to their program purpose, such as construction, or education and training.

This discussion presents spending for gross investment, without adjusting for depreciation.

[2] Historical figures on investment outlays beginning in 1940 may be found in the Budget's *Historical Tables*. The *Historical Tables* are available at *https://whitehouse.gov/omb/historical-tables/*.

[3] A more thorough discussion of research and development funding may be found in the "Research and Development" chapter of this volume.

Table 5–1. COMPOSITION OF FEDERAL INVESTMENT OUTLAYS
(In billions of dollars)

Federal Investment	Actual 2023	Estimate 2024	Estimate 2025
Major public physical capital investment:			
Direct Federal:			
National defense	193.5	210.8	232.8
Nondefense	51.0	71.5	69.6
Subtotal, direct major public physical capital investment	244.5	282.3	302.4
Grants to State and local governments	111.9	132.0	161.1
Subtotal, major public physical capital investment	356.3	414.3	463.5
Conduct of research and development:			
National defense	87.4	93.6	94.9
Nondefense	84.3	89.7	92.6
Subtotal, conduct of research and development	171.7	183.3	187.5
Conduct of education and training:			
Grants to State and local governments	89.0	85.0	74.8
Direct Federal	–82.1	218.1	121.4
Subtotal, conduct of education and training	6.9	303.2	196.2
Total, major Federal investment outlays	**534.9**	**900.8**	**847.2**
MEMORANDUM			
Major Federal investment outlays:			
National defense	281.0	304.4	327.7
Nondefense	254.0	596.4	519.6
Total, major Federal investment outlays	534.9	900.8	847.2
Miscellaneous physical investment:			
Commodity inventories	–1.9	*	*
Other physical investment (direct)	3.0	7.1	6.9
Total, miscellaneous physical investment	1.1	7.1	6.9
Total, Federal investment outlays, including miscellaneous physical investment	536.1	907.9	854.1

*$500 million or less

COMPOSITION OF FEDERAL INVESTMENT OUTLAYS

Major Federal Investment

The composition of major Federal investment outlays is summarized in Table 5–1. The categories include major public physical investment, the conduct of research and development, and the conduct of education and training. Total major Federal investment outlays were $534.9 billion in 2023. They are estimated to increase by 68.4 percent to $900.8 billion in 2024, and decrease by 5.9 percent to $847.2 billion in 2025. For 2023 through 2025, defense investment outlays comprise about 40 percent of total major Federal investment, while non-defense investment comprises about 60 percent. In 2024, defense investment outlays are expected to increase by $23.4 billion, or 8.3 percent, and non-defense investment outlays are expected to increase by $342.4 billion, or 134.8 percent. In 2025, the Budget projects a defense investment increase of $23.3 billion, or 7.7 percent over 2024 and a decrease in non-defense investment of $76.9 billion, or 12.9 percent.

Physical investment:

Outlays for major public physical capital (hereafter referred to as "physical investment") were $356.3 billion in 2023 and are estimated to increase by 16.3 percent to $414.3 billion in 2024. In 2025, outlays for physical investment are estimated to increase by 11.9 percent to $463.5 billion. Physical investment outlays are for construction and renovation, the development or purchase of major equipment, and the purchase or sale of land and structures. Around 65 percent of these outlays are for direct physical investment by the Federal Government, with the remainder being grants to State and local governments for physical investment.

Direct physical investment outlays by the Federal Government are primarily for defense. Defense outlays for physical investment are estimated to be $232.8 billion in 2025, $22 billion higher than in 2024. Outlays for direct physical investment for non-defense purposes are estimated to be $69.6 billion in 2025, a decrease of 2.6 percent from 2024.

Outlays for grants to State and local governments for physical investment are estimated to be $161.1 billion in 2025, a 22 percent increase over the 2024 estimate of $132.0 billion. Grants for physical investment fund transportation programs, sewage treatment plants, community and regional development, public housing, and other State and tribal assistance. Much of this investment originates from funding included in the Infrastructure Investment and Jobs Act (IIJA, Public Law 117-58), which was signed into law on November 15, 2021. The IIJA makes an array of transformational investments in the Nation's infrastructure.

Conduct of research and development:

Outlays for research and development were $171.7 billion in 2023. Outlays are estimated to increase by 6.8 percent to $183.3 billion in 2024, and increase by 2.3 percent in 2025 to $187.5 billion. Roughly half of research and development outlays are for defense, a trend which has remained consistent over the past decade. Physical investment for research and development facilities and equipment is included in the physical investment category.

Non-defense outlays for the conduct of research and development are estimated to be $92.6 billion in 2025, 3.2 percent higher than 2024. Highlights include a roughly $20 billion investment at the Department of Energy's Office of Science, the National Science Foundation, and the Department of Commerce's National Institute for Standards and Testing in research and development activities that support the goals of Public Law 117-167, commonly referred to as the CHIPS and Science Act of 2022. Additionally, the 2025 Budget reflects approximately $3 billion in investments across multiple agencies to fund artificial intelligence research and development activities that focus both on leveraging its benefits and enhancing protections from its risks.

A discussion of research and development funding can be found in the "Research and Development" chapter of this volume.

Conduct of education and training:

Outlays for the conduct of education and training were $6.9 billion in 2023. Outlays are estimated to increase to $303.2 billion in 2024, and decrease in 2025 to $196.2 billion.

Grants to State, local, tribal, and territorial governments for this category were $89.0 billion in 2023. The grants are estimated to decrease by 4.4 percent to $85.0 billion in 2024, and decrease by 12 percent to $74.8 billion in 2025. In 2025, grants are estimated to be slightly over one-third of total investment in education and training. This pattern of spending on grants to State, local, tribal, and territorial governments for education and training is largely explained by changes in spending levels in response to the health and economic crises caused by the COVID-19 pandemic. For example, through the Education Stabilization Fund, which received nearly $166 billion in funding from the American Rescue Plan Act of 2021 (Public Law 117-2), the Department of Education outlayed roughly $20 billion in grants for education and training in 2023 and is estimated to outlay roughly $7 billion in grants for education and training in 2024, before closing out the program and outlaying $0 in 2025.

Direct Federal education and training outlays in 2023 were -$82.1 billion. They are estimated to be $218.1 billion in 2024, and $121.4 billion in 2025. Programs in this category primarily consist of aid for higher education through student financial assistance, loan subsidies, and veterans' education, training, and rehabilitation. This category does not include outlays for education and training of Federal civilian and military employees. Outlays for education and training that are for physical investment and for research and development are in the categories for physical investment and the conduct of research and development.

The negative outlays in this category are explained by changes in accounting for the Federal Direct Student Loan Program. In 2023, outlays for this program were -$189 billion, mainly due to the impacts of loan modifications and reestimates. There were much smaller negative subsidies and reestimates in this program for 2024, yielding total estimated outlays for the Federal Direct Student Loan Program in 2024 of roughly $93 billion. In 2025, outlays for this program are estimated to be $38 billion and are only associated with loan subsidies for the 2025 cohort, as no modifications or reestimates for 2025 have been made.

Major Federal investment outlays will comprise an estimated 11.7 percent of total Federal outlays in 2025 and 2.9 percent of the Nation's gross domestic product. Budget authority and outlays for major Federal investment by subcategory may be found in Table 5–2 at the end of this chapter.

Miscellaneous Physical Investment

In addition to the categories of major Federal investment, miscellaneous categories of investment outlays are shown at the bottom of Table 5–1.

Outlays for commodity inventories are for the purchase or sale of agricultural products pursuant to farm price support programs and other commodities. Outlays for other miscellaneous physical investment are estimated to be $6.9 billion in 2025.

Detailed Table on Investment Spending

Table 5-2 provides data on budget authority as well as outlays for major Federal investment, divided according to grants to State and local governments and direct Federal spending. Miscellaneous investment is not included in this table.

Table 5–2. FEDERAL INVESTMENT BUDGET AUTHORITY AND OUTLAYS: GRANT AND DIRECT FEDERAL PROGRAMS

(In millions of dollars)

Description	Budget Authority			Outlays		
	2023 Actual	2024 Estimate	2025 Estimate	2023 Actual	2024 Estimate	2025 Estimate
GRANTS TO STATE AND LOCAL GOVERNMENTS						
Major public physical investment:						
Construction and rehabilitation:						
Transportation:						
Highways	70,796	71,367	69,334	53,422	62,271	67,726
Mass transportation	22,158	22,222	21,706	23,593	20,474	20,753
Rail transportation	16,293	16,287	16,033	3,378	3,931	7,833
Air and other transportation	12,219	12,221	12,082	5,679	8,477	9,520
Subtotal, transportation	121,466	122,097	119,155	86,072	95,153	105,832
Other construction and rehabilitation:						
Pollution control and abatement	17,254	15,997	16,448	6,084	5,535	9,647
Community and regional development	14,774	8,386	5,971	10,663	16,754	20,400
Housing assistance	6,061	6,260	17,937	5,350	6,771	8,695
Other	1,545	1,002	1,284	1,319	3,592	11,875
Subtotal, other construction and rehabilitation	39,634	31,645	41,640	23,416	32,652	50,617
Subtotal, construction and rehabilitation	161,100	153,742	160,795	109,488	127,805	156,449
Other physical assets	3,876	3,468	3,045	2,370	4,238	4,697
Subtotal, major public physical investment	164,976	157,210	163,840	111,858	132,043	161,146
Conduct of research and development:						
Agriculture	396	396	399	370	370	443
Other	364	406	404	189	224	242
Subtotal, conduct of research and development	760	802	803	559	594	685
Conduct of education and training:						
Elementary, secondary, and vocational education	46,302	46,055	46,155	63,507	55,632	46,496
Higher education	668	668	678	639	796	755
Research and general education aids	959	1,012	1,023	1,057	1,193	1,060
Training and employment	3,637	3,287	3,561	3,244	3,595	3,717
Social services	16,247	18,005	18,073	16,239	19,192	18,124
Agriculture	471	471	495	408	434	558
Other	3,431	3,405	3,330	3,860	4,207	4,136
Subtotal, conduct of education and training	71,715	72,903	73,315	88,954	85,049	74,846
Subtotal, grants for investment	**237,451**	**230,915**	**237,958**	**201,371**	**217,686**	**236,677**
DIRECT FEDERAL PROGRAMS						
Major public physical investment:						
Construction and rehabilitation:						
National defense:						
Military construction and family housing	16,998	16,958	15,424	10,042	13,093	16,665
Atomic energy defense activities and other	4,908	4,597	4,707	3,751	3,833	3,957
Subtotal, national defense	21,906	21,555	20,131	13,793	16,926	20,622
Nondefense:						
International affairs	1,290	1,282	1,292	1,224	1,222	1,425
General science, space, and technology	2,058	1,969	2,039	2,056	2,182	2,143
Water resources projects	6,449	5,974	5,445	4,216	9,289	7,218
Other natural resources and environment	4,932	3,195	3,318	1,963	2,311	2,639
Energy	4,793	5,135	6,964	3,171	6,665	9,693
Postal service	2,938	754	754	1,009	945	945
Transportation	687	679	716	80	219	403
Veterans hospitals and other health facilities	7,335	8,862	7,873	5,822	4,860	4,955
Administration of justice	2,025	2,035	1,277	1,833	2,934	3,033
GSA real property activities	1,585	1,497	11,877	1,136	1,619	3,238
Other construction	4,670	5,555	6,480	4,016	5,509	4,537
Subtotal, nondefense	38,762	36,937	48,035	26,526	37,755	40,229
Subtotal, construction and rehabilitation	60,668	58,492	68,166	40,319	54,681	60,851

Table 5–2. FEDERAL INVESTMENT BUDGET AUTHORITY AND OUTLAYS: GRANT AND DIRECT FEDERAL PROGRAMS—Continued

(In millions of dollars)

Description	Budget Authority			Outlays		
	2023 Actual	2024 Estimate	2025 Estimate	2023 Actual	2024 Estimate	2025 Estimate
Acquisition of major equipment:						
National defense:						
Department of Defense	215,613	210,516	215,788	178,358	192,360	210,322
Atomic energy defense activities	1,758	1,618	1,899	1,427	1,543	1,850
Subtotal, national defense	217,371	212,134	217,687	179,785	193,903	212,172
Nondefense:						
General science and basic research	578	539	530	569	571	566
Postal service	4,710	4,748	4,748	1,948	3,878	3,878
Air transportation	4,748	4,690	6,326	4,271	4,714	5,178
Water transportation (Coast Guard)	1,703	1,607	1,545	1,635	5,232	1,834
Other transportation (railroads)	5	6	11	5	6	10
Hospital and medical care for veterans	3,802	3,912	1,134	3,221	3,958	1,574
Federal law enforcement activities	2,920	3,018	2,931	2,972	3,250	3,044
Department of the Treasury (fiscal operations)	239	283	283	773	1,295	1,940
National Oceanic and Atmospheric Administration	1,756	1,477	1,873	1,452	1,752	1,841
Other	6,793	6,853	7,395	7,314	8,952	9,062
Subtotal, nondefense	27,254	27,133	26,776	24,160	33,608	28,927
Subtotal, acquisition of major equipment	244,625	239,267	244,463	203,945	227,511	241,099
Purchase or sale of land and structures:						
National defense	–42	–33	–35	–48	–27	–35
Natural resources and environment	523	522	525	384	490	516
General government	–41	–307		–41	–307	
Other	162	165	168	–69	–68	–61
Subtotal, purchase or sale of land and structures	602	347	658	226	88	420
Subtotal, major public physical investment	305,895	298,106	313,287	244,490	282,280	302,370
Conduct of research and development:						
National defense:						
Defense military	95,541	90,380	92,536	82,338	88,393	89,483
Atomic energy and other	5,356	5,308	5,544	5,087	5,189	5,430
Subtotal, national defense	100,897	95,688	98,080	87,425	93,582	94,913
Nondefense:						
International affairs	268	252	252	280	252	252
General science, space, and technology:						
NASA	10,841	11,000	10,869	10,609	10,956	11,006
National Science Foundation	7,468	7,289	7,482	6,780	7,580	7,888
Department of Energy	6,585	6,141	6,727	6,029	7,670	7,196
Other general science, space, and technology			190			40
Subtotal, general science, space, and technology	24,894	24,430	25,268	23,418	26,206	26,130
Energy	6,185	7,431	7,507	3,655	4,860	5,542
Transportation:						
Department of Transportation	1,079	1,129	1,144	876	1,112	1,194
NASA	771	764	794	693	757	795
Other transportation	41	41	24	38	55	24
Subtotal, transportation	1,891	1,934	1,962	1,607	1,924	2,013
Health:						
National Institutes of Health	46,356	45,753	48,119	44,045	44,454	44,998
Other health	1,544	1,375	2,757	1,169	1,035	1,310
Subtotal, health	47,900	47,128	50,876	45,214	45,489	46,308
Agriculture	2,258	2,249	2,258	2,192	2,634	2,573
Natural resources and environment	3,521	3,304	3,287	3,187	3,125	3,081
National Institute of Standards and Technology	2,839	2,123	2,009	827	1,399	2,717
Hospital and medical care for veterans	1,684	1,799	1,709	1,751	1,564	1,588
All other research and development	1,668	1,698	1,725	1,576	1,660	1,709
Subtotal, nondefense	93,108	92,348	96,853	83,707	89,113	91,913
Subtotal, conduct of research and development	194,005	188,036	194,933	171,132	182,695	186,826

Table 5–2. FEDERAL INVESTMENT BUDGET AUTHORITY AND OUTLAYS: GRANT AND DIRECT FEDERAL PROGRAMS—Continued

(In millions of dollars)

Description	Budget Authority			Outlays		
	2023 Actual	2024 Estimate	2025 Estimate	2023 Actual	2024 Estimate	2025 Estimate
Conduct of education and training:						
Elementary, secondary, and vocational education	1,767	2,356	2,689	47,134	60,252	10,529
Higher education	–149,334	147,446	88,219	–152,319	132,409	82,750
Research and general education aids	2,747	2,792	2,908	2,779	3,078	2,889
Training and employment	2,527	2,681	10,662	2,323	2,669	2,960
Health	2,468	2,551	2,806	2,515	2,983	2,852
Veterans education, training, and rehabilitation	9,132	9,019	16,253	12,659	13,401	16,053
General science and basic research	1,195	1,157	1,313	859	1,180	1,224
International affairs	790	790	797	890	869	794
Other	1,285	1,326	1,303	1,087	1,295	1,305
Subtotal, conduct of education and training	–127,423	170,118	126,950	–82,073	218,136	121,356
Subtotal, direct Federal investment	**372,477**	**656,260**	**635,170**	**333,549**	**683,111**	**610,552**
Total, Federal investment	**609,928**	**887,175**	**873,128**	**534,920**	**900,797**	**847,229**

6. RESEARCH AND DEVELOPMENT

Scientific discoveries, technological breakthroughs, and innovation are essential to expand the frontiers of what is possible and to meet the challenges and opportunities of the 21st Century. Now more than ever, science, technology, and innovation are instrumental to expanding opportunities for the American people, advancing the health of our communities, tackling the climate crisis, advancing global security and stability, realizing the benefits of artificial intelligence (AI) while managing its risks, and fostering a strong, resilient, and thriving democracy. The President's 2025 Budget is a testament to the Administration's commitment to collaborative investments that support the research, development, and application of technologies that advance American health, security, and competitiveness and keep America at the forefront of responsible innovation. The Budget invests $202 billion in research and development (R&D), a $2 billion increase over the 2023 enacted level and a $41 billion increase in R&D investments from the start of the Administration. The Budget provides $99 billion for basic and applied research, an increase of $2.2 billion above the 2023 enacted level and nearly $13 billion above the Administration's initial investments in these fundamental areas.

The Administration is harnessing the power of innovation to address important national missions that have not traditionally benefited from R&D. The Budget supports transformative research approaches—including those based on the successful model of the Defense Advanced Research Projects Agency (DARPA; $4.4 billion)—to tackle pressing societal challenges in health (ARPA-H; $1.5 billion), energy (ARPA-E; $450 million), and transportation (ARPA-I; $15 million). The Budget seeks to expand R&D to areas where those industries and jobs have not customarily thrived by supporting regional innovation initiatives at the National Science Foundation (NSF) and the Department of Commerce. The Administration is also committed to a dual mandate of leveraging AI for good—to improve the lives of the American people, advance knowledge, and make Government more effective—and providing protection from AI's risks.

CHIPS AND SCIENCE ACT

Public Law 117-167, commonly referred to as the CHIPS and Science Act of 2022 (CHIPS and Science Act) authorized discretionary funding for three science agencies: NSF, the Department of Commerce's National Institute of Standards and Technology (NIST), and the Department of Energy's (DOE) Office of Science. The Budget funds these agencies' toplines at $20.1 billion, collectively – a $1.2 billion increase over the 2023 enacted level – to support American innovation and leadership in research and scientific discovery.

- NSF is funded at $10.2 billion, seven percent higher than the 2023 level, including a 36 percent increase for the Directorate for Technology, Innovation, and Partnerships (TIP) and a 4.5 percent increase for emerging technologies. The Budget also supports NSF's STEM workforce programs, a key CHIPS and Science Act priority.
- The DOE Office of Science is funded at $8.6 billion, six percent higher than the 2023 level, to support cutting-edge research at the national laboratories and universities, build and operate world-class scientific user facilities, identify and accelerate novel technologies for clean energy solutions, provide new computing insight through quantum information, and position the United States to meet the demand for isotopes.
- NIST is funded at $1.5 billion, including targeted investments to advance research and standards development for critical and emerging technologies. This total also includes a $182 million increase over the 2023 level for maintenance, renovations, and improvements at its research campuses.

In addition to the funding at these three agencies, the Department of Commerce is responsible for administering $11 billion in CHIPS and Science Act funding to advance U.S. leadership in semiconductor R&D. As part of this, NIST awarded over $100 million across 29 projects in the CHIPS Metrology program. These projects will help inventors and entrepreneurs more easily scale innovations into commercial products.

PRIORITIES FOR FEDERAL RESEARCH AND DEVELOPMENT

Advancing Safe, Secure, and Trustworthy Artificial Intelligence

AI is one of the most powerful technologies of our time. Foundational research in AI and machine learning (ML) has never been more critical to the understanding, creation, and deployment of AI-powered systems that deliver transformative and trustworthy solutions across our society. To ensure that America leads the way in seizing the promise and managing the risks of AI, the Budget invests in AI programs across many agencies to: 1) equip the Federal Government to use AI technology to better deliver on a wide range of Government missions, 2) mitigate AI risks, and 3) advance public solutions to societal challenges that the private sector will not address on its own.

The Administration has already made significant investments in AI. For example, NSF has awarded 20 National AI Research Institutes and the U.S. Department of Agriculture (USDA) National Institute of Food and Agriculture is supporting five additional AI Institutes through this program. These Institutes represent multisector collaborations among Government, industry, academia, and philanthropy, and are aimed at: 1) advancing fundamental knowledge of AI; 2) using AI to solve real-world problems of importance to the nation; and 3) growing the U.S. AI workforce.

The Budget supports the development of innovative approaches to guide the design of regulatory and enforcement regimes for mitigating AI threats to truth, trust, and democracy; safety and security; privacy, civil rights, and civil liberties; and economic opportunity for all. The Budget bolsters the capacity of the Federal Government to bring in AI-enabling talent and other technological expertise, including the U.S. Digital Service, the Presidential Innovation Fellowship, U.S. Digital Corps, and the Technology Modernization Fund, and the technology offices at the Federal Trade Commission, the Department of Justice, and the Consumer Financial Protection Bureau. In addition, the Budget provides $200 million in mandatory R&D funding that will bolster efforts to harness the capacity of AI to accelerate scientific research across a variety of disciplines at multiple agencies.

The Budget invests in the development and deployment of methods to design, pilot, and assess the results of new approaches to apply AI to improve Government functions and public services. For example, the Budget continues to invest in the Department of Health and Human Services' (HHS) Office of the National Coordinator (ONC) to advance interoperability, improve transparency, and support the access, exchange, and use of electronic health information through the ONC Health Information Technology (IT) Certification Program, which recently established first-of-its-kind transparency requirements for AI and other predictive support algorithms that are part of certified health IT. ONC-certified health IT supports the care delivered by more than 96 percent of hospitals and 78 percent of office-based physicians around the country.

The Budget provides robust investments in AI R&D that span nine focus areas across more than six departments and agencies, including:

- $1.6 billion in investments across the National Institutes of Health (NIH). NIH launched the AI/ML Consortium to Advance Health Equity and Researcher Diversity (AIM-AHEAD) Program in 2021. This program seeks to increase the participation and representation of the researchers and communities that are currently underrepresented in AI/ML modeling and applications through mutually beneficial partnerships;
- $729 million for AI R&D at NSF (a ten percent increase from 2023 enacted), including $30 million for the second year of the National AI Research Resource Pilot, which is aimed at developing a roadmap for standing up a national research infrastructure to broaden access to the resources essential to AI R&D;
- $335 million for AI/ML within DOE, 54 percent above 2023 enacted, to enhance DOE's computing capabilities and support the development of AI testbeds to build foundational models for energy security, national security, and climate resilience as well as continuing support for training new researchers capable of meeting the rising demands for AI talent;
- $310 million for DARPA's AI Forward initiative to research and develop trustworthy technology that operates reliably, interacts appropriately with people, and meets the most pressing national security and societal needs in an ethical manner;
- $50 million at NIST to spearhead development of standards and tests to ensure that AI systems are safe, secure, and trustworthy;
- $37 million for DOE's National Nuclear Security Administration (NNSA) to develop capabilities that assess the potential for AI misuse that enables the development or production of chemical, biological, nuclear, and radiological threats and provides an annual technical assessment of proprietary and open-source large language models; and
- $10 million at the Department of Veterans Affairs (VA) to support medical and prosthetic research.

These investments hold promise for catalyzing groundbreaking advancements across all sectors of society.

Maintaining Global Security and Stability

In the face of immense geopolitical changes and evolving risks, the Budget supports R&D that will create the next generation of national security technologies and capabilities that will promote and protect the health, safety, and prosperity of the American people. At a time when our allies and partners look to American leadership to uphold global security, it is crucial to not only mitigate critical national security risks but also propel the responsible development and adoption of technology at a pace that aligns with the demands of a competitive global environment.

The Budget includes $92.8 billion in Department of Defense (DOD) R&D to support the development of next generation defense capabilities, including in critical and emerging technology areas such as AI and autonomy; quantum information science; biotechnology and biomanufacturing; advanced materials; next generation wireless communication; human-machine interfaces; directed energy, hypersonic system development; integrated sensing and cyber; and microelectronics. Since 2022, the Administration has made significant investments in these critical and emerging technology areas with a focus on technology development, prototype maturation, and the transition of promising prototypes to fully-developed defense capabilities to satisfy military requirements.

Civilian and defense agencies are cooperating to harness science and technology intelligence and develop analytic capabilities to assess U.S. competitiveness. Specifically, NSF and DOD will work together in a central interagency hub to conduct Global Competitive Analysis that will deliver a comprehensive and data-driven view of the competitive dynamics between the U.S., its allies, and its adversaries across the breadth of the technology ecosystem, including technologies and broader policy enablers.

The Budget supports DOE's NNSA science-based program to maintain a safe, secure, and reliable nuclear stockpile, including $683 million for inertial confinement fusion to replicate in a laboratory environment conditions of a nuclear detonation and $880 million for advanced simulation and computing to interpret the vast data from such experiments. The Budget also provides $69 million to conduct early technical assessments of future nuclear capabilities and threats.

DOE's NNSA will mature new capabilities for space situational awareness to reinforce arms control and verification missions in support of current treaties, like the Outer Space Treaty. This work protects our national interests and assets, providing information on activities all the way to the lunar surface and beyond. Specifically, the Budget funds the NNSA Space Monitoring and Verification Program at $35 million, advancing our space-based sensing capability.

Tackling the Climate Crisis and Environmental Impacts

Building on the climate funding and tax benefits enacted in the Infrastructure Investment and Jobs Act (IIJA; Public Law 117-58) and Public Law 117-169, commonly referred to as the Inflation Reduction Act of 2022 (IRA) to spur deployment of currently available climate and clean energy solutions, the Budget prioritizes R&D investments that advance the Administration's climate goals, including by leading the world on next generation technology development, harnessing the power of nature, strengthening and protecting the health of communities, especially those disproportionately impacted by climate change, lowering energy costs for families, protecting biodiversity, and creating good-paying jobs here in the United States.

The Budget supports over $10.7 billion in clean energy innovation activities that are crucial for the nation to achieve net-zero greenhouse gas emissions economy-wide no later than 2050 as embodied in the Long-Term Strategy of the United States: Pathways to Net-Zero Greenhouse Gas Emissions by 2050. Since the start of the Administration, the President has requested, and Congress has enacted, year-over-year increases in the total Government-wide funding for clean energy innovation. The Net-Zero Game Changers Initiative frames 37 innovative technologies, systems, and solutions that will drive significant emissions reductions across sectors. For example, the Budget includes $844 million for a DOE-wide initiative to accelerate the viability of commercial fusion energy, coordinating academia, national laboratories, and the private sector, which supports the Bold Decadal Vision for Commercial Fusion Energy. In addition, DOE's Energy Earthshots initiative aligns climate and energy innovation programs towards a common purpose linking innovation to widespread commercial adoption with the Pathways to Commercial Liftoff effort. The Budget includes $450 million for ARPA-E, which will advance high-impact transformational technologies to cut emissions and make our infrastructure smarter and more resilient, as well as over $3.1 billion for the Office of Energy Efficiency and Renewable Energy to conduct R&D across clean energy sources and uses, ranging from solar and energy to buildings and manufacturing. The Budget also includes $143 million within the DOE Office of Nuclear Energy for five ongoing cost-shared projects to resolve technical, operational, and regulatory challenges and enable future demonstration of a diverse set of advanced reactor designs. The Budget invests $325 million for critical minerals R&D across DOE to advance the goals of increasing domestically-sourced critical minerals, supporting more sustainable extraction, and minimizing supply chain disruptions for products that rely on critical minerals such as batteries for electric vehicles. At NASA, the Budget calls for more than $500 million for green aviation research and development activities, which will lead to the introduction of ultra-efficient U.S.-made commercial airliners in the next decade.

Further, to advance our understanding of climate change and its implications, the Budget supports $4.5 billion in climate research activities, including the U.S. Global Change Research Program's (USGCRP) Decadal Strategic Plan. The Budget also advances, through coordination by USGCRP, the development of actionable climate services consistent with the Federal Framework and Action Plan, to support communities, Governments, and businesses in enhancing resilience and taking action. USGCRP activities in the Budget include:

- $407 million to support DOE's Office of Science in improving the predictability of climate trends and impacts using high performance computing and advances climate modeling.
- $54 million at the Environmental Protection Agency (EPA) to support USGCRP assessments, air and water quality research, environmental assessments of mitigation technologies, and the Creating Resilient Water Utilities initiative;
- $69 million for the U.S. Geological Survey's National and Regional Climate Adaptation Science Centers, including support for interagency climate resilience technical assistance and climate service coordination;
- $16 million for the National Oceanic and Atmospheric Administration's Climate Adaptation Partnerships, which will support collaborative efforts that help communities build equitable climate resilience;
- $150 million at NASA to develop the next generation of Landsat satellites, which will provide important

data for water resource management and climate science; and

- $218 million at the USDA, including $27 million for Climate Hubs.

The Budget supports increased coordination and integration of greenhouse gas measurement and monitoring activities, consistent with the National Strategy to Advance an Integrated U.S. Greenhouse Gas Measurement, Monitoring, and Information System. This includes continued support for multi-agency efforts like the U.S. Greenhouse Gas Center and research to better understand greenhouse gas emissions and removals from natural systems.

The Budget funds R&D efforts to improve analysis for difficult-to-monetize or -quantify policy options and technologies such as ecosystem services, track natural assets through the increasingly developed national system of environmental and economic statistics (i.e., natural capital accounting), support the National Nature Assessment, and advance recommendations in the Nature-Based Solutions Roadmap. Natural capital accounting capabilities and research continue to evolve and grow consistent with the National Strategy to Develop Statistics for Environmental-Economic Decisions and are supported in the Budget within the Department of the Interior's (DOI) United States Geological Survey, USDA's Economic Research Service and Forest Service, the DOE's Energy Information Administration, the Department of Commerce's Bureau of Economic Analysis and National Oceanic and Atmospheric Administration, and the EPA.

The Budget also supports increased investment in R&D that would improve Federal land and water management as risks to natural resources increase due to climate change. The Budget provides $5 million to support the establishment of the Joint Office for Wildfire Science and Technology between USDA's Forest Service and DOI. In line with recommendations from the President's Council of Advisors on Science and Technology and the Wildland Fire Mitigation and Management Commission, this office would lead Forest Service and DOI's development, deployment, and sustainment of technology, science, and data to be used to improve safety, effectiveness, and cost efficiency across the full spectrum of wildland fire management operations. The Budget also provides $30 million for Bureau of Reclamation research and development supporting applied research to increase water conservation and expand water supplies, including $7 million for desalination and water purification.

Achieving Better Health Outcomes for Every Person

The President's Budget makes major investments in R&D activities to achieve better health outcomes in communities across the United States.

The President has set the ambitious goals of cutting the age-adjusted death rate from cancer by at least 50 percent over the next 25 years, preventing more than four million cancer deaths by 2047, and improving the experience of people who are touched by cancer. The Budget robustly funds activities to help the Cancer Moonshot achieve its goal of ending cancer as we know it, including efforts to close the screening gap, understand and address environmental and toxic exposures, decrease the impact of preventable cancers, bring cutting-edge research through the pipeline of patients and communities, and support patients and caregivers.

At more than $3.4 billion in R&D for Cancer Moonshot-related investments, the Budget supports laboratory, clinical, public health, and environmental health research programs that span five focus areas across more than a dozen departments and agencies, including:

- $2.9 billion in discretionary and mandatory resources at HHS supporting Cancer Moonshot activities across the National Cancer Institute, and cancer projects at the Advanced Research Projects Agency for Health (ARPA-H);
- $521 million at EPA to support cancer prevention and environmental justice priorities;
- $45 million for VA's Cancer Moonshot clinical and research initiatives; and
- $30 million for research at DOD and $59 million for the Murtha Cancer Center Research Programs—the APOLLO project, the Framingham Blood Serum Program, and the Cancer Research and Clinical Trials Network.

Since its launch in March 2022, ARPA-H has initiated multiple programs and onboarded 50 program managers as they work towards their ambitious goals. The R&D programs funded by ARPA-H impact cancer and other diseases, conditions, and disruptive health systems and continued funds will allow ARPA-H to successfully launch programs, such as the Novel Innovations for Tissue Regeneration in Osteoarthritis, Precision Surgical Interventions, and Platform Accelerating Rural Access to Distributed & InteGrated Medical care.

The Budget provides $317 million to bolster the capacity to mitigate current and emerging health threats across the Centers for Disease Prevention and Control, including addressing antimicrobial resistance investing in advanced molecular detection, wastewater surveillance and continued support for the Center for Forecasting, and Outbreak Analytics. The Budget will continue to make progress toward ending the HIV epidemic globally with bilateral assistance through the President's Emergency Plan for AIDS Relief (PEPFAR).

To achieve the promise of the President's Unity Agenda, the Budget emphasizes R&D investments to tackle an unprecedented mental health crisis, with resources targeted towards at-risk communities like caregivers, medical professionals, youth, and members of the LGBTQI+ community by providing support for behavioral and mental health for all Americans. The Budget emphasizes suicide prevention and mental health of our veterans with over $135 million for VA Medical Care.

Reducing Barriers and Inequalities While Strengthening Research

The Budget supports workforce development in science, technology, engineering, and mathematics (STEM) all across America with an emphasis on emerging research institutions and historically underserved communities. In addition, the Budget increases funding for work to secure the Nation's research enterprise, make that enterprise more efficient, and increase public access to federally-funded research.

Key workforce efforts include:

- NSF's programs to broaden participation of underrepresented groups in STEM education and research programs, such as Expanding AI Innovation through Capacity Building and Partnerships (ExpandAI) and the Experiential Learning for Emerging and Novel Technologies (ExLENT) program;
- Department of Commerce efforts to nurture STEM talent and develop the EDA's STEM Talent Challenge; and
- The Minority Serving Institution Partnership Program at DOE's NNSA and DOE's Reaching a New Energy Sciences Workforce (RENEW) program.

Multiple agencies are also supporting and building R&D capacity at Historically Black Colleges and Universities (HBCUs), Tribally Controlled Colleges and Universities (TCCUs), and Minority Servicing Institutions (MSIs):

- DOE proposes to build capacity for advancing energy research and developing a new energy workforce at HBCUs, MSIs, Tribal Colleges, Community Colleges and emerging research institutions;
- NSF supports education and research at minority-serving institutions through programs such as HBCU – Excellence in Research, HBCU – Undergraduate Program, Hispanic Serving Institutions Program, and the Tribal Colleges and Universities Program;
- DOD proposes to fund individual grants in research areas important to the DOD, equipment, and cooperative agreements with HBCUs and other minority-serving institutions;
- The Department of Transportation invests in the University Transportation Centers
- NASA supports the Minority University Research & Education Project to build STEM capacity and retain underrepresented students in STEM at minority-serving institutions; and
- The Department of Homeland Security proposes to support summer research experiences for MSI participants in order to advance research areas of importance to DHS and strengthen the talent pool for the homeland security enterprise.

Research security efforts in both the industrial and academic sectors continue to identify and address challenges to protect the Nation's research enterprise. NSF will stand up the SECURE Center, authorized by the CHIPS and Science Act, to serve as a clearinghouse for research security information to share with the research community, to share information and reports on research security risks, and to provide training to the research community. NSF is also identifying ways to use the Growing Research Access for Nationally Transformative Equity and Diversity (GRANTED) program, an initiative to increase participation and competitiveness of researchers and investigators at emerging research institutions, to support research security assistance at HBCUs, MSIs, and TCCUs. At NIH, funding will support the Offices of Data Science to oversee data management and sharing, the responsible use of data, data science training to staff, and new funding programs in data science. These efforts strengthen the data science workforce within NIH and provide a strong foundation for continued growth.

The Budget includes funding at multiple agencies for the infrastructure and capacity to provide free, immediate, and equitable public access to federally-funded research results, while developing mechanisms to incentivize and reward open, reproducible, and secure research practices, in ways that benefit individuals, industry, and innovators everywhere. For example, the Budget proposes investments at NSF to support public access activities, such as those through the Findable, Accessible, Interoperable, and Reusable Research Coordination Networks and Pathways to Enable Open-Source Ecosystems programs, which aim to support best practices in open science through coordination of research projects, development of community standards, advancing educational opportunities, and fostering synthesis and new collaborations. At NASA, the Budget includes funding to advance its Transform to Open Science Initiative, developing training and incentivizing researchers to accelerate adoption of practices that increase public access to the Nation's taxpayer-supported research.

The Budget supports new approaches to achieve agency missions, such as streamlining processes to minimize administrative burdens, engaging new R&D performers, exploring new R&D methods, and forging new partnerships. The Administration's evidence agenda includes the design and implementation of rigorous experiments and evaluations, data sharing agreements, and prototyping exercises to answer critical policy questions by generating comparative evidence about how well different approaches can help us reach national goals more equitably, effectively, and expeditiously, with appropriate privacy protections in place. These efforts include:

- A Census Bureau partnership with the National Telecommunications and Information Administration (NTIA) to understand the economic impacts of broadband infrastructure, adoption, and digital equity by providing detailed, single-year estimates, as well as through its community resilience estimates, which include broadband access as a metric for assessing the capacity of communities to cope with and respond to disasters; and

- NSF's Analytics for Equity Initiative, which pilots a new way to support social, economic, and behavioral sciences research that leverages federal data assets (ensuring privacy is protected and data are secure) and scientific advances in researching equity-related topics for greater.

Bolstering R&D for Future Economic Competitiveness

The Administration prioritizes supporting and expanding applied research, experimental development, pre-commercialization, standards, and related efforts that will facilitate the adoption of a broad range of new technologies. Emerging technology R&D efforts include:

- Robust funding for biotechnology and biomanufacturing research and development, including all components of the pre-commercial pipeline, that support bio in the economy;
- $900 million, an increase of 36 percent from 2023, for NSF's TIP Directorate, which focuses on building partnerships across R&D sectors to translate basic R&D to products and processes that can benefit the American people; and
- $606 million at DOE's Office of Science to integrate supercomputing, AI, and quantum-based technology for developing next-generation high performance computing systems to ensure U.S. leadership while broadening access to leading-edge computing resources by the community.

The Budget builds on regional innovation and resilience by invigorating communities and traditional or emerging industries to spark growth and create good-paying jobs. This builds on the Inflation Reduction Act's R&D payroll tax credit, which incentivizes qualified R&D activities while reducing tax liability for companies. Notable investments include $4 billion in mandatory funding and $41 million in discretionary funding for EDA's Regional Technology and Innovation Hub Program. This funding would enable EDA to establish cutting-edge and strategic regional technology hubs that foster the geographic diversity of innovation and create quality jobs in underserved and vulnerable communities. The Budget also includes $205 million for the Regional Innovation Engines program in NSF's TIP Directorate, which was first proposed by the Administration in 2022 and recently announced awards of up to $160 million each over ten years to 10 teams spanning universities, nonprofits, businesses and other organizations across the United States. Both programs have made important strides and issued initial awards in 2023 and the Budget will drive additional growth to create innovation ecosystems in parts of the Nation that do not have them.

FEDERAL RESEARCH AND DEVELOPMENT DATA

R&D is the collection of efforts directed toward gaining greater knowledge or understanding and applying knowledge toward the production of useful materials, devices, and methods. R&D investments can be characterized as basic research, applied research, development, R&D equipment, or R&D facilities. The Office of Management and Budget has used those or similar categories in its collection of R&D data since 1949. Please note that R&D crosscuts in specific topical areas as mandated by law will be reported separately in forthcoming Supplements to the President's 2025 Budget.

Background on Federal R&D Funding

More than 20 Federal agencies fund R&D in the United States. The character of the R&D that these agencies fund depends on the mission of each agency and on the role of R&D in accomplishing it. Table 6-1 shows agency-by-agency spending on basic research, applied research, experimental development, and R&D equipment and facilities.

Basic research is systematic study directed toward a fuller knowledge or understanding of the fundamental aspects of phenomena and of observable facts without specific applications toward processes or products in mind. Basic research, however, may include activities with broad applications in mind.

Applied research is systematic study to gain knowledge or understanding necessary to determine the means by which a recognized and specific need may be met.

Experimental development is creative and systematic work, drawing on knowledge gained from research and practical experience, which is directed at producing new products or processes or improving existing products or processes. Like research, experimental development will result in gaining additional knowledge.

Research and development equipment includes acquisition or design and production of movable equipment, such as spectrometers, research satellites, detectors, and other instruments. At a minimum, this category includes programs devoted to the purchase or construction of R&D equipment.

Research and development facilities include the acquisition, design, and construction of, or major repairs or alterations to, all physical facilities for use in R&D activities. Facilities include land, buildings, and fixed capital equipment, regardless of whether the facilities are to be used by the Government or by a private organization, and regardless of where title to the property may rest. This category includes such fixed facilities as reactors, wind tunnels, and particle accelerators.

Table 6–1. FEDERAL RESEARCH AND DEVELOPMENT SPENDING
(Mandatory and discretionary budget authority [1], dollar amounts in millions)

	2023 Actual	2024 Estimate [2]	2025 Proposed	Dollar Change: 2024 to 2025	Percent Change: 2024 to 2025
By Agency					
Defense [3]	95,541	90,632	92,757	2,125	2%
Health and Human Services	48,393	47,591	51,364	3,773	8%
Energy	20,790	22,237	23,440	1,203	5%
NASA	11,691	11,797	11,715	-82	-1%
National Science Foundation	7,988	7,800	8,122	322	4%
Agriculture	3,380	3,379	3,283	-96	-3%
Commerce	5,141	3,930	3,926	-4	0%
Veterans Affairs	1,684	1,799	1,709	-90	-5%
Transportation	1,411	1,462	1,513	51	3%
Interior	1,296	1,258	1,330	72	6%
Homeland Security	634	634	544	-90	-14%
Environmental Protection Agency	568	568	614	46	8%
Education	389	446	441	-5	-1%
Smithsonian Institution	347	347	390	43	12%
Other	702	684	601 [4]	-83	-12%
AI Mandatory Proposal	0	0	200	200	....
TOTAL	**199,955**	**194,564**	**201,949** [4]	**7,385**	**4%**
Basic Research					
Defense	2,847	2,519	2,493	-26	-1%
Health and Human Services	23,097	22,748	23,602	854	4%
Energy	6,775	6,324	6,923	599	9%
NASA	5,115	5,417	5,302	-115	-2%
National Science Foundation	6,290	6,134	6,267	133	2%
Agriculture	1,392	1,386	1,383	-3	0%
Commerce	316	316	355	39	12%
Veterans Affairs	683	756	718	-38	-5%
Transportation	....	....	....	....	....
Interior	101	99	105	6	6%
Homeland Security	62	62	62	0	0%
Environmental Protection Agency	....	....	....	....	....
Education	29	28	28	0	0%
Smithsonian Institution	314	314	351	37	12%
Other	2	2	2	0	0%
AI Mandatory Proposal	0	0	93	93	....
SUBTOTAL	**47,023**	**46,105**	**47,684**	**1,579**	**3%**
Applied Research					
Defense	8,013	6,237	6,024	-213	-3%
Health and Human Services	24,819	24,363	27,262	2,899	12%
Energy	6,643	7,086	7,351	265	4%
NASA	1,843	1,948	2,228	280	14%
National Science Foundation	1,178	1,155	1,215	60	5%
Agriculture	1,371	1,372	1,358	-14	-1%
Commerce	1,637	1,495	1,412	-83	-6%
Veterans Affairs	965	1,007	953	-54	-5%
Transportation	981	1,036	1,045	9	1%
Interior	990	955	1,014	59	6%
Homeland Security	161	161	149	-12	-7%
Environmental Protection Agency	441	441	477	36	8%
Education	256	292	290	-2	-1%
Smithsonian Institution	....	....	....	....	....
Other	427	382	346	-36	-9%
AI Mandatory Proposal	0	0	97	97	....
SUBTOTAL	**49,725**	**47,930**	**51,221**	**3,291**	**7%**

Table 6–1. FEDERAL RESEARCH AND DEVELOPMENT SPENDING —Continued

(Mandatory and discretionary budget authority [1], dollar amounts in millions)

	2023 Actual	2024 Estimate [2]	2025 Proposed	Dollar Change: 2024 to 2025	Percent Change: 2024 to 2025
Experimental Development					
Defense [3]	84,681	81,624	84,019	2,395	3%
Health and Human Services	46	58	58	0	0%
Energy	4,499	5,270	5,343	73	1%
NASA	4,654	4,399	4,133	-266	-6%
National Science Foundation	....	....	....	....	....
Agriculture	295	296	334	38	13%
Commerce	2,361	1,627	1,510	-117	-7%
Veterans Affairs	36	36	38	2	6%
Transportation	384	384	391	7	2%
Interior	203	202	209	7	3%
Homeland Security	356	356	283	-73	-21%
Environmental Protection Agency	127	127	137	10	8%
Education	104	126	123	-3	-2%
Smithsonian Institution	....	....	....	....	....
Other	271	298	253	-45	-15%
AI Mandatory Proposal	....	....	....	....	....
SUBTOTAL	**98,017**	**94,803**	**96,831**	**2,028**	**2%**
Facilities and Equipment					
Defense	0	252	221	-31	-12%
Health and Human Services	431	422	442	20	5%
Energy	2,873	3,557	3,823	266	7%
NASA	79	33	52	19	58%
National Science Foundation	520	511	640	129	25%
Agriculture	322	325	208	-117	-36%
Commerce	827	492	649	157	32%
Veterans Affairs	....	....	....	....	....
Transportation	46	42	77	35	83%
Interior	2	2	2	0	0%
Homeland Security	55	55	50	-5	-9%
Environmental Protection Agency	....	....	....	....	....
Education	....	....	....	....	....
Smithsonian Institution	33	33	39	6	18%
Other	2	2	0[4]	-2	-100%
AI Mandatory Proposal	0	0	10	10	....
SUBTOTAL	**5,190**	**5,726**	**6,213[4]**	**487**	**9%**

[1] This table shows funding levels for Departments or Independent agencies with more than $200 million in R&D activities in 2025.

[2] The 2024 Estimate column applies the main 2025 Budget volume approach of using annualized appropriations provided by the 2024 Continuing Resolution.

[3] DOD's contribution to the overall Federal R&D budget includes DOD Research, Development, Test, and Evaluation Budget Activities 6.1 through 6.6 (Basic Research; Applied Research; Advanced Technology Development; Advanced Component Development and Prototypes; System Development and Demonstation; and Management Support).

[4] Does not match the amount published in the 2025 Appendix, but is the correct amount.

7. CREDIT AND INSURANCE

The Federal Government offers direct loans and loan guarantees to support a wide range of activities including home ownership, student loans, small business, farming, energy, infrastructure investment, and exports. In addition, Government-sponsored enterprises (GSEs) operate under Federal charters for the purpose of enhancing credit availability for targeted sectors. Through its insurance programs, the Federal Government insures deposits at depository institutions, guarantees private-sector defined-benefit pensions, and insures against some other risks such as flood and terrorism. These programs are also exposed to climate-related financial risks, which the private sector is increasingly taking into account in the pricing of financial products. For a discussion of climate risks faced by Federal housing loans, please see the "Analysis of Federal Climate Financial Risk Exposure" chapter of this volume.

This chapter discusses the roles of these diverse programs. The first section discusses individual credit programs and GSEs. The second section reviews Federal deposit insurance, pension guarantees, disaster insurance, and insurance against terrorism and other security-related risks. The final section includes a brief analysis of the Troubled Asset Relief Program (TARP).

I. CREDIT IN VARIOUS SECTORS

Housing Credit Programs

Through its main housing credit programs, the Federal Government promotes homeownership among various groups that may face barriers to owning a home, including low- and moderate-income people, veterans, and rural residents. By expanding affordable homeownership opportunities for underserved borrowers, these programs can advance equity. In times of economic crisis, the Federal Government's role and target market can expand dramatically.

Federal Housing Administration

The Federal Housing Administration (FHA) guarantees single-family mortgages that expand access to homeownership for households who may have difficulty obtaining a conventional mortgage. In addition to traditional single-family "forward" mortgages, FHA insures "reverse" mortgages for seniors (Home Equity Conversion Mortgages, described below) and loans for the construction, rehabilitation, and refinancing of multifamily housing, hospitals, and other healthcare facilities.

FHA Single-Family Forward Mortgages

FHA has been a primary facilitator of mortgage credit for first-time and minority homebuyers, a pioneer of products such as the 30-year self-amortizing mortgage, and a vehicle to enhance credit for many low- to moderate-income households. One of the major benefits of an FHA-insured mortgage is that it provides a homeownership option for borrowers who, though they can only make a modest down payment, can show that they are creditworthy and have sufficient income to afford the house they want to buy. First-time homebuyers accounted for 82 percent of new FHA purchase loans in 2023 and, for calendar year (CY) 2022, the low-income homebuyer share was over 40 percent. In the market as a whole, more than half of all Black and Hispanic borrowers who obtained low down payment mortgages (less than 5 percent down) in CY 2022 relied on FHA.

FHA Home Equity Conversion Mortgages

Home Equity Conversion Mortgages (HECMs), or "reverse" mortgages, are designed to support aging in place by enabling elderly homeowners to borrow against the equity in their homes without having to make repayments during their lifetime (unless they sell, refinance, or fail to meet certain requirements). A HECM is known as a "reverse" mortgage because the change in home equity over time is generally the opposite of a forward mortgage. While a traditional forward mortgage starts with a small amount of equity and builds equity with amortization of the loan, a HECM starts with a large equity cushion that declines over time as the loan accrues interest and premiums. The risk of HECMs is therefore weighted toward the end of the mortgage, while forward mortgage risk is concentrated in the first 10 years.

FHA Mutual Mortgage Insurance (MMI) Fund

FHA guarantees for forward and reverse mortgages are administered under the Mutual Mortgage Insurance (MMI) Fund. At the end of 2023, the MMI Fund had $1.38 trillion in total mortgages outstanding and a capital ratio of 10.51 percent, a minor decrease from the 2022 level of 11.11 percent. For more information on the financial status of the MMI Fund, please see the *Annual Report to Congress Regarding the Financial Status of the FHA Mutual Mortgage Insurance Fund, Fiscal Year 2023.*[1]

FHA's new origination volume in 2023 was $209 billion for forward mortgages and $16 billion for HECMs, and the Budget projects $220 billion and $18 billion, respectively, for 2025.

[1] https://www.hud.gov/sites/dfiles/PA/documents/2023FHAAnnualReportMMIFund.pdf

FHA Multifamily and Healthcare Guarantees

In addition to the single-family mortgage insurance provided through the MMI Fund, FHA's General Insurance and Special Risk Insurance (GISRI) loan programs continue to facilitate the construction, rehabilitation, and refinancing of multifamily housing, hospitals, and other healthcare facilities. The credit enhancement provided by FHA enables borrowers to obtain long-term, fixed-rate financing, which mitigates interest rate risk and facilitates lower monthly mortgage payments. This can improve the financial sustainability of multifamily housing and healthcare facilities, and may also translate into more affordable rents and lower healthcare costs for consumers.

GISRI's new origination loan volume for all programs in 2023 was $17 billion and the Budget projects $18 billion for 2025. The total amount of guarantees outstanding on mortgages in the FHA GISRI Fund were $167 billion at the end of 2023.

VA Housing Loan Program

The Department of Veterans Affairs (VA) assists veterans, members of the Selected Reserve, and active duty personnel in purchasing homes in recognition of their service to the Nation. The VA housing loan program effectively substitutes a Federal guarantee for the borrower's down payment, meaning more favorable lending terms for veterans. Under this program, VA does not guarantee the entire mortgage loan, but typically fully guarantees the first 25 percent of losses upon default. In fiscal year 2023, VA guaranteed a total of 320,274 new purchase home loans, providing approximately $119.4 billion in guarantees. VA also guaranteed 5,000 Interest Rate Reduction Refinance loans and veteran borrowers lowered interest rates on their home mortgages through streamlined refinancing. VA provided approximately $144 billion in guarantees for 400,695 VA loans in fiscal year 2023. That followed $257 billion in guarantees for 746,091 VA loans closed in fiscal year 2022.

VA, in cooperation with VA-guaranteed loan servicers, also assists borrowers through home retention options and alternatives to foreclosure. VA intervenes when needed to help veterans and servicemembers avoid foreclosure through loan modifications, special forbearances, repayment plans, and acquired loans, as well as assistance to complete compromised sales or deeds-in-lieu of foreclosure. These standard efforts helped resolve over 96 percent of defaulted VA-guaranteed loans and assisted 145,480 veterans retain homeownership or avoid foreclosure in 2023. These efforts resulted in over $2.5 billion in avoided guaranteed claim payments. VA has responded to the COVID-19 crisis by providing special CARES Act (Public Law 116-136) forbearances to support otherwise-current borrowers through the pandemic. As of September 30, 2023, 24,833 VA borrowers were participating in a special COVID-19 forbearance.

Rural Housing Service

The Rural Housing Service (RHS) at the U.S. Department of Agriculture (USDA) offers direct and guaranteed loans to help very-low- to moderate-income rural residents buy and maintain adequate, affordable housing. RHS housing loans and loan guarantees differ from other Federal housing loan programs in that they are means-tested, making them more accessible to low-income, rural residents. The single family housing guaranteed loan program is designed to provide home loan guarantees for moderate-income rural residents whose incomes are between 80 percent and 115 percent (maximum for the program) of area median income.

RHS has traditionally offered both direct and guaranteed homeownership loans. The direct single family housing loans have been historically funded at $1.2 billion a year, while the single family housing guaranteed loan program, authorized in 1990 at $100 million, has grown into a $30 billion loan program annually. USDA also offers direct and guaranteed multifamily housing loans, as well as housing repair loans.

Education Credit Programs

The Department of Education (ED) direct student loan program is one of the largest Federal credit programs, with $1.34 trillion in Direct Loan principal outstanding in 2023. The Federal student loan programs provide students and their families with the funds to help meet postsecondary education costs. Because funding for the loan programs is provided through mandatory budget authority, student loans are considered separately for budget purposes from other Federal student financial assistance programs (which are largely discretionary), but should be viewed as part of the overall Federal effort to expand access to higher education.

Loans for higher education were first authorized under the William D. Ford program, which was included in the Higher Education Act of 1965 (Public Law 89-329). The direct loan program was authorized by the Student Loan Reform Act of 1993 (subtitle A of title IV of Public Law 103–66). The enactment of the SAFRA Act (subtitle A of title II of Public Law 111–152) ended the guaranteed Federal Financial Education Loan program. On July 1, 2010, ED became the sole originator of Federal student loans through the Direct Loan program.

Under the current direct loan program, the Federal Government partners with over 5,500 institutions of higher education, which then disburse loan funds to students. Loans are available to students and parents of students regardless of income, and only Parent and Graduate PLUS loans include a minimal credit check. There are three types of Direct Loans: Federal Direct Subsidized Stafford Loans, Federal Direct Unsubsidized Stafford Loans, and Federal Direct PLUS Loans, each with different terms.

The Direct Loan program offers a variety of repayment options, including income-driven repayment ones for all student borrowers. Depending on the plan, monthly payments are capped at no more than 5 to 15 percent of borrower discretionary income, with any remaining balance after 10 to 25 years of payments forgiven. In addition, borrowers working in public service professions while making 10 years of qualifying payments are eligible for Public Service Loan Forgiveness.

The Department of Education also operates the Historically Black College and Universities (HBCU) Capital Financing Program. Since fiscal year 1996, the Program has provided HBCUs with access to low-cost capital financing for the repair, renovation, and, in exceptional circumstances, construction or acquisition of educational facilities, instructional equipment, research instrumentation, and physical infrastructure.

Small Business and Farm Credit Programs

The Government offers direct loans and loan guarantees to small businesses and farmers, who may have difficulty obtaining credit elsewhere. It also provides guarantees of debt issued by certain investment funds that invest in small businesses. Two GSEs, the Farm Credit System and the Federal Agricultural Mortgage Corporation, increase liquidity in the agricultural lending market.

Small Business Administration

The Small Business Administration (SBA) ensures that small businesses across the Nation have the tools and resources needed to start, grow, and recover their business. SBA's lending programs complement credit markets by offering creditworthy small businesses access to affordable credit through private lenders when they cannot otherwise obtain financing on reasonable terms or conditions.

In 2023, SBA provided $26 billion in loan guarantees to assist small business owners with access to affordable capital through its largest program, the 7(a) General Business Loan Guarantee program. This program provides access to financing for general business operations, such as operating and capital expenses. In addition, through the 504 Certified Development Company (CDC) and Refinance Programs, SBA supported $6 billion in guaranteed loans for fixed-asset financing and provided the opportunity for small businesses to refinance existing 504 CDC loans. These programs enable small businesses to secure financing for assets such as machinery and equipment, construction, and commercial real estate, and to free up resources for expansion. The Small Business Investment Company (SBIC) Program also supports privately-owned and -operated venture capital investment firms that invest in small businesses. In 2023, SBA supported $4 billion in SBIC venture capital investments. In addition to these guaranteed lending programs, the 7(m) Direct Microloan program supports the smallest of businesses, startups, and underserved entrepreneurs through loans of up to $50,000 made by non-profit intermediaries. In 2023, SBA facilitated a record $52 million in microlending.

Community Development Financial Institutions

Since its creation in 1994, the Department of the Treasury's (Treasury) Community Development Financial Institutions (CDFI) Fund has, through different grant, loan, and tax credit programs, worked to expand the availability of credit, investment capital, and financial services for underserved people and communities by supporting the growth and capacity of a national network of CDFIs, investors, and financial service providers. Today, there are more than 1,480 Certified CDFIs nationwide, including a variety of loan funds, community development banks, credit unions, and venture capital funds. CDFI certification also enables some non-depository financial institutions to apply for financing programs offered by certain Federal Home Loan Banks.

Unlike other CDFI Fund programs, the CDFI Bond Guarantee Program (BGP), enacted through the Small Business Jobs Act of 2010, does not offer grants, but is instead exclusively a Federal credit program. The BGP was designed to provide CDFIs greater access to low-cost, long-term, fixed-rate capital.

Under the BGP, the Treasury provides a 100 percent guarantee on long-term bonds of at least $100 million issued to qualified CDFIs, with a maximum maturity of 30 years. To date, the Treasury has issued nearly $2.5 billion in bond guarantee commitments to 27 CDFIs, over $1.6 billion of which has been disbursed to help finance affordable housing, charter schools, commercial real estate, community healthcare facilities, and other eligible uses in 34 States and the District of Columbia.

Farm Service Agency

Farm operating loans were first offered in 1937 by the newly created Farm Security Administration (FSA) to assist family farmers who were unable to obtain credit from a commercial source to buy equipment, livestock, or seed. Farm ownership loans were authorized in 1961 to provide family farmers with financial assistance to purchase farmland. Presently, FSA assists low-income family farmers in starting and maintaining viable farming operations. Emphasis is placed on aiding beginning and socially disadvantaged farmers. Legislation mandates that a portion of appropriated funds are set aside for exclusive use by those underserved groups.

FSA offers operating loans and ownership loans, both of which may be either direct or guaranteed loans. Operating loans provide credit to farmers and ranchers for annual production expenses and purchases of livestock, machinery, and equipment, while farm ownership loans assist producers in acquiring and developing their farming or ranching operations. As a condition of eligibility for direct loans, borrowers must be unable to obtain private credit at reasonable rates and terms. As FSA is the "lender of first opportunity," default rates on FSA direct loans are generally higher than those on private-sector loans. FSA-guaranteed farm loans are made to more creditworthy borrowers who have access to private credit markets. Because the private loan originators must, in most situations, retain 10 percent of the risk, they exercise care in examining the repayment ability of borrowers. The subsidy rates for the direct programs fluctuate largely because of changes in the interest component of the subsidy rate.

In 2023, there were more than 22,000 direct or guaranteed loan obligations totaling over $4.7 billion. The entire portfolio of outstanding debt as of September 30, 2023, totaled $33 billion, serving 122,000 farmers and ranchers. In 2023, the amount of lending declined in both dollar and volume terms, down 19 and seven percent, respectively. Lending in dollar terms for real estate purchases decreased for both direct loans (decreasing two percent) and guaranteed loans (decreasing 42 percent). Operating loan obligations also fell in dollar terms for guaranteed loans (decreasing 14 percent), but increased for direct loans (increasing six percent). The decline in 2023 obligations was not unexpected, particularly for farm ownership loans where increased real estate values and rising interest rates resulted in decreased demand for land purchases and real estate refinancing. Direct operating loans that provide working capital to farmers and ranchers did see an increase in 2023 as rising interest rates and cost of inputs pressuring farm profits and resulting in an increased need for the favorable rates and terms provided by the direct operating loan program. This cyclicality is typical for farm loan programs and underscores the importance of FSA's Farm Loan Programs as a safety net.

A beginning farmer is an individual or entity who: has operated a farm for not more than 10 years; substantially participates in farm operation; and, for farm ownership loans, the applicant cannot own a farm larger than 30 percent of the average size farm in the county at time of application. If the applicant is an entity, all entity members must be related by blood or marriage, and all members must be eligible beginning farmers. Beginning farmers received 60 percent of direct and guaranteed loans in 2023. Direct and guaranteed loan programs provided assistance totaling $2.7 billion to nearly 13,600 beginning farmers. Additionally in 2023, loans for socially disadvantaged farmers totaled nearly $1.1 billion to nearly 6,000 borrowers, of which $748 million was in the farm ownership program and $339 million in the farm operating program.

The FSA Microloan program increases overall direct and guaranteed lending to small niche producers and minorities. This program dramatically simplifies application procedures for small loans and implements more flexible eligibility and experience requirements. Demand for the micro-loan program continues to grow while delinquencies and defaults remain at or below those of the regular FSA operating loan program.

Energy and Infrastructure Credit Programs

The Department of Energy (DOE) administers four credit programs: Title XVII Innovative Technology Loan Guarantee Program (Title XVII), the Advanced Technology Vehicle Manufacturing (ATVM) Loan Program, the Tribal Energy Loan Guarantee Program, and the Carbon Dioxide Transportation Infrastructure Finance and Innovation Program. Section 1703 of title XVII of the Energy Policy Act of 2005, as amended (Public Law 109–58) authorizes DOE to issue loan guarantees for clean energy projects that employ innovative technologies or are supported by State Energy Financing Institutions to reduce, avoid, or sequester air pollutants or man-made greenhouse gases. To date, under Title XVII, DOE has issued five loan guarantees totaling over $15 billion to support the construction of two new commercial nuclear power reactors, a clean hydrogen production and storage project, and a solar plus storage virtual power plant project. DOE has three active conditional commitments totaling $1.5 billion. DOE is actively working with applicants proceeding to conditional commitment and financial close to utilize the $3.5 billion in appropriated credit subsidy and $73 billion in available loan guarantee authority currently available.

The American Recovery and Reinvestment Act of 2009 (Public Law 111–5) amended section 1705 of Title XVII and appropriated credit subsidy to support loan guarantees on a temporary basis for commercial or advanced renewable energy systems, electric power transmission systems, and leading-edge biofuel projects. Authority for the temporary program to extend new loans expired September 30, 2011. $16 billion in loans and loan guarantees was disbursed via 24 loan guarantees issued prior to the program's expiration.

Public Law 117-169, commonly referred to as the Inflation Reduction Act of 2022 (IRA) further amended section 1706 to the Title XVII program's authorizing statute and appropriated $4.8 billion in credit subsidy to support loan guarantees for projects that retool, repower, repurpose, or replace energy infrastructure and avoid, reduce, or sequester air pollutants or man-made greenhouse gases. Appropriated authority for the section 1706 program expires September 30, 2026. DOE is actively working with applicants toward conditional commitment and financial close.

Section 136 of the Energy Independence and Security Act of 2007 (Public Law 110–140) authorizes DOE to issue loans to support the development of advanced technology vehicles and qualifying components. In 2009, the Congress appropriated $7.5 billion in credit subsidy to support a maximum of $25 billion in loans under ATVM. From 2009 to 2011, DOE issued five loans totaling over $8 billion to support the manufacturing of advanced technology vehicles. Since 2021, DOE has issued 11 conditional commitments totaling over $19 billion, of which two loans have reach financial close. DOE has $4.6 billion in credit subsidy balances with no loan limitation and is actively working with applicants proceeding to conditional commitment and financial close.Title XXVI of the Energy Policy Act of 1992, as amended (Public Law 102-486) authorizes DOE to guarantee up to $20 billion in loans to Indian Tribes for energy development. The Congress has appropriated over $80 million in credit subsidy, cumulatively, to support tribal energy development. DOE issued a revised solicitation in 2022 and is actively working with applicants proceeding to conditional commitment and financial close.

Section 40304 of the Infrastructure Investment and Jobs Act (IIJA; Public Law 117-58) amended Title IX of the Energy Policy Act of 2005 by authorizing DOE to issue loans, loan guarantees, and grants to support the development of carbon dioxide transportation infrastructure (e.g., pipelines). The law provided $3 million for program start-up costs in 2022 and an advance appropriation of $2.1 billion in 2023 budget authority for the cost of loans, loan guarantees, and grants to eligible projects. DOE is actively working to establish the program.

Electric and Telecommunications Loans

Rural Utilities Service (RUS) programs of the USDA provide grants and loans to support the distribution of rural electrification, telecommunications, distance learning, and broadband infrastructure systems.

In 2023, RUS delivered $6.9 billion in direct electrification loans (including $1.87 billion in Federal Financing Bank (FFB) Electric Loans, $900 million in electric underwriting, and $201.5 million rural energy savings loans), $17.1 million in direct and FFB telecommunications loans, and $1.99 billion in Reconnect broadband loans. RUS also helped a rural Kentucky electric utility. As a result, RUS made an operating loan to a local cooperative for $122.8 million, which also unlocked an additional $12.3 million in energy efficiency initiatives.

USDA Rural Infrastructure and Business Development Programs

USDA, through a variety of Rural Development (RD) programs, provides grants, direct loans, and loan guarantees to communities for constructing facilities such as healthcare clinics, police stations, and water systems, as well as to assist rural businesses and cooperatives in creating new community infrastructure (e.g., educational and healthcare networks) and to diversify the rural economy and employment opportunities. In 2023, RD provided $1.1 billion in Community Facility (CF) direct loans, which are for communities of 20,000 or less. The CF programs have the flexibility to finance more than 100 separate types of essential community infrastructure that ultimately improve access to healthcare, education, public safety and other critical facilities and services. RD also provided $1.1 billion in water and wastewater (W&W) direct loans, and guaranteed $2 billion in rural business loans, which will help create and save jobs in rural America. Since 2020, CF and W&W loan guarantees have been for communities of 50,000 or less.

Water Infrastructure

The Environmental Protection Agency's Water Infrastructure Finance and Innovation Act (WIFIA) program accelerates investment in the Nation's water infrastructure by providing long-term, low-cost supplemental loans for projects of regional or national significance. To date, WIFIA has closed 120 loans totaling $19 billion in credit assistance to help finance over $43 billion for water infrastructure projects and create 143,000 jobs. The selected projects demonstrate the broad range of project types that the WIFIA program can finance, including wastewater, drinking water, stormwater, and water reuse projects.

In addition, the WIFIA Program, authorized by the Water Resources Reform and Development Act of 2014, as amended (Public Law 113-121), allows the U.S. Army Corps of Engineers to issue loans and loan guarantees for eligible non-Federal water resources projects. The Consolidated Appropriations Act, 2021 (Public Law 116-260) provided $12 million for the cost of loans and loan guarantees for dam safety projects at non-Federal dams identified in the National Inventory of Dams. The IIJA provided an additional $64 million for this purpose. The Corps of Engineers is actively working to establish this new Federal credit program, including developing implementing regulations.

Transportation Infrastructure

The Department of Transportation (DOT) administers credit programs that fund critical transportation infrastructure projects, often using innovative financing methods. The two predominant programs are the Transportation Infrastructure Finance and Innovation Act (TIFIA) and the Railroad Rehabilitation and Improvement Financing (RRIF) loan programs. DOT's Build America Bureau administers both of these programs, as well as Private Activity Bonds. The Bureau serves as the single point of contact for State and local governments, transit agencies, railroads and other types of project sponsors seeking to utilize Federal transportation innovative financing expertise, apply for Federal transportation credit programs, and explore ways to access private capital in public-private partnerships.

Transportation Infrastructure Finance and Innovation Act (TIFIA)

Established by the Transportation Equity Act for the 21st Century (TEA-21; Public Law 105-178) in 1998, the TIFIA program is designed to fill market gaps and leverage substantial private co-investment by providing supplemental and subordinate capital to transportation infrastructure projects. Through TIFIA, DOT provides three types of Federal credit assistance to highway, transit, rail, intermodal, airport, and transit-oriented development projects: direct loans, loan guarantees, and lines of credit. TIFIA can help advance qualified, large-scale projects that otherwise might be delayed or deferred because of size, complexity, or uncertainty over the timing of revenues. For example, in 2023 the TIFIA program provided a $501 million loan to the I-25 Express Lanes project in Colorado, which will add 52 miles of express toll lanes between Denver and Fort Collins. The IIJA authorized $250 million annually for TIFIA for fiscal years 2022-2026, and the Budget fully reflects the IIJA-authorized level for 2025.

Railroad Rehabilitation and Improvement Financing (RRIF)

Also established by TEA–21 in 1998, the RRIF program provides loans or loan guarantees with an interest rate equal to the Treasury rate for similar-term securities for terms up to 75 years. The RRIF program allows borrowers to pay the subsidy cost of a loan (a "Credit Risk Premium") using non-Federal sources, thereby allowing the program to operate without Federal subsidy appropriations. The RRIF program assists rail infrastructure projects that improve rail safety and efficiency, support economic development and opportunity, or increase the capacity of the national rail network. For example, in 2023 the RRIF program provided a $27.5 million loan to the Double Track Project in Northwest Indiana, to improve connections between the region and Chicago.

International Credit Programs

Through 2023, seven unique Federal agencies provide or have existing portfolios of direct loans, loan guarantees, and insurance to a variety of private and sovereign borrowers: USDA, the Department of Defense, the Department of State, the Treasury, the U.S. Agency for International Development, the Export-Import Bank (ExIm), and the U.S. International Development Finance Corporation (DFC). These programs are intended to level the playing field for U.S. exporters, deliver robust support for U.S. goods and services, stabilize international financial markets, enhance security, and promote sustainable development.

Federal export credit programs provide financing support for American businesses involved in international trade and to counteract unfair foreign trade financing. Various foreign governments provide their exporters official financing assistance, usually through export credit agencies. The U.S. Government has worked since the 1970s to constrain official credit support through a multilateral agreement in the Organisation for Economic Cooperation and Development (OECD). This agreement has established standards for Government-backed financing of exports. In addition to ongoing work in keeping these OECD standards up-to-date, the U.S. Government established the International Working Group on Export Credits to set up a new framework that will include China and other non-OECD countries, which were not previously subject to export credit standards. The process of establishing these new standards, which is not yet complete, advances a congressional mandate to reduce subsidized export financing programs.

Export Support Programs

When the private sector is unable or unwilling to provide financing, ExIm fills the gap for American businesses by equipping them with the financing support necessary to level the playing field against foreign competitors. ExIm support includes direct loans and loan guarantees for creditworthy foreign buyers to help secure export sales from U.S. exporters. It also includes working capital guarantees and export credit insurance to help U.S. exporters secure financing for overseas sales. USDA's Export Credit Guarantee Programs (GSM programs) similarly help to level the playing field. Like programs of other agricultural exporting nations, GSM programs guarantee payment from countries and entities that want to import U.S. agricultural products but cannot easily obtain credit. The GSM 102 program provides guarantees for credit extended with short-term repayment terms not to exceed 18 months.

Exchange Stabilization Fund

Consistent with U.S. obligations in the International Monetary Fund (IMF) regarding global financial stability, the Exchange Stabilization Fund (ESF) managed by the Treasury may provide loans or credits to a foreign entity or government of a foreign country. A loan or credit may not be made for more than six months in any 12-month period unless the President gives the Congress a written statement that unique or emergency circumstances require that the loan or credit be for more than six months. The CARES Act established within the ESF an Economic Stabilization Program with temporary authority for lending and other eligible investments, which included programs or facilities established by the Board of Governors of the Federal Reserve System pursuant to section 13(3) of the Federal Reserve Act. The Consolidated Appropriations Act, 2021 rescinded this authority, though loans and investments already made remain active until obligations are liquidated.

Sovereign Lending and Guarantees

The U.S. Government can extend short-to-medium-term loan guarantees that cover potential losses that might be incurred by lenders if a country defaults on its borrowings; for example, the U.S. may guarantee another country's sovereign bond issuance. The purpose of this tool is to provide the Nation's sovereign international partners access to necessary, urgent, and relatively affordable financing during temporary periods of strain when they cannot access such financing in international financial markets, and to support critical reforms that will enhance long-term fiscal sustainability, often in concert with support from international financial institutions such as the IMF. The goal of sovereign loan guarantees is to help lay the economic groundwork for the Nation's international partners to graduate to an unenhanced bond issuance in the international capital markets. For example, as part of the U.S. response to fiscal crises, the U.S. Government has extended sovereign loan guarantees to Jordan and Iraq to enhance their access to capital markets while promoting economic policy adjustment.

Development Programs

Credit is an important tool in U.S. bilateral assistance to promote sustainable development. The DFC provides loans, guarantees, and other investment tools such as equity and political risk insurance to facilitate and incentivize private-sector investment in emerging markets that will have positive developmental impact, and meet national security objectives.

The Government-Sponsored Enterprises (GSEs)

Fannie Mae and Freddie Mac

The Federal National Mortgage Association (Fannie Mae) created in 1938, and the Federal Home Loan Mortgage Corporation (Fredie Mac) created in 1970, were established to support the stability and liquidity of a secondary market for residential mortgage loans. Fannie Mae's and Freddie Mac's public missions were later broadened to promote affordable housing. The Federal Home Loan Bank (FHLB) System, created in 1932, is comprised of eleven individual banks with shared liabilities. Together they lend money to financial institutions, mainly banks and thrifts, that are involved in mortgage financing to varying degrees, and they also finance some mortgages using their own funds. The mission of the FHLB System is broadly defined as promoting housing finance, and the System also has specific requirements to support affordable housing.

Together these three GSEs currently are involved, in one form or another, with approximately half of residential mortgages outstanding in the U.S. today.

History of the Conservatorship of Fannie Mae and Freddie Mac and Budgetary Effects

Growing stress and losses in the mortgage markets in 2007 and 2008 seriously eroded the capital of Fannie Mae and Freddie Mac. Legislation enacted in July 2008 strengthened regulation of the housing GSEs through the creation of the Federal Housing Finance Agency (FHFA), a new independent regulator of housing GSEs, and provided the Treasury with authorities to purchase securities from Fannie Mae and Freddie Mac.

On September 6, 2008, FHFA placed Fannie Mae and Freddie Mac under Federal conservatorship. The next day, the Treasury launched various programs to provide temporary financial support to Fannie Mae and Freddie Mac under the temporary authority to purchase securities. The Treasury entered into agreements with Fannie Mae and Freddie Mac to make investments in senior preferred stock in each GSE in order to ensure that each company maintains a positive net worth. The cumulative funding commitment through these Preferred Stock Purchase Agreements (PSPAs) with Fannie Mae and Freddie Mac was set at $445.5 billion. In total, as of December 31, 2023, $191.5 billion has been invested in Fannie Mae and Freddie Mac. The remaining commitment amount is $254.1 billion.

The PSPAs also generally require that Fannie Mae and Freddie Mac pay quarterly dividends to the Treasury, though the terms governing the amount of those dividends have changed several times pursuant to agreements between the Treasury and Fannie Mae and Freddie Mac. Notably, changes announced on January 14, 2021, permit the GSEs to suspend dividend payments until they achieve minimum capital levels established by FHFA through regulation. The Budget projects those levels will not be reached during the Budget window and accordingly reflects no dividends through 2034. Through December 31, 2023, the GSEs have paid a total of $301.0 billion in dividend payments to the Treasury on the senior preferred stock.

The Temporary Payroll Tax Cut Continuation Act of 2011 (Public Law 112–78) amended the Housing and Community Development Act of 1992 (Public Law 102-550) by requiring that Fannie Mae and Freddie Mac increase their annual credit guarantee fees on single-family mortgage acquisitions between 2012 and 2021 by an average of at least 0.10 percentage points. This sunset was extended through 2032 by the IIJA. The Budget estimates these fees, which are remitted directly to the Treasury and are not included in the PSPA amounts, will result in deficit reduction of $69.7 billion from 2025 through 2034.

In addition, effective January 1, 2015 FHFA directed Fannie Mae and Freddie Mac to set aside 0.042 percentage points for each dollar of the unpaid principal balance of new business purchases (including but not limited to mortgages purchased for securitization) in each year to fund several Federal affordable housing programs created by the Housing and Economic Recovery Act of 2008 (Public Law 110-289), including the Housing Trust Fund and the Capital Magnet Fund. The 2025 Budget projects these assessments will generate $4.9 billion for the affordable housing funds from 2025 through 2034.

Future of the Housing Finance System

Fannie Mae and Freddie Mac are in their fifteenth year of conservatorship, and the Congress has not yet enacted legislation to define the GSEs' long-term role in the housing finance system. The Administration is committed to housing finance policy that increases the supply of housing that is affordable for low- and moderate-income households, expands fair and equitable access to homeownership and affordable rental opportunities, protects taxpayers, and promotes financial stability. The Administration has a key role in shaping, and a key interest in the outcome of, housing finance reform, and stands ready to work with the Congress in support of these goals.

The Farm Credit System (Banks and Associations)

The Farm Credit System (FCS or System) is a GSE. Its banks and associations constitute a nationwide network of borrower-owned cooperative lending institutions originally authorized by Congress in 1916. Their mission is to provide sound and dependable credit to American farmers, ranchers, producers or harvesters of aquatic products, farm cooperatives, and farm-related businesses. The institutions also serve rural America by providing financing for rural residential real estate; rural communication, energy, and water/wastewater infrastructure; and agricultural exports. In addition, maintaining special policies and programs for the extension of credit to young, beginning, and small (YBS) farmers and ranchers is a legislative mandate for the System.

The financial condition of the System's banks and associations remains fundamentally sound. The ratio of capital to assets was 14.7 percent on September 30, 2023, compared with 14.9 percent on September 30, 2022. An increase in interest rates, which reduced the fair value of existing fixed-rate investment securities, contributed to the decline in the capital-to-assets ratio in 2023. Capital that is available to absorb losses amounted to $72.3 billion, which is mainly composed of retained earnings (high-quality capital). For the first nine months of calendar year 2023, net income equaled $5.5 billion compared with $5.4 billion for the same period the previous year.

Over the 12-month period ended September 30, 2023, System assets grew 6.1 percent, primarily because of higher cash and investment balances and increased loan volume primarily in rural infrastructure, processing and marketing, production and intermediate-term, and real estate mortgage loans. During the same period, nonperforming assets as a percentage of the dollar volume of loans and other property owned was 0.53 percent on September 30, 2023, compared with 0.51 percent on September 30, 2022.

The number of FCS institutions continues to decrease because of intra-System consolidation. As of September 30, 2023, the System consisted of four banks and 59 associations, compared with five banks and 84 associations in September 2011. Of the 67 FCS banks and associations rated, 62 had a rating of 1 or 2 on a safety and soundness scale of 1 to 5 (1 being most safe and sound) and accounted for 99.1 percent of System assets. Five FCS institutions had a rating of 3.

Dollar volume outstanding increased for both total System lending and YBS lending. Total System loan volume outstanding increased by 9.4 percent. Loan volume outstanding to young farmers increased by 6.3 percent, to beginning farmers by 9.6 percent, and to small farmers by 5.3 percent. The growth rate of outstanding loans was lower in 2022 than it was in both 2020 and 2021. While the total number of loans outstanding for the System decreased by 0.6 percent, the number of outstanding loans to young and beginning farmers increased modestly, whereas the number of small farmer loans outstanding contracted slightly.

The dollar volume of loans made in 2023 decreased for the System as a whole and for the YBS categories. The System's total new loan dollar volume decreased by 1.7 percent while new loan volume to young farmers decreased by 12.5 percent, to beginning farmers by 17.9 percent, and to small farmers by 25.3 percent. The number of total System loans made during the year decreased by 17.2 percent. The number of loans to young farmers decreased by 17.1 percent, to beginning farmers by 18.9 percent, and to small farmers by 22.9 percent.

Several factors led to reduced System lending in 2023:

- Rising interest rates and fewer refinanced loans
- Changing economic conditions and less demand for rural properties
- End of the Paycheck Protection Program

The System has recorded strong earnings and capital growth in 2023. The System also faces risks associated with its portfolio concentration in agriculture and rural America, the System, including labor shortages due to a tight labor market, interest expenses and tightening farm profit margins, and regional drought. After reaching record highs in 2022, farm income in 2024 is expected to decline for the second consecutive year and near historical averages.

Federal Agricultural Mortgage Corporation (Farmer Mac)

Farmer Mac was established in 1988 by the Agricultural Credit Act of 1987 (Public Law 100-233) as a federally chartered instrumentality of the United States and an institution of the System to facilitate a secondary market for farm real estate and rural housing loans. Farmer Mac is not liable for any debt or obligation of the other System institutions, and no other System institutions are liable for any debt or obligation of Farmer Mac. The Farm Credit System Reform Act of 1996 (Public Law 104-105) expanded Farmer Mac's role from a guarantor of securities backed by loan pools to a direct purchaser of mortgages, enabling it to form pools to securitize. The Food, Conservation, and Energy Act of 2008 (Public Law 110-246) expanded Farmer Mac's program authorities by allowing it to purchase and guarantee securities backed by rural utility loans made by cooperatives.

Farmer Mac continues to meet core capital and regulatory risk-based capital requirements. As of September 30, 2023, Farmer Mac's total outstanding program volume (loans purchased and guaranteed, standby loan purchase commitments, and AgVantage bonds purchased and guaranteed) amounted to $27.7 billion, which represents an increase of 9.2 percent from the level a year ago. Of total program activity, on-balance-sheet loans and guaranteed securities amounted to $23 billion, and off-balance-sheet obligations amounted to $4.7 billion. Total assets were $28.3 billion, with nonprogram investments (including cash and cash equivalents) accounting for $5.7 billion of those assets. Farmer Mac's net income attributable to common stockholders for the first three quarters of calendar year 2023 was $132 million, compared with $114.4 million for the same period in 2022.

II. INSURANCE PROGRAMS

Deposit Insurance

Federal deposit insurance promotes stability in the U.S. financial system. Prior to the establishment of Federal deposit insurance, depository institution failures often caused depositors to lose confidence in the banking system and rush to withdraw deposits. Such sudden withdrawals caused serious disruption to the economy. In 1933, in the midst of the Great Depression, a system of Federal deposit insurance was established to protect depositors and to prevent bank failures from causing widespread disruption in financial markets.

Today, the Federal Deposit Insurance Corporation (FDIC) insures deposits in banks and savings associations (thrifts) using the resources available in its Deposit Insurance Fund (DIF). The National Credit Union Administration (NCUA) insures deposits (shares) in most credit unions through the National Credit Union Share Insurance Fund (SIF). (Some credit unions are privately insured.) As of September 30, 2023, the FDIC insured $10.6 trillion of deposits at 4,623 commercial banks and thrifts, and as of September 30, 2023, the NCUA insured nearly $1.7 trillion of shares at 4,645 Federal and federally insured State-chartered credit unions.

Since its creation, the Federal deposit insurance system has undergone many reforms. As a result of the 2008 financial crisis, several reforms were enacted to protect both the immediate and longer-term integrity of the Federal deposit insurance system. The Helping Families Save Their Homes Act of 2009 (division A of Public Law 111–22) provided NCUA with tools to protect the SIF and the financial stability of the credit union system. Notably, the Act established the Temporary Corporate Credit Union Stabilization Fund, which has now been closed with its assets and liabilities distributed into the SIF. In addition, the Act:

- Provided flexibility to the NCUA Board by permitting use of a restoration plan to spread insurance premium assessments over a period of up to eight years, or longer in extraordinary circumstances, if the SIF equity ratio falls below 1.2 percent; and
- Permanently increased the Share Insurance Fund's borrowing authority to $6 billion.

The Dodd-Frank Wall Street Reform and Consumer Protection Act of 2010 (Dodd-Frank Act; Public Law 111-203) established new DIF reserve ratio requirements. The Act required the FDIC to achieve a minimum DIF reserve ratio (ratio of the deposit insurance fund balance to total estimated insured deposits) of 1.35 percent by 2020, up from 1.15 percent in 2016. On September 30, 2018, the DIF reserve ratio reached 1.36 percent. However, as of June 30, 2020 the DIF reserve ratio fell to 1.30 percent, below the statutory minimum of 1.35 percent. The decline was a result of strong one-time growth in insured deposits. On September 15, 2020, FDIC adopted a Restoration Plan to restore the DIF reserve ratio to at least 1.35 percent by 2027.

In addition to raising the minimum reserve ratio, the Dodd-Frank Act also:

- eliminated the FDIC's requirement to rebate premiums when the DIF reserve ratio is between 1.35 and 1.5 percent;
- gave the FDIC discretion to suspend or limit rebates when the DIF reserve ratio is 1.5 percent or higher, effectively removing the 1.5 percent cap on the DIF; and
- required the FDIC to offset the effect on small insured depository institutions (defined as banks with assets less than $10 billion) when setting assessments to raise the reserve ratio from 1.15 to 1.35 percent. In implementing the Dodd-Frank Act, the FDIC issued a final rule setting a long-term (i.e., beyond 2028) reserve ratio target of 2 percent, a goal that FDIC considers necessary to maintain a positive fund balance during economic crises while permitting steady long-term assessment rates that provide transparency and predictability to the banking sector.

The Dodd-Frank Act also permanently increased the insured deposit level to $250,000 per account at banks or credit unions insured by the FDIC or NCUA.

Recent Fund Performance

As of September 30, 2023, the FDIC DIF balance stood at $119.3 billion on an accrual basis, a one-year decrease of $6.2 billion. The decline in the DIF balance is primarily a result of bank failures that occurred in early 2023. As a result, the reserve ratio on September 30, 2023, declined by 12 basis points from 1.25 percent one year prior to 1.13 percent.

As of September 30, 2023, the number of insured institutions on the FDIC's "problem list" (institutions with the highest risk ratings) totaled 44, which represented a decrease of 95 percent from December 2010, the peak year for bank failures during the 2008 financial crisis, but an increase of two banks from the year prior. Moreover, the assets held by problem institutions were 87 percent below the level in December 2009, the peak year for assets held by problem institutions.

The NCUA-administered SIF ended September 2023 with assets of $20.9 billion and an equity ratio of 1.27 percent. In December 2023, NCUA continued to maintain the normal operating level of the SIF equity ratio at 1.33 percent of insured shares after, in December 2022, the NCUA Board reduced the ratio from 1.38 to 1.33 percent. If the equity ratio exceeds the normal operating level, a distribution is normally paid to insured credit unions to reduce the equity ratio.

The health of the credit union industry has markedly improved since the 2008 financial crisis. As of September 30, 2023, NCUA reserved $214 million in the SIF to cover potential losses, up 16 percent from the $185 million reserved as of December 31, 2022. The ratio of insured shares in troubled institutions to total insured shares has remained stable from the end of 2022 through September 2023. The ratio increased slightly from 0.29 percent in December 2022 to 0.33 percent in June 2023 before declining to 0.28 percent in September 2023. This is a significant reduction from a high of 5.7 percent in December 2009.

Budget Outlook

The Budget estimates DIF net outlays of -$162.3 billion over the current 10-year budget window (2025–2034). This includes the repayment of $93.3 billion in principal on FFB financing transactions executed in 2023 and 2024 (see below), as well as the current anticipated impact of a special assessment to recover the DIF's estimated losses associated with uninsured depositors following the closures of Silicon Valley Bank and Signature Bank, after the Secretary of the Treasury announced on March 12, 2023, that uninsured depositors would be covered to avoid systemic risk to the financial system. The final rule implementing this special assessment was approved by the FDIC Board of Directors on November 16, 2023. The Budget projects that FDIC's Restoration Plan will remain in effect until 2027, when the DIF is estimated to reach the statutory reserve ratio target of 1.35 percent. The Budget also assumes that the DIF will reach the historic long-run reserve ratio target of 1.5 percent over the 10-year budget window. Although the FDIC has authority to borrow up to $100 billion from the Treasury to maintain sufficient DIF balances, the Budget does not anticipate FDIC utilizing this direct borrowing authority. In 2023, the FDIC engaged in a financing transaction with the FFB to purchase a $50 billion note guaranteed by the FDIC in its corporate capacity as deposit insurer and regulator. The Budget reflects this as an exercise of borrowing authority and reflects additional transactions totalling $43.3 billion in January 2024.

Pension Guarantees

The Pension Benefit Guaranty Corporation (PBGC) insures the pension benefits of workers and retirees in covered defined-benefit pension plans. PBGC operates two legally and financially separate insurance programs: single-employer plans and multiemployer plans.

Single-Employer Insurance Program

When an underfunded single-employer plan terminates, PBGC becomes the trustee and pays benefits, up to a guaranteed level. This typically happens when the employer sponsoring an underfunded plan insured by PBGC goes bankrupt, ceases operation, or can no longer afford to keep the plan going. PBGC's claims exposure is the amount by which guaranteed benefits exceed assets in insured plans. In the near term, the risk of loss stems from financially distressed firms with underfunded plans. In the longer term, loss exposure also results from the possibility that well-funded plans become underfunded due to inadequate contributions, poor investment results, or increased liabilities, and that the firms sponsoring those plans become distressed.

PBGC monitors companies with large, underfunded plans and acts to protect the interests of the pension insurance program's stakeholders where possible. Under its Early Warning Program, PBGC works with plan sponsors to mitigate risks to pension plans posed by corporate transactions or otherwise protect the insurance program from avoidable losses. However, PBGC's authority to manage risks to the insurance program is limited. Most private insurers can diversify or reinsure their catastrophic risks as well as flexibly price these risks. Unlike private insurers, Federal law does not allow PBGC to deny insurance coverage to a defined-benefit plan or adjust premiums according to risk. Both types of PBGC premiums, the flat rate (a per person charge paid by all plans) and the variable rate (paid by underfunded plans), are set in statute.

Claims against PBGC's insurance programs are highly variable. One large pension plan termination may result in a larger claim against PBGC than the termination of many smaller plans. The future financial health of the PBGC will continue to depend largely on the potential termination of a limited number of very large plans. Finally, PBGC's financial condition is sensitive to market risk. Interest rates and equity returns affect not only PBGC's own assets and liabilities, but also those of PBGC-insured plans.

Single-employer plans generally provide benefits to the employees of one employer. When an underfunded single-employer plan terminates, PBGC becomes trustee of the plan, applies legal limits on payouts, and pays benefits. To determine the amount to pay each participant, PBGC considers: a) the benefit that a participant had accrued in the terminated plan; b) the availability of assets from the terminated plan to cover benefits; c) how much PBGC recovers from employers for plan underfunding; and d) the legal maximum benefit level set in statute. The guaranteed benefit limits are indexed (i.e., they increase in proportion to increases in a specified Social Security wage index) and vary based on the participant's age and elected form of payment. For plans terminating in 2024, the maximum guaranteed annual benefit payable as a single life annuity under the single-employer program is $85,295 for a retiree at age 65.

Multiemployer Insurance Program

Multiemployer plans are collectively bargained pension plans maintained by one or more labor unions and more than one unrelated employer, usually within the same or related industries. PBGC does not trustee multiemployer plans. In the Multiemployer Program, the event triggering PBGC's guarantee is plan insolvency (the inability to pay guaranteed benefits when due), whether or not the plan has terminated. PBGC provides insolvent multiemployer plans with financial assistance in the statutorily required form of loans sufficient to pay PBGC guaranteed benefits and reasonable administrative expenses. Since multiemployer plans generally do not receive PBGC assistance until their assets are fully depleted, financial assistance is almost never repaid unless the plan receives special financial assistance under the American Rescue Plan Act of 2021 (ARPA; Public Law 117-2).

Benefits guaranteed under the multiemployer program are calculated based on: a) the benefit a participant would have received under the insolvent plan, subject to; b) the multiemployer guarantee limit set in statute. The guarantee limit depends on the participant's years of service and the level of the benefit accruals. For example, for a participant with 30 years of service, PBGC guarantees 100 percent of the pension benefit up to a yearly amount of $3,960. If the pension exceeds that amount, PBGC guarantees 75 percent of the rest of the pension benefit up to a total maximum guarantee of $12,870 per year for a participant with 30 years of service. This limit has been in place since 2001 and is not adjusted for inflation or cost-of-living increases.

PBGC's FY 2022 Projections Report shows the Multiemployer Program is likely to remain solvent over the 40-year projection period. Prior to the enactment of the ARPA, PBGC's Multiemployer Program was projected to become insolvent in 2026. ARPA amended the Employee Retirement and Income Security Act of 1974 (Public Law 93-406) and established a new Special Financial Assistance program that provides funding from the Treasury's General Fund for lump-sum payments to eligible multiemployer plans. This program allows PBGC to provide funding assistance to eligible plans so they can pay projected benefits at the plan level through 2051. By providing special financial assistance to the most financially troubled multiemployer plans, ARPA significantly extends the solvency of PBGC's Multiemployer Program. ARPA also assists plans by providing funds to reinstate previously suspended benefits.

Disaster Insurance

Flood Insurance

The Federal Government provides flood insurance through the National Flood Insurance Program (NFIP), which is administered by the Department of Homeland Security's Federal Emergency Management Agency (FEMA). Flood insurance is available to homeowners, renters, businesses, and State and local governments in communities that have adopted and enforce minimum floodplain management measures. Coverage is limited to buildings and their contents. As of November 30, 2023, the program had 4.7 million policies worth $1.3 trillion in force in over 22,600 communities.[2]

The Congress established the NFIP in 1968 via the National Flood Insurance Act of 1968 (Title XIII of Public Law 90-448) to make flood insurance coverage widely available, to combine a program of insurance with flood mitigation measures to reduce the Nation's risk of loss from floods, protect the natural and beneficial functions of the floodway,[3] and to reduce Federal disaster-assistance expenditures on flood losses. The NFIP requires participating communities to adopt certain land use ordinances consistent with FEMA's floodplain management regulations and to take other mitigation efforts to reduce flood-related losses in high flood hazard areas ("Special Flood Hazard Areas") identified through partnership with FEMA, States, and local communities. These efforts have resulted in substantial reductions in the risk of flood-related losses nationwide. Legislation enacted in 2012 and 2014 established a Reserve Fund that is available to meet the expected future obligations of the flood insurance program and invest available resources. The Reserve Fund is funded by an assessment and fixed annual surcharge. Legislation also introduced a phase-in to higher full-risk premiums for structures newly mapped into the Special Flood Hazard Area until full-risk rates are achieved, capped annual premium increases at 18 percent for most structures, and created the Office of the Flood Insurance Advocate.

As of April 1, 2023, FEMA has fully implemented NFIP's new pricing approach, Risk Rating 2.0, The approach leverages industry best practices and cutting-edge technology to enable FEMA to deliver rates that are actuarially sound, equitable, and better reflect a property's flood risk. Since the 1970s, rates had been predominantly based on relatively static measurements, emphasizing a property's elevation within a zone on the Flood Insurance Rate Map (FIRM). The 1970s legacy methodology did not incorporate as many flooding variables as today's pricing approach. FEMA is building on years of investment in flood hazard information by incorporating private sector data sets, catastrophe models, and evolving actuarial science. In addition, the 1970s legacy rating methodology did not account for the cost of rebuilding a home. Policyholders with lower-valued homes may have been paying more than their share of the risk while higher -valued homes may have been paying less than their share of the risk. Today's NFIP pricing approach enables FEMA to set rates that are fairer and ensures up-to-date actuarial principles based upon new technology, including modeling. With the implementation of the NFIP's pricing approach, FEMA is now able to equitably distribute premiums across all policyholders based on home value and a property's flood risk.

FEMA's Community Rating System offers discounts on policy premiums in communities that adopt and enforce more stringent floodplain land use ordinances than those identified in FEMA's regulations and/or engage in mitigation activities beyond those required by the NFIP. The discounts provide an incentive for communities to implement new flood protection activities that can help save lives and property when a flood occurs. Further, NFIP offers flood mitigation assistance grants for planning and carrying out activities to reduce the risk of flood damage to structures covered by NFIP, which may include demolition or relocation of a structure, elevation or flood-proofing a structure, and community-wide mitigation efforts that will reduce future flood claims for the NFIP. In particular, flood mitigation assistance grants targeted toward repetitive and severe repetitive loss properties not only help owners of high-risk property, but also reduce the disproportionate drain these properties cause on the National Flood Insurance Fund (NFIF). The IIJA provided significant additional resources of $3.5 billion over five years for the flood mitigation assistance grants. The flood grants are a Justice40 covered program.

Due to the catastrophic nature of flooding, with Hurricanes Harvey, Katrina, and Sandy as notable examples, insured flood damages can far exceed premium revenue and deplete the program's reserves. On those occasions, the NFIP exercises its borrowing authority through the Treasury to meet flood insurance claim obligations. While the program needed appropriations in the early 1980s to repay the funds borrowed during the 1970s, it was able to repay all borrowed funds with interest using only premium dollars between 1986 and 2004. In 2005, however, Hurricanes Katrina, Rita, and Wilma generated more flood insurance claims than the cumulative number of claims paid from 1968 to 2004. Hurricane Sandy in 2012 generated $8.8 billion in flood insurance claims. As a result, in 2013 the Congress increased the borrowing authority for the fund to $30.425 billion. After the estimated $2.4 billion and $670 million in flood insurance claims generated by the Louisiana flooding of August 2016, and Hurricane Matthew in October 2016, respectively, the NFIP used its borrowing authority again, bringing the total outstanding debt to the Treasury to $24.6 billion.

[2] Community - any State or area or political subdivision thereof, or any Indian Tribe or authorized tribal organization, or Alaska Native village or authorized native organization, which has authority to adopt and enforce flood plain management regulations for the areas within its jurisdiction.

[3] A regulatory floodway is the channel of a river or other watercourse and the adjacent land areas that must be reserved in order to discharge the base flood without cumulatively increasing the water surface elevation more than a desig-nated height

In the fall 2017, Hurricanes Harvey and Irma struck the southern coast of the United States, resulting in catastrophic flood damage across Texas, Louisiana, and Florida. To pay claims, NFIP exhausted all borrowing authority. The Congress provided $16 billion in debt cancellation to the NFIP, bringing its debt to $20.525 billion. To pay Hurricane Harvey flood claims, NFIP also received more than $1 billion in reinsurance payments as a result of transferring risk to the private reinsurance market at the beginning of 2017. FEMA continues to mature its reinsurance program and transfer additional risk to the private market. In September 2022 Hurricane Ian hit the southern coast of Florida. Based on FEMA's NFIP claims data as of January 31, 2024, FEMA estimates that Hurricane Ian could potentially result in flood claims losses between $4.9–$5.2 billion, including loss adjustment expenses.

Budget projections rely on both NFIF and Reserve Fund balances to make up for annual deficits between collections from policyholders and NFIF expenses, until 2027-2032 when NFIF would utilize borrowing authority for any shortfalls. FEMA has submitted 17 legislative proposals to reform the NFIP, achieve long-term reauthorization, and better protect policyholders. These proposals include eliminating the debt, reducing borrowing authority, and collecting congressional equalization payments.

The 2022-2026 FEMA Strategic Plan creates a shared vision for the NFIP and other FEMA programs to build a more prepared and resilient Nation. The Strategic Plan outlines a bold vision and three ambitious goals designed to address key challenges the agency faces during a pivotal moment in the field of emergency management: Instill Equity as a Foundation of Emergency Management, Lead Whole of Community in Climate Resilience, and Promote and Sustain a Ready FEMA and Prepared Nation. While the NFIP supports all three goals, it is central to leading whole of community in climate resilience. To that end, FEMA is pursuing initiatives including:

- providing products that clearly and accurately communicate flood risk;
- helping individuals, businesses, and communities understand their risks and the available options like the NFIP to best manage those risks;
- transforming the NFIP into a simpler, customer-focused program that policyholders value and trust; and
- increasing the number of properties covered by flood insurance (either through the NFIP or private insurance).

Crop Insurance

Subsidized Federal crop insurance, administered by USDA's Risk Management Agency (RMA) on behalf of the Federal Crop Insurance Corporation (FCIC), assists farmers in managing yield and revenue shortfalls due to bad weather or other natural disasters. The program is a cooperative partnership between the Federal Government and the private insurance industry. Private insurance companies sell and service crop insurance policies. The Federal Government, in turn, pays private companies an administrative and operating expense subsidy to cover expenses associated with selling and servicing these policies. The Federal Government also provides reinsurance through the Standard Reinsurance Agreement and pays companies an "underwriting gain" if they have a profitable year. For the 2025 Budget, the combined payments to the companies are projected to be $4.51 billion. The Federal Government also subsidizes premiums for farmers as a way to encourage farmers to participate in the program.

The most basic type of crop insurance is catastrophic coverage (CAT), which compensates the farmer for losses in excess of 50 percent of the individual's average yield at 55 percent of the expected market price. The CAT premium is entirely subsidized, and farmers pay only an administrative fee. Higher levels of coverage, called "buy-up," are also available. A portion of the premium for buy-up coverage is paid by FCIC on behalf of producers and varies by coverage level – generally, the higher the coverage level, the lower the percent of premium subsidized. The remaining (unsubsidized) premium amount is owed by the producer and represents an out-of-pocket expense.

For 2023, the four principal crops (corn, soybeans, wheat, and cotton) accounted for over 74 percent of total crop liability, and approximately 89 percent of the total U.S. planted acres of the 10 principal row crops (also including barley, peanuts, potatoes, rice, sorghum, and tobacco) were covered by crop insurance. Producers can purchase both yield- and revenue-based insurance products, which are underwritten on the basis of a producer's actual production history (APH). Revenue insurance programs protect against loss of revenue resulting from low prices, low yields, or a combination of both. Revenue insurance has enhanced traditional yield insurance by adding price as an insurable component.

In addition to price and revenue insurance, FCIC has made available other plans of insurance to provide protection for a variety of crops grown across the United States. For example, "area plans" of insurance offer protection based on a geographic area (most commonly a county), and do not directly insure an individual farm. Often, the loss trigger is based on an index, such as one on rainfall, which is established by a Government entity (for example, the National Oceanic and Atmospheric Administration). One such plan is the pilot Rainfall Index plan, which insures against a decline in an index value covering Pasture, Rangeland, and Forage. These pilot programs meet the needs of livestock producers who purchase insurance for protection from losses of forage produced for grazing or harvested for hay. In 2023, there were over 60,000 Rainfall Index policies earning premiums, covering over 290 million acres of pasture, rangeland, and forage. In 2023, there was also over $16.9 billion in liability for those producers who purchased livestock coverage and $9.5 billion in liability for those producers who purchased coverage for milk.

A crop insurance policy also contains coverage compensating farmers when they are prevented from planting their crops due to weather and other perils. When an insured farmer is unable to plant the planned crop within the planting time period because of excessive drought or moisture, the farmer may file a prevented planting claim, which pays the farmer a portion of the full coverage level. It is optional for the farmer to plant a second crop on the acreage. If the farmer does, the prevented planting claim on the first crop is reduced and the farmer's APH is recorded for that year. If the farmer does not plant a second crop, the farmer gets the full prevented planting claim, and the farmer's APH is held harmless for premium calculation purposes the following year. Buy-up coverage for prevented planting is limited to five percent.

RMA is continuously working to develop new products and to expand or improve existing products in order to cover more agricultural commodities. In late 2022, RMA offered a temporary Transitional and Organic Grower Assistance Program (TOGA) to reduce producers' overall crop insurance premium bill, which incentivizes farmers to transition to organic agricultural systems. The premium benefits of using TOGA included: 10 percentage points of premium subsidy for all crops in transition, $5 per acre premium benefit for certified organic grain and feed crops, and 10 percentage points of premium subsidy for all Whole-Farm Revenue Protection (WFRP) policies covering any number of crops in transition to organic or crops with the certified organic practice. In 2023, RMA introduced five new crop insurance programs for kiwifruit, grapevine, oysters, controlled environment, and weaned calf. Furthermore, the Agency introduced several major program changes: adding a new option to Hurricane Insurance Protection-Wind Index (HIP-WI) for named tropical storm weather events, Margin Protection program expansion, Annual Forage program flexibilities, expansion of enterprise units for specialty crops, and improvements to livestock products. For more information and additional crop insurance program details please reference *RMA's website*.

Farm Credit System Insurance Corporation (FCSIC)

The FCSIC, an independent Government-controlled insurance corporation, insuring payments of principal and interest on FCS obligations for which the System banks are jointly and severally liable. If the Farm Credit System Insurance Fund (Insurance Fund) does not have sufficient funds to ensure payment on insured obligations, System banks will be required to make payments under joint and several liability, as required by section 4.4(a)(2) of the Farm Credit Act of 1971, as amended (12 U.S.C. 2155(a)(2)). The insurance provided by the Insurance Fund is limited to the resources in the Insurance Fund. System obligations are not guaranteed by the U.S. Government.

On September 30, 2023, the assets in the Insurance Fund totaled $7.2 billion. As of September 30, 2023, the Insurance Fund as a percentage of adjusted insured debt was 2.05 percent. This was slightly above the statutory secure base amount of 2.00 percent. From September 30, 2022, to September 30, 2023, the principal amount of outstanding insured System obligations increased by 6.5 percent, from $377.8 billion to $402.3 billion.

Insurance Against Security-Related Risks

Terrorism Risk Insurance

The Terrorism Risk Insurance Program (TRIP) was authorized by the Terrorism Risk Insurance Act of 2002

Chart 7-1. Face Value of Federal Credit Outstanding

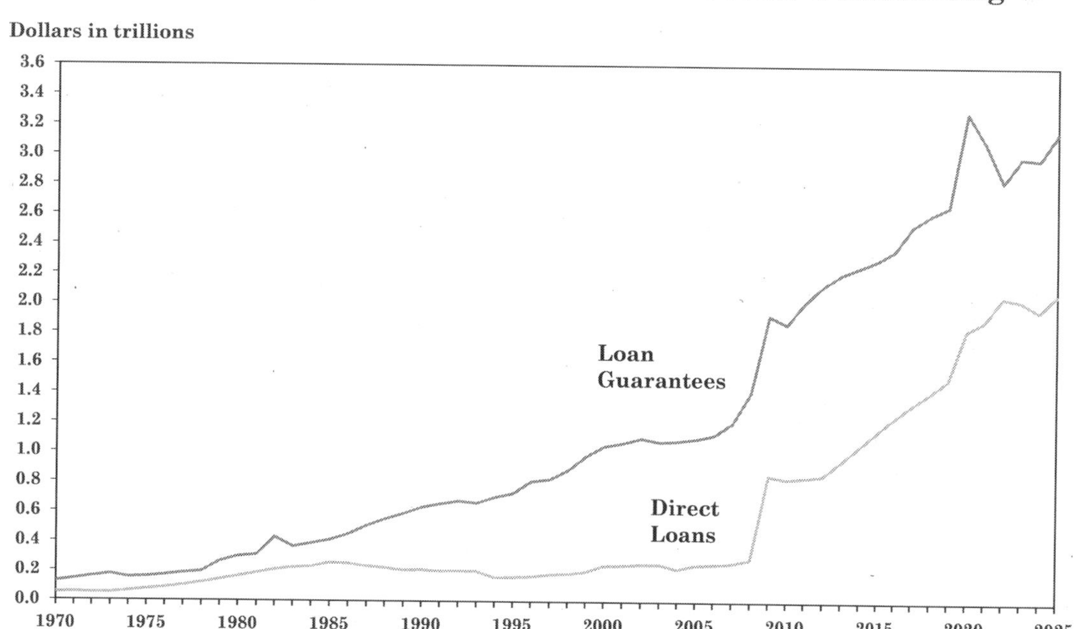

(Public Law 107-297) to ensure the continued availability of property and casualty insurance following the terrorist attacks of September 11, 2001. TRIP was previously intended to expire in 2020, but has been extended. It is currently set to expire on December 31, 2027, and authorizes collections through 2029, after it was reauthorized by the Terrorism Risk Insurance Program Reauthorization Act of 2019 (title V of division I of Public Law 116–94). TRIP's initial three-year authorization established a system of shared public and private compensation for insured property and casualty losses arising from certified acts of foreign terrorism.

The prior reauthorization, the Terrorism Risk Insurance Program Reauthorization Act of 2015 (Public Law 114–1), made several program changes to reduce potential Federal liability. Over the five years after the 2015 extension, the loss threshold that triggers Federal assistance was increased by $20 million each year to $22 million in 2020, and the Government's share of losses above the deductible decreased from 85 to 80 percent over the same period. The 2015 extension also required the Treasury to recoup 140 percent of all Federal payments made under the program up to a mandatory recoupment amount, which increased by $2 billion each year until 2019 when the threshold was set at $37.5 billion. Since January 1, 2020, the mandatory recoupment amount has been indexed to a running three-year average of the aggregate insurer deductible of 20 percent of direct-earned premiums.

The Budget baseline includes the estimated Federal cost of providing terrorism risk insurance, reflecting current law. Using market data synthesized through a proprietary model, the Budget projects annual outlays and recoupment for TRIP. While the Budget does not forecast any specific triggering events, the Budget includes estimates representing the weighted average of TRIP payments over a full range of possible scenarios, most of which include no notional terrorist attacks (and therefore no TRIP payments), and some of which include notional terrorist attacks of varying magnitudes. On this basis, the Budget projects net spending of $393 million over the 2025–2034 period.

Aviation War Risk Insurance

In December 2014, the Congress sunset the premium aviation war risk insurance program, thereby sending U.S. air carriers back to the commercial aviation insurance market for all of their war risk insurance coverage. The National Defense Authorization Act for Fiscal Year 2020 (Public Law 116-92) originally authorized the non-premium program through September 30, 2023, but the passing of the Airport and Airway Extension Act of 2023, Part II (Public Law 118-34) extended the program. It provides aviation insurance coverage for aircraft used in connection with certain Government contract operations by a department or agency that agrees to indemnify the Secretary of Transportation for any losses covered by the insurance.

III. BUDGETARY EFFECTS OF THE TROUBLED ASSET RELIEF PROGRAM (TARP)

This section provides analysis consistent with sections 202 and 203 of the Emergency Economic Stabilization Act of 2008 (EESA; Public Law 110-343), including estimates of the cost to taxpayers and the budgetary effects of TARP transactions as reflected in the Budget. This section also explains the changes in TARP costs, and includes alternative estimates as prescribed under EESA. Under EESA, the Treasury has purchased different types of financial instruments with varying terms and conditions.[4] The Budget reflects the costs of these instruments using the methodology as provided by section 123 of EESA.

The estimated costs of each transaction reflect the underlying structure of the instrument. TARP financial instruments have included direct loans, structured loans, equity, loan guarantees, and direct incentive payments. The costs of equity purchases, loans, guarantees, and loss sharing are the net present value of cash flows to and from the Government over the life of the instrument, per the Federal Credit Reform Act of 1990 (FCRA); as amended (title V of Public Law 93-344, 2 U.S.C. 661 et seq.), with an EESA-required adjustment to the discount rate for market risks. Costs for the incentive payments under TARP housing programs, other than loss sharing under the FHA Refinance program, involve financial instruments without any provision for future returns and are recorded on a cash basis.[5]

Tables 7–10 through 7–16 are available online. Table 7–10 summarizes the cumulative and anticipated activity under TARP, and the estimated lifetime budgetary cost reflected in the Budget, compared to estimates from the 2024 Budget. The direct impact of TARP on the deficit is projected to be $31.5 billion, equal to the $31.5 billion estimate in the 2024 Budget. The total programmatic cost represents the lifetime net present value cost of TARP obligations from the date of disbursement, which remains estimated to be $50.2 billion, a figure that excludes interest on reestimates.[6]

Table 7–11 shows the current value of TARP assets through the actual balances of TARP financing accounts as of the end of each fiscal year through 2023, and pro-

[4] For a more detailed analysis of the assets purchased through TARP and its budgetary effects, please see the "Budgetary Effect of the Troubled Asset Relief Program" chapter included in the *Analytical Perspectives* volume of prior budgets.

[5] Section 123 of EESA provides the Treasury the authority to record TARP equity purchases pursuant to FCRA, with required adjustments to the discount rate for market risks. The Hardest Hit Fund (HHF) and Making Home Affordable (MHA) programs involve the purchase of financial instruments that have no provision for repayment or other return on investment, and do not constitute direct loans or guarantees under FCRA. Therefore, these purchases are recorded on a cash basis. Administrative expenses for TARP are recorded under the Office of Financial Stability and the Special Inspector General for TARP on a cash basis, consistent with other Federal administrative costs, but are recorded separately from TARP program costs.

[6] With the exception of MHA and HHF, all the other TARP investments are reflected on a present value basis pursuant to FCRA and EESA.

jected balances for each subsequent year through 2034.[7] Based on actual net balances in financing accounts at the end of 2009, the value of TARP assets totaled $129.9 billion. As of December 31, 2023, all TARP programs are closed, all TARP assets have been disposed of, and total TARP net asset value has decreased to $0.

Table 7-12 shows the estimated impact of TARP activity on the deficit, debt held by the public, and gross Federal debt following the methodology required by EESA. Direct activity under TARP is expected to increase the 2024 deficit by $2.1 billion, the major components being:

- Administrative expense outlays for TARP are estimated at $7 million in 2024.
- Outlays for the Special Inspector General for TARP are estimated at $11 million in 2024.
- Debt service is estimated at $2.1 billion for 2024 and then expected to decrease to $1.6 billion by 2034, largely due to outlays for TARP housing programs and interest effects. Total debt service will continue over time after TARP winds down, due to the financing of past TARP costs.

Debt net of financial assets due to TARP is estimated to be $40.3 billion as of the end of 2024. This is $0.4 billion higher than the projected debt held net of financial assets for 2024 that was reflected in the 2024 Budget.

Table 7-13 reflects the estimated effects of TARP transactions on the deficit and debt, as calculated on a cash basis. Under cash basis reporting, the 2024 deficit would be $0.3 million lower than the $2.1 billion estimate now reflected in the Budget. However, the impact of TARP on the Federal debt, and on debt held net of financial assets, is the same on a cash basis as under FCRA and therefore these data are not repeated in Table 7-13.

Table 7-14 shows detailed information on upward and downward reestimates to program costs. The current reestimate of $0.4 million reflects a decrease in estimated TARP costs from the 2024 Budget. This decrease was due in large part to interest effects and continued progress winding down TARP investments over the past year.

The 2025 Budget, as shown in Table 7–15, reflects a total TARP deficit impact of $31.5 billion. This is equal to the 2024 Budget projection of $31.5 billion. The estimated 2024 TARP deficit impact reflected in Table 7-15 differs from the programmatic cost of $50.2 billion in the Budget because the deficit impact includes $18.8 billion in cumulative downward adjustments for interest on subsidy reestimates. See footnote 2 in Table 7-15.

Table 7-16 compares the OMB estimate for TARP's deficit impact to the deficit impact estimated by CBO in its "Report on the Troubled Asset Relief Program—April 2023."[8]

CBO estimates the total cost of TARP at $31 billion, based on estimated lifetime TARP disbursements of $444 billion. The Budget reflects a total deficit cost of $31 billion, based on estimated disbursements of $449 billion. CBO and OMB cost estimates for TARP have generally converged over time as TARP equity programs have wound down.

[7] Reestimates for TARP are calculated using actual data through September 30, 2023, and updated projections of future activity. Thus, the full impacts of TARP reestimates are reflected in the 2023 financing account balances.

[8] Available at: https://www.cbo.gov/publication/59091.

8. AID TO STATE AND LOCAL GOVERNMENTS

The analysis in this chapter focuses on Federal spending that is provided to State and local governments, U.S. Territories, and American Indian Tribal governments to help fund programs administered by those entities. This type of Federal spending is known as Federal financial assistance, primarily administered as grants.

In 2023, the Federal Government spent roughly $1.1 trillion, approximately 4 percent of GDP, on aid to State, local, tribal, and territorial governments. The Budget continues to estimate $1.1 trillion in outlays in both 2024 and 2025. Total Federal grant spending to State and local governments is estimated to be 3.7 percent of GDP in 2025.

Federal grants to State and local governments reached a historic high in 2021, at 5.5 percent of GDP, in large part due to significant Federal financial assistance provided in response to the health and economic crisis caused by the COVID-19 pandemic. Outlays remain elevated in 2023, continuing to reflect this assistance, while dipping in 2024 and 2025 as COVID-19 aid programs wind down. At the same time, higher outlays for infrastructure and community development reflect investments made in the Infrastructure Investment and Jobs Act (IIJA; Public Law 117-58), the Bipartisan Safer Communities Act (BSCA; Public Law 117-159), and Public Law 117-169, commonly referred to as the Inflation Reduction Act (IRA).

BACKGROUND AND ANALYSIS

Federal grants are authorized by the Congress in statute, which then establishes the purpose of the grant and how it is awarded. Most often, Federal grants are awarded as direct cash assistance, but Federal grants can also include in-kind assistance—non-monetary aid, such as commodities purchased for the National School Lunch Program—and Federal revenues or assets shared with State and local governments.

In its 2023 State Expenditure Report, the National Association of State Budget Officers (NASBO) estimates that, of the approximately $2.96 trillion[1] in total State spending in State fiscal year 2023[2], 35.3 percent, or $1.04 trillion, came from Federal funds. The NASBO reports that total State expenditures (including general funds, other State funds, bonds and Federal funds) increased 12.3 percent in 2023, with all program areas experiencing growth in State funds.[3]

Table 8-1, below, shows Federal grants spending by decade, actual spending in 2023, and estimated spending in 2024 and 2025. Table 8-2 shows the Budget's funding level for grants in every Budget account, organized by functional category, Budget Enforcement Act (BEA) category, and by Federal Agency.

The Federal Budget classifies grants by general area or function. Of the total proposed grant spending in 2025, 58.2 percent is for health programs, with most of the funding for Medicaid. Beyond health programs, approximately 15.4 percent of Federal aid is estimated to go to income security programs; 9.9 percent to transportation programs; 7.4 percent to education, training, and social services; and 9.1 percent for all other functions.

The Federal Budget also classifies grant spending by BEA category—discretionary or mandatory.[4] Funding for discretionary grant programs is generally determined through annual appropriations acts. Outlays for discretionary grant programs are estimated to account for 30 percent of total grant spending in 2025. Funding for mandatory programs is provided directly in authorizing legislation that establishes eligibility criteria or benefit formulas; funding for mandatory programs is not usually limited by the annual appropriations process. Outlays for mandatory grant programs are estimated to account for 70 percent of total grant spending in 2025. Section B of Table 8-1 shows the distribution of grants between mandatory and discretionary spending.

In 2025, grants provided from discretionary funding are estimated to have outlays of $334 billion, a decrease of roughly 1.8 percent from 2024. The five largest discretionary programs in 2025 are estimated to be Federal-aid Highway programs, with outlays of $52 billion; Tenant-Based Rental Assistance, with outlays of $32 billion; Education for the Disadvantaged (Title I), with outlays of $20 billion; the Community Development Fund, with outlays of $16 billion; and Special Education, with outlays of $14 billion.

In 2025, outlays for mandatory grant programs are estimated to be $761 billion, a decrease of 0.8 percent from spending in 2024, which is estimated to be $768 billion. This estimated decline reflects the winding down of pandemic-related aid programs, as discussed above. Medicaid is by far the largest mandatory grant program with estimated outlays of $587 billion in 2025. After Medicaid, the four largest mandatory grant programs by outlays

[1] "2023 State Expenditure Report." National Association of State Budget Officers, 2023. p. 1, 3.

[2] According to "The Fiscal Survey of States" published by the National Association of State Budget Officers (Fall 2022, p. VI), "Forty-six States begin their fiscal years in July and end them in June. The exceptions are New York, which starts its fiscal year on April 1; Texas, with a September 1 start date; and Alabama and Michigan, which start their fiscal years on October 1."

[3] "2023 State Expenditure Report." National Association of State Budget Officers, 2023. p. 3.

[4] For more information on these categories, see the "Budget Concepts" chapter of this volume.

Table 8–1. TRENDS IN FEDERAL GRANTS TO STATE AND LOCAL GOVERNMENTS

(Outlays in billions of dollars)

	1980	1990	2000	2005	2010	2015	2020	2023	Estimate	
									2024	2025
A. Distribution of grants by function:										
Natural resources and environment	5.4	3.7	4.6	5.9	9.1	7.0	7.2	10.9	38.6	18.0
Agriculture	0.6	1.1	0.7	0.9	0.8	0.7	0.8	0.9	0.9	1.1
Transportation	13.0	19.2	32.2	43.4	61.0	60.8	69.3	87.7	97.3	108.0
Community and regional development	6.5	5.0	8.7	20.2	18.9	14.4	52.5	38.3	72.8	42.6
Education, training, employment, and social services	21.9	21.8	36.7	57.2	97.6	60.5	67.9	92.2	87.5	81.4
Health	15.8	43.9	124.8	197.8	290.2	368.0	493.4	663.7	615.1	637.8
Income security	18.5	36.9	68.7	90.9	115.2	101.1	118.2	166.9	167.2	168.7
Administration of justice	0.5	0.6	5.3	4.8	5.1	3.7	9.4	6.2	8.6	8.8
General government	8.6	2.3	2.1	4.4	5.2	3.8	4.3	9.4	8.3	11.2
Other	0.7	0.8	2.1	2.6	5.3	4.3	6.1	7.2	11.2	17.6
Total	**91.4**	**135.3**	**285.9**	**428.0**	**608.4**	**624.4**	**829.1**	**1,083.4**	**1,107.6**	**1,095.3**
B. Distribution of grants by BEA category:										
Discretionary	53.4	63.5	116.7	182.3	247.4	189.6	259.4	289.1	340.1	334.0
Mandatory	38.0	71.9	169.2	245.7	361.0	434.7	569.7	794.3	767.5	761.4
Total	**91.4**	**135.3**	**285.9**	**428.0**	**608.4**	**624.4**	**829.1**	**1,083.4**	**1,107.6**	**1,095.3**
C. Composition:										
Current dollars:										
Payments for individuals [1]	33.1	77.4	186.5	278.8	391.4	463.4	608.6	816.4	770.7	799.1
Physical capital [1]	22.6	27.2	48.7	60.8	93.3	77.2	85.3	111.9	132.0	161.1
Other grants	35.8	30.7	50.7	88.4	123.7	83.7	135.2	155.1	204.8	135.1
Total	**91.4**	**135.3**	**285.9**	**428.0**	**608.4**	**624.4**	**829.1**	**1,083.4**	**1,107.6**	**1,095.3**
Percentage of total grants:										
Payments for individuals [1]	36.2%	57.2%	65.3%	65.1%	64.3%	74.2%	73.4%	75.4%	69.6%	73.0%
Physical capital [1]	24.7%	20.1%	17.0%	14.2%	15.3%	12.4%	10.3%	10.3%	11.9%	14.7%
Other grants	39.1%	22.7%	17.7%	20.7%	20.3%	13.4%	16.3%	14.3%	18.5%	12.3%
Total	**100.0%**	**100.0%**	**100.0%**	**100.0%**	**100.0%**	**100.0%**	**100.0%**	**100.0%**	**100.0%**	**100.0%**
Constant (FY 2017) dollars:										
Payments for individuals [1]	86.7	130.9	254.1	341.2	432.3	474.5	580.8	679.4	621.9	629.7
Physical capital [1]	61.9	51.6	77.3	83.6	105.9	79.0	79.1	86.1	99.0	117.2
Other grants	157.1	73.4	84.5	120.9	141.9	85.4	124.9	125.9	161.9	103.6
Total	**305.7**	**255.9**	**415.9**	**545.7**	**680.1**	**638.8**	**784.8**	**891.4**	**882.8**	**850.4**
D. Total grants as a percent of:										
Federal outlays:										
Total	15.5%	10.8%	16.0%	17.3%	17.6%	16.9%	12.7%	17.7%	16.0%	15.1%
Domestic programs [2]	22.2%	17.1%	22.0%	23.5%	23.4%	21.2%	15.0%	23.0%	21.2%	20.1%
State and local expenditures	26.4%	18.0%	21.0%	22.9%	25.6%	23.9%	26.1%	28.3%	N/A	N/A
Gross domestic product	3.3%	2.3%	2.8%	3.3%	4.1%	3.5%	3.9%	4.0%	3.9%	3.7%
E. As a share of total State and local gross investments:										
Federal capital grants	34.5%	21.0%	21.3%	21.2%	26.8%	21.7%	19.0%	21.3%	N/A	N/A
State and local own-source financing	65.5%	79.0%	78.7%	78.8%	73.2%	78.3%	81.0%	78.7%	N/A	N/A
Total	**100.0%**	**100.0%**	**100.0%**	**100.0%**	**100.0%**	**100.0%**	**100.0%**	**100.0%**		

N/A: Not available at publishing.

[1] Grants that are both payments for individuals and capital investment are shown under capital investment.

[2] Excludes national defense, international affairs, net interest, and undistributed offsetting receipts.

in 2025 are estimated to be: Child Nutrition programs, which include the School Breakfast Program, the National School Lunch Program and others, $32 billion; Children's Health Insurance Program, $18 billion; the Temporary Assistance for Needy Families program, $16 billion; and the Refundable Premium Tax Credit, $14 billion.

Federal spending by State for major grants may be found in supplemental material available on *the Office of Management and Budget (OMB) website*. This material includes two tables that summarize State-by-State spending for major grant programs, one summarizing obligations for each program by agency and bureau, and another summarizing total obligations across all programs for each State, followed by 46 individual tables showing State-by-State obligation data for each grant program. The programs shown in these State-by-State tables cover the majority of total grants to State and local governments. The sections that follow include highlights of grant proposals from the Budget listed by function.

HIGHLIGHTS

Energy

Building on the more than $15 billion in the IIJA and the IRA funding for the Department of Energy's Office of State and Community Energy Programs and other programs, the Administration is committed to continue creating jobs through support for State and community action to deploy clean energy infrastructure. The Budget invests $1.6 billion in clean energy infrastructure and projects through the Department of Energy, providing more than $385 million to weatherize and decarbonize low-income homes through efficiency and electrification retrofits, and $102 million to support utilities and State and local governments in building a more resilient electrical grid that utilizes clean energy sources. In addition, the Budget provides $95 million to electrify tribal homes and transition tribal colleges and universities to renewable energy.

Natural Resources and Environment

The Budget commits to tackling the climate crisis with urgency by investing in Environmental Protection Agency (EPA) grants to States and Tribes that will support the implementation of on-the-ground efforts in communities across the Nation, such as providing $100 million for the Diesel Emissions Reduction Act (DERA) grant program, which funds grants and rebates to States and tribal governments to reduce harmful emissions from diesel engines, and $70 million for the Targeted Airshed Grants (TAG). Also included is a total of $101 million for two EPA grant programs dedicated to remediating lead contamination in drinking water.

To protect communities from hazardous waste and environmental damage, the Budget also requests $208 million for EPA's Brownfields program to provide technical assistance and grants to communities, including disadvantaged communities, so they can safely clean up and reuse contaminated properties.

Agriculture

The Budget continues to invest in rural communities by providing $10 million in Rural Community Facilities Grants to facilitate the energy transition and modernization of infrastructure. Building on the $2 billion for broadband programs initiated in the IIJA, the Budget further supports rural communities by funding $112 million for the ReConnect Program, which provides grants and loans to deploy broadband to underserved areas, especially tribal areas.

To support tribal communities, the Budget invests $64 million for agriculture research, education and extension grants to tribal institutions; and $2 million to support Native American farmers and ranchers through the Intertribal Technical Assistance Network.

Transportation

The Budget provides robust support for transportation projects that cut commute times, improve safety, reduce freight bottlenecks, better connect communities, and reduce greenhouse gas emissions. Investments include: a total of $800 million for the Rebuilding American Infrastructure with Sustainability and Equity (RAISE) and the National Infrastructure Project Assistance (Mega) competitive grant programs to promote innovative highway, transit, passenger rail, freight, port, and other transportation projects; $250 million for the Consolidated Rail Infrastructure and Safety Improvements competitive grant program; and $2.4 billion for the Capital Investment Grants program, which will advance the construction of new, high-quality transit corridors to reduce travel time and increase economic development.

The Budget provides a total of $78.4 billion for highway, highway safety, and transit formula programs, including $61.3 billion in obligation limitation for the Federal-aid Highway program to modernize and upgrade roads and bridges. It also supports core capital and planning programs, transit research, technical assistance, and data collection with $14.3 billion in Transit Formula Grants, an increase of $645 million above the 2023 enacted level. It also reflects $9.5 billion in advance appropriations provided by the IIJA for bridge replacement and rehabilitation, electric vehicle charging infrastructure, and other programs to improve the safety, sustainability, and resilience of America's highway network.

Building on investments initiated under the IIJA, the Budget supports efforts to modernize America's port and waterway infrastructure, improve supply chain efficiency, and strengthen maritime freight capacity by providing $80 million for the Port Infrastructure Development Program.

Community and Regional Development

The Budget invests in underserved communities by providing $2.9 billion for the Community Development Block Grant program to help communities modernize infrastructure, invest in climate resilience and economic development, create parks and other public amenities, and provide social services. Within this amount, up to $100 million is provided to expand PRO Housing, a competitive program that builds upon ongoing Department of Housing and Urban Development (HUD) research on land use and affordable housing by rewarding State, local, and regional jurisdictions that make progress in removing barriers to affordable housing developments, such as restrictive zoning.

Additionally, to create jobs and drive growth in economically distressed communities across the Nation, the Budget prioritizes continued funding for the U.S. Economic Development Administration (EDA). It requests $41 million for the EDA's Recompete Pilot Program, which provides flexible, place-based funding to communities working to reduce economic distress and prime-age employment gaps by creating good-paying jobs. The Budget also boosts competitiveness and expands career opportunities in persistently distressed communities by investing $25 million in the Good Jobs Challenge to fund high-quality, locally-led workforce systems, and $5 million at the EDA to support grants focused exclusively on the economic development needs of tribal governments and Indigenous communities.

The Budget also includes $4 billion in mandatory funding for EDA's Regional Technology and Innovation Hub Program and $41 million in discretionary funding for smaller grants that enable tech and innovation in underrepresented regions. Together, these investments support cutting-edge technology and foster geographic diversity of technology jobs. The Budget also proposes $1 billion for the Federal Emergency Management Agency's (FEMA) Building Resilient Infrastructure and Communities grant program, which helps States, local communities, Tribes, and Territories build climate resilience. This grant program is one of several climate resilience grant programs, and supports the Administration's resilience goals described in the National Climate Resilience Framework.

Education, Training, Employment, and Social Services

Disruptions caused by the COVID-19 pandemic continue to take a toll on the physical and mental health of students, teachers, and school staff. Recognizing the profound effect of physical and mental health on academic achievement, the Budget includes a $216 million investment to increase the number of counselors, nurses, and mental health professionals in schools, colleges and universities, including $200 million from the BSCA.

To advance the goal of providing a high-quality education to every student, the Budget includes $18.6 billion for Title I schools. Title I, which reaches 90 percent of school districts across the Nation, helps schools provide students from low-income families the learning opportunities they need to succeed. This substantial support for the program reflects a major step toward fulfilling the Administration's commitment to address long-standing funding disparities between under-resourced schools—which disproportionately serve students of color—and their wealthier counterparts.

The Budget also funds voluntary, universal, free preschool for all four million of the Nation's four-year-olds and charts a path to expand preschool to three-year-olds. High-quality preschool would be offered in the setting of the parent's choice—from public schools to child care providers to Head Start. In addition, the Budget increases Head Start funding by $544 million to support the Administration's goal to reach pay parity between Head Start staff and public elementary school teachers with similar qualifications over time. Together these proposals would support healthy child development, help children enter kindergarten ready to learn, and support families by reducing their costs prior to school entry and allowing parents to work.

The Administration is also committed to ensuring that children with disabilities receive the services and support they need to thrive. The Budget provides $14.4 billion for Individuals with Disabilities Education Act (IDEA) grants to States to support special education and related services for students in grades Pre-K through 12. The Budget also invests $545 million in IDEA Grants for Infants and Families to provide early intervention services to infants and toddlers with disabilities. To address nationwide special educator shortages, the Budget also invests $125 million, $10 million above 2023 enacted, in grants for special education and early intervention training.

To increase institutional capacity at Historically Black Colleges and Universities (HBCUs), Tribally Controlled Colleges and Universities (TCCUs), Minority-Serving Institutions (MSIs), and low-resourced institutions, including community colleges, the Budget provides over $1 billion, an increase of $83 million over the 2023 enacted level, for these programs. This funding includes $100 million for four-year HBCUs, TCCUs, and MSIs to increase research and development infrastructure at these institutions.

Health

The Budget includes increased funding to build public health capacity, infrastructure, and data systems and collection at the State and local government levels. It invests in resources for behavioral, mental, and maternal health and supports the health and wellbeing of children.

To combat the substance use crisis, the Budget builds on the accomplishments of grant programs for States, Territories, and Tribes, including the State Opioid Response grant program, by providing additional grant funding for expanded access to prevention, harm reduction, treatment, and recovery support services. In addition, the Budget expands mental health assistance and support services in schools, and expands the Center for Disease Control's suicide prevention program to additional States, tribal, and territorial jurisdictions.

In addition, the Budget proposes a Vaccines for Adults program to provide uninsured adults with access to routine and outbreak vaccines at no cost. The Budget also expands the Vaccines for Children (VFC) program to include all children under age 19 enrolled in the Children's Health Insurance Program (CHIP) and covers the vaccine administration fee for all VFC-eligible uninsured children.

To address racial disparities in maternal and perinatal health and reduce maternal mortality and morbidity rates, the Budget provides funding for the ongoing implementation of the White House Blueprint for Addressing the Maternal Health Crisis. The Budget promotes maternal health equity by expanding Medicaid maternal health support services during the pregnancy and post-partum period by incentivizing States to reimburse a broad range of providers including doulas, community health workers, peer support initiatives, and nurse home visiting programs. Additionally, the Budget eliminates gaps in maternal health insurance coverage by requiring all States to provide continuous Medicaid coverage for 12 months post-partum.

The Budget also provides $350 million within HUD for States, local governments, and nonprofits to reduce lead-based paint and other health hazards, especially in the homes of low-income families with young children. Of that, the Budget proposes $206 million for a new formula grant program to improve efficiency in lead and other home health hazard mitigation efforts.

Income Security

The Budget strengthens families—and the economy—by investing in high-quality child care. The Budget creates a historic new program under which working families with incomes up to $200,000 per year would be guaranteed affordable, high-quality child care from birth until kindergarten, with most families paying no more than $10 a day, and the lowest income families paying nothing. This would provide a lifeline to the parents of more than 16 million children, saving the average family over $600 per month in care costs, per child. In addition, the Budget provides $8.5 billion for the Child Care and Development Block Grant, a $500 million increase over the 2023 enacted level.

The Budget makes a historic investment in lowering housing costs for renters and homebuyers through $185 billion in mandatory spending and tax proposals, a portion of which will be distributed via State and local governments. For instance, the Budget provides $3 billion in mandatory funding for competitive grants to promote and solidify State and local efforts to reform eviction policies by providing access to legal counsel, emergency rental assistance, and other forms of rent relief. In addition to the mandatory and tax proposals, the Budget includes $10 million for the Eviction Protection Grant Program, which provides legal assistance to low-income tenants at risk of or subject to eviction. To increase affordable rental housing supply and homeownership opportunities, the Budget also invests $1.25 billion in the HOME Investment Partnerships Program (HOME).

The Budget further supports households through the Low Income Home Energy Assistance Program (LIHEAP) for States and Territories by providing $4 billion for the program. LIHEAP helps families access home energy and weatherization assistance—vital tools for protecting vulnerable families' health in response to extreme weather and climate change. As part of the Justice40 initiative, Health and Human Services (HHS) plans to continue its efforts to prevent energy shutoffs and increase support for households with young children and older people or high energy burdens. The Budget also proposes to expand LIHEAP to advance the goals of both LIHEAP and the Low Income Household Water Assistance Program (LIHWAP). Specifically, the Budget gives States the option to use a portion of their LIHEAP funds to provide water bill assistance to low-income households.

The Budget also includes $2.5 million for Department of Labor's Women's Bureau to help States expand access to paid leave benefits, including through grants to support States in implementing new paid leave programs and through the creation of a Technical Assistance Hub to share best practices among States.

The Budget also provides competitive grants for States and localities with a focus on improving the child welfare workforce, advancing reforms that would reduce the overrepresentation of children and families of color in the child welfare system, respecting the rights of LGBTQ+ individuals, as well as $195 million for States and community-based organizations to respond to and prevent child abuse, with a focus on Tribes and other underserved populations.

The Budget supports a strong nutrition safety net by providing $8.5 billion for critical nutrition programs, including $7.7 billion for the Special Supplemental Nutrition Program for Women, Infants, and Children, to help vulnerable families put healthy food on the table and address racial disparities in maternal and child health outcomes.

Additionally, the Budget includes several investments to help States modernize and strengthen the Unemployment Insurance (UI) program. The Budget proposes a comprehensive legislative package designed to provide States with tools and resources to combat UI fraud and improper payments, while ensuring equity and accessibility for all claimants. The Budget also includes principles to guide future efforts to reform the UI system, including improving benefit levels and access, scaling UI benefits automatically during recessions, expanding eligibility to reflect the modern labor force, improving State and Federal solvency through more equitable and progressive financing, expanding reemployment services, and further safeguarding the program from fraud.

Administration of Justice

The Budget provides $3.7 billion in discretionary resources to the Department of Justice for State and local grants and $30 billion in mandatory resources to support efforts to hire police officers, reform criminal justice systems, and combat violent crime, as detailed in the President's Safer America Plan. Additionally, the

Budget proposes $100 million for Community Violence Intervention programs, an increase of $50 million over the 2023 enacted level, to bolster evidence-based strategies to reduce gun violence in U.S. communities.

The Administration remains committed to addressing substance use, proposing $429 million in grant funding in the Budget, including $190 million for the Comprehensive Opioid, Stimulant, and Substance Use Program, $95 million to support Drug Courts, and $51 million for anti-drug task forces.

OTHER SOURCES OF INFORMATION ON FEDERAL GRANTS

A number of other sources provide State-by-State spending data and other information on Federal grants but may use a broader definition of grants beyond what is included in this chapter.

The website *Grants.gov* is a primary source of information for communities wishing to apply for grants and other Federal financial assistance. *Grants.gov* hosts all competitive open notices of opportunities to apply for Federal grants.

The *System for Award Management* hosted by the General Services Administration contains detailed Assistance Listings (formerly known as the Catalog of Federal Domestic Assistance) of grant and other assistance programs; discussions of eligibility criteria, application procedures, and estimated obligations; and related information. The *Assistance Listings* are available on the internet at *SAM.gov*.

Current and updated grant receipt information by State and local governments and other non-Federal entities can be found on *USASpending.gov*. This public website includes additional detail on Federal spending, including contract and loan information.

The *Federal Audit Clearinghouse* maintains an online database that provides public access to audit reports conducted under OMB guidance located at 2 CFR part 200, Uniform Administrative Requirements, Cost Principles, and Audit Requirements for Federal Awards. Information is available for each audited entity, including the amount of Federal money expended by program and whether there were audit findings.

The Bureau of Economic Analysis in the Department of Commerce produces the monthly *Survey of Current Business*, which provides data on the national income and product accounts, a broad statistical concept encompassing the entire economy. These accounts, which are available at *https://apps.bea.gov/scb/*, include data on Federal grants to State and local governments.

In addition, information on grants and awards can be found through individual Federal Agencies' websites:[5]

- USDA Current Research Information System, *https://cris.nifa.usda.gov/*
- Department of Defense Medical Research Programs, *https://cdmrp.health.mil/*
- Department of Education, Institute of Education Sciences, Funded Research Grants and Contracts, *https://www2.ed.gov/fund/*
- HHS Grants, *https://www.hhs.gov/grants/*
- HHS Tracking Accountability in Government Grants System, *https://taggs.hhs.gov/*
- National Institutes of Health Grants and Funding, *https://grants.nih.gov/*
- HUD Grants, *https://hud.gov/program_offices/cfo/gmomgmt/grantsinfo*
- DOJ Grants, *https://www.justice.gov/grants*
- DOL Employment and Training Administration, Grants Awarded, *https://dol.gov/agencies/eta/grants/awards*
- Department of Transportation Grants, *https://www.transportation.gov/grants*
- EPA Grants, *https://www.epa.gov/grants*
- National Science Foundation Awards, *https://nsf.gov/awardsearch/*
- Small Business Innovation Research and Small Business Technology Transfer Awards, *https://www.sbir.gov/sbirsearch/award/all*

[5] *https://www.cfo.gov/wp-content/uploads/2021/Managing-for-Results-Performance-Management-Playbook-for-Federal-Awarding-Agencies.pdf*

9. SOCIAL INDICATORS

The social indicators presented in this chapter illustrate in broad terms how the Nation is faring in selected areas.[1] Indicators are drawn from six domains: economic, demographic, socioeconomic, health, safety and civic, and environment and energy. The indicators shown in the tables in this chapter were chosen in consultation with statistical and data experts from across the Federal Government. These indicators are only a subset of the vast array of available data on conditions in the United States. In choosing indicators for these tables, priority was given to measures that are broadly relevant to Americans and consistently available over an extended period. Such indicators provide a current snapshot, while also making it easier to draw comparisons and establish trends.

The measures in these tables are influenced to varying degrees by many Government policies and programs, as well as by external factors beyond the Government's control. They do not measure the impacts of Government policies. Instead, they provide a quantitative picture of the baseline on which future policies are set and useful context for prioritizing budgetary resources.

Economic.—Over the entire period since 1960, the primary pattern has been one of economic growth and rising living standards. Real GDP per person has tripled as technological advancements and accumulation of human and physical capital increased the Nation's productive capacity. The stock of physical capital including consumer durable goods, like cars and appliances, was $70.2 trillion in 2022. However, national savings, which is a key determinant of future prosperity as it supports capital accumulation, remains low relative to historical standards, standing at 1.6 percent of GDP in 2022, down from 10.9 percent in 1960. The labor force participation rate, also critical for growth, has generally been decreasing since 2000, with the aging of the population contributing to the decline.

Meanwhile, the structure of the economy has also changed over time as a result of technological change, foreign competition, and an increasingly educated workforce. Foreign trade has expanded, and the United States has experienced persistent trade deficits since the early 1980s, reaching $951.2 billion in 2022. By the same year, goods-producing industries accounted for 19.6 percent of total private goods and services, measured in value added as a percentage of GDP, while the remaining 80.4 percent came from services-producing industries. This composition has been affected by longer-term trends in the economy, such as the expanded breadth of the service sector spurred by computerization and the Internet.

The COVID-19 pandemic was the worst pandemic experienced by the U.S. in a century. It disrupted economic activity, leading to temporary declines in most economic indicators. Real GDP per person decreased by 2.6 percent in 2020 before exceeding pre-pandemic levels in 2021. The unemployment rate, which had been trending downward after the Great Recession, jumped to 8.1 percent in 2020 before recovering to 3.6 percent in 2023, one of the lowest unemployment rates since 1970. The employment-population ratio, which had only partly recovered following the Great Recession, dropped sharply to 56.8 percent in 2020. In 2023, it stood at 60.3 percent, almost reaching its pre-pandemic level but still below its high of 64.4 in 2000. The labor force participation rate fell during the COVID-19 pandemic but did not see as large of a drop as during the Great Recession. Although the labor force participation rate increased from 2021 to 2023, it remains below pre-pandemic levels.

Demographic.—The U.S. population steadily increased from 1970 to 2023, growing from 204 million to 334.9 million. The foreign-born population has rapidly increased, more than quadrupling from 9.7 million in 1960 to 44.7 million in 2018. The U.S. population is getting older, due in part to the aging of the baby boomers, improvements in medical technology, and declining birth rates. From 1970 to 2019, the share of the population aged 65 and over increased from 9.8 to 16.5 percent, and the percentage of Americans aged 85 and over increased from 0.7 to 2.0. In contrast, the proportion of the population aged 17 and younger declined from 28.0 percent in 1980 to 22.3 percent in 2019.

The composition of American households and families has evolved considerably over time. The share of Americans aged 15 and over who have ever married has declined from 78.0 percent in 1960 to 65.9 percent in 2023. Average family size has also fallen during the same period from 3.7 to 3.2 members per family household. Declining average family size is a pattern that is typical among developed countries. Births to unmarried women aged 15 to 17 reached a turning point in 1990 after increasing for two decades. From 1990 to 2022, the number of births per 1,000 unmarried women aged 15 to 17 fell from 29.6 to 5.6, the lowest level on record. Single parent households comprised 9.1 percent of all households in 2010, up from only 4.4 percent in 1960. Since 2010, the percentage has been declining and was 7.4 percent in 2023.

Socioeconomic.—Education is a critical component of the Nation's economic growth and competitiveness, while also benefiting society in areas such as health, crime, and civic engagement. Between 1960 and 1980, the percentage of 25- to 34-year-olds who have graduated from high school increased from 58.1 to 84.2 percent, a gain of 13 percentage points per decade. Over the next 42 years, the high school attainment rate has since increased by approximately eight percentage points to 92.7 percent. The

[1] The public can also access the social indicators data, along with data visualizations, at *Performance.gov*.

percentage of 25- to 34-year-olds who have graduated from college continues to rise, from only 11.0 percent in 1960 to 39.8 percent in 2022. While the share of the population with a graduate degree has risen, the percentage of graduate degrees in science and engineering fell by one-third in the period between 1960 and 1980, from 16.5 percent to 11.2 percent. However, since 2010 this decline has largely reversed, with science and engineering degrees rising to 15.9 percent of all graduate degrees in 2022.

Although national prosperity has grown considerably over the past 50 years, these gains have not been shared equally. Real disposable income per capita more than tripled since 1960, while for the median household, real income increased by only 34.4 percent since 1970, and much of those gains took place prior to 2000. This inequality is also reflected in how the distribution of income has changed over time. From 1980 to 2021, the adjusted gross income share for the top one percent of taxpayers increased from 8.5 to 26.3 percent, while the share of the lower 50 percent of taxpayers fell from 17.7 to 10.4 percent. During the COVID-19 pandemic, real disposable income increased, in part from financial assistance from the Government, and the personal savings rate rose to 15.4 percent in 2020 from 7.4 in 2019. As pandemic-era Government programs ended and households spent down savings, real disposable income decreased, and the personal savings rate fell to 4.5 in 2023.

From 2000 to 2010, the poverty rate, the percentage of food-insecure households, and the percentage of Americans receiving benefits from the Supplemental Nutrition Assistance Program (SNAP) increased, with most of this increase taking place during and after the Great Recession. Before the pandemic, the poverty rate had recovered to its pre-recession level, while food insecurity and the percentage of the population on SNAP had declined. The COVID-19 pandemic led to increases in the poverty rate and the percentage of Americans receiving SNAP benefits, and in 2022, the percentage of food-insecure households increased sharply to 12.8 percent.

After increasing from 1990 to 2005, homeownership rates among households with children fell to a low of 59.5 percent in 2015 following the 2008 housing crisis but increased to 64 percent in 2021. The share of families with children and severe housing cost burdens more than doubled from eight percent in 1980 to 17.9 percent in 2010, before falling to 13.3 percent in 2019. This increased slightly to 14.7 in 2021 following the pandemic. The percentage of families with children and inadequate housing steadily decreased from a high of nine percent in 1980 to a low of 4.9 percent in 2019. The downward trend was partially reversed by the pandemic, and the percentage increased to 5.6 percent in 2021.

Health.—The United States has by far the most expensive health care system in the world. National health expenditures as a share of GDP increased from five percent in 1960 to nearly 20 percent in 2020 during the beginning of the COVID-19 pandemic before dropping to 17.3 percent in 2022. This upward trend in health care spending coincides with improvements in medical technologies that have improved health. However, the level of per capita health care spending in the United States is far greater than in other Organization for Economic Cooperation and Development (OECD) countries that have experienced comparable health improvements.[2] Average private health insurance premiums paid by an individual or family with private health insurance increased by 80 percent from 2000 to 2022, after adjusting for inflation.

Some key indicators of national health have improved since 1960. Infant mortality fell from 26 per 1,000 live births in 1960 to 5.6 in 2022, with a rapid decline occurring in the 1970s. Life expectancy at birth increased by nine years, from 69.7 in 1960 to 78.7 in 2010. However, life expectancy decreased to 78.6 in 2017, with increased unintentional drug overdoses contributing to this decline,[3] before increasing again to 78.8 in 2019. Life expectancy dropped to 76.4 in 2021 as a result of the COVID-19 pandemic but increased to 77.5 in 2022.

Improvements in health-related behaviors among Americans have been mixed. Although the percentage of adults who smoked cigarettes in 2022 was approximately one-third of what it was in 1970, rates of obesity have soared. In 1980, 15.0 percent of adults and 5.5 percent of children were obese; in 2020, 42.4 percent of adults and 19.3 percent of children were obese. Adult obesity continued to rise even as the share of adults engaging in regular physical activity increased from 15 percent in 2000 to almost 26 percent in 2022.

Safety and Civic.—The last four decades have witnessed a remarkable decline in crime. From 1980 to 2022, the property crime rate dropped by 79 percent while the murder rate fell by 38 percent. The downward decline in the murder rate ended in 2010 at 4.8. The murder rate has since risen and jumped during the pandemic to 6.8 in 2021, before falling slightly in 2022. The prison incarceration rate increased more than five-fold from 1970 through 2010, before declining by 30 percent from 2010 through 2021.

Road transportation has become safer. Safety belt use increased by 21 percentage points from 2000 to 2023, and the annual number of highway fatalities has been trending downward since 1970 despite the increase in the population, although improvements were partially reversed during and after the COVID-19 pandemic.

Charitable giving among Americans, measured by the average charitable contribution per itemized tax return, has generally increased over the past 50 years.[4] There was a sharp drop in charitable giving from 2005 to 2010 following the Great Recession, and average charitable giving per itemized tax return jumped in 2018, likely as a result of tax changes stemming from the Tax Cuts and Jobs Act (Public Law 115-97) that resulted in fewer itemizing taxpayers. Americans also give of their time,

[2] Squires, D. and C. Anderson (2015). U.S. Health Care from a Global Perspective: Spending, Use of Services, Prices and Health in 13 Countries, The Commonwealth Fund.

[3] National Center for Health Statistics (2018). Health, United States, 2017: With special feature on mortality. Hyattsville, MD.

[4] This measure includes charitable giving only among those who claim itemized deductions. As such, it is impacted by modifications to tax legislation as well as the characteristics of individuals who itemize.

and almost one-quarter of Americans 16 and older volunteered in 2021.

In recent years, the number of military personnel on active duty has fallen to its lowest levels since at least 1960. The highest count of active duty military personnel was 3.1 million in 1970, which was reached during the Vietnam War. It now stands at 1.3 million. The number of veterans has declined from 28.6 million in 1980 to 18.3 million in 2023.

Environment and Energy.—Gross annual greenhouse gas emissions have remained high, peaking in the mid-2000s before decreasing. The annual mean atmospheric CO2 concentration—a measure of CO2 stored in the atmosphere—has increased, largely at an increasing rate, since 1960. Substantial progress has been made on air quality in the United States, with the concentration of particulate matter falling 42 percent from 2000 to 2022 and ground level ozone falling by 28 percent from 1980 to 2022. As of 2023, 93.4 percent of the population served by community water systems received drinking water in compliance with applicable Federal water quality standards, which has remained relatively stable since 2000.

Technological advances and a shift in production patterns mean that Americans use less than half as much energy per real dollar of GDP as they did 50 years ago, and per capita energy consumption is at its lowest since the 1960s despite rising population and income levels. From 2005 to 2022, coal production fell by almost 50 percent. This decrease in coal production coincided with increases in the production of natural gas, petroleum, and renewable energy, as well as new regulatory proposals and requirements. Renewable energy production has been increasing over time, with 21.3 percent of total electricity generated from renewable sources in 2022.

Table 9–1. SOCIAL INDICATORS

(Calendar years)

		1960	1970	1980	1990	2000	2005	2010	2015	2016	2017	2018	2019	2020	2021	2022	2023
	Economic																
	General Economic Conditions																
1	Real GDP per person (chained 2017 dollars)	19,364	25,922	31,869	40,191	49,915	54,015	54,189	58,364	58,968	60,002	61,418	62,606	60,983	64,410	65,420	66,750
2	Real GDP per person change, 5-year annual average (%)	0.8	2.4	2.6	2.3	3.1	1.6	0.1	1.5	1.6	1.6	1.8	1.8	0.9	1.8	1.8	1.7
3	Consumer Price Index [1]	12.3	16.2	34.3	54.5	71.7	81.4	90.9	98.8	100.0	102.1	104.6	106.5	107.8	112.9	121.9	127.0
4	Private goods producing (%)	N/A	N/A	N/A	N/A	N/A	N/A	N/A	N/A	N/A	19.8	20.1	19.5	18.6	18.9	19.6	N/A
5	Private services producing (%)	N/A	N/A	N/A	N/A	N/A	N/A	N/A	N/A	N/A	80.2	79.9	80.5	81.4	81.1	80.4	N/A
6	New business starts (thousands) [2]	N/A	N/A	440	493	446	519	380	422	444	440	443	454	457	476	N/A	N/A
7	Business failures (thousands) [3]	N/A	N/A	369	434	405	431	441	384	388	399	403	419	444	485	N/A	N/A
8	International trade balance (billions of dollars; + surplus / - deficit) [4]	3.5	2.3	-19.4	-80.9	-369.7	-716.5	-503.1	-490.8	-479.5	-516.9	-578.6	-559.4	-652.9	-841.6	-951.2	N/A
	Jobs and Unemployment																
9	Labor force participation rate (%)	59.4	60.4	63.8	66.5	67.1	66.0	64.7	62.7	62.8	62.9	62.9	63.1	61.7	61.7	62.2	62.6
10	Employment (millions)	65.8	78.7	99.3	118.8	136.9	141.7	139.1	148.8	151.4	153.3	155.8	157.5	147.8	152.6	158.3	161.0
11	Employment-population ratio (%)	56.1	57.4	59.2	62.8	64.4	62.7	58.5	59.3	59.7	60.1	60.4	60.8	56.8	58.4	60.0	60.3
12	Payroll employment change - December to December, SA (millions)	-0.4	-0.4	0.3	0.3	1.9	2.5	1.0	2.7	2.3	2.1	2.3	2.0	-9.3	7.2	4.5	3.1
13	Payroll employment change - 5-year annual average, NSA (millions)	0.7	2.0	2.7	2.4	2.9	0.4	-0.7	2.3	2.5	2.5	2.5	2.4	0.1	0.4	1.2	1.4
14	Civilian unemployment rate (%)	5.5	4.9	7.1	5.6	4.0	5.1	9.6	5.3	4.9	4.4	3.9	3.7	8.1	5.3	3.6	3.6
15	Unemployment plus marginally attached and underemployed (%)	N/A	N/A	N/A	N/A	7.0	8.9	16.7	10.4	9.6	8.5	7.7	7.2	13.6	9.4	6.9	6.9
16	Receiving Social Security disabled-worker benefits (% of population) [5]	0.9	2.0	2.8	2.5	3.7	4.5	5.5	5.8	5.7	5.6	5.5	5.4	5.2	5.0	4.8	4.6
	Infrastructure, Innovation, and Capital Investment																
17	Nonfarm business output per hour (average 5 year % change) [6]	1.8	2.1	1.3	1.5	2.9	3.1	2.3	0.7	0.9	1.0	1.1	1.4	2.1	2.3	1.7	1.7
18	Corn for grain production (million bushels)	3,907	4,152	6,639	7,934	9,915	11,112	12,425	13,601	15,148	14,604	14,420	13,661	14,111	15,074	13,730	15,234
19	Real net stock of fixed assets and consumer durable goods (billions of chained 2017 dollars)	N/A	N/A	N/A	N/A	N/A	N/A	57,870	62,064	63,141	64,183	65,374	66,595	67,710	69,039	70,165	N/A
20	Population served by secondary wastewater treatment or better (%) [7]	N/A	41.6	56.4	63.7	71.4	74.3	72.0	N/A	N/A	N/A	N/A	N/A	N/A	N/A	N/A	N/A
21	Electricity net generation (kWh per capita)	4,201	7,485	10,077	12,171	13,473	13,724	13,337	12,722	12,628	12,417	12,798	12,586	12,096	12,379	12,693	N/A
22	Patents for invention, U.S. origin (per million population) [8]	N/A	231	164	190	301	253	348	440	445	464	442	509	496	453	N/A	N/A
23	Net national saving rate (% of GDP)	10.9	8.5	7.1	3.8	6.0	2.9	-0.6	3.6	2.5	2.8	3.1	3.2	1.5	1.4	1.6	N/A
24	R&D spending (% of GDP) [9]	2.53	2.45	2.21	2.55	2.61	2.49	2.70	2.72	2.79	2.84	2.94	3.12	3.40	N/A	N/A	N/A
	Demographic																
	Population																
25	Total population (millions) [10]	N/A	204.0	227.2	249.6	282.2	295.5	309.3	320.7	323.1	325.1	326.8	328.3	331.5	332.0	333.3	334.9
26	Foreign born population (millions) [11]	9.7	9.6	14.1	19.8	31.1	37.5	40.0	43.3	43.7	44.5	44.7	N/A	N/A	N/A	N/A	N/A
27	17 years and younger (%) [10]	N/A	N/A	28.0	25.7	25.7	24.9	24.0	23.0	22.8	22.6	22.5	22.3	N/A	N/A	N/A	N/A
28	65 years and older (%) [10]	N/A	9.8	11.3	12.5	12.4	12.4	13.1	14.9	15.2	15.6	16.0	16.5	N/A	N/A	N/A	N/A
29	85 years and older (%) [10]	N/A	0.7	1.0	1.2	1.5	1.6	1.8	2.0	2.0	2.0	2.0	2.0	N/A	N/A	N/A	N/A
	Household Composition																
30	Ever married (% of age 15 and older) [12]	78.0	75.1	74.1	73.8	71.9	70.9	69.3	68.2	67.8	68.0	67.7	67.6	67.2	66.5	65.9	65.9
31	Average family size [13]	3.7	3.6	3.3	3.2	3.2	3.1	3.2	3.1	3.1	3.1	3.1	3.1	3.2	3.1	3.1	3.2
32	Births to unmarried women age 15-17 (per 1,000 unmarried women age 15-17)	N/A	17.1	20.6	29.6	23.9	19.4	16.8	9.6	8.6	7.7	7.1	6.6	6.1	5.6	5.6	N/A
33	Single parent households (%)	4.4	5.2	7.5	8.3	8.9	8.9	9.1	8.8	8.7	8.4	8.3	7.9	7.7	8.1	8.1	7.4
	Socioeconomic																
	Education																
34	High school graduates (% of age 25-34) [14]	58.1	71.5	84.2	84.1	83.9	86.4	87.2	89.7	90.1	90.9	91.4	91.7	N/A	92.5	92.7	N/A

Table 9–1. SOCIAL INDICATORS—Continued

(Calendar years)

		1960	1970	1980	1990	2000	2005	2010	2015	2016	2017	2018	2019	2020	2021	2022	2023
35	College graduates (% of age 25-34)[15]	11.0	15.5	23.3	22.7	27.5	29.9	31.1	34.1	34.9	35.6	36.2	36.9	N/A	39.1	39.8	N/A
36	Reading achievement score (age 17)[16]	N/A	285	285	290	288	283	287	N/A	N/A	N/A	N/A	N/A	N/A	N/A	N/A	N/A
37	Math achievement score (age 17)[17]	N/A	304	298	305	308	305	306	N/A	N/A	N/A	N/A	N/A	N/A	N/A	N/A	N/A
38	Science and engineering graduate degrees (% of total graduate degrees)[18]	16.5	17.2	11.2	14.7	12.6	12.7	12.1	15.0	16.3	17.0	16.9	16.5	16.7	16.5	15.9	N/A
39	Receiving special education services (% of age 3-21 public school students)	N/A	N/A	10.1	11.4	13.3	13.7	13.0	13.2	13.4	13.7	14.1	14.3	14.5	14.7	N/A	N/A
	Income, Savings, and Inequality																
40	Real median income: all households (2021 dollars)[19]	N/A	55,490	56,580	61,500	67,470	66,780	64,300	68,410	70,840	72,090	73,030	78,250	76,660	76,330	74,580	N/A
41	Real disposable income per capita (chained 2017 dollars)	13,387	18,797	22,842	28,878	35,424	38,396	40,361	43,179	43,659	44,710	46,059	47,225	50,039	51,519	48,317	50,106
42	Adjusted gross income share of top 1% of all taxpayers	N/A	N/A	8.5	14.0	20.8	21.2	18.9	20.7	19.7	21.0	20.9	20.1	22.2	26.3	N/A	N/A
43	Adjusted gross income share of lower 50% of all taxpayers	N/A	N/A	17.7	15.0	13.0	12.9	11.7	11.3	11.6	11.3	11.6	11.5	10.2	10.4	N/A	N/A
44	Personal saving rate (% of disposable personal income)	10.1	12.8	11.1	8.4	4.3	2.2	5.9	5.8	5.4	5.8	6.4	7.4	15.4	11.4	3.3	4.5
45	Foreign remittances (billions of 2021 dollars)[20]	N/A	N/A	N/A	N/A	41.7	43.5	46.0	50.3	51.4	52.1	53.5	55.8	54.1	55.8	53.8	N/A
46	Poverty rate (%)[21]	22.2	12.6	13.0	13.5	11.3	12.6	15.1	13.5	12.7	12.3	11.8	10.5	11.5	11.6	11.5	N/A
47	Food-insecure households (% of all households)[22]	N/A	N/A	N/A	N/A	10.5	11.0	14.5	12.7	12.3	11.8	11.1	10.5	10.5	10.2	12.8	N/A
48	Supplemental Nutrition Assistance Program (% of population on SNAP)	N/A	3.3	9.5	8.2	6.1	8.9	13.1	14.3	13.7	13.0	12.5	11.6	12.0	12.5	12.4	12.6
49	Median wealth of households, age 55-64 (in thousands of 2022 dollars)[23]	99	N/A	195	226	310	396	245	N/A	211	N/A	N/A	246	N/A	N/A	364	N/A
	Housing																
50	Homeownership among households with children (%)[24]	N/A	N/A	N/A	63.6	67.5	68.4	65.5	59.5	60.5	61.5	62.4	63.3	63.7	64.0	N/A	N/A
51	Families with children and severe housing cost burden (%)[25]	N/A	N/A	8	10	11	14.5	17.9	15.1	15.0	15.0	14.2	13.3	14.0	14.7	N/A	N/A
52	Families with children and inadequate housing (%)[26]	N/A	N/A	9	9	7	5.4	5.3	6.3	5.8	5.3	5.1	4.9	5.2	5.6	N/A	N/A
	Health																
	Health Status																
53	Life expectancy at birth (years)	69.7	70.8	73.7	75.4	76.8	77.6	78.7	78.7	78.7	78.6	78.7	78.8	77.0	76.4	77.5	N/A
54	Infant mortality (per 1,000 live births)	26.0	20.0	12.6	9.2	6.9	6.9	6.1	5.9	5.9	5.8	5.7	5.6	5.4	5.4	5.6	N/A
55	Low birthweight [2,500 gms] (% of babies)	7.7	7.9	6.8	7.0	7.6	8.2	8.2	8.1	8.2	8.3	8.3	8.3	8.2	8.5	8.6	N/A
56	Disability (% of age 5-17)[27]	N/A	N/A	N/A	N/A	N/A	N/A	N/A	N/A	N/A	N/A	N/A	11.9	13.7	11.7	13.4	N/A
57	Disability (% of age 18 and over)[28]	N/A	N/A	N/A	N/A	N/A	N/A	8.9	9.5	8.6	8.7	10.2	9.0	8.8	8.8	9.3	N/A
58	Disability (% of age 65 and over)[28]	N/A	N/A	N/A	N/A	N/A	N/A	22.6	21.6	18.2	19.5	21.9	19.3	18.4	18.9	18.5	N/A
	Health Behavior																
59	Engaged in regular physical activity (% of age 18 and older)[29]	N/A	N/A	N/A	N/A	15.0	16.6	20.7	21.6	22.7	24.5	24.2	N/A	25.5	N/A	25.6	N/A
60	Obesity (% of age 20-74 with BMI 30 or greater)[30]	13.4	N/A	15.0	23.2	30.5	34.3	35.7	N/A	39.6	N/A	42.4	N/A	42.4	N/A	N/A	N/A
61	Obesity (% of age 2-19)[31]	N/A	N/A	5.5	10.0	13.9	15.4	16.9	N/A	18.5	N/A	19.3	N/A	19.3	N/A	N/A	N/A
62	Cigarette smokers (% of age 18 and older)	N/A	37.1	33.1	25.3	23.1	20.8	19.3	15.3	15.7	14.1	13.9	14.2	12.7	11.7	11.7	N/A
63	Heavier drinker (% of age 18 and older)[32]	N/A	N/A	N/A	N/A	4.3	4.8	5.2	5.0	5.3	5.3	5.1	N/A	6.3	N/A	6.4	N/A
	Access to Health Care																
64	Total national health expenditures (% of GDP)	5.0	6.9	8.9	12.1	13.3	15.5	17.2	17.3	17.6	17.6	17.4	17.5	19.5	18.2	17.3	N/A
65	Average total single premium per enrolled employee at private-sector establishments (2021 dollars)[33]	N/A	N/A	N/A	N/A	4,176	5,537	6,139	6,817	6,888	7,040	7,246	7,390	7,485	7,380	7,028	N/A

Table 9–1. SOCIAL INDICATORS—Continued

(Calendar years)

		1960	1970	1980	1990	2000	2005	2010	2015	2016	2017	2018	2019	2020	2021	2022	2023
66	Average health insurance premium paid by an individual or family (2021 dollars) [34]	N/A	N/A	N/A	N/A	2,035	2,972	3,457	4,005	4,129	4,155	4,177	4,049	4,012	3,843	3,656	N/A
67	Persons without health insurance (% of age 18-64) [35]	N/A	N/A	N/A	N/A	18.9	19.3	22.3	12.8	12.4	12.8	13.2	14.5	13.9	12.6	12.4	N/A
68	Persons without health insurance (% of age 17 and younger) [35]	N/A	N/A	N/A	N/A	12.6	9.3	7.8	4.5	5.1	5.0	5.2	5.1	5.0	4.1	4.2	N/A
69	Vaccination coverage by age 24 months among children (% with recommended vaccine series) [36]	N/A	N/A	N/A	N/A	N/A	N/A	65.9	68.3	69.7	69.8	70.1	70.1	67.9	N/A	N/A	N/A
	Safety and Civic																
	Crime																
70	Property crimes (per 100,000 households) [37]	N/A	N/A	49,610	34,890	19,043	15,947	12,541	11,072	11,859	10,838	10,817	10,138	9,446	9,034	10,188	N/A
71	Violent crime victimizations (per 100,000 population age 12 or older) [38]	N/A	N/A	4,940	4,410	3,749	2,842	1,928	1,858	1,967	2,060	2,319	2,100	1,639	1,647	2,347	N/A
72	Murder rate (per 100,000 persons) [39]	5.1	7.9	10.2	9.4	5.5	5.6	4.8	4.9	5.4	5.3	5.0	5.1	6.5	6.8	6.3	N/A
73	Prison incarceration rate (state and federal institutions, rate per 100,000 persons) [40]	118.8	95.8	144.4	308.7	491.4	513.4	519.7	474.1	465.2	456.7	446.9	434.5	368.2	362.3	N/A	N/A
	National Security																
74	Military personnel on active duty (thousands) [41]	2,475	3,065	2,051	2,044	1,384	1,389	1,431	1,314	1,301	1,307	1,317	1,339	1.347	1.348	1,317	1,286
75	Veterans (thousands)	22,534	27,647	28,640	27,320	26,605	24,830	23,014	21,397	21,043	20,660	20,342	19,938	19,398	18,957	18,592	18,250
	Transportation Safety																
76	Safety belt use (%)	N/A	N/A	N/A	N/A	70.7	81.7	85.1	88.5	90.1	89.7	89.6	90.7	90.3	90.4	91.6	91.9
77	Highway fatalities [42]	36,399	52,627	51,091	44,599	41,945	43,510	32,999	35,484	37,806	37,473	36,835	36,355	39,007	42,939	42,795	N/A
	Civic and Cultural Engagement																
78	Average charitable contribution per itemized tax return (current dollars) [43]	2,316	2,298	2,650	3,332	4,703	4,813	4,097	5,084	5,289	5,465	11,234	10,958	13,174	17,736	N/A	N/A
79	Voting for President (% of voting age population) [44]	63.4	57.0	55.1	56.4	52.1	56.7	58.3	N/A	55.7	N/A	N/A	N/A	62.8	N/A	N/A	N/A
80	Persons volunteering (% age 16 and older) [45]	N/A	N/A	N/A	20.4	N/A	28.8	26.3	24.9	N/A	30.3	N/A	30.0	N/A	23.2	N/A	N/A
81	Attendance at visual or performing arts activity, including movie-going (% age 18 and older) [46]	N/A	N/A	71.9	72.1	69.8	63.9	68.4	66.5	N/A	65.3	N/A	N/A	64.9	N/A	58.0	N/A
82	Creating and performing art (% age 18 and older) [47]	N/A	N/A	49.4	49.7	37.4	38.7	53.0	N/A	44.0	52.6	42.0	N/A	42.7	N/A	51.4	N/A
83	Reading: Novels or short stories, poetry, or plays (not required for work or school; % age 18 and older) [46]	N/A	N/A	56.4	54.2	46.6	49.2	47.0	43.1	N/A	44.2	N/A	N/A	39.9	N/A	39.6	N/A
	Environment and Energy																
	Air Quality and Greenhouse Gases																
84	Ground level ozone (ppm) [48]	N/A	N/A	0.093	0.087	0.081	0.080	0.072	0.067	0.069	0.068	0.069	0.065	0.065	0.067	0.067	N/A
85	Particulate matter 2.5 (ug/m3) [49]	N/A	N/A	N/A	N/A	13.5	12.9	10.1	8.6	7.8	8.1	8.3	7.7	8.1	8.5	7.8	N/A
86	Annual mean atmospheric CO2 concentration (Mauna Loa, Hawaii; ppm) [50]	316.9	325.7	338.8	354.5	369.7	380.0	390.1	401.0	404.4	406.8	408.7	411.7	414.2	416.5	418.5	421.1
87	Gross greenhouse gas emissions (million metric tons CO2 equivalent) [51]	N/A	N/A	N/A	6,487.3	7,369.2	7,477.4	7,058.2	6,737.4	6,578.4	6,561.8	6,754.8	6,617.9	6,026.0	6,340.2	N/A	N/A
88	Net greenhouse gas emissions, including sinks (million metric tons CO2 equivalent)	N/A	N/A	N/A	5,606.4	6,533.4	6,696.3	6,307.2	6,065.5	5,763.1	5,787.6	5,989.7	5,913.9	5,249.8	5,586.0	N/A	N/A
89	Gross greenhouse gas emissions per capita (metric tons CO2 equivalent)	N/A	N/A	N/A	25.59	25.73	24.95	22.52	20.76	20.13	19.96	20.45	19.94	17.92	18.73	N/A	N/A
90	Gross greenhouse gas emissions per 2012$ of GDP kg CO2 equivalent)	N/A	N/A	N/A	0.6992	0.5609	0.5018	0.4510	0.3874	0.3721	0.363	0.363	0.3477	0.3256	0.3233	N/A	N/A
91	Population that receives drinking water in compliance with standards (%) [52]	N/A	N/A	N/A	N/A	90.8	88.5	92.2	91.1	91.2	92.8	91.0	91.9	93.1	92.4	93.2	93.4

Table 9–1. SOCIAL INDICATORS—Continued

(Calendar years)

		1960	1970	1980	1990	2000	2005	2010	2015	2016	2017	2018	2019	2020	2021	2022	2023
	Energy																
92	Energy consumption per capita (million Btu)	243	322	335	330	343	332	308	295	291	289	298	294	268	281	284	N/A
93	Energy consumption per 2017$ GDP (thousand Btu per 2017$)	12.6	12.4	10.5	8.2	6.9	6.1	5.7	5	4.9	4.8	4.8	4.7	4.4	4.4	4.3	N/A
94	Electricity net generation from renewable sources, all sectors (% of total) [53]	19.7	16.4	12.4	11.8	9.4	8.8	10.4	13.3	14.9	17.0	16.9	17.6	19.5	19.8	21.3	N/A
95	Coal production (million short tons)	434	613	830	1,029	1,074	1,131	1,084	897	728	775	756	706	535	577	594	N/A
96	Natural gas production (dry) (trillion cubic feet) [54]	12.2	21.0	19.4	17.8	19.2	18.1	21.3	27.1	26.6	27.3	30.8	33.9	33.8	34.5	36.4	N/A
97	Petroleum production (million barrels per day)	8.0	11.3	10.2	8.9	7.7	6.9	7.6	12.8	12.4	13.1	15.3	17.1	16.5	16.7	17.8	N/A
98	Renewable energy production (quadrillion Btu)	1.8	2.3	3.4	3.9	4.1	4.2	5.9	6.8	7.2	7.5	7.7	7.8	7.5	7.8	8.3	N/A

N/A = Not Availabe

[1] Adjusted CPI-U. 2016=100.

[2] New business starts are defined as firms with positive employment in the current year and no paid employment in any prior year of the LBD. Employment is measured as of the payroll period including March 12th.

[3] Business failures are defined as firms with employment in the prior year that have no paid employees in the current year.

[4] Calculated as the value of U.S. exports of goods and services less the value of U.S. imports of goods and services, on a balance of payments basis. This balance is a component of the U.S. International Transactions (Balance of Payments) Accounts.

[5] Gross prevalence rate for persons receiving Social Security disabled-worker benefits among the estimated population insured in the event of disability at end of year. Gross rates do not account for changes in the age and sex composition of the insured population over time.

[6] Values for prior years have been revised from the prior version of this publication.

[7] Data correspond to years 1972, 1982, 1992, 1996, 2000, 2004, 2008, and 2012.

[8] Patent data adjusted by OMB to incorporate total population estimates from U.S. Census Bureau.

[9] The data point for 2018 is estimated and may be revised in the next report of this time series. The R&D to GDP ratio data reflect the methodology introduced in the 2013 comprehensive revision of the GDP and other National Income and Product Accounts by the U.S. Bureau of Economic Analysis (BEA). In late July 2013, BEA reported GDP and related statistics that were revised back to 1929. This GDP methodology treats R&D as investment in all sectors of the economy, among other methodological changes. For further details see NSF's InfoBrief "R&D Recognized as Investment in U.S. Gross Domestic Product Statistics: GDP Increase Slightly Lowers R&D-to-GDP Ratio" at http://www.nsf.gov/statistics/2015/nsf15315/nsf15315.pdf.

[10] Data sources and values for 2020 to 2023 have been updated relative to the prior version of this publication. Differences observed between 2019 and 2020 may be due in part to the change in data sources and not necessarily reflective of trends in the data. For examplê, the data for 2010 to 2019 are based on the population estimates released for July 1, 2020 and have not yet been adjusted to account for the results of the 2020 Census. Because the data for 2020 take the results of the 2020 Census into account, this results in an "error of closure" between the data for 2019 and 2020 whereby differences are inherent to the two sources of data and not necessarily reflective of demographic trends.

[11] Data source for 1960 to 2000 is the decennial census; data source for 2006, 2010, 2011, 2012, 2013, 2014, 2015, 2016, and 2017 is the American Community Survey.

[12] For 1960, age 14 and older.

[13] Average size of family households. Family households are those in which there is someone present who is related to the householder by birth, marriage, or adoption.

[14] For 1960, includes those who have completed 4 years of high school or beyond. For 1970 and 1980, includes those who have completed 12 years of school or beyond. For 1990 onward, includes those who have completed a high school diploma or the equivalent.

[15] For 1960 to 1980, includes those who have completed 4 or more years of college. From 1990 onward, includes those who have a bachelor's degree or higher.

[16] Data correspond to years 1971, 1980, 1990, 1999, 2004, and 2012. Beginning with 2004, data are based on revised assessments that, among other changes, includes students tested with accommodations.

[17] Data correspond to years 1973, 1982, 1990, 1999, 2004, and 2012. Beginning with 2004, data are based on revised assessments that, among other changes, includes students tested with accommodations.

[18] Science and engineering degrees include majors with a 2020 Classification of Instructional Programs (CIP) designation in the areas of computer and information sciences, engineering and engineering technologies, biological and biological sciences, mathematics and statistics, physical science, or science technologies.

[19] Beginning with 2013, data are based on redesigned income questions. The source of the 2013 data is a portion of the CPS ASEC sample which received the redesigned income questions, approximately 30,000 addresses. For more information, please see the report Income and Poverty in the United States: 2014, U.S. Census Bureau, Current Population Reports, P60-252. Beginning in 2017, the data reflect the implementation of an updated processing system. For more information, please see the report Income and Poverty in the United States: 2018, U.S. Census Bureau, Current Population Reports P60-266.

[20] Foreign remittances, referred to as 'personal transfers' in the U.S. International Transactions (Balance of Payments) Accounts, consist of all transfers in cash or in kind sent by the foreign-born population resident in the United States to households resident abroad. Adjusted by OMB to 2016 dollars using the CPI-U.

[21] The poverty rate does not reflect noncash government transfers. The CPS ASEC has undergone changes to the processing system and questionnaire over time. Estimates from 2017 onward reflect the implementation of an updated processing system. The most recent changes to the questionnaire occurred in 2014. For more information, please see the report Poverty in the United States: 2022, U.S. Census Bureau, Current Population Reports, P60–280.

[22] Food-insecure classification is based on reports of three or more conditions that characterize households when they are having difficulty obtaining adequate food, out of a total of 10 questions for households without children and 18 questions for households with children.

[23] Data values shown are 1962, 1983, 1989, 2001, 2004, 2010, 2013, 2016, 2019, and 2022. For 1962, the data source is the SFCC; for subsequent years, the data source is the SCF.

[24] Data for even years was interpolated.

[25] Expenditures for housing and utilities exceed 50 percent of reported income. Data for even years was interpolated.

[26] Inadequate housing has moderate to severe problems, usually poor plumbing, or heating or upkeep problems. Data for even years was interpolated.

[27] Disability in children aged 5-17 is defined by responses in 13 core functioning domains: 1) seeing, 2) hearing, 3) mobility, 4) self-care, 5) communication, 6) learning, 7) remembering, 8) concentrating, 9) accepting change, 10) controlling behavior, 11) making friends, 12) anxiety, and 13) depression. Children who were reported to have "a lot of difficulty" or "cannot do at all" to at least one of the first 11 domains or "daily" to domains 12 or 13 are classified in the "disability" category.

[28] Disability is defined by level of difficulty in six domains of functioning: 1) vision, 2) hearing, 3) mobility, 4) communication, 5) cognition, and 6) self-care. Persons indicating "a lot of difficulty," or "cannot do at all/unable to do" in at least one domain are classified in "disability" category.

[29] Starting with 2020 data, regular physical activity is defined as participation in leisure-time aerobic and muscle-strengthening activities that meet the 2018 Physical Activity Guidelines for Americans. Aerobic guidelines for adults recommend at least 150 to 300 minutes a week of moderate-intensity, or 75 to 150 minutes a week of vigorous-intensity, or an equivalent combination of moderate- and vigorous-intensity aerobic activity. Muscle-strengthening guidelines for adults recommend activities of moderate or greater intensity involving all major muscle groups on 2 days a week or more. Before 2020, regular physical activity was based on the 2008 federal physical activity guidelines for adults that recommended at least 150 minutes (2 hours and 30 minutes) a week of moderate-intensity, or 75 minutes (1 hour and 15 minutes) a week of vigorous-intensity aerobic physical activity, or an equivalent combination of moderate- and vigorous-intensity aerobic activity. The 2008 federal physical activity guidelines also recommend that adults perform muscle-strengthening activities that are moderate or high intensity and involve all major muscle groups on 2 or more days a week. Due to the redesign of the National Health Interview Survey in 2019, use caution when comparing 2020 and 2022 data with data from previous years.

[30] BMI refers to body mass index. The 1960, 1980, 1990, 2000, 2005, 2010, 2014, 2016, 2018 data correspond to survey years 1960-1962, 1976-1980, 1988-1994, 1999-2000, 2005-2006, 2009-2010, 2013-2014, 2015-2016, and 2017-2018, respectively.

Table 9–1. SOCIAL INDICATORS—Continued

(Calendar years)

	1960	1970	1980	1990	2000	2005	2010	2015	2016	2017	2018	2019	2020	2021	2022	2023

31 Percentage at or above the sex-and age-specific 95th percentile BMI cutoff points from the 2000 CDC growth charts. The 1980, 1990, 2000, 2005, 2010, 2014, 2016, 2018 data correspond to survey years 1976-1980, 1988-1994, 1999-2000, 2005-2006, 2009-2010, 2013-2014, 2015-2016, and 2017-2018, respectively.

32 Heavier drinking is based on self-reported responses to questions about average alcohol consumption and is defined as, on average, more than 14 drinks per week for men and more than 7 drinks per week for women.

33 Includes only employees of private-sector establishments that offer health insurance. Adjusted to 2021 dollars by OMB.

34 Unpublished data. This is the mean total private health insurance premium paid by an individual or family for the private coverage that person is on. If a person is covered by more than one plan, the premiums for the plans are added together. Those who pay no premiums towards their plans are included in the estimates. In 2019 the National Health Interview Survey (NHIS) questionnaire was redesigned to better meet the needs of data users. Therefore, estimates based on NHIS from 2019 moving forward may not be strictly comparable to those prior to 2019. Adjusted to 2021 dollars by OMB.

35 A person was defined as uninsured if he or she did not have any private health insurance, Medicare, Medicaid, CHIP (1999-2021), state-sponsored, other government-sponsored health plan (1997-2021), or military plan. Beginning in 2014, a person with health insurance coverage through the Health Insurance Marketplace or state-based exchanges was considered to have private coverage. A person was also defined as uninsured if he or she had only Indian Health Service coverage or had only a private plan that paid for one type of service such as accidents or dental care. In 1993-1996 Medicaid coverage is estimated through a survey question about having Medicaid in the past month and through participation in Aid to Families with Dependent Children (AFDC) or Supplemental Security Income (SSI) programs. In 1997 to 2021, Medicaid coverage is estimated through a question about current Medicaid coverage. Beginning in the third quarter of 2004, a Medicaid probe question was added to reduce potential errors in reporting Medicaid status. Persons under age 65 with no reported coverage were asked explicitly about Medicaid coverage. In 2019 the National Health Interview Survey (NHIS) questionnaire was redesigned to better meet the needs of data users. Therefore, estimates based on NHIS from 2019 moving forward may not be strictly comparable to those prior to 2019.

36 Data are reported by birth year. Data for the 2015 birth year are from survey years 2016, 2017, and 2018; data for the 2016 birth year are from survey years 2017, 2018, and 2019; data for the 2017 birth year are from survey years 2018, 2019, and 2020; data for the 2018 birth year are from survey years 2019, 2020, and 2021. Recommended vaccine series consists of 4 or more doses of either the diphtheria, tetanus toxoids, and pertussis vaccine (DTP), the diphtheria and tetanus toxoids vaccine (DT), or the diphtheria, tetanus toxoids, and acellular pertussis vaccine (DTaP); 3 or more doses of any poliovirus vaccine; 1 or more doses of a measles-containing vaccine (MCV); 3 or more doses or 4 or more doses of Haemophilus influenzae type b vaccine (Hib) depending on Hib vaccine product type (full series Hib); 3 or more doses of hepatitis B vaccine; 1 or more doses of varicella vaccine; and 4 or more doses of pneumococcal conjugate vaccine (PCV). Data are reported by birth year. Data for the 2010 birth year are from survey years 2011, 2012, and 2013; data for the 2015 birth year are from survey years 2016, 2017, and 2018; data for the 2016 birth year are from survey years 2017, 2018, and 2019; data for the 2017 birth year are from survey years 2018, 2019, and 2020; data for the 2018 birth year are from survey years 2019, 2020, and 2021; data for the 2019 birth year are from survey years 2020, 2021, and 2022; data for the 2020 birth year are considered preliminary and are from survey years 2021 and 2022 (data from survey year 2023 are not yet available). Recommended vaccine series consists of 4 or more doses of either the diphtheria, tetanus toxoids, and pertussis vaccine (DTP), the diphtheria and tetanus toxoids vaccine (DT), or the diphtheria, tetanus toxoids, and acellular pertussis vaccine (DTaP); 3 or more doses of any poliovirus vaccine; 1 or more doses of a measles-containing vaccine (MCV); 3 or more doses or 4 or more doses of Haemophilus influenzae type b vaccine (Hib) depending on Hib vaccine product type (full series Hib); 3 or more doses of hepatitis B vaccine; 1 or more doses of varicella vaccine; and 4 or more doses of pneumococcal conjugate vaccine (PCV).

37 Property crimes, including burglary, motor vehicle theft, and other theft, reported by a sample of households. Every 10 years, the National Crime Victimization Survey (NCVS) sample is redesigned to reflect changes in the population. To permit cross-year comparisons that were inhibited by the 2016 sample redesign, BJS created a revised data file. Estimates for 2016 are based on the revised file and replace previously published estimates. For more information, see Criminal Victimization, 2016 (Revised), available at https://bjs.ojp.gov/redirect-legacy/content/pub/pdf/cv16re.pdf.

38 Violent crimes include rape and sexual assault, robbery, aggravated assault, and simple assault. Includes crimes both reported and not reported to law enforcement. Due to methodological changes in the enumeration method for NCVS estimates from 1993 to present, use caution when comparing 1980 and 1990 criminal victimization estimates to future years. Estimates from 1995 and beyond include a small number of victimizations, referred to as series victimizations, using a new counting strategy. High-frequency repeat victimizations, or series victimizations, are six or more similar but separate victimizations that occur with such frequency that the victim is unable to recall each individual event or describe each event in detail. Including series victimizations in national estimates can substantially increase the number and rate of violent victimization; however, trends in violence are generally similar regardless of whether series victimizations are included. See Methods for Counting High-Frequency Repeat Victimizations in the National Crime Victimization Survey, NCJ 237308, BJS web, April 2012 for further discussion of the new counting strategy and supporting research. Every 10 years, the National Crime Victimization Survey (NCVS) sample is redesigned to reflect changes in the population. To permit cross-year comparisons that were inhibited by the 2016 sample redesign, BJS created a revised data file. Estimates for 2016 are based on the revised file and replace previously published estimates. For more information, see Criminal Victimization, 2016 (Revised), available https://bjs.ojp.gov/redirect-legacy/content/pub/pdf/cv16re.pdf.

39 Estimates of the murder rate per 100,000 persons are taken from the FBI's Uniform Crime Reporting (UCR) Program. Estimates for 2021 and 2022 are based on a revised statistical methodology and may not be directly comparable to the murder rates estimated for previous years.

40 For the purposes of this report, the prison incarceration rate is a "custody plus privates"-based rate, meaning that it includes all persons held in state or federal publicly operated prison facilities and private facilities contracted to state or federal departments of corrections, but does NOT include prisoners housed in local jails with the exception of those housed in the six combined prison/jail system states (Alaska, Connecticut, Delaware, Hawaii, Rhode Island, Vermont). Prisoners of all sentence length and statuses are included in this report. This statistic corresponds to the prison incarceration rate published by BJS in its annual Corrections Populations in the United States, YYYY bulletin. (Prior to 1977, the National Prisoners Statistics (NPS) Program reports were based on custody population (not including either private prisons or jails). Beginning in 1977, BJS changed the official statistic for the prison population to a jurisdiction count, so rates prior to 1977 should not be compared directly to those published after 1977. As stated, the estimate provided does not include prisoners held in local jails, although under the pure definition of jurisdiction (legal authority over the person regardless of where s/he is held), prisoners in jails would be included.)

41 For all years, the actuals reflect Active Component only excluding full-time Reserve Component (RC) members and RC mobilized to active duty.

42 Note: A traffic fatality is defined as a death that occurs within 30 days after a traffic crash.

43 Charitable giving reported as itemized deductions on Schedule A.

44 Data correspond to years 1964, 1972, 1980, 1992, 1996, 2000, 2004, 2008, 2012, 2016, and 2020. The voting statistics in this table are presented as ratios of official voting tallies, as reported by the U.S. Clerk of the House, to population estimates from the Current Population Survey.

45 Indicator reflects the estimated share of Americans who volunteered through an organization at least once in the previous year. The figure for 1990 refers to an estimate from the May 1989 Current Population Survey (CPS) Multiple Job Holding, Flexitime, and Volunteer Work Supplement. Figures for 2002-2015 refer to estimates from the CPS Volunteering Supplement sponsored by the Corporation for National and Community Service annually in September. From 2017 on, figures refer to estimates from the CPS Civic Engagement and Volunteering (CEV) Supplement sponsored by the Corporation for National and Community Service dba AmeriCorps biennially in September. The increase between 2015 and 2017 likely reflects order effects related to transitioning from the Volunteering to CEV supplement questionnaire. All CEV data and documentation is publicly available at http://data.americorps.gov. Estimates for 2023 will be published in late 2024.

46 The 1980, 1990, 2000, 2005, and 2010 data come from the 1982, 1992, 2002, 2008, and 2012 waves of the Survey of Public Participation in the Arts, respectively. The 2017 and 2022 data come from the Survey of Public Participation in the Arts. Data from all other years are from the Arts Basic Survey. Survey items may have slight variations across years.

47 The 1980, 1990, 2000, 2005, and 2010 data come from the 1982, 1992, 2002, 2008, and 2012 waves of the Survey of Public Participation in the Arts, respectively. The 2017 and 2022 data come from the Survey of Public Participation in the Arts. Data from all other years are from the Arts Basic Survey. The wording and placement of questions differed across survey years, and the indicator for arts creation in future years will strive for greater consistency.

48 Ambient ozone concentrations based on 132 monitoring sites meeting minimum completeness criteria.

49 Ambient PM2.5 concentrations based on 361 monitoring sites meeting minimum completeness criteria.

50 2023 annual mean value is preliminary.

51 The gross emissions indicator does not include emissions and sinks from the Land Use, Land Use Change and Forestry sector. Emissions or sequestration of CO_2, as well as emissions of CH_4 and N_2O, can occur from management of lands in their current use or as lands are converted to other land uses.. Gross emissions are therefore more indicative of trends in energy consumption and efficiency than are net emissions. See https://www.epa.gov/ghgemissions/inventory-us-greenhouse-gas-emissions-and-sinks

52 Percent of the population served by community water systems that receive drinking water that meets all applicable health - based drinking water standards.

53 Includes net generation from solar thermal and photovoltaic (PV) energy at utility-scale facilities. Does not include distributed (small-scale) solar thermal or photovoltaic generation.

54 Dry natural gas is also known as consumer-grade natural gas.

10. LEVERAGING FEDERAL STATISTICS TO STRENGTHEN EVIDENCE-BASED DECISION-MAKING

The Federal statistical system provides the gold-standard for impartial, trusted Federal statistics, foundational to informing decisions across the public and private sectors. The Executive Branch, the Congress, businesses, and members of the public rely upon the Federal statistical system to provide objective, credible, and reliable data to address key questions pertaining to the economy, education, employment, health, and well-being of the Nation and its citizens. Accurate, timely, and relevant statistical data and products are also critical inputs for other evidence builders, such as researchers and evaluators, and are used in decision-making by Government programs that affect the lives and livelihoods of all people who need services and information.

Addressing ever-expanding information needs of the Nation efficiently and effectively requires more seamless collaboration within the Federal statistical system and across the broader data and evidence ecosystem. Made up of over 100 agencies, units, and programs, as well as officials across the Government, the various parts of the Federal statistical system continue to work together to become more seamless in support of key evidence-building needs. For example, the Federal statistical system is engaging in shared decision-making; using common frameworks, tools, and best practices; and using shared infrastructure, services, and capacities when feasible.

To fulfill these shared system-wide requirements, as well as the critical individual missions of the Federal statistical agencies, units, and programs, enhanced support for the work of the Federal statistical system is needed. The remainder of this chapter provides 1) an overview of the Federal statistical system; 2) a discussion of efforts to move toward a more seamless statistical system; 3) a description of system-wide statistical capacity and infrastructure needs and opportunities; 4) highlights of new and revamped critical Government-wide statistical standards and guidance; 5) priorities and budgets of each of the 16 Recognized Statistical Agencies and Units; and 6) recent achievements of Statistical Officials. For more information on the Budget's related investments in other evidence-building capacity and program evaluation, see the "Building and Using Evidence to Improve Government Effectiveness" chapter in this volume.

An Overview of the Federal Statistical System

Federal statistics have informed decision-making in the United States since its founding. The first constitutionally mandated census of population and housing was in 1790.[1] The 1790 Census planted the seeds for what is referred to today as the Federal statistical system. Over the 19th Century, the system continued to blossom into a specialized and decentralized, yet interconnected network of agencies, units, programs, and officials across the Government addressing emerging information demands of the Nation, including in the fields of tax, agriculture, education, and labor. The 20th Century presented new policy needs leading to further expansion of the Federal statistical system that included the fields of commerce, health, energy, justice, transportation, and more.

Today, the Federal statistical system collects and transforms data into useful, objective information and makes it readily and equitably available to stakeholders, while protecting the responses of individual data providers. Federal, State, local, territorial, and tribal governments, as well as businesses and the public, all trust this information to be credible and reliable, and use it to make informed decisions. The Federal statistical system includes the following entities and officials:

- *Office of the U.S. Chief Statistician*. Led by the U.S. Chief Statistician, this office in the Office of Management and Budget (OMB) is statutorily responsible for coordinating the Federal statistical system to ensure its efficiency and effectiveness, as well as the objectivity, impartiality, utility, and confidentiality of information collected for statistical purposes.[2] The office develops and maintains statistical policies and standards, promulgates regulations, identifies priorities for improving statistical programs and methodologies, assesses statistical agency budgets, reviews and approves collections of information from statistical agencies and units, and leads U.S. participation in international statistical activities.

- *24 Statistical Officials*. Each Chief Financial Officers Act (CFO Act) agency[3] has designated a senior staff person in the agency to be the Statistical Official with the authority and responsibility to advise on statistical policy, techniques, and procedures, and to champion statistical data quality and confidentiality. At the 11 CFO Act agencies that contain a Recognized Statistical Agency or Unit, the head of the agency or unit has been designated the Statistical Official, as required by the Foundations for Evidence-Based Policymaking Act of 2018 (Evidence Act).[4]

- *16 Recognized Statistical Agencies and Units*. OMB currently recognizes 16 statistical agencies and units under the Confidential Information Protection and Statistical Efficiency Act of 2002, as amended

[1] Carroll Wright, Comm'r of Labor, *The History and Growth of the United States Census* 11, S. Doc. No. 194 (1900), available at *https://census.gov/history/pdf/wright-hunt.pdf*.

[2] 44 U.S.C. 3504(e).

[3] See 31 U.S.C. 901(b) (defining CFO Act agencies).

[4] Public Law 115-435, 132 Stat. 5529 (2019).

(CIPSEA; 44 U.S.C. 3561-3583). OMB-recognized agencies or units are organizational units of the Executive Branch whose activities are predominantly the collection, compilation, processing, or analysis of information for statistical purposes. These agencies cover topics such as the economy, workforce, energy, agriculture, foreign trade, education, housing, crime, transportation, and health.

- *Other Statistical Programs*. In addition to the 16 recognized statistical agencies and units, there are approximately 100 other statistical programs that produce and disseminate statistics in support of other mission areas. Often, these programs also conduct a variety of evidence-building functions, such as program evaluation, policy and program analysis, and provision of funding and support for research.[5]
- *Interagency Council on Statistical Policy (ICSP)*. The ICSP,[6] led by the U.S. Chief Statistician, supports the Federal statistical system's vision to operate seamlessly. Membership includes the Statistical Officials and heads of each recognized statistical agency and unit (for a total of 30 unique members, including the Chief Statistician). Working together, the members of the ICSP set strategic goals for modernizing the statistical system, ensuring data quality and confidentiality, attaining and providing safe and appropriate data access, as well as enhancing coordination and collaboration across the system.
- *Federal Committee on Statistical Methodology (FCSM)*. The FCSM was founded in 1975 by the Office of the U.S. Chief Statistician to assist in carrying out the office's role in setting and coordinating statistical policy.[7] The FCSM serves as a resource for OMB, ICSP, and the Federal statistical system to inform decision-making on matters of statistical policy, and to provide technical assistance, expertise, and resources on methodological and statistical challenges that affect Federal data.[8] The FCSM is currently composed of 23 members from across the Federal statistical system, appointed by the U.S. Chief Statistician based on their individual expertise in statistical methods.

The figure on the next page depicts each of the entities that form the interconnected network that is the Federal statistical system. Each provides value by advancing its specific mission and set of responsibilities. Coordination and collaboration enhance the value of each entity and the system as a whole.

[5] A full listing is included in the Annual Reports to Congress on Statistical Programs of the United States Government, which are available at *https://whitehouse.gov/omb/information-regulatory-affairs/statistical-programs-standards/*.

[6] 44 U.S.C. 3504(e)(8).

[7] More information about the FCSM is available at *https://www.fcsm.gov/about/*.

[8] Resources include the *Framework for Data Quality*, *Data Protection Toolkit*, and *Equitable Data Toolkit*.

Moving Towards a More Seamless Federal Statistical System

As the challenges facing the Nation continue to evolve and become more complex, so does the information required to inform decisions. Addressing the new information needs of the Nation efficiently and effectively requires coordination and collaboration within the Federal statistical system and across a broad set of data partners and users in the data and evidence ecosystem. The system must be more seamless to meet the increasingly-complex needs and demands for various types of data and access to that data, and to do that efficiently and effectively.

Many challenges continue to present themselves, such as *long-term downward trends in survey response*; increased risk of re-identification of confidential information; increased need for more blended data products where data from surveys, administrative forms, *private sector data*, and program records are all combined to generate evidence;[9] and the *potential for artificial intelligence (AI) to both solve urgent challenges and exacerbate societal harms*. While each of the Federal statistical agencies, units, and programs has found innovative ways to address challenges individually, a successful future for the whole Federal statistical system will require more seamless collaboration across the system and across the broader data and evidence ecosystem.

It is not sufficient for individual statistical agencies, units, or programs to focus solely on their individual missions. The vision for the Federal statistical system is to operate as a seamless system, as stewards of much of the Nation's most sensitive data, enabling greater evidence building, civic engagement, and public and private sector decision-making. The system is working together to address cross-system challenges more seamlessly via advancing shared decision-making and communications; using common frameworks, guidelines, techniques, tools, and best practices; using shared infrastructure, services and capacities when feasible; integrating data across agencies and missions; and ensuring a common experience for data users.

Recognizing the potential efficiencies and advancements that could flow from unifying the whole Federal statistical system's infrastructure and expertise, the Office of the Chief Statistician, leaders across the Federal statistical system, the Administration, and the Congress have all sought ways to require, encourage, and expand coordination and collaboration across Government. For example, the Confidential Information Protection and Statistical Efficiency Act of 2018 (CIPSEA 2018), as amended by Title III of the Evidence Act, requires the adoption of common frameworks for activities such as acquiring existing Federal data (e.g., administrative or program data) for statistical uses, protecting confidential statistical data, and providing expanded access to nonpublic data for statistical purposes. Other provisions of the Evidence Act, as expanded upon by OMB guidance,

[9] See for example presentations in the linked data track at the 2022 FCSM Research and Policy Conference, which are available at *https://fcsm.gov/events/2022-fcsm-conference/*.

Chart 10–1 THE DECENTRALIZED FEDERAL STATISTICAL SYSTEM

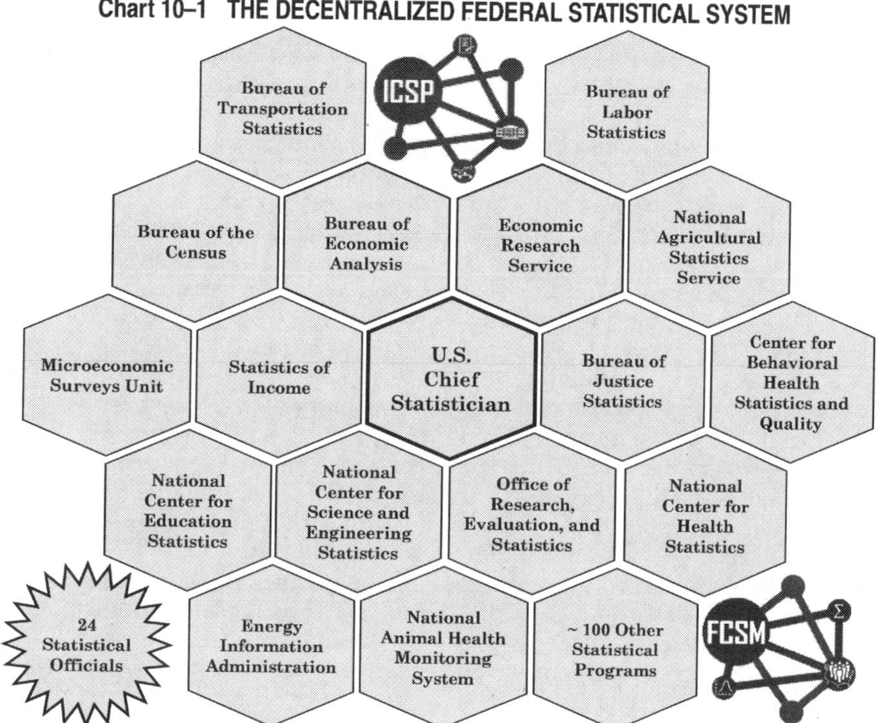

require agency Statistical Officials to facilitate coordination of statistical activities and serve on the ICSP, leading shared decision-making for the Federal statistical system.

Expanded Partnerships, Collaboration, and Engagement

In line with the vision to become more seamless, one collaborative effort across statistical agencies and other Federal agencies is focused on addressing a long-standing barrier to improving the efficiency and comparability of statistical business data. Since enactment of CIPSEA of 2002, the Census Bureau, Bureau of Economic Analysis (BEA), and Bureau of Labor Statistics (BLS) have had statutory responsibility to find efficiencies and reduce reporting burdens on the public by sharing business data, much of which is intermingled with tax data. However, a provision in the Internal Revenue Code limits sharing tax data in a manner that has significantly limited their efforts. The Census Bureau, BEA, BLS, and Departments of Commerce and the Treasury are working on a legislative proposal to remove this statutory barrier in order to increase efficiency and improve statistical products built on shared statistical business data. This was identified as a priority in the 2024 Green Book, Treasury's companion volume with the President's Budget.

In addition to collaborating with each other, statistical agencies and units are also collaborating with external and internal partners, to ensure the system's future success. For example, recognizing the risk of making decisions based on outdated data but not having the resources to make necessary updates, the Bureau of Transportation Statistics (BTS) initiated a partnership with the Department of Energy, other Department of Transportation agencies, and the Census Bureau to restore the more than 20-year-old Vehicle Inventory and Use Survey (VIUS). More agencies have now expressed interest to be part of the next VIUS and to partner with BTS on the first Electric Vehicle Inventory and Use Survey (eVIUS).[10] Additionally, the National Center for Heath and Statistics (NCHS) is modernizing the National Vital Statistics System by working with jurisdictional partners for production use of Fast Health Interoperability Resources (FHIR) to enable bi-directional exchange of mortality data between various jurisdictions and NCHS. FHIR will produce reliable, timely, and high-quality mortality data for critical public health surveillance and research.

The system will also continue to rely on its traditional means of engagement with external stakeholders, such as Federal advisory committees (e.g., the *Federal Economic Statistics Advisory Committee*, the *Bureau of Labor Statistics Technical Advisory Committee*, and the *National Center for Health Statistics Board of Scientific Counselors*), public comment opportunities, and focus groups or listening sessions. Across the Federal statistical system, agencies, the ICSP, and the Office of the U.S. Chief Statistician are building and implementing strategies to more regularly and effectively engage and obtain critical input from members of the public on their work, including data needs and user-friendly, relevant data products. For example, in seeking and implementing projects for the National Secure Data Service (NSDS) demonstration project, the National Center for Science and Engineering Statistics (NCSES) employed the capabilities and infrastructure of NCSES's recently established America's DataHub Consortium, including creating a new *Idea Bank* to receive project ideas from the public. For this ef-

[10] The Department of Transportation anticipates acting during 2024.

fort, NCSES also participated in other broad stakeholder engagement, outreach, and collaboration efforts with Federal agencies, the National AI Research Resource Task Force, and the State Network of Chief Data Officers, among others.

Forthcoming CIPSEA 2018 Regulations and Guidance

The future success of the Federal statistical system as a lynchpin for evidence building will also require significant growth by recognized statistical agencies and units in how they acquire data and make data safely accessible for public and private sector uses. As required by CIPSEA 2018, OMB, through the Office of the Chief Statistician, is developing three regulations. The Trust Regulation, which was published as a proposed rule in August 2023 and is discussed in more detail below, proposes measures to strengthen OMB-recognized statistical agencies and units as the trusted intermediaries of data, ensuring the objectivity, credibility, relevance, confidentiality, and exclusive statistical use of confidential statistical data.[11] The next two regulations will aim to promote consistent, comparable implementation of policies: 1) to make more Federal data assets accessible to OMB-recognized statistical agencies and units for the purposes of developing evidence;[12] and 2) to safely and securely expand access to data assets of OMB-recognized statistical agencies and units, while protecting such assets from inappropriate access and use.[13] OMB expects to develop and issue future guidance outlining the process by which an agency may be designated an OMB-recognized statistical agency or unit. Getting such policies and regulations right is important to the seamlessness and success of the Federal statistical system.

Building Statistical Capacity and Investing in Essential Statistical Infrastructure

Statistical agency, unit, and program contributions—both individual and collective—are necessary to maintain a strong Federal statistical system and to support the broader data and evidence ecosystem as needs constantly evolve. Accurate, timely, and relevant statistical products are critical inputs for other evidence builders, such as researchers and evaluators, and also for decision-making by Government programs that affect the lives and livelihoods of all people who need services and information. Statistical capacity is required to support these diverse needs efficiently, equitably, and effectively. Statistical products are also a public good; they help businesses and members of the public access services and make informed decisions, and their value increases the more they are trusted and used. Statistical infrastructure is essential to improving agency mission delivery, enabling modernization, and promoting reliability. However, like bridges and roads, statistical infrastructure requires ongoing maintenance and updating.

Individually, Federal statistical agencies, units, and programs regularly assess their work and advance the methods used for collection, analysis, protection, and dissemination of their statistical products. They also ensure robust security and information technology (IT) infrastructure is in place to facilitate their work. For example, the Statistics of Income Division of the Internal Revenue Service continued to make progress improving and updating its IT infrastructure. This included implementing a GitLab-based project control system for all its major programs, replacing aged hardware, completing necessary work on cloud-based infrastructure to facilitate system back-ups, implementing new system access logging and data encryption requirements, and ensuring IT management practices align with Federal Information Security Modernization Act (FISMA) requirements. Additionally, many agencies are exploring ways to take advantage of AI to support evidence-based policy and process improvements on behalf of the American people, while ensuring that official statistics are used correctly by AI and that the public receives accurate and trustworthy information. Several other agency-specific examples are highlighted later in this chapter. Without ongoing investments in the statistical infrastructure at each of the OMB-recognized statistical agencies and units, as well as throughout the Federal Government more broadly, the quality and relevance of Federal statistics begins to deteriorate.

Ongoing investments and advancements are also needed at a system-wide level, such as shared infrastructure, services, and capacities, as well as common frameworks, guidelines, techniques, tools, and best practices. For example, CIPSEA 2018 contemplates advancements such as common frameworks for inventorying data, protecting data, acquiring data from other agencies, and disseminating data securely. Executing such common frameworks requires increased interagency engagement when developing new policies or procedures. Several system-wide advancement examples are highlighted in the next section.

Highlights of Recent Significant Advancements Across the Federal Statistical System

Trust Regulation Proposed Rule. Trust is the backbone for the use of Federal statistics for evidence building. Trust in Federal statistics and the producers of Federal statistics underpins the value of those statistics, and each entity within the Federal statistical system must be diligent in upholding this trust. For individuals and entities to provide their data, they must trust the system to protect the confidentiality and exclusively statistical use of the information they provide. Similarly, for consumers of Federal statistical data and products to rely on Federal statistics, they must trust that Federal statistics are free from bias, generated with quality data, and reliable. *Statistical Policy Directive No. 1* identifies four fundamental responsibilities for OMB-recognized statistical agencies and units: 1) relevance and timeliness; 2) accuracy and credibility; 3) objectivity; and 4) confidentiality and exclusive statistical use of data. These four fundamental responsibilities align very closely with the five core values and other aspects of the United Nations' Fundamental Principles of Official Statistics. Importantly, Statistical Policy Directive No. 1 also directs other Federal agencies, including parent departments containing statistical agencies and units, to

---

[11] 44 U.S.C. 3563.

[12] 44 U.S.C. 3581(c).

[13] 44 U.S.C. 3582(b).

support, enable, and facilitate statistical agencies and units in meeting these responsibilities, emphasizing the importance of statistical autonomy to maintain trust of data providers, users, and the public.

CIPSEA 2018 incorporated those four fundamental responsibilities, and the corresponding responsibilities of other agencies, into statute. The codification of these responsibilities also signifies their criticality to the statistical infrastructure. By upholding these core responsibilities, agencies ensure the trustworthiness of the Federal statistical system—a necessity as the system takes an expanded role in the generation of evidence to support policy and program decisions. Any doubts or uncertainty about the system could introduce negative effects on markets, investments, economic growth, and job creation. As required by CIPSEA 2018, OMB will promulgate a regulation on the fundamental responsibilities of recognized statistical agencies and units, commonly known as the Trust Regulation. In August 2023, the Notice of Proposed Rulemaking was published in the Federal Register. The comment period closed in October 2023. OMB expects to issue the final regulation in 2024.

Standard Application Process. The Evidence Act required the Federal statistical system to develop a Standard Application Process (SAP) for researchers and other data users to access non-public, restricted use, statistical data for purposes of evidence building. The SAP portal was launched in December 2022 to serve as a single "front door" to apply for restricted access to confidential statistical data from any OMB-recognized statistical agency or unit. It is meaningfully advancing evidence building by increasing safe access to data in a less burdensome and more transparent way for data users.

As of December 2023, the SAP Data Catalog currently includes metadata across over 1,400 datasets available from recognized statistical agencies and units. In its first year of operation, over 525 applications were received through the SAP Portal. The ICSP's SAP Governance Board is responsible for overseeing this system-wide shared service and is working a number of actions to further advance the SAP. The SAP portal demonstrates the strength of the Federal statistical system seamlessly working together and can serve as a launching pad for additional collaboration in support of evidence building by both Federal and non-federal stakeholders.

Federal Statistical Research Data Center (FSRDC). The FSDRC program provides access to confidential, restricted-use statistical data from multiple statistical agencies and units via partner research institutions across the United States and virtual access. In 2023, the *ICSP's FSRDC Executive Committee adopted a new three-prong strategic action plan* to increase equitable access to data, by improving research training support, expanding financial assistance, and enhancing virtual access. This plan aligns the FSRDC program with the obligations of recognized statistical agencies and units to expand secure access to statistical data as codified in CIPSEA 2018.

Aligned with this strategic action plan, one of the NSDS's pilot projects will conduct a landscape analysis of FSRDC user demand and unmet needs, and identify opportunities to expand access beyond the FSRDC's traditional user base, focusing particularly on data users at minority-serving institutions, State and local government, and non-profit institutions. This project will inform not only the FSRDC program, but also how a future NSDS may be designed for broader data access. The FSRDC program is important part of the Federal statistical system's data access ecosystem and expanding access to its critical statistical data resources will ensure a more seamless system overall.

StatsPolicy.gov. In April 2023, the Federal statistical system launched a new public facing website, *StatsPolicy.gov*. The website presents a new avenue to share key information, resources, and news about the Federal statistical system, ICSP, and the Office of the U.S. Chief Statistician.

New Infrastructure Opportunities and Capacity-Development Needs

Envisioning a National Secure Data Service (NSDS). In its final report, the Commission on Evidence-based Policymaking recommended establishing a National Secure Data Service "to facilitate access to data for evidence building while ensuring privacy and transparency in how those data are used."[14]

The NSDS is envisioned as an added capacity for the Federal statistical system to support (not supplant) ongoing work within the individual agencies, and to provide a system-wide capacity to aid with coordination, data sharing, data linkage, shared research and development, and other functions. While the specifics for an NSDS are still being determined, the Federal statistical system would support a future NSDS that would provide shared services for innovation in data linkage, data access, and enhanced confidentiality protections. *Public Law 117-167*, commonly referred to as the CHIPS and Science Act of 2022, authorized the National Science Foundation's National Center for Science and Engineering and Statistics (NCSES) to launch an NSDS Demonstration project.[15] NCSES has worked closely with the Office of the U.S. Chief Statistician and the ICSP to develop demonstration projects that will inform decisions about the form a future NSDS will take, which functions are needed and can be most effective, and what innovations can support an NSDS.[16]

Fourteen NSDS demonstration projects were awarded in 2023 and the first months of 2024. These projects include conducting a systematic review of privacy-preserving technologies, identifying and highlighting new opportunities for using interoperable health data, and creating and validating synthetic data, among others. Some of the projects already awarded will conclude as early as 2024, at which point NCSES and the ICSP will begin to analyze lessons learned from these projects. Lessons learned from these projects and additional projects in the coming years will inform future Federal investments in

[14] Comm'n on Evidence-Based Policymaking, *The Promise of Evidence-Based Policymaking* 1 (Sept. 7, 2017), available at *https://www2.census.gov/adrm/fesac/2017-12-15/Abraham-CEP-final-report.pdf*.

[15] 42 U.S.C. 19085(b).

[16] More information about the development of the NSDS is available at *https://ncses.nsf.gov/about/national-secure-data-service-demo*.

the NSDS and move the Federal statistical system toward establishing an NSDS envisioned by the Commission on Evidence-Based Policymaking and providing solutions as recommended by Advisory Committee on Data for Evidence Building.[17]

Increasing Capacity for the Statistical Officials. The effectiveness of the U.S. statistical and evidence-building infrastructure is supported by the capabilities, capacity, and resources available to the 24 Statistical Officials to serve their agencies. Pursuant to *OMB Memorandum M-19-23, Phase 1 Implementation of the Foundations for Evidence-Based Policymaking Act of 2018: Learning Agendas, Personnel, and Planning Guidance*, an agency's Statistical Official has the authority and responsibility to advise on, direct, and coordinate statistical policy, techniques, and procedures across the agency, and to provide leadership on confidentiality across all departmental data assets. This work is to be done in collaboration with Federal data partners, such as the Chief Data Officer (CDO), Evaluation Officer, Senior Agency Official for Privacy, Chief Information Officer, and Chief Artificial Intelligence Officer. The Statistical Official must be an active participant on the ICSP and the agency's Data Governance Body. To promote the ability of Statistical Officials to meet these responsibilities, agencies will pursue a foundational investment of no less than two full-time equivalent (FTE) positions to support this work. In 2023, the ICSP established a subcommittee focused on Statistical Official roles and responsibilities to further develop, coordinate, support, and communicate standards, policies, and procedures related to the role of the Statistical Official.

Investing in New and Revamped Critical Government-Wide Statistical Standards and Guidance

Pursuant to the Paperwork Reduction Act of 1995 (Public Law 104-13), the Office of the U.S. Chief Statistician develops statistical policies, guidance, standards, and best practices and maintains them through periodic review and revision, to ensure their relevance.[18] Much of this work is accomplished through interagency coordination, including across the Federal statistical system, in collaboration with the ICSP and through public engagement. Over the last year, the Office of the U.S. Chief Statistician disseminated several updates to and made progress on advancing other statistical policies, guidance, standards, and best practices. Below are a few highlights.

Federal Standards for Collecting and Reporting Race and Ethnicity

First, reflecting a top priority of the Office of the U.S. Chief Statistician and the Federal statistical system, in 2022, the Office of the U.S. Chief Statistician *launched a formal review of Statistical Policy Directive No. 15: Standards for Maintaining, Collecting, and Presenting Data on Race and Ethnicity (SPD 15)*. SPD 15 provides minimum standards for race and ethnicity that ensure the ability to compare data across Federal agencies and also to understand how well Federal programs serve a diverse America. The Office of the U.S. Chief Statistician is leading a revision process, similar to those used for other trusted statistical standards, to help ensure the rigor, validity, objectivity, and impartiality of the resulting revisions. This process includes convening an interagency technical working group to ensure perspectives from across the Executive Branch are incorporated into the recommendations for any revision.

This working group, which includes participants from more than 20 agencies across the Federal Government, convened in Summer 2022 to begin developing a set of recommendations for improving the quality and usefulness of Federal race and ethnicity data. Because SPD 15 is designed, in part, to clarify how well Federal programs serve racially and ethnicity diverse populations, this working group used multiple approaches for engaging with communities and members of the public from across the United States to inform their recommendations for revisions.

First, OMB published a set of initial proposals developed by the working group based on existing research in a Federal Register Notice (FRN) in January 2023. The FRN received over 20,000 *written public comments* over a 90-day period. Second, the working group conducted a listening tour that included a tribal consultation and three virtual town halls open to the public. More than 200 town hall attendees spoke to share their perspectives and more than 3,500 callers joined to listen. Third, the working group hosted over 90 *biweekly listening sessions* from September 2022 through September 2023 to give members of the public the opportunity to meet with members of the working group and share their input. The working group heard directly from over 100 speakers on a variety of topics during the listening sessions. Fourth, the working group engaged with scholars and technical experts at various professional association conferences and convenings. Finally, the working group launched *spd15revision.gov* to provide information and updates about the revision process. The working group has been reviewing and synthesizing the comments received through its many outreach efforts to issue final recommendations based on relevant research and public feedback. OMB expects to release an update to SPD 15 by no later than Summer 2024.

Core-Based Statistical Areas

Related to *Statistical Policy Directive No. 7: Metropolitan Statistical Areas*, in July 2023, OMB published *Bulletin No. 23-01: Revised Delineations of Metropolitan Statistical Areas, Micropolitan Statistical Areas, And Combined Statistical Areas, and Guidance on Uses of these Areas*. OMB first published a delineation of Core-Based Statistical Areas (CBSAs) following the 1950 census in order to provide the Federal statistical system with a consistent geographic framework for official statistics. This most recent update to the CBSAs is the first update to use population data from the 2020 Decennial Census. It is also the first update published following

---

[17] Advisory Comm. on Data for Evidence Building, *Year 2 Report* (Oct. 14, 2022), available at *https://www.bea.gov/system/files/2022-10/acdeb-year-2-report.pdf*.

[18] 44 U.S.C. 3504(e).

enactment of the Metropolitan Areas Protection and Standardization Act of 2021, which recognized the importance of maintaining the objective statistical basis of the CBSAs by requiring OMB to "ensure that any change to the standards of core-based statistical area . . . delineations shall . . . not be influenced by any non-statistical considerations such as impact on program administration or service delivery."[19]

Standard Occupational Classification System

In December 2023, the Office of the U.S. Chief Statistician and the interagency Standard Occupational Classification Policy Committee (SOCPC) launched the 2028 revision process for *Statistical Policy Directive No. 10: Standard Occupational Classification (SOC) System*. The SOC provides meaningful statistics on the labor market and economy broadly by ensuring that occupational data collected and published across recognized statistical agencies and units are consistent and comparable. The SOCPC is responsible for reviewing and maintaining the SOC and for providing recommendations to the U.S. Chief Statistician for possible revisions. The SOCPC expects to solicit public feedback on the SOC as part of its work and to help inform its recommendations. OMB plans to issue the final 2028 SOC sometime ahead of 2028.

North American Industry Classification System and Product Classification System

In September 2023, the Office of the U.S. Chief Statistician and the interagency Economic Classification Policy Committee (ECPC) initiated planning for the 2027 revision process for *Statistical Policy Directive No. 8: North American Industry Classification System* (NAICS), as well as the North American Product Classification System (NAPCS).[20] The NAICS is a standard classification of business establishments enabling measurement of U.S. industrial output across 20 sectors of the economy. The NAPCS is a hierarchical classification for products (goods and services). The NAICS and NAPCS ensure that industry and product data are collected and published across recognized statistical agencies and units in a consistent and comparable way. The ECPC is responsible for reviewing and maintaining the NAICS and NAPCS and for providing recommendations to the U.S. Chief Statistician for possible revisions. The ECPC will solicit public feedback as part of its work and to help inform its recommendations.

Relevant to this work and in response to Executive Order 14081, "Advancing Biotechnology and Biomanufacturing Innovation for a Sustainable, Safe, and Secure American Bioeconomy," the Office of the U.S. Chief Statistician convened an interagency technical working group in December 2022, charged with developing a set of recommendations for bioeconomy-related revisions to the NAICS and NAPCS. To inform this work, OMB published a *request for information in the Federal Register* in April 2023 seeking input from interested communities, researchers, and the public. The working group also conducted listening sessions. This input informed the set of recommended revisions provided to the U.S. Chief Statistician and the ECPC in September 2023. The working group continues to meet to report on Federal agency use of NAICS and NAPCS and to further develop recommendations for revisions to the NAPCS. In turn, the ECPC will use these insights in their review and revision process for the 2027 NAICS and NAPCS. OMB plans to issue the final 2027 NAICS and NAPCS sometime ahead of 2027.

Natural Capital Accounting and Environmental Economic Statistics

OMB, through the Office of Information and Regulatory Affairs, jointly led the development of the *National Strategy for Statistics for Environmental Economic Decisions* (National Strategy) with the Office of Science and Technology Policy and the Department of Commerce, published in January 2023. This strategy was the product of a policy working group representing 27 agencies across the Executive Branch, and incorporated feedback from the public received in response to a *Federal Register notice*. Execution of this 15-year strategy will result in a new, reliable, regularly updated statistical series of data that will connect the environment and the economy to better inform decisions about the environment. To meet these goals and develop comparable, consistent statistical series, the plan envisions the Office of the U.S. Chief Statistician playing a leading role in coordinating this work across the Executive Branch, as well as developing relevant statistical classification systems.

To begin the technical work, in October 2023, the Office of the U.S. Chief Statistician launched an Environmental-Economic Accounting interagency technical working group focused on building economic classifications for what the National Strategy names as Phase I natural capital accounts, plus "Forests" from Phase II.[21] The working group expects to solicit public feedback as part of its work and new account classifications will be consistent with international statistical standards, particularly those of the United Nations Standard National Accounts and System of Environmental-Economic Accounting. A first major product of this working group will be recommendations for new account classifications to the U.S. Chief Statistician by the end of 2025.

The Office of the U.S. Chief Statistician and BEA are also leading technical cooperation for the U.S. under a *trilateral Agreement* among the U.S., Australia, and Canada to work on natural capital accounting topics of common interest to their respective national economic accounts. This is reflective of international interest in more explicitly measuring humans' relationships with the environment.

Best Practices for Collecting Sexual Orientation and Gender Identity Data on Federal Surveys

Federal surveys play a vital role in generating the data that the public, businesses, and Government agencies need to make informed decisions. Measuring the sexual orientation and gender identity of the population in Federal

[19] 44 U.S.C. 3504(e)(10)(B).

[20] More information on NAICS is available at *https://www.census.gov/naics/*. More information on NAPCS is available at *https://www.census.gov/naics/napcs/*.

[21] Off. of Sci. & Tech. Pol'y, Off. of Mgmt. & Budget, and Dep't of Com, *National Strategy to Develop Statistics for Environmental Economic Decisions* (Jan. 2023), available at *https://www.whitehouse.gov/wp-content/uploads/2023/01/Natural-Capital-Accounting-Strategy-final.pdf*.

surveys improves understanding of the LGBTQI+ population and supports evidence-based policymaking. Changes in terminology, among other social changes, could impact the ways sexual orientation and gender identity (SOGI) data should be collected to meet the purposes of various surveys, so measurement practices for SOGI data need to be flexible and adapt over time to maintain usefulness.

In January 2023, the Office of the U.S. Chief Statistician published *Recommendations on the Best Practices for the Collection of SOGI Data on Federal Statistical Surveys*, fulfilling the requirement of Section 11(e) of Executive Order 14075, "Advancing Equality for Lesbian, Gay, Bisexual, Transgender, Queer, and Intersex Individuals." This report includes recommendations that were built on a long history of robust Federal effort to develop and refine SOGI measurement best practices. It highlights the importance of continual learning, offers best practices for including SOGI items on Federal statistical surveys, provides example approaches for collecting and reporting SOGI information, offers guidance on how to safeguard SOGI data, and concludes with a summary of challenges that warrant further research.

Highlights of 2025 Recognized Statistical Agency and Unit Budget Proposals

Each of the 16 OMB-recognized statistical agencies and units plays an important role in the Federal statistical system, leading development and dissemination of Federal statistical products and services, and coordinating with other agencies and units to promote a more cohesive seamless system. The collective priorities reflected in the Budget demonstrate the commitment of those Recognized Statistical Agencies and Units to advancing not only their own missions, but the more coordinated future of the Federal statistical system.

- *Bureau of the Census (Census Bureau), Department of Commerce*. Funding is requested to support ongoing core programs and to: 1) continue a multiyear process of transforming its organization and operations from a survey-centric model to a data-centric model that blends survey data with administrative and alternative digital data sources; 2) use resources for developing new data products, improving data methods and quality, investing in crosscutting research techniques, and investing in Enterprise technology; 3) integrate its programs into its data ingest and collection for the Enterprise initiative, which provides common capabilities for data collection and ingest to programs across the Enterprise; 4) launch the design and integration phase for the 2030 Census program; 5) establish an annual Puerto Rico Economic Program and strengthen current population estimates, as well as establish and maintain infrastructure supporting the intercensal population estimates; 6) modernize and increase the household sample of the Survey of Income and Program Participation; 7) support a focus on privacy enhancing technology and protecting Americans' privacy against AI threats; and 8) onboard surveys into the new dissemination system and advance support tools.
- *Bureau of Economic Analysis (BEA), Department of Commerce*. Funding is requested to: 1) support core programs, including the production the National, Regional, and International Economic Accounts, which include of some of the Nation's most critical economic statistics, such as Gross Domestic Product and international trade in services; 2) support research on new, emerging, and important topics in the economy, including global value chains, the distribution of personal income and consumption expenditures, the digital economy, the space economy, and health care; 3) support research that will explore new and innovated methods, including the use of data science techniques; and 4) develop a new system of U.S. Environmental-Economic Accounts to systematically measure the contribution of environmental economic activities to economic growth.
- *Bureau of Justice Statistics (BJS), Department of Justice*. Funding is requested to support ongoing data collections and to: 1) explore new uses of current BJS data; 2) identify and use new administrative data sources; 3) create new efficiencies to collect and disseminate timely and high-quality data, including the development of a real-time crime dashboard to collect, standardize, and publish crime data online in a form that can be accessed and interpreted by a wide variety of audiences; 4) implement the capability to conduct rapid response surveys to allow for more timely research using commercial probability-based online survey panels; 5) implement a Survey of Formerly Incarcerated Persons; 6) develop a Corporate Crime Database; 7) conduct a survey of State Sentencing Commissions; 8) implement the Law Enforcement Calls for Service data collection; 9) conduct a Census of Problem-Solving Courts; 10) conduct a Survey of Digital Evidence Analysis; and 11) develop a two-phase, nationally-representative Survey of Law Enforcement Leadership to examine the existing policies and roles of first-line supervisors within law enforcement agencies.
- *Bureau of Labor Statistics (BLS), Department of Labor*. Funding is requested to support and maintain core programs and to: 1) produce gold-standard data and analyses; 2) understand changes in the economy while safeguarding respondent confidentiality; 3) ensure data are released appropriately; 4) pursue new technologies and non-traditional data sources; and 5) identify efficiencies to improve data accuracy, lower respondent burden, increase survey responses, and better reach its customers, while providing its diverse customer base high-quality data for decision-making.
- *Bureau of Transportation Statistics (BTS), Department of Transportation*. Funding is requested to support core programs and to: 1) to develop methods and tools to improve the ability of transportation infra-

structure asset owners to assess climate change vulnerability of their assets and projects, identify evidence-based approaches to resilience improvements, and estimate their financial risks associated with the impact of climate change through the Climate Change Vulnerability Study; 2) implement parts of the Ocean Shipping Reform Act of 2022; 3) advance Statistical Official functions; 4) identify new statistical methods to estimate system-wide freight flows at the county level; and 5) implement the SAP.

- *Center for Behavioral Health Statistics and Quality (CBHSQ), Department of Health and Human Services.* Funding is requested to support ongoing, core programs and to further support CBHSQ's implementation of the SAP by: 1) using the SAP portal to process all incoming data requests; 2) designating researchers as CIPSEA agents upon completion of confidentiality training and submission of completed and notarized Designated Agent Form; and 3) reviewing all output received from either the NCHS Research Data Center or FSRDC program to ensure it meets disclosure requirements as stipulated by the agency's *Guidelines for SAMHSA RDC Data Users*.
- *Economic Research Service (ERS), Department of Agriculture.* Funding is requested to support core programs and to: 1) continue its work on democratizing data by engaging with external partners, such the Extension Foundation, State agencies, academic institutions, and other organizations; and 2) understand how ERS data are used, constraints with using the data, and ways to encourage greater access across diverse stakeholder groups. This work will extend previous pilot efforts to ensure more equitable and diverse access to ERS data.
- *Energy Information Administration (EIA), Department of Energy.* Funding is requested to continue delivering the critical data, analysis, forecasts, and long-term energy outlooks on which its stakeholders rely, and to: 1) field a pilot collection to measure the extent of utility disconnections resulting from arrears in customer payment in response to stakeholder interest in developing evidence to measure equity and energy insecurity; 2) release official statistics from the pilot collection in 2025; 3) join the FSRDC program, which will facilitate EIA's data access in conjunction with the SAP; and 4) move forward with a next-generation energy model to improve scenario analysis for decarbonization pathways.
- *Microeconomic Surveys Unit, Board of Governors of the Federal Reserve Board (FRB).* Funding is requested to support ongoing, core programs and to improve the Survey of Consumer Finance by enhancing survey content, reducing respondent burden, and increasing data quality.
- *National Agricultural Statistics Service (NASS), Department of Agriculture.* Funding is requested to support core programs and to: 1) serve as co-lead (with ERS) of the Inflation Reduction Act (IRA) Greenhouse Gas (GHG) Quantification Action Area team, to improve the temporal and spatial coverage of national conservation activity data for official USDA GHG Inventory reporting and modeling for the Agriculture and Forestry sector; 2) lead the effort to establish the USDA IRA Conservation Data Team Enclave in the Research, Education and Economics (REE) CIPSEA Azure Cloud, which is specifically designed for use by the Interagency Conservation Practices Data Team and will enable team members to process and integrate the diverse data sources contributing to the Conservation Practice Data Series; 3) contribute to climate-related activities across USDA including a White House Interagency Technical Working Group on Measurement, Monitoring, Reporting and Verification of GHGs for the Agriculture and Forestry sector to coordinate and accelerate Federal efforts to enhance measurement and monitoring of GHG emissions and removals from the atmosphere; 4) participate in the Agriculture Innovation Mission for Climate Summit, the REE Climate Research Strategy Team, the USDA Global Change Task Force, and the USDA Climate Adaptation Team; 5) participate in the SAP Technical Working Group; and 6) transition all agency data access requests to the SAP.
- *National Animal Health Monitoring System (NAHMS), Department of Agriculture.* Funding is requested to provide support for NAHMS ongoing activities and to: 1) collect data that will inform and support various animal health programs of the Animal and Plant Health Inspection Service; 2) pursue modernization efforts to increase efficiencies and timeliness; 3) partner with other statistical agencies to conduct statistical activities such as partnering with ERS to support questionnaire design for an upcoming study of the U.S. broiler industry; 4) support information collections on the health and productivity of the U.S. poultry and dairy population; and 5) explore opportunities to work with new and underserved aquaculture and livestock producer populations.
- *National Center for Education Statistics (NCES), Department of Education.* Funding is requested to provide support for NCES ongoing activities and to: 1) add findings to its Equity in Education Dashboard, which compiles key findings and trends on the current state of educational equity in the United States; 2) add items to the Integrated Postsecondary Education Data System (IPEDS) Admissions survey in 2025–2026 to better understand equity in early decision and early admission processes, and to better study non-first-time students; and 3) participate in interagency work related to the SAP through extensive participation in the SAP Technical Working

Group focused on the SAP Portal and co-chairing the SAP Policy and Budget sub-working group.

- *National Center for Health Statistics (NCHS), Department of Health and Human Services*. Funding is requested to support its base programs and to: 1) track detailed health and demographic information about the U.S. population, providing policymakers with the information needed to support evidence-based decision-making, track progress, and measure disparities; 2) monitor key health indicators by supporting its ongoing surveys and data collection systems, which obtain information from personal interviews, healthcare records, physical examinations, lab tests, and vital event registrations; 3) offer the Virtual Data Enclave as a new mode for researchers to remotely access NCHS's restricted-use data without the burden of traveling to a physical FSRDC; and 4) launch the NCHS Data Query System, which will make data discovery faster and easier by providing web users access to health statistics from many data collection systems in one central repository and will promote health equity research by allowing the audience to filter national statistics by factors that influence health, such as demographic, socioeconomic, and geographic characteristics.

- *National Center for Science and Engineering Statistics (NCSES), National Science Foundation*. Funding is requested to provide support for ongoing activities and to: 1) develop evidence-building infrastructure activities for Government-wide shared services including the SAP; 2) continue implementation of the NSDS Demonstration projects, including continued support for the establishment of a secure compute environment for secure data linking and testing privacy preserving technologies; 3) support methodological research and data collections to improve quality and reporting for understanding the science and engineering enterprise in a global context; 4) continue data collection and research of the Nation's skilled technical workforce and its relevance to economic recovery and industries of the future, including AI, cybersecurity, and the bioeconomy; 5) develop robust metadata to link to non-NCSES data sets; 6) plan for the potential implementation of findings from feasibility studies and topical module development efforts for the NCSES surveys; and 7) implement user experience improvements to the National Science Board's Science and Engineering Indicators suite of reports.

- *Office of Research, Evaluation, and Statistics (ORES), Social Security Administration*. Funding is requested to support core programs and to: 1) conduct research on Social Security programs and their beneficiaries, including publishing papers in the Social Security Bulletin; 2) provide policymakers and the public with objective, scientific, and methodologically sound information and analysis; 3) automate

Table 10–1. 2023–2025 BUDGET APPROPRIATIONS FOR RECOGNIZED STATISTICAL AGENCIES AND UNITS[1]
(In millions of dollars)

Agency	Actual 2023	Estimates 2024	Estimates 2025
Bureau of the Census[2]	1,503.9	1,503.9	1,596.6
Bureau of Economic Analysis	130.0	130.0	138.5
Bureau of Justice Statistics	42.0	42.0	42.0
Bureau of Labor Statistics	698.0	698.0	711.5
Bureau of Transportation Statistics[3]	29.3	29.5	38.8
Center for Behavioral Health Statistics and Quality, SAMHSA	122.0	122.0	122.0
Economic Research Service	92.6	92.6	98.0
Enery Information Administration	135.0	135.0	135.0
Microeconomic Surveys Unit, FRB[4]	3.4	4.5	18.5
National Agricultural Statistics Service[5]	211.1	211.1	195.0
National Animal Health Monitoring System, APHIS	3.9	3.9	4.0
National Center for Education Statistics	369.8	382.4	382.4
Statistics	138.5	144.8	144.8
Assessment	223.5	228.3	228.3
National Assessment Governing Board	7.8	9.3	9.3
National Center for Health Statistics	187.4	187.4	187.4
National Center for Science and Engineering Statistics, NSF	88.9	91.2	96.9
Office of Research, Evaluation, and Statistics, SSA	40.0	41.3	41.4
Statistics of Income Division, IRS	41.7	45.6	52.2

[1] Reflects any rescissions and sequestration.
[2] Agency Total includes discretionary and mandatory funds.
[3] 2023, 2024, and 2025 estimates reflect an allocation account from the Highway Trust Fund.
[4] 2025 estimate reflects funding for the Survey of Consumer Finance.

and modernize the production of statistical publications; 4) utilize the expertise of researchers around the United States through grants and contracts, such as the Retirement and Disability Research Consortium; 5) provide objective, secure data and statistics while protecting privacy through strict adherence to disclosure review policies; and 6) work on ICSP initiatives to implement requirements of the Evidence Act.

- *Statistics of Income Division (SOI), Department of the Treasury*. Funding is requested to support ongoing statistical programs, which released more than 640 tables and datasets to the public in 2023, and to: 1) make progress on projects that will expand access to tax data through the release of synthetic datasets, pilot a validation server process, stand-up a new service to provide tabulated tax data in support of program evaluation for Federal, State, local or tribal governments, and provide support and oversight for research conducted under SOI's Joint Statistical Research Program; 2) produce and release data describing new clean energy tax credits that will be reported for the first time on tax returns filed in 2024; 3) develop in house capacity to generate and deploy new disclosure limitation tools, based on principles of differential privacy; 4) make progress in developing statistical estimates that can help users understand the impact of tax policies and tax administration practices on taxpayers across a range of demographic groups; 5) explore the use of AI-related tools such as natural language processing, to automate manual processes and derive information from non-traditional data sources; 6) expand the availability of tax data to the Census Bureau and the FSRDC program; and 7) modernize SOI's web pages and products, develop division-specific branding, and expand user-engagement activities.

Recent Highlights and Achievements of Statistical Officials

Each Statistical Official has an important role to play not only for their own agency, but also the more seamless future of the Federal statistical system. As noted previously, effective expansion of the U.S. statistical and evidence-building infrastructure will require increasing the capabilities, capacity, and resources for the 24 Statistical Officials to serve their agencies and departments, and will require an initial investment of no less than two FTE positions to support these responsibilities. Some agencies may still be staffing the function to meet this initial minimum investment level.

The accomplishments of the Statistical Officials are varied in content and scope, and are expected to grow over the coming years. Nevertheless, in their current capacity, the Statistical Officials engage in projects with real-life impacts on the Federal statistical system, the Federal Government, and the American people. Statistical Officials' 2023 impact is detailed in *Statistical Officials Highlights and Achievements*. A few examples include:

- The Statistical Officials, such as at the Departments of Commerce, Defense, Interior, State, Transportation, the Treasury, and the Small Business Administration are evaluating strategies for the use of AI in Federal statistics to support evidence-based policy and process improvements on behalf of the American people.
- The General Services Administration (GSA) Statistical Official worked with the GSA Office of Evidence and Analysis to develop a Data Quality Index pilot project to gauge the data quality of Government-wide data assets and target areas for improvement.
- The Environmental Protection Agency (EPA) Statistical Official provided guidance on the development of statistical surveys, conducted statistical analysis to support agency decision-making, and developed new statistical products to support key EPA priorities, including addressing climate change and advancing environmental justice. For example, EPA finalized new statistical estimates of the Social Cost of Greenhouse Gases to inform agency decisions via evidence on the social benefits of mitigating climate change-inducing pollution.

Conclusion

Realizing the full potential of Federal statistics for effective evidence building requires ongoing, robust investments and growth in both agency-specific and system-wide statistical capacity and infrastructure. Such investments are enhanced by effective collaboration and coordination across the Federal statistical system. Ongoing investments in system-wide statistical capacity and infrastructure must be made to meet the increasing demands for data access and the new challenges to the public trust that arise in the context of the evolving data landscape.

11. ANALYSIS OF FEDERAL CLIMATE FINANCIAL RISK EXPOSURE

I. EXECUTIVE SUMMARY[1]

Climate change impacts are being felt across the United States, including in the form of increasingly costly disasters and slower but notable changes in drought, heat, and precipitation. These changes pose financial risks to the services and programs of the Federal Government. As directed by the President in Executive Order 14030, "Climate-Related Financial Risk", the Office of Management and Budget is working with Federal Agencies to conduct assessments of the Government's climate financial risk exposure and is taking steps to reduce these risks to both the Government and the Nation. This chapter presents two detailed assessments of climate financial risk to agency programs, specifically the U.S. Department of Agriculture's (USDA) Livestock Forage Disaster Program; and the Department of Agriculture Forest Service (USDA FS) and U.S. Department of the Interior (DOI) wildland fire suppression programs. The chapter also includes additional agency highlights that demonstrate various approaches currently being employed to assess physical climate risk to agency programs, facilities, and services. This year's chapter on Federal climate financial risk notes:

- The USDA estimates that due to increased drought fueled by climate change, the Agency could see up to double the number of ranchers seeking assistance under the Livestock Forage Disaster Program by the end of the century compared to today. This corresponds to $800 million more per year in Federal expenditures, by the end of the century.
- The USDA FS and DOI estimate that climate-fueled wildland fires could burn an additional 3.2 million acres of federally owned forests—an increase of 86 percent compared to today—by the end of the century, increasing expected suppression costs to $4.7 billion per year—compared to an average of $3.4 billion currently. Federal Agencies are taking action to reduce these risks through a range of climate risk management programs and investments, and developing new decision support tools and analytical capabilities.
- Building on over $50 billion in historic climate resilience investment provided by the Infrastructure Investment and Jobs Act (Public Law 117-58) and the Inflation Reduction Act of 2022 (Public Law 117-169), this year's Budget also invests in the development of new analytical capabilities to characterize and manage the financial risks posed by climate change; responds to wildland fire assessment findings by bolstering the wildland fire workforce and expanding hazardous fuels reduction efforts; invests in flood hazard mapping; and continues funding for a range of Agencies' technical assistance programs that provide decision-relevant information to help communities, States, and Tribes manage their climate financial risks.

[1] The 2025 Climate Financial Risk *Analytical Perspectives* Chapter was authored by a collaborative team of Federal officials from the Assessments of Federal Financial Climate Risk Interagency Working Group. The Office of Management and Budget is deeply appreciative of the Interagency Working Group's contributions, including the following individuals who authored sections of the chapter: Lead Chapter Editors & Authors (Christopher Clavin (OMB), Bryan Parthum (EPA), Robert Richardson (OMB)); USDA Livestock Forage Disaster Program (Aaron Hronzencik (USDA ERS)); USDA Forest Service & DOI Wildland Fire Suppression (Jeffrey Prestemon (USDA FS Southern Research Station), Jeffrey Morisette (USDA FS Rocky Mountain Research Station), Erin Belval (USDA FS Rocky Mountain Research Station), Jennifer Costanza (USDA FS Southern Research Station), Shannon Kay (USDA FS Rocky Mountain Research Station), Karin Riley (USDA FS Rocky Mountain Research Station, Karen Short (USDA FS Rocky Mountain Research Station)); HUD Commercial Loan Climate Risk Assessment (Ian Feller (HUD), Elayne Weiss (HUD)); DOE Managing Climate Risk at DOE Sites (Craig Zamuda (DOE), Steve Bruno (DOE)); Exploratory Analyses on Federal Lending Portfolio of Single-Family Housing (Nathalie Herman (OMB), Michael Craig (HUD), MingChao Chen (GinnieMae), Alex Masri (USDA)); EPA Managing Physical Climate Risk at Superfund Sites (David Nicholas (EPA)); DOD Managing Climate Risks at DOD Sites (Kathleen White (DOD), Shubhra Mistra (DOD)); New Analytical Capabilities (Quentin Cummings (FEMA), Karen Marsh (FEMA), Casey Zuzak (FEMA), Jesse Rozelle (FEMA), Julian Reyes (OSTP/US Global Change Research Program), Stacy Aguilera-Peterson (OSTP/US Global Change Research Program))

II. INTRODUCTION

Climate change is already affecting people and communities across the United States, including through the effects of climate-related extreme weather events. Human activities are affecting climate system processes in ways that alter the intensity, frequency, and/or duration of many weather and climate extremes, including extreme heat, extreme precipitation and flooding, agricultural and hydrological drought, and wildfire.[2] The impacts of climate change to the Nation's economy, communities, and

[2] Leung, L.R., Terando, A. , Joseph, R., Tselioudis, G., Bruhwiler, L.M., Cook, B., Deser, C., Hall, A., Hamlington, B.D., Hoell, A., Hoffman, F.M., Klein, S., Naik, V., Pendergrass, A.G., Tebaldi, C., Ullrich, P.A., & Wehner, M.F. (2023). Ch. 3. Earth systems processes. In: *Fifth National Climate Assessment*. Crimmins, A. R., Avery, C. W., Easterling, D. R., Kunkel, K. E., Stewart, B. C., & Maycock, T. K., Eds. U.S. Global Change Research Program, Washington, DC, USA. *https://doi.org/10.7930/NCA5.2023.CH3*

households continue to be realized through a range of increased costs, from goods and services such as healthcare, food, and insurance, to the costs of repairing and recovering from extreme weather events and natural disasters.[3] These effects are felt across the Nation, with their collective impacts projected to reduce economic output and labor productivity across sectors and regions—particularly in places that have historical or cultural connections to, or dependence on, natural resources.[4]

Some communities are at higher risk of negative impacts from climate change due to social and economic inequities caused by environmental injustice and ongoing systemic discrimination, exclusion, underinvestment, and disinvestment. Many such communities are also already overburdened by the cumulative effects of adverse environmental, health, economic, or social conditions. Climate change worsens these long-standing inequities, contributing to persistent disparities in the resources needed to prepare for, respond to, and recover from climate impacts.[5] Not only are the risks and impacts of climate change disproportionately concentrated in low-income communities and communities of color, as well as in Tribal Nations, but these communities also often face a steeper road to recovery when disaster strikes.[6]

Further, the frequency of intense extreme weather events with significant financial impacts has increased. Forty years ago, the United States experienced, on average, one billion-dollar disaster every four months, adjusting to 2022 dollars.[7] Today, the Nation experiences a billion-dollar disaster every three weeks.[8] Weather-related disasters currently result in at least $150 billion per year in average direct damages, and the frequency and intensity of such disasters are expected to increase in the near term.[9] Each of these extreme events typically causes direct economic losses through damages to homes, buildings, and infrastructure; disruptions in services; and impacts to social and health-related outcomes that often exacerbate existing inequities.[10] These effects are expected to increase costs to public programs, including those provided by the Federal Government, posing additional challenges to public budgets that fail to account for the risks posed by climate change.[11,12]

Notable Federal Climate Risk Reduction and Resilience Action Since the Publication of the 2024 Budget

Action is being taken across governments, sectors, and regions to identify, assess, and mitigate the risks that climate change poses to operations, assets, and the economy. In the past year alone, the Federal Government has made great strides in understanding the economic risks climate effects are already having—and will have—on the Nation's infrastructure, social safety nets, public health, national security, and the ability to prepare for and respond to the impacts of natural disasters to protect American lives and livelihoods. Under the Infrastructure Investment and Jobs Act (Public Law 117-58) (IIJA) and the Inflation Reduction Act of 2022 (Public Law 117-169) (IRA), the Administration has invested over $50 billion to help communities advance climate resilience, increase the resilience of the grid and critical infrastructure, reduce flood risk to communities across the Nation, and invest in conservation to advance resilience. Further, since the publication of last year's *Analytical Perspectives*, the Administration has continued to take a whole-of-Government approach to make historic investments that increase the Nation's resilience to climate change impacts. Notable highlights include the following:

In September 2023, the Administration published the first-ever *National Climate Resilience Framework*, which provides a vision for climate resilience across the Nation and identifies opportunities for action to reduce climate risk across sectors. Consistent with Executive Order 14030 and this report, the National Climate Resilience *Framework* recognizes the need for continued research and development of modeling capabilities to integrate projections of climate change using models of changes

[3] Hsiang, S., Greenhill, S., Martinich, J., Grasso, M., Schuster, R. M., Barrage, L., Diaz, D. B., Hong, H., Kousky, C., Phan, T., Sarofim, M. C., Schlenker, W., Simon, B., & Sneeringer, S. E. (2023). Ch. 19. Economics. In: Fifth National Climate Assessment. Crimmins, A. R., Avery, C. W., Easterling, D. R., Kunkel, K. E., Stewart, B. C., & Maycock, T. K., Eds. U.S. Global Change Research Program, Washington, DC, USA. *https://doi.org/10.7930/NCA5.2023.CH19*

[4] *Ibid.*

[5] Jay, A.K., Crimmins, A.R., Avery, C.W., Dahl, T.A., Dodder, R.S., Hamlington, B.D., Lustig, A., Marvel, K., Méndez-Lazaro, P.A., Osler, M.S., Terando, A., Weeks, E.S., & Zycherman, A. (2023). Ch. 1. Overview: Understanding risks, impacts, and responses. In: *Fifth National Climate Assessment*. Crimmins, A. R., Avery, C. W., Easterling, D. R., Kunkel, K. E., Stewart, B. C., & Maycock, T. K., Eds. U.S. Global Change Research Program, Washington, DC, USA. *https://doi.org/10.7930/NCA5.2023.CH1*

[6] National Climate Resilience Framework. (2023). The White House, Washington, DC, USA. *https://www.whitehouse.gov/wp-content/uploads/2023/09/National-Climate-Resilience-Framework-FINAL.pdf*

[7] Marvel, K., Su, W., Delgado, R., Aarons, S., Chatterjee, A., Garcia, M. E., Hausfather, Z., Hayhoe, K., Hence, D. A., Jewett, E. B., Robel, A., Singh, D., Tripati, A., & Vose, R. S. (2023). Ch. 2. Climate trends. In: *Fifth National Climate Assessment*. Crimmins, A. R., Avery, C. W., Easterling, D. R., Kunkel, K. E., Stewart, B. C., & Maycock, T. K., Eds. U.S. Global Change Research Program, Washington, DC, USA. *https://doi.org/10.7930/NCA5.2023.CH2*

[8] *Ibid.*

[9] Hsiang, S., Greenhill, S., Martinich, J., Grasso, M., Schuster, R. M., Barrage, L., Diaz, D. B., Hong, H., Kousky, C., Phan, T., Sarofim, M. C., Schlenker, W., Simon, B., & Sneeringer, S. E. (2023). Ch. 19. Economics. In: *Fifth National Climate Assessment*. Crimmins, A. R., Avery, C. W., Easterling, D. R., Kunkel, K. E., Stewart, B. C., & Maycock, T. K., Eds. U.S. Global Change Research Program, Washington, DC, USA. *https://doi.org/10.7930/NCA5.2023.CH19*

[10] Environmental Protection Agency. (2021). Climate Change and Social Vulnerability in the United States. *https://www.epa.gov/system/files/documents/2021-09/climate-vulnerability_september-2021_508.pdf*

[11] Dolan, F., Price, C.C., Lempert, R.J., Patel, K.V., Sytsma, T., Park, H.M., De Leon, F., Bond, C.A., Miro, M.E., & Lauland, A. (2023). The Budgetary Effects of Climate Change and Their Potential Influence on Legislation: Recommendations for a Model of the Federal Budget. Santa Monica, CA: RAND Corporation. *https://www.rand.org/pubs/research_reports/RRA2614-1.html*

[12] For the purposes of this chapter, "Analysis of Federal Climate Financial Risk Exposure,", "financial climate risk" refers to the budgetary risks borne by the Federal Government through the administration of programs and policies.

in land use, demographics, and the built environment, to support risk-informed decision making.

In June 2023, in response to Executive Order 14030, the U.S. Department of the Treasury's Federal Insurance Office released the *Insurance Supervision and Regulation of Climate-Related Risks* report that provides a comprehensive set of 20 recommendations to incorporate climate-related risks into insurance regulation and supervision. The report commends and encourages continued collaboration with the National Association of Insurance Commissioners and state insurance regulators for the nascent and growing efforts to incorporate climate-related risks in regulation and supervision.

In November 2023, the Office of Management and Budget (OMB) published Memorandum M-24-03, *Advancing Climate Resilience through Climate-Smart Infrastructure Investments and Implementation Guidance for the Disaster Resiliency Planning Act*. This memorandum recommends tangible steps Agencies can take to enhance the climate resilience of infrastructure that is being built in communities across the Nation, and as required by the Disaster Resiliency Planning Act, provides guidance to Federal Agencies on addressing the risks that natural hazards and climate change pose to the Federal Government's facilities.

The White House Council on Environmental Quality and OMB provided revised instructions to Principal Agencies[13] to incorporate a data-driven assessment of climate risk in all Agencies' Climate Adaptation Plans. These updated Climate Adaptation Plans, scheduled to be published in 2024, use a climate science-informed approach to plan and implement climate adaptation measures that safeguard Federal investments and manage risks due to the observed and expected changes in climate that are relevant to agency missions and programs.

Recent Costs of Climate-Related Disaster Impacts and Historic Investments to Continue Reducing National Climate Risk and Enhancing Resilience

In the last five years (2019-2023), there have been notable climate-related financial impacts to the Government due to disasters and preparing for disasters. For the built environment, notable impacts include:

- The Federal Emergency Management Agency (FEMA) obligated $97.8 billion from the Disaster Relief Fund between 2019 and 2023 for natural disasters;
- The U.S. Department of Housing and Urban Development (HUD)'s Community Development Block Grant Disaster Recovery program obligated $37.5 billion to support long-term housing, economic development, and infrastructure recovery needs; and
- The U.S. Army Corps of Engineers obligated $3.6 billion for its disaster response and recovery efforts.

This level of financial support needed to restore the built environment emphasizes the need for forward-looking designs that reduce physical climate risk and avoid locking in land use and infrastructure designs that are based on historical climate assumptions.[14] Policies like the Federal Flood Risk Management Standard and its implementation across the Government are essential tools to manage development and reduce the risk of future flood damages.[15]

Wildland fire management activities, including hazardous fuels treatments (e.g., prescribed fire) and suppression operations, are also important for disaster preparedness and response. The number, extent, and intensity of catastrophic wildfires has increased in recent decades, leading to significant economic damages. The economic burden of wildfires on the United States economy includes wildfire-induced damages and losses as well as the management costs to suppress and mitigate ignitions and fire spread. These trends are notable due to the following:

- The annualized burden of wildfires in the United States is estimated to be in the tens to hundreds of billions of dollars per year.[16,17] Federal expenditures on wildland fire management are substantial and they have increased steadily over the past three decades.
- More recently, between 2019 and 2023, USDA FS and DOI obligated over $16.5 billion toward suppression operations.
- These costs continue a trend where, since 1989, annual suppression costs have more than tripled in inflation-adjusted terms, which has been partly driven by climate change impacts.[18]

[13] Executive Order 14057, "Catalyzing Clean Energy Industries and Jobs Through Federal Sustainability" 86 FR 70935 (December 13, 2021) defines Principal Agencies to include the Departments of State, the Treasury, Defense (including the United States Army Corps of Engineers), Justice, the Interior, Agriculture, Commerce, Labor, Health and Human Services, Housing and Urban Development, Transportation, Energy, Education, Veterans Affairs, and Homeland Security; the Environmental Protection Agency; the Small Business Administration; the Social Security Administration; the National Aeronautics and Space Administration; the Office of Personnel Management; the General Services Administration; and the National Archives and Records Administration.

[14] Chu, E.K., Fry, M.M., Chakraborty, J., Cheong, S.-M., Clavin, C., Coffman, M., Hondula, D.M., Hsu, D., Jennings, V.L., Keenan, J.M., Kosmal, A., Muñoz-Erickson, T.A., & Jelks, N.T.O. (2023). Ch. 12. Built environment, urban systems, and cities. In: *Fifth National Climate Assessment*. Crimmins, A. R., Avery, C. W., Easterling, D. R., Kunkel, K. E., Stewart, B. C., & Maycock, T. K., Eds. U.S. Global Change Research Program, Washington, DC, USA. *https://doi.org/10.7930/NCA5.2023.CH12*

[15] See recent Federal Flood Risk Management Standard proposed rules at FEMA and HUD.

[16] Thomas, D., Butry, D., Gilbert, S., Webb, D., & Fung, J. (2017). The costs and losses of wildfires: A literature review. NIST Special Publication 1215. Gaithersburg, MD: National Institute of Standards and Technology. *https://doi.org/10.6028/NIST.SP.1215*

[17] Wildland Fire Mitigation and Management Commission. (2023) ON FIRE: The Report of the Wildland Fire Mitigation and Management Commission. *https://www.usda.gov/sites/default/files/documents/wfmmc-final-report-09-2023.pdf*

[18] CBO. (2022) Wildfires. *https://www.cbo.gov/system/files/2022-06/57970-Wildfires.pdf*

Additional investment in wildland fire management and mitigation could help society avoid some of the large losses associated with catastrophic wildfire by reducing the intensity of and damage from future fires.[19]

While these programs represent only a select set of disaster assistance and recovery programs and activities, they highlight that climate-related extreme weather events have significant fiscal impacts that are expected to increase in future years unless continued action is taken to reduce exposure and manage Federal programs' vulnerability to expected changes in climate conditions.

Notable Climate Financial Risk Findings from the Fifth National Climate Assessment

The *Fifth National Climate Assessment* (NCA5)—the Nation's preeminent source of authoritative information on the risks, impacts, and responses to climate change—was published in November 2023. NCA5 documents observed and projected vulnerabilities, risks, and impacts associated with climate change across the United States and provides examples of response actions underway in many communities. NCA5 includes an economics chapter for the first time, in addition to analyses on a range of other societal and economic sectors and regional-focused analyses.

NCA5 finds that future changes in the climate are expected to impose substantial new costs to the United States economy and harm economic opportunities for most Americans, including through increased costs of healthcare, food, and insurance. Over the next few decades, climate change is projected to continue causing increased ecosystem disruptions, water stress, agricultural losses, and further disruptions to supply chains.[19,20] A rise in extreme heat is expected to lead to lost labor hours—particularly for workers of color, low-income individuals, and those without a high school diploma—with projected wages lost due to unsafe heat ranging from $19 billion to $46 billion annually by 2050.[21] In the long term, the Nation faces relocation costs and damages to property due to flooding, wildfires, drought, and other perils; disruptions to food systems from drought or extreme rain events; risks to loss of life or property from wildfires; substantial health costs that disproportionately hit the most marginalized or disadvantaged; and challenges for public budgets with programs that rely on historical climate assumptions for estimating revenues or outlays.

Specifically, with regard to economic impacts, NCA5 finds that, to date, direct economic impacts of climate change have already been observed. For example, weather-related disasters result in at least $150 billion in costs to the United States per year (in 2022 dollars) through effects such as infrastructure damage, worker injuries, and crop losses. Future impacts are expected to be more significant and apparent. These effects are estimated to be non-linear and subject to sudden increases and decreases resulting from both direct and complex interactions between climate hazards and economic sectors.[22] NCA5 provides *sample future economic impact estimates*, such as finding that GDP growth would be expected to be 0.13 percentage points lower per year per one degree of global temperature warming, and that by the end of the century, the aggregate effect of multisector impacts ranges from 0.1 percent GDP growth to 1.7 percent GDP loss for a low emissions scenario and 1.5 percent to 5.6 percent GDP loss for a high emissions scenario. For context, the so-called Great Recession of 2007-2009 was associated with a 4.3 percent GDP loss in the United States,[23] and it was unprecedented in the post-war era for its severity and duration.[24] These figures and the rest of the NCA5 findings underline that economic impacts of climate change are expected to vary by location and sector, and are projected to impact all levels of Government budgeting through changes in revenues, spending, and borrowing costs.

Chapter Scope

To improve the Federal Government's capabilities to assess and reduce the risk that climate change poses to the Government and the economy, the President signed Executive Order 14030, "Climate-Related Financial Risk" on May 20, 2021.[25] Section 6(b) of Executive Order 14030 directs "[t]he Director of OMB and the Chair of the Council of Economic Advisers, in consultation with the Director of the National Economic Council, the National Climate Advisor, and the heads of other Agencies as appropriate, [to] develop and publish annually, within the President's Budget, an assessment of the Federal Government's climate risk exposure." Additionally, Section 6(c) of the Executive Order directs "[t]he Director of OMB [to] improve the accounting of climate-related Federal ex-

[19] Hsiang, S., Greenhill, S., Martinich, J., Grasso, M., Schuster, R. M., Barrage, L., Diaz, D. B., Hong, H., Kousky, C., Phan, T., Sarofim, M. C., Schlenker, W., Simon, B., & Sneeringer, S. E. (2023). Ch. 19. Economics. In: *Fifth National Climate Assessment*. Crimmins, A. R., Avery, C. W., Easterling, D. R., Kunkel, K. E., Stewart, B. C., & Maycock, T. K., Eds. U.S. Global Change Research Program, Washington, DC, USA. *https://doi.org/10.7930/NCA5.2023.CH19*

[20] Kosmal, A., A.R. Crimmins, F.J. Dóñez, L.W. Fischer, J. Finzi Hart, D.L. Hoover, B.A. Scott, and L.I. Sperling, 2023: Focus on risks to supply chains. In: *Fifth National Climate Assessment*. Crimmins, A.R., C.W. Avery, D.R. Easterling, K.E. Kunkel, B.C. Stewart, and T.K. Maycock, Eds. U.S. Global Change Research Program, Washington, DC, USA. *https://doi.org/10.7930/NCA5.2023.F4*

[21] Hayden, M. H., Schramm, P. J., Beard, C. B., Bell, J. E., Bernstein, A. S., Bieniek-Tobasco, A., Cooley, N., Diuk-Wasser, M., Dorsey, M. K., Ebi, K. L., Ernst, K. C., Gorris, M. E., Howe, P. D., Khan, A. S., Lefthand-Begay, C., Maldonado, J., Saha, S., Shafiei, F., Vaidyanathan, A., & Wilhelmi, O. V. (2023). Ch. 15. Human health. In: *Fifth National Climate Assessment*. Crimmins, A. R., Avery, C. W., Easterling, D. R., Kunkel, K. E., Stewart, B. C., & Maycock, T. K., Eds. U.S. Global Change Research Program, Washington, DC, USA. *https://doi.org/10.7930/NCA5.2023.CH15*

[22] Burke, M., S.M. Hsiang, & E. Miguel. (2015). Global non-linear effect of temperature on economic production. *Nature, 527* (7577), 235–239. *https://doi.org/10.1038/nature15725*

[23] Rich, R. (2013). The Great Recession. Federal Reserve History. *https://www.federalreservehistory.org/essays/great-recession-of-200709*

[24] Schanzenbach, D. W., Nunn, R., Bauer, L., Boddy, D., & Nantz, G. (2016). Nine facts about the Great Recession and tools for fighting the next downturn. The Hamilton Project, The Brookings Institution. *https://www.brookings.edu/wp-content/uploads/2016/07/fiscal_facts.pdf*

[25] Executive Order 14030, "Climate-Related Financial Risk", 86 FR 27967 (May 20, 2021). *https://www.federalregister.gov/documents/2021/05/25/2021-11168/climate-related-financial-risk*

penditures, where appropriate, and reduce the Federal Government's long-term fiscal exposure to climate-related financial risk through formulation of the President's Budget and oversight of budget execution." Building on the assessments of climate-related financial risk published in the *2023* and *2024* Budgets, this chapter meets the requirements of Executive Order 14030 Sections 6(b) and (c) for 2025.[26]

For 2025, this chapter presents a wide range of Federal agency climate risk assessments and management approaches prepared by the Assessments of Federal Financial Climate Risk Interagency Working Group. It is intended to provide a demonstration of the various approaches currently being employed to assess physical climate risk to agency programs, facilities, and services, including two analyses that provide detailed projections of quantified financial risks to agency programs. These qualitative and quantitative assessments are organized into five themes: 1) disaster preparedness and response, 2) risks to long-term infrastructure, 3) social safety net and human health, 4) national security, and 5) highlights of new climate risk assessment capabilities and decision support tools, including those recently published alongside the *Fifth National Climate Assessment*. This year's assessment does not address risks to Government revenues and does not address risks posed by transitioning the economy to clean energy sources (i.e., transition risk). Further, this chapter is not intended to provide a comprehensive whole-of-Government assessment of physical or transition risks of climate change.

[26] The analyses presented in this chapter are complementary to the climate-related projections for gross domestic product (GDP) and the debt based on long-term budget projections that are published in Chapter 3, "Long-Term Budget Outlook". Chapter 3 meets the requirements of Section 6(a) of Executive Order 14030, which states that "[t]he Director of OMB, in consultation with the Secretary of the Treasury, the Chair of the Council of Economic Advisers, the Director of the National Economic Council, and the National Climate Advisor, shall identify the primary sources of Federal climate-related financial risk exposure and develop methodologies to quantify climate risk within the economic assumptions and the long-term budget projections of the President's Budget."

III. FEDERAL ACTIONS TO IDENTIFY, ASSESS, AND REDUCE CLIMATE FINANCIAL RISK

Disaster Preparedness and Response

This section provides details on two risk assessments included in this chapter: 1) an overview of the climate financial risk associated with the U.S. Department of Agriculture (USDA)'s Livestock Forage Disaster Program, and 2) an update on projected wildland fire suppression costs due to climate change impacts on lands managed by the USDA Forest Service and the bureaus of the U.S. Department of the Interior (DOI).

U.S. Department of Agriculture: The Climate Financial Risk of the Livestock Forage Disaster Program

Climate change is already impacting many sectors of the United States economy.[27] The agricultural sector is particularly vulnerable to the impacts of climate change as crop yields, forage availability, and farm profits depend on evolving climatic conditions.[28,29] The Federal Government administers a variety of programs to support climate change resilience and climate risk mitigation within the agricultural sector.[30] Several of these programs, such as the USDA Farm Service Agency's (USDA-FSA) Livestock Forage Disaster Program (LFP), aim to compensate ranchers against drought risk. The LFP, and other Federal programs like it, constitute a financial climate risk for the Federal Government,[31] as projections of climate in the United States suggest that drought conditions are likely to become more frequent and intense for many regions in the future.[32,33,34,35]

The LFP was initially established by the 2008 Farm Bill and provides compensation to livestock producers

[27] Jay, A.K., Crimmins, A.R., Avery, C.W., Dahl, T.A., Dodder, R.S., Hamlington, B.D., Lustig, A., Marvel, K., Méndez-Lazaro, P.A., Osler, M.S., Terando, A., Weeks, E.S., & Zycherman, A. (2023). Ch. 1. Overview: Understanding risks, impacts, and responses. In: *Fifth National Climate Assessment*. Crimmins, A. R., Avery, C. W., Easterling, D. R., Kunkel, K. E., Stewart, B. C., & Maycock, T. K., Eds. U.S. Global Change Research Program, Washington, DC, USA. *https://doi.org/10.7930/NCA5.2023.CH1*

[28] Hsiang, S., R. Kopp, A. Jina, J. Rising, M. Delgado, S. Mohan, D. J. Rasmussen, R. Muir-Wood, P. Wilson, M. Oppenheimer, K. Larsen, & T. Houser. (2017). Estimating economic damage from climate change in the United States. *Science, 356*, 6345, 1362-1369. *https://doi.org/10.1126/science.aal4369*

[29] Malikov, E., Miao, R., & Zhang, J. (2020). Distributional and temporal heterogeneity in the climate change effects on U.S. agriculture. *Journal of Environmental Economics and Management, 104*, 102386. *https://doi.org/10.1016/j.jeem.2020.102386*

[30] Baldwin, K., Williams, B., Tsiboe, F., Effland, A., Turner, D., Pratt, B., Jones, J., Toossi, S., & Hodges, L. (2023). U.S. Agricultural Policy Review, 2021. USDA Economic Research Service, Economic Information Bulletin Number 254, February 2023. *https://doi.org/10.22004/ag.econ.333549*

[31] Hrozencik, R. A., Perez-Quesada, G., & Bocinsky, K. (2024). The stocking impact and financial-climate risk of the Livestock Forage Disaster Program (Report No. ERR-329). U.S. Department of Agriculture, Economic Research Service. *https://ers.usda.gov/publications/pub-details/?pubid=108371*

[32] Lehner, F., Coats, S., Stocker, T. F., Pendergrass, A. G., Sanderson, B. M., Raible, C. C., & Smerdon, J. E. (2017). Projected drought risk in 1.5 C and 2 C warmer climates. *Geophysical Research Letters, 44*(14), 7419-7428. *https://doi.org/10.1002/2017GL074117*

[33] Leng, G., & Hall, J. (2019). Crop yield sensitivity of global major agricultural countries to droughts and the projected changes in the future. *Science of the Total Environment, 654*, 811-821. *https://doi.org/10.1016/j.scitotenv.2018.10.434*

[34] Zhao, T., & Dai, A. (2017). Uncertainties in historical changes and future projections of drought. Part II: model-simulated historical and future drought changes. *Climatic Change, 144*, 535-548. *https://doi.org/10.1007/s10584-016-1742-x*

[35] Climate change also poses financial risks for individuals and firms, these risks are not considered here.

Chart 11-1. Total Annual Nominal and Real LFP Payments, 2008-2022

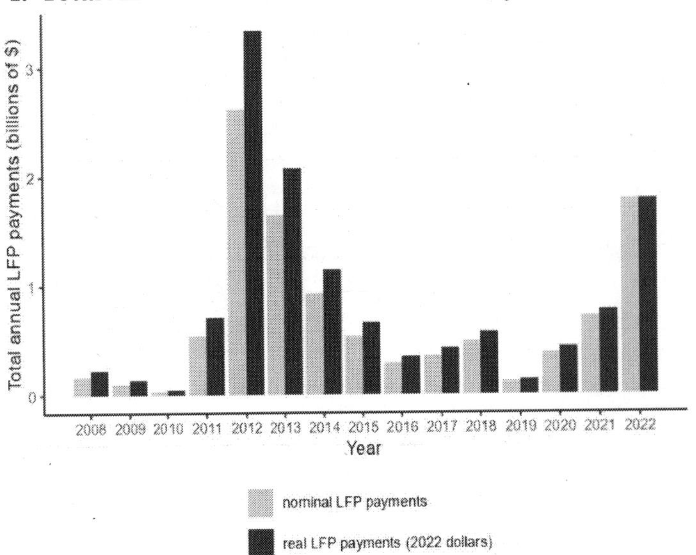

Source: USDA, Economic Research Service using data provided by USDA-FSA. Note: nominal payments represent the value of the payment in the year provided, and real payments represented inflation-adjusted amounts in 2022 dollars.

experiencing losses in forage due to drought.[36,37] LFP payments cover feed costs for a variety of livestock species, ranging from beef cattle to reindeer, on a per-animal basis for eligible expected losses due to drought. USDA-FSA annually sets species-specific per-animal payment rates as well as county-level eligible grazing periods. LFP payment rates are set to reflect feed costs and generally aim to cover 60 percent of monthly per-animal feed expenditures. To be eligible for LFP payments, the county that a livestock producer operates within must experience drought conditions exceeding a specified threshold during the county's eligible grazing period.[38] County-level drought conditions are classified weekly by the U.S. Drought Monitor (USDM), which designates five levels of increasing drought severity ranging from D0: Abnormally Dry to D4: Exceptional Drought.

Chart 11-1 plots annual aggregate LFP payments, in nominal and real values, between 2008 and 2022, highlighting the potential financial climate risk posed by the program, especially during periods of severe drought. Specifically, LFP payments peaked to more than $3 billion (in 2022 dollars) in 2012, when many livestock production regions of the United States were affected by unprecedented levels of drought severity. Not only was this the first drought since 1988 that impacted almost the entire Corn Belt, it also was unique in how quickly it developed and intensified.[39] Financial climate risks are particularly pertinent to the LFP as eligibility and program payments are a function of drought severity. If projected increases in drought incidence and severity are realized, then the Federal Government's budgetary expenditures associated with the LFP may also increase substantially.

Modeling the financial climate risk of the LFP involves integrating projections of future drought conditions, under differing emissions scenarios, with historical data relating drought severity and duration to LFP payments. Recently, researchers have raised questions regarding classifications of drought in a changing climate, suggesting that classifications of drought based on long-term historical climate conditions, e.g., USDM's classifications,[40] may bias current and future drought assessments toward classifying a region as experiencing drought when more recent climatic data would suggest that a region is not experiencing drought compared to more recent dry or arid

[36] Livestock producers also face risks of losses from the impacts of wildfires. However, the LFP only indemnifies producers if the wildfire occurred on Federally managed grazing land.

[37] MacLachlan, M., Ramos, S., Hungerford, A., & Edwards, S. (2018). *Federal Natural Disaster Assistance Programs for Livestock Producers, 2008-16* (No. 1476-2018-5471). *https://doi.org/10.22004/ag.econ.276251*

[38] Livestock producers become eligible for one month of LFP payments if the county where they operate experiences eight or more weeks of continuous severe drought (D2) during the eligible grazing period. Producers become eligible for additional months of LFP payments when experiencing more severe drought. For example, producers experiencing at least one week of exceptional drought (D4) during the eligible grazing period are eligible for four months of LFP payments.

[39] Fuchs, B., Umphlett, N., Timlin, M. S., Ryan, W., Doesken, N., Angel, J., Kellner, O., Hillaker, H. J., Knapp, M., Lin, X., Foster, S., Andresen, J., Pollyea, A., Spoden, G., Guinan, P., Akyüz, A., Rogers, J. C., Edwards, L. M., Todey, D., ... & Bergantino, T. (2012). From Too Much to Too Little: How the central US drought of 2012 evolved out of one of the most devastating floods on record in 2011. National Drought Mitigation Center, National Integrated Drought Information System. *https://drought.gov/documents/too-much-too-little-how-central-us-drought-2012-evolved-out-one-most-devastating-floods*

[40] It is important to note that the USDM was created to be a single measure to index drought conditions that impact many different sectors, not only agriculture.

Chart 11-2. Projected LFP Payments, 2023-2100

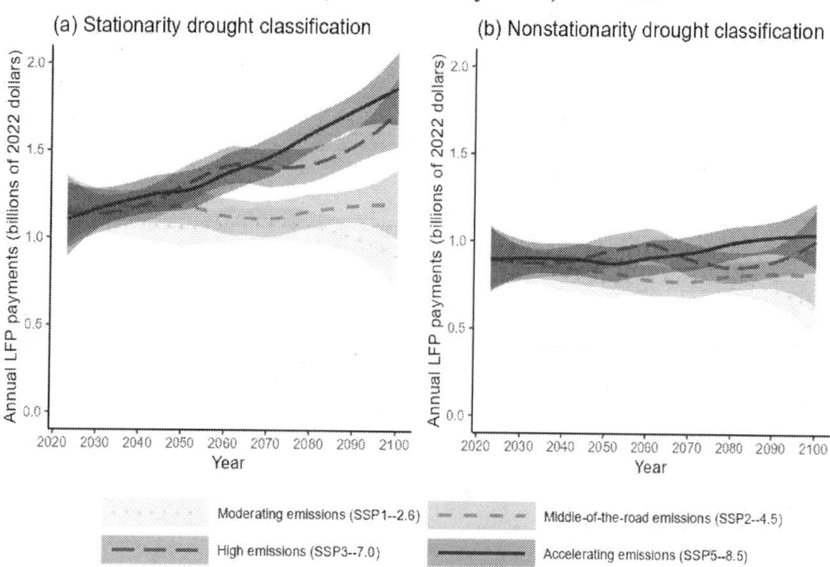

Source: USDA, Economic Research Service using data provided by USDA, Farm Service Agency, parameter estimates generated by econometric modeling and projections of future drought conditions across differing emissions scenarios and models.

conditions.[41,42] To address these drought classification issues, the LFP financial climate risk model uses medium- and long-term climatic data to construct alternative drought classifications. This analysis presents alternative drought classifications to represent their potential impact on LFP payments; however, neither this assessment nor its results take a position on broader considerations and consequences of modifying classifications of drought.

Chart 11-2 presents projections of future aggregate annual LFP payments and 95 percent confidence intervals through 2100 across a range of emissions scenarios and two methods for classifying drought. The left panel shows projected LFP expenditures under longer-term, historical climate data (60+ years) used to define drought classifications (stationarity drought classification). The right panel plots projected LFP expenditures for the case where drought classifications are instead based on decadally updated 30-year climate "normals" (non- stationarity drought classification). In each panel, average annual LFP expenditures are presented for four different climate scenarios, with 95 percent confidence intervals.[43]

Modeling results, presented in the left panel of Chart 11-2, suggest that under higher GHG emissions scenarios (high/SSP3-7.0 and accelerating/SSP5-8.5) and stationarity drought classification, annual Federal Government expenditures on the LFP may increase by more than 100 percent, or more than $800 million per year (in 2022 dollars), by the end of the century compared to average aggregate annual expenditures between 2014 and 2022 (in 2022 dollars). In the middle-of-the-road emissions scenarios (SSP2-4.5), model results indicate that Federal Government LFP expenditures may increase by 65 percent, or more than $400 million per year (in 2022 dollars), by the end of the century. These projected increases in LFP payments are relatively small compared to current Federal Government expenditures associated with the Federal Crop Insurance Program (FCIP). For example, average annual Federal Government expenditures for FCIP exceeded $8 billion over the 2011 to 2021 time period.[44] However, given that FCIP premium rates (before subsidies) are set to be actuarily fair, projected percent

[41] Hoylman, Z. H., Bocinsky, R. K., & Jencso, K. G. (2022). Drought assessment has been outpaced by climate change: empirical arguments for a paradigm shift. *Nature Communications*, 13, 1, 2715. *https://doi.org/10.1038/s41467-022-30316-5*

[42] Parker B., Lisonbee, J., Ossowski, E., Prendeville, H., Todey, D. (2023). Drought Assessment in a Changing Climate: Priority Actions & Research Needs. U.S. Department of Commerce, National Oceanic and Atmospheric Administration, Office of Oceanic and Atmospheric Research, National Integrated Drought Information System. NOAA Technical Report OAR CPO-002. *https://drought.gov/sites/default/files/2023-11/Drought-Assessment-Changing-Climate-Report-11-2023_0.pdf*

[43] These parameter estimates are then combined with projected future drought conditions in the United States, which distill future climate conditions into USDM classifications and months of LFP eligibility using eight different climate change models. For each climate change model, annual aggregate LFP payments are generated by multiplying econometric model parameters by the number of LFP eligible months projected by the model for each county and summing across counties. Annual results from each climate model are then aggregated and confidence intervals estimated using locally weighted (LOESS, locally weighted scatterplot smoothing) regression techniques. See Cleveland, W. S., & Devlin, S. J. (1988). Locally weighted regression: an approach to regression analysis by local fitting. Journal of the American Statistical Association, 83, 403, 596-610. *https://doi.org/10.1080/01621459.1988.10478639*

[44] GAO (Government Accountability Office). (2023). Farm Bill: Reducing Crop Insurance Costs Could Fund Other Priorities. GAO-23-106228. February 16, 2023. *https://gao.gov/products/gao-23-106228*

increases in FCIP expenditures under climate change are generally smaller than those predicted for the LFP.[45]

When drought classification methods update decadally to reflect changing climate patterns, the model results demonstrate that the financial climate risk of LFP diminishes (right panel of Chart 11-2). Specifically, in higher emissions scenarios (high/SSP3-7.0 and accelerating/SSP5-8.5), annual Federal Government expenditures related to LFP may increase by more than 25 percent, or approximately $200 million (in 2022 dollars), by the end of the century compared to average aggregate annual expenditures between 2014 and 2022 (in 2022 dollars). In the middle-of-the-road emissions scenario, the model results indicate that Federal Government LFP expenditures may increase by 14 percent, or approximately $200 million per year (in 2022 dollars), by the end of the century. Comparing projections of future LFP payments generated under stationary and non-stationary drought classification methods highlights the importance of drought classification methods in characterizing the climate financial risk of LFP. Specifically, if the methods used to classify drought do not adjust as the future climate changes (e.g., aridification), then LFP constitutes a potentially larger financial climate risk to the Federal Government's budget, particularly in higher emissions scenarios. However, using methods to classify drought for LFP eligibility that adapt to evolving climate patterns diminishes the financial climate risk of the LFP to the Federal Government, particularly in lower emissions scenarios.

The modeling results presented in Chart 11-2, both left and right panels, rely on several key assumptions. The most restrictive of these assumptions is that the United States livestock sector will not adapt to evolving climatic conditions by changing production practices or relocating production to regions less impacted by drought. This is a strong assumption given the possibility that producers may adapt to changing patterns of drought.[46] Any livestock sector adaptation to climate change and drought would decrease future financial climate risk of LFP. Additionally, modeling results do not incorporate potential changes in LFP payment rates through time that may be influenced by persistent and severe drought conditions. Specifically, USDA-FSA determines LFP payments rates based on forage and feed prices. If future drought conditions impact larger commodity markets (e.g., corn), and those goods' prices rise more than overall inflation, then LFP payment rates will increase to reflect higher costs of feed and forage. These LFP payment adjustments potentially increase the financial climate risk of the program as drought conditions would lead to larger Government expenditures to fund the program. Given the countervailing impacts of these two key modeling assumptions—and the many other avenues of uncertainty when projecting LFP payments into the future—the results presented in Chart 11-2 constitute neither an upper nor lower bound on future LFP payments.

U.S. Department of Agriculture Forest Service and U.S. Department of the Interior: Update on Projected Wildland Fire Suppression Costs due to Climate Change Impacts

Climate change is anticipated to raise land and ocean temperatures globally, change precipitation patterns, and drive changes in land use, including in the United States, and this change is likely to lead to shifts in the rate, severity, and extent of wildfire on Federal lands. Relevant to the Budget, such changes bring with them the expectation that spending to suppress wildfires and manage wildfire hazards, including emergency spending and spending necessary to rebuild or replace Federal infrastructure lost to wildfires, would generally change as the climate changes.[47] This report extends similar work done in 2016 and 2021-2022, with the 2021-2022 work published in the 2023 Budget. Similar to that work, USDA FS evaluates how changes to climate in the United States could lead to changes in annual spending to suppress wildfires on USDA FS and DOI managed lands by the middle and the end of the current century without holistic changes to the wildland fire mitigation and management. USDA FS builds on the previous analyses by refining the models to improve fit, updating data on wildfire suppression expenditures through 2019 (from 2005 for the USDA FS and 2013 for DOI), increasing the spatial resolution of the observations for suppression and wildfire, increasing the time span of historical wildfire to Fiscal Years 1993 through 2019, and expanding consideration of the potential drivers of wildfires. Similar to the 2023 Budget report, USDA FS developed statistical models of wildfire and its associated spending based on historical data on climate and wildfire.

In the current effort, USDA FS assembled an expanded set of climate projections by five global climate models (GCMs) and two warming scenarios (representative concentration pathway (RCP) 4.5 and RCP8.5) through 2099 for the continental United States (CONUS) at the 1/24th-degree grid scale.[48] This resulted in ten potential scenarios for both historical (1993-2019) and future (2020-2099) time periods.[49] Compared to the previous efforts, this effort refined spatial resolution of the resulting wildfire projections for USDA FS to the National Forest level

[45] Crane-Droesch, B. A., Marshall, E., Rosch, S., Riddle, A., Cooper, J., & Wallander, S. (2019). Climate change and agricultural risk management into the 21st century. *Economic Research Report-Economic Research Service, USDA*, (266). *https://ers.usda.gov/webdocs/publications/93547/err-266.pdf*

[46] Rojas-Downing, M. M., Nejadhashemi, A. P., Harrigan, T., & Woznicki, S. A. (2017). Climate change and livestock: Impacts, adaptation, and mitigation. *Climate Risk Management*, *16*, 145-163. *https://doi.org/10.1016/j.crm.2017.02.001*

[47] It is important to note that total costs from wildfires are much larger than Federal Government expenditures on preparedness and fire suppression.

[48] Area burned on FS lands in Alaska comprised less than 0.06 percent of historical wildfire for FS. Further, USDA FS lacked for this study monthly data on projected climate corresponding to the two national forests in the State, precluding projections of wildfire using climate data. Hence, in the current study, USDA FS does not model or consider FS spending in Alaska.

[49] See accompanying white paper for more details on the methods underlying this assessment.

Table 11–1. PROJECTED INCREASES IN AREA BURNED AND SUPPRESSION EXPENDITURES FOR FOREST SERVICE AND DEPARTMENT OF THE INTERIOR

Model	Time Period	Forest Service (FS)	Department of the Interior (DOI)	Combined (FS + DOI)
Area Burned	Mid-Century	98% [42%, 306%]	77% [43%, 163%]	86% [44%, 234%]
Area Burned	Late-Century	232% [29%, 2,488%]	171% [71%, 635%]	205% [73%, 1,399%]
Suppression Expenditures	Mid-Century	42% [20%, 84%]	31% [17%, 55%]	40% [19%, 81%]
Suppression Expenditures	Late-Century	81% [71%, 283%]	58% [26%, 173%]	76% [16%, 265%]

Detailed projections of increases in area burned and suppression spending, by USDA FS and DOI and combined, percentage changes from modeled historical area burned (2013-2019) and spending (2013-2019) for mid-century (2041-2059) and late century (2081-2099) projections. Lower (5th) and upper (95th) percentile bounds for a 90 percent uncertainty band are shown in brackets. Large upper tails are connected to the exponential functional form of area burned and to the wildfire outcomes generated from the climate predictions of the Hadley Centre Global Environment Model version 2 climate model (HadGEM2-ES365), which projects substantially hotter and drier conditions under both RCP 4.5 and 8.5 compared to the majority of the climate models included in this analysis.

(from the region level)[50], accounted for the negative feedback effect of historical wildfire on current period fire by introducing temporal lags to national forest wildfire models, and refined the DOI spatial resolution to the region by bureau level (from the region level Department-wide). Uncertainty in the area burned and suppression spending for each climate projection was quantified using Monte Carlo (bootstrapping) simulations, where the regression models used to project area burned and suppression costs are fit using a random sample of historical data for each iteration of the bootstrap. Overall uncertainty about climate was captured by projecting wildfires and suppression spending under the ten projections (5 GCMs x 2 RCP scenarios). The ten projections differed widely in their projected futures (by intention), with GCMs selected to capture a range of plausible futures in two climate dimensions: temperature and precipitation.[51] Additionally, this analysis identifies a single baseline for historical burned areas and suppression spending with which to compare future projections. The baseline is provided by modeled (or backcast) historical area burned and spending for 1999-2019. Future projections for 2020-2099 were then modeled for the area burned and suppression spending.[52]

Results show that the median area burned per year, across both USDA FS and DOI lands and across all climate projections, is projected to be 86 percent higher by mid-century (average from 2041-2059 projections) and 205 percent higher by late-century (average from 2081-2099 projections). Applying these percentage changes to historical area burned, area burned is projected to rise from the 2013-2019 average of 3.77 million acres per year to 7.02 million acres by mid-century and 11.49 million acres by late-century. Similarly, annual spending of both USDA FS and DOI are projected to rise. Compared to historical backcast spending (2013-2019) expenditures per year will rise by 40 percent by mid-century and 76 percent by late-century. Applying these percentage increases to observed historical spending, USDA FS projects that total Federal spending for USDA FS and the DOI will rise from a historical average of $3.35 billion per year (in 2022 dollars) to a projected $4.69 billion per year in mid-century and $5.9 billion per year by late century (see Table 11-1).

It bears emphasizing that this analysis only considers suppression expenditures by USDA FS and DOI, not additional wildfire-related damages in terms of losses to property, natural resources, human health, or other economic costs, nor suppression expenditures by other private and public entities. As such, the analysis covers a subset of all economic impacts generated by wildfire occurring on Federally managed lands in the CONUS. It is also important to note that not all wildfires need or receive management, and smaller or less intensive fires may result in more area burned but less suppression costs. Additionally, hazardous fuels were not directly modeled and, therefore, this analysis does not account for ongoing Federal efforts to address and mitigate associated risks. Even with these caveats, the models provide evidence that both wildfire areal extent and suppression expenditures are expected to increase with climate change. The modeling results show that increases in area burned could plausibly triple and inflation-adjusted suppression spending could nearly double, in this century.

[50] The lagged wildfire negative association included in the statistical models for the national forests cannot indicate whether a specific parcel within a national forest would be subject to reburning within a specific time span. However, the statistical result for the national forests implies that historical wildfire reduces current period wildfire, with implications for suppression spending.

[51] Langner, L. L., Joyce, L. A., Wear, D. N., Prestemon, J. P., Coulson, D., & O'Dea, C. B. (2020). Future scenarios: A technical document supporting the USDA Forest Service 2020 RPA Assessment. Gen. Tech. Rep. RMRS-GTR-412. Fort Collins, CO: U.S. Department of Agriculture, Forest Service, Rocky Mountain Research Station. 34 p. *https://doi.org/10.2737/RMRS-GTR-412*

[52] Using backcast data allows for consistent projections of magnitude changes in wildfire and suppression spending, reducing the effects of the biases contained in the underlying global climate models with respect to wildfire and spending.

Risks to Long-Term Infrastructure

This section provides highlights of forthcoming analysis and Federal agency efforts to address climate risk to the Federal Government's investments in physical assets: 1) an overview of ongoing assessments by the U.S. Department of Housing and Urban Development's commercial loan portfolio, and 2) a widespread accounting of the U.S. Department of Energy assets and infrastructure in the face of climate change.

U.S. Department of Housing and Urban Development: Commercial Loan Climate Risk Assessment Plans for 2026+

HUD's Federal Housing Administration (FHA) insures single family and commercial portfolios of mortgages and seeks to proactively manage credit risk, including from current and future climate-related natural disasters. This includes managing the credit risk of FHA's multifamily and healthcare (collectively "commercial") loan portfolios, which, as of month end August 2023, had nearly 15,000 loans totaling $162 billion in unpaid principal balances (UPB).[53] To better understand the effect of climate change on the multifamily and healthcare loan portfolios, and quantify these values for the public, HUD is developing several budget impact analyses in 2024 to present in the 2026 budget. Climate change poses several risks to HUD's commercial portfolio; most notably, buildings with chronic damage from coastal or riverine flooding, or acute damage from physical natural disasters, may experience reduced market values. When these borrowers default, whether due to economic causes or physical disasters, HUD's recoveries on lender claims will be lower, increasing the costs of these loan programs. The analyses described below evaluate the degree to which FHA's commercial portfolios are at risk of climate-related impact and identify the dollar value of projected gains or losses.

HUD FHA's Office of Risk Management and Regulatory Affairs (Risk) regularly estimates the budgetary impacts of three commercial loan portfolios: 1) multifamily housing, 2) nursing home, assisted living, board and care, and 3) hospitals. For these calculations, Risk maintains financial models that forecast the probability of prepayment by the borrower, probability of insurance claim payment by FHA (due to borrower default), and probability of recovery on claimed loans/properties. These models allow Risk to produce reports for audits, budgets, portfolio management, and ad hoc policy analyses.

These models use a series of factors to forecast loan performance, including:

1. Loan characteristics (e.g., term, interest rates, etc.);
2. Borrower characteristics (e.g., default history, physical inspection score, etc.);
3. Borrower financial statements; and
4. Macroeconomic projections (e.g., vacancy rate, median household income, etc.).

These models undergo annual updates to incorporate the latest historical loan performance data and forecasted macroeconomic projections, as well as adjustments to the underlying methodology, if appropriate. These updates are evaluated and approved by HUD FHA's Model Risk Governance Board, overseen by OMB, and audited by HUD's Office of Inspector General. Given the maturity and independent oversight of these models, HUD will use them as the starting point for the planned climate analyses.

Notably, these models do not include the impact of natural hazard risk, such as whether the property would be covered by hazard insurance, or the effects of climate change on natural hazard risk. Therefore, HUD proposes three novel analyses to incorporate physical climate risk into its models:

- *Approach 1: Simplified natural disaster cost calculation:* incorporate physical natural disaster hazards into FHA's loan forecasting models and calculate the costs to FHA's commercial loan portfolios.
- *Approach 2: Historical loss data aggregation:* In tandem with Approach 1, HUD plans to attribute historical claims and losses to historical natural disasters, consistent with standard econometric modeling techniques.
- *Approach 3: Advanced forecast of budgetary impacts:* FHA plans to develop an advanced budgetary forecast by incorporating robust climate data regarding transitional, chronic, and catastrophic risks into its loan performance models. Specifically, HUD will obtain property-level climate risk data for the probability of natural disasters, such as hurricanes, floods, and wildfires; the Approach will incorporate time-varying macroeconomic forecasts on the transitional risks related to climate changes.

In Fiscal Year 2024, FHA is assessing the feasibility of these approaches for analyzing climate risks to its commercial loan portfolio. Results from one or more of these analyses are expected to be included in the Fiscal Year 2026 Budget chapter on climate-related financial risk.

U.S. Department of Energy: Managing Climate Risk at Department of Energy Sites

The U.S. Department of Energy (DOE) is committed to leading Federal efforts to manage the short- and long-term effects of climate change and extreme weather on its mission, policies, programs, and operations. In October 2021, DOE issued its *Climate Adaptation and Resilience Plan* (CARP) to meet the goals of Executive Order 14008: Tackling the Climate Crisis at Home and Abroad, and to make climate adaptation and resilience an essential element of the work DOE does.

The financial impact of climate change on DOE's sites has been significant. Since 2000, DOE sites reported 31

[53] These multifamily and healthcare Government loan programs are negative subsidy and self-funded. Therefore, they do not require or receive annual appropriations from Congress.

separate events each costing the Department over $1 million, with an aggregated cost of $518 million. Future damage costs are projected to increase without mitigation and adaptation. Facilities are vulnerable to a range of hazards, including extreme precipitation events, inland and coastal flooding, wildfires, and extreme temperatures. These major damages have impacted DOE's mission and affected a range of sites, facilities, and infrastructure. Climate hazards vary across the DOE locations. For example, from June to August 2011, a wildfire burned virtually unchecked in the Jemez Mountains near Los Alamos National Laboratory, and the fire's intensity and proximity to the Laboratory resulted in a nine-day closure for all non-essential personnel. The Las Conchas fire, the largest recorded wildfire in New Mexico history, burned 154,000 acres, including some Los Alamos National Laboratory land, and direct Laboratory damages were estimated at $15.7 million, not including lost productivity.[54] In September 2013, Los Alamos received 450 percent of historical average rainfall, leading to ground saturation. The unusually heavy precipitation event caused $17.4 million in damages to environmental restoration infrastructure, monitoring gages, roadways and storm water control structures on the National Laboratory property alone.[55] In February 2015, severe winter weather, including an historic ice storm, hit the Y-12 National Security Complex in Tennessee. The storm caused significant damage to the facility, resulting in costs totaling $13.6 million.[56] The storm was characterized by freezing rain and ice accumulation, which caused widespread power outages and damage to infrastructure. In August 2020, the West Hackberry site of the Strategic Petroleum Reserve in southern Louisiana suffered considerable damages from Hurricane Laura totaling $35 million. Other sites have suffered damages from severe winter weather events, flooding, and other hazards.

In response to the CARP requirements, DOE's sites developed *Vulnerability Assessment and Resilience Plans* (VARPs) in 2021 to understand their individual site risks and the resilience actions necessary to mitigate the projected impacts of climate change. In this process, sites identified critical assets, analyzed historic climate events and damages, projected future climate hazards and associated risks, and developed sets of resilience solutions that respond to the identified risks. The VARP methodology (described in further detail in the *white paper* accompanying this chapter), follows a nine-step process where a multidisciplinary planning team identifies critical assets and infrastructure that are integral to their site's mission, identifies regional climate hazards, and forecasts the projected impacts of these hazards on their critical assets and infrastructure.

DOE's recent advances that address site-based climate vulnerability assessments and implement VARPs, include:

- *Incorporating Climate Risks in VARP Methodology.* Climate risks are projected to vary on a regional basis.[57] For example, many sites in the Midwest are projected to experience increased drought and extreme weather, while the Northeast, Southeast, and Southern Great Plains sites are projected to experience increased heat waves and storm activity. The Northwest and Southwest sites may experience increased heat, extreme precipitation, and wildfire. Coastal facilities, particularly along the Gulf and East Coast, may experience a combination of more extreme storm events, such as hurricanes, along with sea level rise and storm surge. Based on historical events and climate projections, the DOE sites most at risk are located in the Northwest, Southwest, and Southeast.

Table 11–2. EXAMPLES OF RESILIENCE SOLUTIONS IDENTIFIED BY DOE SITES AND THE CLIMATE HAZARD(S) THEY ADDRESS

Resilience Solution	Climate Hazard Addressed
Implement advanced cooling for transformers, cooling centers for workers	Heatwave
Install microgrid/battery storage infrastructure	Drought, Wildfire
Bury aboveground power lines	Strong Wind
Controlled burns and vegetation management	Wildfire
Reduce water intensity of operations, recycle water	Drought
Install seawalls, floodwalls, levees, or wetlands restoration	Riverine and Coastal Flooding, Tsunami
Install onsite renewable electricity generation with backup battery storage	All hazards

[54] DOE. (2015). Climate Change and the Los Alamos National Laboratory: The Adaptation Challenge. PNNL-24097. Richland, Washington, Pacific Northwest National Laboratory. *https://pnnl.gov/main/publications/external/technical_reports/PNNL-24097.pdf*

[55] *Ibid.*

[56] National Oceanic and Atmospheric Administration, National Weather Service. (2015). February 20-21, 2015 Historic Ice Storm. Nashville, Tennessee Weather Forecast Office. *https://weather.gov/ohx/20150221*

[57] Current VARP methodology encourages the use of historical weather data and projections of climate impacts. The methodology encourages the use of RCP 4.5 and 8.5 emission scenarios, and for DOE sites to use the National Climate Assessment regional chapters as the basis for projections. Additional resources such as the U.S. Climate Resilience Toolkit, the Climate Explorer, and resources from Climate Impact Labs are referenced in the appendix of the VARP methodology.

- *Resilience Solution Identification and Implementation.* To address their projected vulnerabilities, DOE sites identified resilience solutions in their VARPs. To aid sites in this, DOE partnered with the National Oceanic and Atmospheric Administration (NOAA) to provide technical assistance and access to a climate adaptation strategies tool, which provided actions grouped by hazard and asset. The three most common solution categories were upgrades to heating, ventilation, and air conditioning systems (19 percent), operational/managerial improvements (19 percent), and energy and water improvements (16 percent). Examples of common DOE resilience solutions can be found in Table 11-2 along with the climate hazard they address.

- *Further Advancing DOE Site Resilience and Needed Capabilities.* DOE's resilience planning has taken a major step forward to increasing understanding of the risks to mission and operations, as well as site resilience planning. The resilience solutions currently identified are a significant step forward for DOE, as many site-specific hazards, vulnerabilities, solutions, and implementation plans had not been previously characterized. In 2024, DOE plans to prioritize sites' identification of comprehensive solution sets, including prioritized implementation plans. DOE will assess the need for additional technical tools, support, and the sharing of best practices. Just as important, however, is the need to identify or create new tools that enable sites to model the financial costs and benefits and return-on-investment of various solutions. Such tools would enable sites to monetize and prioritize investments, and to compare and contrast the costs and benefits of investing in different types of resilience solutions versus taking no action.

Social Safety Net and Human Health

This section provides an overview of analysis prepared in response to Executive Order 14030's requirements to address climate-related financial risk in Federal agency underwriting standards and loan terms of Federal lending programs, and highlights from the Environmental Protection Agency, Office of Land and Emergency Management's efforts to manage physical risks at Superfund sites.

Update on Exploratory Analyses on Federal Lending Portfolio of Single-Family Housing

Executive Order 14030, Section 5(c) directs the Secretary of Agriculture, the Secretary of Housing and Urban Development, and the Secretary of Veterans Affairs "to consider approaches to better integrate climate-related financial risk into underwriting standards, loan terms and conditions, and asset management and servicing procedures, as related to their Federal lending policies and programs." OMB accordingly established the 5(c) Task Force under the Federal Credit Policy Council, with HUD, USDA, and the U.S. Department of Veterans Affairs (VA) (lending Agencies) to conduct initial analyses and to create a replicable framework for assessing climate risk in Federal lending programs. Last year marked the first time that the Federal Government had undertaken the task of broadly examining how climate-related financial risks could impact Federal lending across multiple Agencies and evaluating the limitations of current tools used to calculate those risks.

The 5(c) Task Force had determined that the first step to considering new approaches for integrating climate-related financial risk in various lending programs is to understand the nature and extent of risks to the single-family guaranteed housing programs at each Federal Agency. These programs include:

- USDA's Rural Development (RD) Single-Family Housing Guaranteed Loan Program (SFHG);
- HUD FHA Single-Family Mortgage Insurance Program;
- HUD's Government National Mortgage Association (Ginnie Mae) Mortgage-Backed Security (MBS) guarantee program; and
- VA's Loan Guaranty program.

In 2021, Federal lending programs for single-family housing had a cumulative outstanding exposure of \$2.1 trillion, and this exposure has increased to \$2.3 trillion as of 2023.

In order to gain a better understanding of the cost of climate change to the Federal lending portfolio, as well as the limitations of today's climate financial risk tools, OMB and the lending Agencies conducted three exploratory analyses to evaluate retrospective, current, and future climate risk.[58] It was concluded that the analysis was limited by today's climate financial risk models that failed to include a broad range of climate events. As a result, the risk is likely underestimated. Results do not represent official Government estimates of the projected losses. Instead, results were presented as illustrative test cases to highlight where further research is needed to address data gaps and methodologies and improve modeling.

It was determined that further analyses needed to be conducted, as other variables such as granularity and the inclusion of other climate events might better capture the severity of the risk. Consequently, this year, the Agencies continued to explore methodologies and refine analyses to better account for climate-related financial risks to the SFHG programs.

This year's analysis makes significant advances towards quantifying past losses to the Federal single family guarantee portfolio. Limitations still exist and should continue to be addressed in the next iteration of the ret-

[58] Retrospective climate risk refers to expected losses from past exposure using data originations from 2004-2017. Current risk analysis calculates expected annual loss (EAL) using data from the FEMA NRI database, as well as the Agencies' self-reported unpaid principal balance (UPB) estimates. Future climate risk is a 30-year lookout analysis that uses an industry standard tool to determine expected losses in the Agencies' mortgage portfolios that could occur given different scenarios of world events, economic trends, and climate change impacts.

Chart 11-3. Expected Annual Loss by Disaster Type, Year-Over-Year Comparison

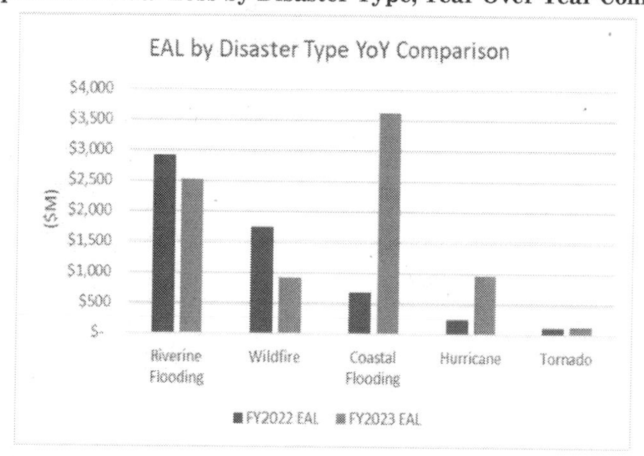

rospective analysis. However, further analyses need to be conducted as more granularity, data availability, and refinements to the assumptions might well change the severity of expected losses.

Retrospective Risk

To examine past risk, the lending Agencies executed a more refined retrospective analysis. The Agencies elected to pilot a mortgage-level analysis developed by HUD. This analysis offers several critical methodological improvements compared to the previous report including the generation of a total cost estimation for the mortgage insurance portfolio. The analysis is based on a ten percent sample of internal FHA data containing originations from 2004 to 2017 and publicly available disaster data from FEMA's Open Data portal consisting of 320 total declared major disasters for that time period. The retrospective analysis demonstrated that mortgages with disaster exposure are 1.14 to 1.21 times more likely to end in claims during each of the first three years post-disaster compared to mortgages without disaster exposure. The claims costs simulations calculate a difference in expected claims of $1.2 billion attributable to major disasters for the studied period. This is approximately 1.5 percent of the $80 billion in total claims paid on the FHA portfolio over this same period. Unfortunately, data and resource limitations prohibited the same calculation for the USDA and VA portfolios; however, Agencies intend to work to gather data components for those portfolios in the next iteration. As discussed further below, since climate change is expected to increase the frequency and severity of wildfires as well as the intensity of hurricanes, this risk is likely to grow over time.

Current Risk

To examine current risk, the Agencies used last year's novel expected annual loss (EAL) calculation developed using portions of the FEMA National Risk Index (NRI) database, as well as their own self-reported UPB estimates. Compared with the Fiscal Year 2022 analysis, the Fiscal Year 2023 analysis includes three main changes: 1) the assessment is based on the outstanding Ginnie Mae guaranty portfolio as of March 2023, which has increased in total volume by 4.6 percent from last year's analysis with the composition of loans insured by FHA, VA, and RD remaining mostly unchanged; 2) the latest NRI release used includes additional historical data, census tract data, and a major methodology overhaul for its coastal flooding and Historical Loss Ratio models; and 3) the Agencies conducted a supplementary analysis of recent originations. Calculations for each Agency were tabulated for five select hazards: 1) hurricanes, 2) coastal flooding, 3) riverine flooding, 4) wildfires, and 5) tornadoes[59] (see Chart 11-3). This risk assessment determined that for the Ginnie Mae portfolio, which represents an amalgam of the three Agencies' portfolios, the total EAL from climate-related events amount for the combined portfolio increased from 0.27 percent to 0.38 percent of the total portfolios. Additionally, coastal flooding and riverine flooding emerged as the top two natural disaster risks to the Agencies with EAL for these two climate events, accounting for 74 percent to 77 percent of EALs (see Chart 11-3).

Compared to the historical portfolio, EAL for wildfire has increased in recent origination cohorts[60] (2018-2022), indicating a growing risk due to wildfires (see Table 11-3). EAL for wildfire as a share of total cohort EAL increased by 3.9% between 2018 and 2022, while the share for other disaster types decreased during that period. It is important to note that this analysis does not include the impact of natural disasters on issuer performance or the impact

[59] Tornados have a complex and subtle relation to climate change. Tornados, as part of severe convective storms, are highly localized event and observed after the event, as opposed to modeled, which makes it difficult to link directly or attribute to global climate trends. See National Academies of Sciences, Engineering, and Medicine. (2016). Attribution of Extreme Weather Events in the Context of Climate Change. Washington, DC: The National Academies Press. *https://doi.org/10.17226/21852*

[60] Cohort analysis is based on a calendar year.

Table 11–3. EXPECTED ANNUAL LOSS BY DISASTER TYPE
(As a percentage of total cohort)

Disaster Type	2018 Cohort	2019 Cohort	2020 Cohort	2021 Cohort	2022 Cohort	% Change from 2018 to 2022
Riverine Flooding	34.0%	33.3%	30.3%	29.3%	30.9%	–3.1%
Wildfire	8.8%	9.9%	11.6%	12.3%	12.7%	3.9%
Coastal Flooding	42.2%	42.1%	44.5%	45.4%	42.2%	–0.0%
Hurricane	13.1%	12.9%	12.0%	11.5%	12.6%	–0.5%
Tornado	1.9%	1.9%	1.6%	1.5%	1.7%	–0.2%
Total Cohort	100.0%	100.0%	100.0%	100.0%	100.0%	

of climate change on investors' appetite for the Ginnie Mae MBS program.

Future Risk

With regard to future risk, the Agencies conducted another prospective analysis of the impact of climate events to a simulated Federal housing portfolio over the next 30 years. For this analysis, the Agencies ran the portion of their overall portfolio backed by Ginnie Mae, which constitutes about 87 percent of the overall portfolios of the three Agencies, through an industry-standard proprietary model. This model projects the expected loss in the lending Agencies' mortgage portfolios that could occur for different scenarios of world events, economic trends, and some climate impacts. The most recent iteration of the model includes the addition of climate risk assumptions consistent with a range of scenarios, including those from Central Banks comprising the Network for Greening the Financial System. The Agencies used this model to estimate losses to each Agency under two assumptions of future economic conditions (a 50th percentile baseline scenario and a 96th percentile severe adverse scenario) and then compared losses in these scenarios with and without climate shocks occurring. Federal researchers found that the model showed little risk, which is not considered an official Government estimate of projected losses; this analysis is considered preliminary and partial due to limitations in the analytical methods available. For example:

- The projected climate shocks are based on the FEMA-designated natural disasters for riverine and coastal floods, hurricanes, typhoons, and tornadoes, rather than global climate modeling.[61] The magnitude of the impact of other natural disasters that are not accounted for in this model—such as wildfires and winter storm events—is unknown and warrants further analysis.
- The modeling is agnostic to the varying insurance structures by program, which guarantee different amounts of losses through claims to lenders/issuers, and ignores that insurance and Federal and state disaster relief are effectively shifting portfolio hazard risk onto State and Federal entities. The analysis was conducted at the state level due to data limitations.
- Each program has unique coverage and policy requirements, which may change the overall Federal Government exposure to the respective portfolios.

In the next phase of the 5(c) workstream, the Task Force will improve upon existing tools and methodologies, as well as determine new tools that are needed to identify, assess, and respond to the risk climate change poses to the portfolios. The Task Force is planning to engage NOAA and DOE National Laboratories climate modeling experts in tool design and development, leverage the latest in climate modeling capabilities, and engage stakeholders, including climate-related data and analytics providers, non-profit organizations, and academia.

To refine and expand this analysis, the 5(c) Task Force continues to recommend the following key next steps:

- building expertise and learning within the interagency through a Climate Data Working Group that relies on the latest climate and hazard models and defining appropriate data sources for current and future climate risk analysis, as well as relevant data sets for consideration;
- developing or procuring the necessary skills and resources in order to improve quantitative capabilities in a rapidly evolving landscape;
- determining an appropriate cadence for repeating and refining the analyses, based on the availability of budget resources and workload requirements;
- sharing lessons learned on risk analysis with other programs within the Agencies, and more broadly with other Federal lending and guarantee programs;
- engaging with NOAA, the DOE National Laboratories, and private sector stakeholders through conversations on current practices and challenges posed by climate change in the financial and housing sectors and identifying appropriate foundational data sets for climate financial risk models that are temporal as well as spatial;

[61] The weather shocks follow a static probability table derived from the historical experience. No linkage was made to climate warming, and there was no drift in probabilities in the future due to a climate change scenario or view. However, there was one climate warming scenario/trajectory that was built into the financial risk model. This trajectory impacts on the future economic variables (GDP growth, interest rates change, prepayment speeds etc.) that ultimately drive the calculation of the dollar expected loss.

- analyzing options suggested by academics, industry groups, and other stakeholders for managing increasing risks from climate change;
- expanding the pool of assets to be analyzed by working with Government-sponsored enterprises and appropriate Agencies on identifying a pool of Federally owned or subsidized housing assets to conduct rigorous analysis of current and future climate risk; and,
- coordinating across Agencies to identify programs, funding, and procedures to disclose and manage climate risk reduction for the housing pool.

U.S. Environmental Protection Agency: Managing Physical Climate Risk at Superfund Sites

The U.S. Environmental Protection Agency (EPA) Office of Land and Emergency Management (OLEM) proactively manages current and anticipated impacts of climate change on hazardous waste site remediation programs. Under the Comprehensive Environmental Response, Compensation, and Liability Act of 1980 (CERCLA, or commonly, Superfund) (Public Law 96-510), as amended, EPA has authority at private-party sites as the lead Agency to carry out response actions to protect human health and the environment with respect to releases of hazardous substances, pollutants, or contaminants.[62] The Superfund program is EPA's primary program to remediate sites contaminated by release of hazardous substances. Activities include establishing a National Priorities List, investigating sites for inclusion on the list, determining their priority, and conducting and supervising cleanup and other remedial actions related to the physical risks at the site, many of which are inseparable from climate change. These risks include extreme weather events that threaten remediation systems, such as increased intensity of hurricane winds, flooding, and drought. EPA also assesses site resilience when there have been changes in site-level conditions that were not considered in initial site design conditions, such as increased stormwater intrusion, or a technological problem, such as an increased risk of power loss, that can arise in the system or site infrastructure due to changes in climate. EPA OLEM is taking action to address these known physical risks. Consistent with CERCLA, the National Oil and Hazardous Substances Pollution Contingency Plan (NCP),[63] as well as agency policy and guidance documents, OLEM is integrating climate resilience in the Superfund cleanup process.

Since 2021, OLEM has made significant progress in assessing site remedy protectiveness and anticipating the impacts of climate change to hazardous waste site remediation programs. These efforts have emphasized integrating adaptation efforts across the site cleanup and waste management programs. As a direct response to manage physical risks of climate change on Superfund sites, in 2021, OLEM published national program guidance[64] on considering climate resilience in Superfund site management. This guidance established policies that encourage regional site managers to consider potential impacts of extreme weather events and changing climate conditions at Superfund sites to ensure the long-term integrity and resilience of actions taken at the site.

Site changes and vulnerabilities, in some cases, involve climate-related changes that are more gradual, such as sea level rise, seasonal changes in precipitation or temperatures, increasing risk of floods, increasing intensity and frequency of hurricanes and wildfires, and melting of permafrost in northern regions. If the original remedial action selected in a record of decision (ROD) requires climate resilience-related changes, they are to be documented in an explanation of significant difference or ROD amendment consistent with the provisions in CERCLA (e.g., § 117) and the NCP (e.g., 40 CFR §300.435). Additionally, the guidance requires regional site managers to assess the vulnerability of a remedial action's components, including its associated site infrastructure and evaluate whether the long-term integrity of a selected remedy may be impaired by adverse effects of climate change. Based on any potential vulnerabilities identified above, regional site managers generally should evaluate adaptation measures that increase the system's resilience to a changing climate and ensure continued protectiveness of human health and the environment.

The following provide examples of vulnerability assessment methods and climate resilience case studies produced by OLEM:

- *Rocky Mountain Arsenal Site Case Study*: The *Rocky Mountain Arsenal site* in Commerce City, Colorado is vulnerable to wildfires and the threats they pose to the site's existing infrastructure and buildings for system maintenance and groundwater treatment. The site is in the wildland-urban interface, which implies additional risks of wildfires to surrounding communities. In December 2021, a wildfire quickly spread across more than 6,000 acres due to an unusually high amount of dry grass acting as fuel, a low amount of recent snowfall, and wind gusts exceeding 100 miles per hour. In response to the identified remedy vulnerabilities to climate change and to adapt to these changing conditions, the site undergoes periodic prescribed burns conducted to expend potential wildfire fuels in a controlled a manner. This practice also helps maintain the desired perennial grasses providing habitat for native and migratory wildlife, prevents onsite growth of invasive plant species, and fosters local biodiversity.
- *Port Hadlock Site Case Study*: The *Port Hadlock site* borders Port Townsend Bay, a marine inlet off the Olympic Peninsula in Washington. Due to its coastal location, the covered landfill is vulnerable to erosion associated with tidal action and storm surge. EPA Region 10 site managers, in collaboration with Department of Defense partners, have responded to these risks through site inspections and remedy

[62] 42 U.S.C. §9604(a)(1).

[63] 40 C.F.R. Part 300.

[64] EPA Memorandum OLEM Dir. No. 9355.1-120, Consideration of Climate Resilience in the Superfund Cleanup Process for Non-Federal National Priorities List Site. *https://semspub.eda.gov/work/HQ/100002993.pdf*

reviews that allow for more precise repairs to the landfill cap and armor rock replacement. In addition to addressing these climate-related risks at the site, these resilience measures provide improved habitat for shellfish rebound, reduce shellfish-related control costs, proactive investments, and sustainable planning.

National Security

This section provides a highlight from the U.S. Department of Defense on the policy, programs, and analytical capabilities currently being implemented to respond to national security risks posed by current and future climate change impacts.

U.S. Department of Defense: Managing Climate Risks at U.S. Department of Defense Sites

Climate change is adversely affecting the U.S. Department of Defense's (DOD's) national security-related missions and operations by amplifying operational demands on the force, degrading installations and infrastructure, and increasing health risks to service members. The risks of climate change to DOD strategies, plans, capabilities, missions, and equipment, as well as those of United States allies and partners, are growing.[65] DOD has been forced to absorb billions of dollars in recovery costs from extreme weather events typical of those fueled by climate change. This includes: $1 billion to rebuild Offutt Air Force Base, Nebraska after historic floods; $3 billion to rebuild Camp Lejeune, North Carolina after Hurricane Florence; and $5 billion to rebuild Tyndall Air Force Base, Florida after Hurricane Michael. Most recently, estimates show that an extreme precipitation event at the U.S. Military Academy, West Point, NY in July 2023 caused more than $200 million in damages.

DOD is responding to climate change with a myriad of policy and planning efforts to reduce risk to national security. DOD's predominant approaches enhance resilience to the effects of climate change through adaptation, in order to reduce DOD's operational and installation energy demand. DOD's existing policy for adaptation and resilience dates to the release of the DOD 2014 Climate Change Adaptation Roadmap and the establishment of *DOD Directive (DODD) 4715.21, Climate Change Adaptation and Resilience*, in 2016. DODD 4715.21 (updated in 2018) establishes policy and assigns responsibilities to provide the DOD with the resources necessary to assess and manage risks associated with the impacts of climate change. This involves deliberate preparation, close cooperation, and coordinated planning by DOD to:

- Facilitate Federal, State, local, Tribal, private sector, and nonprofit sector efforts to improve climate preparedness and resilience, and to implement the *DOD 2014 Climate Change Adaptation Roadmap* and its successor 2021 *DOD Climate Adaptation Plan*;
- Help safeguard United States economic, infrastructure, environment, and natural resources; and
- Provide for the continuity of DOD operations, services, and programs.

Climate Adaptation to Enhance National Security Resilience

The financial and national security consequences of failing to adapt to climate change will only compound over time, due to lost military capability, weakened alliances, weakened international stature, degraded infrastructure, and missed opportunities for technical innovation and economic growth. Since the release of the *DOD 2014 Climate Change Adaptation Roadmap*, DOD policy has required that all operations, planning activities, business processes, and resource allocation decisions include climate change considerations. The purpose of doing so is to ensure the military forces of the United States retain operational advantage under all conditions, leveraging efficiency and resilience to ensure our forces are agile, capable, and effective. Climate change adaptation must align with and support DOD's warfighting requirements.

The DOD climate adaptation framework for current and future force decisions laid out in the 2021 *DOD Climate Adaptation Plan* provides an update to the 2014 Roadmap and has five major lines of effort: 1) climate-informed decision-making, 2) train and equip a climate-ready force, 3) resilient built and natural infrastructure, 4) supply chain resilience and innovation, and 5) enhance adaptation and resilience through collaboration. Four enablers support and integrate these efforts: continuous monitoring and data analytics, aligning incentives to reward innovation, climate literacy, and environmental justice.

All actions in the DOD Climate Adaptation Plan are dependent on the outcomes of the first line of effort, climate-informed decision-making. Climate considerations must continue becoming an integral element of DOD's enterprise-wide resource allocation and operational decision-making processes. Climate assessments must be based on the best available, validated, and actionable climate science that informs the most likely climate change outcomes. Climate data sources must be continuously monitored and updated—with consideration of the operational impact—to account for the rapid rate of climate change and its impacts. Examples of assets supporting climate-informed decision-making include the DOD Climate Assessment Tool (DCAT), DOD Regionalized Sea Level (DRSL) Database, and the issuance of guidance on climate parameters for wargames. DCAT is discussed below, and other examples are provided in the accompanying *white paper*.

The DOD Climate Assessment Tool (*DCAT*), developed in accordance with Section 326 of National Defense Authorization Act of 2020 and released in 2021, integrates climate risk into DOD's risk management processes by assessing climate exposure at more than 2,300 DOD locations around the globe, including all major installa-

[65] Department of Defense, Office of the Undersecretary for Policy (Strategy, Plans, and Capabilities). (2021). Department of Defense Climate Risk Analysis. Report Submitted to National Security Council. *https://media.defense.gov/2021/Oct/21/2002877353/-1/-1/0/DOD-CLIMATE-RISK-ANALYSIS-FINAL.PDF*

tions (per 10 USC 2721 and DODI 4165.14, Real Property Inventory and Forecasting) and locations of interest identified by the Military Departments. The climate hazards addressed in DCAT are coastal flooding, riverine flooding, extreme temperature, drought, energy demand, land degradation, wildfire, and historical extreme conditions, supported by 33 indicators providing more granular information on specific conditions (e.g., coastal flood extent, five-day maximum temperature). DCAT aggregates exposure across these eight hazards and, for all but historical extreme conditions, provides information on how these hazards are projected to change over the 21st century.

DCAT contains exploratory visualizations and automated reports, along with screening-level inundation mapping of projected coastal flooding associated with changing sea levels (from DRSL). For riverine flooding, the initial release incorporated the freeboard approach of the Federal Flood Risk Management Standard (FFRMS). A second FFRMS method is being added in 2024: the 0.2 percent annual exceedance probability level for flood inundation. DCAT reports climate exposure information and mapping information critical to climate risk management and long-term planning, such as the exposure of its almost 670,000 buildings, structures, and linear structures. GIS analyses allow DOD to understand current and future exposure by class of facilities (e.g., percentage and type of buildings impacted by flooding in a future scenario). DCAT reports also include context for past extreme weather events by providing information sourced from NOAA about the damages they inflicted on counties containing installations.

New Analytical Capabilities

Each of the prior sections demonstrated an increasing need for Federal-wide and agency-specific analytical capabilities to identify relevant projections of the physical impacts of climate change. Ensuring these capabilities are usable, available, and accessible to the public is essential to managing climate risk to the Nation. This section provides a discussion of recent and forthcoming analytical capabilities provided by the Federal Emergency Management Agency and decision support tools published alongside NCA5.

Climate Risk Analytical Tools from the Federal Emergency Management Agency

Providing relevant, reliable, and actionable data in a usable format is a hallmark responsibility of the Federal Government. To fulfill this responsibility, FEMA produces data in an accessible format to improve awareness and understanding of climate risks, and to help people anticipate, prepare for, and adapt to future-based risks. Through interagency and private-sector collaborations, FEMA has published three tools that help emergency managers, community leaders and the public develop strategies for resilience:[66]

- The *Climate Risk and Resilience Portal (ClimRR)*[67] provides dynamical downscaled climate datasets to support analysis and data-driven planning for future climate risks. ClimRR hazards include maximum and minimum temperature, cooling and heating degree days, heat index, precipitation/lack of precipitation, wind speed, and fire weather index, all downscaled to 12 km grid cells for CONUS and most of Alaska under two potential future warming scenarios (RCP8.5 and RCP4.5). In 2024, ClimRR will include new projection data for coastal and inland flooding, available for 200m grid cells and displayed by hydrologic unit code (HUC) 12 watersheds, and begin to provide datasets that are downscaled to a finer resolution of 4 km grid cells for CONUS, and all of Alaska and Puerto Rico.
- The *Resilience Analysis & Planning Tool (RAPT)* is a browser-based GIS tool to examine the interplay of population demographics, infrastructure and hazards, weather, and risk. RAPT includes over 100 pre-loaded data layers[68] and easy-to-use analysis tools for data-driven decision making for all phases of emergency management. Additionally, RAPT includes the FEMA Community Resilience Challenges Index (CRCI), a composite index of 22 resilience indicators that have been used in multiple peer-reviewed research methodologies.
- The *National Risk Index (NRI)* is an index that assesses risk at a census tract-level for 18 natural hazards[69] and helps planners and emergency managers at the local, regional, state, and Federal levels, as well as other decision makers and interested members of the general public, better understand the natural hazard risks to their communities. It is one component of the methodology that is used to implement the Community Disaster Resilience Zones Act (CDRZ). The NRI and the Climate and Economic Justice Screening Tool help determine which census tracts are most in need of assistance for resilience-building projects and CDRZ designation.
- *Climate Informed NRI.* FEMA is expanding the NRI by developing a prototype platform to project how climate change and future conditions will change the impact of natural hazards through the mid- and late-century. Coastal flooding, drought, heatwave,

[66] These tools and their associated data are meant for planning purposes only.

[67] ClimRR was developed by the Center for Climate Resilience and Decision Science at Argonne National Laboratory in collaboration with AT&T and FEMA.

[68] RAPT includes data layers on population and community characteristics (e.g., population with a disability, mobile homes as a percentage of housing), infrastructure (e.g., hospitals, high hazard dams, places of worship), and hazards (e.g., real-time national weather service weather data, flood hazard zones, and sea level rise). RAPT data comes from authoritative sources, including U.S. Census Bureau, Homeland Infrastructure Foundation-Level Data, NOAA, USGS. Additional data can also be added to RAPT for more tailored analysis.

[69] These include avalanche, coastal flooding, cold wave, drought, earthquake, hail, heatwave, hurricane, ice storm, landslide, lightning, riverine flooding, strong wind, tornado, tsunami, volcanic activity, wildfire, and winter weather.

hurricane wind, and wildfire are included in the prototype. The Climate Informed NRI, anticipated to be released in 2024, describes climate change impact metrics by deriving Climate Informed Adjustment Factors (CIAF) from the ClimRR, RAPT, and the NRI.[70] This factor is a multiplicative adjustment that is applied to the Expected Annual Loss (EAL), as calculated in the NRI. To calculate the CIAF, a climate variable that is highly correlated with an aspect of current losses is used. Finally, the platform will calculate the other projected metrics, such as the Scores and Ratings index, relative to the present hazard levels and thresholds.

The Fifth National Climate Assessment Interactive Atlas and Climate Mapping for Resilience and Adaptation Updates

As described in the *National Climate Resilience Framework*, the Federal Government has published and is updating a range of analytical tools. These analytical capabilities are needed by a range of stakeholders, including architects and engineers, farmers and ranchers, and municipal government officials that are incorporating climate risks in updates to their general plans. NCA5 is the preeminent source of authoritative information on the risks, impacts, and responses to climate change in the United States. This section presents highlights of new analytical tools published alongside NCA5—specifically, the *NCA5 Atlas* and new updates to the *Climate Mapping for Resilience and Adaptation portal*—and includes additional technical background on downscaling methods employed in NCA5.

- *NCA5 Atlas*: To make the downscaled climate projections more accessible for the public, the U.S. Global Change Research Program published the *NCA5 Interactive Atlas* (NCA5 Atlas). The NCA5 Atlas provides digital access to downscaled climate projections of physical climate data (temperature and precipitation) used in NCA5. It will include projections of future sea-level rise in the near future. The NCA5 Atlas is an extension of NCA5, offering interactive maps that show projections of future conditions in United States. While the NCA5 is a static report, the NCA5 Atlas allows users to access and explore climate data for locations across the United States, even if those data were not explicitly presented in NCA5. Projections in the NCA5 Atlas are from GCMs that participated in CMIP6. To make the CMIP6 projections more relevant at regional-to-local scales, results from global models were spatially downscaled using statistical methods documented by LOCA2 and STAR-ESDM.
- *CMRA Updates*: With updated projections from the NCA5, the *U.S. Climate Resilience Toolkit* and *Climate Mapping for Resilience and Adaptation* (CMRA) portal has been updated and leveraged as primary knowledge-sharing hubs that are intended to support the development and co-production of adaptation and resilience solutions by sharing real-world case studies on resilience-building efforts. Using the NCA5 data as a foundation, the CMRA portal has been updated to represent the latest climate risks. For example, a new hazard topic, extreme cold, will be added to the popular dashboard of real-time climate-related hazards. The user experience has been improved on CMRA, including explaining that checking past and projected future climate is one of the first steps in protecting a community from climate hazards. CMRA reports will also better link to FEMA's NRI and *NOAA's Billion-Dollar Weather and Climate Disasters* site,[71] providing additional context of climate risks. Along with the NCA5 Atlas, these tools represent implementation pilots of the Climate Resilience Information System (CRIS), which will provide the information infrastructure needed for easy and consistent access to observed climatologies, climate projections, and other decision-relevant climate-related data. Collectively, these online resources represent a major opportunity to better support communities in localizing climate hazard data with other relevant information, such as infrastructure and socio-economic conditions.

[70] Additional details on the underlying data sources and methodology for the Climate Informed NRI are provided in the accompanying white paper.

[71] NOAA's National Centers for Environmental Information tracks the number and types of weather and climate disasters where overall damages/costs reached or exceeded one billion dollars.

IV. REDUCING CLIMATE-RELATED FINANCIAL RISK IN THE 2025 BUDGET

This chapter represents the Government's third published assessment of climate-related fiscal risk in the President's Budget since the release of Executive Order 14030. The 2023 Budget included assessments of fiscal risk due to crop insurance, the National Flood Insurance Program, flood risk to Federal facilities, and wildland fire suppression costs. In the 2024 Budget, illustrative analyses demonstrated advances in combined flood modeling and damage assessment of Federal facilities and projected heating and cooling demands, which could affect the Low-Income Home Energy Assistance Program. Additionally, it presented a new mandatory proposal to provide incentives to farmers to plant cover crops, which was a direct response to the prior year's assessment results.

This section addresses section 6(c) of Executive Order 14030, which calls for OMB to reduce the Government's long-term fiscal exposure to climate-related risk through the Budget. Building on the work conducted in prior years and the agency assessments and highlights presented in this chapter, the 2025 Budget includes a series of investments that directly respond to assessment findings. Table 11-4 includes a listing of notable examples of investments in reducing fiscal exposure to climate-related risk in the 2025 Budget. These examples, while not comprehensive,

Table 11–4. NOTABLE INVESTMENTS IN REDUCING FISCAL EXPOSURE TO CLIMATE-RELATED RISK IN THE 2025 BUDGET

Theme	Agency	Objective	Amount (in $ millions)
Reducing risk exposure	USDA FS and DOI	Invest in wildland fire management workforce by supporting permanent, comprehensive pay reform and expanding workforce capacity, health services, and Government housing.	$522
	USDA FS and DOI	Establish a new Joint Office for Wildlife Science & Technology and continue investing in the Joint Fire Sciences Program.	$13
	DOE	Invest in the Federal Energy Management Program to provide technical and financial assistance to Federal Agencies to advance Federal facility resilience.	$64
	EPA	Support Tribes in performing direct implementation of EPA prorams and authorities in Indian Country, with a focus on reducing vulnerability to climate change impacts.	$13
	EPA	Provide grants to municipalities or intermunicipal, interstate, or State agencies for planning, designing, or constructing projects that increase the resilience of publicly owned treatment works to natural hazards through the Clean Water Infrastructure Resiliency and Sustainability Program.	$25
	EPA	Assist public water systems serving small and underserved communities in the planning, design, construction, implementation, operation, or maintenance of a drinking water program or project that increases resilience to natural hazards, including climate change, through the Drinking Water Infrastructure Resilience and Sustainability Program.	$65
	U.S. Bureau of Reclamation	Support for the U.S. Bureau of Reclamation (USBR) for the WaterSMART program, through which Reclamation funds projects to conserve and use water more efficiently and build long-term resilience to drought.	$ 65
	USBR	Provide emergency drought relief for federally recognized Indian Tribes for near-term drought relief to mitigate drought impacts for Tribes impacted by the operation of a Reclamation water projects.	$ 9
	DOE	Invest in scientific developments and public-private partnerships to support the development and use of AI technologies to advance climate modeling, increase the nation's resilience to climate impacts and address climate risks.	$ 10
Develop technical capacity within the Federal Government to model and assess physical asset risk and connect those models to understand potential impacts of Federal program expenditures	U.S. Geological Survey (USGS)	Work with FEMA to study and develop methods that project future disaster-related outlays due to coastal hazards and hurricane events.	$ 2
	U.S. Department of Transportation	Conduct a study to develop methods and tools to improve the ability of transportation infrastructure asset owners to assess the climate change vulnerability of their assets and projects, identify evidence-based approaches to resilience improvements, and estimate financial risks associated with the impact of climate change.	$ 4
Investments to accompany the release of National Climate Resilience Framework, including discretionary resources to advance the development and public use of Federal climate services	FEMA	Investments in the Building Resilient Infrastructure and Communities grant program paid for out of the Disaster Relief Fund.	$ 1,000
	FEMA	Support for the flood hazard mapping program.	$ 517
	NOAA	Support for advances in the Climate Mapping for Resilience and Adaptation (CMRA) portal assessment tool ($2 million) and accelerate the development of the Climate Resilience Information System (CRIS) ($5 million).	$ 7
	USDA	Continued support of the USDA Climate Hubs.	$ 22
	USGS	Invest in the National and Regional Climate Adaptation Science Centers.	$ 69
	DOE	Create a multi-office extreme heat community initiative that will design and scale.	$ 105
	Corporation for National and Community Service	Invest in the American Climate Corps (ACC) by providing funding to support an ACC hub at AmeriCorps and grow the number of ACC volunteers.	$ 38
	EPA	Support of the Climate Adaptation Program, which funds targeted assistance to States, Tribes and Indigenous peoples, territories, local governments, communities, and businesses to bolster climate resilience efforts.	$ 20
	U.S. Department of Health and Human Services	Fund the Office of Climate Change and Health Equity, which aims to protect the health of people throughout the US in the face of climate change, especially those experiencing a higher share of exposures and impacts.	$ 5

highlight the range of investments the Administration continues to make that reduce the Nation's exposure and risk to climate change impacts.

Investments in the 2025 Budget build on a historic level of over $50 billion in funding from both the Infrastructure Investment and Jobs Act (Public Law 117-58) and the Inflation Reduction Act of 2022 (Public Law 117-169) that is directly increasing the Nation's resilience to climate change impacts, and reducing the fiscal risk of the Federal Government to these impacts in the future. Notable examples of these investments are highlighted in Table 11-5.

Table 11–5. NOTABLE INVESTMENTS IN REDUCING FISCAL EXPOSURE TO CLIMATE-RELATED RISK IN THE INFRASTRUCTURE INVESTMENT AND JOBS ACT AND THE INFLATION REDUCTION ACT

	Agency	Objective	Amount (in $ millions)
Investments in funding from IIJA and IRA	EPA	Fund EPA's Environmental and Climate Justice Community Change Grants program to support community-driven projects that deploy clean energy, strengthen climate resilience, and build community capacity to respond to environmental and climate justice challenges.	$ 2,000
	NOAA	Increase coastal resilience, building natural infrastructure, and protecting coastal natural resources.	$ 2,600
	USDA FS and DOI	Invest in wildland fire and hazardous fuels management programs to expand efforts to reduce wildfire risk, prepare for and respond to catastrophic wildfires, and support post-fire recovery.	$ 6,900
	DOE	Support DOE's efforts to strengthen and modernize the electric grid, increasing reliability of service and reducing impacts of extreme weather events.	$ 3,900

V. CONCLUSION

This chapter of the 2025 Budget presents assessments and program highlights of climate financial risk exposure and an expanded view of both future risks due to climate change impacts and actions that the Government is taking now to reduce these risks. These efforts, called for in Executive Order 14030, are directly responding to the latest scientific conclusions that sectors across the economy, including public-sector budgets, need to adapt to a changing climate in order to be sustainable. New analytical capabilities presented here build on the physical asset risk and Federal expenditure analytical approaches presented in the 2024 Budget, and continue to address the need for additional technical capabilities. Lastly, the Budget proposals highlighted in this chapter directly respond to this year or prior years' climate risk exposure assessments, and aim to advance the Administration's goal to enhance the Nation's climate resilience.

MANAGEMENT PRIORITIES

12. DELIVERING A HIGH-PERFORMANCE GOVERNMENT

Introduction

The American people deserve a high-performing, effective Government—one that sets and meets ambitious goals for protecting individuals and communities, modernizes infrastructure and services, invests in children, and takes care of the most vulnerable. And like all high-performing organizations, the Federal Government has developed a set of management routines that drive a results-oriented culture and help organizations deliver prioritized, transparent outcomes. Grounded in proven, evidence-based management practices of high-performing public and private sector organizations, the Federal Government's approach to delivering a more effective and efficient Government is operationalized through the ***Federal Performance Framework*** (*"the Framework"*)[1]—a system of management routines that are focused on defining mission success, engaging senior leaders to review progress using the best available data and evidence, and reporting results transparently to the public.

Since taking office, the Administration has been committed to using the Framework—originally authorized by Congress in 1993 with the Government Performance and Results Act of 1993 (GPRA; Public Law 103-62), and updated in 2010 with the GPRA Modernization Act of 2010 (GPRAMA; Public Law 111-352)—to improve the lives of the American people, including disadvantaged communities that have been historically underserved, marginalized, and adversely affected by persistent poverty and structural inequality. Federal agencies are continuing to apply and mature these performance management practices and routines, shifting the Government's focus from programs to people; from the means of Government to its ends; and from rules to values. Moreover, this systems-focused approach allows the Federal Government to align its budget and resources to its performance framework, operating concurrently and in coordination with one another to help ensure that agencies' organizational goals and objectives are resourced efficiently, effectively, and with accountability.

This Chapter offers an annual review of the Framework's approach to organizational health and organizational performance management, and its application to date by the Administration to improve outcomes and deliver a high-performance Government. Actions by the Administration and investments supported by the President's 2025 Budget to advance the Framework are detailed, including a section summarizing insights and themes from the work by Federal agencies to implement frameworks and routines for measuring, monitoring, and assessing organizational health and organizational performance in the context of evolving Agency work environments.[2]

[1] *OMB Circular A-11, Part 6 – The Federal Performance Framework for Improving Program and Service Delivery.*

[2] *OMB Memorandum M-23-15, Measuring, Monitoring, and Improving Organizational Health and Organizational Performance in the Context of Evolving Agency Work Environments.*

THE FEDERAL PERFORMANCE FRAMEWORK: HARDWIRING A FOCUS ON RESULTS AND IMPLEMENTATION

Overview of the Framework

At its core, the Framework and its associated practices and routines provide a set of tools that enable organizations to ensure the means of government are effectively and efficiently applied to deliver results for the people of the United States—the ends of Government. Originally seeking to apply leading organizational management practices from the private sector to Government, the Framework's foundations are grounded in the GPRAMA, updating and modernizing the original 1993 GPRA while incorporating lessons learned from public and private sector management practices after over three decades of implementation.

The GPRAMA reinforced core organizational performance and management routines and practices for Federal agencies by creating an updated statutory framework with a renewed focus on organizational strategic planning, priority goal setting that engages leadership, and enhanced public reporting of progress and results achieved on a central website (*Performance.gov*). It shifted focus from a "supply-side" approach of producing information towards a "demand-driven" model that centered on supporting leadership in identifying and accomplishing their top priorities within the framework; created and clarified roles and responsibilities including that of Agency Chief Operating Officer (COO), Performance Improvement Officer (PIO), and Goal Leader; aligned strategic planning with presidential election cycles; emphasized the use of performance information and evidence for decision-making by agency leadership while seeking to minimize reporting and compliance burdens; and established a formal body chaired by the Office of Management and Budget (OMB) and comprised of the PIOs from major Federal agencies to support cross-agency collaboration and best practice sharing.

Chart 12-1. Policy Framework: Federal Performance Management Cycle

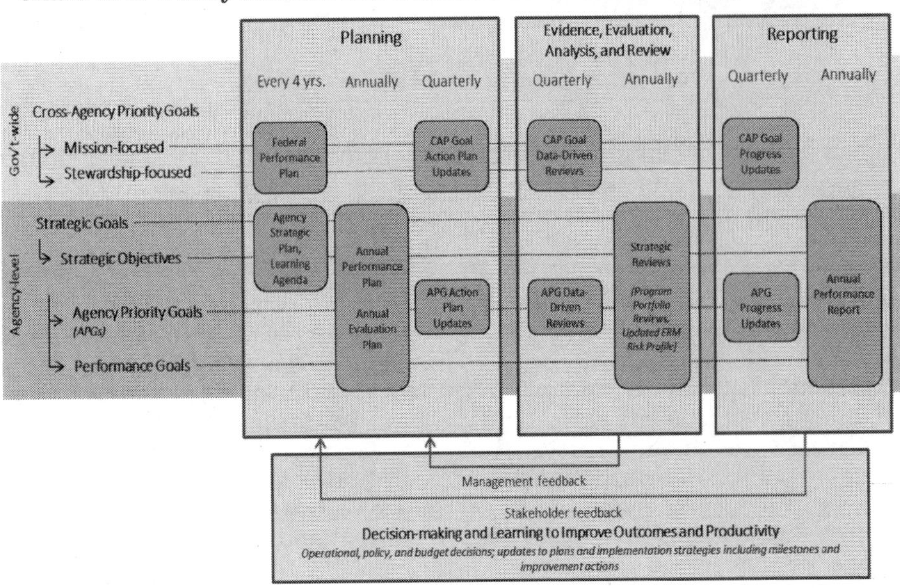

Key Principles and Practices

The Federal Performance Framework provides the foundation of organizational routines for the coordination and integration of various analytical management skillsets and decision-support capabilities to work in concert to improve agency performance and program service delivery. This approach rests on the following proven practices and principles:

- engaging leaders;
- defining mission success through strategic planning and priority goal setting;
- routines of regular, recurring data-driven performance reviews that incorporate a broad range of qualitative and quantitative inputs and evidence;
- expanding impact through strategic planning and strategic reviews;
- strengthening agency management capabilities, capacity, collaboration and integration; and
- communicating performance results and information effectively.

Federal Performance Management Cycle

The Framework's major provisions create a cycle of performance management routines that govern organizational planning and goal setting, data-driven reviews of progress against those goals, and reporting for agencies to use to drive organizational performance and management improvements. See Chart 12-1. Importantly, its construction across four-year, annual, and quarterly cycles provides a key mechanism for maximizing the organizational learning that stems from the management routines of data-driven reviews. Agencies translate the longer-term strategic goals and objectives in their Strategic Plans to programmatic performance goals, including Agency Priority Goals (APGs), in the Agency Performance Plan (APP). The APP communicates the agency's strategic objectives and performance goals with other elements of the agency's budget request, detailing how goals will be achieved, identifying priorities among the goals, and describing mechanisms to monitor progress, which is subsequently reported annually in the Agency Performance Report (APR) for the most recently completed fiscal year performance period. With a two-year coverage period that is reviewed and updated annually by the agency, the APP complements the longer-term planning in the Agency Strategic Plan with shorter and intermediate-term operational planning horizons for the organization. This gives agencies the opportunity to revise implementation strategies and programmatic operations in order to address and overcome identified barriers or challenges to deliver on their missions.

Since GPRAMA's enactment in 2010, the Framework has continued to evolve to accommodate the coordination and integration of additional Government-wide, management-focused legislation and initiatives that have been introduced to improve overall organizational performance by applying increasingly specialized decision-support functions and skillsets. Such flexibility embedded into the Framework's design enables the mutability needed to support shifts in both approach and emphasis in order to meet the organizational and management needs of changing internal or external environments and priorities of leadership. Notably, in 2023 concepts of organizational health were introduced to be considered in concert with the organizational performance of Federal agencies as articulated in OMB Memorandum M-23-15. The integration of organizational health strengthened the Framework by establishing a set of metrics and routines that acknowledges the interconnectedness of, and relationships across, the organizational dimensions of health, performance, and work environments while helping facilitate management actions and responses that can position Federal agencies to build the resilience, capacity, and capabilities they need to meet the demands of dynamic operating environments.[3]

[3] See the "Delivering a High-Performance Government" chapter of the 2024 *Analytical Perspectives* volume of the President's Budget for a more detailed discussion on the Framework's evolution to date, evidence in support of the Framework's organizational practices, as well as inherent challenges associated with the Framework—some of which are common to implementing any system for organizational performance management across complex organizations.

DEFINING SUCCESS THROUGH ROUTINES OF ORGANIZATIONAL GOAL SETTING AND DATA-DRIVEN PERFORMANCE REVIEWS TO DRIVE RESULTS IN EXECUTION

Routines of Strategic Planning and Priority Goal Setting

Strategic planning and Priority Goal setting are common tools that were designed to set and communicate the direction of an organization. The Agency Strategic Plan defines the agency mission, long-term strategic goals and objectives, strategies planned to achieve those goals and objectives, and the approaches it will use to monitor its progress in addressing specific national problems, needs, challenges, and opportunities related to its mission. At the beginning of each new Presidential term, and concurrent with the preparation of the President's Budget, each Federal agency produces a revised four-year Strategic Plan which sets out the long-term objectives the agency hopes to accomplish. By defining from the start of a new administration what strategic priorities and objectives the agency aims to achieve, what actions the Agency will take to realize those priorities, and how the Agency will deal with challenges and risks that may hinder progress, each new administration can benefit from the deliberateness of sound planning, resourcing and stakeholder communication that will be needed to drive effectiveness in the multi-year execution efforts to follow.

Agency Priority Goals (APGs) complement agencies' strategic planning activities. They reflect Administration-aligned agency commitments in near-term, performance improvement outcomes while advancing progress towards longer-term, outcome-focused strategic goals and objectives within each agency's four-year Strategic Plan. Agency heads establish these implementation-focused priority goals every two years and use clearly identified Goal Leaders, Deputy Goal Leaders, and quarterly metrics and milestones to manage progress. Agency Deputy Secretaries (or equivalent), in their role as COO, lead quarterly data-driven performance reviews to overcome barriers and accelerate performance results.

Routines of Data-Driven Performance Reviews

Conducting routine, data-driven performance reviews led by agency leaders on a set of the agency's performance improvement priorities is a management practice proven to produce better results. Incorporating a range of quantitative and qualitative evidence with regular reviews provides a mechanism for agency leaders to review the organization's performance and bring together the people, resources, and analysis needed to drive progress on agency priorities of both mission-focused and management goals. Frequent, data-driven performance reviews reinforce the agency's priorities and establish an agency culture of continuous learning and improvement, sending a signal throughout the organization that agency leaders are focused on effective and efficient implementation to improve the delivery of results. Planning activities related to Agency Learning Agendas, Annual Evaluation Plans, and Capacity Assessments required by the Foundations for Evidence-Based Policymaking Act of 2018 (Evidence Act; Public Law 115-435) reinforce this same culture of learning and improvement that is cultivated by the data-driven performance review.

It is the Framework's application of data-driven performance review routines, and the use of performance information and evidence, that underscores the Federal Government's fundamental approach to monitoring, assessing, and driving improvements to agency organizational health and organizational performance. At the Departmental-level, the two primary routines of frequent, data-driven performance reviews at the core of the Framework are:

- the quarterly, data-driven performance review of APGs and other organizational priorities to drive progress toward achieving agency goals; and
- the annual, data-driven strategic review of agency strategic objectives to inform decision-making, budget formulation, and near-term agency actions, as well as preparation of the annual APP and APR.

The following sub-sections detail efforts over the past year on the part of Federal agencies in applying these key organizational routines and practices to drive performance and management improvements towards tangible outcomes for the American public.

APGs: Retrospective on the 2022-2023 Cycle

Over the past two years, Federal agencies used the routines of their quarterly, data-driven performance reviews to achieve a broad array of performance improvements and outcomes across a portfolio of 90 APGs that spanned over 200 key indicators and milestones covering the fiscal years 2022-2023 APG cycle. First announced in March

2022, concurrent with the President's 2023 Budget, agencies' priority goal setting efforts reflected alignment of both strategic objectives and the Administration's policy priorities. These priorities included, in particular, continued agency work to meet the health, welfare, and economic challenges of the COVID-19 pandemic, advance equity, and address climate change. Joint APGs were also encouraged in areas where programs from multiple agencies must work together to achieve a common outcome. Setting joint priority goals served as a policy response designed to address the simple fact that many of the most pressing challenges facing Government do not fit neatly within the boundaries of a single agency, bureau, division, or office. Using the routines and structure of the Framework provided agencies with a management and governance mechanism for facilitating the collaboration and coordination required to drive successful implementation.

With the performance period for the 2022-2023 APGs ending on September 30, 2023, over 80 percent of the 2022-2023 APG goal teams either achieved their stated performance objectives or realized performance improvements above prior year baseline levels, as they advanced near-term outcomes across key Administration priorities. Below is a sampling of more specific performance improvements and accomplishments achieved by APG goal teams during the ***2022-2023 APG cycle.***

- To *complete the critical building blocks needed for the deployment of a national network of electric vehicle (EV) chargers under the IIJA*, the Departments of Energy (DOE) and Transportation (DOT) joint APG goal team oversaw and assisted with the development and review of EV Infrastructure Deployment Plans from all 50 States, Puerto Rico, and the District of Columbia. Based on the review and recommendations of the Joint Office of Energy and Transportation, the Federal Highway Administration approved all plans in September 2022, which collectively unlocked $1.5 billion in funding to begin building out convenient, reliable, affordable, and equitable EV charging corridors along over 75,000 miles of the highway system. Moreover, the joint APG goal team exceeded its performance goal target of increasing the number of public EV charging ports to 160,000 by the end of calendar year 2023.
- To *ensure all Americans have access to high-speed, affordable, and reliable broadband*, with a focus on communities in the greatest need, the Departments of Agriculture (USDA) and Commerce (DOC) partnered together on a joint goal to fund projects that when implemented, will provide broadband to at least 550,000 additional households. Achieving over 98 percent of the goal's 550,000 households mark, the team's efforts made significant progress towards the joint goal, an ambitious target established at the start of the performance period. With these efforts, more American households have access to high-speed internet enabling them to do their jobs, participate equally in school learning, access health care, and stay connected.
- To make progress in *phasing down the production and consumption of hydrofluorocarbons (HFCs)*—potent greenhouse gases many of which have global warming potentials hundreds to thousands of times that of carbon dioxide—the Environmental Protection Agency (EPA) reached their performance goal of reducing the annual consumption of HFCs by 10 percent below baseline levels of 303.9 million metric tons of carbon dioxide equivalent (MMTCO2e). At the end of the goal period, the EPA estimated it will have achieved an HFCs consumption level of 253.4 MMTCO2e within the United States.
- To *strengthen Federal cybersecurity*, the Cybersecurity and Infrastructure Security Agency (CISA) at the Department of Homeland Security's (DHS) worked with Federal agencies to bring 84 percent of Federal agencies under *Binding Operational Directive 22-01's* (Reducing the Significant Risk of Known Exploited Vulnerabilities) requirements for using automated reporting of Continuous Diagnostics and Mitigation data—exceeding the agency's targeted level of performance by 34 percent. Defined in 44 U.S.C. 3552, binding operational directives are compulsory directions to Federal agencies and Executive Branch departments for purposes of safeguarding Federal information and information systems. Binding Operation Directive 22-01 established a CISA-managed catalog of known exploited vulnerabilities that carry significant risk to the Federal enterprise, and put in place requirements for agencies to remediate any such vulnerabilities included in the catalog. Such centralized reporting provides CISA with increased visibility at the Federal Enterprise Level, identifying cross-agency threats and vulnerabilities in order to take action to safeguard systems.
- To enable the *study of every phase in the history of our universe*, ranging from the first luminous glows after the Big Bang, to the formation of other stellar systems capable of supporting life on planets like Earth, to the evolution of our own solar system, the National Aeronautics and Space Administration (NASA) successfully commissioned the James Webb Space Telescope, the most powerful and complex space telescope ever built, and began Webb's second year of science observations.
- To support the *critical and urgent recruitment and hiring needs across Government* to effectively implement the Infrastructure Investment and Jobs Act (IIJA; Public Law 117-58), the Office of Personnel Management (OPM) exceeded its goal of helping agencies fill over 75 percent of IIJA-surge hiring positions, surpassing its IIJA-related hiring goals of 5,800 positions. These efforts supported hiring in mission-critical areas that ranged from engineers and scientists, to information technology and human

resources specialists, construction management, and project management.

- To *reduce disparities in attainment of high-quality degrees and credentials*, the Department of Education (ED) saw notable performance improvement towards an ambitious goal of increasing the number and diversity of higher education grant applicants from community colleges, Historically Black Colleges and Universities, Tribally Controlled Colleges and Universities, and Minority Serving Institutions. While the goal team fell just short of their aspirational goal of a five percent increase, this measure continues as a key performance indicator in the Department's Strategic Plan to drive ongoing management actions, assessments, and monitoring.

APGs: Prospective on the 2024-2025 Cycle

Federal agencies continue to build upon the successes and performance outcomes achieved over previous two-year cycles while charting new and even more ambitious priority performance goals. On the heels of the 2022-2023 APG cycle, agencies in December 2023 established 79 new, two-year performance commitments to be achieved during the fiscal year 2024-2025 cycle that started on October 1, 2023. Several cross-cutting themes are reflected in the 2024-2025 portfolio, representative of both the role and purpose of priority goal setting routines within the Framework.

- ***Continuation of goal areas with more ambitious performance improvement gains.*** Over two thirds of APGs continue implementation of priorities from the 2022-2023 cycle where the goal remains a priority policy area to the agency head, agency leadership, and the Administration. For example, the Department of Labor continues its efforts focused on *Strengthening America's Safety Net for Workers*, to increase intrastate first payments of unemployment benefits made within 21 days by at least 10 percent (relative to the 2023 level), towards the regulatory target of 87 percent. The National Science Foundation (NSF) is continuing to *Improve Representation in the Scientific Enterprise* by making changes that will lead to an increase in proposal submissions led by individuals from underrepresented groups and from underserved communities at emerging research institutions. And the Department of the Interior (DOI) is continuing its work to *Improve Tribal Land into Trust Processing*, seeking to reduce the average time of processing land into trust applications from 779 days to 650 days by September 30, 2025. Efforts by the agency and goal team build on progress made in recent years to support both the principles and the guidelines established in the Indian Reorganization Act, and reaffirmed in the Indian Self-Determination and Education Assistance Act.

- ***Deliver on Recent Legislative Accomplishments.*** Agencies aligned their 2024-2025 APG setting efforts to complement and support the implementation of major legislative accomplishments of the Administration—from delivering tangible, programmatic impacts in areas supported by the IIJA and Public Law 117-167, commonly referred to as the CHIPS and Science Act of 2022 (CHIPS Act), to Public Law 117-169, commonly referred to as the Inflation Reduction Act of 2022 (IRA). For example, USDA and DOC are continuing their collaboration on their joint goal to expand access to high-speed broadband for more Americans, setting an ever-more ambitious goal to fund projects that, when completed, will provide more than six million households and other locations with *reliable and affordable access to high-quality internet service* by September 30, 2025 – a major initiative of the IIJA. The DOC has also set a goal to advance U.S. national security and economic competitiveness by *building domestic semiconductor manufacturing capacity* through investing in the development of a range of semiconductor facilities and upstream suppliers, implementing parts of the CHIPS Act.

- ***Align with Administration Priority Policy Areas.*** APGs are supporting implementation of IIJA, CHIPS Act, and IRA programs while also advancing or aligning to other priority policy areas of the Administration. New APGs from the Departments of Veterans Affairs (VA) and Housing and Urban Development (HUD) will advance complementary efforts to tackle aspects of homelessness in America. By September 30, 2025, HUD seeks to *make homelessness rare, brief, and non-recurring* by reducing the number of people experiencing unsheltered homelessness by seven percent, as measured in the January 2025 Point-in-Time count, while actions by the VA *aim to place at least 76,000 unique Veterans into permanent housing and ensure that at least 90 percent of at-risk Veterans are prevented from becoming homeless*. The Department of Health and Human Services (HHS) commits to improve health outcomes for those affected by behavioral health conditions through increasing access to and utilization of critical prevention, crisis intervention, treatment, and recovery services. By September 30, 2025, HHS will *reduce emergency department visits for acute alcohol use, mental health conditions, suicide attempts, and drug overdose by 10 percent*, compared to the 2023 levels.

- ***Tool for Advancing "Joint Agency" Implementation Efforts.*** Agencies again established APGs in areas where inter-agency coordination and collaboration is needed to achieve the end result, leveraging the benefits of shared strategy development and implementation in order to strengthen their ability to deliver on desired outcomes. For example, DOE and DOT are again partnering on their joint APG *to deploy electric vehicle (EV) charging infrastructure under the IIJA towards a national network of at least 500,000 EV-chargers by 2030 so that everyone can ride and drive electric*. And continuing a trend that dates back several APG cycles, the Department of State (State) and the U.S. Agency for International Development (USAID) have designated several joint APGs, including efforts to *achieve and sustain control of the HIV epidemic and end HIV/AIDS as a public health threat*, and *combat global climate change by advancing climate resilient, net-zero emissions development globally*.

- ***Advance President Management Agenda (PMA) Priorities.*** APGs are being used to accelerate progress on delivering tangible impacts that advance commitments in support of the PMA. For example, aligned to PMA Priority Area 1, *Strengthening and Empowering the Federal Workforce*, the Department of Defense (DOD) is using the APG structure to organize its efforts to *improve recruitment and retention of its civilian workforce and shape an appropriately skilled and ready workforce* for the future, in addition to other contributions. And aligned to PMA Priority Area 2, *Delivering Excellent, Equitable, and Secure Federal Services and Customer Experience*, HHS has developed a Department-wide APG wherein *every operating division within HHS will pursue substantial projects to improve services to the American people*, from streamlining grant applications and overhauling public communications tools to building foundational capacity through training, customer identification, journey mapping, and sharing leading practices on the use of performance data and evidence to make decisions. DHS has also established an APG to *advance customer experience efforts within the Transportation Security Administration*, one of the Department's designated High-Impact Service Providers.

Common across these themes and the portfolio of priority goal setting efforts is a continued, concerted emphasis on evidence to develop sound theories of change for what success looks like, along with valid performance measures and milestones that comprise the more detailed implementation action plans and strategies to achieve those goals. From using evidence that supports scaling-up an intervention, a suite of interventions that are likely to advance outcomes, or where the use of selected measures is grounded in an evidence-based theory of change, the Administration is pushing agencies and goal teams to use a portfolio of evidence and tools in their implementation action plans to help them accomplish their goals. As the performance period of the 2024-2025 APG cycle advances, progress towards these goals is available on Performance.gov—with data and progress reported publicly each quarter.

2023 Strategic Reviews: Policy and Focus

Agencies' annual, internal strategic reviews provide a critical organizational learning opportunity for agency management on the implementation of programs supporting strategic objectives. Following agencies' internal assessments, OMB convenes Strategic Review Meetings that provide a forum for agency leadership and OMB to discuss, using evidence, progress in the implementation of Agency Strategic Plans while aligning these management discussions to a timeline that informs the President's Budget development, and future strategic planning, evidence-building, and management efforts by agencies.

Building on the 2022 Strategic Reviews—which represented the first year of reviews since the establishment of the new strategic goal and objective frameworks, learning agendas, and performance and evaluation plans in March 2022—the 2023 Strategic Review sessions and the processes that drive them continued as key tools to implement Administration priorities and jointly align resources, management activities, and evidence to deliver results for the Nation. Throughout the past summer, OMB met with the leadership of the larger Federal agencies to explore a range of operational, programmatic, and management questions, all with the shared, fundamental charge of delivering on the Government's commitments with accountability to the American people.

- How can the Federal Government better help people calling into the 988 Suicide & Crisis Lifeline connect with trained counselors who can offer immediate assistance?
- How might the Government help address the challenge of teacher shortages across the Nation?
- How can the ManufacturingUSA network increase the competitiveness of U.S. manufacturing via new authorities from the CHIPS Act?

These types of issues were at the forefront of the 2023 Strategic Review meetings to assess progress against agency strategic goals and objectives—the Federal Government's "Bottom Line." Like meetings past, the 2023 meetings were designed to bring together senior leadership from OMB, policy councils, and agencies to review progress towards achieving over 400 strategic goals and objectives, including assessments of the impacts from enterprise risk management reviews, and findings and contributions from agency learning agendas. These reviews played a key role in identifying the subset of strategic objectives that would be designated by agencies as either an area of Noteworthy Progress or a Focus Area for Improvement in their Agency Performance Report.[4]

In addition to reviewing progress against strategic objectives, agendas for the 2023 Strategic Review meetings included a limited number of "Deep Dive" topics while implementation of OMB Memorandum M-23-15 also factored prominently, and is discussed more in-depth in the following section. Deep Dive topics focused on one to two substantive policy, management, or evidence-building areas in which collaboration and coordination between OMB and the agency were critical to make meaningful gains. Such cross-agency Deep Dives brought key agency leaders to the meeting table to synthesize the performance data and evidence needed to inform what concrete actions and interventions are necessary to deliver on the outcomes committed to by agency leadership. Moreover,

[4] For additional information on OMB's policies governing strategic reviews and the categorization of strategic objectives, see Circular A-11, Part 6, Section 260.

Deep Dive topics not only allowed for more substantive engagement by management officials on big picture outcomes —like more robust behavioral health care access and the barriers that inhibit such access—but the continuity of OMB's engagement across agencies facilitated the surfacing of common themes which demand shared policy solutions across the Federal enterprise.

For example, the 2023 Strategic Reviews connected OMB, OPM, and agency leaders identifying action items on a wide range of human capital issues: from law enforcement hiring at DHS, to talent management within the DOD, and succession planning at the DOE's National Nuclear Security Agency. These routines served to not only sharpen and expedite our delivery of outcomes for Americans, but also helped us maintain a ready and capable Federal enterprise.

Spotlight on the 2023 Strategic Review Meetings: Extending Participation in Data-Driven Reviews to Representatives External to the Organization

Interagency collaboration can be strengthened when an agency expands, where relevant, participation in their data-driven review to representatives that are external to the organization based on shared contributions towards achieving the agency's goals and objectives.

Where a 2023 Strategic Review Deep Dive topic had a nexus to workforce and human capital, the meetings included senior leadership from OPM. This marked a first where representatives from an organization external to the agency and the Executive Office of the President (EOP) participated in the Strategic Review Meetings—a leading practice for using the data-driven review to strengthen interagency collaboration where contributions towards goals and outcomes are shared by more than one agency. This approach to advancing interagency collaboration complements similar efforts that have been applied within the Federal Performance Framework to date, from Cross-Agency Priority (CAP) Goals to joint Priority Goal setting in previous two-year APG cycles.

Based on the experiences of this summer's 2023 Strategic Review meetings, along with other data-driven reviews, the following is a list of criteria and practices developed to help agencies consider when to extend participation in their data-driven review meetings, to include relevant representatives external to the organization.

- **Clear Value-Proposition.** Certain programmatic policy areas or priorities may be strengthened through shared strategy development, implementation, or problem-solving that require collaboration and coordination across multiple agencies to achieve a common outcome. Agencies should consider extending participation in their data-driven reviews in such instances where a strong, clear value-proposition exists.

- **Policy and Management Alignment.** Agencies should consider extending participation in their data-driven reviews to achieve policy and management alignment, leveraging complementary or shared authorities, roles, expertise, and resources from the relevant external organization. Expanding participation allows the agency to better apply the expertise of the relevant external organization to the specific context or circumstances that may be impeding achievement of an agency goal or accelerate progress.

- **Roles and Responsibilities.** When external representatives will participate in the data-driven review, staff responsible for organizing the review should ensure that participants' roles and responsibilities are identified and agreed to in advance of the meeting's discussion.

- **Accessing Common or Shared Data.** Access to relevant agency data on the goals, areas, or topics to be discussed in the data-driven review meeting is critical to ensuring all participants can effectively contribute to the meeting discussion. When external representatives will participate in the data-driven review, providing access to common or shared IT infrastructure and data collection systems in advance of the meeting will help ensure representatives external to the organization are appropriately staffed, informed, and prepared to substantively engage during the data-driven review.

- **Pre-Meeting Management and Staffing: Preparation, Planning, and Communication.** Introducing the participation of representatives external to the organization increase the coordination and touch-points needed for a successful data-driven review. Staff planning, preparation, and communication leading up to the data-driven amongst identified points of contacts from participating organizations is critical to help ensure an effective meeting discussion. For example, clear communications that include staff from all organizations will ensure common understanding on relevant details of the meeting (i.e., meeting purpose, intent, desired outcomes, time, location, and attendees). Preparing and sharing read-ahead materials and analysis will also help meeting principals and senior leaders involved understand the complexity of the topics and issue(s) at hand, facilitating their substantive engagement during the meeting to enable joint problem solving.

- **Actioning Post-Meeting Follow-ups.** Assign a meeting participant(s) to take notes during the data-driven review meeting, documenting any agreed-upon action items that are identified during the review to guide post-meeting follow-on efforts. Dissemination of follow-on actions to meeting participants offers a guide for structuring the coordination and collaboration needed across organizations to drive progress on performance improvement, and overcome performance or other management barriers moving forward.

All effective organizations require a set of management routines to assess their performance and remain accountable to meeting the outcomes and deliverables promised to their stakeholders. The Framework's Strategic Review process applies a leading organizational management practice of high-performing private and public sector organizations to do just that, but with a "Bottom Line" that ranges from being able to support veteran mental health, to expanding broadband access for every American. Over the course of the past year, agencies applied routines of data-driven performance reviews to make measurable progress, and report on, their strategic goals and objectives. They also provided the Administration with a key management mechanism for reviewing the organizational health and organizational performance frameworks and approaches that enable agencies' continued ability to deliver on their statutory missions, to which the discussion in this chapter now turns.

IMPLEMENTING FRAMEWORKS AND ROUTINES FOR MEASURING, MONITORING, AND ASSESSING ORGANIZATIONAL HEALTH AND ORGANIZATIONAL PERFORMANCE

Establishing a Consistent Approach and Vocabulary

OMB Memorandum M-23-15, outlined new guidance to help ensure that agency decisions regarding their work environments are aimed to continually improve their organization's health and organizational performance. It established a common and consistent approach for heads of Federal Departments and agencies to regularly take stock of the organizational health and organizational performance of operating units (with particular focus at the component-level), and use those insights to make decisions on agency work environments. The policies and guidance outlined in OMB Memorandum M-23-15 reinforced that organizational health and organizational performance should be the foundation for an agency's operational decisions—ensuring managers and leaders alike give close attention to strong, sustainable organizational health and culture over time, while also applying lessons learned and evidence to sustain high-performing, innovative organizations. To that end, OMB Memorandum M-23-15 directed agencies to:

- make updates to Work Environment plans based on previously-submitted agency reentry plans to reflect their post-pandemic posture;
- establish organizational routines at the major operating unit level of agencies to assess and implement these workplace policy changes on an ongoing basis; and
- identify a more coordinated and integrated set of indicators to measure, monitor, and improve organizational health and organizational performance, and that could serve as the evidence-base for decisions.

OMB Memorandum M-23-15 also advanced a common vernacular—defining and articulating concepts of organizational health, organizational performance, work environment, and their corresponding frameworks which sit at the intersection of this integrated approach to enable the identification and assessment of relationships across these organizational dimensions of Federal agencies to inform decision-making. Its guidance was incorporated into the Framework as part of this past summer's 2023 revision and update to Part 6 of OMB Circular A-11. By strengthening the institutionalization of these policies and approach into agencies core management frameworks, practices and operations, the Administration continues to make strides that better position Federal agencies to be resilient for the future to deliver Federal services and programs for the people and communities we serve.

The remainder of this section provides an overview of the actions and efforts taken by the Administration since the release of OMB Memorandum M-23-15 to advance implementation of its policies, with particular focus on frameworks and routines for monitoring and assessing organizational health and organizational performance. See the "Strengthening the Federal Workforce" chapter of this volume for more information and further discussion on agency work environments, including lessons learned from national workplace trends and the public health emergency.

Identifying Organizational Health 'Frontiers' with Organizational Health Scans

In OMB Memorandum M-23-15, OMB committed to provide major Federal agencies with analysis assessing intra- and inter-agency trends of select organizational-level indicators and indices of engagement, performance confidence, and other measures related to organizational health within 60 days following issuance of the Memorandum. A joint agency collaboration between OMB, OPM, and GSA, these Organizational Health Scans—a first-of-its-kind product—provided each agency's senior leadership team and the implementation leads of agency-identified major operating units with insights on current indices and indicators related to their organizational health and performance, offering a roadmap for additional inquiry and assessment to direct future action and planning.

The analysis presented to agencies in these Organizational Health Scans included several elements. First, the scans illustrated and assessed trends of select organizational-level indices of engagement, performance confidence, and other areas related to organizational health using data from the Federal Employee Viewpoint Survey (FEVS). Recognizing the implicit power that the standardized indicators in the FEVS have to provide natural comparison values, the scans were designed to show the "relativeness" in these indices and indicators across a Department's major organizational division and work units. In short, they provided a reference point or anchor to facilitate judgements through comparisons on what could otherwise be viewed as abstract, absolute numbers. Borrowing from principles underlying data

Chart 12-2. Example Organizational Health Dashboard Being Used at USAID

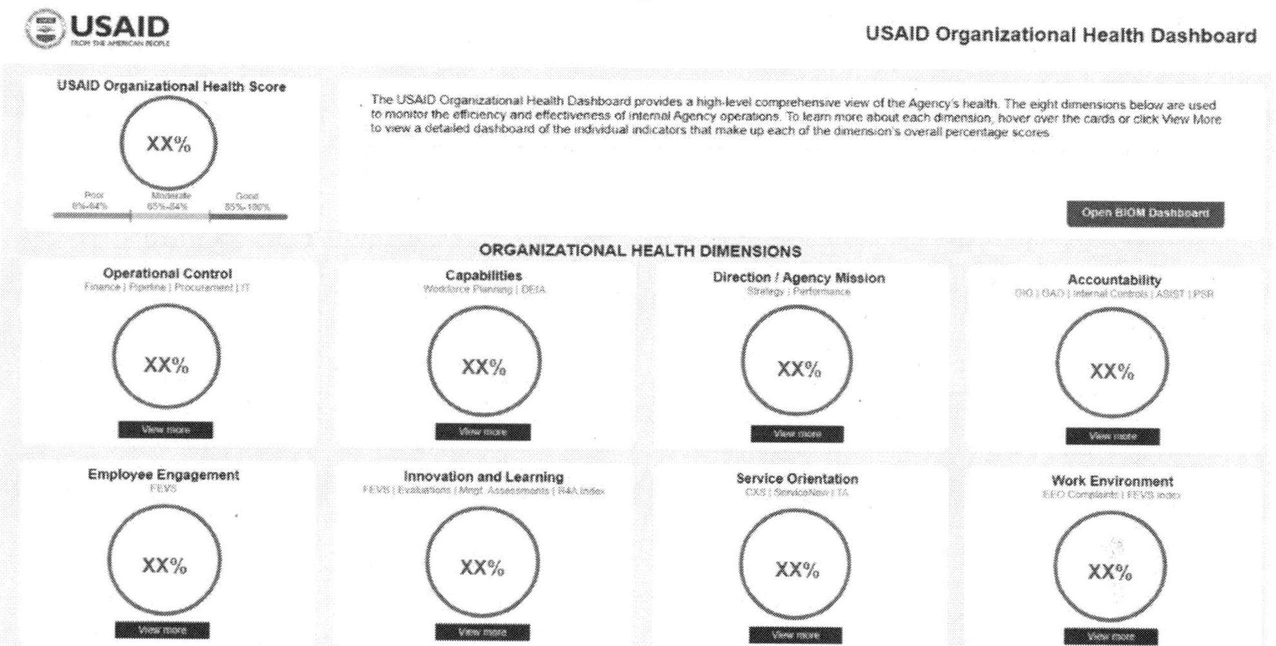

envelopment analysis techniques, scans presented each agency's organizational work units with scores in the top 10 and bottom 10 of organizational units, and at different levels of an agency's organizational structure. This presentation served to create a hypothetical organizational health"frontier" across an agency's top 10 scoring organizational units from which leaders and managers at other units could learn. Scans also included parallel insights on mission-support services using GSA's annual Customer Satisfaction Survey data, as well as showed workforce attrition summaries using information from OPM's Enterprise Human Resources Integration database. Scans of organizational health were presented to and socialized with agency leadership through various management-focused governance bodies, including the President's Management Council (PMC), the Chief Human Capital Officers (CHCO) Council, and Performance Improvement Officer (PIO) Council, and distributed on a timeline aligned with the 2023 Strategic Reviews.

Sustaining this joint OMB, OPM, and GSA collaboration to produce additional Organizational Health Scans in the future that reflect subsequent, comparable data remains a priority for 2024.

Identifying Leading and Innovative Practices from Organizational Health and Organizational Performance Implementation Efforts

Leveraging the Framework's existing routine of annual, data-driven strategic reviews, OMB's leadership conducted Strategic Review meetings in summer 2023 with the Deputy Secretaries of major agencies in their role as COO. As previously detailed above, these meetings not only reviewed progress on Agency Strategic Plans, but also discussed agencies' approaches to strengthening organizational health and organizational performance to advance implementation of OMB Memorandum M-23-15. Through those meetings, several themes emerged which are being applied in practice across Federal agencies and are highlighted below.

- ***Developing Integrated Business Systems.*** Effectively strengthening agencies' organizational health, organizational performance, and work environment plans in line with the Administration's policies demands a degree of business systems capabilities at the enterprise level that can integrate data analytics across performance indicators and other evidence. For example, ***Pulse***—DOD's authoritative performance management analytics platform—is an ecosystem of applications and dashboards in the agency's ***Advana*** (Advanced Analytics), a multi-domain, enterprise-wide data, analytics, and AI platform to provide military and civilian decision-makers and analysts at all levels access to authoritative, enterprise data and structured analytics in a scalable, reliable, and secure environment. Pulse integrates performance data and other analytics to track implementation of the Department's National Defense Strategy, Strategic Management Plan's priority metrics, Performance Improvement Initiatives, and Business Health Metrics (BHM). It leverages data from existing DOD business systems, allowing DOD to integrate performance improvement priorities into a unifying framework to show how they are performing against the Secretary's and Deputy Secretary's strategic priorities for proactive monitoring of agency performance.

- ***Developing and Using Dashboards to Present Performance Indicators and Data.*** To strengthen support for decision-making by executive leadership, many agencies continue to adapt and mature their dashboard and related data visualization capabilities—a leading private-sector best practice that that OMB has encouraged for agency's strategic review analysis for the past several years. Dashboards allow leadership a fast, unified, and comprehensive view of the organization's performance and health across multiple areas and indicators simultaneously, enabling leaders and managers alike to explore potential connections and relationships across key performance data. Agencies from DOD, DOE, EPA, and USAID (see Chart 12-2), to many others, are using integrated, coordinated visualization displays and dashboards to support leadership decision-making across various dimensions related to the health and performance of their organizations. See the "Strengthening the Federal Workforce" chapter for a complementary discussion on the development and use of workforce-related dashboards.
- ***Developing and Using Composite Indicators and Indices.*** A number of agencies are advancing promising work to incorporate into their organizational health and organizational performance frameworks composite measures, or indices, for performance monitoring and assessment purposes. In general terms, a composite indicator is created by compiling individual indicators into a single index based on an underlying model that informs their aggregation in order to measure multidimensional concepts which cannot be captured by a single indicator.[5] For example, GSA is using its Acquisition Excellence Composite Metric—which is an index of various acquisition performance indicators—as an important component contributing to GSA's broader agency-wide framework and overall ability to measure and assess organizational health and performance.

Encouraging and promising work is occurring across agencies, reflective of a thoughtful and deliberateness in both planning and execution in their approach to advance this priority management policy. The discussion now shifts to efforts to build capacity, capability, and socialize leading practices and promising innovations Government-wide.

Building Agency Capacity and Analytical Capabilities for Data-Driven Management that Strengthens Organizational Health and Organizational Performance

OMB continues to focus on building the analytical capacity of agencies so that they may put into practice elements of the Framework and apply its data-driven management principles across all aspects of their approach to organizational health and organizational performance. From investments in the President's 2025 Budget, to workshops hosted by the Performance Improvement Council (PIC) and an interagency community of practice, strengthening the capacity and capabilities of Federal agencies to do this work remains a concerted priority.

Investments in the President's 2025 Budget

The President's 2025 Budget makes investments that continue to build agency capacity and analytical capabilities for data-driven management that strengthens organizational health and organizational performance. For example, highlights include:

- Increases in FTE capacity at both ED and HUD to implement organizational health and organizational performance frameworks, and the monitoring and assessment of major operating units within them.
- Increases in FTE capacity for additional performance and program analysis within DOC's Departmental Management office to implement management reforms recommended by external auditors, including the U.S. Government Accountability Office and Office of Inspector General.
- The President's 2025 Budget also supports an organizational study of ED's Office of Federal Student Aid to provide recommendations and analysis for how the Office could be better organized in order to improve their service delivery.

Expanding the Knowledge Base by Sharing Leading, Innovative Practices through Workshops, Symposia, and a Community of Practice

In partnership with agencies, OMB has been leading actions to apply resources from the President's Budget process to our strongest asset—the talent and skillsets of the Federal workforce who are leading the execution of programs and policies every day for the American people.

[5] For more information on composite indicators, see e.g., the Organisation for Economic Co-operation and Development's (OECD) *Handbook on Constructing Composite Indicators: Methodology and User Guide*, 2008.

For example, the PIC's workshop series hosted each spring and fall and open to all Government employees, provided trainings that enhanced the skills of over 2,300 participants in 2023, covering a range of topics from "Responsible Collection and Use of DEIA Data," "Organizational Change Management," and "Negotiating Data Sharing Agreements," to "Tools and Resources for Federal Enterprise Risk Management (ERM)," and "Data Visualization: Using Data to Tell a Story." Attendee feedback collected by post-workshop questionnaires showed that over 92 percent of participants expressed satisfaction with the workshops they attended, and 88 percent reported that using information they learned during the workshop could enhance their contributions to their work unit or organization.

OMB established an Organizational Health and Performance Community of Practice following the release of OMB Memorandum M-23-15. This effort led immediate, near-term implementation of organizational health and organizational performance frameworks while providing a forum for mobilizing a collective focus government-wide where agencies could develop and share their own leading, innovative practices and approaches. The underlying work of the Community of Practice will continue in 2024 as the forum transitions facilitation of such interagency learning to other established bodies, including the various executive management councils and PIC-sponsored workshop series.

Additionally, OMB is collaborating with OPM to produce a forthcoming Organizational Health and Performance Toolkit. The toolkit initiative is designed to help agencies develop and use action plans for monitoring organizational effectiveness and apply data-informed decisions to strengthen mission success.

OMB is further partnering with GSA and the National Academy of Public Administration (NAPA) to examine emerging workforce trends and provide promising strategies for Federal agencies to enhance organizational health and performance. The results of this effort will be used to update NAPA's 2018 Report, *Strengthening Organizational Health and Performance in Government*,[6] and will include three NAPA-organized symposia throughout the course of 2024 focused on various aspects of organizational health and performance assessment from the perspective of State, local, nonprofit, and private sectors.

Finally, promising work to identify and build an evidence base using performance measurement and other tools occurred throughout 2023. These efforts help chart a focus for future evidence-building work moving forward. For example, a joint VA/OMB study[7] used mixed effects multivariate regression methodology to assess and validate a positive relationship between employee engagement at VA healthcare facilities and patient experience. Initial findings from this study showed that a 10 percent employee engagement increase was associated with a four percent increase in overall hospital ratings, and three percent increase in patient trust.

A 10 percent employee engagement increase was associated with a 4 percent increase in overall hospital rating, and 3 percent increase in patient trust.

The promising correlation from this study's findings suggests simultaneous increases in the employee engagement index and trust, and holds encouraging potential for application Government-wide as relationships between employee engagement and customer satisfaction in Government are further examined.

With the issuance of OMB Memorandum M-23-15, the Administration established Government-wide policies and guidance that require agencies to consider dimensions related to the organizational health of their major operating units as part of constructing an integrated framework of organizational health and organizational performance—thereby strengthening agencies' ability to continue delivering on their mission while responding to changes in their internal and external operating environments. The institutionalization of these principles in both the Framework and OMB guidance, as well as through the agency actions detailed above, reinforces the Administration's north star that guides every decision agencies make about their operations: delivering results for the American people.

[6] NAPA's 2018 report Strengthening Organizational Health and Performance in Government: A White Paper by the Standing Panel on Executive Organization and Management, is available online at NAPA's website.

[7] For further reading, see the November 7, 2023 Performance.gov blog post "VA Study Demonstrates a Promising, Potential Relationship Between Employee Engagement and Customer Satisfaction in Government," including an overview of the methodology employed in the case study.

FACILITATING INTERAGENCY COLLABORATION AND ADVANCING GOVERNMENT-WIDE MANAGEMENT PRIORITIES THROUGH THE PRESIDENT'S MANAGEMENT AGENDA (PMA)

The *President's Management Agenda (PMA)* lays out a long-term vision for improving the Federal Government's ability to deliver agency mission outcomes, provide excellent service, and effectively steward taxpayer dollars. Under the leadership and direction of *Priority Area Leaders*, each priority area of the PMA is advanced through Strategies supported by Strategy Leads who oversee the development and execution of more defined goals organized into a select number of Cross-Agency Priority (CAP) Goals. Focused on implementation, defining metrics and milestones, and piloting innovative approaches to address stated goals, interagency teams work collaboratively with interagency forums, including the PMC, executive management councils, and communities of practice, to ensure that collaborative, values-driven approaches developed through the PMA create lasting change.

Long-term in nature and designed to drive the cross-Government collaboration needed to tackle management challenges affecting multiple agencies, the Administration leverages the CAP Goals as a mechanism to coordinate and publicly track implementation of PMA priorities and strategies across Federal agencies—with teams reporting on progress quarterly through public updates to Performance.gov to foster accountability and build public trust. This system-wide focus affords opportunities to identify issues early, resolve conflicts across discrete lines of effort, and provide the training and guidance needed for agency practitioners while incorporating data-management and evidence-building strategies, along with other capacity-building strategies to advance the Administration's management priorities.

Highlights and updates on accomplishments to date across the PMA's three Priority Areas are provided on *Performance.gov*. A more in-depth discussion of Priority Area Two—Delivering Excellent, Equitable, and Secure Federal Services and Customer Experience—follows in the section below.

Improving Government Through Delivery of Secure Federal Services and Excellent Customer Experience (CX)

Federal services have not always been designed with the public's needs and priorities in mind, nor have these services always kept up with these needs. Poorly designed and delivered Government services result in inequitable outcomes and are a cost to the Nation; it can mean that veterans can't connect to the resources and benefits they have earned, small business owners cannot access financing to grow their businesses, new mothers and infants lack critical nutrition supports, and disaster survivors face mountains of paperwork to rebuild their homes.

During his first year in office, the President signed Executive Order 14058, "Transforming Federal Customer Experience and Service Delivery to Rebuild Trust in Government," directing a whole-of-Government effort to design and deliver an equitable, effective, and accountable Government that delivers results for all Americans. Since then, more than 17 Federal agencies have taken actions to deliver simple, seamless and secure customer experiences. The President's 2025 Budget includes more than $500 million to strengthen activities focused on modernizing services, reducing administrative burdens, and piloting new online tools and technologies. Importantly, the Budget targets efforts on deepening the expertise, capacity, and capabilities that Federal agencies need to meaningfully engage and better serve their customers—the American people.

The President's 2025 Budget directs funding for customer experience, including service design efforts and digital service delivery improvements, at all 17 Federal agencies that maintain the 38 High Impact Service Providers (HISPs) designated by OMB. These efforts are a continuation of Executive Order 14058 commitments, cross-agency life experience work, and core customer experience management activities as directed in OMB Circular A-11, Section 280. Specifically, the Budget supports more than 15 CX teams within Federal agencies, bureaus, and offices. Building on existing CX teams at HHS and DHS, the Budget invests in the creation of complementary and dedicated teams within the Administration for Children and Families, Customs and Border Protection, and the Federal Emergency Management Agency. A new Departmental-level team at the Patent and Trademark Office will develop enterprise strategies to improve customer experience for America's inventors. The Budget makes additional investments in expanding CX teams, including those at the Internal Revenue Service, the Social Security Administration, ED's Office of Federal Student Aid, and DOI's Bureau of Indian Affairs. The Budget will also support the retention and hiring of more than 170 full-time equivalent (FTEs) individuals with customer experience and digital service delivery training, skills, and experience. This talent can lead customer experience activities across Federal agencies, including engaging with and learning from customers, mapping customer journeys, identifying pain points, analyzing quantitative and qualitative feedback, and leading iterative design sprints to power service improvements.

The Federal Government interacts with millions of people each day and provides vital services during some of the most critical moments in people's lives. Whether claiming retirement benefits, seeking assistance following military service or rebuilding after a hurricane, Americans expect Government services to be responsive to their needs. But too often, people have to navigate a tangled web of Government websites, offices, and phone numbers to access the services they depend on. The "life experience" organizing framework requires a new model of the Federal delivery system working together—within agencies, across agencies, even across levels of Government—driven by customer (human-centered design) research, rather than within bureaucratic silos, to solve problems. The President's 2025 Budget dedicates more than $30 million to bolster interagency life experience projects that enable more efficient administration of Federally-funded benefits programs, simplify the Medicare enrollment process, and equip new parents with diapers, clothing and information on supportive services. At least 14 Federal agencies will play a role in implementing these multi-agency projects. The Budget also provides an additional $27 million for the Health Resources and Services Administration (HRSA) to support workforce needs and development within the Healthy Start program, which could include building on lessons learned from ongoing life experience pilot projects at HRSA.

Designing Federal services with the public's needs and priorities in mind requires a clear understanding of both how Government service providers are performing today, and of what is needed to improve their capacity to better deliver for Americans in the future. To that end, the President's 2025 Budget facilitates customer research activities, including those related to the launch and continuation of pilot projects. For example, the Budget provides $5 million to support a customer experience technical assistance pilot for farmers and ranchers applying for farm loans. Other pilots supported by the President's 2025 Budget include Direct File of Federal tax returns, the expansion of the Special Supplemental Nutritional Program for Women, Infants, and Children (WIC), online shopping, and a unified Federal certification platform for small businesses.

Since 2018, designated HISPs have worked as a cohort to build trust in Government by improving service delivery one customer interaction at a time. The Administration understands that the majority of the more than 400 million individuals, families, businesses, and organizations that access Federal information and services do so online and increasingly from mobile devices. The President's 2025 Budget invests significantly in building the capacity of agencies to design and develop high-quality digital experiences and to continue to implement the 21st Century Integrated Digital Experience Act (21st Century IDEA Act; Public Law 115-336). This includes approximately $55 million for eleven Federal agencies to more effectively deliver critical government services through priority projects, including recruiting talent with key digital service skills, identified through CX Action Plans. The Budget also encourages 10 agencies to further innovate by bringing on teams from the Technology Transformation Service at GSA. The infusion of customer experience and digital service talent and further investments in Federal websites and digital services will help users find the information and support they need during pivotal moments such as applying for naturalization or for retirement benefits, during routine interactions to renew a passport or make a student loan payment, and, when inspiration strikes, apply for a digital pass to take in one of the Nation's majestic national parks or wildlife refuges.

Coordinating the Federal Interagency Permitting Process to Deliver Federal Infrastructure Projects On Time, On Task, and On Budget

With the passage of the IIJA, IRA, and the CHIPS Act, the United States is making a once-in-a-generation investment in America's infrastructure and competitiveness that will create good-paying union jobs, grow the U.S. economy, invest in communities, and combat climate change. The Administration has been breaking ground on projects to rebuild our roads and bridges, deliver clean and safe water, clean up legacy pollution, expand access to high-speed internet, and build a clean energy economy that is unlocking access to economic opportunity, creating good-paying jobs, boosting domestic manufacturing, and growing America's economy from the middle up and bottom out—not the top-down.

To make the most of these historic investments and ensure the timely and sound delivery of critical infrastructure projects, the Administration released *The Biden-Harris Permitting Action Plan to Rebuild America's Infrastructure, Accelerate the Clean Energy Transition, Revitalize Communities, and Create Jobs (Permitting Action Plan)* and OMB Memorandum M-23-14, Implementation Guidance for the Biden-Harris Permitting Action Plan, to strengthen and accelerate Federal environmental review and permitting. The Administration is committed to ensuring that processes are effective, efficient, timely, and transparent, guided by the best available science to promote positive environmental and community outcomes, and shaped by early and meaningful public engagement. Agencies are currently implementing the Permitting Action Plan and focused on accelerating smart permitting through early cross-agency coordination; establishing clear timeline goals and tracking key project information; engaging in early and meaningful outreach and communication with States, Tribal Nations, Territories, and local communities; improving agency responsiveness, technical assistance and support; and using resources and the environmental review process to improve impact.

The Federal Permitting Improvement Steering Council is also leveraging its expanded authorities under the IIJA to provide agencies with additional resources to hire more permitting experts and acquire vital systems and tools to increase the efficiency and effectiveness of infrastructure permitting review and authorizations, meet project review timelines, improve coordination among agencies, and accelerate information sharing and troubleshooting. The Administration convened sector-specific teams of experts that are advancing the responsible build-out and modernization of U.S. infrastructure by facilitating interagency coordination on siting, permitting, supply chain, and related issues. Federal agencies are also utilizing the *Federal Permitting Dashboard* to increase transparency and accountability by tracking key project information, including timetables and milestones, for infrastructure projects. Taken together, these actions are helping to strengthen supply chains, lower costs for families, grow the clean energy economy, revitalize communities across the Nation, support well-paying jobs, and accelerate and deliver infrastructure investments on time, on task, and on budget.

Spotlight on the Transportation Security Administration (TSA): Understanding Drivers of the Passenger Experience to Improve the Customer Experience of the Flying Public

In Spring 2023, TSA's Customer Service Branch (CSB) carried out its second Passenger Experience Survey (PES), collecting feedback from over 13,000 respondents at 16 airports on the American-traveling public's experience interacting with TSA's screening workforce. This survey effort built upon the lessons learned from TSA's pilot deployment of the PES in 2019 at five airports. In conducting the survey, CSB engaged with local TSA officials to gain support for the approach, trained employees on survey administration practices, and provided airport-specific analysis to close the loop post-survey. Results of the survey were overwhelmingly positive across multiple dimensions for how the TSA's screening workforce interacts with the traveling public to provide excellent customer service in performing its security mission.

Specifically, analysis of respondent data from the 2023 PES revealed ***93 percent of respondents were satisfied*** with their experience the day of security screening, and

Chart 12-3. Snapshot of the 2023 PES Results

93% of participants reported they were satisfied with their experience at the security checkpoint

94% of participants reported they are confident in the ability of the TSA Officers to keep air travel safe

78% of participants reported no challenges at checkpoint

95% of participants reported the TSA Officers they interacted with were professional

95% of the participants reported they were treated with respect by TSA Officers the day they took the survey

91% of the participants reported that they found their wait time reasonable

94 percent were confident in the ability of TSA officers to keep air travel safe. See Chart 12-3. For comparison and context, the American Customer Satisfaction Index reports a good customer satisfaction score is between 75-85 percent. Additional analysis revealed that drivers of professionalism, respect, and the explanation of screening requirements by TSA agents superseded wait time in impacting travelers' confidence in TSA.

Moreover, the five airports that hosted both rounds of the PES showed an 18 percent improvement in traveler's understanding why additional screening was required, when compared to 2019 data. See Chart 12-4.

What changed between 2019 and 2023, and why were there such significant performance improvements on this question? In 2020, TSA created a "CX Demystified" briefing which is now included in all new hire training, suggestive of a promising link between the strength of CX training and field outcomes. The incorporation of CX-related training for all new hires at the agency also helped reinforce a CX-oriented culture within the organization that emphasizes CX is part of everyone's job, and helps enhance TSA's security mission.

What's next? The results of this PES will inform TSA's first Agency Priority Goal (APG) focused on customer experience and their upcoming CX Strategic Roadmap. Additional analysis of survey results is also being planned to identify the strength of relationships across other questions and their drivers, including exploring potential connections with other indicators of organizational health and organizational performance from related datasets, such as the FEVS.

COMMUNICATING PERFORMANCE RESULTS AND INFORMATION TRANSPARENTLY

To improve the usefulness of program information through reporting modernization, a central website— *Performance.gov*—makes finding and consuming performance information easier for the public, the Congress, delivery partners, agency employees, and other stakeholders. First established in 2010, Performance.gov continues to offer an online window to Federal performance management efforts, helping to improve accountability by providing one centralized reporting location to find information on agency goals along with regular progress updates towards achieving APGs and

Chart 12-4. Longitudinal Results Among the 5 Airports Participating in both the 2019 and 2023 Studies.

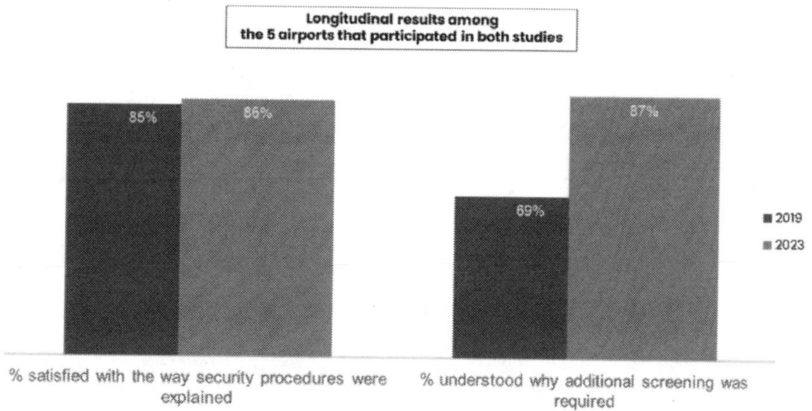

CAP Goals, which are being used to implement and drive progress on the PMA.

The Administration has continued to develop the Performance.gov platform as a primary means to inform the public on the management initiatives and performance improvements major Federal agencies are making, allowing for an increased and expanded ability to communicate directly with the American public. For example, in December 2023, a redesigned homepage was introduced to improve the user experience in navigating the website to track the Federal Government's goals and objectives. Organized under the site's "Data" heading in its top navigational bar, additional datasets continue to be added that allow for and encourage stakeholders to interact with some of the same information that is available to managers and leaders within the Federal Government. CX post-transaction feedback data being collected by HISPs is available and updated quarterly, while results of the Customer Satisfaction Survey measuring the satisfaction of Federal employees with their human capital, contracting, financial management, and information technology services provided internally by their agencies is updated annually.

Also introduced to the website this past year were the long-collected U.S. Social Indicators that illustrate in broad terms how the Nation is faring across six selected domains: economic, demographic and civic, socioeconomic, health, security and safety, and environment and energy. Although they reflect just a subset of the vast array of available data on conditions in the U.S. and do not directly measure the effects of Government policies, they offer a quantitative picture of the progress towards some of the ultimate ends that Government policy is intended to promote. U.S. Social Indicators will continue to be updated on Performance.gov, while the "Social Indicators" chapter of this volume provides further reading.

Moreover, site traffic has increased steadily over the years—even throughout Administration transitions—while these and other enhancements to the site continue to make performance information more transparent. Below is a "by the numbers" summary on the reach of Performance.gov content in 2023:

- Over 14.1 million social media impressions throughout five outreach initiatives designed to celebrate Federal performance management and civil service.
- Over 2,000 attendees from Federal, State, and nonprofit entities participated in five webinars covering the PMA, APGs, and CX-topics.
- Over 106,000 views across 32 published news blogs on the site.
- Over 10,000 social media followers interested in keeping up with the Federal Government's progress to achieve performance outcomes.
- Over 465,000 unique views of the Performance.gov website.

Setting clear goals, showing the public plans to achieve those goals, and then being transparent about our results is fundamental to building trust with the American public. With planned future site updates and initiatives including accompanying social media channels, the Administration continues to support the evolution of Performance.gov from a site that is not just a GPRAMA-compliance tool, but one that builds trust in Government by communicating performance results effectively and offering a unified, comprehensive view of Federal performance and management. Visit Performance.gov to learn more about Federal agencies' efforts to deliver a smarter, leaner, and more effective government. A complementary site, *Evaluation.gov*, offers a comprehensive view of agency evidence-building plans and associated program evaluation activities and resources.

Conclusion

Effective organizations develop and implement a framework or system for organizational performance management—a series of management routines, processes, and practices that can be applied for engaging senior leadership, articulating a vision of what success looks like for the organization, and mechanisms to regularly assess performance against those stated goals, objectives, and priorities using data and evidence. To that end, the Federal Government is no different, having developed a set of management routines that at their core drive a results-oriented culture within the Government and help Federal agencies deliver prioritized, transparent outcomes.

Delivering the high-performance Government that the American people deserve demands an integrated framework and approach to public management and governance that can facilitate the coordination and application of an increasingly sophisticated array of skillsets, tools, disciplines, and routines to manage the organizational complexities of Federal agencies. This commitment to good Government—using a multi-disciplinary array of management skillsets and tools incorporated within the Federal Performance Framework to strive toward an equitable, effective, and accountable Government that delivers results for all—has been evident since the start of the Administration. From guiding the sustained, effective implementation of major, historic legislation enacted under the Administration—such as the IIJA, IRA, and CHIPS Act—to advancing efforts to fulfill the goals of the PMA, the Framework and its routines are being used to improve outcomes for the American public while ensuring transparency into agencies' performance and management activities through a central reporting website at *Performance.gov*.

The Administration's actions and efforts reflect a concerted, coordinated management approach to achieving the outcomes of Government. Implementation of the Framework and its application since 2010 are leading to increased use of data and performance information to drive the decision-making needed for organizational performance improvement at Federal agencies—particularly where previous systems were less effective.[8] As Federal managers have an important obligation to ensure that tax payer dollars deliver equitable and effective results for all Americans, the Framework is a proven tool and means for achieving those ends.

[8] Moynihan, Donald, and Alexander Kroll. (2021). "Tools of Control? Comparing Congressional and Presidential Performance Management Reforms." *Public Administration Review*, 81(4): 599–609.

13. BUILDING AND USING EVIDENCE TO IMPROVE GOVERNMENT EFFECTIVENESS

Introduction

January 2024 marked the five-year anniversary of the Foundations for Evidence-Based Policymaking Act of 2018 (Evidence Act; Public Law 115-435), and the third year since the Presidential Memorandum on Restoring Trust in Government Through Scientific Integrity and Evidence-Based Policymaking. Much has been accomplished in this short time, including further development of a Federal evidence and evaluation infrastructure that reaches both across Government and within agencies. The Administration is using evidence to advance key priorities and has undertaken new and groundbreaking efforts to further develop the evidence ecosystem. The Budget sustains and enhances investments in evidence-based programs, demonstrating the Administration's commitment to using evidence for responsible investments in America. The Budget also supports agency capacity to build and use evidence through targeted investments in key areas.

Despite this notable progress, work remains to achieve the full potential of an evidence-based Government. Leaders at all levels must increase their demand for and use of evidence so that it becomes a routine part of decision-making and implementation. More of Government must embrace a true learning mindset, which means asking tough questions, considering new possibilities, and testing and innovating to uncover more effective and efficient paths. The world continues to change and evolve rapidly, and as new priorities emerge, the Federal Government must be capable of building and using the evidence needed to address the challenges facing the Nation. Evidence-based policymaking is on an upward trajectory in the United States, but this work has always been a long-term proposition as both evidence-building and evidence application matures and spreads. The Government should celebrate its progress, while also recognizing what remains undone and continuing to push forward for the kind of government Americans deserve. Evidence generation and use are not optional activities, and investing in evidence should not be seen as competing with other priorities or jeopardizing programmatic outcomes. Rather, relying on evidence to inform decision-making at all levels is a way to ensure that the Government optimizes its choices and best serves the American people.

The Federal Evidence and Evaluation Infrastructure

Implementation of the Evidence Act across the Federal Government has contributed to a stronger, more coordinated evidence and evaluation infrastructure. This includes the introduction of strategic evidence planning processes, the development of evaluation policies, and the appointment of senior leaders and leadership bodies responsible for agencies' evaluation functions. Importantly, this infrastructure serves to improve coordination agency-wide, while acknowledging and strengthening the distributed structure that fosters capacity building within component offices or directorates, incorporates program-specific subject matter expertise, and ensures independence in evidence generation. While the Evidence Act requires that the 24 Chief Financial Officers (CFO) Act agencies designate Evaluation Officers and develop agency-wide Learning Agendas, Annual Evaluation Plans, and Evaluation Policies, many small or independent agencies, in addition to a number of components within CFO Act agencies, have adopted these roles and activities as well.

Over a remarkably short period of time, Federal agencies have established the leadership, processes, and routines needed to build up the systems and structures required by Title I of the Evidence Act. While opportunities remain to meet the Act's ambitious goals, the groundwork has been laid to increase and improve the generation and use of evidence in policymaking. The *Evaluation.gov website* provides a unified access point for the key components of this new evidence and evaluation infrastructure, ensuring transparency and information sharing. The central elements of the systems and structures include:

- *Learning Agendas*. A *Learning Agenda* is a multi-year strategic evidence-building plan. By thinking strategically about evidence needs, agencies can prioritize those questions that, when answered, can inform consequential decisions and high-priority functions, while limiting ad hoc and uncoordinated analytic efforts and the associated inefficient use of scarce resources. The process of developing the Learning Agenda (i.e., engaging stakeholders, reviewing available evidence, developing questions, planning and undertaking evidence-building activities, disseminating and using results, and refining questions based on the evidence generated) may be equally, if not more, beneficial than the resulting document itself. Agencies execute their Learning Agendas through the initiation and conduct of the identified evidence-building activities to build the evidence needed to inform programs, policies, regulations, and operations. Learning Agendas also signal priority evidence needs to the broader research community.

- *Annual Evaluation Plans*. The *Annual Evaluation Plan* describes the significant evaluation activities that each agency plans to conduct in the subsequent fiscal year. The Annual Evaluation Plan primarily includes those activities that meet the Evidence Act's definition of evaluation, "an assessment using systematic data collection and analysis of one or more programs, policies, and organizations intended to assess their effectiveness and efficiency." Agencies define which evaluations are considered "significant," generally focusing on evaluations that address priority questions on the Learning Agenda, are noteworthy in scope or alignment with Administration or agency priorities, or are required by statute. The annual process of planning for and identifying significant evaluations provides opportunities to improve coordination and ensure adequate lead time to plan for complex studies, including necessary data access and/or data collection.

- *Capacity Assessment for Statistics, Evaluation, Research, and Analysis ("Capacity Assessment")*. Every four years, as part of the preparation of each agency's Strategic Plan, the Evaluation Officer, in conjunction with the Statistical Official, Chief Data Officer, and other agency personnel, leads the effort to conduct and provide an assessment of the coverage, quality, methods, effectiveness, and independence of the statistics, evaluation, research, and analysis efforts of the agency. Agencies completed their first *Capacity Assessments* in 2022, and a number of agencies have developed annual processes to review and update their assessment. The Capacity Assessments serve to identify and inform areas of strength and areas in need of further development in order to align organizational evidence-building capacity to agency evidence needs. For many agencies, the initial Capacity Assessment provides a baseline against which agencies are able to monitor changes over time as they further build capacity.
- *Evaluation Policies*. Nearly all of the 24 CFO Act agencies, as well as a number of small or independent agencies, have issued agency-wide *evaluation policies* that align with the evaluation standards articulated in *OMB Memorandum M-20-12, Phase 4 Implementation of the Foundations for Evidence-Based Policymaking Act of 2018: Program Evaluation Standards and Practices*. These standards include relevance and utility, rigor, independence and objectivity, transparency, and ethics. Many agencies have also incorporated an equity standard that integrates the definition from *Executive Order 13985, "Advancing Racial Equity and Support for Underserved Communities Through the Federal Government,"* to ensure the use of equitable evaluation methods.
- *The Evidence Team at OMB*. This team of senior-level subject matter experts, situated within the Office of Management and Budget (OMB) Office of Performance and Personnel Management, coordinates and supports evidence-building and use across the Federal Government with a particular focus on program evaluation. Through supporting the Evaluation Officer Council, engaging with the Federal evaluation community, and developing guidance and resources, the *Evidence Team* advances the goal of better integrating evidence and rigorous evaluation in budget, management, operational, and policy decisions. The Team leads implementation of Title I of the Evidence Act, executes a range of cross-agency evidence-building projects, and leads efforts in areas like evaluation procurement and hiring to support and improve the Federal evaluation ecosystem.
- *Evaluation Officers*. All CFO Act agencies have identified *Evaluation Officers* to lead the implementation of Title I of the Evidence Act across the organization and improve agency coordination of and capacity for evaluation. These senior leaders serve as their agency's champion for evaluation, responsible for advancing and advising on program evaluation across their respective agencies. Consistent with OMB guidance, Evaluation Officers are expected to have demonstrated, senior-level technical expertise in evaluation methods and practices.
- *Evaluation Officer Council*. The *Evaluation Officer Council* (EOC), chaired by the OMB Evidence Team Lead, convenes monthly to bring together Evaluation Officers and their deputies. Through the EOC, members exchange knowledge; consult with and advise OMB on issues that affect evaluation functions including evaluator competencies, program evaluation practices, and evaluation capacity building; coordinate and collaborate on areas of common interest (including development of deliverables required under Title I of the Evidence Act); and serve in a leadership role for the broader Federal evaluation community.
- *Interagency Council on Evaluation Policy (ICEP)*. Co-chaired by an agency representative on a rotating basis and a representative from the OMB Evidence Team, the mission of *ICEP* is to enhance the value and contributions of Federal evaluations to improve Government operations and delivery of Government services. ICEP members are Federal employees who are technical experts in one or more aspects of evaluation. ICEP provides skilled consultation through office hours, host professional development opportunities, and develop and share resources to support the Federal evaluation community.

More information on the evidence and evaluation infrastructure can be found in *OMB Memorandum M-19-23, Phase 1 Implementation of the Foundations for Evidence-Based Policymaking Act of 2018: Learning Agendas, Personnel, and Planning Guidance* and *OMB Memorandum M-21-27, Evidence-Based Policymaking: Learning Agendas and Annual Evaluation Plans*.

Sustaining and Enhancing Investments in Evidence-Based Programs in the 2025 Budget

One of the important aspects of the evidence framework is using the best available science and data to inform resource allocation decisions. Evidence-based policies and programs are the expectation, essential to the Nation's democracy in a time of limited resources. The examples here demonstrate the value of investments in evidence-building by showcasing how that evidence has informed policies to improve the lives of Americans. While the process of building a robust evidence base may take time, when those findings are translated into action, programs are more effective and the public can trust in Government's ability to bring about its intended goals. The 2025 Budget demonstrates the Administration's commitment to investing in evidence-based programs and policies across a range of Federal agencies and functions, even with caps on discretionary spending. The following are a few examples of such 2025 investments:

- Evidence has informed many programs and activities underway to support the Administration's goal of protecting and expanding access to high-quality health care and creating healthier communities. Improving the health and well-being of all Americans is a whole-of-Government effort, and the Department of Health and Human Services (HHS) plays a central role. The Budget invests in several evidence-based programs at HHS, including its investments supporting teen pregnancy prevention. The President's Budget includes $101 million for the Teen Pregnancy Prevention program which has been the subject of rigorous evaluations since 2010, and it will continue to build the evidence base on these approaches. Reflecting a robust *evidence portfolio*, these evaluations have included impact studies of new and innovative approaches, as well as replication studies of programs previously showing positive outcomes. Importantly, the President's Budget does not fund the Sexual Risk Avoidance Education Program, which uses an abstinence-only approach that prior evidence has shown to be ineffective in reducing the incidence of pregnancy and sexually transmitted infections, including HIV, in adolescents.

- Reflecting the evidence in the area of early childhood and maternal well-being, the President's Budget includes $600 million to support the Maternal, Infant, and Early Childhood Home Visiting (MIECHV) Program, which provides funding for States, territories, and tribal entities to implement evidence-based home visiting programs and to continue to build evidence. The birth of a child and the immediate years following can be challenging for any parent. Decades of literature have demonstrated home visiting is a strategy that can improve outcomes across vital domains like child development, school readiness, maternal health, child health, and reductions in maltreatment. MIECHV builds on the decades-long portfolio of evidence on effective approaches in early childhood home visiting. This robust *literature* documents that home visits as an intervention approach to work with families and young children can lead to improved outcomes across domains such as child development and school readiness, maternal health, child health, and reductions in child maltreatment. As noted above, efforts continue to build and add to this rigorous evidence base.

- Understanding and implementing effective workforce development strategies based on rigorous evidence are central to the Administration's approach to supporting the American workforce. At the Department of Labor (DOL), the President's Budget continues to invest in *evidence-based workforce development programs*. These investments include $388 million for the Reemployment Services and Eligibility Assessment Grants program, as well as a $335 million investment in Registered Apprenticeships. Also at DOL, the President's Budget includes an investment of $50 million in the Sectoral Employment through Career Training for Occupational Readiness (SECTOR) program, reflecting the strong evidence base on sector strategies, which have demonstrated an ability to improve employment outcomes for low-income workers. Sector-based training programs target key sectors of the economy with high local demand. Several rigorous evaluations found evidence that sector-based programs, such as *Project Quest* and *Year Up*, result in large and enduring impacts on worker earnings. Evidence suggests that programs that employ strategies such as sector-specific training across job types or provide participants with non-occupational support services may increase overall program effectiveness. Finally, the 2025 Budget includes enhanced levels of funding for DOL's Strengthening Community College (SCC) and Reentry Employment Opportunities (REO) interventions, both of which show promising evidence of effectiveness and help further build the evidence base.

- The Department of Education (ED) continues to invest in evidence-based strategies. The Budget proposes to double the investment in Postsecondary Student Success Grants from $50 million to $100 million, part of the Fund for the Improvement of Postsecondary Education (FIPSE). These programs fund grants to implement, scale, and rigorously evaluate evidence-based activities to support data-driven decisions and actions to improve student outcomes. In particular, funding through this program may be used to expand student access to *evidence-based support services* such as academic advising, mentoring, and tutoring to increase overall college attainment and completion rates. In addition, the Budget funds a $200 million investment, $50 million above 2023 enacted levels, for Full Service Community Schools (FSCS), which requires grantees to implement evidence-based activities, evaluate the effectiveness of their projects, and comply with any evaluations of FSCS conducted by the Institute of Education Sciences. Existing *literature* demonstrates that Full Service Community Schools successfully advance academic achievement and improve student attendance by implementing a common set of evidence-based practices. The Budget sustains support at $43 million for School Climate Transformation Grants at ED, which funds evidence-based activities. These grants to State Educational Agencies and Local Educational Agencies are intended to develop and adopt, or expand to more schools, multi-tiered systems of support, such as Positive Behavioral Interventions and Supports, that guide the selection, integration, and implementation of evidence-based practices for improving school climate and supporting student social and emotional well-being.

- The Budget also invests $940 million, $50 million above 2023 enacted levels, for English Language Acquisition (ELA) grants, which help implement evidence-based practices that improve outcomes for English learners. The Budget sustains funding for the American History and Civics Education program, which funds grants that promote evidence-based instructional methods and professional development programs in American history, civics and government, and geography, particularly those methods and programs that benefit students from low-income backgrounds and underserved students. And finally, the Budget sustains funding in Javits Gifted and Talented Education grants, which by statute, give priority awards to projects that include evidence-based activities or that develop new information to improve the capacity of schools to operate gifted and talented education programs or to assist schools in identifying and serving underserved students.
- The Budget includes $4 billion for the Department of Housing and Urban Development's (HUD) Continuum of Care program, which incentivizes grantees to commit to using the evidence-based Housing First approach. The Housing First approach emphasizes rapid placement and stabilization of people experiencing homelessness in permanent housing without imposing service participation requirements or preconditions and is proven to offer greater long-term housing stability, especially for people experiencing chronic homelessness, who have higher service needs. The evidence supporting the effectiveness of these strategies draws on over two decades of *research and evaluation*, including randomized controlled trials. In 2016, results from HUD's *Family Options Study* found that "assignment to the SUB [permanent housing subsidies] group more than halved most forms of residential instability, improved multiple measures of adult and child well-being, and reduced food insecurity." More recently, a 2020 *systematic review* of Housing First programs lends further support to the effectiveness of this approach for decreasing homelessness.
- The Budget invests in critical nutrition assistance programs administered by the Department of Agriculture's Food and Nutrition Service (FNS) that are informed by a robust portfolio of evidence. Recent efforts in outreach and to modernize the Special Supplemental Nutrition Program for Women, Infants, and Children (WIC) have contributed to increased program enrollment and participation. The President's Budget funds WIC at $7.697 billion this year to fully fund participation in the program. To address unanticipated growth in the program, the Budget includes an emergency contingency fund that will pay out additional funds when there are unanticipated cost pressures. The strong *evidence base* supporting the benefits of WIC for critical maternal and child health outcomes underscores the importance of protecting this program. Strong evidence also demonstrates the value of the Summer Electronic Benefit Transfer Program for Children (Summer EBT), which the Congress authorized as a permanent program in December 2022. *Evaluators* using random assignment to test the impact of these benefits on food insecurity found that the benefits contributed to significant reductions to very low food security among children. The Budget supports Summer EBT benefits and State and Indian Tribal Organization administrative expenses to launch implementation of this new benefit.

Supporting Agency Capacity to Build and Use Evidence

Generating a robust evidence base that can be used to inform major policy initiatives and associated investments requires ongoing, consistent investments in the capacity and infrastructure needed to enable that work. To that end, the President's Budget directs funds to sustain and, in key areas, enhance agency capacity to carry out evidence-building activities and rigorous evaluations. In addition to financial resources, agencies require skilled leadership and staff, continued investments in generating quality and timely data, improvements in data availability and data sharing, and robust knowledge management systems that ensure decisionmakers can tap into available data and evidence.

The Budget includes investments to sustain and build critical capacity for evidence in agencies, including for qualified staff, specific evaluation efforts, and related activities. This capacity is essential to building evidence on Administration priorities and overarching strategies to deliver for the American public. For example, at the Department of Justice, the President's Budget continues and enhances prior commitments to build critical capacity to support program evaluation activities, and includes funding for an Evidence Lead within the Justice Management Division to continue the Department's progress in implementing and executing activities from its Learning Agenda and Annual Evaluation Plans. The 2025 Budget also includes investments at the Department of the Treasury for staffing and other capacity dedicated to program evaluation activities. At the Office of Personnel Management (OPM), the President's Budget continues prior commitments to build critical capacity to support program evaluation activities, includes funding for priority evaluations of the Paid Parental Leave Program and implementation of the new Postal Service Health Benefits Program, and sustains staffing with qualified evaluators to execute these activities. Similarly, the President's Budget sustains critical research and evaluation resources at HUD's Office of Policy Development and Research at 2024 Budget levels. This signifies the importance of maintaining HUD's research capacity to build and use evidence to inform housing and community development programs and policy. The Budget also proposes $2.6 million for a new independent program evaluation fund at the Department of the Interior (DOI), which will allow DOI to execute rigorous evaluations to build evidence in priority areas.

Building needed evidence requires resources, including staff and funding for program evaluation activities. However, effectively executing evidence-building activities relies upon a number of other factors that enable evidence generation and use, including having the necessary authorities to do this work. The 2025 Budget also continues essential authorities for evaluating and improving Federal programs. For example, the Budget maintains the authority for DOL to set aside up to 0.75 percent of appropriations so that there may be sufficient funds for conducting significant and rigorous evaluations, and it continues to provide DOL's Chief Evaluation Office the authority to carry out grants and demonstration projects to test innovative strategies for building evidence. The Budget also includes measures to further support evidence-building offices; it requests passage of an Evaluation Funding Flexibility general provision which would give DOL's Chief Evaluation Office and Bureau of Labor Statistics and HHS's Office of the Assistant Secretary for Planning and Evaluation and Office of Planning, Research and Evaluation in the Administration for Children and Families the ability to use evaluation funds over a greater period of time to support strategic, long-term, and flexible evaluation planning. The 2025 President's Budget expands Medicaid maternal health support services during the pregnancy and post-partum period by incentivizing States to reimburse a broad range of providers including doulas, community health workers, peer support initiatives, and nurse home visiting programs. Importantly, this new benefit is being coupled with rigorous program evaluation in order to assess the effects of these changes on maternal health and other key outcomes.

With respect to improvements in data availability and data sharing, the 2025 President's Budget makes critical investments in the data infrastructure needed to execute priority evidence-building activities. For example, the Budget increases investment for the Census Bureau's Survey of Income and Program Participation, a preeminent source of longitudinal data on the economic well-being of American households, to ensure the stability and usefulness of this critical data source for future evidence-building opportunities. The Budget also invests in Department of Transportation data collections to inform road safety by improving understanding of the causal factors for large and medium truck crashes. The Administration also supports efforts to more effectively use administrative data for evidence-building, including employment and earnings data. Expanding secure access to critical data sources, like the National Directory of New Hires, among others, will unleash their full potential to help the Federal Government build the evidence it needs to better serve the American people. At OPM, the President's 2025 Budget sustains critical investments to build and enhance data systems and increase analytic capacity to better use Federal workforce data. Federal human capital data are critical to understanding the Government's workforce, and to building evidence on how to attract, hire, develop, and retain the talent needed to deliver for the American people.

Leveraging Evidence to Improve Outcomes for the American People

In his first week in office, President Biden issued a *Presidential Memorandum on Restoring Trust in Government Through Scientific Integrity and Evidence-Based Policymaking*, stating that "it is the policy of my Administration to make evidence-based decisions guided by the best available science and data." At its heart, this Presidential Memorandum reflects the Administration's belief that in order to achieve its goals as a Federal Government, it must ground all of its work in science and facts. Evidence is not just a "nice to have," it is an essential component of all that the Government does, and it must leverage evidence in order to make progress on the Administration's priorities and for the Nation more broadly. This commitment to evidence is also demonstrated by requirements for the generation and use of data and evidence across the Administration's priorities. For example, Executive Order 13985 emphasizes the need for equitable data to support data-driven efforts to address equity, and *Executive Order 14058, "Transforming Federal Customer Experience and Service Delivery to Rebuild Trust in Government*," requires plans for rigorously testing whether changes lead to measurable improvements. Agencies are actively working to integrate evidence-building in their efforts to address key Administration priorities, including equity, customer experience and service delivery, infrastructure, and climate.

Over five years since the passage of the Evidence Act, there is growing enthusiasm and continued progress across the Federal Government to harness the law's call to build and use evidence to effectively serve all Americans. No place is that call more urgent and important than in supporting the mental health needs of those individuals who have served the Nation. Ensuring the health and well-being of veterans, particularly their mental health, is a priority for the Administration, and the Veterans Health Administration (VHA) is committed to building evidence on what works to meet the mental health needs of and prevent suicide among the Nation's veterans. As discussed in the Department's 2024 Annual Evaluation Plan and forthcoming 2025 Annual Evaluation Plan, VHA is executing a set of evaluations that all seek to answer the question, "What strategies work best to prevent suicide among veterans?" Three programs are being evaluated: the Veterans Sponsorship Initiative, a public-private partnership that connects transitioning service members/veterans to sponsors in their post-military hometowns to help with reintegration; the Caring Letters program, which provides letters to veterans following a call to the Veterans Crisis Line; and the Reach Out, Stay Strong, Essentials program, an evidence-based, telehealth intervention for preventing perinatal depression among racially and ethnically diverse low-income women at high risk for perinatal depression. Through VHA's evaluations of the Veteran Sponsorship Initiative, the Caring Letters program, and the Reach Out, Stay Strong, Essentials program, VHA is demonstrating its dedication to building and using evidence to better serve those who have served.

The Administration is also committed to building evidence in areas that cut across agencies, including new and emerging priorities. Some of these evidence priorities have been articulated in cross-Government Learning Agendas, including the *President's Management Agenda Learning Agenda*, the *American Rescue Plan Equity Learning Agenda*, and the *Federal Evidence Agenda on LGBTQI+ Equity*. The questions from these Learning Agendas are displayed in the *Learning Agenda Questions Dashboard* on Evaluation.gov, along with all of agencies' individual Learning Agenda questions. Agencies are now doing the hard work of beginning to answer some of the questions on these cross-Government Learning Agendas to further build evidence on Administration priorities. As additional crosscutting priorities emerge, the development of a Government-wide Learning Agenda provides a productive mechanism to promote sustained engagement and collaboration in generating evidence to address some of the most complex challenges and new frontiers.

One leading example is the American Rescue Plan (ARP) National Evaluation, which aims to look systematically across a selected subset of ARP programs and provide an integrated account of whether, how, and to what extent their implementation served to achieve their intended outcomes, particularly with respect to advancing equity. The Office of Evaluation Sciences (OES) at the General Services Administration (GSA) is supporting that work in partnership with the OMB Evidence Team, the ARP Implementation Team, and other agency partners. This study is a groundbreaking approach to addressing the need for cross-agency and cross-program collaboration to build evidence related to overlapping investments in communities toward shared goals. Based on extensive document reviews, robust engagement with agency program staff, and consultation with subject matter experts conducted during the first phase of this work, plans for three in-depth evaluations and four program-specific analyses have been developed. The in-depth evaluations will cover State coordination across ARP programs serving low-income families with children, equitable implementation of ARP housing programs, and integration of funding to increase equitable access to behavioral health crisis services. Program-specific analyses will explore equity and effectiveness of emergency housing vouchers, the effect of employee-targeted child care stabilization funds on labor market outcomes for child care workers, the effect of the postpartum Medicaid extension on enrollment, health care utilization, and outcomes for postpartum women, and how State spending on Medicaid home- and community-based services affected equitable access to services. Additionally, plans are underway for a public-facing user-friendly website that will bring together information about 32 ARP programs and related evidence-building activities, as well as the evaluations and analyses conducted for the study.

Another example is the Federal Evidence Agenda on LGBTQI+ Equity, which includes a *Learning Agenda to Advance LGBTQI+ Equity*. The priority questions raised in this Learning Agenda cover such topics as health, healthcare, and access to care; housing stability and security; economic security and education; and safety, security, and justice. Together, these questions will help the Federal Government determine what additional evidence is needed to more effectively advance equity for and improve the well-being of LGBTQI+ people. Since the Administration released the Federal Evidence Agenda on LGBTQI+ Equity in January 2023, agencies have developed Sexual Orientation and Gender Identity (SOGI) Data Action Plans that articulate how each agency will work strategically to build evidence on these priority questions outlined in the Federal Evidence Agenda. For example, the U.S. Census Bureau has proposed the American Community Survey (ACS) Methods Panel: 2024 Sexual Orientation and Gender Identity (SOGI) Test to conduct a test of SOGI questions on the ACS. The ACS is a critically important survey that provides detailed social, economic, housing, and demographic data about America's communities. It is widely used by Federal agencies and external researchers to answer critical questions. This is just one example, and as agencies continue to implement their SOGI Data Action Plans and build much needed evidence, the Government's understanding of effective strategies to advance LGBTQI+ Equity will continue to grow.

More broadly, evidence is being used to advance equity for all Americans in other contexts. For example, with equity as its through line, the *Analytics for Equity Initiative*, first announced during the *Year of Evidence for Action*, is now in progress. Led by the National Science Foundation in partnership with the White House Office of Science and Technology Policy (OSTP), OMB, and other Federal agencies, the Initiative links interested researchers directly with Federal agencies seeking to answer research questions captured in their Learning Agendas in five equity-related research themes. The goal of this effort is to fund researchers to produce rigorous empirical evidence and research in equity-related topics aligned to agency Learning Agendas, so that Federal agencies and other organizations can increase the impact of equity-focused evidence-based strategies. Phase 1 projects were awarded in thematic areas that include equity of access to STEM research and education opportunities, environmental stressors and equity, equity in human services delivery and outcomes, health equity in the wake of climate change, and equity considerations for workplace safety and workers. The Budget supports continuation of Analytics for Equity, including Phase 2 projects that would fund researchers to conduct larger-scale research and analyses and develop research papers, evidence-based reports, memos, and policy papers discussing the potential implications of research findings for Federal programs.

New Efforts to Bolster the Evidence and Evaluation Landscape

Significant progress has been made to meet the Evidence Act's ambitions of strengthening the Federal evidence and evaluation landscape. As with any major paradigm shift, there is a need to build new routines and processes to reflect, take stock, and consider where further change is needed. For example, the increased focus on evaluation and its potential to meet priority evidence needs has highlighted opportunities for Government-wide solutions to improve access to the expertise that high quality evaluation requires. Similarly, as agencies improve their capacity to plan and conduct evaluations, senior leaders must be equipped to harness the evidence these evaluations produce and put the findings into action. The new and emerging activities described here are intended to meet these needs and continue to strengthen capacity across the Government for evidence-building and use.

Improving Agency Routines for Evidence Planning through Spring Briefings

In spring 2023, OMB initiated a new annual review process on evidence-building activities through Evidence Spring Briefings with each CFO Act agency. As described in OMB Circular No. A-11, Section 290, these Evidence Briefings provided an opportunity for agencies to:

- provide updates on the status of evidence-building activities included in their Learning Agendas and Annual Evaluation Plans;
- discuss progress made, challenges encountered, and changes to activities on those plans; and
- as available, share interim or final results of evaluations or other activities with OMB.

The Briefings reflected the Evidence Act's emphasis on working across functional siloes and brought together staff from across agencies and OMB. For example, from OMB, these briefings included program examiners, the Evidence Team members directly overseeing Evidence Act implementation, and staff responsible for related functions around performance and personnel management. For agencies, Evaluation Officers were encouraged to include relevant staff from their operating divisions or sub-agencies, and many chose to do so, allowing for deeper discussion of specific evaluations and other evidence-building projects. While following the direction noted in A-11, agencies worked collaboratively with OMB to develop agency-specific agendas, each tailored to the unique contexts, needs, and opportunities in each agency.

In these 24 Briefings, agencies provided updates on putting evidence-building plans into action. Agencies listed hundreds of learning activities either completed or underway, including numerous evaluations, that had been initiated across agencies to address priority questions. The updates also described the many activities that were planned or in development, as well as questions where agencies were still working to identify specific projects or activities to provide the evidence needed. With respect to implementing their Annual Evaluation Plans, agencies noted that most 2022 evaluations were either completed or well underway, with 2023 and 2024 evaluations in the planning phase. The types of evaluations being conducted varied across agencies, with a number of agencies starting with formative evaluations to inform design of anticipated outcome or impact evaluations. Agencies also underscored the numerous evaluations and studies underway that are not included in Annual Evaluation Plans because of how each agency has defined "significant"—an important nuance for those seeking to understand the full scope of Federal evaluation activity.

Many agencies emphasized how integrating evidence planning into strategic planning processes has improved understanding of and demand for evidence across the agency. Agencies noted that the Learning Agenda and Annual Evaluation Plan development process provides opportunities for internal and external engagement and input, improves coordination and collaboration with agency components by "breaking down silos," and increases collaboration with other Evidence Act Officials, such as Chief Data Officers and Statistical Officials. A number of agencies described the work underway within agency components to develop component-specific Learning Agendas to guide their evidence-building activities, thus demonstrating the value that agency leadership and staff at all levels have found in participating in the strategic evidence planning process. Additionally, agencies described their process for revisiting, refining, and updating their Learning Agenda to reflect shifting priorities. Increased demand for evidence from policymakers and agency leadership was exemplified through requests for timely evidence to inform policy and program design, a strong push for disaggregated data to inform efforts related to equity, greater interest in evidence and data analysis to inform operational decisions, and a focus on grantee evaluation capacity and requirements for evidence-building.

The Briefings provided an opportunity for agencies to describe the critical investments that have been made in evidence-building and evaluation capacity, including key hires of qualified evaluators. Agencies underscored the importance of having skilled staff with strong education, training, and experience in program evaluation for making progress in implementing the agency's Learning Agenda and related evaluation activities. Agencies also described the various approaches taken to improve general understanding of evaluation, including staff development opportunities, launching evidence and evaluation communities of practice, and providing workshops and office hours. Agencies also pointed to investments in the development of information and data systems to improve data sharing, better align disparate data systems, and make available data more "legible." Agencies highlighted the need to make data and evidence accessible and understandable to leadership, which many agencies are working to address by building communication channels to support evidence use, including data and evidence dashboards and evidence repositories or "exchanges" where reports are made available.

The 2023 Evidence Spring Briefings were a critical moment for OMB and agencies to come together and take stock of progress on implementing activities on agency Learning Agendas and Annual Evaluation Plans. This dedicated time to discuss evaluation and evidence-building across functional areas was useful in driving continued progress. OMB collected feedback from all briefing participants – in OMB and agencies – and the response was overwhelmingly positive, with near unanimous agreement that these briefings were helpful and that they should continue going forward. To that end, the August 2023 update of OMB Circular No. A-11 continued the requirement that agencies participate in an Evidence Spring Briefing in 2024.

Improving Agency Access to Evaluation Expertise

Agencies have long faced challenges in identifying and connecting with highly skilled contractors to meet critical evaluation needs. A multiyear partnership between the OMB Evidence Team and GSA to address this concern has led to an innovative solution: a *Program Evaluation Services Subgroup* on GSA's Multiple Award Schedule (MAS) to strengthen Federal infrastructure for high-quality program evaluation. The subgroup, which launched on July 20, 2023, under MAS Special Item Number (SIN) 541611, gathers together qualified, pre-vetted contractors that can be selected by Federal agencies to respond to requests for the design and execution of program evaluations. The subgroup helps agencies find qualified contractors for evaluations and related studies, which allows them to tap into the expertise needed for high-quality evaluations that meet Federal evidence-building needs. Contractor applications to the subgroup are reviewed by a panel of Federal evaluation experts, and those contractors with documented expertise and experience in program evaluation are invited to join. Federal agencies now can target solicitations for evaluations and evaluation-related projects to contractors with verified expertise in program evaluation, which should lead to higher quality evaluations and more useful information for agency leaders.

Another advance in the evidence and evaluation landscape is the development of the Evidence Project Portal on Evaluation.gov. The Evidence Project Portal is intended to help Federal agencies broaden their reach and connect with external researchers to address Learning Agenda questions or other key evidence needs. Through the Portal, agencies can more easily connect with the external research community, get help identifying external researcher talent with relevant expertise, and receive coaching on effective ways to describe and scope evidence-building projects. External researchers will be able to view well defined projects where Federal agencies are looking for support and connect directly with agency staff. GSA sponsored the first Portal project, which resulted in a successful match with a researcher, and more projects are in the pipeline for 2024 and beyond.

Qualified Evaluation Officers and program evaluation staff with the appropriate skills and technical expertise are essential to a healthy and high-functioning Federal evaluation ecosystem. Recruiting, hiring, and retaining staff with program evaluation experience requires the right tools and a commitment to building and sustaining this critical workforce. Recognizing this, the OMB Evidence Team is developing an online library of evaluator position descriptions that will be available for all agencies to access. The library will also include sample language for program evaluation job postings at various GS-levels, and resources to assist agencies through their hiring process, including example interview questions and prompts for writing samples. This library will help agencies recruit and retain the qualified talent needed to design, oversee, and execute their program evaluation activities.

Improving Leadership Understanding of, and Demand for, Evidence

The value of evidence is only realized when it is used to improve policies, programs, and operations and brought into the decision-making processes at all levels. That can only happen when agency leaders – both career and political – demand evidence and can understand and apply that information to their decisions. To foster a culture of evidence-based decision-making across the Federal Government, it is important to acknowledge the need to equip leaders at all levels with the skills to demand, understand, and apply complex evidence and data to achieve their mission. To address this need, the OMB Evidence Team has partnered with the Federal Executive Institute (FEI) at OPM to provide the Evidence-Based Decision-Making Leadership Academy (the Academy) for Senior Executives. Across six half-day sessions, the Academy aims to provide senior career leaders with the tools needed to ground their decision-making in the best available evidence while also building a learning culture within their agencies. The first cohort of the Academy, launched in November 2023, includes executives from nine different agencies who represent diverse functions, including budget and performance, legislative affairs, human capital, grants, and civil rights, among others. Demand for this initial pilot cohort far exceeded the available slots, which indicates that leaders see value in pursuing this kind of training. At the conclusion of the Academy, these Senior Executives will leave with an action plan for how they will apply what they have learned to advance evidence-based decision-making in their agencies.

Using evidence in decision-making requires an understanding of different forms of evidence and the types of questions they answer, including questions for the purpose of program evaluation. Too often evidence generation and use stall because agency staff at all levels – from leadership to frontline workers – do not fully understand the value that an approach like program evaluation can bring to their work. In response, OMB launched the *Federal Evaluation Toolkit*, a set of curated, technical resources to help Federal agency staff at all levels better understand evaluation – what it is, why it is important, and how it can help them execute their missions more effectively. There are many high-quality tools and resources available that provide guidance on all aspects of evaluation from planning to execution to dissemination and use. The Federal

Evaluation Toolkit pulls together a single set of curated, high-quality resources from across Federal agencies and external entities, making it easier for Federal staff to find the information they need. Hosted on *Evaluation.gov*, the Federal Evaluation Toolkit covers such topics as Evaluation 101, the purpose of evaluation, working with evaluators, and using evaluation findings, and will be updated with new resources over time.

OMB is also committed to increasing the evaluation capacity of the Federal workforce in other ways, including through its long-running Evidence and Evaluation Community of Practice Workshop Series. In place since 2017, this series of workshops highlights agency speakers sharing findings from recent evaluation studies, new analytic tools and methods, and discussions of agency evaluation policies. These workshops bring together evaluators and evaluation allies from across Federal agencies to learn from one another, share experiences and expertise, and strengthen the Federal evaluation community. Complementing these workshops are a series of professional development opportunities hosted by the ICEP, including networking events and topical workshops. Routinely drawing 100 to 150 participants to each session, these workshops have reached Federal staff across all CFO Act agencies and many small or independent agencies and cultivated a Community of Practice for hundreds of Federal evaluators. Participant feedback on the workshops consistently finds that attendees view the content as a helpful source of insights that will enhance their contributions to their own office. Together, these opportunities play an important role in elevating, educating, and nurturing the Federal evaluation workforce.

Future Directions for the Federal Evidence Agenda

As the Administration looks ahead and anticipates coming priorities for the Federal evidence agenda, there are a number of areas where it will be critical to demonstrate how agencies are delivering on their objectives and generating evidence that can inform policies to address complex challenges. There are emerging priorities associated with recent historic investments in technology and infrastructure that merit complementary historic prioritization of evidence-building and evidence utilization. Agencies also must prioritize and adopt new ways of learning that allow for faster and more responsive evidence generation. While examples from both Federal agencies and the private sector are helpful starting points, a broader cultural shift in the Government is needed to foster curiosity and a willingness to be as open about what is and, importantly, is not working.

Addressing Emerging Priorities

The Administration is embarking on a series of investments in industrial policy, including American semiconductor manufacturing, and posing new opportunities to assess the effectiveness of these investments and learn how to best target resources to achieve the shared goal of positioning U.S. workers, communities, and businesses for success in the 21st Century. To that end, in its Notice of Funding Opportunity (NOFO) for the CHIPS Incentives Program – Commercial Fabrication Facilities, the National Institute of Standards and Technology included a commitment to conducting rigorous evaluation activities to assess the outcomes related to funds awarded under the NOFO for projects that aim to improve domestic production capacity, mitigate environmental impacts, and increase economic opportunity in communities.

The Administration is also committed to rebuilding America's critical infrastructure, and the Infrastructure Investment and Jobs Act (Public Law 117-58) is a critical tool for directing investments in communities across the Nation in striving toward that goal. Doing this work requires a skilled workforce, and included in these investments are new and novel approaches to develop the workforce of the 21st Century. Agencies including the Departments of Commerce, Energy, and Transportation have launched programs that require awardees to implement such approaches as Registered Apprenticeships, job matching, training, and wraparound supports to advance workforce development in infrastructure sectors. As these infrastructure projects continue to take shape, learning about the impact and outcomes of these workforce development investments will be important for future efforts. Planning from the outset for implementation, outcome, and impact evaluations is critical to ensure that agencies are asking the right questions, gathering the right data, and carrying out rigorous analyses that can generate evidence with the widest possible relevance and usefulness.

More recently, *Executive Order 14110, "Safe, Secure, and Trustworthy Development and Use of Artificial Intelligence*," established a Government-wide approach to govern the development and use of artificial intelligence (AI) safely and responsibly, guided by a set of principles and priorities. As noted in the Executive Order, AI holds extraordinary potential for both promise and peril, and it is imperative that the Nation seeks to harness AI's potential for good, recognizing the many benefits it can deliver for the American people. However, realizing these benefits requires systematic examination of the extent to which the Federal Government's uses of AI achieve their intended outcomes and enable mission success. Agencies will need to ask – and answer – evaluation questions such as: what is the impact of using AI on improved teacher productivity, student learning, and patient outcomes, as compared to current activities? Agencies must also evaluate the impacts of AI as it is deployed to improve targeting of Government benefits and/or increase the reach of its programs.

Promoting a Culture of Experimentation and Learning

Fully embracing evidence-based policymaking requires wide-scale adoption of experimentation and learning. True learning organizations are open to new ideas, unafraid to ask challenging questions, experiment with new ways of doing business, embrace data and results—no matter how surprising or uncomfortable—and make changes based on what has been uncovered. Several Federal agencies have a rich history of experimentation and learning in order to improve results. In some cases, this experimentation is mandated by statute, enabling agencies to test different models and approaches and assess their outcomes using rigorous program evaluation. In many parts of the Government, however, agencies are still largely reluctant to experiment and embed regular evaluation in their operations and mission execution even when it is allowable and feasible. The hesitation is understandable; program leaders are often afraid of uncovering poor results or calling longstanding practices into question, and concerned about the consequences of sharing negative findings. A culture of experimentation challenges agencies to overcome inertia and biases that favor the status quo. When agencies adopt a learning and improvement mindset, the insights that result allow agencies to execute their missions and operations more effectively.

The Federal Government already has some leading examples to guide what experimentation and learning in agencies can look like. Authorized by the Patient Protection and Affordable Care Act (Public Law 111-148), the Center for Medicare and Medicaid Innovation, known as the CMS Innovation Center or CMMI, was established to identify ways to improve healthcare quality and reduce costs in the Medicare, Medicaid, and Children's Health Insurance Program. It does this by launching models that test new ways to provide better and more affordable care and couples those models with rigorous evaluation to assess short-term impacts. Since its creation over 10 years ago, CMMI has tested more than 50 models, providing evidence on approaches to improving quality of care, and using that evidence to share lessons learned and best practices throughout the U.S. health care system. CMMI's approach of coupling innovation with rigorous evaluation is an example of how the Federal Government can use evidence to improve programs.

At DOL, activities are underway to leverage evidence to implement and test innovations in existing programs. For example, the Employment and Training Administration will soon launch the Sectoral Training for Low-Income Older Adults Demonstration. This Demonstration will test whether sectoral strategies, which have shown evidence of effectiveness in other populations, increase employment and earnings for older workers with low incomes, including from underrepresented populations. Using a rigorous randomized controlled trial, the Demonstration will test whether sector-focused occupational skills training plus on-the-job training (i.e., the innovation) is more effective in increasing employment and earnings compared to standard services offered through the traditional Senior Community Service Employment Program. In executing this Demonstration, DOL is using existing evidence to innovate and test, with the goal of improving outcomes for this critical population within the workforce.

Experimentation to test new ways of doing Government business is also reflected in the work of the Office of Evaluation Sciences (OES) at GSA. With a mission to build and use evidence to better serve the public, OES works directly with agencies to implement and test new programs or program changes often using experimental methods. A recent example of OES's work includes an evaluation of a new intervention in Idaho to increase applications to the Homeowner Assistance Fund, a program operated by Treasury that provides funds to eligible homeowners to assist with mortgage payments and other qualified expenses related to housing and avoid housing displacement from the COVID-19 pandemic. A rapid evaluation showed that sending mailers to eligible individuals did not increase applications, enabling the State to make real-time decisions to shift resources away from these mailers to other forms of outreach. This example highlights how a willingness to test new approaches coupled with an openness to results – good or bad – can allow evidence to be used to improve the delivery of services for the American people.

Fundamentally, the Federal Government can serve communities and the American public better if agencies understand what is working well, what is not working well, and how agencies can do better. Regular and iterative experimentation will uncover new, effective approaches and support comprehensive understanding of what is and is not working as intended. At times, this approach will result in incremental improvements, while at other times, it may lead to a major change in direction with dramatic results. Integrating evaluation to enable continuous learning makes better use of taxpayer dollars by efficiently providing the insights needed to make small tweaks, system-wide adjustments, or, when warranted, wholesale change. However, adopting a culture of evidence throughout the Federal Government requires that leaders and staff feel safe questioning deeply-held assumptions, embracing experimentation, demanding regular measurement and analysis, taking time to understand results that may surprise them, and incorporating results into decisions as a matter of course. The Evidence Act provides statutory tools to create a framework for agencies to ask the tough questions that can drive this work through their Learning Agendas and Annual Evaluation Plans. Future efforts should leverage these tools and their associated routines to help agencies normalize innovation and celebrate taking risks, while recognizing that failure often leads to novel insights, necessary adjustments, and beneficial changes.

Conclusion

Five years after passage of the Evidence Act and nearly three years since the Presidential Memorandum on evidence-based policymaking, OMB and agencies have made notable gains in building evidence and evaluation capacity. The Federal Government must continue the hard work, collaboration, and commitment to ensure that evidence is routinely integrated into mission delivery and operations. Emerging priorities and once-in-a-generation investments will also require attention, collaboration, and renewed commitments across the Federal evidence ecosystem. Moving from incremental progress to transformational change requires widespread adoption of a culture of learning and experimentation throughout the Federal Government. Embracing this culture is what drives progress in building evidence and using it to improve the lives of Americans and their communities. With a shared commitment to this work, the future of the Federal evidence agenda is bright.

14. STRENGTHENING THE FEDERAL WORKFORCE

"Our Nation's future depends on ensuring our public servants have good jobs with competitive pay and benefits, along with the resources they need to accomplish their work. It also depends on the next generation of smart, dedicated people answering the call of public service and joining their ranks, helping deliver the promise of America to more of our citizens." —President Biden, *Public Service Recognition Week Proclamation, 2023*

There are more than four million dedicated public servants, civilian and military, who serve in the Federal Government in almost every occupation and in duty stations across the Nation and around the world. Through their work, these public servants implement the laws and policies enacted by elected leaders and provide the critical connective tissue between the Nation's democratic process and the lives of its residents.

This chapter describes the Administration's continued commitment to secure an equitable, effective, and accountable Federal workforce to accomplish this critical task. It outlines the current state of the Federal workforce; provides historical and contemporary analysis on key workforce trends; and highlights growing investments and initiatives that are positioning the Federal Government as a competitive, model employer and aligning its assets to ensure excellent service delivery and strong performance.

The roadmap to realize this vision is the *President's Management Agenda* (PMA). The initiatives advanced under the first priority of the PMA, Strengthening and Empowering the Federal Workforce, are bringing a new level of strategic focus and visibility to the workforce. The Administration's workforce agenda emphasizes a whole of Government approach with cross-agency collaboration to meet common challenges and share leading practice. It marshals agencies' significant workforce data to build evidence that advances its understanding of the current and future civil servants that Government will need to meet the mission today and into the future. Above all, it invests in people, in particular through new approaches to assess and fill urgent talent needs at all levels within agencies, as well as elevating innovative practices and scaling promising initiatives.

The Budget reflects the importance of this set of commitments, by making historic workforce investments to:

- Build and sustain professional, well-trained, and sufficiently resourced human resources (HR) functions within agencies and engage HR workforces as a strategic asset.
- Strengthen the Federal Government's internship programs and career talent pipelines through regulatory changes, meeting students and jobseekers where they are, utilizing the latest technologies, and leveraging the new centralized internship portal.
- Sustain a suite of workforce data tools and dashboards to equip Agency leaders with timely insights around bringing qualified applicants into Government more efficiently (especially in mission-critical occupations (MCOs) such as technology roles), addressing attrition and improving employee engagement levels, and improving diversity, equity, inclusion, and accessibility (DEIA).
- Sustain the success of the Infrastructure Investment and Jobs Act (IIJA; Public Law 117-58) hiring surge and drive an ongoing Artificial Intelligence (AI), Cyber, and Tech Hiring Surge to supercharge capacity in critical, emerging talent needs through cross-agency collaboration and cross-agency hiring actions.
- Bring implementation of Federal management and Federal workforce priorities closer to the people through investment in Federal Executive Board (FEB) reforms, including a new FEB Fellowship program designed to enhance regional recruitment efforts by building new talent pipelines and serving as Federal ambassadors across the United States.

These investments are aligned with the following four key strategies in the PMA to strengthen and empower the Federal workforce. In addition to setting near-term milestones, these investments and initiatives lay the groundwork for longer term progress to position the workforce for the future.

Strategy 1: Attract and hire the most qualified employees, who reflect the diversity of our country, in the right roles across the Federal Government

Through collaboration under the banner of the PMA, agencies have developed and deployed a new suite of tools and practices to assess their capacity needs, attract the best talent, enable Agency missions and service delivery to the American public, and hire a workforce that reflects the diversity of the Nation. This comprehensive approach to hiring reform takes stock of the Federal Government's assets, identifies areas for priority action, and launches new tools to empower agencies to collaborate to meet acute talent needs.

Assessing Government's Talent Needs: The State of the Federal Workforce

The total Federal workforce is composed of approximately 4.3 million employees, with 2.2 million Federal civilian employees and 2.1 million military personnel. See Tables 14-1 and 14-2 for distribution across agen-

Table 14–1. FEDERAL CIVILIAN EMPLOYMENT IN THE EXECUTIVE BRANCH

(Civilian employment as measured by full-time equivalents (FTE) in thousands, excluding the Postal Service)

Agency	Actual		Estimate		Change: 2024 to 2025	
	2022	2023	2024	2025	FTE	Percent
Cabinet agencies						
Agriculture	85.0	88.0	92.5	93.9	1.4	1.6%
Commerce	41.0	41.3	44.6	45.4	0.8	1.9%
Defense--Military Programs	772.3	775.1	796.4	795.4	-0.9	-0.1%
Education	4.1	4.1	4.2	4.4	0.2	5.9%
Energy	14.8	15.7	16.3	17.5	1.1	7.0%
Health and Human Services	79.2	81.3	86.3	87.5	1.3	1.5%
Homeland Security	202.8	212.0	206.4	217.6	11.2	5.4%
Housing and Urban Development	8.1	8.4	8.8	9.0	0.2	2.6%
Interior	61.9	63.0	64.9	66.2	1.3	2.0%
Justice	115.0	114.6	119.7	123.2	3.5	2.9%
Labor	14.9	15.7	15.6	15.9	0.3	1.9%
State	30.0	29.9	30.6	30.9	0.3	0.8%
Transportation	53.1	54.2	55.6	58.1	2.5	4.6%
Treasury	94.4	98.7	99.1	106.8	7.8	7.8%
Veterans Affairs	411.6	433.7	458.2	448.2	-10.0	-2.2%
Other agencies -- excluding Postal Service						
Bureau of Consumer Financial Protection	1.6	1.7	1.8	1.9	0.1	4.3%
Corps of Engineers--Civil Works	23.0	24.9	24.7	24.7	....	....
Environmental Protection Agency	14.2	15.0	15.0	15.4	0.4	2.6%
Equal Employment Opportunity Commission	2.0	2.2	2.2	2.2	....	....
Federal Communications Commission	1.4	1.5	1.6	1.6	....	....
Federal Deposit Insurance Corporation	5.9	6.3	7.1	7.2	0.1	1.8%
Federal Trade Commission	1.1	1.2	1.4	1.4	0.1	4.0%
General Services Administration	11.7	12.3	13.3	13.6	0.3	2.0%
International Assistance Programs	6.1	6.4	6.8	7.0	0.2	2.8%
National Aeronautics and Space Administration	17.7	17.8	17.9	17.1	–0.8	–4.6%
National Archives and Records Administration	2.7	2.7	3.0	3.0	*	0.1%
National Credit Union Administration	1.1	1.2	1.3	1.3	*	0.3%
National Labor Relations Board	1.2	1.2	1.3	1.3	*	4.0%
National Science Foundation	1.5	1.5	1.6	1.6	*	2.1%
Nuclear Regulatory Commission	2.7	2.8	3.0	2.9	–*	–1.7%
Office of Personnel Management[1]	2.6	2.7	2.7	2.8	*	1.5%
Securities and Exchange Commission	4.5	4.7	5.0	5.2	0.2	3.0%
Small Business Administration	8.0	6.5	7.1	5.6	–1.5	–20.7%
Smithsonian Institution	4.7	4.7	5.0	5.0	*	*
Social Security Administration	58.2	58.8	58.0	59.7	1.7	3.0%
Tennessee Valley Authority	10.4	10.9	10.9	10.9	....	....
U.S. Agency for Global Media	1.6	1.6	1.7	1.7	–*	–1.5%
Other Defense--Civil Programs	1.1	1.0	1.2	1.2	–*	–0.1%
Total, Executive Branch civilian employment	2,185.8	2,238.0	2,306.1	2,327.9	21.8	0.9%

* 50 or less.

[1] Includes transfer of functions to the General Services Administration and to other agencies.

cies. Using data from the Bureau of Labor Statistics on full-time, full-year employees, Table 14-3 breaks out all Federal and private sector jobs into 22 occupational groups to illustrate the compositional differences between the Federal and private workforces. Charts 14-4 and 14-5 present trends in educational levels for the Federal and private sector workforces over the past two decades, demonstrating a continuation in the advanced educational attainment of Federal employees. Chart 14-6 shows the trends in average age in both the Federal and private sectors, reflecting the average age of Federal employees to be significantly higher than the average age of private sector employees. Charts 14-7 and 14-8 show the location of Federal employees in 1978 and again in 2023. Chart 14-9 reflects the changing nature of work, comparing the number of employees in each General Schedule grade in 1950 versus 2023, showing an almost complete shift from lower-grade to higher-grade types of work.

Table 14–2. TOTAL FEDERAL EMPLOYMENT
(As measured by Full-Time Equivalents)

Description	2023 Actual	2024 Estimate	2025 Estimate	Change: 2024 to 2025	
				FTE	PERCENT
Executive Branch Civilian:					
All Agencies, Except Postal Service	2,238,006	2,306,140	2,327,905	21,765	0.9%
Postal Service [1]	572,186	559,423	549,746	–9,677	–1.8%
Subtotal, Executive Branch Civilian	2,810,192	2,865,563	2,877,651	12,088	0.4%
Executive Branch Uniformed Military:					
Department of Defense [2]	1,340,750	1,321,067	1,307,837	–13,230	–1.0%
Department of Homeland Security (USCG)	40,006	43,051	40,656	–2,395	–5.9%
Commissioned Corps (DOC, EPA, HHS)	9,939	10,012	10,112	100	1.0%
Subtotal, Uniformed Military	1,390,695	1,374,130	1,358,605	–15,525	–1.1%
Subtotal, Executive Branch	4,200,887	4,239,693	4,236,256	–3,437	–0.1%
Legislative Branch [3]	33,251	35,575	36,017	442	1.2%
Judicial Branch	32,606	33,104	33,963	859	2.5%
Grand Total	4,266,744	4,308,372	4,306,236	–2,136	–*

* Less than 0.1%.
[1] Includes Postal Rate Commission.
[2] Includes activated Guard and Reserve members on active duty. Does not include Full-Time Support (Active Guard & Reserve (AGRSs)) paid from Reserve Component appropriations.
[3] FTE data not available for the Senate (positions filled were used for actual year and extended at same level).

Americans continue to answer the call to serve by applying for Federal employment and engaging with Federal recruiters. In calendar year 2023, USAJOBS.gov hosted over 440,000 job announcements, facilitated over 1 billion job searches, and enabled individuals to begin more than 22.9 million applications for Federal jobs. Further, over one million jobseekers made their resumes searchable in the USAJOBS.gov Agency Talent Portal, and agencies created over 6,000 recruitment campaigns and posted over 850 recruitment events to attract jobseekers to their announcements.

With such a large workforce, spread across hundreds of Agency components and thousands of duty stations, deploying new tools to benchmark shared talent needs is a key success for the Workforce Priority. As part of the growing suite of workforce data tools, the Office of Personnel Management (OPM) launched a *Mission-Critical Occupations (MCO) Dashboard* to provide the public and Agency leaders a new depth of insight into Government-wide and Agency-identified MCO hiring. The dashboard assesses progress on hiring for top priorities and provides illustration of opportunities for cross-agency collaboration to leverage pooled hiring, as discussed below.

Reaching Early Career Talent

A critical workforce priority for the Administration is recruiting and hiring the next generation of Federal leaders. As illustrated in Chart 14-6, the Federal workforce is significantly older on average than the private sector workforce, and building a deeper pipeline of workers at the beginning of their careers will ensure that the Government can meet its mission without interruption as workers retire. Reaching this population requires a specialized set of tools, and revitalizing Federal internship programs is one of the most impactful approaches to strengthening this pipeline. OPM and the Office of Management and Budget (OMB) are providing the President's Management Council comparative data on internships across agencies to spur cross-agency learning and prioritize investment in growing the total number of Federal internships. In tandem, the Budget sustains investments under the PMA to develop new resources to help agencies enhance their internship programs and increase access for jobseekers.

In 2023, OPM's USAJOBS team began developing a USAJOBS Career Explorer tool. Jobseekers, including interns, will be able to input their interests into the tool and receive results for the top ten Federal job series that align. A public-facing version with over 500 Federal occupations will launch in 2024, providing jobseekers with a practical lens to see themselves in public service.

After releasing early career talent hiring guidance in January 2023, OPM launched a new Federal Intern Experience Program in June 2023 to complement agencies' existing intern programs with a standardized, high-quality professional development experience. The program features high-quality training, mentorship opportunities, executive speakers, showcases for intern work, and a hub for intern network building. Additionally, the OPM USAJOBS team is building a new Pathways Intern Conversion database to launch in 2024. This database will provide Pathways interns additional options to find full-time position opportunities if their Agency is unable to hire them directly.

These tools reflect the importance of building cross-agency collaboration around Federal internships as an entry point into public service overall. Leveraging platforms like the Recruitment and Outreach Community of Practice, agencies can coordinate the timing of their internship postings to *https://intern.usajobs.gov/* to

Table 14–3. OCCUPATIONS OF FEDERAL AND PRIVATE SECTOR WORKFORCES
(Grouped by Average Private Sector Salary)

Occupational Groups	Percent	
	Federal Workers	Private Sector Workers
Highest Paid Occupations Ranked by Private Sector Salary		
Lawyers and judges	2.2%	0.6%
Engineers	4.9%	2.2%
Scientists and social scientists	4.5%	0.9%
Managers	13.7%	15.3%
Pilots, conductors, and related mechanics	2.6%	0.5%
Doctors, nurses, psychologists, etc.	8.7%	6.9%
Miscellaneous professionals	16.8%	10.8%
Administrators, accountants, HR personnel	4.5%	1.5%
Inspectors	1.2%	0.4%
Total Percentage	**59.0%**	**39.0%**
Medium Paid Occupations Ranked by Private Sector Salary		
Sales including real estate, insurance agents	0.9%	5.5%
Other miscellaneous occupations	4.4%	5.5%
Automobile and other mechanics	2.0%	2.9%
Law enforcement and related occupations	8.3%	0.8%
Office workers	1.9%	5.3%
Social workers	1.6%	0.6%
Drivers of trucks and taxis	0.6%	3.2%
Laborers and construction workers	2.8%	9.9%
Clerks and administrative assistants	12.1%	9.5%
Manufacturing	2.4%	7.3%
Total Percentage	**36.8%**	**50.3%**
Lowest Paid Occupations Ranked by Private Sector Salary		
Other miscellaneous service workers	2.1%	5.2%
Janitors and housekeepers	1.3%	2.1%
Cooks, bartenders, bakers, and wait staff	0.8%	3.4%
Total Percentage	**4.2%**	**10.6%**

Source: 2018–2023 Current Population Survey, IPUMS-CPS, University of Minnesota, www.ipums.org.
Notes: Federal workers exclude the military and Postal Service, but include all other Federal workers in the Executive, Legislative, and Judicial Branches. However, the vast majority of these employees are civil servants in the Executive Branch. Private sector workers exclude the self-employed. Neither category includes State and local government workers. This analysis is limited to full-time, full-year workers, i.e. those with at least 1,500 annual hours of work.

provide candidates the widest possible array of options to explore Federal careers. Looking further ahead, there may be new opportunities to apply the proven approaches of pooled hiring and shared certificates to cross-agency internship pools so that intern applicants can apply to a single posting and be considered by multiple agencies.

Additionally, the Administration is working to make it easier for agencies to incorporate interns and recent graduates into their early career talent strategies through a substantial updating of the Pathways Program regulations. These updates, which are on track to be released by OPM in 2024, aim to make the programs more user-friendly for agencies and provide more streamlined options for Pathways interns, recent graduates, and Presidential Management Fellows (PMFs) to be hired permanently. In 2024, OPM will provide agencies an analysis of the business case for early career talent to support their increasing early career talent positions in strategic workforce plans.

Another investment in growing pipelines for early career talent is through Registered Apprenticeships. Federal agencies are working to identify occupations where vacancies can be filled through adoption of the proven Registered Apprenticeship model, leveraging lessons-learned from programs like the Cybersecurity Apprenticeship Program for Veterans, which is meeting acute talent needs at the Department of Veterans Affairs, while simultaneously building economic opportunities for veterans. Expanding the use of Registered Apprenticeships beyond their traditional application in the skilled trades is a unique opportunity for the Federal Government to grow its own skilled talent and support a critical nationwide skills development initiative.

The Administration continues to apply these tools in innovative ways to engage early career talent. To reach new pools of early career talent reflecting the Nation's diversity, OPM partnered with Hampton University to pilot a series of career readiness events called "Level Up to

Public Service." These one-day, hands-on convenings highlighted the value of public service and showcased Federal internship opportunities for college and high school students and helped participants build Federal resumes and USAJOBS profiles, while hearing reflections from current Federal employees. OPM plans to replicate the Level Up to Public Service program pilot at other minority serving institutions in 2024 and will provide agencies with technical assistance and resources to support their efforts to recruit diverse talent through the Talent Sourcing for America campaign.

Given the paramount importance of deepening early career talent pipelines to meet key workforce priorities, the Administration is continuing to work with agencies to ensure that they have the tools and resources they need to sustain investments in early career talent in a changing and challenging budgetary environment.

Strengthening Hiring Systems

It should be straightforward for the public to bring their talents to the Federal civil service, and agencies should have personnel systems that allow them to hire this talent effectively and expeditiously. The Administration is committed to making this a reality and addressing real concerns raised by applicants and hiring managers alike. OPM's *Hiring Manager Satisfaction Dashboard*, a workforce data tool launched under the PMA, illustrates longstanding frustrations among hiring managers with the timeliness of the hiring process and the skills alignment of those referred for consideration. Under the banner of the PMA, the Administration has been driving a new level of collaboration and coordination between agencies to address this challenge and improve the hiring process for applicants and for agencies.

To support strategic coordination within agencies around hiring, the Budget sustains investments in Agency talent teams, which serve as hubs within agencies to leverage workforce data to meet talent needs and foreground applicant experience. All 24 Chief Financial Officers (CFO) Act agencies have stood up talent teams, and some of those agencies have also established talent teams at the sub-component/department level. A robust 250-member Talent Team community of practice, led by OPM, shares lessons learned and best practices to support the expansion of innovative hiring operations.

To provide additional centralized support, OPM established a new Hiring Experience (HX) Group to support agencies and their talent teams and to drive a significant reimagining of Federal hiring that emphasizes cross-agency collaboration and leverages the Federal Government's size to unlock economies of scale. HX is centralizing hiring actions for mission-critical occupations, such as Information Technology (IT) Product Managers and Grants Management Specialists, which allow applicants to apply once for roles at many agencies and allow agencies to select qualified candidates from a single shared certificate. Some of these pooled actions leverage investments in rigorous assessments, such as the Subject Matter Expert-Qualifications Assessment (SME-QA) and other competency-based tools, and engage support from subject matter experts and HR specialists in agencies to maximize value and distribute costs. Over 300 selections have been made from HX's first six Government-wide actions, and HX will launch at least eight more actions in 2024.

Additionally, OPM's new Talent Pools feature on the USAJOBS Agency Talent Portal provides a central hub for both OPM-led cross-Government actions and Agency-led shared certificates under the Competitive Service Act of 2015 (Public Law 114-137). In 2023, four agencies shared seven hiring actions, enabling another 93 pooled hiring selections to be made across nine agencies. To build on this proof of concept, HX is positioned to identify and elevate clusters of agencies with similar talent needs and provide them consultative support to dramatically scale cross-agency hiring. Work completed in 2023 is just the beginning of a significant reorientation in Federal hiring. HX will continue integrating feedback and lessons-learned from agencies to improve, scale, and institutionalize pooled hiring.

The Administration continues its work to improve how agencies vet their civilian, military, and contractor personnel. During 2023, the Administration launched new training standards for background investigators and adjudicators, authorized the expansion of continuous vetting beyond national security sensitive personnel, and continued to transition from legacy software to the eApp platform, a more user-friendly and integrated approach for individuals entering the personnel vetting process. The 2025 Budget provides support for agencies to drive further improvements as directed in the Trusted Workforce 2.0 Implementation Strategy. Among other goals, agencies will continue to enroll their non-sensitive personnel into continuous vetting, expand data collection for enhanced performance metrics, update training and internal processes to reflect reform progress, and adopt additional personnel vetting shared services.

There is still work ahead to continue to make Federal hiring more nimble, flexible, and user-friendly. One new opportunity is by easing conversion pathways for term employees. Term employees are current public servants engaged on fixed duration assignments, but agencies are generally unable to convert them to permanent positions. Instead, they must apply for competitive service roles with no additional status beyond the general public despite their experience and the investments agencies have made in their development. One model to address this is the Land Management Workforce Flexibility Act of 2015 (Public Law 114-47), which enabled agencies to more easily convert land management employees who were initially hired through competitive hiring processes and have strong performance assessments into permanent roles, securing a key tool to recruit and retain talent.

Reaching Talent in New Places

The Administration continues to identify new strategies to reach talent outside of traditional recruiting methods. One such example is the Administration's ongoing work to reimagine the Federal Executive Board (FEB) program. The Budget secures resources to complete the strategic shift, known as FEB Forward, that began with the 60th anniversary of the FEB program in 2021. These resources will build on key activities completed in 2023, including:

- establishing a tri-governance structure between OPM, OMB, and GSA to provide guidance for the program's rejuvenated vision, structure, and strategic objectives;
- transferring all FEB staff from an array of Agency sponsors into a single, coordinated program office at OPM with a stable, centralized funding model;
- onboarding an SES Executive Director to lead the program; and
- reorganizing FEBs into regions, each managed by a GS-15 Regional Director, ensuring comprehensive national coverage.

Expanding FEB coverage areas and resources will allow FEB members and staff to maintain essential engagement with local Federal agencies to assist in sharing talent needs and to channel these insights to the center of Government to inform workforce strategy. In support of this aim, FEB leaders are designing a professional development fellowship, modeled after the State Department's Diplomat in Residence Program, through which Federal employees can be detailed to a FEB office to drive strategic outreach to colleges and universities, build new talent pipelines, and serve as Federal ambassadors across the Nation.

Even as departments and agencies collaborate to broaden their recruitment through pooled hiring and shared certificates, the Federal Government also needs the flexibility to be targeted and tactical in filling jobs in a specific location. One fruitful opportunity is examining public notice requirements. Currently, Agencies are required to post job opportunities nationally, resulting in an applicant pool spread throughout the United States for a duty station in a specific geography. Candidates may overstate their willingness to relocate, which increases the costs and timeline to fill a vacancy. The planned 2024 updates to the Pathways Program regulations would allow Agencies to enhance targeted recruitment for internships and recent graduates by using a focused USAJOBS custom posting, and lessons from this change may serve to provide direction for broader adoption.

Further, the Government is reaching new pools of talent by embracing the economy-wide trend toward hiring on the basis of skills, which will allow Americans without traditional four-year degrees to demonstrate their qualification for Federal roles while also improving tightness of fit between new hires and their work. The Administration favors a flexible approach to add skills-based methods to Federal Government hiring alongside existing authorities. In September 2023, OPM released a *skills-based hiring handbook* to help agencies incorporate a skills lens into Federal hiring, drawing on surveys of 90,000 Federal employees from more than 300 job series. OMB and OPM will work with agencies to target adoption of skills-based hiring in high-need occupational categories. Where agencies continue to use specific educational credentials in hiring, they must be thoughtful to avoid setting overly onerous or excessive requirements that do not clearly link to the work that the role requires.

Putting it all Together in Talent Surges

Over the last two years, the Administration coordinated among seven departments and agencies to drive surge hiring for more than 90 key occupations needed to implement the IIJA, including engineers, scientists, project managers, IT and HR specialists, and construction managers. The Federal Government hired 3,000 IIJA-targeted positions in fiscal year 2022, exceeded its fiscal year 2023 goal with over 3,400 selections, and has hired an additional 394 positions in the first quarter of fiscal year 2024—totaling 6,877 selections Government-wide to date.

Building on this experience and leveraging the suite of tools launched under the PMA, the Administration is launching an AI, Cyber, and Tech Hiring Surge. In August 2023, the Administration released its National Cyber Workforce and Education Strategy, which includes a pillar focused on strengthening Federal cyber capacity co-led by OMB and the Office of the National Cyber Director. Additionally, OPM has transmitted to the Congress for its consideration a package of legislative proposals, developed in concert with OMB and ONCD, to strengthen the personnel system for cyber professionals that includes a new classification and pay system, enhanced flexibility for agencies in selecting candidates for cyber positions, and other policies to increase the Federal Government's competitiveness as an employer. In October, the President signed Executive Order 14110, "Safe, Secure, and Trustworthy Development and Use of Artificial Intelligence." Executive Order 14110 commits to rapidly hiring AI and AI-enabling talent through a whole-of-Government collaboration including OMB, the White House Office of Science and Technology Policy (OSTP), the United States Digital Service (USDS), and OPM.

Agencies collaborating to advance these critical Administration priorities are deploying the practices launched under the PMA. Investments in human capital data tools—especially the MCO Dashboard and OPM's new authenticated Cyber Dashboard—are proving essential to assessing the scope of Government-wide hiring and identifying agencies with overlapping needs for proactive collaboration. The Tech-to-Gov initiative, a workstream of the Federal Cyber Workforce Working Group that is supporting Executive Order 14110, has held two virtual career fairs coinciding with OPM-led pooled hiring actions to attract technology professionals and channel them into jobs. To integrate lessons learned from engagement with jobseekers, agencies are developing shared plain-language, market-oriented position descriptions and titles to ensure that applicants can understand how their experience aligns with Federal needs.

Strategy 2: Make every Federal job a good job, where all employees are engaged, supported, heard, and empowered, with opportunities to learn, grow, join a union and have an effective voice in their workplaces through their union, and thrive throughout their careers

The Administration believes that a constructive employer-employee relationship is essential to sustaining a Federal workforce that delivers for Americans. From Day One, the Administration committed to rebuilding this relationship by making critical investments in its people and its workplaces.

These investments in recent years are paying dividends. The 2023 installment of OPM's annual Federal Employee Viewpoints Survey (FEVS) found that employee engagement tied a five-year high of 72 percent positive overall, and improvements continued across several key metrics. Employees' perception of the integrity of leadership (Leaders Lead) increased two percentage points to 61 percent. Employees' feelings of motivation and competency in the workplace (Intrinsic Work Experience) increased one percentage point to 74 percent. The factor measuring trust, respect, and support between employees and their supervisors remained at a high of 80 percent positive.

Led by OPM, agencies are retooling their approach to employee wellness programming including Employee Assistance Programs designed to support Federal employees through a wide range of wellbeing challenges.

As part of the growing culture of human capital data, in September 2023, OPM released a new FEVS Dashboard to CFO Act agencies to help them leverage the rich insights from the FEVS survey. The OPM FEVS Dashboard is a dynamic and user-friendly data visualization tool that allows Agency human capital professionals to review year-by-year trends and outliers, surface promising practices, and provide leadership with actionable insights on key indicators related to organizational health and performance. OPM will expand dashboard access to all FEVS participating agencies in 2024.

Pay and Benefits

The Budget reflects an average pay increase of 2.0 percent for civilian employees. This increase builds on the average pay increases of 5.2 percent for 2024, 4.6 percent for 2023, and 2.7 percent for 2022. It illustrates the Administration's continued strong commitment to the civil service, reflecting the need to attract the talent necessary to serve Americans and recognizing the fiscal constraints Federal agencies face.

In addition to year-to-year pay increases, the Administration is pursuing structural reforms to enhance the competitiveness of the Federal pay system. The Administration is committed to addressing the challenges caused by long-standing career Senior Executive Service and higher-graded General Schedule (GS) pay compression, as well as blue collar Federal Wage grade pay limitations. Addressing pay compression is a critical component of attracting and retaining experienced talent in roles with significant market competition. The Administration has identified several potential responses, and looks forward to working with the Congress to advance them to ensure that the Federal Government has the targeted tools needed to secure a skilled workforce. These potential responses include: increasing Executive Schedule official rates (while maintaining the senior political appointee pay freeze), which are tethered to SES, GS, and other senior-level employee pay caps, and modifying how the rates are adjusted each year; removing current ceilings in the Federal Wage System (FWS) wage schedules and establishing a statutory minimum for annual pay rate adjustments; repealing the aggregate pay rate limitation that caps the total amount of Title 5 allowances, differentials, bonuses awards, and other similar payments an employee may receive in a calendar year; and raising the special rate limitation for certain categories of employees to provide competitive salaries, particularly for cyber, STEM, and healthcare professions. The Administration also continues to support targeted, strategic use of a variety of pay flexibilities, such as special salary rate requests and recruitment, relocation, and retention incentives, to meet talent goals. Several of these elements are reflected in the cyber workforce legislative proposal discussed above. Additionally, OPM will be working with agencies in 2024 on targeted pay flexibilities to support the Federal cyber and specialized technology workforce.

The Administration is continuing to carefully track Federal civilian pay and incentives in comparison to comparable roles in the private sector and will work to mitigate attrition risk within the existing workforce. For example, in 2023, OPM issued proposed regulations to provide agencies with access to higher payment limitations for recruitment and relocation incentives without requesting approval from OPM. Table 14-4 summarizes total pay and benefit costs. Chart 14-1 illustrates the long-term trends between the Federal and private sector pay rates. The differential between Federal civilian pay and private sector pay has expanded in the past three decades over this period, creating attrition risk within the existing workforce and reducing the competitiveness of Federal jobs.

The Federal Employees Health Benefits (FEHB) Program offered 157 plan options in 2024 for 8.2 million Federal civilian employees, annuitants, and their families, as well as certain tribal employees and their families. OPM's Retirement Services processed almost 100,000 new retirement cases and about 27,000 survivor claims. Average processing time for new retirement cases dropped from 89 days in October 2022 to 69 days in November 2023. The new retirement case inventory in November 2023 (15,826) is the lowest it has been since December 2017.

Civil Service Diversity, Equity, Inclusion, and Accessibility

Since the 2021 release of Executive Order 14035, "Diversity, Equity, Inclusion, and Accountability in the Federal Workforce," it has been the policy of the Administration that the Federal Government be a model for DEIA where all employees are treated with dignity and respect. Throughout 2023, agencies have been driving implementation of strategic and customized Agency action plans to drive forward Executive Order 14035's core goals, with coordination from the Chief Diversity Officers Executive Council, launched in 2022.

To track progress in this work, in 2022, OPM updated the FEVS to include a DEIA Index. In 2023, 71 percent of respondents reported positive perceptions of Agency practices related to DEIA, an increase of two percentage points from the DEIA score of 69 percent in baseline year 2022. All four distinct factors (DEIA) increased for 2023. OPM is leveraging this Index to further strengthen the growing suite of workforce data tools through a new DEIA Dashboard launched in April 2023. The DEIA Dashboard, available to all 24 CFO Act agencies, is helping agencies implement DEIA-focused programs, practices, and policies while improving data collection, use, and sharing.

Looking ahead, OPM will continue to release the *DEIA Annual Report* to provide a recurring snapshot of the diversity of the Federal workforce and to highlight accomplishments aligned to the Government-wide Strategic Plan to Advance DEIA in the Federal Workforce. Additionally, to advance pay equity in Government-wide pay systems, in 2024, OPM issued final regulations that prohibit agencies from relying on a candidate's non-Federal salary history when setting initial pay.

OPM data from September 2023 provides a snapshot of the Federal civilian workforce. Civilian employees self-identified as 59.5 percent White; 18.4 percent Black; 10.1 percent Hispanic of all races; 6.8 percent Asian/Pacific Islander; 1.6 percent Native American/Alaskan Native; and 2.2 percent more than one race. Men comprise 54.2 percent of all permanent Federal employees, and women represent 45.8 percent, which is up from 44.1 percent in September 2020. Veterans make up 28.5 percent of the Federal workforce, which is significantly higher than the percentage in the private sector non-agricultural workforce. One-fifth of all Federal employees self-identify as having a disability, which includes 2.2 percent who possess a "targeted disability," such as blindness. See Table 14-5 for trends in these categories since 2016.

The Federal workforce has an average age of 47 years. Over 28 percent of employees are older than 55, while 8.7 percent of employees are younger than 30, a modest increase from 8.4 percent in September 2020. Chart 14-6 illustrates the Federal Government's consistently higher average age than the private sector, and Chart 14-2 shows a widening gap between the older and younger worker cohorts at the 24 CFO Act agencies since 2007. This gap is especially pronounced in some career fields, such as information technology, as illustrated in Chart 14-3. The decline in the Federal workforce under the age of 30 became more acute after 2010, when Federal internships and hiring programs for recent graduates became subject to new restrictions. The Administration's proposed updates to the Pathways Program regulations, discussed above in Strategy 1, seek to enhance the opportunities to bring early career talent into the Federal workforce.

Chart 14-1. Federal vs. Private pay differential (1980 normalized to 0)

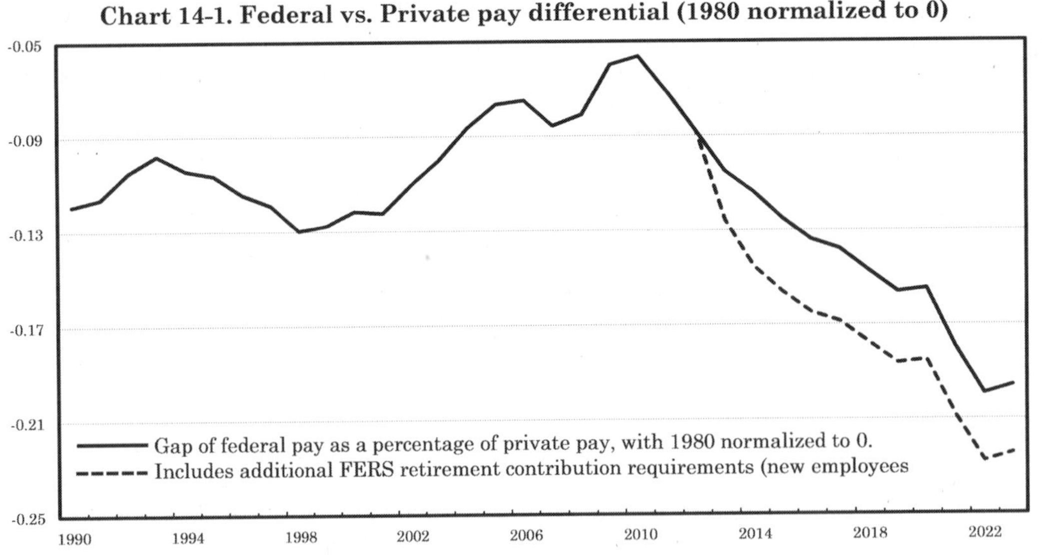

For newly hired federal employees, FERS contributions increased 2.3pp for employees hired in 2013 and an additional 1.3pp for employees hired in 2014 or after.

Sources: Public Laws, Executive Orders, Office of Personnel Management, OPM Memoranda from federal websites, Congressional Budget Office, and Bureau of Labor Statistics.
Notes: Federal pay is for civilians and includes base and locality pay. Private pay is measured by the Employment Cost Index wages and salaries, private industry workers series.

CHART 14-2. Potential Retirees to Younger than 30 Employees, Federal Workforce (CFO Act Agencies)

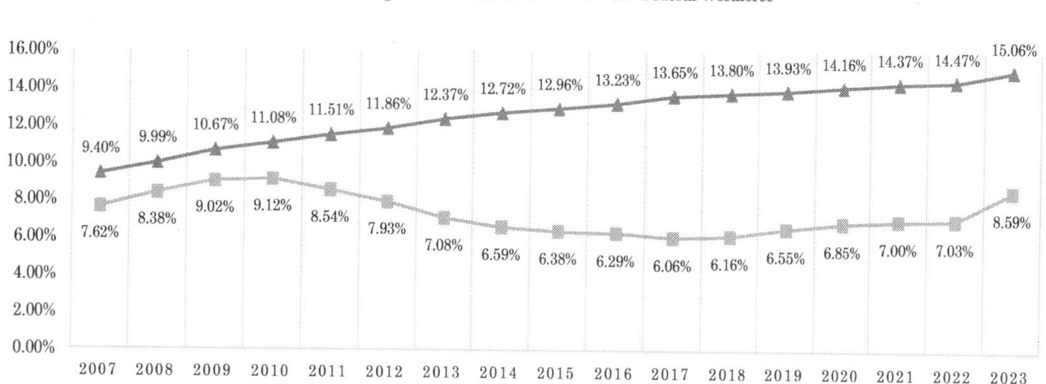

Source: FedScope FY 2007-2023 (Annual September Employment Cube)
Data Filter: Job Series excludes nulls, Work Schedule includes only "F", Work status includes only Non-Season Full-Time Permanent, Age Cohort excludes less than 20 and unspecified, 24 CFO Act Agencies Only
Data Range: FY 2007-2023, Age Cohorts 20-29, 60+

Chart 14-3. Potential Retirees to Younger than 30 Employees, Federal IT Workforce vs. Federal Workforce (24 CFO Act Agencies)

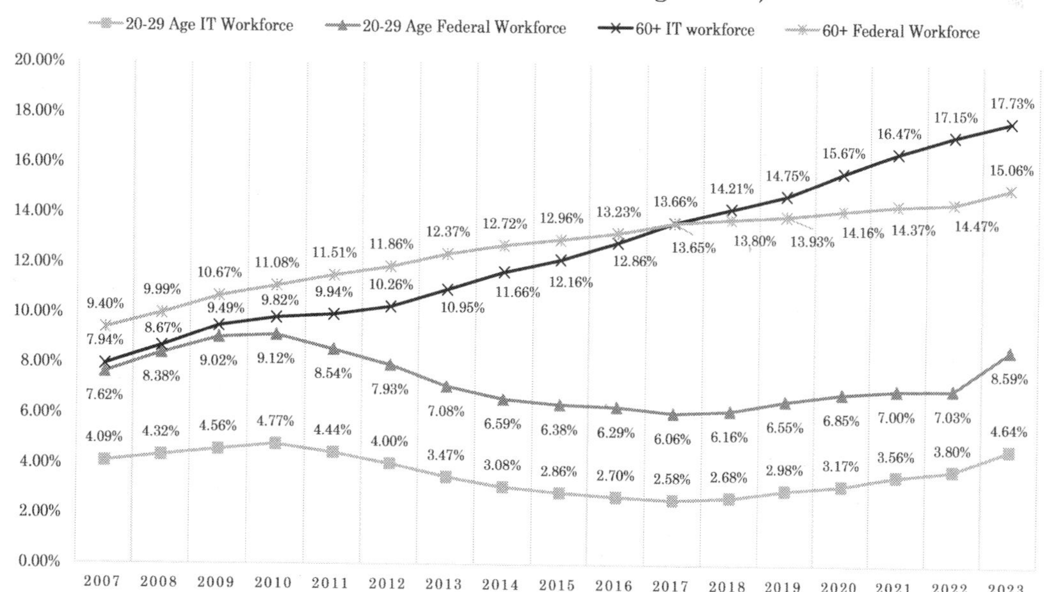

Source: FedScope FY 2007-2023 (Annual September Employment Cube)
Data Filter: Job Series excludes nulls, Work Schedule includes only "F", Work status includes only Non-Season Full-Time Permanent, Age Cohort excludes less than 20 and unspecified, IT Workforce is 2210 occupational series, 24 CFO Act Agencies Only
Data Range: FY 2007-2023, Age Cohorts 20-29, 60+

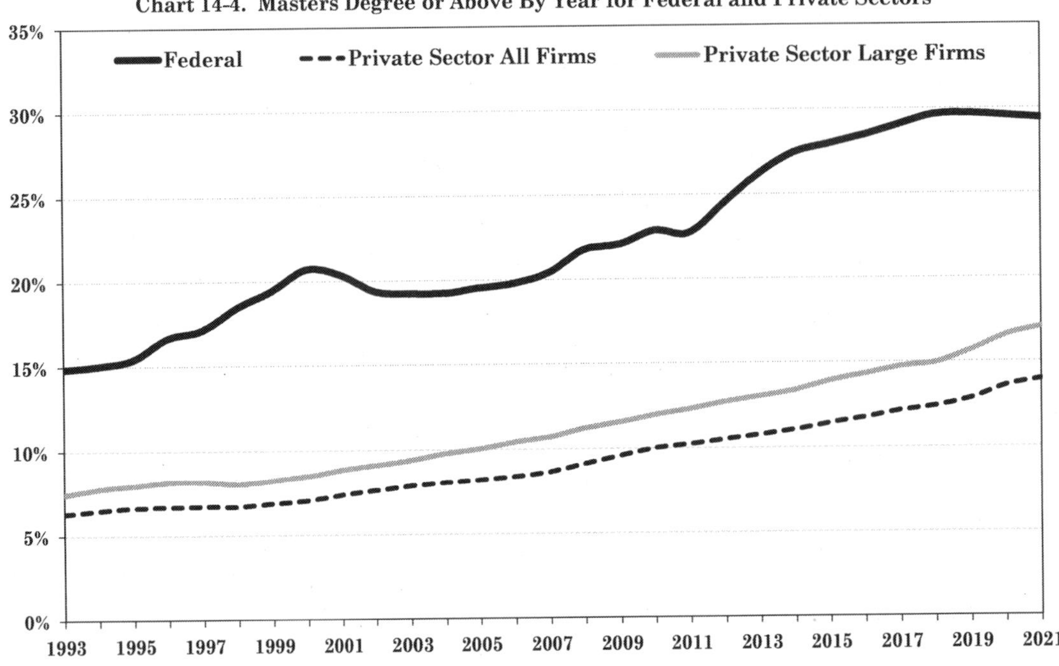

Source: 1992-2023 Current Population Survey, IPUMS-CPS, University of Minnesota, www.ipums.org.
Notes: Federal excludes the military and Postal Service, but includes all other Federal workers. Private Sector excludes the self-employed. Neither category includes State and local government workers. Large firms have at least 1,000 workers. This analysis is limited to full-time, full-year workers, i.e. those with at least 1,500 annual hours of work and presents three-year averages.

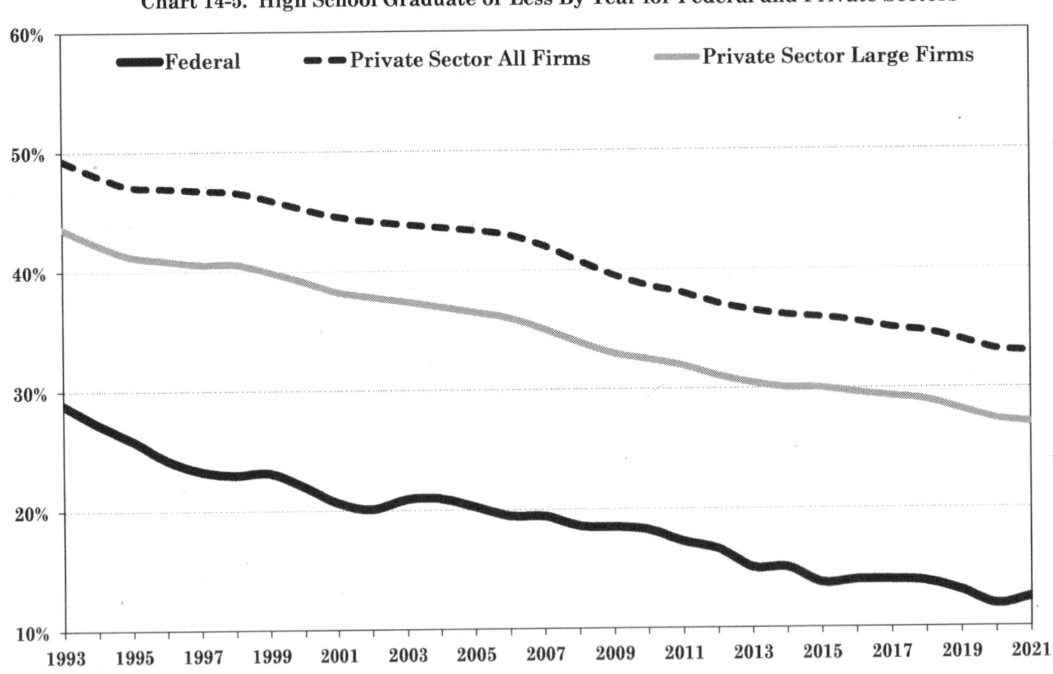

Source: 1992-2023 Current Population Survey, IPUMS-CPS, University of Minnesota, www.ipums.org.
Notes: Federal excludes the military and Postal Service, but includes all other Federal workers. Private Sector excludes the self-employed. Neither category includes State and local government workers. Large firms have at least 1,000 workers. This analysis is limited to full-time, full-year workers, i.e. those with at least 1,500 annual hours of work and presents three-year averages.

Table 14–4. PERSONNEL PAY AND BENEFITS

(In millions of dollars)

Description	2023 Actual	2024 Estimate	2025 Estimate	Change: 2024 to 2025	
				Dollars	Percent
Civilian Personnel Costs:					
Executive Branch (excluding Postal Service):					
Pay	242,139	264,136	275,123	10,987	4.2%
Benefits	116,817	120,092	127,869	7,777	6.5%
Subtotal	358,956	384,228	402,992	18,764	4.9%
Postal Service:					
Pay	43,309	43,878	44,434	556	1.3%
Benefits	15,674	17,256	17,595	339	2.0%
Subtotal	58,983	61,134	62,029	895	1.5%
Legislative Branch:					
Pay	2,840	3,045	3,271	226	7.4%
Benefits	1,091	1,186	1,303	117	9.9%
Subtotal	3,931	4,231	4,574	343	8.1%
Judicial Branch:					
Pay	3,736	4,223	4,431	208	4.9%
Benefits	1,388	1,486	1,515	29	2.0%
Subtotal	5,124	5,709	5,946	237	4.2%
Total, Civilian Personnel Costs	426,994	455,302	475,541	20,239	4.4%
Military Personnel Costs					
Department of Defense--Military Programs:					
Pay	118,168	123,447	129,616	6,169	5.0%
Benefits	62,314	70,892	70,104	-788	-1.1%
Subtotal	180,482	194,339	199,720	5,381	2.8%
All other Executive Branch uniform personnel:					
Pay	4,234	4,378	4,733	355	8.1%
Benefits	746	807	852	45	5.6%
Subtotal	4,980	5,185	5,585	400	7.7%
Total, Military Personnel Costs	185,462	199,524	205,305	5,781	2.9%
Grand total, personnel costs	**612,456**	**654,826**	**680,846**	**26,020**	**4.0%**
ADDENDUM					
Former Civilian Personnel:					
Pensions	106,353	112,392	116,763	4,371	3.9%
Health benefits	14,495	15,236	16,182	946	6.2%
Life insurance	43	43	44	1	2.3%
Subtotal	120,891	127,671	132,989	5,318	4.2%
Former Military Personnel:					
Pensions	76,240	79,390	82,045	2,655	3.3%
Health benefits	12,044	11,509	11,293	-216	-1.9%
Subtotal	88,284	90,899	93,338	2,439	2.7%
Total, Former Personnel	209,175	218,570	226,327	7,757	3.5%

Table 14–5. HIRING TRENDS SINCE 2016

Federal Civilian Workforce	SEPT 2016	SEPT 2017	SEPT 2018	SEPT 2019	SEPT 2020	SEPT 2021	SEPT 2022	SEPT 2023
Total Federal Workforce Count[1]	2,097,038	2,087,747	2,100,802	2,132,812	2,181,106	2,191,011	2,180,296	2,258,821
Average Age (in years)	47.1	47.2	47.1	47.1	47.0	47.0	47.0	46.9
Total Under 30	7.88%	7.55%	7.76%	8.07%	8.39%	8.33%	8.30%	8.74%
Total 55 and Over	28.16%	28.79%	28.99%	29.17%	29.11%	28.98%	28.70%	28.29%
Male	56.70%	56.60%	56.44%	56.27%	55.90%	55.56%	55.03%	54.19%
Female	43.29%	43.38%	43.52%	43.72%	44.10%	44.44%	44.97%	45.81%
All Disabilities	9.46%	10.49%	12.38%	13.89%	15.33%	17.01%	18.37%	20.45%
Targeted Disabilities[2]	1.10%	2.69%	2.66%	2.61%	2.56%	2.52%	2.54%	2.21%
Veteran	29.33%	29.43%	29.34%	29.15%	28.78%	28.37%	29.35%	28.45%
American Indian or Alaskan Native	1.71%	1.69%	1.66%	1.63%	1.62%	1.62%	1.62%	1.57%
Asian	5.86%	5.99%	6.10%	6.01%	6.17%	6.49%	6.70%	6.80%
Black/African American	17.91%	18.15%	18.21%	18.02%	18.06%	18.19%	18.25%	18.44%
Native Hawaiian or Pacific Islander	0.49%	0.51%	0.52%	0.52%	0.54%	0.56%	0.57%	0.58%
More Than One Race	1.47%	1.60%	1.73%	1.82%	1.91%	2.01%	2.11%	2.24%
Hispanic/Latino (H/L)	8.46%	8.75%	9.08%	9.14%	9.33%	9.53%	9.75%	10.10%
White	64.04%	63.26%	62.63%	61.22%	60.86%	61.20%	60.53%	59.54%

Source: U.S. Office of Personnel Management

[1] Total count varies slightly from other sources because of date and data collection method.

[2] These totals are included in the "All Disabilities" category.

Civil Service Protection

The Administration remains committed to protecting, empowering, and rebuilding the career Federal workforce that has served the Nation since the passage of the Pendleton Act in 1883. Shortly after inauguration, the President issued Executive Order 14003, "Protecting the Federal Workforce," revoking the previous administration's creation of a Schedule F excepted service category that undermined the foundation of a merit-based civil service and the core protections for career civil servants. The Administration has repeatedly supported codifying the protections provided by Executive Order 14003 in statute and will continue to work with the Congress on this proposal. Further, in 2024, OPM anticipates finalizing new regulations to reinforce and clarify longstanding civil service protections and merit systems principles. OPM's proposed regulations would protect employees from involuntary loss of their earned civil service protections for reasons unrelated to poor performance or conduct. The regulations will interpret "confidential, policy-determining, policy-making, or policy-advocating" and "confidential or policy-determining" to describe positions of the character generally excepted from civil service protections to mean noncareer, political appointments. They would set additional procedures for moving positions from the competitive to excepted service or within the excepted service in order to support good administration, add transparency, and provide employees with a right of appeal to the Merit Systems Protection Board under certain circumstances. Americans deserve a Federal workforce selected and retained for its merit, skill, and experience not favoritism or political loyalties.

Strategy 3: Reimagine and build a roadmap to the future of Federal work informed by lessons from the pandemic and nationwide workforce and workplace trends

During the COVID-19 pandemic, hundreds of thousands of Federal employees worked countless hours, in-person and on-site, to continue delivering the vast Federal services that the American people count on despite the risk present in the community. Over the course of 2022 and 2023, agencies brought nearly all other employees back to their regular pre-pandemic duty stations, by carefully managing space, resources, mission needs, and public health guidance. As of January 2024, in excess of 80 percent of Federal work is performed in-person at employees' assigned job sites, either at a Federal facility or at postings around the Nation as required to fulfill Agency missions.

In the wake of the pandemic, Federal agencies continue to evaluate their work environment policies and build toward a durable, long-term work environment posture that maintains a focus on delivering results for Americans and reflects new rhythms of work across the economy that have necessitated a thoughtful redesign of norms around hybrid work. In general, agencies are moving towards a posture whereby hybrid teams are working in-person at least half of the time, on average. This balanced approach recognizes the vital importance of in-person collaboration, while still ensuring flexibilities are in place so that the Government can attract and retain top talent. It engages with the vast diversity of occupations across the Federal Government, recognizing that work modality and duty station vary immensely across the workforce. The Budget assumes resources to complete this transition in a thoughtful, intentional, data-informed manner. It will build on current investments such as OPM's free "Thriving in a Hybrid Work Environment" training that was completed by more than 25,000 Federal employees.

To ensure that agencies continue to improve organizational health and organizational performance in a post-pandemic work environment and sustain a singular focus on service delivery, OMB released OMB Memorandum M-23-15, Measuring, Monitoring, and Improving Organizational Health and Organizational Performance in the Context of Evolving Agency Work Environments, in April 2023. Memorandum M-23-15 included a call for agencies to "substantially increase meaningful in-person work at Federal offices, particularly at headquarters and equivalents" where hybrid work is mostly concentrated. Agencies were directed to develop updated Work Environment Plans over the summer 2023 that considered how best to accomplish this given the unique circumstances, missions, and customers of each Agency. OMB has continued to monitor Agency implementation and collaborate with agencies on areas of common concern in executing this shift, including commuter benefits, reopening cafeterias, modernizing workspaces, human capital data standards, and other implementation components.

Work environment is one component of organizational health and performance frameworks (explored further in Chapter 12, "Delivering a High-Performance Government," of this volume), and the Administration continues to make investments to hone work environment policies using the same research and evidence-based approach that drives the broader framework. The Administration has engaged the National Academy of Public Administration to expand on its 2018 report, Strengthening Organizational Health and Performance in Government. Additionally, OPM is conducting and disseminating three research studies on the future of work, assessing the effect of telework, remote work, and hybrid work on hiring, engagement, and retention, as well as a project to improve accessibility of organizational health and organizational performance data for Agency leaders through toolkits and dashboards.

The Administration has made critical investments to ensure that Federal employees have the tools to succeed in this new equilibrium. In March 2023, OPM released a memorandum on "Advancing Future of the Workforce Policies and Practices to Support Mission Delivery," which outlined a strategic vision for the future of the Federal workforce that is inclusive, agile, and engaged, and possesses the right skills to enable mission delivery. It identifies five priority areas for which OPM will provide support to agencies to realize the future state: Policy and Resources, Research and Evaluation, Training and Technical Assistance, Data Analytics, and Stakeholder Engagement. To do this, OPM has detailed the key steps for the Agency action strategies into a Future of the Workforce Playbook, which provides implementation strategies for new innovations and existing authorities and practices that have not been fully utilized.

Additionally, the Administration is investing in innovative, next-generation workspaces to support agencies as they build toward durable norms informed by the lessons of the pandemic. In 2023, the General Services Administration (GSA) launched the Workplace Innovation Lab to share best practices and spur creative thinking and cross-agency collaboration related to the workplace of the future. The lab offers a variety of workspaces, collaboration spaces, and conference rooms, with deeply integrated technology assets and modular flexibility, all in a Federal building equipped with an access control system and on-site security personnel. In its first nine months of operation, employees from 13 different agencies booked more than 22,000 hours of reservations. Through careful measurement of customers' work patterns and regular customer surveying, GSA is using the lab to generate insights to inform the design of Federal workspaces throughout the Nation.

Further, GSA has launched six Federal coworking test sites in Tacoma, WA; San Francisco, CA; Denver, CO; Kansas City, MO; Chicago, IL; and Philadelphia, PA. These move-in ready spaces complement existing Agency office space, provide a venue for proactive cross-agency collaboration in regions, and illustrate opportunities for cost-savings. GSA also released an updated menu of contracts and solutions to support Agency planning for hybrid work. As GSA continues to test and assess design, technologies, and operations, it will diffuse leading practice and help position the Government as a competitive employer with a workplace model that ensures quality service delivery.

Additional information on the Administration's efforts to inform workforce and workplace policies through advancing implementation of organizational health and organizational performance frameworks is discussed in the "Delivering a High-Performance Government" chapter of this volume.

Strategy 4: Build the personnel system and support required to sustain the Federal Government as a model employer able to effectively deliver on a broad range of agency missions

Strengthening the HR workforce is essential to unlocking the full value of PMA and other workforce initiatives. The Government's 47,000 HR professionals are the "gateway to public service," and a strong, effective, and strategically-oriented HR workforce is essential to meeting all other workforce goals. The Budget supports investments in the HR workforce and in OPM to realize this critical strategy to embed the work of the PMA across the Government for years to come.

Inattention to HR workforce development and resources is reflected in low satisfaction scores from HR customers. GSA's annual Mission Support Customer Satisfaction survey consistently measures satisfaction with human capital services as ranking last among enabling functions (Financial Management, Acquisitions, and IT) from 2018 to 2022. Attrition and difficulty with hiring has compounding effects because the absence of HR staff adds time and complexity to the hiring process to backfill HR positions and other critical occupations. To reverse this trend, the Administration is making targeted investments to ensure that Agency HR workforces possess the technical acumen and strategic vision to deliver on urgent hiring and management needs.

To expand foundational HR training and work towards Government-wide certification standards, OPM has created an executive position to coordinate Federal workforce development efforts. OPM has provided new no-cost trainings to HR practitioners including technical assistance modules aimed at improving Delegated Examining certification pass rates and trainings to help practitioners implement skills-based hiring. OPM has begun to develop web-based career tools for HR practitioners including an HR career growth website. To expand the recruitment pipeline, the Chief Human Capital Officers (CHCO) Council has developed intern and early career development program concepts focused on Federal human capital management processes and requirements. Agencies are coordinating on efforts to build career paths in the Federal HR workforce by drafting a new career pathing model and launching a career pathing pilot at nine agencies. Driven by data and evidence, this focus on the HR workforce is building momentum with Government-wide efforts to strengthen human capital results for the whole of Government.

The Administration is supporting investments in OPM to meet these human capital needs. In the fall of 2023, OPM renamed its former Employee Services division as Workforce Policy and Innovation to reflect the Agency's elevation of its Government-wide, strategic human capital role and to transform its Agency HR policy and operations support roles through improved customer engagement and increased awareness of critical Agency perspectives. This change aligns with OPM's 2022-2026 Strategic Plan (Strategy 4) and the 2021 National Academy of Public Administration (NAPA) Report on "Elevating Human Capital: Reframing the U.S. Office of Personnel Management's Leadership Imperative." This realignment brings together the newly established FEB Operations Center, the Hiring Experience (HX) group, and the planned Center for Innovation in Federal Talent designed to provide human capital management leadership to agencies through demonstration projects, pilots, and identification of leading practices across the Federal Government. Additionally, several human capital policy areas such as leadership development and training, workforce flexibilities, and workplace culture were re-mapped to best align with customer Agency needs and contemporary employer practices.

Now halfway through its Strategic Plan focused on transforming the Agency, OPM has continued to make marked progress in investing in its internal Agency enablers, like talent and skills, while also building new capabilities to better support the Federal workforce at large. OPM has created a stronger employee culture and experience, as evidenced through increased FEVS Employee Engagement results, while also on-boarding key senior executives to advance contemporary civil service talent practices. At the same time, OPM launched a Data Strategy and has delivered new customer experience enhancements from hiring innovations and products, new data dashboards, forward-leaning policy, and tools for employee and annuitant beneficiaries. OPM's transformation will continue to focus on growing OPM capabilities to provide a more seamless customer experience and delivering on the next wave of modernization initiatives.

Looking Ahead

In addition to some of the near-term actions the PMA implementation team and agencies have begun to tackle across the PMA strategy areas, the PMA's designating the Federal Workforce as its number one priority has brought a heightened level of attention and investment to long-standing and long-term Federal workforce challenges. Even as the Administration works to embed the leading practices advanced under the PMA in Agency operations, this work has surfaced a further set of strategic questions for the future of the Federal workforce.

Opportunity: How does Government define work responsibilities?

Even before the COVID-19 pandemic, workplaces were experiencing profound shifts in how work is defined and completed. Across the economy, barriers between traditional functions and divisions have eroded; workflow has become more collaborative and more integrated with technology; and new jobs are constantly appearing and rapidly becoming essential components of the enterprise. These changes are shaping expectations among employees, and employers are moving quickly to position themselves on the leading edge of their sectors. The COVID-19 pandemic served to accelerate some of these shifts and left many employers asking strategic questions around not only how work is defined but also employees' relationships to work and the workplace.

The Administration appreciates the need to respond nimbly and incorporate leading practices into workforce management. However, some of the broader shifts are incongruent with the Government's long-standing, traditional approach to classifying and describing work and occupations. OPM will launch a review, in coordination with agencies, that includes consideration of whether the General Schedule's formal classification of positions effectively and efficiently provides hiring managers and HR professionals with the ability to recruit and hire talent with the skills needed for the future. This level of responsiveness to future organizational needs is especially critical given the extreme diversity of roles in Federal service and the accelerating pace of changes in the private sector – including emerging roles in areas such as AI, post-quantum cryptography, virtual reality, and cybersecurity – and the need for the workforce to flex, adapt, and evolve around skills and taskings that will change over time. A sustained and strategic initiative will explore, identify, and incorporate skills-based competencies to create new or modify existing occupational series reflecting emerging needs.

In support of this shift, and in alignment with the broader skills-based objectives discussed above, the Administration will encourage agencies to advertise for jobs using plain language and market-relevant titles and position descriptions that connect with today's workforce without interpretation. This will provide greater clarity for jobseekers, allow the Government to compete directly with other sectors, and increase the accessibility of Federal employment to jobseekers without personal or network connections to current Federal employment. It can help current civil servants, managers, and the HR workforce thoughtfully align individual employees' responsibilities with the core missions of their Agency.

To help drive this effort forward, agencies can coordinate action by creating and updating work and position descriptions, as well as desirable aptitudes and skills, for newly-emerging and rapidly-evolving roles, and sharing these with peers in other agencies. For example, Executive Order 14110 tasks OPM and OMB, including the USDS, to collaborate to develop position descriptions for a variety of emerging AI roles (as well as roles that enable integration of AI and other technological advances) to relieve individual agencies of that responsibility and to support strong cross-agency alignment. The Federal Cyber Workforce Working Group, implementing the Federal components of the National Cyber Workforce and Education Strategy, is driving a similar activity for critical cyber roles. Even roles outside the technologist domain, such as permitting project manager, benefit from consistent, cross-agency alignment on responsibilities and duties.

Alongside improving classification, in order to compete for talent in the marketplace, the Government must build capacity to assess candidate's skills and aptitudes in meaningful ways that are tightly mapped to how it defines work. As Federal agencies move away from using applicant self-assessments, they must develop and share validated assessment processes more quickly so they can be embedded into the hiring process. Quality assessments, like those used for SME-QA or the Department of Homeland Security's Cybersecurity Talent Management System (CTMS), can be costly to develop and slow to validate, presenting a significant barrier to scale. Looking ahead, agencies must act in a coordinated manner to distribute costs and share effective assessments across hiring teams. Federal leaders should work collaboratively to explore opportunities to expand trusted assessment options, leverage leading practices from the broader marketplace, and build internal capacity to deploy them quickly. Further, Federal leaders may consider how to deploy automation or AI in the Federal HR arena, such as reviewing resumes or assessing skills, in coordination with broader policy and requirements. OMB is engaging across agencies implementing Executive Order 14110 to develop and socialize assessments for Federal AI roles as well as to explore automation with appropriate parameters and guardrails.

Federal agencies also must recognize that career development and advancement is an essential component of structuring work in an appealing and effective manner. In addition to support for professional development offerings in skills that are tightly aligned with Federal needs, Government must ensure that all Federal positions have thoughtful structural position management and career paths integrated into their workforce plans. As agencies develop new skills frameworks, for example, there are new opportunities to integrate skills maturity models and crosswalk with professional development investments to ensure that Federal employees have tools and pathways to grow their skills and deepen their contributions throughout their careers.

Opportunity: How can Government build internal capacity for recruiting and hiring the talent Americans need in every Agency?

Many of the key approaches advancing under the PMA—such as pooled hiring or shared data tools—are centralized activities. Ensuring that the momentum built through this PMA is sustained and embedded deeply in Agency operations and culture will require adoption of its practices by a highly decentralized group of Federal leaders. The Budget's sustained investments in Agency talent teams are already providing a critical bulwark in agencies, but Government must consider how to ensure that every Agency and Agency component has the internal capacity to apply new tools discussed in this chapter, integrate these practices through thoughtful change management, and drive strategic human capital planning.

The Federal Government's HR function needs to be more strategic and engaged at a leadership level on Agency-wide strategy and decision-making. Over the last 20 years, the senior HR professionals in private corporations have increasingly been elevated into strategic leadership roles. Similarly, HR professionals across the Government must be equipped to serve as true strategic partners in achieving each Agency's mission. OPM's HR Workforce Development proposal, discussed above under PMA Workforce Priority Strategy Four, is an important launching point in this work, and will build a new HR workforce competency framework leveraging lessons from successful efforts to elevate the procurement function in the past decade. As the HR Workforce Development proposal advances, Federal leaders may consider whether the current classification standards for HR roles are aligned with this elevated lens. Recognizing the critical role that an empowered and adept HR workforce has in meeting all of Government's human capital needs, it will be essential to build strong pipelines and upward career mobility to ensure that investments in the HR workforce become self-reinforcing.

In supporting and elevating the frontline HR workforce, there will be a growing imperative to integrate a user-focused, customer-service mindset as OPM, GSA, and other agencies continue to develop new tools, templates, guidance, and authorities for Agency use. The Administration's work to socialize and drive adoption of the growing suite of human capital dashboards from OPM and GSA discussed in this chapter is a strong illustration of this approach. Looking ahead, all such tools—new hiring authorities, assessments, data, templates, and best practices—should be thoughtfully designed for easy application by the HR workforce at the component and subcomponent level, with accessible guidance on when and how they should be used by other management and workforce enablers and decision-makers. Adopting this mindset will reinforce a core related goal: ensuring that a user-focused orientation pervades applicant experience as well.

As leaders work to raise the profile of the HR function in Government, HR leaders must be on the lookout for opportunities to integrate a strategic human capital lens into other functional domains. The CHCO Council is a crucial tool for cross-agency collaboration around workforce issues. Looking ahead, in addition to ensuring that CHCOs are partnering with other "C-suite" leaders in their agencies—such as Chief Information Officers, Chief Financial Officers, and Chief Data Officers—the CHCO Council as a body can also explore new opportunities to support the human capital management dimensions of the other CXO councils serving these roles. There may also be opportunities to align recurrent review processes by leveraging the Human Capital Operating Plan review process, to reinforce and better inform OMB's annual Strategic Reviews of Agency Strategic Plans.

Chart 14-6. Average Age by Year for Federal and Private Sectors

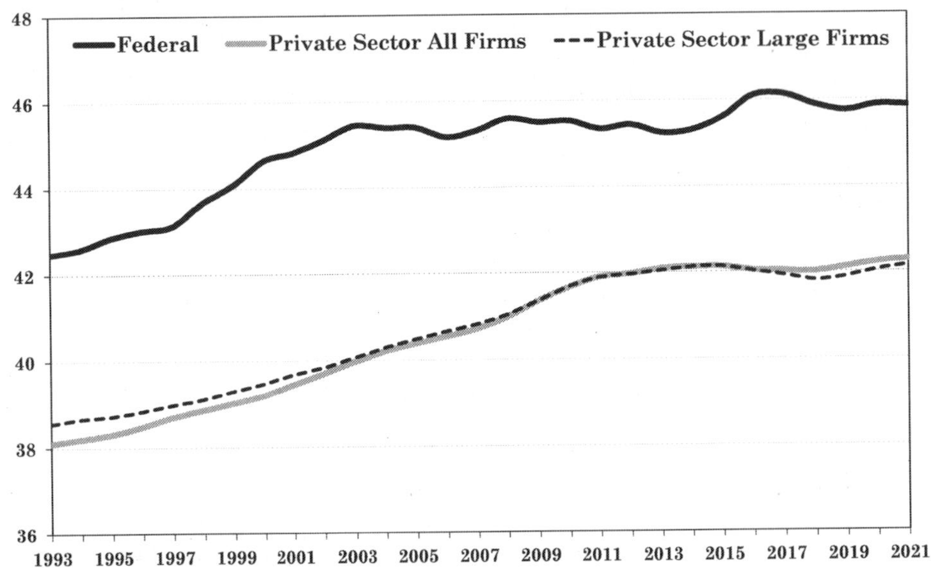

Source: 1992-2023 Current Population Survey, IPUMS-CPS, University of Minnesota, www.ipums.org.
Notes: Federal excludes the military and Postal Service, but includes all other Federal workers. Private Sector excludes the self-employed. Neither category includes State and local government workers. Large firms have at least 1,000 workers. This analysis is limited to full-time, full-year workers, i.e. those with at least 1,500 annual hours of work and presents three-year averages.

Chart 14-7. Government-wide On-Board U.S. Distribution, October 1978

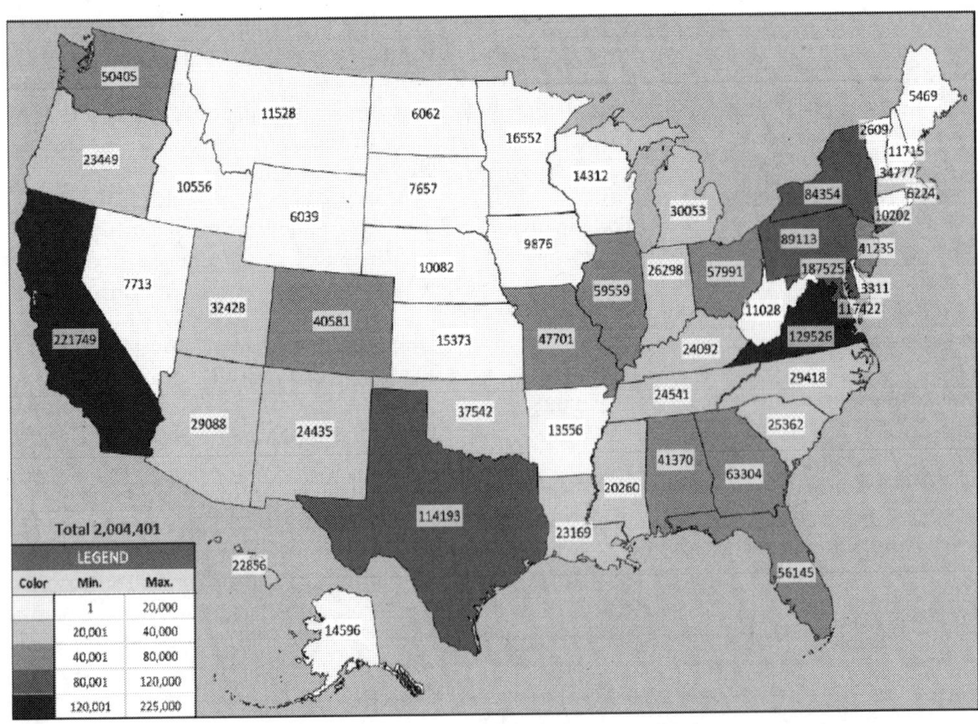

Source: Office of Personnel Management

Chart 14-8. Government-wide On-Board US Distribution, September 2023

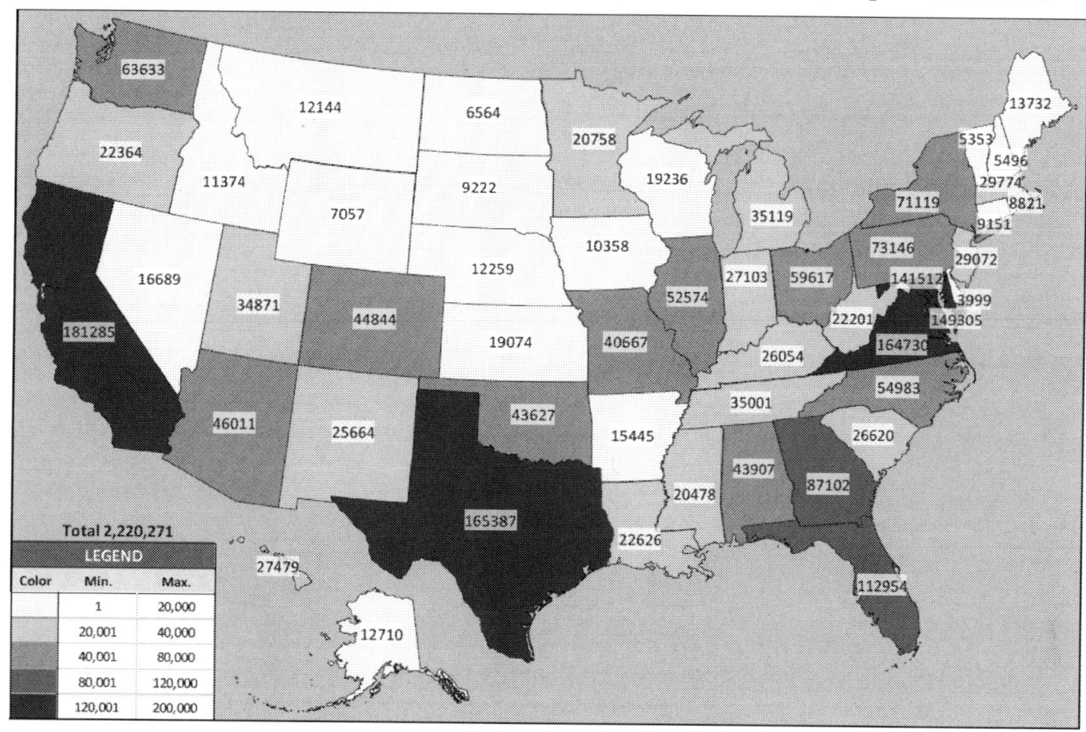

Source: Office of Personnel Management

Chart 14-9. The Changing General Schedule Workforce

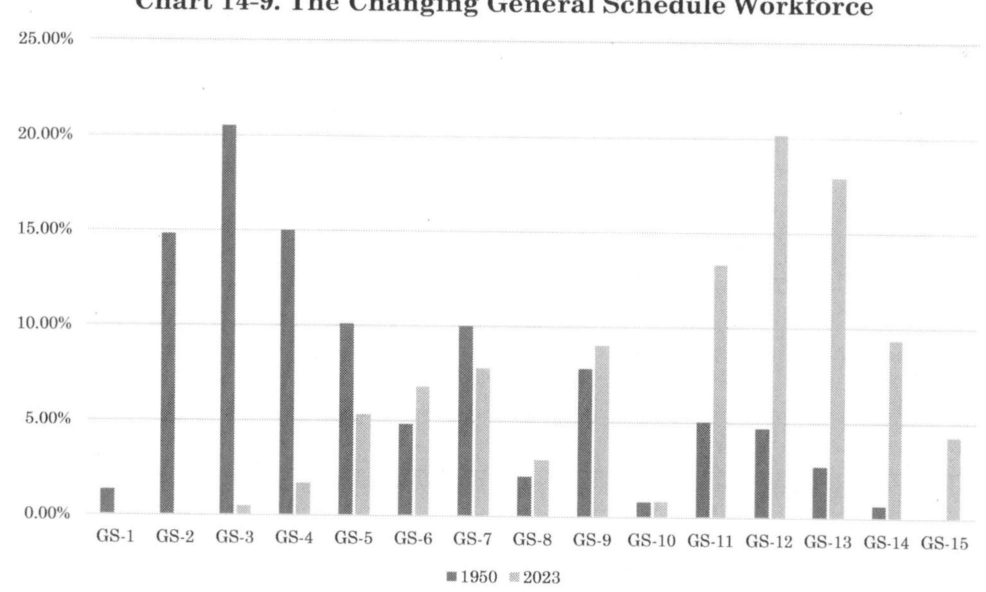

Source: Office of Personnel Management

15. INFORMATION TECHNOLOGY AND CYBERSECURITY FUNDING

Information Technology Priorities

Technology serves as a foundation of the Federal Government's ability to deliver on its mission. The Administration is leading the Federal enterprise on the technology issues of our time—stopping foreign intrusions into Federal agencies, balancing difficult trade-offs in digital identity and artificial intelligence, redefining security expectations for software and the cloud, and maximizing the impact of taxpayer dollars to drive digital transformation across the Government to deliver a better customer experience for the American people. The Budget supports launching tech policy that meets today's expectations and results in technology that is secure by design, allowing Federal agencies to deliver on their missions safely, reliably, and easily. The Administration is focused on understanding where agencies are on their information technology (IT) modernization journeys, determining the right investments to support secure technology integration and innovation, and planning when to implement these updates to ensure both year-over-year technological advances and progress against overarching agency timelines for achieving digital transformation. The Budget proposes spending $75 billion on IT at civilian agencies in 2025, which will be used to deliver simple, seamless, and secure Government services. The President's Budget also supports the implementation of Federal laws that enable agency technology planning, oversight, funding, and accountability practices, as well as Office of Management and Budget (OMB) guidance to agencies on the strategic use of IT to enable mission outcomes.

OMB continues to focus on five strategic priorities, all enabled by a strong Federal workforce. The priorities include:

Cybersecurity—Departments and agencies will continue to increase the safety and security of public services, implementing the requirements contained in *Executive Order 14028*, "Improving the Nation's Cybersecurity," the Federal Zero Trust Strategy, and the National Cyber Strategy.

To guide agencies in addressing these critical efforts in the 2025 Budget, OMB and the Office of the National Cyber Director jointly released *OMB Memorandum M-23-18*, Administration Cybersecurity Priorities for the FY 2025 Budget.

This memo directed Federal agencies to prioritize funding consistent with the five pillars outlined in the National Cybersecurity Strategy: defend critical infrastructure; disrupt and dismantle threat actors; shape market forces to drive security and resilience; invest in a resilient future; and forge international partnerships to pursue shared goals. Collectively, these efforts will support key efforts in the National Cyber Strategy and its implementation plan, and drive Strategic Objective 1.5, Modernize Federal Defenses.

Artificial Intelligence—Managing artificial intelligence (AI) technologies that present tremendous promise to improve public services and increase the efficiency of Federal Government operations. However, because the Federal Government makes decisions and takes actions that have profound impact on the public, agencies have a distinct responsibility to identify and manage AI risks because of the role they play in society. To seize the promise and manage the risks of AI, the Administration issued *Executive Order 14110*, "Safe, Secure, and Trustworthy Development and Use of Artificial Intelligence," and released a corresponding publicly-commented-on draft OMB policy on the use of AI in Federal agencies—the most significant set of actions any government has ever taken on AI safety, security, and trust. The Executive Order establishes new standards for AI safety and security, protects Americans' privacy, advances equity and civil rights, and stands up for consumers and workers. The Executive Order also promotes innovation and competition which advances American leadership around the world across these and a number of other critical facets of responsible AI. The President's Budget funds the implementation of these historic actions, through which the Federal Government will lead by example and provide a global model for the responsible use of AI.

IT Modernization—Adopting modern technologies, retiring legacy systems, employing methods of continuous improvement, and scaling them across Government, so that the Government can run more effectively and improve the delivery and reliability of trusted services. The President's Budget includes an additional $75 million for the Technology Modernization Fund (TMF), an innovative funding model that reimagines how the Government uses IT to deliver a simple, seamless, and secure digital experience to the American public. The TMF, a complement to the annual budget process, allows agencies to quickly access funding for critical IT modernization projects. Funds are invested in the most promising projects that have a high likelihood of success and a measurable impact on advancing key priorities, such as modernizing high priority systems, strengthening the cybersecurity of Federal agencies, and improving public-facing digital products and services. TMF investments are diverse and far-reaching, and reflect the Administration's strong commitment to improving the American public's interactions with the Government. Such investments have assisted veterans and their families by enabling access to digital service records and benefits; farmers and consumers by streamlining produce inspection to safeguard the food supply; and retirement and disability beneficiaries by securing systems that protect their personal information.

Table 15–1. ESTIMATED 2025 CIVILIAN FEDERAL IT SPENDING AND PERCENTAGE BY AGENCY
(In millions of dollars)

Agency	2025	Percent of Total
Department of Homeland Security	11,116	14.8%
Department of Health and Human Services	9,884	13.2%
Department of the Treasury	9,067	12.1%
Department of Veterans Affairs	8,833	11.8%
Department of Energy	5,511	7.3%
Department of Justice	4,446	5.9%
Department of Transportation	4,361	5.8%
Department of State	3,267	4.3%
Department of Agriculture	2,914	3.9%
Department of Commerce	2,893	3.9%
Social Security Administration	2,459	3.3%
National Aeronautics and Space Administration	2,171	2.9%
Department of the Interior	2,042	2.7%
Department of Education	1,690	2.2%
Department of Labor	953	1.3%
General Services Administration	888	1.2%
Department of Housing and Urban Development	539	0.7%
Environmental Protection Agency	439	0.6%
U.S. Agency for International Development	383	0.5%
Small Business Administration	328	0.4%
U.S. Army Corps of Engineers	252	0.3%
National Science Foundation	201	0.3%
Nuclear Regulatory Commission	186	0.2%
Office of Personnel Management	158	0.2%
National Archives and Records Administration	147	0.2%
Total	**75,128**	**100.0%**

This analysis excludes the Department of Defense.

The TMF is a catalyst to address technology modernization needs and show what's possible across Government – and to scale lessons learned.

Digital-First Public Experience—Delivering a simple, seamless, and secure experience to the American public that meets 21st century expectations. Digital is now the default way the public interacts with the Government and more than ever, digital experience is central to Federal agencies' mission delivery. The President's Budget reflects funding for multiyear implementation efforts to improve digital experiences per the requirements outlined in OMB Memorandum M-23-22, Delivering a Digital-First Public Experience, the 21st Century Integrated Digital Experience Act (Public Law 115-336), and Executive Order 14058, "Transforming Federal Customer Experience and Service Delivery to Rebuild Trust in Government." OMB Memorandum M-23-22, issued in September 2023, provides a robust policy framework for the next decade of digital modernization across Government and gives Federal agencies a roadmap for delivering online information and services that meet today's expectations. The policy guidance outlines analytics, accessibility, branding, content, design, search, and digitization as key pillars of digital experience. The President's Budget reflects funding across these pillars, with an emphasis on funding to deduplicate web content, modernize the front-end design of websites and digital services, and improve the accessibility of websites and digital services. OMB also released OMB Memorandum M-24-08, Strengthening Digital Accessibility and the Management of Section 508 of the Rehabilitation Act, which provides agencies with guidance on what further steps agencies can take to improve digital accessibility.

Data as a Strategic Asset—Powering intelligent Government operations and citizen services by harnessing accurate, available, and actionable data to drive key insights into the decision-making process. OMB initially released the Federal Data Strategy (FDS) in 2019 as a foundational document for enabling agencies to use and manage Federal data to serve the American people. The FDS provides a consistent framework of principles and practices that are intended to guide agencies as they continue to use and manage data as a resource and strategic asset. The FDS provides an overarching and iterative approach to data stewardship through the release of action plans that support the implementation of the strategy over an eight-year period.

Federal Spending on IT

As shown in Table 15-1, the President's Budget for IT at civilian Federal agencies is estimated to be $75 billion in 2025. Chart 15-1 shows trending information for Federal

CHART 15-1. TRENDS IN FEDERAL CIVILIAN IT SPENDING

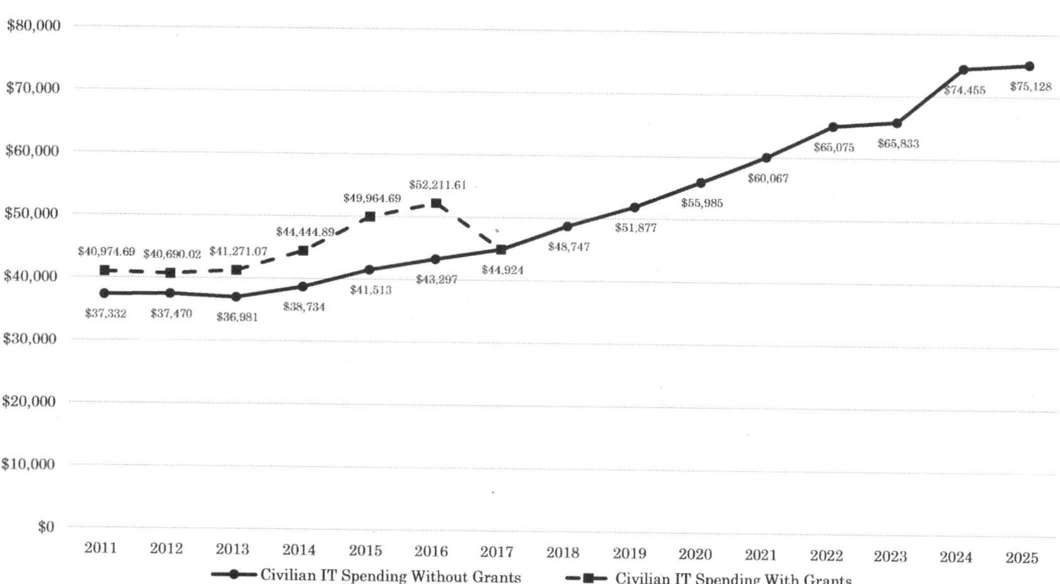

civilian IT spending from 2021 forward. The President's Budget includes funding for 4,446 investments at 25 agencies. These investments support the three IT Portfolio areas shown in Chart 15-2. As outlined in OMB Circular A-11, Section 55—Information Technology Investments, agencies are required to determine major IT investment designations based on several factors including whether the investment under consideration has significant program or policy implications; has high executive or public visibility; has high development, high operating, and/or high maintenance costs; or requires special management attention because of its importance to the agency's mission or critical functions. Of the 4,446 IT investments, 595 have been designated as major IT investments. For each designated major IT investment, agencies are required to submit a business case analysis which provides additional transparency regarding the major investment's cost, schedule, risk, and performance. OMB also requires that each reporting agency Chief Information Officer (CIO) provide additional risk ratings for each major IT investment reported on the IT Dashboard website. Throughout the fiscal year, agency CIOs are required to continuously reassess how risks for their major IT investments are being managed and mitigated.

Federal Spending on Cybersecurity

Cybersecurity is a top priority for the Administration. The Nation's adversaries continue to employ novel and sophisticated methods in an effort to compromise Federal systems. With the release of *Executive Order 14028*, "Improving the Nation's Cybersecurity," on May 12, 2021, the Administration initiated a paradigm shift for cybersecurity. The Executive Order sets a framework to aggressively change the cybersecurity strategy and culture across the Federal enterprise to ultimately center around leading industry practices. Through implementation of Executive Order 14028, Federal agencies are enhancing the protection of Federal systems through modernization of cybersecurity defenses, improving information sharing between the Federal Government and the private sector, and strengthening the United States' ability to rapidly respond to incidents when they occur. Agencies can no longer rely on a perimeter-based approach or "digital walls" to keep sophisticated actors from gaining unauthorized access to Federal systems. The Administration is focused on making Federal systems more defensible by adopting zero trust principles, a security strategy premised on the idea that trust is never granted implicitly but must be continually evaluated.

To that end, OMB has released several Government-wide policies that align to the zero trust vision outlined in Executive Order 14028. On January 26, 2022, OMB released *OMB Memorandum M-22-09*, Moving the U.S. Government Toward Zero Trust Cybersecurity Principles, or the Federal Zero Trust Strategy. The strategy requires agencies to invest in technology that is built and deployed with security foremost in mind and move towards a zero trust architecture that provides the vigilance to detect malicious behaviors and react quickly. The Federal Zero Trust Strategy and associated agency implementation plans delineate meaningful milestones in implementing a zero trust architecture.

In September 2022, OMB took new actions to address potential security gaps in the software supply chain. By issuing *OMB Memorandum M-22-18*, Enhancing the Security of the Software Supply Chain through Secure Development Practices, the Administration focused agencies on shifting to exclusively utilizing software developed with appropriate security practices in place. The Memorandum focuses on minimizing the risks associated

CHART 15-2. 2025 CIVILIAN IT INVESTMENT PORTFOLIO SUMMARY

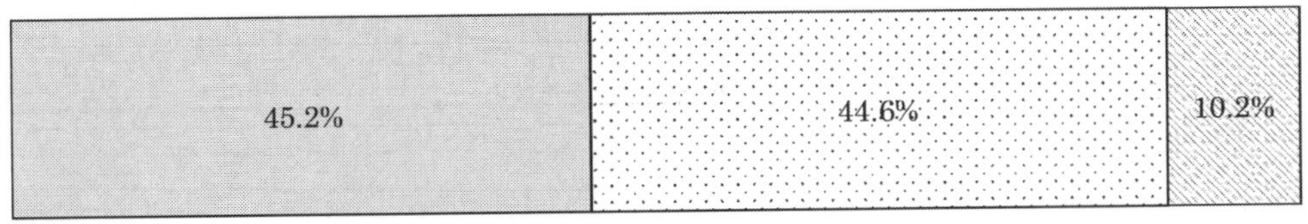

with running unvetted technologies on agency networks, increasing the resilience of Federal technology against cyber threats.

In addition, OMB will carry forward the vision—not just the actions—laid out in Executive Order 14028. The cyber landscape is rapidly evolving, and the Government will continue to discover new threats and tactics that our adversaries intend to use against us. This is why agencies must build upon the strategic direction of Executive Order 14028 and take actions to secure Federal systems against all present and future threats as they become known. For example, the Administration recognized the future threat that quantum computers may pose to the Federal Government, and consequently published *OMB Memorandum M-23-02*, Migrating to Post-Quantum Cryptography, which establishes requirements for agencies to prioritize and identify where they are using cryptography within their most sensitive systems that are vulnerable to decryption by a future quantum computer. This guidance will help prepare the Government for an inevitable shift in security that could ultimately expose securely encrypted secrets to foreign adversaries if we do not act decisively.

In the three years since the release of Executive Order 14028, Federal agencies have made considerable progress towards a more cyber-secure future. Agencies are implementing higher levels of encryption, using the best methods in the industry to verify legitimate users, and utilizing toolsets that create constant vigilance within Federal systems. These efforts to adopt technologies and practices that enhance cybersecurity defenses and ensuring the human capital to maintain these endeavors will and must continue. The President's Budget includes approximately $13 billion of budget authority for civilian cybersecurity-related activities.

Federal Spending on Artifical intelligence

Advances in AI are creating groundbreaking opportunities, while changing the nature of work and organizational management. To benefit from the opportunities created by AI while mitigating its risks, the Administration is committed to advancing its management of AI and significantly expanding AI talent in the Federal Government. The Budget provides $70 million for Federal agencies to establish agency Chief AI Officers accountable for their agency's use of AI and to establish minimum safeguards for agency use of AI. This includes significant additional AI management funding for the Departments of State, Agriculture, Commerce, Energy, Homeland Security, Housing and Urban Development, Interior, Justice, Transportation, and the Treasury, as well as the Environmental Protection Agency, the National Science Foundation, and the U.S. Agency for International Development. The Budget also proposes $300 million in mandatory funding to increase agency funding for AI, both to address major risks from, as well as to advance its use for public good. In addition to this funding, the Budget includes an additional $40 million for the U.S. Digital Service, General Services Administration, and Office of Personnel Management to support the National AI Talent Surge that will rapidly increase agencies' recruitment and hiring of AI talent, fill urgent gaps at key agencies with highly qualified fellows, and expand Government-wide AI training programs to upskill the existing workforce.

Table 15–2. ESTIMATED CIVILIAN FEDERAL CYBERSECURITY SPENDING BY AGENCY

(In millions of dollars)

Organization	2023	2024	2025
Civilian CFO Act Agencies	**10,728**	**11,210**	**12,325**
Department of Agriculture	230	239	233
Department of Commerce	460	458	420
Department of Education	218	261	268
Department of Energy	765	731	971
Department of Health and Human Services	915	1,043	1,120
Department of Homeland Security	2,997	2,995	3,152
Department of Housing and Urban Development	57	112	99
Department of Justice	1,083	1,052	1,162
Department of Labor	79	80	79
Department of State	569	736	686
Department of the Interior	161	161	205
Department of the Treasury	966	1,064	1,225
Department of Transportation	399	399	472
Department of Veterans Affairs	669	655	952
Environmental Protection Agency	37	37	65
General Services Administration	104	132	113
National Aeronautics and Space Administration	217	201	185
National Science Foundation	308	296	294
Nuclear Regulatory Commission	39	39	40
Office of Personnel Management	50	89	117
Small Business Administration	21	33	35
Social Security Administration	301	314	361
U.S. Agency for International Development	83	82	72
Non-CFO Act Agencies	**549.0**	**613.4**	**674.3**
Access Board	0.8	0.9	0.9
African Development Foundation	2.4	3.1	3.8
American Battle Monuments Commission	0.8	1.7	2.0
Armed Forces Retirement Home	0.3	0.3	0.3
Chemical Safety and Hazard Investigation Board	0.7	0.8	0.8
Commission on Civil Rights	0.6	0.6	0.6
Commodity Futures Trading Commission	12.9	14.1	18.1
Consumer Financial Protection Bureau	29.3	30.0	30.5
Consumer Product Safety Commission	3.8	3.2	3.6
Corporation for National and Community Service	6.8	8.3	7.5
Council of the Inspectors General on Integrity and Efficiency	1.1	0.8	0.8
Court Services and Offender Supervision Agency	4.0	4.0	4.0
Defense Nuclear Facilities Safety Board	3.3	3.8	3.6
Denali Commission	1.0	1.0	1.0
Election Assistance Commission	2.3	2.3	9.1
Equal Employment Opportunity Commission	9.7	9.6	9.6
Export-Import Bank of the United States	4.4	5.3	6.3
Farm Credit Administration	4.0	4.0	4.4
Federal Communications Commission	20.9	22.1	28.4
Federal Deposit Insurance Corporation	97.5	115.0	122.9
Federal Election Commission	8.0	8.2	8.7
Federal Energy Regulatory Commission	24.9	28.4	30.7
Federal Labor Relations Authority	0.4	0.4	0.4
Federal Maritime Commission	0.2	0.6	0.2
Federal Mediation and Conciliation Service	1.6	1.7	1.7
Federal Retirement Thrift Investment Board	28.6	28.6	31.7
Federal Trade Commission	19.4	19.4	18.9
Institute of Museum and Library Services	0.7	0.9	0.9
International Development Finance Corporation	7.9	8.9	10.7
International Trade Commission	6.3	7.6	7.8
Merit Systems Protection Board	0.5	0.5	1.5

Table 15–2. ESTIMATED CIVILIAN FEDERAL CYBERSECURITY SPENDING BY AGENCY—Continued

(In millions of dollars)

Organization	2023	2024	2025
Millennium Challenge Corporation	1.7	2.4	2.6
National Archives and Records Administration	10.1	9.8	20.7
National Council on Disability	0.5	0.5	1.1
National Credit Union Administration	13.2	17.4	17.4
National Endowment for the Arts	3.4	5.1	2.6
National Endowment for the Humanities	1.1	1.6	1.4
National Gallery of Art	4.0	4.1	4.4
National Labor Relations Board	3.8	3.8	4.7
National Mediation Board	2.1	2.2	2.3
National Transportation Safety Board	5.3	6.8	7.4
Nuclear Waste Technical Review Board	0.4	0.7	0.5
Occupational Safety and Health Review Commission	1.1	1.2	1.2
Office of Government Ethics	0.7	0.7	0.9
Office of Special Counsel	1.1	1.1	1.3
Peace Corps	12.3	12.3	20.3
Pension Benefit Guaranty Corporation	27.0	32.9	28.3
Postal Regulatory Commission	1.5	2.5	2.2
Presidio Trust	0.7	0.7	0.7
Privacy and Civil Liberties Oversight Board	2.0	2.1	2.1
Railroad Retirement Board	1.9	3.4	4.2
Securities and Exchange Commission	67.5	70.0	70.0
Selective Service System	0.5	0.5	0.5
Smithsonian Institution	15.6	15.6	15.9
Surface Transportation Board	2.8	2.9	3.5
Tennessee Valley Authority	48.8	63.4	60.2
Trade and Development Agency	1.3	1.3	1.3
U.S. Agency for Global Media	6.0	6.0	10.7
U.S. Army Corps of Engineers	4.0	2.4	10.2
United States AbilityOne Commission	0.3	0.3	0.3
United States Holocaust Memorial Museum	2.8	3.0	3.0
United States Institute of Peace	0.6	0.7	0.7
Total	**11,277.0**	**11,823.7**	**12,999.7**

Table 15–3. NIST FRAMEWORK FUNCTION CIVILIAN CFO ACT AGENCY FUNDING TOTALS

(In millions of dollars)

NIST Framework Function	2024	2025
Identify	3,172	3,553
Protect	1,140	1,243
Detect	4,875	5,179
Respond	1,365	1,563
Recover	317	296
Sector Risk Management & Human Capital	341	491
Total	**11,210**	**12,325**

This analysis excludes Department of Defense spending.

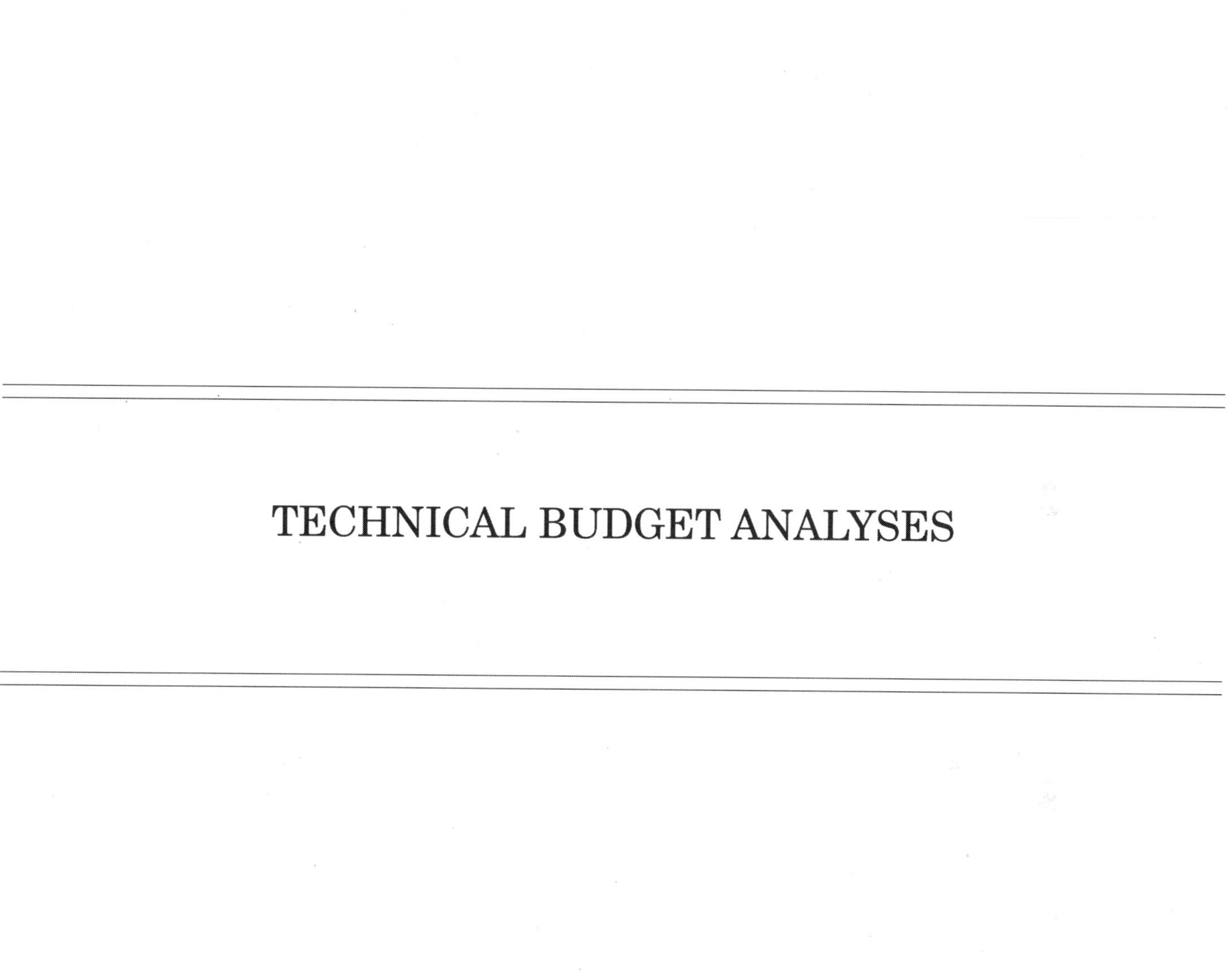

TECHNICAL BUDGET ANALYSES

16. BUDGET CONCEPTS

The budget system of the United States Government provides the means for the President and the Congress to decide how much money to spend, what to spend it on, and how to raise the money they have decided to spend. Through the budget system, they determine the allocation of resources among the agencies of the Federal Government and between the Federal Government and the private sector. The budget system focuses primarily on dollars, but it also allocates other resources, such as Federal employment. Budget decisions made affect the Nation as a whole, State and local governments, and individual Americans. Many decisions have worldwide significance. The Congress and the President enact budget decisions into law. The budget system ensures that these laws are carried out.

This chapter provides an overview of the budget system and explains some of the more important budget concepts. It includes summary dollar amounts to illustrate major concepts. Other chapters of the budget documents discuss these concepts and more detailed amounts in greater depth.

The following section discusses the budget process, covering formulation of the President's Budget, action by the Congress, and execution of enacted budget laws. The next section provides information on budget coverage, including a discussion of on-budget and off-budget amounts, functional classification, presentation of budget data, types of funds, and full-cost budgeting. Subsequent sections discuss the concepts of receipts and collections, budget authority, and outlays. These sections are followed by discussions of Federal credit; surpluses, deficits, and means of financing; Federal employment; and the basis for the budget figures. A glossary of budget terms appears at the end of the chapter.

Various laws, enacted to carry out requirements of the Constitution, govern the budget system. The chapter refers to the principal ones by title throughout the text and gives complete citations in the section just preceding the glossary.

THE BUDGET PROCESS

The budget process has three main phases, each of which is related to the others:

1. Formulation of the President's Budget;
2. Action by the Congress; and
3. Execution of enacted budget laws.

Formulation of the President's Budget

The Budget of the United States Government consists of several volumes that set forth the President's fiscal policy goals and priorities for the allocation of resources by the Government. The primary focus of the Budget is on the budget year—the next fiscal year for which the Congress needs to make appropriations, in this case 2025. (Fiscal year 2025 will begin on October 1, 2024, and end on September 30, 2025.) The Budget also covers the nine years following the budget year in order to reflect the effects of budget decisions over the longer term. It includes the funding levels provided for the current year, in this case 2024, which allows the reader to compare the President's Budget proposals with the most recently enacted levels. The Budget also includes data on the most recently completed fiscal year, in this case 2023, so that the reader can compare budget estimates to actual accounting data.

In a normal year (excluding transitions between administrations), the President begins the process of formulating the budget by establishing general budget and fiscal policy guidelines, usually by late spring of each year. Based on these guidelines, the Office of Management and Budget (OMB) works with the Federal agencies to establish specific policy directions and planning levels to guide the preparation of their budget requests.

During the formulation of the budget, the President, the Director of OMB, and other officials in the Executive Office of the President continually exchange information, proposals, and evaluations bearing on policy decisions with the Secretaries of the Departments and the heads of the other Government agencies. Decisions reflected in previously enacted budgets—including the one for the fiscal year in progress, reactions to the last proposed budget (which the Congress is considering at the same time the process of preparing the forthcoming budget begins), and evaluations of program performance—all influence decisions concerning the forthcoming budget, as do projections of the economic outlook, prepared jointly by the Council of Economic Advisers, OMB, and the Department of the Treasury.

Agencies normally submit their budget requests to OMB, where analysts review them and identify issues that OMB officials need to discuss with the agencies. OMB and the agencies resolve many issues themselves. Others require the involvement of White House policy officials and the President. This decision-making process is usually completed by late December. At that time, the final stage of developing detailed budget data and the preparation of the budget documents begins.

The decision-makers must consider the effects of economic and technical assumptions on the budget estimates. Interest rates, economic growth, the rate of inflation, the unemployment rate, and the number of people eligible for various benefit programs, among other factors, affect Government spending and receipts. Small changes in these assumptions can alter budget estimates by many billions of dollars. (The "Economic Assumptions" chapter of this volume provides more information on this subject.)

Thus, the budget formulation process involves the simultaneous consideration of the resource needs of individual programs, the allocation of resources among the agencies and functions of the Federal Government, and the total outlays and receipts that are appropriate in light of current and prospective economic conditions.

The law governing the President's Budget requires the transmittal of the following fiscal year's Budget to the Congress on or after the first Monday in January but not later than the first Monday in February of each year. The budget is usually scheduled for transmission to the Congress on the first Monday in February, giving the Congress eight months to act on the budget before the fiscal year begins. However, because a significant portion of budget formulation depends on analyzing current year funding levels, budget timing can be affected by the timing of enactment of appropriations for the current year. In addition, in years when a Presidential transition has taken place, the timeline for budget release is commonly extended to allow the new administration sufficient time to take office and formulate its budget policy. While there is no specific timeline set for this circumstance, the detailed budget is usually completed and released in April or May. However, in order to aid the congressional budget process (discussed below), new administrations often release a budget blueprint that contains broad spending outlines and descriptions of major policies and priorities earlier in the year.

Congressional Action[1]

The Congress considers the President's Budget proposals and approves, modifies, or disapproves them. It can change funding levels, eliminate programs, or add programs not requested by the President. It can add or eliminate taxes and other sources of receipts or make other changes that affect the amount of receipts collected.

The Congress does not enact a budget as such. Through the process of adopting a planning document called a budget resolution, the Congress agrees on targets for total spending and receipts, the size of the deficit or surplus, and the debt limit. The budget resolution provides the framework within which individual congressional committees prepare appropriations bills and other spending and receipts legislation. The Congress provides funding for specified purposes in appropriations acts each year. It also enacts changes each year in other laws that affect spending and receipts.

In making appropriations, the Congress does not vote on the level of outlays (spending) directly, but rather on budget authority, which is the authority provided by law to incur financial obligations that will result in outlays. In a separate process, prior to making appropriations, the Congress usually enacts legislation that authorizes an agency to carry out particular programs, authorizes the appropriation of funds to carry out those programs, and, in some cases, limits the amount that can be appropriated for the programs. Some authorizing legislation expires after one year, some expires after a specified number of years, and some is permanent. The Congress may enact appropriations for a program even though there is no specific authorization for it or its authorization has expired.

The Congress begins its work on its budget resolution shortly after it receives the President's Budget. Under the procedures established by the Congressional Budget Act of 1974 (Congressional Budget Act), the Congress decides on budget targets before commencing action on individual appropriations. The Congressional Budget Act requires each standing committee of the House and Senate to recommend budget levels and report legislative plans concerning matters within the committee's jurisdiction to the Budget Committee in each body. The House and Senate Budget Committees then each design and report, and each body then considers, a concurrent resolution on the budget. The Act calls for the House and Senate to resolve differences between their respective versions of the congressional budget resolution and adopt a single budget resolution by April 15 of each year.

In the report on the budget resolution, the Budget Committees allocate the total on-budget budget authority and outlays set forth in the resolution to the Appropriations Committees and the other committees that have jurisdiction over spending. These committee allocations are commonly known as "302(a)" allocations, in reference to the section of the Congressional Budget Act that provides for them. The Appropriations Committees are then required to divide their 302(a) allocations of budget authority and outlays among their subcommittees. These subcommittee allocations are known as "302(b)" allocations. There are procedural hurdles associated with considering appropriations bills that would breach an Appropriations subcommittee's 302(b) allocation. Similar procedural hurdles exist for considering legislation that would cause the 302(a) allocation for any committee to be breached. The Budget Committees' reports may discuss assumptions about the level of funding for major programs. While these assumptions do not bind the other committees and subcommittees, they may influence their decisions.

Budget resolutions may include "reserve funds," which permit adjustment of the resolution allocations as necessary to accommodate legislation addressing specific matters, such as healthcare or tax reform. Reserve funds are most often limited to legislation that is deficit neutral, including increases in some areas offset by decreases in

[1] For a fuller discussion of the congressional budget process, see Bill Heniff Jr., *Introduction to the Federal Budget Process* (Congressional Research Service Report 98–721), and Robert Keith and Allen Schick, *Manual on the Federal Budget Process* (Congressional Research Service Report 98–720, archived).

others. The budget resolution may also contain "reconciliation directives" (discussed further below).

Since the concurrent resolution on the budget is not a law, it does not require the President's approval. However, the Congress considers the President's views in preparing budget resolutions, because legislation developed to meet congressional budget allocations does require the President's approval. In some years, the President and the joint leadership of the Congress have formally agreed on plans to reduce the deficit. These agreements were then reflected in the budget resolution and legislation passed for those years.

If the Congress does not pass a budget resolution, the House and Senate typically adopt one or more "deeming resolutions" in the form of a simple resolution or as a provision of a larger bill. A deeming resolution may serve nearly all functions of a budget resolution, except it may not trigger reconciliation procedures in the Senate.

Once the Congress approves the budget resolution, it turns its attention to enacting appropriations bills and authorizing legislation. The Appropriations Committee in each body has jurisdiction over annual appropriations. These committees are divided into subcommittees that hold hearings and review detailed budget justification materials prepared by the Executive Branch agencies within the subcommittee's jurisdiction. After a bill has been drafted by a subcommittee, the full committee and the whole House, in turn, must approve the bill, sometimes with amendments to the original version. The House then forwards the bill to the Senate, where a similar review follows. If the Senate disagrees with the House on particular matters in the bill, which is often the case, the two bodies form a conference committee (consisting of some Members of each body) to resolve the differences. The conference committee revises the bill and returns it to both bodies for approval. When the revised bill is agreed to, first in the House and then in the Senate, the Congress sends it to the President for approval or veto.

Since 1977, when the start of the fiscal year was established as October 1, there have been only three fiscal years (1989, 1995, and 1997) for which the Congress agreed to and enacted every regular appropriations bill by that date. When one or more appropriations bills are not enacted by this date, the Congress usually enacts a joint resolution called a "continuing resolution" (CR), which is an interim or stop-gap appropriations bill that provides authority for the affected agencies to continue operations at some specified level until a specific date or until the regular appropriations are enacted. Occasionally, a CR has funded a portion or all of the Government for the entire year.

The Congress must present these CRs to the President for approval or veto. In some cases, Congresses have failed to pass a CR or Presidents have rejected CRs because they contained unacceptable provisions. Left without funds, Government agencies were required by law to shut down operations—with exceptions for some limited activities—until the Congress passed a CR or appropriations bill the President would approve. Previous shutdowns have ranged in duration from just one day to several weeks.

The Congress also provides budget authority in laws other than appropriations acts. In fact, while annual appropriations acts fund the majority of Federal programs, they account for only about a third of the total spending in a typical year. Authorizing legislation controls the rest of the spending, which is commonly called "mandatory spending." A distinctive feature of these authorizing laws is that they provide agencies with the authority or requirement to spend money without first requiring the Appropriations Committees to enact funding. This category of spending includes interest the Government pays on the public debt and the spending of several major programs, such as Social Security, Medicare, Medicaid, unemployment insurance, and Federal employee retirement. Almost all taxes and most other receipts also result from authorizing laws.

Some authorizing legislation making changes to laws that affect receipts or mandatory spending may be developed under a unique set of procedures known as reconciliation. The budget resolution often includes reconciliation directives, which direct each designated authorizing committee to report amendments to the laws under the committee's jurisdiction that would achieve changes in the levels of receipts or mandatory spending controlled by those laws. These directives specify the dol-

BUDGET CALENDAR

The following timetable highlights the scheduled dates for significant budget events during a normal budget year:

Between the 1st Monday in January and the 1st Monday in February	President transmits the budget
Six weeks later	Congressional committees report budget estimates to Budget Committees
April 15	Action to be completed on congressional budget resolution
May 15	House consideration of annual appropriations bills may begin even if the budget resolution has not been agreed to.
June 10	House Appropriations Committee to report the last of its annual appropriations bills.
June 15	Action to be completed on "reconciliation bill" by the Congress.
June 30	Action on appropriations to be completed by House
July 15	President transmits Mid-Session Review of the Budget
October 1	Fiscal year begins

lar amount of changes that each designated committee is expected to achieve, but do not specify which laws are to be changed or the changes to be made. However, the Budget Committees' reports on the budget resolution frequently discuss assumptions about how the laws would be changed. Like other assumptions in the report, they do not bind the committees of jurisdiction but may influence their decisions. A reconciliation instruction may also specify the total amount by which the statutory limit on the public debt is to be changed.

The committees subject to reconciliation directives draft the implementing legislation. Such legislation may, for example, change the tax code, revise benefit formulas or eligibility requirements for benefit programs, or authorize Government agencies to charge fees to cover some of their costs. Reconciliation bills are typically omnibus legislation, combining the legislation submitted by each reconciled committee in a single act.

The Senate considers such omnibus reconciliation acts under expedited procedures that limit total debate on the bill. To offset the procedural advantage gained by expedited procedures, the Senate places significant restrictions on the substantive content of the reconciliation measure itself, as well as on amendments to the measure. Any material in the bill that is extraneous or that contains changes to the Federal Old-Age and Survivors Insurance and the Federal Disability Insurance programs is not in order under the Senate's expedited reconciliation procedures. Non-germane amendments are also prohibited. Reconciliation acts, together with appropriations acts for the year, are usually used to implement broad agreements between the President and the Congress on those occasions where the two branches have negotiated a comprehensive budget plan. Reconciliation acts have sometimes included other matters, such as laws providing the means for enforcing these agreements.

Budget Execution

Government agencies may not spend or obligate more than the Congress has appropriated, and they may use funds only for purposes specified in law. The Antideficiency Act prohibits agencies from spending or obligating funds in advance or in excess of an appropriation, unless specific authority to do so has been provided in law. The Antideficiency Act also requires the President to apportion the budgetary resources available for most executive branch agencies. The President has delegated this authority to OMB. Some apportionments are by time periods (usually by quarter of the fiscal year), some are by projects or activities, and others are by a combination of both. Agencies may request OMB to reapportion funds during the year to accommodate changing circumstances. This system helps to ensure that funds do not run out before the end of the fiscal year.

During the budget execution phase, the Government sometimes finds that it needs more funding than the Congress has appropriated for the fiscal year because of unanticipated circumstances. For example, more might be needed to respond to a severe natural disaster. Under such circumstances, the Congress may enact a supplemental appropriation.

On the other hand, the President may propose to reduce a previously enacted appropriation, through a "rescission" or "cancellation" of those funds. How the President proposes this reduction determines whether it is considered a rescission or a cancellation. A rescission is a reduction in previously enacted appropriations proposed pursuant to the Impoundment Control Act (ICA). The ICA allows the President, using the specific authorities in that Act, to transmit a "special message" to the Congress to inform Members of these proposed rescissions, at which time the funding can be withheld from obligation for up to 45 days on the OMB-approved apportionment. Agencies are instructed not to withhold funds without the prior approval of OMB. If the Congress does not act to rescind these funds within the 45-day period, the funds are made available for obligation.

The President can also propose reductions to previously enacted appropriations outside of the ICA; in these cases, these reductions are referred to as cancellations. Cancellation proposals are not subject to the requirements and procedures of the ICA and amounts cannot be withheld from obligation. The 2025 President's Budget includes $12.9 billion in proposed cancellations.

COVERAGE OF THE BUDGET

Federal Government and Budget Totals

The budget documents provide information on all Federal agencies and programs. However, because the laws governing Social Security (the Federal Old-Age and Survivors Insurance and the Federal Disability Insurance trust funds) and the Postal Service Fund require that the receipts and outlays for those activities be excluded from the budget totals and from the calculation of the deficit or surplus, the budget presents on-budget and off-budget totals. The off-budget totals include the Federal transactions excluded by law from the budget totals. The on-budget and off-budget amounts are added together to derive the totals for the Federal Government. These are sometimes referred to as the unified or consolidated budget totals.

It is not always obvious whether a transaction or activity should be included in the budget. Where there is a question, OMB normally follows the recommendation of the 1967 President's Commission on Budget Concepts to be comprehensive of the full range of Federal agencies, programs, and activities. In recent years, for example, the budget has included the transactions of the Affordable Housing Program funds, the Universal Service Fund, the Public Company Accounting Oversight Board, the Securities Investor Protection Corporation, Guaranty Agencies Reserves, the National Railroad Retirement Investment Trust, the United Mine Workers Combined

Table 16–1. TOTALS FOR THE BUDGET AND THE FEDERAL GOVERNMENT
(In billions of dollars)

	2023 Actual	Estimate	
		2024	2025
Budget authority			
Unified	6,482	6,949	7,484
On-budget	5,246	5,628	6,080
Off-budget	1,236	1,321	1,404
Receipts:			
Unified	4,441	5,082	5,485
On-budget	3,247	3,842	4,201
Off-budget	1,194	1,240	1,284
Outlays:			
Unified	6,135	6,941	7,266
On-budget	4,914	5,629	5,870
Off-budget	1,221	1,312	1,396
Deficit (–) / Surplus (+):			
Unified	–1,694	–1,859	–1,781
On-budget	–1,666	–1,788	–1,669
Off-budget	–27	–72	–112

Benefits Fund, the Federal Financial Institutions Examination Council, Electric Reliability Organizations (EROs) established pursuant to the Energy Policy Act of 2005, the Corporation for Travel Promotion, and the National Association of Registered Agents and Brokers.

In contrast, the budget excludes tribal trust funds that are owned by Indian Tribes and held and managed by the Government in a fiduciary capacity on the Tribes' behalf. These funds are not owned by the Government, the Government is not the source of their capital, and the Government's control is limited to the exercise of fiduciary duties. Similarly, the transactions of Government-sponsored enterprises, such as the Federal Home Loan Banks, are not included in the on-budget or off-budget totals. Federal laws established these enterprises for public policy purposes, but they are privately owned and operated corporations. Nevertheless, because of their public charters, the budget discusses them and reports summary financial data in the Budget *Appendix* and in some detailed tables.

The budget also excludes the revenues from copyright royalties and spending for subsequent payments to copyright holders where: 1) the law allows copyright owners and users to voluntarily set the rate paid for the use of protected material; and 2) the amount paid by users of copyrighted material to copyright owners is related to the frequency or quantity of the material used. The budget excludes license royalties collected and paid out by the Copyright Office for the retransmission of network broadcasts via cable collected under 17 U.S.C. 111 because these revenues meet both of these conditions. The budget includes the royalties collected and paid out for license fees for digital audio recording technology under 17 U.S.C. 1004, since the amount of license fees paid is unrelated to usage of the material.

The *Appendix* includes a presentation for the Board of Governors of the Federal Reserve System for information only. The amounts are not included in either the on-budget or off-budget totals because of the independent status of the System within the Government. However, the Federal Reserve System transfers its net earnings to the Treasury, and the budget records them as receipts.

The "Coverage of the Budget" chapter of this volume provides more information on this subject.

How the Budget Measures Costs

A budget is a financial plan for allocating resources—deciding how much the Federal Government should spend in total, program by program, and for the parts of each program, and deciding how to finance the spending. The budgetary system provides a process for proposing policies, making decisions, implementing these policies, and reporting the results. The budget needs to measure costs accurately so that decision makers can compare the cost of a program with its benefits, the cost of one program with another, and the cost of one method of reaching a specified goal with another. Furthermore, these costs need to be fully included in the budget up front, when the spending decision is made, so that executive and congressional decision makers have the necessary information and the incentive to take the total costs into account when setting priorities. Finally, the budget needs to differentiate between transactions that allocate resources—and therefore represent a cost to the Government—and transactions that finance those costs. (See "Means of Financing" later in this chapter for additional details.)

For most programs, the most transparent and easily comparable measure of cost to the Government (or value, in terms of revenues) are cash outlays and cash receipts. The budget records these outlays and receipts in full, as they occur; this approach is often referred to as "cash budgeting" or "the cash budget." In addition to facilitating comparisons between competing programs, cash budgeting has the benefit of producing intuitive aggregate totals, as the difference between spending and revenue in a given year is equal to that year's deficit or surplus. The cash budget also aligns with the requirements of the recording statute (31 U.S.C. 1501), which directs agencies to record their obligations in full, against available resources, as they are incurred. The primary exception to the cash budget is provided for Federal credit programs. (See "Federal Credit" later in this chapter for additional details.)

Unlike private sector accounting, or most State and local government budgeting, the Federal budget does not differentiate between capital and operating costs. The budget records capital investment on a cash basis, and it requires the Congress to provide budget authority before an agency can obligate the Government to make a cash outlay. However, the budget measures only costs, and the benefits with which these costs are compared, based on policy makers' judgment, must be presented in supplementary materials. By these means, the budget allows the total cost of capital investment to be compared up front in a rough way with the total expected future net benefits; this is similar to the way in which policy makers are able to compare operating costs with the benefits of that spending. In addition, such a comparison of total costs with benefits is consistent with the formal method of cost-benefit analysis of capital projects in Government, in which the full cost of a capital asset as the cash is paid out is compared with the full stream of future benefits (all in terms of present values). (The "Federal Investment" chapter of this volume provides more information on capital investment.)

Functional Classification

The functional classification system is used to organize budget authority, outlays, and other budget data according to the major purpose served—such as agriculture, transportation, income security, and national defense. There are 20 major functions, 17 of which are concerned with broad areas of national need and are further divided into subfunctions. For example, the Agriculture function comprises the subfunctions Farm Income Stabilization and Agricultural Research and Services. The functional classification meets the Congressional Budget Act requirement for a presentation in the budget by national needs and agency missions and programs. The remaining three functions—Net Interest, Undistributed Offsetting Receipts, and Allowances—enable the functional classification system to cover the entire Federal budget.

The following criteria are used in establishing functional categories and assigning activities to them:

- A function encompasses activities with similar purposes, emphasizing what the Federal Government seeks to accomplish rather than the means of accomplishment, the objects purchased, the clientele or geographic area served (except in the cases of functions 450 for Community and Regional Development, 570 for Medicare, 650 for Social Security, and 700 for Veterans Benefits and Services), or the Federal agency conducting the activity (except in the case of subfunction 051 in the National Defense function, which is used only for defense activities under the Department of Defense—Military).
- A function must be of continuing national importance, and the amounts attributable to it must be significant.
- Each basic unit being classified (generally the appropriation or fund account) usually is classified according to its primary purpose and assigned to only one subfunction. However, some large accounts that serve more than one major purpose are subdivided into two or more functions or subfunctions.

In consultation with the Congress, the functional classification is adjusted from time to time as warranted. Detailed functional tables, which provide information on Government activities by function and subfunction, are available in the *Analytical Perspectives* volume online.

Agencies, Accounts, Programs, Projects, and Activities

Various summary tables in the *Analytical Perspectives* volume of the Budget provide information on budget authority, outlays, and offsetting collections and receipts arrayed by Federal agency. A table that lists budget authority and outlays by budget account within each agency and the totals for each agency of budget authority, outlays, and receipts that offset the agency spending totals is available in the *Analytical Perspectives* volume online. The *Appendix* provides budgetary, financial, and descriptive information about programs, projects, and activities by account within each agency.

Types of Funds

Agency activities are financed through Federal funds and trust funds.

Federal funds comprise several types of funds. Receipt accounts of the ***general fund***, which is the greater part of the budget, record receipts not earmarked by law for a specific purpose, such as income tax receipts. The general fund also includes the proceeds of general borrowing. General fund appropriation accounts record general fund expenditures. General fund appropriations draw from general fund receipts and borrowing collectively and, therefore, are not specifically linked to receipt accounts.

Special funds consist of receipt accounts for Federal fund receipts that laws have designated for specific purposes and the associated appropriation accounts for the expenditure of those receipts.

Public enterprise funds are revolving funds used for programs authorized by law to conduct a cycle of business-type operations, primarily with the public, in which outlays generate collections.

Intragovernmental funds are revolving funds that conduct business-type operations primarily within and between Government agencies. The collections and the outlays of revolving funds are recorded in the same budget account.

Trust funds account for the receipt and expenditure of monies by the Government for carrying out specific purposes and programs in accordance with the terms of a statute that designates the fund as a trust fund (such as the Highway Trust Fund) or for carrying out the stipulations of a trust where the Government itself is the beneficiary (such as any of several trust funds for gifts and donations for specific purposes). ***Trust revolving funds*** are trust funds credited with collections earmarked by law to carry out a cycle of business-type operations.

The Federal budget meaning of the term "trust," as applied to trust fund accounts, differs significantly from its private-sector usage. In the private sector, the beneficiary of a trust usually owns the trust's assets, which are managed by a trustee who must follow the stipulations of the trust. In contrast, the Federal Government owns the assets of most Federal trust funds, and it can raise or lower future trust fund collections and payments, or change the purposes for which the collections are used, by changing existing laws. There is no substantive difference between a trust fund and a special fund or between a trust revolving fund and a public enterprise revolving fund.

However, in some instances, the Government does act as a true trustee of assets that are owned or held for the benefit of others. For example, it maintains accounts on behalf of individual Federal employees in the Thrift Savings Fund, investing them as directed by the individual employee. The Government accounts for such funds in ***deposit funds***, which are not included in the budget. (The "Trust Funds and Federal Funds" chapter of this volume provides more information on this subject.)

RECEIPTS, OFFSETTING COLLECTIONS, AND OFFSETTING RECEIPTS

In General

The budget records amounts collected by Government agencies two different ways. Depending on the nature of the activity generating the collection and the law that established the collection, they are recorded as either:

Governmental receipts, which are compared in total to outlays (net of offsetting collections and offsetting receipts) in calculating the surplus or deficit; or

Offsetting collections or ***offsetting receipts***, which are deducted from gross outlays to calculate net outlay figures. These amounts are recorded as offsets to outlays so that the budget totals represent governmental rather than market activity and reflect the Government's net transactions with the public. They are recorded in one of two ways, based on interpretation of laws and longstanding budget concepts and practice. They are offsetting collections when the collections are authorized by law to be credited to expenditure accounts. Otherwise, they are deposited in receipt accounts and called offsetting receipts.

Offsetting collections and offsetting receipts result from any of the following types of transactions:

- ***Business-like transactions or market-oriented activities with the public***—these include voluntary collections from the public in exchange for goods or services, such as the proceeds from the sale of postage stamps, the fees charged for admittance to recreation areas, and the proceeds from the sale of Government-owned land; and reimbursements for damages. The budget records these amounts as *offsetting collections from non-Federal sources* (for offsetting collections) or as *proprietary receipts* (for offsetting receipts).
- ***Intragovernmental transactions***—collections from other Federal Government accounts. The budget records collections by one Government account from another as *offsetting collections from Federal sources* (for offsetting collections) or as *intragovernmental receipts* (for offsetting receipts). For example, the General Services Administration rents office space to other Government agencies and records their rental payments as offsetting collections from Federal sources in the Federal Buildings Fund. These transactions are exactly offsetting and do not affect the surplus or deficit. However, they are an important accounting mechanism for allocating costs to the programs and activities that cause the Government to incur the costs.
- ***Voluntary gifts and donations***—gifts and donations of money to the Government, which are treated as offsets to budget authority and outlays.
- ***Offsetting governmental transactions***—collections from the public that are governmental in nature and should conceptually be treated like Federal revenues and compared in total to outlays (e.g., tax receipts, regulatory fees, compulsory user charges, custom duties, license fees) but are required by law or longstanding practice to be misclassified as offsetting. The budget records amounts from non-Federal sources that are governmental in nature as *offsetting governmental collections* (for offsetting collections) or as *offsetting governmental receipts* (for offsetting receipts).

Governmental Receipts

Governmental receipts are collections that result from the Government's exercise of its sovereign power to tax or otherwise compel payment. Sometimes they are called receipts, budget receipts, Federal receipts, or Federal revenues. They consist mostly of individual and corporation income taxes and social insurance taxes, but also include excise taxes, compulsory user charges, regulatory fees, customs duties, court fines, certain license fees, and deposits of earnings by the Federal Reserve System. Total receipts for the Federal Government include both on-budget and off-budget receipts (see Table 16–1, "Totals for the Budget and the Federal Government," which appears earlier in this chapter.) The "Governmental Receipts" chapter of this volume provides more information on governmental receipts.

Offsetting Collections

Some laws authorize agencies to credit collections directly to the account from which they will be spent and, usually, to spend the collections for the purpose of the account without further action by the Congress. Most revolving funds operate with such authority. For example, a permanent law authorizes the Postal Service to use collections from the sale of stamps to finance its operations without a requirement for annual appropriations. The budget records these collections in the Postal Service Fund (a revolving fund) and records budget authority in an amount equal to the collections. In addition to revolving funds, some agencies are authorized to charge fees to defray a portion of costs for a program that are otherwise financed by appropriations from the general fund and usually to spend the collections without further action by the Congress. In such cases, the budget records the offsetting collections and resulting budget authority in the program's general fund expenditure account. Similarly, intragovernmental collections authorized by some laws may be recorded as offsetting collections and budget authority in revolving funds or in general fund expenditure accounts.

Sometimes appropriations acts or provisions in other laws limit the obligations that can be financed by offsetting collections. In those cases, the budget records budget authority in the amount available to incur obligations, not in the amount of the collections.

Offsetting collections credited to expenditure accounts automatically offset the outlays at the expenditure account level. Where accounts have offsetting collections, the budget shows the budget authority and outlays of the account both gross (before deducting offsetting collections) and net (after deducting offsetting collections). Totals for the agency, subfunction, and overall budget are net of offsetting collections.

Offsetting Receipts

Collections that are offset against gross outlays but are not authorized to be credited to expenditure accounts are credited to receipt accounts and are called offsetting receipts. Offsetting receipts are deducted from budget authority and outlays in arriving at total net budget authority and outlays. However, unlike offsetting collections credited to expenditure accounts, offsetting receipts do not offset budget authority and outlays at the account level. In most cases, they offset budget authority and outlays at the agency and subfunction levels.

Proprietary receipts from a few sources, however, are not offset against any specific agency or function and are classified as undistributed offsetting receipts. They are deducted from the Government-wide totals for net budget authority and outlays. For example, the collections of rents and royalties from outer continental shelf lands are undistributed because the amounts are large and for the most part are not related to the spending of the agency that administers the transactions and the subfunction that records the administrative expenses.

Similarly, two kinds of intragovernmental transactions—agencies' payments as employers into Federal employee retirement trust funds and interest received by trust funds—are classified as undistributed offsetting receipts. They appear instead as special deductions in computing total net budget authority and outlays for the Government rather than as offsets at the agency level. This special treatment is necessary because the amounts are so large they would distort measures of the agencies' activities if they were attributed to the agency.

User Charges

User charges are fees assessed on individuals or organizations for the provision of Government services and for the sale or use of Government goods or resources. The payers of the user charge must be limited in the authorizing legislation to those receiving special benefits from, or subject to regulation by, the program or activity beyond the benefits received by the general public or broad segments of the public (such as those who pay income taxes or customs duties). Policy regarding user charges is established in OMB Circular A–25, "User Charges." The term encompasses proceeds from the sale or use of Government goods and services, including the sale of natural resources (such as timber, oil, and minerals) and proceeds from asset sales (such as property, plant, and equipment). User charges are not necessarily dedicated to the activity they finance and may be credited to the general fund of the Treasury.

The term "user charge" does not refer to a separate budget category for collections. User charges are classified in the budget as receipts, offsetting receipts, or offsetting collections according to the principles explained previously.

See the "Offsetting Collections and Offsetting Receipts" chapter of this volume for more information on the classification of user charges.

BUDGET AUTHORITY, OBLIGATIONS, AND OUTLAYS

Budget authority, obligations, and outlays are the primary benchmarks and measures of the budget control system. The Congress enacts laws that provide agencies with spending authority in the form of budget authority. Before agencies can use these resources—obligate this budget authority—OMB must approve their spending plans. After the plans are approved, agencies can enter into binding agreements to purchase items or services or to make grants or other payments. These agreements are recorded as obligations of the United States and deducted from the amount of budgetary resources available to the agency. When payments are made, the obligations are liquidated and outlays recorded. These concepts are discussed more fully below.

Budget Authority and Other Budgetary Resources

Budget authority is the authority provided in law to enter into legal obligations that will result in immediate or future outlays of the Government. In other words, it is the amount of money that agencies are allowed to commit to be spent in current or future years. Government officials may obligate the Government to make outlays only to the extent they have been granted budget authority.

In deciding the amount of budget authority to request for a program, project, or activity, agency officials estimate the total amount of obligations they will need to incur to achieve desired goals and subtract the unobligated balances available for these purposes. The amount of budget authority requested is influenced by the nature of the programs, projects, or activities being financed. For current operating expenditures, the amount requested usually covers the needs for the fiscal year. For major procurement programs and construction projects, agencies generally must request sufficient budget authority in the first year to fully fund an economically useful segment of a procurement or project, even though it may be obligated over several years. This full funding policy is intended to ensure that the decision-makers take into account all costs and benefits at the time decisions are made to provide resources. It also avoids sinking money into a procurement or project without being certain if or when future funding will be available to complete the procurement or project, as well as saddling future agency budgets with must-pay bills to complete past projects.

Budget authority takes several forms:

- ***Appropriations***, provided in annual appropriations acts or other laws, permit agencies to incur obligations and make payments;
- ***Borrowing authority***, usually provided in permanent law, permits agencies to incur obligations but requires them to borrow funds, usually from the general fund of the Treasury, to make payments;
- ***Contract authority***, usually provided in permanent law, permits agencies to incur obligations in advance of a separate appropriation of the cash for payments or in anticipation of the collection of receipts that can be used for payments; and
- ***Spending authority from offsetting collections***, usually provided in permanent law, permits agencies to credit offsetting collections to an expenditure account, incur obligations, and make payments using the offsetting collections.

Because offsetting collections and offsetting receipts are deducted from gross budget authority, they are referred to as negative budget authority for some purposes, such as Congressional Budget Act provisions that pertain to budget authority.

Authorizing statutes usually determine the form of budget authority for a program. The authorizing statute may authorize a particular type of budget authority to be provided in appropriations acts, or it may provide one of the forms of budget authority directly, without the need for further appropriations.

An appropriation may make funds available from the general fund, special funds, or trust funds. An appropriations act may also authorize the spending of offsetting collections credited to expenditure accounts, including revolving funds. Borrowing authority is usually authorized for business-like activities where the activity being financed is expected to produce income over time with which to repay the borrowing with interest. The use of contract authority is traditionally limited to transportation programs.

New budget authority for most Federal programs is normally provided in annual appropriations acts. However, new budget authority is also made available through permanent appropriations under existing laws and does not require current action by the Congress. Much of the permanent budget authority is for trust funds, interest on the public debt, and the authority to spend offsetting collections credited to appropriation or fund accounts. For most trust funds, the budget authority is appropriated automatically under existing law from the available balance of the fund and equals the estimated annual obligations of the funds. For interest on the public debt, budget authority is provided automatically under a permanent appropriation enacted in 1847 and equals interest outlays.

Annual appropriations acts generally make budget authority available for obligation only during the fiscal year to which the act applies. However, they frequently allow budget authority for a particular purpose to remain available for obligation for a longer period or indefinitely (that is, until expended or until the program objectives have been attained). Typically, budget authority for current operations is made available for only one year, and budget authority for construction and some research projects is available for a specified number of years or indefinitely. Most budget authority provided in authorizing statutes, such as for most trust funds, is available indefinitely. If budget authority is initially provided for a limited period of availability, an extension of availability would require enactment of another law (see "Reappropriation" later in this chapter).

Budget authority that is available for more than one year and not obligated in the year it becomes available is carried forward for obligation in a following year. In some cases, an account may carry forward unobligated budget authority from more than one prior year. The sum of such amounts constitutes the account's ***unobligated balance***. Most of these balances had been provided for specific uses, such as the multiyear construction of a major project, and so are not available for new programs. A small part may never be obligated or spent, primarily amounts provided for contingencies that do not occur or reserves that never have to be used.

Amounts of budget authority that have been obligated but not yet paid constitute the account's ***unpaid obligations***. For example, in the case of salaries and wages, one to three weeks elapse between the time of obligation and the time of payment. In the case of major procurement and construction, payments may occur over a period of several years after the obligation is made. Unpaid obligations (which are made up of accounts payable and undelivered orders) net of the accounts receivable and unfilled customers' orders are defined by law as the ***obligated balances***. Obligated balances of budget authority at the end of the year are carried forward until the obligations are paid or the balances are cancelled. (A general law provides that the obligated balance of budget authority that was made available for a definite period is automatically cancelled five years after the end of the period.) Due to such flows, a change in the amount of budget authority available in any one year may change the level of obligations and outlays for several years to come. Conversely, a change in the amount of obligations incurred from one year to the next does not necessarily result from an equal change in the amount of budget authority available for that year and will not necessarily result in an equal change in the level of outlays in that year.

The Congress usually makes budget authority available on the first day of the fiscal year for which the appropriations act is passed. Occasionally, the appropriations language specifies a different timing. The language may provide an ***advance appropriation***—budget authority that does not become available until one fiscal year or more beyond the fiscal year for which the appropriations act is passed. ***Forward funding*** is budget authority that is made available for obligation beginning in the last quarter of the fiscal year (beginning on July 1) for the financing of ongoing grant programs during the next fiscal year. This kind of funding is used mostly for education programs, so that obligations for education grants can be made prior to the beginning of the next school year. For certain benefit programs funded by annual appropriations, the appropriation provides for ***advance funding***—budget authority that is to be charged to the appropriation in the succeeding year, but which authorizes obligations to be incurred in the last quarter of the current fiscal year if necessary to meet benefit payments in excess of the specific amount appropriated for the year. When such authority is used, an adjustment is made to increase the budget authority for the fiscal year in which it is used and to reduce the budget authority of the succeeding fiscal year.

Provisions of law that extend into a new fiscal year the availability of unobligated amounts that have expired or would otherwise expire are called ***reappropriations***. Reappropriations of expired balances that are newly available for obligation in the current or budget year count as new budget authority in the fiscal year in which the balances become newly available. For example, if a 2025 appropriations act extends the availability of unobligated budget authority that expired at the end of 2024, new budget authority would be recorded for 2025. This scorekeeping is used because a reappropriation has exactly the same effect as allowing the earlier appropriation to expire at the end of 2024 and enacting a new appropriation for 2025.

The Federal Government uses budget enforcement mechanisms to control revenues, spending, and deficits (see the "Budget Process" chapter of this volume for a detailed discussion of the budget enforcement framework). For purposes of budget enforcement, the budget classifies budget authority as ***discretionary*** or ***mandatory***. This classification indicates whether an appropriations act or authorizing legislation controls the amount of budget authority that is available. Generally, budget authority is discretionary if provided in an appropriations act and mandatory if provided in authorizing legislation. However, the budget authority provided in appropriations acts for certain specifically identified programs is also classified as mandatory by OMB and the congressional scorekeepers. This is because the authorizing legislation for these programs entitles beneficiaries—persons, households, or other levels of government—to receive payment, or otherwise legally obligates the Government to make payment and thereby effectively determines the amount of budget authority required, even though the payments are funded by a subsequent appropriation.

Sometimes, budget authority is characterized as current or permanent. Current authority requires the Congress to act on the request for new budget authority for the year involved. Permanent authority becomes available pursuant to standing provisions of law without appropriations action by the Congress for the year involved. Generally, budget authority is current if an annual appropriations act provides it and permanent if authorizing legislation provides it. By and large, the current/permanent distinction has been replaced by the discretionary/mandatory distinction, which is similar but not identical. Outlays are also classified as discretionary or mandatory according to the classification of the budget authority from which they flow (see "Outlays" later in this chapter).

The amount of budget authority recorded in the budget depends on whether the law provides a specific amount or employs a variable factor that determines the amount. It is considered ***definite*** if the law specifies a dollar amount (which may be stated as an upper limit, for example, "shall not exceed ..."). It is considered ***indefinite*** if, instead of specifying an amount, the law permits the amount to be determined by subsequent circumstances. For example, indefinite budget authority is provided for interest on the public debt, payment of claims and judgments awarded by the courts against the United States, and many entitlement programs. Many of the laws that authorize collections to be credited to revolving, special, and trust funds make all of the collections available for expenditure for the authorized purposes of the fund, and such authority is considered to be indefinite budget authority because the amount of collections is not known in advance of their collection.

Obligations

Following the enactment of budget authority and the completion of required apportionment action, Government agencies incur obligations to make payments (see earlier discussion under "Budget Execution"). Agencies must record obligations when they incur a legal liability that will result in immediate or future outlays. Such obligations include the current liabilities for salaries, wages, and interest; and contracts for the purchase of supplies and equipment, construction, and the acquisition of office space, buildings, and land. For Federal credit programs, obligations are recorded in an amount equal to the estimated subsidy cost of direct loans and loan guarantees (see "Federal Credit" later in this chapter).

Outlays

Outlays are the measure of Government spending. They are payments that liquidate obligations (other than most exchanges of financial instruments, of which the repayment of debt is the prime example). The budget records outlays when obligations are paid, in the amount that is paid.

Agency, function and subfunction, and Government-wide outlay totals are stated net of offsetting collections and offsetting receipts for most budget presentations.

(Offsetting receipts from a few sources do not offset any specific function, subfunction, or agency, as explained previously, but only offset Government-wide totals.) Outlay totals for accounts with offsetting collections are stated both gross and net of the offsetting collections credited to the account. However, the outlay totals for special and trust funds with offsetting receipts are not stated net of the offsetting receipts. In most cases, these receipts offset the agency, function, and subfunction totals but do not offset account-level outlays. However, when general fund payments are used to finance trust fund outlays to the public, the associated trust fund receipts are netted against the bureau totals to prevent double-counting budget authority and outlays at the bureau level.

The Government usually makes outlays in the form of cash (currency, checks, or electronic fund transfers). However, in some cases agencies pay obligations without disbursing cash, and the budget nevertheless records outlays for the equivalent method. For example, the budget records outlays for the full amount of Federal employees' salaries, even though the cash disbursed to employees is net of Federal and State income taxes withheld, retirement contributions, life and health insurance premiums, and other deductions. (The budget also records receipts for the amounts withheld from Federal employee paychecks for Federal income taxes and other payments to the Government.) When debt instruments (bonds, debentures, notes, or monetary credits) are used in place of cash to pay obligations, the budget records outlays financed by an increase in agency debt. For example, the budget records the acquisition of physical assets through certain types of lease-purchase arrangements as though a cash disbursement were made for an outright purchase. The transaction creates a Government debt, and the cash lease payments are treated as repayments of principal and interest.

The budget records outlays for the interest on the public issues of Treasury debt securities as the interest accrues, not when the cash is paid. A small portion of Treasury debt consists of inflation-indexed securities, which feature monthly adjustments to principal for inflation and semiannual payments of interest on the inflation-adjusted principal. As with fixed-rate securities, the budget records interest outlays as the interest accrues. The monthly adjustment to principal is recorded, simultaneously, as an increase in debt outstanding and an outlay of interest.

Most Treasury debt securities held by trust funds and other Government accounts are in the Government account series. The budget normally states the interest on these securities on a cash basis. When a Government account is invested in Federal debt securities, the purchase price is usually close or identical to the par (face) value of the security. The budget generally records the investment at par value and adjusts the interest paid by Treasury and collected by the account by the difference between purchase price and par, if any.

For Federal credit programs, outlays are equal to the subsidy cost of direct loans and loan guarantees and are recorded as the underlying loans are disbursed (see "Federal Credit" later in this chapter).

The budget records refunds of receipts that result from overpayments by the public (such as income taxes withheld in excess of tax liabilities) as reductions of receipts, rather than as outlays. However, the budget records payments to taxpayers for refundable tax credits (such as earned income tax credits) that exceed the taxpayer's tax liability as outlays. Similarly, when the Government makes overpayments that are later returned to the Government, those refunds to the Government are recorded as offsetting collections or offsetting receipts, not as governmental receipts.

Not all of the new budget authority for 2025 will be obligated or spent in 2025. Outlays during a fiscal year may liquidate obligations incurred in the same year or in prior years. Obligations, in turn, may be incurred against budget authority provided in the same year or against unobligated balances of budget authority provided in prior years. Outlays, therefore, flow in part from budget authority provided for the year in which the money is spent and in part from budget authority provided for prior years. The ratio of a given year's outlays resulting from budget authority enacted in that or a prior year to the original amount of that budget authority is referred to as the outlay rate for that year.

As shown in the accompanying chart, $5,728 billion of outlays in 2025 (79 percent of the outlay total) will be made from that year's $7,484 billion total of proposed new budget authority (a first-year outlay rate of 77 percent). Thus, the remaining $1,538 billion of outlays in 2025 (21 percent of the outlay total) will be made from budget authority enacted in previous years. At the same time, $1,756 billion of the new budget authority proposed for 2025 (23 percent of the total amount proposed) will not lead to outlays until future years.

As described earlier, the budget classifies budget authority and outlays as discretionary or mandatory. This classification of outlays measures the extent to which actual spending is controlled through the annual appropriations process. About 28 percent of total outlays in 2023 ($1,718 billion) were discretionary and the remaining 72 percent ($4,416 billion in 2023) were mandatory spending and net interest. Such a large portion of total spending is mandatory because authorizing rather than appropriations legislation determines net interest ($658 billion in 2023) and the spending for a few programs with large amounts of spending each year, such as Social Security ($1,348 billion in 2023) and Medicare ($839 billion in 2023).

The bulk of mandatory outlays flow from budget authority recorded in the same fiscal year. This is not necessarily the case for discretionary budget authority and outlays. For most major construction and procurement projects and long-term contracts, for example, the budget authority available at the time the projects are initiated covers the entire estimated cost of the project even though the work will take place and outlays will be made over a period extending beyond the year for which the budget authority is enacted. Similarly, discretionary budget authority for most education and job training activities is appropriated for school or program years that begin in the fourth quarter of the fiscal year. Most of these funds result in outlays in the year after the appropriation.

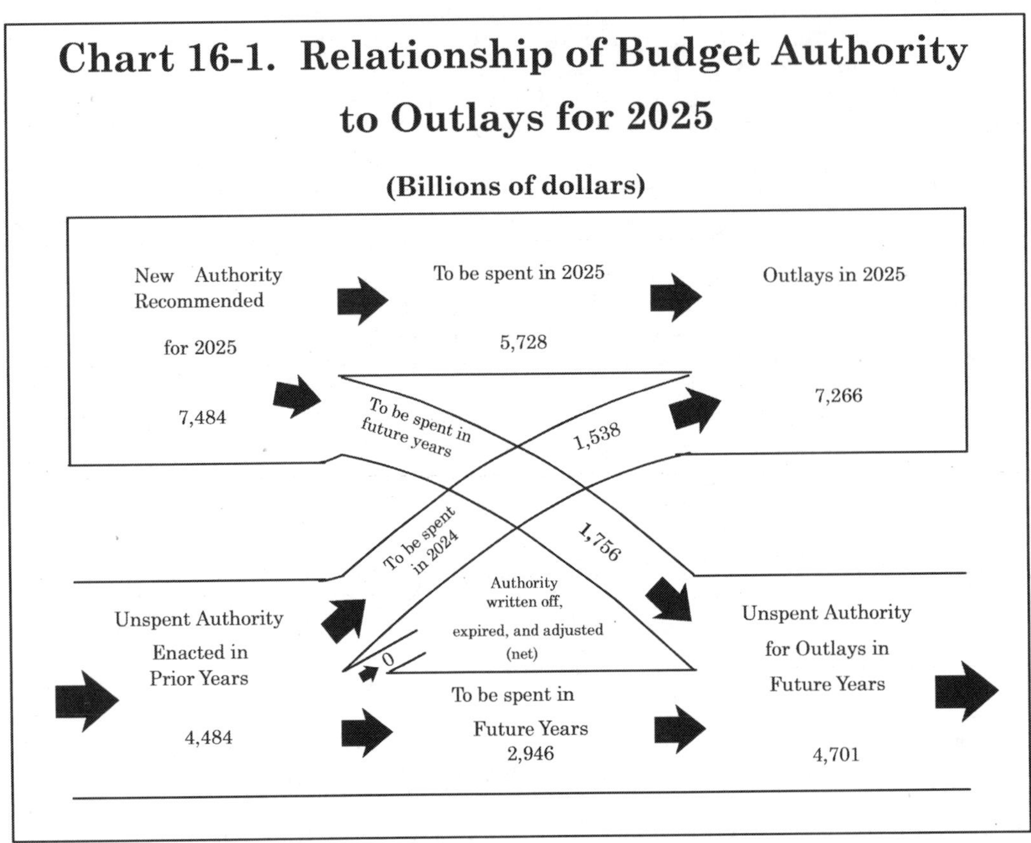

FEDERAL CREDIT

Some Government programs provide assistance through direct loans or loan guarantees. A ***direct loan*** is a disbursement of funds by the Government to a non-Federal borrower under a contract that requires repayment of such funds with or without interest and includes economically equivalent transactions, such as the sale of Federal assets on credit terms. A ***loan guarantee*** is any guarantee, insurance, or other pledge with respect to the payment of all or a part of the principal or interest on any debt obligation of a non-Federal borrower to a non-Federal lender.

Under the budgetary treatment specified by the Federal Credit Reform Act of 1990, as amended (FCRA), the budget records obligations and outlays for direct loans and loan guarantees up front, for the net cost to the Government, rather than recording the cash flows year by year over the term of the loan. By differentiating between the net cost to the Government (which represents an allocation of resources) and the cash flows associated with the direct loan or loan guarantee (which represents the financing of that cost), FCRA treatment allows the comparison of direct loans and loan guarantees to each other, and to other methods of delivering assistance, such as grants, on an apples-to-apples basis.

The cost of direct loans and loan guarantees, sometimes called the "subsidy cost," is estimated as the present value of expected payments to and from the public over the term of the loan, discounted using appropriate Treasury interest rates.[2] Similar to most other kinds of programs, agencies can make loans or guarantee loans only if the Congress has appropriated funds sufficient to cover the subsidy costs, or provided a limitation in an appropriations act on the amount of direct loans or loan guarantees that can be made.

The budget records the subsidy cost to the Government arising from direct loans and loan guarantees—the budget authority and outlays—in ***credit program accounts***. When a Federal agency disburses a direct loan or when a non-Federal lender disburses a loan guaranteed by a Federal agency, the program account disburses or outlays an amount equal to the estimated present value cost, or subsidy, to a non-budgetary ***credit financing account***. The financing accounts record the actual transactions with the public. For a few programs, the estimated subsidy cost is negative because the present value of expected Government collections exceeds the present value of expected payments to the public over the term of the loan. In such cases, the financing account pays the estimated subsidy cost to the program's negative subsidy receipt account, where it is recorded as an offsetting receipt. In a few cases, the offsetting receipts of credit accounts are

[2] Present value is a standard financial concept that considers the time-value of money. That is, it accounts for the fact that a given sum of money is worth more today than the same sum would be worth in the future because interest can be earned.

dedicated to a special fund established for the program and are available for appropriation for the program.

The agencies responsible for credit programs must reestimate the subsidy cost of the outstanding portfolio of direct loans and loan guarantees each year. If the estimated cost increases, the program account makes an additional payment to the financing account equal to the change in cost. If the estimated cost decreases, the financing account pays the difference to the program's downward reestimate receipt account, where it is recorded as an offsetting receipt. FCRA provides permanent indefinite appropriations to pay for upward reestimates.

If the Government modifies the terms of an outstanding direct loan or loan guarantee in a way that increases the cost as the result of a law or the exercise of administrative discretion under existing law, the program account records obligations for the increased cost and outlays the amount to the financing account. As with the original subsidy cost, agencies may incur modification costs only if the Congress has appropriated funds to cover them. A modification may also reduce costs, in which case the amounts are generally returned to the general fund, as the financing account makes a payment to the program's negative subsidy receipt account.

Credit financing accounts record all cash flows arising from direct loan obligations and loan guarantee commitments. Such cash flows include all cash flows to and from the public, including direct loan disbursements and repayments, loan guarantee default payments, fees, and recoveries on defaults. Financing accounts also record intragovernmental transactions, such as the receipt of subsidy cost payments from program accounts, borrowing and repayments of Treasury debt to finance program activities, and interest paid to or received from the Treasury. The cash flows of direct loans and of loan guarantees are recorded in separate financing accounts for programs that provide both types of credit. The budget totals exclude the transactions of the financing accounts because they do not represent an allocation of resources by the Government; rather, they affect the means of financing a budget surplus or deficit (see "Credit Financing Accounts" in the next section). The budget documents display the transactions of the financing accounts, together with the related program accounts, for information and analytical purposes.

The budgetary treatment of direct loan obligations and loan guarantee commitments made prior to 1992 was grandfathered in under FCRA. The budget records these on a cash basis in ***credit liquidating accounts***, the same as they were recorded before FCRA was enacted. However, this exception ceases to apply if the direct loans or loan guarantees are modified as described above. In that case, the budget records the subsidy cost or savings of the modification, as appropriate, and begins to account for the associated transactions under FCRA treatment for direct loan obligations and loan guarantee commitments made in 1992 or later.

Under the authority provided in various acts, certain activities that do not meet the definition in FCRA of a direct loan or loan guarantee are reflected pursuant to FCRA. For example, the Emergency Economic Stabilization Act of 2008 (EESA) created the Troubled Asset Relief Program (TARP) under the Department of the Treasury, and authorized Treasury to purchase or guarantee troubled assets until October 3, 2010. Under the TARP, Treasury purchased equity interests in financial institutions. Section 123 of the EESA provides the Administration the authority to treat these equity investments on a FCRA basis, recording outlays for the subsidy as is done for direct loans and loan guarantees. The budget reflects the cost to the Government of TARP direct loans, loan guarantees, and equity investments consistent with the FCRA and Section 123 of EESA, which requires an adjustment to the FCRA discount rate for market risks. Similarly, Treasury equity purchases under the Small Business Lending Fund are treated pursuant to the FCRA, as provided by the Small Business Jobs Act of 2010. The Coronavirus Aid, Relief, and Economic Security (CARES) Act authorized certain investments in programs and facilities established by the Federal Reserve. Section 4003 of the CARES Act provided that these amounts be treated in accordance with FCRA.

BUDGET DEFICIT OR SURPLUS AND MEANS OF FINANCING

When outlays exceed receipts, the difference is a deficit, which the Government finances primarily by borrowing. When receipts exceed outlays, the difference is a surplus, and the Government automatically uses the surplus primarily to reduce debt. The Federal debt held by the public is approximately the cumulative amount of borrowing to finance deficits, less repayments from surpluses, over the Nation's history.

Borrowing is not exactly equal to the deficit, and debt repayment is not exactly equal to the surplus, because of the other transactions affecting borrowing from the public, or other means of financing, such as those discussed in this section. The factors included in the other means of financing can either increase or decrease the Government's borrowing needs (or decrease or increase its ability to repay debt). For example, the change in the Treasury operating cash balance is a factor included in other means of financing. Holding receipts and outlays constant, increases in the cash balance increase the Government's need to borrow or reduce the Government's ability to repay debt, and decreases in the cash balance decrease the need to borrow or increase the ability to repay debt. In some years, the net effect of the other means of financing is minor relative to the borrowing or debt repayment; in other years, the net effect may be significant.

Borrowing and Debt Repayment

The budget treats borrowing and debt repayment as a means of financing, not as receipts and outlays. If borrowing were defined as receipts and debt repayment as outlays, the budget would always be virtually balanced by definition. This rule applies both to borrowing in the form of Treasury securities and to specialized borrowing in the form of agency securities. The rule reflects the commonsense understanding that lending or borrowing is just an exchange of financial assets of equal value—cash for Treasury securities—and so is fundamentally different from, say, paying taxes, which involve a net transfer of financial assets from taxpayers to the Government.

In 2023, the Government borrowed $1,982 billion from the public, bringing debt held by the public to $26,236 billion. This borrowing financed the $1,694 billion deficit in that year, as well as the net impacts of the other means of financing, such as changes in cash balances and other accounts discussed below.

In addition to selling debt to the public, the Department of the Treasury issues debt to Government accounts, primarily trust funds that are required by law to invest in Treasury securities. Issuing and redeeming this debt does not affect the means of financing, because these transactions occur between one Government account and another and thus do not raise or use any cash for the Government as a whole.

(See the "Federal Borrowing and Debt" chapter of this volume for a fuller discussion of this topic.)

Exercise of Monetary Power

Seigniorage is the profit from coining money. It is the difference between the value of coins as money and their cost of production. Seigniorage reduces the Government's need to borrow. Unlike the payment of taxes or other receipts, it does not involve a transfer of financial assets from the public. Instead, it arises from the exercise of the Government's power to create money and the public's desire to hold financial assets in the form of coins. Therefore, the budget excludes seigniorage from receipts and treats it as a means of financing other than borrowing from the public. The budget also treats proceeds from the sale of gold as a means of financing, since the value of gold is determined by its value as a monetary asset rather than as a commodity.

Credit Financing Accounts

The budget records the net cash flows of credit programs in credit financing accounts. These accounts include the transactions for direct loan and loan guarantee programs, as well as the equity purchase programs under TARP that are recorded on a credit basis consistent with Section 123 of EESA. Financing accounts also record equity purchases under the Small Business Lending Fund consistent with the Small Business Jobs Act of 2010, and certain investments in programs and facilities established by the Federal Reserve consistent with Section 4003 of the CARES Act. Credit financing accounts are excluded from the budget because they are not allocations of resources by the Government (see "Federal Credit" earlier in this chapter). However, even though they do not affect the surplus or deficit, they can either increase or decrease the Government's need to borrow. Therefore, they are recorded as a means of financing.

Financing account disbursements to the public increase the requirement for Treasury borrowing in the same way as an increase in budget outlays. Financing account receipts from the public can be used to finance the payment of the Government's obligations and therefore reduce the requirement for Treasury borrowing from the public in the same way as an increase in budget receipts.

Deposit Fund Account Balances

The Treasury uses non-budgetary accounts, called deposit funds, to record cash held temporarily until ownership is determined (for example, earnest money paid by bidders for mineral leases) or cash held by the Government as agent for others (for example, State and local income taxes withheld from Federal employees' salaries and not yet paid to the State or local government or amounts held in the Thrift Savings Fund, a defined contribution pension fund held and managed in a fiduciary capacity by the Government). Deposit fund balances may be held in the form of either invested or uninvested balances. To the extent that they are not invested, changes in the balances are available to finance expenditures without a change in borrowing and are recorded as a means of financing other than borrowing from the public. To the extent that they are invested in Federal debt, changes in the balances are reflected as borrowing from the public (in lieu of borrowing from other parts of the public) and are not reflected as a separate means of financing.

United States Quota Subscriptions to the International Monetary Fund (IMF)

The United States participates in the IMF primarily through a quota subscription. Financial transactions with the IMF are exchanges of monetary assets. When the IMF temporarily draws dollars from the U.S. quota, the United States simultaneously receives an equal, offsetting, interest-bearing, Special Drawing Right (SDR)-denominated claim in the form of an increase in the U.S. reserve position in the IMF. The U.S. reserve position in the IMF increases when the United States makes deposits in its account at the IMF when the IMF temporarily uses members' quota resources to make loans and decreases when the IMF returns funds to the United States as borrowing countries repay the IMF (and the cash flows from the reserve position to the Treasury letter of credit).

The U.S. transactions with the IMF under the quota subscriptions do not increase the deficit in any year, and the budget excludes these transfers from budget outlays and receipts, consistent with the budgetary treatment for exchanges of monetary assets recommended by the President's Commission on Budget Concepts in 1967. The only exception is that interest earnings on U.S. deposits in its IMF account are recorded as offsetting receipts. Other exchanges of monetary assets, such as deposits of cash in Treasury accounts at commercial banks, are likewise not included in the Budget. However, the Congress has historically expressed interest in showing some kind of budgetary effect for U.S. transactions with the IMF.[3]

[3] For a more detailed discussion of the history of the budgetary treatment of U.S. participation in the quota and New Arrangements to Borrow (NAB), see pages 139-141 in the *Analytical Perspectives* volume of the 2016 Budget. As discussed in that volume, the budgetary treatment of the U.S. participation in the NAB is similar to the quota. See pages 85-86 of the *Analytical Perspectives* volume of the 2018 Budget for a more complete discussion of the changes made to the budgetary presentation of quota increases in Title IX of the Department of State, Foreign Operations, and Related Programs Appropriations Act, 2016.

FEDERAL EMPLOYMENT

The Budget includes information on civilian and military employment. It also includes information on related personnel compensation and benefits and on staffing requirements at overseas missions. The "Strengthening the Federal Workforce" chapter of this volume provides employment levels measured in full-time equivalents (FTEs). Agency FTEs are the measure of total hours worked by an agency's Federal employees divided by the total number of one person's compensable work hours in a fiscal year.

BASIS FOR BUDGET FIGURES

Data for the Past Year

The past year column (2023) generally presents the actual transactions and balances as recorded in agency accounts and as summarized in the central financial reports prepared by the Department of the Treasury for the most recently completed fiscal year. Occasionally, the Budget reports corrections to data reported erroneously to Treasury but not discovered in time to be reflected in Treasury's published data. In addition, in certain cases the Budget has a broader scope and includes financial transactions that are not reported to Treasury (see the "Comparison of Actual to Estimated Totals" chapter of this volume for a summary of these differences).

Data for the Current Year

The current year column (2024) includes estimates of transactions and balances based on the amounts of budgetary resources that were available when the Budget was prepared. In cases where the Budget proposes policy changes effective in the current year, the data will also reflect the budgetary effect of those proposed changes.

Data for the Budget Year

The Budget year column (2025) includes estimates of transactions and balances based on the amounts of budgetary resources that are estimated to be available, including new budget authority requested under current authorizing legislation, and amounts estimated to result from changes in authorizing legislation and tax laws.

The Budget *Appendix* generally includes the appropriations language for the amounts proposed to be appropriated under current authorizing legislation. In a few cases, this language is transmitted later because the exact requirements are unknown when the budget is transmitted. The *Appendix* generally does not include appropriations language for the amounts that will be requested under proposed legislation; that language is usually transmitted later, after the legislation is enacted. Some tables in the budget identify the items for later transmittal and the related outlays separately. Estimates of the total requirements for the Budget year include both the amounts requested with the transmittal of the budget and the amounts planned for later transmittal.

Data for the Outyears

The Budget presents estimates for each of the nine years beyond the budget year (2026 through 2034) in order to reflect the effects of budget decisions on objectives and plans over a longer period.

Allowances

The budget may include lump-sum allowances to cover certain transactions that are expected to increase or decrease budget authority, outlays, or receipts but are not, for various reasons, reflected in the program details. For example, the budget might include an allowance to show the effect on the budget totals of a proposal that would affect many accounts by relatively small amounts, in order to avoid unnecessary detail in the presentations for the individual accounts.

Baseline

The Budget baseline is an estimate of the receipts, outlays, and deficits or surpluses that would occur if no changes were made to current laws and policies during the period covered by the Budget. Its construction is governed by rules codified in BBEDCA. The baseline assumes, with limited exceptions, that receipts and mandatory spending, which generally are authorized on a permanent basis, will continue in the future consistent with current law and policy. Funding for discretionary programs is inflated from the most recent enacted appropriations using specified inflation rates. In certain cases, adjustments to the BBEDCA baseline are needed to better represent the deficit outlook under current policy and to serve as a more appropriate benchmark against which to measure policy changes; this presentation is colloquially referred to as the "adjusted baseline." (The "Current Services Estimates" chapter of this volume provides more information on the baseline and adjustments in the 2025 Budget baseline.)

Baseline outlays represent the amount of resources that the Government would use over the period covered by the Budget on the basis of laws currently enacted.

The baseline serves several useful purposes:

- It may warn of future problems, either for Government fiscal policy as a whole or for individual tax and spending programs.
- It may provide a starting point for formulating the President's Budget.
- It may provide a benchmark against which the President's Budget and alternative proposals can be compared to assess the magnitude of proposed changes.

PRINCIPAL BUDGET LAWS

The Budget and Accounting Act of 1921 created the core of the current Federal budget process. Before enactment of this law, there was no annual centralized budgeting in the Executive Branch. Federal Government agencies usually sent budget requests independently to congressional committees with no coordination of the various requests in formulating the Federal Government's budget. The Budget and Accounting Act required the President to coordinate the budget requests for all Government agencies and to send a comprehensive budget to the Congress. The Congress has amended the requirements many times and portions of the Act are codified in Title 31, United States Code. The major laws that govern the budget process are as follows:

Article 1, section 8, clause 1 of the Constitution, which empowers the Congress to lay and collect taxes.

Article 1, section 9, clause 7 of the Constitution, which requires appropriations in law before money may be spent from the Treasury and the publication of a regular statement of the receipts and expenditures of all public money.

Antideficiency Act (codified in Chapters 13 and 15 of Title 31, United States Code), which prescribes rules and procedures for budget execution.

Balanced Budget and Emergency Deficit Control Act of 1985, as amended, which establishes limits on discretionary spending and provides mechanisms for enforcing mandatory spending and discretionary spending limits.

Chapter 11 of Title 31, United States Code, which prescribes procedures for submission of the President's budget and information to be contained in it.

Congressional Budget and Impoundment Control Act of 1974, as amended (Public Law 93–344). This Act comprises the:

- ***Congressional Budget Act of 1974, as amended***, which prescribes the congressional budget process;
- ***Impoundment Control Act of 1974, as amended***, which controls certain aspects of budget execution; and
- ***Federal Credit Reform Act of 1990, as amended (2 U.S.C. 661–661f)***, which the Budget Enforcement Act of 1990 included as an amendment to the Congressional Budget Act to prescribe the budget treatment for Federal credit programs.

Chapter 31 of Title 31, United States Code, which provides the authority for the Secretary of the Treasury to issue debt to finance the deficit and establishes a statutory limit on the level of the debt.

Chapter 33 of Title 31, United States Code, which establishes the Department of the Treasury as the authority for making disbursements of public funds, with the authority to delegate that authority to executive agencies in the interests of economy and efficiency.

Government Performance and Results Act of 1993, as amended (Public Law 103–62), which emphasizes managing for results. It requires agencies to prepare strategic plans, annual performance plans, and annual performance reports.

Statutory Pay-As-You-Go Act of 2010, which establishes a budget enforcement mechanism generally requiring that direct spending and revenue legislation enacted into law not increase the deficit.

GLOSSARY OF BUDGET TERMS

Account refers to a separate financial reporting unit used by the Federal Government to record budget authority, outlays and income for budgeting or management information purposes as well as for accounting purposes. All budget (and off-budget) accounts are classified as being either expenditure or receipt accounts and by fund group. Budget (and off-budget) transactions fall within either of two fund groups: 1) Federal funds and 2) trust funds. (Cf. Federal funds group and trust funds group.)

Accrual method of measuring cost means an accounting method that records cost when the liability is incurred. As applied to Federal employee retirement benefits, accrual costs are recorded when the benefits are earned rather than when they are paid at some time in the future. The accrual method is used in part to provide data that assists in agency policymaking, but not used in presenting the overall budget of the United States Government.

Advance appropriation means appropriations of new budget authority that become available one or more fiscal years beyond the fiscal year for which the appropriation act was passed.

Advance funding means appropriations of budget authority provided in an appropriations act to be used, if necessary, to cover obligations incurred late in the fiscal year for benefit payments in excess of the amount specifically appropriated in the act for that year, where the budget authority is charged to the appropriation for the program for the fiscal year following the fiscal year for which the appropriations act is passed.

Agency means a Department or other establishment of the Government.

Allowance means a lump-sum included in the budget to represent certain transactions that are expected to increase or decrease budget authority, outlays, or receipts but that are not, for various reasons, reflected in the program details.

Balanced Budget and Emergency Deficit Control Act of 1985, as amended (BBEDCA) refers to legislation that altered the budget process, primarily by replacing the earlier fixed targets for annual deficits with a Pay-As-You-Go requirement for new tax or mandatory spending legislation and with caps on annual discretionary funding. The Statutory Pay-As-You-Go Act of 2010, which is a standalone piece of legislation that did not directly amend the BBEDCA, reinstated a statutory pay-as-you-go rule for revenues and mandatory spending legislation, and the Fiscal Responsibility Act of 2023 (Public Law 118-5), which did amend BBEDCA, reinstated discretionary caps on budget authority through 2025.

Balances of budget authority means the amounts of budget authority provided in previous years that have not been outlayed.

Baseline means a projection of the estimated receipts, outlays, and deficit or surplus that would result from continuing current law or current policies through the period covered by the budget.

Budget means the Budget of the United States Government, which sets forth the President's comprehensive financial plan for allocating resources and indicates the President's priorities for the Federal Government.

Budget authority (BA) means the authority provided by law to incur financial obligations that will result in outlays. (For a description of the several forms of budget authority, see "Budget Authority and Other Budgetary Resources" earlier in this chapter.)

Budget Control Act of 2011 refers to legislation that, among other things, amended BBEDCA to reinstate discretionary spending limits on budget authority through 2021 and restored the process for enforcing those spending limits. The legislation also increased the statutory debt ceiling; created a Joint Select Committee on Deficit Reduction that was instructed to develop a bill to reduce the Federal deficit by at least $1.5 trillion over a 10-year period; and provided a process to implement alternative spending reductions in the event that legislation achieving at least $1.2 trillion of deficit reduction was not enacted.

Budget resolution—see concurrent resolution on the budget.

Budget totals mean the totals included in the budget for budget authority, outlays, receipts, and the surplus or deficit. Some presentations in the budget distinguish on-budget totals from off-budget totals. On-budget totals reflect the transactions of all Federal Government entities except those excluded from the budget totals by law. Off-budget totals reflect the transactions of Government entities that are excluded from the on-budget totals by law. Under current law, the off-budget totals include the Social Security trust funds (Federal Old-Age and Survivors Insurance and Federal Disability Insurance Trust Funds) and the Postal Service Fund. The budget combines the on- and off-budget totals to derive unified (i.e. consolidated) totals for Federal activity.

Budget year refers to the fiscal year for which the budget is being considered, that is, with respect to a session of the Congress, the fiscal year of the Government that starts on October 1 of the calendar year in which that session of the Congress begins.

Budgetary resources mean amounts available to incur obligations in a given year. The term comprises new budget authority and unobligated balances of budget authority provided in previous years.

Cap means the legal limits for each fiscal year under BBEDCA on the budget authority and outlays (only if applicable) provided by discretionary appropriations.

Cap adjustment means either an increase or a decrease that is permitted to the statutory cap limits for each fiscal year under BBEDCA on the budget authority and outlays (only if applicable) provided by discretionary appropriations only if certain conditions are met. These conditions may include providing for a base level of funding, a designation of the increase or decrease by the Congress, (and in some circumstances, the President) pursuant to a section of the BBEDCA, or a change in concepts and definitions of funding under the cap. Changes in concepts and definitions require consultation with the Congressional Appropriations and Budget Committees.

Cash equivalent transaction means a transaction in which the Government makes outlays or receives collections in a form other than cash or the cash does not accurately measure the cost of the transaction. (For examples, see the section on "Outlays" earlier in this chapter.)

Collections mean money collected by the Government that the budget records as a governmental receipt, an offsetting collection, or an offsetting receipt.

Concurrent resolution on the budget refers to the concurrent resolution adopted by the Congress to set budgetary targets for appropriations, mandatory spending legislation, and tax legislation. These concurrent resolutions are required by the Congressional Budget Act of 1974, and are generally adopted annually.

Continuing resolution means an appropriations act that provides for the ongoing operation of the Government in the absence of enacted appropriations.

Cost refers to legislation or administrative actions that increase outlays or decrease receipts. (Cf. savings.)

Credit program account means a budget account that receives and obligates appropriations to cover the subsidy cost of a direct loan or loan guarantee and disburses the subsidy cost to a financing account.

Current services estimate—see Baseline.

Debt held by the public means the cumulative amount of money the Federal Government has borrowed from the public and not repaid.

Debt held by the public net of financial assets means the cumulative amount of money the Federal Government has borrowed from the public and not repaid, minus the current value of financial assets such as loan assets, bank deposits, or private-sector securities or equities held by the Government and plus the current value of financial liabilities other than debt.

Debt held by Government accounts means the debt the Department of the Treasury owes to accounts within the Federal Government. Most of it results from the surpluses of the Social Security and other trust funds, which are required by law to be invested in Federal securities.

Debt limit means the maximum amount of Federal debt that may legally be outstanding at any time. It includes both the debt held by the public and the debt held by Government accounts, but without accounting for offsetting financial assets. When the debt limit is reached, the Government cannot borrow more money until the Congress has enacted a law to increase the limit.

Deficit means the amount by which outlays exceed receipts in a fiscal year. It may refer to the on-budget, off-budget, or unified budget deficit.

Direct loan means a disbursement of funds by the Government to a non-Federal borrower under a contract that requires the repayment of such funds with or without interest. The term includes the purchase of, or participation in, a loan made by another lender. The term also includes the sale of a Government asset on credit terms of more than 90 days duration as well as financing arrangements for other transactions that defer payment for more than 90 days. It also includes loans financed by the Federal Financing Bank (FFB) pursuant to agency loan guarantee authority. The term does not include the acquisition of a federally guaranteed loan in satisfaction of default or other guarantee claims or the price support "loans" of the Commodity Credit Corporation. (Cf. loan guarantee.)

Direct spending—see mandatory spending.

Disaster funding means a discretionary appropriation that is enacted that the Congress designates as being for disaster relief. Such amounts are a cap adjustment to the limits on discretionary spending under BBEDCA. The total adjustment for this purpose cannot exceed a ceiling for a particular year that is defined as the total of the average funding provided for disaster relief over the previous 10 years (excluding the highest and lowest years) and the unused amount of the prior year's ceiling (excluding the portion of the prior year's ceiling that was itself due to any unused amount from the year before). Disaster relief is defined as activities carried out pursuant to a determination under section 102(2) of the Robert T. Stafford Disaster Relief and Emergency Assistance Act.

Discretionary spending means budgetary resources (except those provided to fund mandatory spending programs) provided in appropriations acts. (Cf. mandatory spending.)

Emergency requirement means an amount that the Congress has designated as an emergency requirement. Such amounts are not included in the estimated budgetary effects of PAYGO legislation under the requirements of the Statutory Pay-As-You-Go Act of 2010, if they are mandatory or receipts. Such a discretionary appropriation that is subsequently designated by the President as an emergency requirement results in a cap adjustment to the limits on discretionary spending under BBEDCA, when such limits are in place.

Entitlement refers to a program in which the Federal Government is legally obligated to make payments or provide aid to any person who, or State or local government that, meets the legal criteria for eligibility. Examples include Social Security, Medicare, Medicaid, and the Supplemental Nutrition Assistance Program (formerly Food Stamps).

Federal funds group refers to the moneys collected and spent by the Government through accounts other than those designated as trust funds. Federal funds include general, special, public enterprise, and intragovernmental funds. (Cf. trust funds group.)

Financing account means a non-budgetary account (an account whose transactions are excluded from the budget totals) that records all of the cash flows resulting from post-1991 direct loan obligations or loan guarantee commitments. At least one financing account is associated with each credit program account. For programs that make both direct loans and loan guarantees, separate financing accounts are required for direct loan cash flows and for loan guarantee cash flows. (Cf. liquidating account.)

Fiscal year means the Government's accounting period. It begins on October 1 and ends on September 30, and is designated by the calendar year in which it ends.

Forward funding means appropriations of budget authority that are made for obligation starting in the last quarter of the fiscal year for the financing of ongoing grant programs during the next fiscal year.

General fund means the accounts in which are recorded governmental receipts not earmarked by law for a specific purpose, the proceeds of general borrowing, and the expenditure of these moneys.

Government-sponsored enterprises mean private enterprises that were established and chartered by the Federal Government for public policy purposes. They are classified as non-budgetary and not included in the Federal budget because they are private companies, and their securities are not backed by the full faith and credit of the Federal Government. However, the budget presents statements of financial condition for certain Government sponsored enterprises such as the Federal National Mortgage Association. (Cf. off-budget.)

Intragovernmental fund—see Revolving fund.

Liquidating account means a budget account that records all cash flows to and from the Government resulting from pre-1992 direct loan obligations or loan guarantee commitments. (Cf. financing account.)

Loan guarantee means any guarantee, insurance, or other pledge with respect to the payment of all or a part of the principal or interest on any debt obligation of a non-Federal borrower to a non-Federal lender. The term does not include the insurance of deposits, shares, or other withdrawable accounts in financial institutions. (Cf. direct loan.)

Mandatory spending means spending controlled by laws other than appropriations acts (including spending for entitlement programs) and spending for the Supplemental Nutrition Assistance Program, formerly food stamps. Although the Statutory Pay-As-You-Go Act of 2010 uses the term direct spending to mean this, mandatory spending is commonly used instead. (Cf. discretionary spending.)

Means of financing refers to borrowing, the change in cash balances, and certain other transactions involved in financing a deficit. The term is also used to refer to the debt repayment, the change in cash balances, and certain other transactions involved in using a surplus. By definition, the means of financing are not treated as receipts or outlays and so are non-budgetary.

Obligated balance means the cumulative amount of budget authority that has been obligated but not yet outlayed. (Cf. unobligated balance.)

Obligation means a binding agreement that will result in outlays, immediately or in the future. Budgetary resources must be available before obligations can be incurred legally.

Off-budget refers to transactions of the Federal Government that would be treated as budgetary had the Congress not designated them by statute as "off-budget." Currently, transactions of the Social Security trust funds and the Postal Service are the only sets of transactions that are so designated. The term is sometimes used more broadly to refer to the transactions of private enterprises that were established and sponsored by the Government, most especially "Government-sponsored enterprises" such as the Federal Home Loan Banks. (Cf. budget totals.)

Offsetting collections mean collections that, by law, are credited directly to expenditure accounts and deducted from gross budget authority and outlays of the expenditure account, rather than added to receipts. Usually, they are authorized to be spent for the purposes of the account without further action by the Congress. They result from business-like transactions with the public, including payments from the public in exchange for goods and services, reimbursements for damages, and gifts or donations of money to the Government and from intragovernmental transactions with other Government accounts. The authority to spend offsetting collections is a form of budget authority. (Cf. receipts and offsetting receipts.)

Offsetting receipts mean collections that are credited to offsetting receipt accounts and deducted from gross budget authority and outlays, rather than added to receipts. They are not authorized to be credited to expenditure accounts. The legislation that authorizes the offsetting receipts may earmark them for a specific purpose and either appropriate them for expenditure for that purpose or require them to be appropriated in annual appropriation acts before they can be spent. Like offsetting collections, they result from business-like transactions or market-oriented activities with the public, including payments from the public in exchange for goods and services, reimbursements for damages, and gifts or donations of money to the Government and from intragovernmental transactions with other Government accounts. (Cf. receipts, undistributed offsetting receipts, and offsetting collections.)

On-budget refers to all budgetary transactions other than those designated by statute as off-budget. (Cf. budget totals.)

Outlay means a payment to liquidate an obligation (other than the repayment of debt principal or other disbursements that are "means of financing" transactions). Outlays generally are equal to cash disbursements, but also are recorded for cash-equivalent transactions, such as the issuance of debentures to pay insurance claims, and in a few cases are recorded on an accrual basis such as interest on public issues of the public debt. Outlays are the measure of Government spending.

Outyear estimates mean estimates presented in the budget for the years beyond the budget year of budget authority, outlays, receipts, and other items (such as debt).

Overseas Contingency Operations/Global War on Terrorism (OCO/GWOT) means a discretionary appropriation that is enacted that the Congress and, subsequently, the President have so designated on an account by account basis. Such a discretionary appropriation that is designated as OCO/GWOT results in a cap adjustment to the limits on discretionary spending under BBEDCA, when such limits are in place. Funding for these purposes has most recently been associated with the wars in Iraq and Afghanistan.

Pay-as-you-go (PAYGO) refers to requirements of the Statutory Pay-As-You-Go Act of 2010 that result in a sequestration if the estimated combined result of new legislation affecting direct spending or revenue increases the on-budget deficit relative to the baseline, as of the end of a congressional session.

Public enterprise fund—see Revolving fund.

Reappropriation means a provision of law that extends into a new fiscal year the availability of unobligated amounts that have expired or would otherwise expire.

Receipts mean collections that result from the Government's exercise of its sovereign power to tax or otherwise compel payment. They are compared to outlays in calculating a surplus or deficit. (Cf. offsetting collections and offsetting receipts.)

Revolving fund means a fund that conducts continuing cycles of business-like activity, in which the fund charges for the sale of products or services and uses the proceeds to finance its spending, usually without requirement for annual appropriations. There are two types of revolving funds: Public enterprise funds, which conduct business-like operations mainly with the public, and intragovernmental revolving funds, which conduct business-like operations mainly within and between Government agencies. (Cf. special fund and trust fund.)

Savings refers to legislation or administrative actions that decrease outlays or increase receipts. (Cf. cost.)

Scorekeeping means measuring the budget effects of legislation, generally in terms of budget authority, receipts, and outlays, for purposes of measuring adherence to the Budget or to budget targets established by the Congress, as through agreement to a Budget Resolution.

Sequestration means the cancellation of budgetary resources. The Statutory Pay-As-You-Go Act of 2010 requires such cancellations if revenue or direct spending legislation is enacted that, in total, increases projected deficits or reduces projected surpluses relative to the baseline. The Balanced Budget and Emergency Deficit Control Act of 1985, as amended, requires annual across-the-board cancellations to selected mandatory programs through 2031.

Special fund means a Federal fund account for receipts or offsetting receipts earmarked for specific purposes and the expenditure of these receipts. (Cf. revolving fund and trust fund.)

Statutory Pay-As-You-Go Act of 2010 refers to legislation that reinstated a statutory pay-as-you-go requirement for new tax or mandatory spending legislation. The law is a standalone piece of legislation that cross-references BBEDCA but does not directly amend that legislation. This is a permanent law and does not expire.

Subsidy means the estimated long-term cost to the Government of a direct loan or loan guarantee, calculated on a net present value basis, excluding administrative costs and any incidental effects on governmental receipts or outlays.

Surplus means the amount by which receipts exceed outlays in a fiscal year. It may refer to the on-budget, off-budget, or unified budget surplus.

Supplemental appropriation means an appropriation enacted subsequent to a regular annual appropriations act, when the need for additional funds is too urgent to be postponed until the next regular annual appropriations act.

Trust fund refers to a type of account, designated by law as a trust fund, for receipts or offsetting receipts dedicated to specific purposes and the expenditure of these receipts. Some revolving funds are designated as trust funds, and these are called trust revolving funds. (Cf. special fund and revolving fund.)

Trust funds group refers to the moneys collected and spent by the Government through trust fund accounts. (Cf. Federal funds group.)

Undistributed offsetting receipts mean offsetting receipts that are deducted from the Government-wide totals for budget authority and outlays instead of being offset against a specific agency and function. (Cf. offsetting receipts.)

Unified budget includes receipts from all sources and outlays for all programs of the Federal Government, including both on- and off-budget programs. It is the most comprehensive measure of the Government's annual finances.

Unobligated balance means the cumulative amount of budget authority that remains available for obligation under law in unexpired accounts. The term "expired balances available for adjustment only" refers to unobligated amounts in expired accounts.

User charges are charges assessed for the provision of Government services and for the sale or use of Government goods or resources. The payers of the user charge must be limited in the authorizing legislation to those receiving special benefits from, or subject to regulation by, the program or activity beyond the benefits received by the general public or broad segments of the public (such as those who pay income taxes or custom duties).

17. COVERAGE OF THE BUDGET

The Federal budget is the central instrument of national policy making. It is the Government's financial plan for proposing and deciding the allocation of resources to serve national objectives. The budget provides information on the cost and scope of Federal activities to inform decisions and to serve as a means to control the allocation of resources. When enacted, it establishes the level of public goods and services the Government provides.

Federal Government activities can be either "budgetary" or "non-budgetary." Those activities that involve direct and measurable allocation of Federal resources are budgetary. The payments to and from the public resulting from budgetary activities are included in the Budget's accounting of outlays and receipts. Federal activities that do not involve direct and measurable allocation of Federal resources are non-budgetary and are not included in the Budget's accounting of outlays and receipts. More detailed information about outlays and receipts may be found in the "Budget Concepts" chapter of this volume.

The Budget documents include information on some non-budgetary activities because they can be important instruments of Federal policy and provide insight into the scope and nature of Federal activities. For example, the Budget documents show the transactions of the Thrift Savings Program (TSP), a collection of investment funds managed by the Federal Retirement Thrift Investment Board (FRTIB). Despite the fact that the FRTIB is budgetary and one of the TSP funds is invested entirely in Federal securities, the transactions of these funds are non-budgetary because current and retired Federal employees own the funds. The Government manages these funds only in a fiduciary capacity.

The Budget also includes information on cash flows that are a means of financing Federal activity, such as for credit financing accounts. However, to avoid double-counting, means of financing amounts are not included in the estimates of outlays or receipts because the costs of the underlying Federal activities are already reflected in the deficit.[1] This chapter provides details about the budgetary and non-budgetary activities of the Federal Government.

Budgetary Activities

The Federal Government has used the unified budget concept—which consolidates outlays and receipts from Federal funds and trust funds, including the Social Security trust funds—since 1968, starting with the 1969 Budget. The 1967 President's Commission on Budget Concepts (the Commission) recommended the change to include the financial transactions of all of the Federal Government's programs and agencies. Thus, the budget includes information on the financial transactions of all 15 Executive Departments, all independent agencies (from all three branches of Government), and all Government corporations.[2]

The Budget shows outlays and receipts for on-budget and off-budget activities separately to reflect the legal. Although there is a legal distinction between on-budget and off-budget activities, there is no difference conceptually. Off-budget Federal activities reflect the same governmental roles as on-budget activities and result in outlays and receipts. Like on-budget activities, the Government funds and controls off-budget activities. The "unified budget" reflects the conceptual similarity between on-budget and off-budget activities by showing combined totals of outlays and receipts for both.

Many Government corporations are entities with business-type operations that charge the public for services at prices intended to allow the entity to be self-sustaining, although some operate at a loss to provide subsidies to specific recipients. Often, these entities are more independent than other agencies and have limited exemptions from certain Federal personnel requirements to allow for flexibility.

All accounts in Table 26-1, "Federal Budget by Agencies and Accounts," of this volume are budgetary. The majority of budgetary accounts are associated with the Departments or other entities that are clearly Federal agencies. Some budgetary accounts reflect Government payments to entities that the Government created or chartered as private or non-Federal entities. Some of these entities receive all or a majority of their funding from the Government. These include the Corporation for Public Broadcasting, Gallaudet University, Howard University, the Legal Services Corporation, the National Railroad Passenger Corporation (Amtrak), the Smithsonian Institution, the State Justice Institute, and the United States Institute of Peace. A related example is the Standard Setting Body, which is not a federally created entity but, since 2003, has received a majority of funding through a federally mandated assessment on public companies under the Sarbanes-Oxley Act of 2022 (Public Law 107-204). Although the Federal payments to these entities are budgetary, the entities themselves are non-budgetary.

[1] For more information on means of financing, see the "Budget Deficit or Surplus and Means of Financing" section of the "Budget Concepts" chapter of this volume.

[2] Government corporations are Government entities that are defined as corporations pursuant to the Government Corporation Control Act, as amended (31 U.S.C. 9101), or elsewhere in law. Examples include the Commodity Credit Corporation, the Export-Import Bank of the United States, the Federal Crop Insurance Corporation, the Federal Deposit Insurance Corporation, the Millennium Challenge Corporation, the U.S. International Development Finance Corporation, the Pension Benefit Guaranty Corporation, the Tennessee Valley Authority, the African Development Foundation (22 U.S.C. 290h-6), the Inter-American Foundation (22 U.S.C. 290f), the Presidio Trust (16 U.S.C. 460bb note).

Whether the Government created or chartered an entity does not alone determine its budgetary status. The Commission recommended that the budget be comprehensive, but it also recognized that proper budgetary classification required weighing all relevant factors regarding establishment, ownership, and control of an entity while erring on the side of inclusiveness. Generally, entities that are primarily Government owned or controlled are classified as budgetary. The Office of Management and Budget (OMB) determines the budgetary classification of entities in consultation with the Congressional Budget Office (CBO) and the Budget Committees of the Congress.

One recent example of a budgetary classification was for the Financial Oversight and Management Board for Puerto Rico, created in June 2016 by the Puerto Rico Oversight, Management, and Economic Stability Act (Public Law 114–187). By statute, this oversight board is not a Department, agency, establishment, or instrumentality of the Federal Government, but is an entity within the territorial government financed entirely by the territorial government. Because the flow of funds from the Territory to the oversight board is mandated by Federal law, the Budget reflects the allocation of resources by the territorial government to the territorial entity as a receipt from the territorial government and an equal outlay to the oversight board, with net zero deficit impact. Because the oversight board itself is not a Federal entity, its operations are not included in the Budget.

Another example involves the National Association of Registered Agents and Brokers (NARAB; 15 U.S.C. 6751-64), established by statute in 2015. NARAB allows for the adoption and application of insurance licensing, continuing education, and other nonresident producer qualification requirements on a multi-State basis. In other words, NARAB streamlines the ability of a nonresident insurer to become a licensed agent in another State. In exchange for providing enhanced market access, NARAB collects fees from its members. In addition to being statutorily established—which in itself is an indication that the entity is governmental for budget purposes—NARAB's board of directors is appointed by the President and confirmed by the Senate. It must also submit bylaws and an annual report to the Department of the Treasury and its primary function involves exercising a regulatory function.

Off-budget Federal activities.—Despite the Commission's recommendation that the budget be comprehensive, every year since 1971 at least one Federal program or agency has been presented as off-budget because of a legal requirement.[3] The Government funds such off-budget Federal activities and administers them according to Federal legal requirements. However, their net costs are excluded, by law, from the rest of the Budget totals, also known as the "on-budget" totals.

Off-budget Federal activities currently consist of the U.S. Postal Service and the two Social Security trust funds: Old-Age and Survivors Insurance and Disability Insurance. Social Security has been classified as off-budget since 1986 and the Postal Service has been classified as off-budget since 1990.[4] Other activities that were designated in law as off-budget at various times before 1986 have been classified as on-budget by law since at least 1985 as a result of the Balanced Budget and Emergency Deficit Control Act of 1985, as amended (Public Law 99–177). Activities that were off-budget at one time, but that are now on-budget, are classified as on-budget for all years in historical budget data.

Social Security is the largest single program in the unified budget and it is classified by law as off-budget; as a result, the off-budget accounts constitute a significant part of total Federal spending and receipts. Table 17–1 divides total Federal Government outlays, receipts, and the surplus or deficit between on-budget and off-budget amounts. Within this table, the Social Security and Postal Service transactions are classified as off-budget for all years to provide a consistent comparison over time.

Non-Budgetary Activities

The Government characterizes some important Government activities as non-budgetary because they do not involve the direct allocation of resources.[5] These activities can affect budget outlays or receipts even though they have non-budgetary components.

Federal credit programs: budgetary and non-budgetary transactions.—Federal credit programs make direct loans or guarantee private loans to non-Federal borrowers. The Federal Credit Reform Act of 1990 (FCRA; 2 U.S.C. 661-661f) established the current budgetary treatment for credit programs. Under FCRA, the budgetary cost of a credit program, known as the "subsidy cost," is the estimated lifetime cost to the Government of a loan or a loan guarantee on a net present value basis, excluding administrative costs.

Outlays equal to the subsidy cost are recorded in the Budget up front, as they are incurred—for example, when a loan is made or guaranteed. Credit program cash flows to and from the public are recorded in non-budgetary financing accounts and the information is included in Budget documents to provide insight into the program size and costs. For more information about the mecha-

[3] While the term "off-budget" is sometimes used colloquially to mean non-budgetary, the term has a meaning distinct from non-budgetary. Off-budget activities would be considered budgetary, absent legal requirement to exclude these activities from the budget totals.

[4] See 42 U.S.C. 911 and 39 U.S.C. 2009a, respectively. The off-budget Postal Service accounts consist of the Postal Service Fund, which is classified as a mandatory account, and the Office of the Inspector General and the Postal Regulatory Commission, both of which are classified as discretionary accounts. The Postal Service Retiree Health Benefits Fund is an on-budget mandatory account with the Office of Personnel Management. The off-budget Social Security accounts consist of the Federal Old-Age and Survivors Insurance Trust Fund and the Federal Disability Insurance Trust Fund, both of which have mandatory and discretionary funding.

[5] Tax expenditures, which are discussed in the "Tax Expenditures" chapter of this volume, are an example of Government activities that could be characterized as either budgetary or non-budgetary. Tax expenditures refer to the reduction in tax receipts resulting from the special tax treatment accorded certain private activities. Because tax expenditures reduce tax receipts and receipts are budgetary, tax expenditures clearly have budgetary effects. However, the size and composition of tax expenditures are not explicitly recorded in the budget as outlays or as negative receipts and, for this reason, tax expenditures might be considered a special case of non-budgetary transactions.

nisms of credit programs, see the "Budget Concepts" chapter of this volume. More detail on credit programs is in the "Credit and Insurance" chapter of this volume.

Deposit funds.—Deposit funds are non-budgetary accounts that record amounts held by the Government temporarily until ownership is determined (such as earnest money paid by bidders for mineral leases) or held by the Government as an agent for others (such as State income taxes withheld from Federal employees' salaries and not yet paid to the States). The largest deposit fund is the Government Securities Investment Fund (G-Fund) which is part of the TSP, the Government's defined contribution retirement plan. The FRTIB manages the fund's investment for Federal employees who participate in the TSP (which is similar to private-sector 401(k) plans). The Department of the Treasury holds the G-Fund assets, which are the property of Federal employees, only in a fiduciary capacity; the transactions of the Fund are not resource allocations by the Government and are therefore non-budgetary.[6] For similar reasons, Native American-owned funds that are held and managed in a fiduciary capacity are also excluded from the Budget.

Government-Sponsored Enterprises (GSEs).—GSEs are privately owned and therefore distinct from Government corporations. The Federal Government has chartered GSEs such as the Federal National Mortgage Association (Fannie Mae), the Federal Home Loan Mortgage Corporation (Freddie Mac), the Federal Home Loan Banks, the Farm Credit System, and the Federal Agricultural Mortgage Corporation, to provide financial intermediation for specified public purposes. Although federally chartered to serve public-policy purposes, GSEs are classified as non-budgetary because they are intended to be privately owned and controlled—with any public benefits accruing indirectly from the GSEs' business transactions. Estimates of the GSEs' activities can be found in a separate chapter of the Budget *Appendix*, and their activities are discussed in the "Credit and Insurance" chapter of this volume.

In September 2008, in response to the financial market crisis, the director of the Federal Housing Finance Agency (FHFA)[7] placed Fannie Mae and Freddie Mac into conservatorship for the purpose of preserving the assets and restoring the solvency of these two GSEs. As conservator, FHFA has broad authority to direct the operations of these GSEs. However, these GSEs remain private companies with boards of directors and management responsible for their day-to-day operations. The Budget continues to treat these two GSEs as non-budgetary private entities in conservatorship rather than as Government agencies. By contrast, CBO treats these GSEs as budgetary Federal agencies. Both treatments include budgetary and non-budgetary amounts.

While OMB reflects all of the GSEs' transactions with the public as non-budgetary, the payments from the Treasury to the GSEs are recorded as budgetary outlays and dividends received by the Treasury are recorded as budgetary receipts. Under CBO's approach, the subsidy costs of Fannie Mae's and Freddie Mac's past credit activities are treated as having already been recorded in the Budget estimates; the subsidy costs of future credit activities will be recorded when the activities occur. Lending and borrowing activities between the GSEs and the public apart from the subsidy costs are treated as non-budgetary by CBO, and Treasury payments to the GSEs are intragovernmental transfers (from Treasury to the GSEs) that net to zero in CBO's budget estimates.

Overall, both the Budget's accounting and CBO's accounting present Fannie Mae's and Freddie Mac's gains and losses as Government receipts and outlays, which reduce or increase Government deficits. The two approaches, however, reflect the effect of the gains and losses in the Budget at different times.

Other federally created non-budgetary entities.—In addition to the GSEs, the Federal Government has created a number of other entities that are classified as non-budgetary. These include federally funded research and development centers (FFRDCs), non-appropriated fund instrumentalities (NAFIs), and other entities; some of these are non-profit entities and some are for-profit entities.[8]

FFRDCs are entities that conduct agency-specific research under contract or cooperative agreement. Some FFRDCs were created to conduct research for the Department of Defense but are administered by colleges, universities, or other non-profit entities. Despite this non-budgetary classification, many FFRDCs receive direct resource allocation from the Government and are included as budget lines in various agencies. Examples of FFRDCs include the Center for Naval Analyses and the Jet Propulsion Laboratory.[9] Even though FFRDCs are non-budgetary, Federal payments to the FFRDC are budget outlays. In addition to Federal funding, FFRDCs may receive funding from non-Federal sources.

[6] The administrative functions of the FRTIB are carried out by Government employees and included in the budget totals.

[7] FHFA is the regulator of Fannie Mae, Freddie Mac, and the Federal Home Loan Banks.

[8] Although most entities created by the Federal Government are budgetary, the Congress and the President have chartered, but not necessarily created, approximately 100 non-profit entities that are non-budgetary. These include patriotic, charitable, and educational organizations under Title 36 of the U.S. Code and foundations and trusts chartered under other titles of the Code. Title 36 corporations include the American Legion; the American National Red Cross; Big Brothers—Big Sisters of America; Boy Scouts of America; Future Farmers of America; Girl Scouts of the United States of America; the National Academy of Public Administration; the National Academies of Sciences, Engineering, and Medicine; and Veterans of Foreign Wars of the United States. Virtually all of the non-profit entities chartered by the Government existed under State law prior to the granting of a Government charter, making the Government charter an honorary rather than governing charter. A major exception to this is the American National Red Cross. Its Government charter requires it to provide disaster relief and to ensure compliance with treaty obligations under the Geneva Convention. Although any Government payments (whether made as direct appropriations or through agency appropriations) to these chartered non-profits, including the Red Cross, would be budgetary, the non-profits themselves are classified as non-budgetary. On April 29, 2015, the Subcommittee on Immigration and Border Security of the Committee on the Judiciary in the U.S. House of Representatives adopted a policy prohibiting the Congress from granting new Federal charters to private, non-profit organizations.

[9] The National Science Foundation maintains a list of FFRDCs at *https://nsf.gov/statistics/ffrdc/*.

NAFIs are entities that support an agency's current and retired personnel. Nearly all NAFIs are associated with the Departments of Defense, Department of Homeland Security (Coast Guard), and Department of Veterans Affairs. Most NAFIs are located on military bases and include the Armed Forces exchanges (which sell goods to military personnel and their families), recreational facilities, and childcare centers. NAFIs are financed by proceeds from the sale of goods or services and do not receive direct appropriations; thus, they are characterized as non-budgetary, but any agency payments to the NAFIs are recorded as budget outlays.

A number of entities created by the Government receive a significant amount of non-Federal funding. Non-Federal individuals or organizations significantly control some of these entities. These entities include Gallaudet University, Howard University, Amtrak, and the Universal Services Administrative Company, among others. Most of these entities receive direct appropriations or other recurring payments from the Government. The appropriations or other payments are budgetary and included in Table 26-1. However, many of these entities are themselves non-budgetary. Generally, entities that receive a significant portion of funding from non-Federal sources but are not controlled by the Government are non-budgetary.

Regulation.—Federal Government regulations often require the private sector or other levels of government to make expenditures for specified purposes that are intended to have public benefits, such as workplace safety and pollution control. Although the Budget reflects the Government's cost of conducting regulatory activities, the costs imposed on the private sector as a result of regulation are treated as non-budgetary and not included in the Budget. The annual Regulatory Plan and the semi-annual Unified Agenda of Federal Regulatory and Deregulatory Actions describe the Government's regulatory priorities and plans.[10] OMB regularly publishes reports summarizing agency estimates of the costs and benefits of Federal regulation.[11]

Monetary policy.—As a fiscal policy tool, the budget is used by elected Government officials to promote economic growth and achieve other public policy objectives. Monetary policy is another tool that governments use to promote economic policy objectives. In the United States, the Federal Reserve System—which is composed of a Board of Governors and 12 regional Federal Reserve Banks—conducts monetary policy. The Federal Reserve Act provides that the goal of monetary policy is to "maintain long-run growth of the monetary and credit aggregates commensurate with the economy's long run potential to increase production, so as to promote effectively the goals of maximum employment, stable prices, and moderate long-term interest rates."[12] The Full Employment and Balanced Growth Act of 1978 (Humphrey-Hawkins Act; Public Law 95-523) reaffirmed the dual goals of full employment and price stability.[13]

By law, the Federal Reserve System is a self-financing entity that is independent of the Executive Branch and subject only to broad oversight by the Congress. Consistent with the recommendations of the Commission, the effects of monetary policy and the actions of the Federal Reserve System are non-budgetary, with exceptions for the transfer to the Treasury of excess income generated through its operations. The Federal Reserve System earns income from a variety of sources including interest on Government securities, foreign currency investments and loans to depository institutions, and fees for services (e.g., check clearing services) provided to depository institutions. The Federal Reserve System remits to the Treasury any excess income over expenses annually. For the fiscal year ending September 2023, Treasury recorded $581 million in receipts from the Federal Reserve System. In addition to remitting excess income to the Treasury, the Dodd-Frank Wall Street Reform and Consumer Protection Act requires the Federal Reserve to transfer a portion of its excess earnings to the Consumer Financial Protection Bureau (CFPB).[14]

The Board of Governors of the Federal Reserve is a Federal Government agency, but because of its independent status, its budget is not subject to Executive Branch review and is included in the Budget *Appendix* for informational purposes only. The Federal Reserve Banks are subject to Board oversight and managed by boards of directors chosen by the Board of Governors and member banks, which include all national banks and State banks that choose to become members. The budgets of the regional Banks are subject to approval by the Board of Governors and are not included in the Budget *Appendix*.

[10] The most recent Regulatory Plan and introduction to the Unified Agenda issued by the General Services Administration's Regulatory Information Service Center are available at *https://reginfo.gov/* and at *https://gpo.gov/*.

[11] *https://whitehouse.gov/omb/information-regulatory-affairs/reports/#ORC*.

[12] See 12 U.S.C. 225a.

[13] See 15 U.S.C. 3101 et seq.

[14] See 12 U.S.C. 5497.

18. GOVERNMENTAL RECEIPTS

This chapter presents the Budget's estimates of taxes and governmental receipts, taking into account the effects of tax legislation enacted in 2023, discusses the provisions of those enacted laws, and introduces the Administration's additional receipt proposals.

ESTIMATES OF GOVERNMENTAL RECEIPTS

Governmental receipts are taxes and other collections from the public that result from the exercise of the Federal Government's sovereign or governmental powers. The difference between governmental receipts and outlays is the surplus or deficit.

The Federal Government also collects income from the public through market-oriented activities. Collections from these activities are subtracted from gross outlays, rather than added to taxes and other governmental receipts, and are discussed in the "Offsetting Collections and Offsetting Receipts" chapter of this volume.

Total governmental receipts (hereafter referred to as "receipts") are estimated to be $5,081.5 billion in 2024, an increase of $640.6 billion or 14.4 percent from 2023. The estimated increase in 2024 is largely due to increased individual income tax collections, along with higher corporation income tax and social insurance and retirement receipts. Receipts in 2024 are estimated to be 18.0 percent of Gross Domestic Product (GDP), which is higher than in 2023 when receipts were 16.5 percent of GDP.

Receipts in the 2025 Budget are estimated to rise to $5,484.9 billion in 2025, an increase of $403.4 billion or 7.9 percent relative to 2024. Receipts are projected to grow at an average annual rate of 5.6 percent between 2025 and 2029, rising to $6,829.9 billion. Receipts are projected to rise to $8,639.2 billion in 2034, growing at an average annual rate of 4.8 percent between 2029 and 2034. This growth is largely due to assumed increases in incomes resulting from both real economic growth and inflation, along with tax reforms.

As a share of GDP, receipts are projected to increase slightly from 18.0 percent in 2024 to 18.7 percent in 2025, and to increase steadily to 20.3 percent in 2034.

Table 18–1. RECEIPTS BY SOURCE--SUMMARY
(In billions of dollars)

	2023 Actual	Estimate										
		2024	2025	2026	2027	2028	2029	2030	2031	2032	2033	2034
Individual income taxes	2,176.5	2,503.4	2,679.2	2,975.8	3,178.3	3,369.1	3,549.0	3,734.4	3,925.3	4,128.7	4,340.6	4,574.5
Corporation income taxes	419.6	612.8	668.1	720.6	703.5	710.2	741.3	770.0	806.4	859.1	881.7	904.7
Social insurance and retirement receipts	1,614.5	1,720.5	1,896.8	1,935.6	2,017.4	2,118.9	2,203.9	2,300.0	2,397.5	2,494.5	2,627.0	2,735.0
(On-budget)	*(420.7)*	*(480.5)*	*(612.4)*	*(593.4)*	*(620.6)*	*(651.9)*	*(678.0)*	*(709.4)*	*(741.1)*	*(771.7)*	*(812.6)*	*(850.3)*
(Off-budget)	*(1,193.8)*	*(1,240.0)*	*(1,284.4)*	*(1,342.2)*	*(1,396.8)*	*(1,467.0)*	*(1,525.8)*	*(1,590.5)*	*(1,656.4)*	*(1,722.7)*	*(1,814.4)*	*(1,884.7)*
Excise taxes	75.8	99.7	109.9	112.5	113.0	112.6	114.9	117.9	118.2	119.8	121.6	122.4
Estate and gift taxes	33.7	29.0	32.6	34.8	52.6	56.8	61.0	65.3	69.4	74.7	80.4	86.6
Customs duties	80.3	81.4	60.7	52.5	52.9	54.5	56.6	58.8	61.2	53.4	55.6	57.7
Miscellaneous receipts	40.6	34.7	37.6	41.0	68.5	87.5	103.3	118.0	131.4	142.7	151.2	158.4
Total, receipts	**4,440.9**	**5,081.5**	**5,484.9**	**5,872.7**	**6,186.2**	**6,509.6**	**6,829.9**	**7,164.4**	**7,509.5**	**7,872.9**	**8,258.1**	**8,639.2**
(On-budget)	*(3,247.2)*	*(3,841.5)*	*(4,200.6)*	*(4,530.5)*	*(4,789.5)*	*(5,042.6)*	*(5,304.1)*	*(5,573.9)*	*(5,853.1)*	*(6,150.1)*	*(6,443.7)*	*(6,754.5)*
(Off-budget)	*(1,193.8)*	*(1,240.0)*	*(1,284.4)*	*(1,342.2)*	*(1,396.8)*	*(1,467.0)*	*(1,525.8)*	*(1,590.5)*	*(1,656.4)*	*(1,722.7)*	*(1,814.4)*	*(1,884.7)*
Total receipts as a percentage of GDP	16.5	18.0	18.7	19.2	19.4	19.6	19.8	19.9	20.0	20.1	20.2	20.3

LEGISLATION ENACTED IN 2023 THAT AFFECTS GOVERNMENTAL RECEIPTS

Two laws were enacted during 2023 that affect receipts. The major provisions of those laws that have a significant impact on receipts are described below.[1]

FISCAL RESPONSIBILITY ACT of 2023 (Public Law 118–5)

The Act, which was signed into law on June 3, 2023, rescinds funding previously provided to the Internal Revenue Service for enforcement activities, operations

[1] In the discussions of enacted legislation, years referred to are calendar years, unless otherwise noted.

support, business systems modernization, and taxpayer services, which had been expected to reduce the tax gap by improving taxpayer compliance. Rescinding these resources results in reduced income tax receipts.

AIRPORT AND AIRWAY EXTENSION ACT of 2023, PART II (Public Law 118–34)

The Act, which was signed into law on December 26, 2023, temporarily extends specific Federal Aviation Administration programs and activities through March 8, 2024, including the authority to collect various taxes and fees into the Airport and Airway Trust Fund, such as taxes on aviation fuel and airline tickets.

ADJUSTMENTS TO THE BALANCED BUDGET AND EMERGENCY DEFICIT CONTROL ACT (BBEDCA) BASELINE

An adjusted baseline provides a realistic measure of the deficit outlook before new policies are enacted. This Budget does so by adjusting the BBEDCA baseline to reflect the full cost of enacting two discretionary measures that have effects on governmental receipts. The BBEDCA baseline, which is commonly used in budgeting and is defined in statute, reflects, with some exceptions, the projected receipt levels under current law.

Internal Revenue Service (IRS). The Inflation Reduction Act of 2022 (IRA) provided nearly $80 billion in mandatory funding to the IRS to complement the agency's annual discretionary appropriations. The Fiscal Responsibility Act of 2023 rescinded approximately $1.4 billion of that funding. The adjusted baseline for the Budget reflects an additional $20.2 billion rescission of the IRA funding, consistent with the 2024 appropriations topline agreement announced in January 2024.

Unemployment Insurance. The Bipartisan Budget Act of 2018 established an adjustment to discretionary base funding for program integrity efforts through Reemployment Services and Eligibility Assessments. The Budget proposes funding through 2034 which results in a reduction in State unemployment taxes.

Table 18–2. ADJUSTMENTS TO THE BALANCED BUDGET AND EMERGENCY DEFICIT CONTROL ACT (BBEDCA) BASELINE ESTIMATES OF GOVERNMENTAL RECEIPTS

(In billions of dollars)

	2024	2025	2026	2027	2028	2029	2030	2031	2032	2033	2034	2025–2029	2025–2034
BBEDCA baseline receipts	4,963.7	5,086.7	5,426.2	5,765.2	6,076.2	6,379.2	6,703.7	7,029.6	7,341.1	7,691.8	8,034.1	28,733.4	65,533.7
Adjustments to BBEDCA baseline:													
Effects of IRS rescission consistent with the recently announced 2024 topline agreement	....	....	....	....	....	–3.0	–42.7	–50.4	–17.5	–8.2	–4.8	–3.0	–126.6
Effects of Unemployment Insurance Reemployment Services and Eligibility Assessments discretionary cap adjustment	....	....	–*	–*	–*	–*	–*	–*	–*	–*	–*	–*	–0.2
Total, adjustments to BBEDCA baseline	....	....	–*	–*	–*	–3.1	–42.7	–50.4	–17.5	–8.3	–4.8	–3.1	–126.8
Adjusted baseline receipts	**4,963.7**	**5,086.7**	**5,426.2**	**5,765.1**	**6,076.1**	**6,376.1**	**6,660.9**	**6,979.2**	**7,323.5**	**7,683.6**	**8,029.3**	**28,730.3**	**65,406.9**

*Less than $50 million.

BUDGET PROPOSALS

The 2025 Budget proposes a series of revenue raisers directed at wealthy people and large corporations. The Budget aims to replace counterproductive tax laws that reward offshoring and profit shifting with provisions that encourage job creation at home and put an end to the worldwide race to the bottom on corporate tax rates. It also includes a set of measures to make sure the wealthiest Americans and corporations pay their fair share in taxes while ensuring that no one making $400,000 per year or less will pay a penny more in new taxes. These proposals affecting governmental receipts are included in the table that follows. Descriptions of proposals can be found in the Department of the Treasury's *General Explanations of the Administration's Fiscal Year 2025 Revenue Proposals.*[2]

[2] Available at this link: https://home.treasury.gov/policy-issues/tax-policy/revenue-proposals.

Table 18–3. EFFECT OF BUDGET PROPOSALS

(In millions of dollars)

	2024	2025	2026	2027	2028	2029	2030	2031	2032	2033	2034	2025–2029	2025–2034
Reform business taxation:													
Raise the corporate income tax rate to 28 percent	74,646	122,474	125,105	128,114	128,624	128,353	129,396	137,888	144,919	150,028	155,040	632,670	1,349,941
Increase the corporate alternative minimum tax rate to 21 percent	10,050	13,543	11,759	12,264	12,675	13,119	13,672	14,238	14,800	15,379	15,980	63,360	137,429
Increase the excise tax rate on repurchase of corporate stock and close loopholes	3,863	15,344	14,980	14,936	15,184	15,792	16,458	17,167	17,912	18,691	19,502	76,236	165,966
Tax corporate distributions as dividends	0	110	160	170	180	190	200	210	230	240	250	810	1,940
Limit tax avoidance through inappropriate leveraging of parties to divisive reorganizations	....	279	826	1,614	2,550	3,569	4,645	5,769	6,937	8,150	9,408	8,838	43,747
Limit losses recognized in liquidation transactions	....	30	50	52	54	56	57	59	61	63	65	242	547
Prevent basis shifting by related parties through partnerships	....	3,851	5,537	3,999	2,325	563	–177	–215	–275	–341	–402	16,275	14,865
Conform definition of "control" with corporate affiliation test	....	447	651	667	681	695	709	719	727	733	736	3,141	6,765
Strengthen limitation on losses for noncorporate taxpayers	....	1,185	2,241	2,519	2,666	12,901	14,735	10,543	9,789	9,621	9,526	21,512	75,726
Expand limitation on deductibility of employee remuneration in excess of $1 million[1]	....	37,169	19,015	30,421	34,951	31,354	28,057	22,148	20,594	22,385	25,760	152,910	271,854
Prevent prison facility rent payments from contributing to qualification as a REIT	....	....	....	....	....	....	....	....	....	....	....	....	....
Subtotal, reform business taxation	88,559	194,432	180,324	194,756	199,890	206,592	207,752	208,526	215,694	224,949	235,865	975,994	2,068,780
Reform international taxation:													
Revise the global minimum tax regime, limit inversions, and make related reforms	8,875	27,920	35,889	34,589	34,819	36,215	37,719	39,261	40,846	42,483	44,178	169,432	373,919
Adopt the undertaxed profits rule		9,596	14,541	14,065	14,389	14,181	14,088	13,837	13,752	13,916	13,948	66,772	136,313
Repeal the deduction for foreign-derived intangible income:													
Repeal the deduction for foreign-derived intangible income	....	13,938	17,669	14,213	14,639	15,078	15,531	15,997	16,477	16,971	17,480	75,537	157,993
Provide additional support for research and experimentation expenditures	....	–13,938	–17,669	–14,213	–14,639	–15,078	–15,531	–15,997	–16,477	–16,971	–17,480	–75,537	–157,993
Subtotal, repeal the deduction for foreign-derived intangible income	....	....	....	....	....	....	....	....	....	....	....	....	....
Revise the rules that allocate Subpart F income and GILTI between taxpayers to ensure that Subpart F income and GILTI are fully taxed	....	106	196	225	250	272	294	313	332	349	366	1,049	2,703
Require a controlled foreign corporation's taxable year to match that of its majority U.S. shareholder	....	....	....	....	....	....	....	....	....	....	....	....	....
Limit foreign tax credits from sales of hybrid entities	....	343	535	484	446	418	397	381	370	362	357	2,226	4,093
Restrict deductions of excessive interest of members of financial reporting groups	....	2,691	4,281	4,038	3,918	3,910	4,002	4,113	4,219	4,341	4,481	18,838	39,994
Conform scope of portfolio interest exclusion for 10-percent shareholders to other tax rules	....	64	54	39	22	5	....	....	....	....	....	184	184
Treat payments substituting for partnership effectively connected income as U.S. source dividends	....	....	....	....	....	....	....	....	....	....	....	....	....
Expand access to retroactive qualified electing fund elections	....	1	2	4	5	6	6	7	8	8	9	18	56
Reform taxation of foreign fossil fuel income:													
Modify foreign oil and gas extraction income and foreign oil related income rules	....	184	310	318	329	340	352	363	377	393	409	1,481	3,375
Modify tax rule for dual capacity taxpayers	....	3,908	6,582	6,735	6,966	7,214	7,458	7,703	7,994	8,332	8,671	31,405	71,563
Subtotal, reform taxation of foreign fossil fuel income	....	4,092	6,892	7,053	7,295	7,554	7,810	8,066	8,371	8,725	9,080	32,886	74,938
Provide tax incentives for locating jobs and business activity in the United States and remove tax deductions for shipping jobs overseas:													
Provide tax credit for inshoring jobs to the United States	....	–3	–6	–6	–7	–7	–8	–8	–8	–9	–9	–29	–71

Table 18–3. EFFECT OF BUDGET PROPOSALS—Continued

(In millions of dollars)

	2024	2025	2026	2027	2028	2029	2030	2031	2032	2033	2034	2025–2029	2025–2034
Remove tax deductions for shipping jobs overseas	....	3	6	6	7	7	8	8	8	9	9	29	71
Subtotal, provide tax incentives for locating jobs and business activity in the United States and remove tax deductions for shipping jobs overseas	....	....	....	....	....	....	....	....	....	....	....	....	....
Subtotal, reform international taxation	8,875	44,813	62,390	60,497	61,144	62,561	64,316	65,978	67,898	70,184	72,419	291,405	632,200
Support housing and urban development:													
Make permanent the new markets tax credit and formalize allocation incentives for investing in areas of higher distress	....	....	–97	–278	–483	–716	–990	–1,290	–1,602	–1,796	–1,866	–1,574	–9,118
Provide a neighborhood homes credit	....	–270	–1,145	–1,829	–1,963	–2,099	–2,183	–2,253	–2,304	–2,371	–2,428	–7,306	–18,845
Expand and enhance the low-income housing credit	....	–84	–354	–980	–1,918	–2,961	–4,010	–5,054	–6,090	–7,118	–8,077	–6,297	–36,646
Subtotal, support housing and urban development	....	–354	–1,596	–3,087	–4,364	–5,776	–7,183	–8,597	–9,996	–11,285	–12,371	–15,177	–64,609
Modify energy taxes:													
Eliminate fossil fuel tax preferences:													
Repeal the enhanced oil recovery credit	....	....	....	....	....	....	....	....	....	....	....	....	....
Repeal the credit for oil and natural gas produced from marginal wells	....	19	34	26	14	4	....	....	....	....	....	97	97
Repeal expensing of intangible drilling costs	....	1,790	2,652	1,971	1,234	478	204	265	334	406	448	8,125	9,782
Repeal the deduction for costs paid or incurred for any qualified tertiary injectant used as part of tertiary recovery method	....	6	8	9	9	9	9	9	9	9	9	41	86
Repeal the exception to passive loss limitations provided to working interests in oil and natural gas properties	....	5	9	8	8	8	8	7	7	7	7	38	74
Repeal the use of percentage depletion with respect to oil and natural gas wells	....	880	1,476	1,493	1,521	1,562	1,611	1,671	1,741	1,820	1,900	6,932	15,675
Increase geological and geophysical amortization period for independent producers	....	65	251	414	455	448	439	432	419	395	360	1,633	3,678
Repeal expensing of mine exploration and development costs	....	148	220	164	102	39	17	22	28	34	38	673	812
Repeal percentage depletion for hard mineral fossil fuels	....	57	103	112	122	128	136	145	148	148	153	522	1,252
Repeal capital gains treatment for royalties	....	26	54	56	54	53	52	53	50	49	48	243	495
Repeal the exemption from the corporate income tax for fossil fuel publicly traded partnerships	....	....	....	....	....	....	75	148	186	220	251	....	880
Repeal the Oil Spill Liability Trust Fund and Superfund excise tax exemption for crude oil derived from bitumen and kerogen-rich rock[1]	....	115	160	166	172	179	183	186	192	198	200	792	1,751
Repeal accelerated amortization of air pollution control equipment	....	12	30	47	62	77	91	103	101	90	79	228	692
Subtotal, eliminate fossil fuel tax preferences	....	3,123	4,997	4,466	3,753	2,985	2,825	3,041	3,215	3,376	3,493	19,324	35,274
Eliminate drawbacks on petroleum taxes that finance the Oil Spill Liability Trust Fund and Superfund[1]	....	149	202	206	210	213	216	218	222	224	227	980	2,087
Impose digital asset mining energy excise tax[1]	....	107	302	533	670	744	832	935	1,052	1,197	1,361	2,356	7,733
Subtotal, modify energy taxes	....	3,379	5,501	5,205	4,633	3,942	3,873	4,194	4,489	4,797	5,081	22,660	45,094
Strengthen taxation of high-income taxpayers:													
Apply the net investment income tax to pass-through business income of high-income taxpayers	8,496	38,302	29,950	31,931	34,819	37,435	39,950	42,143	43,986	46,126	48,579	172,437	393,221
Increase the net investment income tax rate and additional Medicare tax rate for high-income taxpayers	8,394	42,920	31,327	32,285	34,710	37,224	39,822	42,450	44,963	47,602	50,487	178,466	403,790
Increase the top marginal income tax rate for high-income earners	9,871	75,419	31,189	13,798	14,939	15,859	16,818	17,833	18,885	19,997	21,187	151,204	245,924
Reform the taxation of capital income	....	18,031	23,713	25,164	26,417	27,624	29,050	30,727	32,158	33,758	41,941	120,949	288,583

Table 18–3. EFFECT OF BUDGET PROPOSALS—Continued

(In millions of dollars)

	2024	2025	2026	2027	2028	2029	2030	2031	2032	2033	2034	2025–2029	2025–2034
Impose a minimum income tax on the wealthiest taxpayers	....	....	50,310	56,387	59,430	60,451	59,974	59,331	53,057	50,215	53,513	226,578	502,668
Subtotal, strengthen taxation of high-income taxpayers	26,761	174,672	166,489	159,565	170,315	178,593	185,614	192,484	193,049	197,698	215,707	849,634	1,834,186
Modify rules relating to retirement plans:													
Prevent excessive accumulations by high-income taxpayers in tax-favored retirement accounts and make other reforms	....	6,926	6,142	3,402	1,992	1,278	931	776	724	726	759	19,740	23,656
Subtotal, modify rules relating to retirement plans	....	6,926	6,142	3,402	1,992	1,278	931	776	724	726	759	19,740	23,656
Support workers, families, and economic security:													
Expand the child credit, and make permanent full refundability and advanceability[2]	–5,409	–209,890	–11,210	–7,769	–11,376	–11,586	–11,827	–12,157	–12,372	–12,717	–9,120	–251,831	–310,024
Restore and make permanent the American Rescue Plan expansion of the earned income tax credit for workers without qualifying children[2]	–388	–15,330	–15,770	–15,998	–16,126	–16,310	–16,451	–16,503	–16,587	–16,695	–16,783	–79,534	–162,553
Make permanent the Inflation Reduction Act expansion of health insurance premium tax credits[2]	....	....	–14,884	–21,751	–23,366	–24,699	–26,308	–27,059	–28,489	–30,481	–32,535	–84,700	–229,572
Make the adoption tax credit refundable and allow certain guardianship arrangements to qualify[2]	....	–2	–2,642	–1,420	–1,186	–1,183	–1,180	–1,186	–1,187	–1,173	–1,182	–6,433	–12,341
Make permanent the income exclusion for forgiven student debt[2]	....	....	–2	–17	–37	–234	–252	–270	–290	–311	–333	–290	–1,746
Extend tax-preferred treatment to certain Federal and tribal scholarship and education loan programs	....	–62	–104	–114	–120	–123	–127	–130	–133	–134	–136	–523	–1,183
Increase the employer-provided childcare tax credit for businesses	....	–19	–37	–38	–40	–41	–43	–43	–44	–44	–44	–175	–393
Improve the design of the work opportunity tax credit to promote longer-term employment	....	85	93	22	12	9	7	5	4	3	2	221	242
Provide tax credits for certain first-time homebuyers and home sellers[2]	–710	–28,517	–14,066	–5,005	218	69	....	....	....	....	....	–47,301	–47,301
Subtotal, support workers, families, and economic security	–6,507	–253,735	–58,622	–52,090	–52,021	–54,098	–56,181	–57,343	–59,098	–61,552	–60,131	–470,566	–764,871
Modify estate and gift taxation:													
Improve tax administration for trusts and decedents' estates	....	9	79	83	96	112	130	150	174	199	227	379	1,259
Limit duration of generation-skipping transfer tax exemption	....	....	....	....	....	....	....	....	....	....	....	....	....
Modify income, estate, gift, and generation-skipping transfer tax rules for certain trusts	....	1,290	2,625	5,032	6,855	8,871	10,566	10,749	11,608	12,587	13,567	24,673	83,750
Revise rules for valuation of certain property	....	331	955	1,025	1,139	1,225	1,296	1,390	1,493	1,613	1,745	4,675	12,212
Subtotal, modify estate and gift taxation	....	1,630	3,659	6,140	8,090	10,208	11,992	12,289	13,275	14,399	15,539	29,727	97,221
Close loopholes:													
Tax carried (profits) interests as ordinary income	....	397	661	659	657	664	677	691	705	719	733	3,038	6,563
Repeal deferral of gain from like-kind exchanges	....	680	1,870	1,926	1,984	2,044	2,104	2,169	2,232	2,300	2,369	8,504	19,678
Require 100 percent recapture of depreciation deductions as ordinary income for certain depreciable real property	....	41	128	267	417	579	755	946	1,151	1,373	1,611	1,432	7,268
Modify depreciation rules for purchases of general aviation passenger aircraft	....	46	141	206	217	207	175	142	125	117	116	817	1,492
Limit use of donor advised funds to avoid a private foundation payout requirement	....	65	61	42	27	14	11	12	12	13	13	209	270
Exclude payments to disqualified persons from counting toward private foundation payout requirement	....	1	2	1	1	1	1	....	....	....	....	6	7
Extend the period for assessment of tax for certain Qualified Opportunity Fund investors	11	26	19	15	11	10	9	6	2	....	....	81	98
Impose ownership diversification requirement for small insurance company election	....	272	908	1,023	1,097	1,165	1,235	1,310	1,395	1,497	1,587	4,465	11,489
Expand pro rata interest expense disallowance for business-owned life insurance	....	609	618	646	668	691	717	748	780	813	850	3,232	7,140

Table 18–3. EFFECT OF BUDGET PROPOSALS—Continued
(In millions of dollars)

	2024	2025	2026	2027	2028	2029	2030	2031	2032	2033	2034	2025–2029	2025–2034
Modify rules for insurance products that fail the statutory definition of a life insurance contract	....	3	10	12	14	17	19	22	26	29	33	56	185
Limit tax benefits for private placement life insurance and similar contracts	....	140	208	288	387	505	651	825	1,032	1,276	1,567	1,528	6,879
Correct drafting errors in the taxation of insurance companies under the Tax Cuts and Jobs Act of 2017	....	77	105	111	107	73	56	47	39	35	32	473	682
Define the term "ultimate purchaser" for purposes of diesel fuel exportation[1]	....	7	9	11	13	15	19	21	23	26	28	55	172
Limit the deduction for the transfer of property to the value of property actually included in income	....	85	128	130	136	141	147	154	159	167	173	620	1,420
Reform excise taxes on business aviation[1]	....	44	106	169	235	300	322	325	329	332	336	854	2,498
Subtotal, close loopholes	11	2,493	4,974	5,506	5,971	6,426	6,898	7,418	8,010	8,697	9,448	25,370	65,841
Improve tax administration:													
Enhance accuracy of tax information:													
Expand the Secretary's authority to require electronic filing for forms and returns	....	....	....	....	....	....	....	....	....	....	....	....	....
Improve information reporting for reportable payments subject to backup withholding	....	41	95	161	221	231	241	252	263	275	301	749	2,081
Subtotal, enhance accuracy of tax information	....	41	95	161	221	231	241	252	263	275	301	749	2,081
Amend the centralized partnership audit regime to permit the carryover of a reduction in tax that exceeds a partner's tax liability	....	–5	–5	–6	–6	–7	–7	–7	–7	–8	–8	–29	–66
Incorporate chapters 2/2A in centralized partnership audit regime proceedings	....	....	....	....	....	....	....	....	....	....	....	....	....
Allow partnerships to resolve audits earlier	....	127	49	8	8	9	9	10	10	10	10	201	250
Modify requisite supervisory approval of penalty included in notice	....	148	152	154	160	162	175	171	178	185	194	776	1,679
Modify the requirement that general counsel review certain offers in compromise	....	6	15	10	2	2	2	2	2	2	2	35	45
Simplify foreign exchange gain or loss rules and exchange rate rules for individuals	....	–1	–2	–3	–3	–3	–3	–3	–3	–4	–4	–12	–29
Modernize reporting with respect to foreign tax credits to reduce burden and increase compliance	....	–10	–31	–34	–34	–34	–35	–35	–36	–39	–40	–143	–328
Authorize limited sharing of business tax return information to measure the economy more accurately	....	....	....	....	....	....	....	....	....	....	....	....	....
Expand TIN matching and improve child support enforcement	....	....	....	....	....	....	....	....	....	....	....	....	....
Clarify that information previously disclosed in a judicial or administrative proceeding is not return information	....	2	2	2	2	2	2	2	2	2	2	10	20
Require earlier electronic filing deadlines for certain information returns	....	175	153	129	118	106	75	59	41	43	45	681	944
Allow the Tax Court to review all evidence in innocent spouse relief cases	....	....	....	....	....	....	....	....	....	....	....	....	....
Permit electronically provided notices	....	....	....	....	....	....	....	....	....	....	....	....	....
Reform Federal grants to low-income taxpayer clinics													
Subtotal, improve tax administration	....	483	428	421	468	468	459	451	450	466	502	2,268	4,596
Improve tax compliance:													
Address taxpayer noncompliance with listed transactions:													
Extend statute of limitations for listed transactions	....	23	51	64	78	76	74	73	72	70	69	292	650
Impose liability on shareholders to collect unpaid income taxes of applicable corporations	....	492	513	534	556	579	604	630	658	686	716	2,674	5,968
Subtotal, address taxpayer noncompliance with listed transactions	....	515	564	598	634	655	678	703	730	756	785	2,966	6,618
Impose an affirmative requirement to disclose a position contrary to a regulation	....	9	11	11	12	14	14	15	15	16	18	57	135

Table 18–3. EFFECT OF BUDGET PROPOSALS—Continued

(In millions of dollars)

	2024	2025	2026	2027	2028	2029	2030	2031	2032	2033	2034	2025–2029	2025–2034
Require employers to withhold tax on failed nonqualified deferred compensation plans ...	....	206	215	225	235	245	256	267	279	291	304	1,126	2,523
Extend to six years the statute of limitations for certain tax assessments ...	....	....	....	....	....	....	....	....	....	....	....	....	....
Increase the statute of limitations on assessment of the COVID-related paid leave and employee retention tax credits[2] ...	42	557	1,624	1,327	218	....	....	....	....	....	....	3,726	3,726
Impose penalties for inaccurate or fraudulent employment tax returns[2] ...	....	1,704	95	45	11	....	....	....	....	....	....	1,855	1,855
Expand and increase penalties for noncompliant return preparation and e-filing and authorize IRS oversight of paid preparers:													
Expand and increase penalties for return preparation and e-filing[2] ...	....	40	53	49	50	55	60	66	72	78	85	247	608
Grant authority to IRS for oversight of paid preparers[2] ...	....	28	51	70	87	98	100	100	99	98	97	334	828
Subtotal, expand and increase penalties and oversight for return preparation and e-filing ...	....	68	104	119	137	153	160	166	171	176	182	581	1,436
Make repeated willful failure to file a tax return a felony for those with significant tax liability ..	....	....	....	....	....	....	....	....	....	....	....	....	....
Expand IRS summons authority for large partnerships ...	....	143	244	255	265	276	288	300	313	326	340	1,183	2,750
Address compliance in connection with tax responsibilities of expatriates ...	....	....	1	2	3	4	5	5	4	4	4	10	32
Define control of the payment of wage ...													
Subtotal, improve tax compliance ...	42	3,202	2,858	2,582	1,515	1,347	1,401	1,456	1,512	1,569	1,633	11,504	19,075
Modernize rules, including those for digital assets:													
Apply the wash sale rules to digital assets and address related party transactions ...	....	1,034	1,774	2,151	2,313	2,515	2,776	2,979	3,201	3,433	3,650	9,787	25,826
Modernize rules treating loans of securities as tax-free to include other asset classes and address income inclusion ...	....	....	....	....	....	....	....	....	....	....	....	....	....
Provide for information reporting by certain financial institutions and digital asset brokers for purposes of exchange of information ...	....	239	279	297	316	334	357	382	403	427	451	1,465	3,485
Require reporting by certain taxpayers of foreign digital asset accounts ...	....	375	439	466	497	526	561	600	634	671	708	2,303	5,477
Amend the mark-to-market rules to include digital assets ...	....	8,047	–58	–64	–70	–77	–85	–94	–103	–113	–125	7,778	7,258
Subtotal, modernize rules, including those for digital assets ...	....	9,695	2,434	2,850	3,056	3,298	3,609	3,867	4,135	4,418	4,684	21,333	42,046
Improve benefits tax administration:													
Rationalize funding for post-retirement medical and life insurance benefits ...	....	....	....	....	....	....	....	....	....	....	....	....	....
Clarify tax treatment of on-demand pay arrangements ...	....	....	....	....	....	....	....	....	....	....	....	....	....
Amend the excise tax on employment-based group health plans ...	....	....	....	....	....	....	....	....	....	....	....	....	....
Subtotal, improve benefits tax administration ..	....	....	....	....	....	....	....	....	....	....	....	....	....
Strengthen program integrity:													
Extend mandatory funding provided to the IRS through fiscal year 2034[2] ...	....	....	–2,673	–2,822	–2,177	–648	27,973	42,108	51,231	60,198	63,520	–8,320	236,710
Subtotal, strengthen program integrity ...	....	....	–2,673	–2,822	–2,177	–648	27,973	42,108	51,231	60,198	63,520	–8,320	236,710
Other initiatives:													
Extend surprise billing protections to ground ambulances[2] ...	....	....	72	99	102	111	114	118	125	130	137	384	1,008
Improve access to behavioral healthcare in the private insurance market[2] ...	....	....	....	–2,464	–3,420	–3,585	–3,753	–3,914	–4,136	–4,343	–4,564	–9,469	–30,179
Require coverage of three primary care visits and three behavioral health visits without cost-sharing[2] ...	....	....	....	–4,787	–4,448	–1,689	–1,016	–1,075	–1,131	–1,192	–1,259	–10,924	–16,597
Limit cost-sharing for insulin at $35 per month[2]	....	–552	–441	–83	....	....	....	....	....	....	....	–1,076	–1,076
Require 12 months of Medicaid postpartum coverage[2] ...	....	82	86	90	92	95	96	106	114	120	126	445	1,007

Table 18–3. EFFECT OF BUDGET PROPOSALS—Continued

(In millions of dollars)

	2024	2025	2026	2027	2028	2029	2030	2031	2032	2033	2034	2025–2029	2025–2034
Expand the continuous eligibility requirement for all children in Medicaid and CHIP from 12 to 36 months[2]	....	10	16	22	27	27	29	23	21	16	15	102	206
Provide continuous eligibility for children in Medicaid and CHIP from birth until they turn age 6[2]	....	....	11	17	18	18	18	11	9	11	10	64	123
Prohibit enrollment fees and waiting periods in CHIP[2]	....	8	5	7	6	7	6	1	–2	–2	–2	33	34
Increase civil penalties for labor law violations	....	150	200	250	250	250	250	250	300	300	300	1,100	2,500
Establish Electronic Visa Update System user fee	....	7	7	8	8	8	8	8	8	8	8	38	78
Fund Unemployment Insurance program integrity	....	....	....	....	–6	–5	–10	–11	–11	–18	–16	–11	–77
Increase FHLB contribution to the Affordable Housing Program [1]	....	284	284	284	284	284	284	284	284	284	284	1,420	2,840
Subtotal, other initiatives	....	–11	240	–6,557	–7,087	–4,479	–3,974	–4,199	–4,419	–4,686	–4,961	–17,894	–40,133
Total, effects of budget proposals	**117,741**	**187,625**	**372,548**	**376,368**	**391,425**	**409,712**	**447,480**	**469,408**	**486,954**	**510,578**	**547,694**	**1,737,678**	**4,199,792**

[1] Net of income offsets.

[2] This proposal affects both receipts and outlays. The net effect is shown above. The outlay effects included in these estimates are as follows:

	2024	2025	2026	2027	2028	2029	2030	2031	2032	2033	2034	2025–2029	2025–2034
Expand the child credit, and make permanent full refundability and advanceability	–80	–186,320	–39,499	–8,623	–8,187	–8,188	–8,200	–8,261	–8,176	–8,195	–4,858	–250,817	–288,507
Restore and make permanent the American Rescue Plan expansion of the earned income tax credit for workers without qualifying children	–2	–13,779	–14,068	–13,955	–14,097	–14,288	–14,439	–14,504	–14,610	–14,722	–14,815	–70,187	–143,277
Make permanent the Inflation Reduction Act expansion of health insurance premium tax credits	....	....	–9,333	–13,774	–14,785	–15,571	–16,469	–16,991	–17,789	–18,865	–19,948	–53,463	–143,525
Make the adoption tax credit refundable and allow certain guardianship arrangements to qualify	....	....	–2,653	–1,481	–1,252	–1,253	–1,254	–1,265	–1,273	–1,268	–1,282	–6,639	–12,981
Make permanent the income exclusion for forgiven student debt	....	....	....	–2	–2	–23	–27	–29	–30	–32	–35	–27	–180
Provide tax credits for certain first-time homebuyers and home sellers	....	–11,287	–6,246	–2,943	....	....	....	....	....	....	....	–20,476	–20,476
Increase the statute of limitations on assessment of the COVID-related paid leave and employee retention tax credits	10	144	434	372	72	....	....	....	....	....	....	1,022	1,022
Impose penalties for inaccurate or fraudulent employment tax returns	....	596	10	....	....	....	....	....	....	....	....	606	606
Expand and increase penalties for return preparation and e-filing	....	24	29	21	19	20	22	24	26	28	30	113	243
Grant authority to IRS for oversight of paid preparers	....	10	17	18	21	24	24	24	23	21	21	90	203
Extend mandatory funding provided to the IRS through fiscal year 2034	....	....	–2,673	–2,822	–2,177	–3,694	–14,718	–18,803	–19,485	–19,803	–20,128	–11,366	–104,303
Extend surprise billing protections to ground ambulances	....	....	15	21	21	25	24	24	25	26	27	82	208
Improve access to behavioral healthcare in the private insurance market	....	....	....	–628	–865	–916	–949	–969	–1,035	–1,071	–1,122	–2,409	–7,555
Require coverage of three primary care visits and three behavioral health visits without cost-sharing	....	....	....	–1,047	–965	–343	–182	–198	–206	–215	–224	–2,355	–3,380
Limit cost-sharing for insulin at $35 per month	....	–143	–106	–17	....	....	....	....	....	....	....	–266	–266
Require 12 months of Medicaid postpartum coverage	....	82	86	90	91	93	93	102	109	113	118	442	977
Expand the continuous eligibility requirement for all children in Medicaid and CHIP from 12 to 36 months	....	10	16	22	27	27	29	23	21	16	15	102	206
Provide continuous eligibility for children in Medicaid and CHIP from birth until they turn age 6	....	....	11	18	18	19	18	12	10	11	11	66	128
Prohibit enrollment fees and waiting periods in CHIP	....	8	6	7	7	7	7	1	–1	–1	–1	35	40
Total, outlay effect of receipt proposals	–72	–210,655	–73,954	–44,723	–42,054	–44,061	–56,021	–60,810	–62,391	–63,957	–62,191	–415,447	–720,817

Table 18–4. RECEIPTS BY SOURCE
(In millions of dollars)

Source	2023 Actual	Estimate										
		2024	2025	2026	2027	2028	2029	2030	2031	2032	2033	2034
Individual income taxes:												
Federal funds	2,176,481	2,509,847	2,639,014	2,914,692	3,145,351	3,325,202	3,498,159	3,687,199	3,886,788	4,070,009	4,272,723	4,490,657
Legislative proposal, not subject to PAYGO	....	−11,218	−57,936	−42,460	−42,397	−44,058	−44,237	−19,960	−8,710	−3,371	583	952
Legislative proposal, subject to PAYGO	....	4,737	98,146	103,537	75,345	87,944	97,095	95,986	85,849	76,892	74,627	87,415
Amounts included in the adjusted baseline	....	....	....	....	....	....	−2,025	−28,812	−38,655	−14,813	−7,340	−4,553
Total, Individual income taxes.	**2,176,481**	**2,503,366**	**2,679,224**	**2,975,769**	**3,178,299**	**3,369,088**	**3,548,992**	**3,734,413**	**3,925,272**	**4,128,717**	**4,340,593**	**4,574,471**
Corporation income taxes:												
Federal funds	419,584	519,502	466,990	453,088	440,013	454,095	483,991	507,896	523,766	552,877	559,674	570,438
Legislative proposal, not subject to PAYGO	....	....	....	....	....	....	1,021	13,879	18,293	20,027	22,240	22,237
Legislative proposal, subject to PAYGO	....	93,279	201,090	267,533	263,473	256,128	257,289	262,137	276,013	288,848	300,700	312,257
Amounts included in the adjusted baseline	....	....	....	....	....	....	−1,021	−13,879	−11,717	−2,689	−903	−229
Total, Corporation income taxes	**419,584**	**612,781**	**668,080**	**720,621**	**703,486**	**710,223**	**741,280**	**770,033**	**806,355**	**859,063**	**881,711**	**904,703**
Social insurance and retirement receipts (trust funds):												
Employment and general retirement:												
Old-age survivors insurance (off-budget)	1,020,442	1,060,152	1,098,053	1,147,768	1,195,671	1,256,085	1,306,007	1,361,261	1,417,618	1,474,423	1,552,821	1,613,039
Legislative proposal, not subject to PAYGO	....	−130	−114	−369	−1,642	−2,005	−1,654	−1,604	−1,679	−1,760	−1,843	−1,934
Disability insurance (off-budget)	173,313	180,040	186,460	194,904	203,039	213,298	221,774	231,157	240,728	250,373	263,686	273,912
Legislative proposal, not subject to PAYGO	....	−22	−19	−63	−279	−340	−280	−272	−285	−299	−312	−328
Hospital Insurance	357,762	384,393	398,836	415,342	433,379	455,812	474,815	495,926	517,602	539,662	569,563	593,099
Legislative proposal, not subject to PAYGO	....	11,218	57,936	42,460	42,397	44,058	46,262	48,772	51,328	54,060	57,178	60,459
Legislative proposal, subject to PAYGO	....	16,972	84,852	61,093	66,740	72,032	76,021	79,997	84,013	88,131	92,794	98,407
Railroad retirement:												
Social security equivalent account	2,912	2,633	2,648	2,692	2,739	2,785	2,833	2,881	2,929	2,978	3,028	3,087
Rail pension & supplemental annuity	3,718	3,592	3,610	3,683	3,755	3,828	3,901	4,152	4,273	4,352	4,620	4,761
Total, Employment and general retirement	1,558,147	1,658,848	1,832,262	1,867,510	1,945,799	2,045,553	2,129,679	2,222,270	2,316,527	2,411,920	2,541,535	2,644,502
On-budget	*(364,392)*	*(418,808)*	*(547,882)*	*(525,270)*	*(549,010)*	*(578,515)*	*(603,832)*	*(631,728)*	*(660,145)*	*(689,183)*	*(727,183)*	*(759,813)*
Off-budget	*(1,193,755)*	*(1,240,040)*	*(1,284,380)*	*(1,342,240)*	*(1,396,789)*	*(1,467,038)*	*(1,525,847)*	*(1,590,542)*	*(1,656,382)*	*(1,722,737)*	*(1,814,352)*	*(1,884,689)*
Unemployment insurance:												
Deposits by States [1]	41,276	44,867	46,727	48,932	51,100	52,710	52,604	53,865	57,166	57,610	59,301	63,083
Legislative proposal, not subject to PAYGO	....	....	....	....	....	−5	−4	−9	−10	−10	−16	−14
Legislative proposal, subject to PAYGO	....	....	....	....	....	−1	−1	−1	−1	−1	−2	−2
Amounts included in the adjusted baseline	....	....	....	−3	−8	−14	−21	−20	−22	−23	−28	−26
Federal unemployment receipts	7,797	9,053	9,613	10,454	11,295	10,853	11,221	12,905	12,409	13,020	13,637	14,265
Railroad unemployment receipts	331	156	33	37	56	123	209	215	158	137	179	230
Total, Unemployment insurance	49,404	54,076	56,373	59,420	62,443	63,666	64,008	66,955	69,700	70,733	73,071	77,536

Table 18–4. RECEIPTS BY SOURCE—Continued

(In millions of dollars)

Source	2023 Actual	Estimate										
		2024	2025	2026	2027	2028	2029	2030	2031	2032	2033	2034
Other retirement:												
Federal employees retirement - employee share	6,883	7,589	8,152	8,647	9,140	9,648	10,167	10,701	11,243	11,798	12,364	12,928
Non-Federal employees retirement	22	30	30	29	29	29	28	28	27	27	27	27
Total, Other retirement	6,905	7,619	8,182	8,676	9,169	9,677	10,195	10,729	11,270	11,825	12,391	12,955
Total, Social insurance and retirement receipts (trust funds)	**1,614,456**	**1,720,543**	**1,896,817**	**1,935,606**	**2,017,411**	**2,118,896**	**2,203,882**	**2,299,954**	**2,397,497**	**2,494,478**	**2,626,997**	**2,734,993**
On-budget	*(420,701)*	*(480,503)*	*(612,437)*	*(593,366)*	*(620,622)*	*(651,858)*	*(678,035)*	*(709,412)*	*(741,115)*	*(771,741)*	*(812,645)*	*(850,304)*
Off-budget	*(1,193,755)*	*(1,240,040)*	*(1,284,380)*	*(1,342,240)*	*(1,396,789)*	*(1,467,038)*	*(1,525,847)*	*(1,590,542)*	*(1,656,382)*	*(1,722,737)*	*(1,814,352)*	*(1,884,689)*
Excise taxes:												
Federal funds:												
Alcohol	9,501	9,645	9,608	9,593	9,588	9,644	9,700	9,755	9,813	9,876	9,950	10,037
Tobacco	10,299	9,706	8,578	8,345	8,298	8,190	8,062	7,966	7,849	7,734	7,621	7,497
Transportation fuels	–15,234	–5,763	–3,646	–1,120	–1,084	–1,020	–999	–983	–967	–944	–923	–906
Legislative proposal, subject to PAYGO	....	....	9	12	15	18	21	25	28	31	34	37
Telephone and teletype services	303	253	209	170	144	121	99	80	63	48	35	25
Indoor tanning services	66	63	61	60	58	57	55	54	53	51	50	49
Corporate stock repurchase	1,687	6,922	7,391	7,217	7,195	7,315	7,607	7,928	8,270	8,629	9,004	9,394
Other Federal fund excise taxes	–1,442	3,114	3,914	3,915	3,944	4,008	4,116	4,238	4,364	4,500	4,641	4,787
Legislative proposal, subject to PAYGO	....	2,977	12,029	12,003	12,253	12,609	13,159	13,786	14,467	15,195	15,986	16,827
Total, Federal funds	5,180	26,917	38,153	40,195	40,411	40,942	41,820	42,849	43,940	45,120	46,398	47,747
Trust funds:												
Transportation	42,216	43,974	43,480	43,261	42,749	42,211	41,294	40,893	40,300	39,419	38,705	38,188
Airport and airway	22,277	19,900	20,215	20,693	21,290	22,066	22,907	23,847	24,863	25,954	27,080	28,250
Legislative proposal, subject to PAYGO	....	....	58	139	222	308	395	422	427	432	436	442
Sport fish restoration and boating safety	575	626	635	645	654	665	675	685	697	708	720	733
Tobacco assessments	11	....	....	....	....	....	....	....	....	....	....	....
Black lung disability insurance	295	308	294	261	225	189	143	110	105	109	115	119
Inland waterway	95	114	114	113	113	113	113	112	112	112	112	111
Superfund	1,205	2,174	2,330	2,412	2,497	2,580	2,663	2,745	2,830	2,923	3,012	3,086
Legislative proposal, subject to PAYGO	....	....	231	317	328	339	349	357	364	374	382	388
Oil spill liability	347	537	542	547	550	555	558	558	558	560	560	560
Legislative proposal, subject to PAYGO	....	....	116	158	160	163	165	166	167	170	171	171
Vaccine injury compensation	220	289	290	292	294	297	301	304	307	310	312	315
Leaking underground storage tank	205	191	189	188	185	181	176	174	169	163	158	154
Supplementary medical insurance	2,797	4,263	2,800	2,800	2,800	1,483	2,800	4,117	2,800	2,800	2,800	1,483
Patient-centered outcomes research	379	422	449	472	491	516	543	570	601	632	666	702
Total, Trust funds	70,622	72,798	71,743	72,298	72,558	71,666	73,082	75,060	74,300	74,666	75,229	74,702
Total, Excise taxes	**75,802**	**99,715**	**109,896**	**112,493**	**112,969**	**112,608**	**114,902**	**117,909**	**118,240**	**119,786**	**121,627**	**122,449**
Estate and gift taxes:												
Federal funds	33,668	29,035	31,277	33,195	48,791	51,128	53,451	56,127	60,122	64,730	69,522	74,678
Legislative proposal, subject to PAYGO	....	....	1,346	1,556	3,839	5,652	7,535	9,183	9,317	9,939	10,890	11,884
Total, Estate and gift taxes	**33,668**	**29,035**	**32,623**	**34,751**	**52,630**	**56,780**	**60,986**	**65,310**	**69,439**	**74,669**	**80,412**	**86,562**

Table 18–4. RECEIPTS BY SOURCE—Continued

(In millions of dollars)

Source	2023 Actual	Estimate										
		2024	2025	2026	2027	2028	2029	2030	2031	2032	2033	2034
Customs duties and fees:												
Federal funds	78,251	79,191	58,414	50,207	50,527	52,024	54,002	56,114	58,417	50,530	52,553	54,547
Trust funds	2,087	2,193	2,257	2,321	2,411	2,502	2,594	2,695	2,801	2,904	3,007	3,115
Total, Customs duties and fees	**80,338**	**81,384**	**60,671**	**52,528**	**52,938**	**54,526**	**56,596**	**58,809**	**61,218**	**53,434**	**55,560**	**57,662**
Miscellaneous receipts:												
Federal funds:												
Miscellaneous taxes	1,139	826	828	829	830	832	824	825	826	828	828	831
Legislative proposal, subject to PAYGO	....	....	379	379	379	379	379	379	379	379	379	379
Deposit of earnings, Federal Reserve System	581	....	....	....	25,007	40,027	51,401	61,671	71,135	79,067	84,788	89,768
Transfers from the Federal Reserve	721	763	811	832	855	877	901	925	951	976	1,003	1,029
Fees for permits and regulatory and judicial services	22,840	23,584	25,959	29,352	31,759	35,666	40,006	44,430	48,332	51,933	54,631	56,738
Legislative proposal, subject to PAYGO	....	....	7	7	8	8	8	8	8	8	8	8
Fines, penalties, and forfeitures	14,004	8,322	8,325	8,256	8,282	8,317	8,346	8,373	8,402	8,432	8,460	8,495
Legislative proposal, subject to PAYGO	....	....	150	200	250	250	250	250	250	300	300	300
Refunds and recoveries	–25	–10	–10	–10	–10	–10	–10	–10	–10	–10	–10	–10
Total, Federal funds	39,260	33,485	36,449	39,845	67,360	86,346	102,105	116,851	130,273	141,913	150,387	157,538
Trust funds:												
United Mine Workers of America, combined benefit fund	11	6	5	5	4	4	3	3	3	2	2	2
Defense cooperation	452	139	142	145	148	151	155	158	161	164	168	171
Fees for permits and regulatory and judicial services	8	10	10	10	10	10	10	10	10	10	10	10
Fines, penalties, and forfeitures	887	1,082	1,031	969	984	992	1,010	996	988	635	629	630
Total, Trust funds	1,358	1,237	1,188	1,129	1,146	1,157	1,178	1,167	1,162	811	809	813
Total, Miscellaneous receipts	**40,618**	**34,722**	**37,637**	**40,974**	**68,506**	**87,503**	**103,283**	**118,018**	**131,435**	**142,724**	**151,196**	**158,351**
Total, budget receipts	**4,440,947**	**5,081,546**	**5,484,948**	**5,872,742**	**6,186,239**	**6,509,624**	**6,829,921**	**7,164,446**	**7,509,456**	**7,872,871**	**8,258,096**	**8,639,191**
On-budget	*(3,247,192)*	*(3,841,506)*	*(4,200,568)*	*(4,530,502)*	*(4,789,450)*	*(5,042,586)*	*(5,304,074)*	*(5,573,904)*	*(5,853,074)*	*(6,150,134)*	*(6,443,744)*	*(6,754,502)*
Off-budget	*(1,193,755)*	*(1,240,040)*	*(1,284,380)*	*(1,342,240)*	*(1,396,789)*	*(1,467,038)*	*(1,525,847)*	*(1,590,542)*	*(1,656,382)*	*(1,722,737)*	*(1,814,352)*	*(1,884,689)*

[1] Deposits by States cover the benefit part of the program. Federal unemployment receipts cover administrative costs at both the Federal and State levels. Railroad unemployment receipts cover both the benefits and administrative costs of the program for the railroads.

[2] Represents employer and employee contributions to the civil service retirement and disability fund for covered employees of Government-sponsored, privately owned enterprises and the District of Columbia municipal government.

19. OFFSETTING COLLECTIONS AND OFFSETTING RECEIPTS

I. INTRODUCTION AND BACKGROUND

The Government records money collected in one of two ways. It is either recorded as a governmental receipt and included in the amount reported on the receipts side of the budget or it is recorded as an offsetting collection or offsetting receipt, which reduces (or "offsets") the amount reported on the outlay side of the budget. Governmental receipts are discussed in the previous chapter of this volume, "Governmental Receipts." The first section of this chapter broadly discusses offsetting collections and offsetting receipts. The second section discusses user charges, which consist of a subset of offsetting collections and offsetting receipts and a small share of governmental receipts. The third section describes the user charge proposals in the 2025 Budget.

Offsetting collections and offsetting receipts are recorded as offsets to spending so that the budget totals for receipts and (net) outlays reflect the amount of resources allocated by the Government through collective political choice, rather than through the marketplace.[1] This practice ensures that the budget totals measure the transactions of the Government with the public, and avoids the double counting that would otherwise result when one account makes a payment to another account and the receiving account then spends the proceeds. Offsetting receipts and offsetting collections are recorded in the budget in one of two ways, based on interpretation of laws and longstanding budget concepts and practice. They are offsetting collections when the collections are authorized to be credited to expenditure accounts. Otherwise, they are deposited in receipt accounts and called offsetting receipts.

There are two sources of offsetting receipts and offsetting collections: from the public and from other budget accounts. Like governmental receipts, offsetting receipts and offsetting collections from the public reduce the deficit or increase the surplus. In contrast, offsetting receipts and offsetting collections resulting from transactions with other budget accounts, called intragovernmental transactions, exactly offset the payments made by these accounts, with no net impact on the deficit or surplus.[2] In 2023, offsetting receipts and offsetting collections from the public were $1,057 billion, while receipts and collections from intragovernmental transactions were $1,478 billion, for a total of $2,535 billion Government-wide.

As described above, intragovernmental transactions are responsible for the majority of offsetting collections and offsetting receipts, when measured by the magnitude of the dollars collected. Examples of intragovernmental transactions include interest payments to funds that hold Government securities (such as the Social Security trust funds), general fund transfers to civilian and military retirement pension and health benefits funds, and agency payments to funds for employee health insurance and retirement benefits. Although receipts and collections from intragovernmental collections exactly offset the payments themselves, with no effect on the deficit or surplus, it is important to record these transactions in the budget to show how much the Government is allocating to fund various programs. For example, in the case of civilian retirement pensions, Government agencies make accrual payments to the Civil Service Retirement and Disability Fund on behalf of current employees to fund their future retirement benefits; the receipt of these payments to the Fund is shown in a single receipt account. Recording the receipt of these payments is important because it demonstrates the total cost to the Government today of providing this future benefit.

Offsetting receipts and collections from the public comprise approximately one-third of total offsetting collections and offsetting receipts, when measured by the magnitude of the dollars collected. Most of the funds collected through offsetting collections and offsetting receipts from the public arise from business-like transactions with the public. Unlike governmental receipts, which are derived from the Government's exercise of its sovereign power, these offsetting collections and offsetting receipts arise primarily from voluntary payments from the public for goods or services provided by the Government. They are classified as offsets to outlays for the cost of producing the goods or services for sale, rather than as governmental receipts. These activities include the sale of postage stamps, land, timber, and electricity; charging fees for services provided to the public (e.g., admission to National parks); and collecting premiums for healthcare benefits (e.g., Medicare Parts B and D). As described above, treating offsetting collections and offsetting receipts as offsets to outlays ensures the budgetary totals represent governmental rather than market activity.

A relatively small portion ($21.5 billion in 2023) of offsetting collections and offsetting receipts from the public is derived from the Government's exercise of its sovereign power. From a conceptual standpoint, these should be classified as governmental receipts. However, they are classified as offsetting rather than governmental receipts either because this classification has been specified in law or because these collections have traditionally been classi-

[1] Showing collections from business-type transactions as offsets on the spending side of the budget follows the concept recommended by the Report of the President's Commission on Budget Concepts in 1967 and is discussed in the "Budget Concepts" chapter of this volume.

[2] For the purposes of this discussion, "collections from the public" include collections from non-budgetary Government accounts, such as credit financing accounts and deposit funds. For more information on these non-budgetary accounts, see the "Coverage of the Budget" chapter of this volume.

Table 19–1. OFFSETTING COLLECTIONS AND OFFSETTING RECEIPTS FROM THE PUBLIC

(In billions of dollars)

	Actual 2023	Estimate	
		2024	2025
Offsetting collections (credited to expenditure accounts):			
User charges:			
Postal Service stamps and other Postal Service fees (off-budget)	77.1	79.6	82.1
Sale of energy:			
Tennessee Valley Authority	54.6	53.5	54.4
Bonneville Power Administration	4.3	4.1	4.3
Deposit Insurance	51.1	19.7	108.2
Employee contributions for employees and retired employees health benefits funds	19.5	21.3	22.6
Pension Benefit Guaranty Corporation fund	11.0	13.6	12.0
Federal Crop Insurance Corporation Fund	7.2	7.0	6.6
Defense Commissary Agency	4.6	4.9	5.0
Passenger Security Fee	3.1	2.8	6.6
Patent and Trademark fees	4.0	4.1	4.5
National Flood Insurance Fund	3.8	3.9	4.1
All other user charges	41.8	37.5	39.9
Subtotal, user charges	282.1	251.9	350.2
Other collections credited to expenditure accounts:			
Commodity Credit Corporation fund	5.6	6.6	7.1
Supplemental Security Income (collections from the States)	3.1	3.4	3.5
Other collections	63.0	6.1	6.8
Subtotal, other collections	71.7	16.1	17.4
Subtotal, offsetting collections	353.8	268.0	367.6
Offsetting receipts (deposited in receipt accounts):			
User charges:			
Medicare premiums	142.2	152.9	165.8
Outer Continental Shelf rents, bonuses, and royalties	6.9	8.4	7.8
Immigration fees	5.9	7.0	7.5
Spectrum auction, relocation, and licenses	--	0.4	--
All other user charges	36.8	34.2	35.0
Subtotal, user charges deposited in receipt accounts	191.9	203.0	216.1
Other collections deposited in receipt accounts:			
Military assistance program sales	52.7	41.4	42.6
Interest received from credit financing accounts	45.4	55.9	55.4
Government-sponsored enterprise (GSE) guarantee fees	6.2	6.4	6.5
Student loan receipt of negative subsidy and downward reestimates	346.6	4.9	0.2
All other collections deposited in receipt accounts	60.8	61.2	53.5
Subtotal, other collections deposited in receipt accounts	511.7	169.8	158.2
Subtotal, offsetting receipts	703.5	372.8	374.4
Total, offsetting collections and offsetting receipts from the public	1,057.3	640.7	742.0
Total, offsetting collections and offsetting receipts excluding off-budget	980.0	561.2	659.9
ADDENDUM:			
User charges that are offsetting collections and offsetting receipts[1]	473.9	454.8	566.3
Other offsetting collections and offsetting receipts from the public	583.4	185.9	175.6

[1] Excludes user charges that are classified on the receipts side of the budget. For total user charges, see Table 19–3.

Table 19–2. SUMMARY OF OFFSETTING RECEIPTS BY TYPE

(In millions of dollars)

Receipt Type	Actual 2023	Estimate					
		2024	2025	2026	2027	2028	2029
Intragovernmental	1,049,755	1,152,858	1,202,416	1,283,032	1,237,404	1,304,391	1,395,599
Receipts from non-Federal sources:							
Proprietary	688,694	355,171	357,635	369,938	424,763	419,204	462,929
Offsetting governmental	14,836	17,606	16,743	17,396	17,821	18,215	18,621
Total, receipts from non-Federal sources	703,530	372,777	374,378	387,334	442,584	437,419	481,550
Total, offsetting receipts	1,753,285	1,525,635	1,576,794	1,670,366	1,679,988	1,741,810	1,877,149

fied as offsets to outlays. Most of the offsetting collections and offsetting receipts in this category derive from fees from Government regulatory services or Government licenses, and include, for example, charges for regulating the nuclear energy industry, bankruptcy filing fees, and immigration fees.[3]

The final source of offsetting collections and offsetting receipts from the public is gifts. Gifts are voluntary contributions to the Government to support particular purposes or reduce the amount of Government debt held by the public.

The spending associated with the activities that generate offsetting collections and offsetting receipts from the public is included in total or "gross outlays." Offsetting collections and offsetting receipts from the public are subtracted from gross outlays to the public to yield "net outlays," which is the most common measure of outlays cited and generally referred to as simply "outlays."[4] For 2023, gross outlays to the public were $7,192 billion, or 26.7 percent of GDP and offsetting collections and offsetting receipts from the public were $1,057 billion, or 3.9 percent of GDP, resulting in net outlays of $6,135 billion or 22.7 percent of GDP. Government-wide net outlays reflect the Government's net disbursements to the public and are subtracted from governmental receipts to derive the Government's deficit or surplus. For 2023, governmental receipts were $4,442, or 16.5 percent of GDP, and the deficit was $1,693 billion, or 6.3 percent of GDP.

Although both offsetting collections and offsetting receipts are subtracted from gross outlays to derive net outlays, they are treated differently when it comes to accounting for specific programs and agencies. Offsetting collections are usually authorized to be spent for the purposes of an expenditure account and are generally available for use when collected, without further action by the Congress. Therefore, offsetting collections are recorded as offsets to spending within expenditure accounts, so that the account total highlights the net flow of funds.

Like governmental receipts, offsetting receipts are credited to receipt accounts, and any spending of the receipts is recorded in separate expenditure accounts. As a result, the budget separately displays the flow of funds into and out of the Government. Offsetting receipts may or may not be designated for a specific purpose, depending on the legislation that authorizes their collection. If designated for a particular purpose, the offsetting receipts may, in some cases, be spent without further action by the Congress. When not designated for a particular purpose, offsetting receipts are credited to the general fund, which

[3] This category of receipts is known as "offsetting governmental receipts." Some argue that regulatory or licensing fees should be viewed as payments for a particular service or for the right to engage in a particular type of business. However, these fees are conceptually much more similar to taxes because they are compulsory, and they fund activities that are intended to provide broadly dispersed benefits, such as protecting the health of the public. Reclassifying these fees as governmental receipts could require a change in law, and because of conventions for scoring appropriations bills, would make it impossible for fees that are controlled through annual appropriations acts to be scored as offsets to discretionary spending.

[4] Gross outlays to the public are derived by subtracting intragovernmental outlays from gross outlays. For 2023, gross outlays were $8,670 billion and intragovernmental outlays were $1,478 billion.

Table 19–3. GROSS OUTLAYS, USER CHARGES, OTHER OFFSETTING COLLECTIONS AND OFFSETTING RECEIPTS FROM THE PUBLIC, AND NET OUTLAYS

(In billions of dollars)

	Actual 2023	Estimate	
		2024	2025
Gross outlays to the public	7,192.0	7,581.6	8,007.9
Offsetting collections and offsetting receipts from the public:			
User charges [1]	473.9	454.8	566.3
Other	583.4	185.9	175.6
Subtotal, offsetting collections and offsetting receipts from the public	1,057.3	640.7	742.0
Net outlays	6,134.7	6,940.9	7,266.0

[1] $4.8 billion of the total user charges for 2023 were classified as governmental receipts, and the remainder were classified as offsetting collections and offsetting receipts. $4.8 billion and $4.9 billion of the total user charges for 2024 and 2025 are classified as governmental receipts, respectively.

contains all funds not otherwise allocated and which is used to finance Government spending that is not financed out of dedicated funds. In some cases where the receipts are designated for a particular purpose, offsetting receipts are reported in a particular agency and reduce or offset the outlays reported for that agency. In other cases, the offsetting receipts are "undistributed," which means they reduce total Government outlays, but not the outlays of any particular agency.

Table 19-1 summarizes offsetting collections and offsetting receipts from the public. The amounts shown in the table are not evident in the commonly cited budget measure of outlays, which is already net of these collections and receipts. For 2025, the table shows that total offsetting collections and offsetting receipts from the public are estimated to be $742 billion, or 2.5 percent of GDP. Of these, an estimated $368 billion are offsetting collections and an estimated $374 billion are offsetting receipts. Table 19–1 also identifies those offsetting collections and offsetting receipts that are considered user charges, as defined and discussed below.

As shown in the table, major offsetting collections from the public include proceeds from Postal Service sales, electrical power sales, loan repayments to the Commodity Credit Corporation for loans made prior to enactment of the Federal Credit Reform Act, and Federal employee payments for health insurance. As also shown in the table, major offsetting receipts from the public include premiums for Medicare Parts A, B and D, proceeds from military assistance program sales, rents and royalties from Outer Continental Shelf oil extraction, and interest income.

Tables 19–2 and 19–3 provide further detail about offsetting receipts, including both offsetting receipts from the public (as summarized in Table 19–1) and intragovernmental transactions. Table 19–5, "Offsetting Receipts by Type," and Table 19–6, "Offsetting Collections and Offsetting Receipts, Detail—2025 Budget," which is a complete listing by account, are available in the *Analytical Perspectives* volume online. In total, offsetting receipts are estimated to be $1,577 billion in 2025; $1,202 billion are from intragovernmental transactions and $374 billion are from the public. The offsetting receipts from the public consist of proprietary receipts ($358 billion), which are those resulting from business-like transactions such as the sale of goods or services, and offsetting governmental receipts, which, as discussed above, are derived from the exercise of the Government's sovereign power and, absent a specification in law or a long-standing practice, would be classified on the receipts side of the budget ($17 billion).

II. USER CHARGES

User charges or user fees[5] refer generally to those monies that the Government receives from the public for market-oriented activities and regulatory activities. In combination with budget concepts, laws that authorize user charges determine whether a user charge is classified as an offsetting collection, an offsetting receipt, or a governmental receipt. Almost all user charges, as defined below, are classified as offsetting collections or offsetting receipts; for 2025, only an estimated 0.9 percent of user charges are classified as governmental receipts. As summarized in Table 19–3, total user charges for 2025 are estimated to be $571 billion with $566 billion being offsetting collections or offsetting receipts, and accounting for more than three-quarters of all offsetting collections and offsetting receipts from the public.[6]

Definition. In this chapter, user charges refer to fees, charges, and assessments levied on individuals or organizations directly benefiting from or subject to regulation by a Government program or activity, where the payers do not represent a broad segment of the public such as those who pay income taxes.

Examples of business-type or market-oriented user charges and regulatory and licensing user charges include those charges listed in Table 19–1 for offsetting collections and offsetting receipts. User charges exclude certain offsetting collections and offsetting receipts from the public, such as payments received from credit programs, and interest, and also exclude payments from one part of the Federal Government to another. In addition, user charges do not include dedicated taxes (such as taxes paid to social insurance programs or excise taxes on gasoline) or customs duties, fines, penalties, or forfeitures.

Alternative definitions. The definition for user charges used in this chapter follows the definition used in OMB Circular No. A–25, "User Charges," which provides policy guidance to Executive Branch Agencies on setting the amount for user charges. Alternative definitions may be used for other purposes. Much of the discussion of user charges below—their purpose, when they should be levied, and how the amount should be set—applies to these alternative definitions as well.

A narrower definition of user charges could be limited to proceeds from the sale of goods and services, excluding the proceeds from the sale of assets, and to proceeds that are dedicated to financing the goods and services being provided. This definition is similar to one the House of Representatives uses as a guide for purposes of committee jurisdiction. (See the Congressional Record, January 3, 1991, p. H31, item 8.) The definition of user charges could be even narrower by excluding regulatory fees and focusing solely on business-type transactions. Alternatively,

[5] In this chapter, the term "user charge" is generally used and has the same meaning as the term "user fee." The term "user charge" is the one used in OMB Circular No. A–11, "Preparation, Submission, and Execution of the Budget"; OMB Circular No. A–25, "User Charges"; and the "Budget Concepts" chapter. In common usage, the terms "user charge" and "user fee" are often used interchangeably, and in A Glossary of Terms Used in the Federal Budget Process, GAO provides the same definition for both terms.

[6] User charge totals presented in this chapter include collections from accounts classified as containing user fee data. OMB accounts are classified as containing user fee data if more than half of collections are estimated to include user charges. Consequently, totals may include collections that are not user charges in accounts that meet the threshold and exclude user charges in accounts that do not meet the threshold.

the user charge definition could be broader than the one used in this chapter by including beneficiary- or liability-based excise taxes.[7]

What is the purpose of user charges? User charges are intended to improve the efficiency and equity of financing certain Government activities. Charging users for activities that benefit a relatively limited number of people reduces the burden on the general taxpayer, as does charging regulated parties for regulatory activities in a particular sector.

User charges that are set to cover the costs of production of goods and services can result in more efficient resource allocation within the economy. When buyers are charged the cost of providing goods and services, they make better cost-benefit calculations regarding the size of their purchase, which in turn signals to the Government how much of the goods or services it should provide. Prices in private, competitive markets serve the same purposes. User charges for goods and services that do not have special social or distributional benefits may also improve equity or fairness by requiring those who benefit from an activity to pay for it and by not requiring those who do not benefit from an activity to pay for it.

When should the Government impose a charge? Discussions of whether to finance spending with a tax or a fee often focus on whether the benefits of the activity accrue to the public in general or to a limited group of people. In general, if the benefits of spending accrue broadly to the public or include special social or distributional benefits, then the program should be financed by taxes paid by the public. In contrast, if the benefits accrue to a limited number of private individuals or organizations and do not include special social or distributional benefits, then the program should be financed by charges paid by the private beneficiaries. For Federal programs where the benefits are entirely public or entirely private, applying this principle can be relatively easy. For example, the benefits from national defense accrue to the public in general, and according to this principle should be (and are) financed by taxes. In contrast, the benefits of electricity sold by the Tennessee Valley Authority accrue primarily to those using the electricity, and should be (and predominantly are) financed by user charges.

In many cases, however, an activity has benefits that accrue to both public and private groups, and it may be difficult to identify how much of the benefits accrue to each. Because of this, it can be difficult to know how much of the program should be financed by taxes and how much by fees. For example, the benefits from recreation areas are mixed. Fees for visitors to these areas are appropriate because the visitors benefit directly from their visit, but the public in general also benefits because these areas protect the Nation's natural and historic heritage now and for posterity. For this reason, visitor recreation fees generally cover only part of the cost to the Government of maintaining the recreation property. Where a fee may be appropriate to finance all or part of an activity, the extent to which a fee can be easily administered must be considered. For example, if fees are charged for entering or using Government-owned land then there must be clear points of entry onto the land and attendants patrolling and monitoring the land's use.

What amount should be charged? When the Government is acting in its capacity as sovereign and where user charges are appropriate, such as for some regulatory activities, current policy supports setting fees equal to the full cost to the Government, including both direct and indirect costs. When the Government is not acting in its capacity as sovereign and engages in a purely business-type transaction (such as leasing or selling goods, services, or resources), market price is generally the basis for establishing the fee.[8] If the Government is engaged in a purely business-type transaction and economic resources are allocated efficiently, then this market price should be equal to or greater than the Government's full cost of production.

Classification of user charges in the budget. As shown in the note to Table 19–3, most user charges are classified as offsets to outlays on the spending side of the budget, but a few are classified on the receipts side of the budget. An estimated $4.9 billion of user charges in 2025 are classified on the receipts side and are included in the governmental receipts totals described in the previous chapter, "Governmental Receipts." They are classified as receipts because they are regulatory charges collected by the Federal Government by the exercise of its sovereign powers. Examples include filing fees in the United States courts and agricultural quarantine inspection fees.

The remaining user charges, an estimated $566 billion in 2025, are classified as offsetting collections and offsetting receipts on the spending side of the Budget. As discussed above in the context of all offsetting collections and offsetting receipts, some of these user charges are collected by the Federal Government by the exercise of its sovereign powers and conceptually should appear on the receipts side of the budget, but they are required by law or a long-standing practice to be classified on the spending side.

[7] Beneficiary- and liability-based taxes are terms taken from the Congressional Budget Office, "The Growth of Federal User Charges," August 1993, and updated in October 1995. Gasoline taxes are an example of beneficiary-based taxes. An example of a liability-based tax is the excise tax that helps fund the hazardous substance superfund in the Environmental Protection Agency. This tax is paid by industry groups to finance environmental cleanup activities related to the industry activity but not necessarily caused by the payer of the fee.

[8] Policies for setting user charges are promulgated in OMB Circular No. A–25: "User Charges" (July 8, 1993).

III. USER CHARGE PROPOSALS

As shown in Table 19–1, an estimated $368 billion of user charges for 2025 will be credited directly to expenditure accounts and will generally be available for expenditure when they are collected, without further action by the Congress. An estimated $374 of user charges for 2025 will be deposited in offsetting receipt accounts and will be available to be spent only according to the legislation that established the charges.

As shown in Table 19–4, the Administration is proposing new or increased user charges that would, in the aggregate, increase collections by an estimated $212 million in 2025 and an estimated total of $21 billion from 2026 through 2034. These estimates reflect only the amounts to be collected; they do not include related spending. Each proposal is classified as either discretionary or mandatory, as those terms are defined in the Balanced Budget and Emergency Deficit Control Act of 1985, as amended (BBEDCA). "Discretionary" refers to user charges controlled through annual appropriations acts and generally under the jurisdiction of the appropriations committees in the Congress. "Mandatory" refers to user charges controlled by permanent laws and under the jurisdiction of the authorizing committees. These and other terms are discussed further in the "Budget Concepts" chapter of this volume.

A. Discretionary User Charge Proposals

1. Offsetting collections

Department of Health and Human Services

Food and Drug Administration (FDA): Increase export certification user fee cap. Firms exporting products from the United States are often asked by foreign customers or foreign governments to supply a "certificate" for products regulated by the FDA to document the product's regulatory or marketing status. The proposal increases the maximum user fee cap from $175 per export certification to $600 to meet FDA's true cost of issuing export certificates and to ensure better and faster service for American companies that request the service.

Increase tobacco product user fee. Currently, FDA's regulation of all tobacco products is financed through user fees collected from six product categories: cigarettes, roll your own tobacco, snuff, chewing tobacco, cigars, and pipe tobacco. This proposal would expand FDA's tobacco user fees and include user fee assessments on e-cigarettes and other electronic nicotine delivery systems (ENDS) manufacturers, which currently do not pay user fees, and increase the current limitation on total tobacco user fee collections by $114 million in 2025. To ensure that resources keep up with new tobacco products, the proposal would also index future collections to inflation. The expansion of tobacco user fees will strengthen FDA's ability to respond to the growth of newer products such as e-cigarettes through investments in regulatory science, enforcement, and premarket review of product applications.

Department of the Interior

Bureau of Land Management (BLM): Establish onshore oil and gas inspection fees. The Budget proposes new inspection fees for oil and gas leases that are subject to inspection by BLM. The fees would be based on the number of oil and gas wells per lease or unit, providing for costs to be shared equitably across the industry. In 2025, BLM will spend $51 million on managing its compliance inspection program. Inspection costs include, among other things, the salaries and travel expenses of inspectors. The proposed fees will generate approximately $51 million in 2025, thereby fully offsetting the Bureau's cost of compliance inspections and requiring energy developers on Federal lands to fund the majority of inspection-related compliance costs incurred by BLM.

Department of State

Establish the National Museum of American Diplomacy (NMAD) goods and services fee. This new user fee will enable the Department of State to charge fees for goods and services, including visitor and outreach services, programs, conference activities, use of venue, museum shop proceeds, and food services, on a cost-recovery basis, to outside organizations for programs and conference activities held at NMAD.

Commodity Futures Trading Commission (CFTC)

Establish CFTC user fee. The Budget proposes an amendment to the Commodity Exchange Act (Public Law 74–675) authorizing the CFTC to collect user fees to fund the Commission's activities, like other Federal financial and banking regulators. Fee funding would shift the costs of services provided by CFTC from the general taxpayer to the primary beneficiaries of CFTC oversight. Contingent upon enactment of legislation authorizing the CFTC to collect fees, the Administration proposes that collections begin in 2025 to offset a portion of CFTC's annual appropriation.

2. Offsetting receipts

Department of State

Extend Western Hemisphere Travel Initiative surcharge. The Administration proposes to permanently extend the authority for the Department of State to collect the Western Hemisphere Travel Initiative surcharge. The surcharge was initially enacted by the Passport Services Enhancement Act of 2005 (Public Law 109–167) to cover the Department's costs of meeting increased demand for passports, which resulted from the implementation of the Western Hemisphere Travel Initiative.

Increase Border Crossing Card (BCC) fee. The Budget includes a proposal to allow the fee charged for BCC minor applicants to be set administratively, rather than statutorily, at one-half the fee charged for processing an adult border crossing card. Administrative fee setting will allow the fee to better reflect the associated cost of service, consistent with other fees charged for consular services. As a result of this change, annual BCC fee collections beginning in 2025 are projected to increase by $5 million (from $1 million to $6 million).

Increase Machine-Readable Visa (MRV) fee. The Budget includes a proposal to authorize the Department of State to account for the cost of other consular services not otherwise subject to a fee or surcharge when setting the amount of the MRV fee.

B. Mandatory User Charge Proposals

Offsetting receipts

Department Health and Human Services

Provide authority for the Secretary to collect and expend re-survey fees from long-term care facilities within the Survey and Certification Program that require a revisit survey. The Budget proposes to provide CMS permanent authority to charge long-term care facilities fees for any revisits required to validate the correction of deficiencies identified during initial certification, recertification, complaint, facility-reported incident, or prior revisit surveys. The collections would supplement the CMS Program Management funding for the Survey and Certification program.

Department of Homeland Security

Extend expiring Customs and Border Protection (CBP) fees. The Budget proposes to extend the Merchandise Processing Fee beyond its current expiration date of September 30, 2031 to September 30, 2033, and makes permanent the rate increase (from 0.21 percent ad valorem to 0.3464 percent ad valorem) enacted in section 503 of the U.S.–Korea Free Trade Agreement Implementation Act (Public Law 112–41). It also proposes to extend fees statutorily set under the Consolidated Omnibus Budget Reconciliation Act of 1985 (COBRA) and the Express Consignment Courier Facilities (ECCF) fee created under the Trade Act of 2002 (Public Law 107–210) beyond their current expiration date of September 30, 2031 to September 30, 2033.

Customs and Border Protection (CBP) User Fee Facilities. The Budget proposes authority for CBP to recover all of its costs associated with providing immigration and agriculture services at User Fee Facilities. Current law authorizes charging a fee for customs services at User Fee Facilities; however, there is an increased need for CBP to recover the costs of immigration and agriculture services that can be clearly segregated from the customs services provided at User Fee Facilities.

C. User Charge Proposals that are Governmental Receipts

Department of Homeland Security

Establish Electronic Visa Update System user fee. The Budget proposes to establish a user fee for the Electronic Visa Update System (EVUS), a CBP program to collect biographic and travel-related information from certain non-immigrant visa holders prior to traveling to the United States. This process will complement the existing visa application process and enhance CBP's ability to make pre-travel admissibility and risk determinations. CBP proposes to establish a user fee to fund the costs of establishing, providing, and administering the system.

Table 19–4. USER CHARGE PROPOSALS[1]
(Estimated collections in millions of dollars)

	2025	2026	2027	2028	2029	2030	2031	2032	2033	2034	2025-2029	2025-2034
OFFSETTING COLLECTIONS AND OFFSETTING RECEIPTS												
DISCRETIONARY:												
Offsetting collections												
Department of Health and Human Services												
Food and Drug Administration:												
Increase export certification user fee cap	5	5	5	6	6	6	6	7	7	7	27	60
Increase tobacco product user fee	114	117	119	122	125	128	131	134	137	140	597	1,267
Department of the Interior												
Bureau of Land Management: Establish onshore oil and gas inspection fees	51	51	51	51	51	51	51	51	51	51	255	510
Department of State												
Establish the National Museum of American Diplomacy rental fee	*	*	*	*	*	*	*	*	*	*	*	*
Commodity Futures Trading Commission (CFTC)												
Establish CFTC user fee	25	116	118	121	123	126	128	131	133	136	503	1,157
Offsetting receipts												
Department of State												
Extend Western Hemisphere Travel Initiative surcharge	---	---	530	542	554	567	580	593	607	621	1,626	4,594
Increase Border Crossing Card fee	3	3	3	3	3	3	3	3	3	3	15	30
Increase Machine-Readable Visa fee	---	---	143	285	285	285	285	285	285	285	713	2,138
Subtotal, discretionary user charge proposals	198	292	969	1,130	1,147	1,166	1,184	1,204	1,223	1,243	3,736	9,756
MANDATORY:												
Offsetting receipts												
Department of Health and Human Services												
Provide authority for the Secretary to collect and expend re-survey fees	---	14	14	15	15	15	16	16	17	---	58	122
Department of Homeland Security												
Extend expiring Customs and Border Protection (CBP) fees	---	---	---	---	---	---	---	5,628	5,115	5,276	---	16,019
Expand CBP user fee facilities costs	7	7	7	7	8	8	8	8	8	9	36	77
Subtotal, mandatory user charge proposals	7	21	21	22	23	23	24	5,652	5,140	5,285	94	16,218
Subtotal, user charge proposals that are offsetting collections and offsetting receipts	205	313	990	1,152	1,170	1,189	1,208	6,856	6,363	6,528	3,830	25,974
GOVERNMENTAL RECEIPTS												
Department of Homeland Security												
Establish Electronic Visa Update System user fee	7	7	8	8	8	8	8	8	8	8	38	78
Total, user charge proposals	212	320	998	1,160	1,178	1,197	1,216	6,864	6,371	6,536	3,868	26,052

* $500,000 or less

[1] A positive sign indicates an increase in collections.

20. TAX EXPENDITURES

The Congressional Budget Act of 1974 (Public Law 93-344) requires that a list of "tax expenditures" be included in the Budget. Tax expenditures are defined in the law as "revenue losses attributable to provisions of the Federal tax laws which allow a special exclusion, exemption, or deduction from gross income or which provide a special credit, a preferential rate of tax, or a deferral of tax liability." These exceptions may be viewed as alternatives to other policy instruments, such as spending or regulatory programs.

Identification and measurement of tax expenditures depends crucially on the baseline tax system against which the actual tax system is compared. The tax expenditure estimates presented in this document are patterned on a comprehensive income tax, which defines income as the sum of consumption and the change in net wealth in a given period of time.

An important assumption underlying each tax expenditure estimate reported below is that other parts of the Tax Code remain unchanged. The estimates would be different if tax expenditures were changed simultaneously because of potential interactions among provisions. For that reason, this document does not present a grand total for the estimated tax expenditures.

Tax expenditures relating to the individual and corporate income taxes are estimated for 2023–2033 using two methods of accounting: current tax receipt effects and present value effects. The present value approach provides estimates of the receipt effects for tax expenditures that generally involve deferrals of tax payments into the future.

TAX EXPENDITURES IN THE INCOME TAX

Tax Expenditure Estimates

All tax expenditure estimates and descriptions presented here are based upon current tax law enacted as of July 31, 2023, and reflect the economic assumptions from the Midsession Review of the 2024 Budget. In some cases, expired or repealed provisions are listed if their tax receipt effects occur in 2023 or later.

The total receipt effects for tax expenditures for 2023–2033 are displayed according to the Budget's functional categories in Table 20-1. Descriptions of the specific tax expenditure provisions follow the discussion of general features of the tax expenditure concept.

Two baseline concepts—the normal tax baseline and the reference tax law baseline—are used to identify and estimate tax expenditures.[1] For the most part, the two concepts coincide. However, items treated as tax expenditures under the normal tax baseline, but not the reference tax law baseline, are indicated by the designation "normal tax method" in the tables. The receipt effects for these items are zero using the reference tax law. The alternative baseline concepts are discussed in detail below.

Table 20-2 ranks the major tax expenditures by the size of their 2024–2033 receipt effect. The first column provides the number of the provision in order to cross reference this table to Tables 20-1, as well as to the descriptions below. Some tax expenditure provisions increase governmental outlays in addition to leading to revenue losses. These outlay estimates are reported in Table 20-4. The tax expenditure tables discussed herein can be obtained for current and previous years from the Department of the Treasury (Treasury) website.[2]

Interpreting Tax Expenditure Estimates

The estimates shown for individual tax expenditures in Tables 20-1 and 20-2 do not necessarily equal the increase in Federal receipts (or the change in the budget balance) that would result from repealing these special provisions, for the following reasons.

First, eliminating a tax expenditure may have incentive effects that alter economic behavior. These incentives can affect the resulting magnitudes of the activity, or the consequences of other tax provisions or Government programs. For example, if capital gains were taxed at higher ordinary income tax rates, capital gain realizations would be expected to decline, which could result in lower tax receipts depending on the elasticity of the capital gains tax rates. Such behavioral effects are not reflected in the estimates.

Second, tax expenditures are interdependent even without incentive effects. Repeal of a tax expenditure provision can increase or decrease the tax receipts associated with other provisions. For example, even if behavior does not change, repeal of an itemized deduction could increase the receipt costs from other deductions because some taxpayers would be moved into higher tax brackets. Alternatively, repeal of an itemized deduction could lower the receipt cost from other deductions if taxpayers are led to claim the standard deduction instead of itemizing. Similarly, if two provisions were repealed simultaneously,

[1] These baseline concepts are thoroughly discussed in Special Analysis G of the 1985 Budget, where the former is referred to as the pre-1983 method and the latter the post-1982 method.

[2] *https://home.treasury.gov/policy-issues/tax-policy/tax-expenditures*. Table numbering within this chapter may not match the Treasury website.

the increase in tax liability could be greater or less than the sum of the two separate tax expenditures, because each is estimated assuming that the other remains in force. In addition, the estimates reported in Table 20-1 are the totals of corporate and individual income tax receipt effects and do not reflect any possible interactions between corporate and individual income tax receipts. Total income tax receipts are broken down into corporate and individual income tax expenditures, which are presented as separate tables on the Treasury website.[3] For this reason, the estimates in Table 20-1 should be regarded as approximations.

Finally, some of the reported estimates reflect the cumulative effects of several pieces of legislation enacted over time to expand and modify provisions targeting a particular economic activity or groups of taxpayers. Each successive enacted piece of legislation may have increased or decreased tax expenditures depending on how an existing provision was modified. As an example, Public Law 117-169, commonly referred to as the the Inflation Reduction Act of 2022 (IRA), modified and extended several energy provisions. The tax expenditure estimates associated with these energy provisions capture the receipt effects of prior law and the adjustments introduced in the IRA.

Present-Value Estimates

The annual value of tax expenditures for tax deferrals is reported on a cash basis in all tables except Table 20-3. Cash-based estimates reflect the difference between taxes deferred in the current year and incoming receipts received due to deferrals of taxes from prior years. Although such estimates are useful as a measure of cash flows into the Government, they do not accurately reflect the true economic cost of these provisions. For example, for a provision where activity levels have changed over time, so that incoming tax receipts from past deferrals are greater than deferred receipts from new activity, the cash-basis tax expenditure estimate can be negative, despite the fact that in present-value terms, current deferrals have a real cost to the Government (i.e., taxpayers). Alternatively, in the case of a newly enacted deferral provision, a cash-based estimate can overstate the real effect on receipts to the Government because the newly deferred taxes will ultimately be received.

Discounted present-value estimates of receipt effects are presented in Table 20-3 for certain provisions that involve tax deferrals or other long-term receipt effects. These estimates complement the cash-based tax expenditure estimates presented in the other tables.

The present-value estimates represent the receipt effects, net of future tax payments that follow from activities undertaken during calendar year 2023 which, cause the deferrals or other long-term receipt effects. For instance, a pension contribution in 2023 would cause a deferral of tax payments on wages in 2023 and on pension fund earnings on this contribution (e.g., interest) in later years. In some future year, however, the 2023 pension contribution and accrued earnings will be paid out and taxes will be due; these receipts are included in the present-value estimate. In general, this conceptual approach is similar to the one used for reporting the budgetary effects of credit programs, where direct loans and guarantees in a given year affect future cash flows.

Tax Expenditure Baselines

A tax expenditure is an exception to baseline provisions of the tax structure that usually results in a reduction in the amount of tax owed. The Congressional Budget Act of 1974, which mandated the tax expenditure budget, did not specify the baseline provisions of the tax law. As noted previously, deciding whether provisions are exceptions, therefore, is a matter of judgment. As in prior years, most of this year's tax expenditure estimates are presented using two baselines: the normal tax baseline and the reference tax law baseline. Tax expenditures may take the form of credits, deductions, special exceptions and allowances.

The normal tax baseline is patterned on a practical variant of a comprehensive income tax, which defines income as the sum of consumption and the change in net wealth in a given period of time. The normal tax baseline allows personal exemptions, a standard deduction, and deduction of expenses incurred in earning income. It is not limited to a particular structure of tax rates, or by a specific definition of the taxpaying unit.

The reference tax law baseline is also patterned on a comprehensive income tax, but it is closer to existing law. Reference tax law tax expenditures are limited to special exceptions from a generally provided tax rule that serves programmatic functions in a way that is analogous to spending programs. Provisions under the reference tax law baseline are generally tax expenditures under the normal tax baseline, but the reverse is not always true.

Both the normal tax and reference tax law baselines allow several major departures from a pure comprehensive income tax. For example, under the normal tax and reference tax law baselines:

- Income is taxable only when it is realized in exchange. Thus, the deferral of tax on unrealized capital gains is not regarded as a tax expenditure. Accrued income would be taxed under a comprehensive income tax.
- There is a separate corporate income tax.
- Tax rates on noncorporate business income vary by level of income.
- Individual tax rates, including brackets, standard deduction, and personal exemptions, are allowed to vary with marital status.
- Values of assets and debt are not generally adjusted for inflation. A comprehensive income tax would adjust the cost basis of capital assets and debt for changes in the general price level. Thus, under a comprehensive income tax baseline, the failure to take account of inflation in measuring depreciation,

[3] Estimates of total corporate and individual income tax expenditures for 2023–2033 are presented as Tables 2A and 2B on the Treasury website: *https://home.treasury.gov/policy-issues/tax-policy/tax-expenditures.*

capital gains, and interest income would be regarded as a negative tax expenditure (i.e., a tax penalty), and failure to take account of inflation in measuring interest costs would be regarded as a positive tax expenditure (i.e., a tax subsidy).

- The base erosion and anti-abuse tax (BEAT) for multinational corporations is treated as a minimum tax and considered part of the rate structure.

Although the reference tax law and normal tax baselines are generally similar, areas of difference include:

- *Tax rates*. The separate schedules applying to the various taxpaying units and the Alternative Minimum Tax are treated as part of the baseline rate structure under both the reference tax law and normal tax methods.
- *Income subject to tax*. Income subject to tax is defined as gross income less the costs of earning that income. Under the reference tax law, gross income excludes gifts defined as receipts of money or property that are not consideration in an exchange, and excludes most transfer payments from the Government.[4] The normal tax baseline additionally excludes gifts between individuals from gross income, but all cash transfer payments from the Government to individuals are counted in gross income, and exemptions of such transfers from tax are identified as tax expenditures. The costs of earning income are generally deductible in determining taxable income under both the reference tax law and normal tax baselines.[5]
- *Capital recovery*. Under the reference tax law baseline no tax expenditures arise from accelerated depreciation. Under the normal tax baseline, the depreciation allowance for property is computed using estimates of economic depreciation.

Descriptions of Income Tax Provisions

Descriptions of the individual and corporate income tax expenditures reported on in this document follow. These descriptions relate to current law as of July 31, 2023.

National Defense

1. ***Exclusion of benefits and allowances to armed forces personnel.***—Under the baseline tax system, all compensation, including dedicated payments and in-kind benefits, should be included in taxable income because they represent accretions to wealth that do not materially differ from cash wages. As an example, a rental voucher of $100 is (approximately) equal in value to $100 of cash income. In contrast to this treatment, certain housing and meals, in addition to other benefits provided military personnel, either in cash or in kind, as well as certain amounts of pay related to combat service, are excluded from income subject to tax.

International Affairs

2. ***Exclusion of income earned abroad by U.S. citizens.***—Under the baseline tax system, all compensation received by U.S. citizens and residents is properly included in their taxable income. It makes no difference whether the compensation is a result of working abroad or whether it is labeled as a housing allowance. In contrast to this treatment, U.S. tax law allows U.S. citizens and residents who live abroad, work in the private sector, and satisfy a foreign residency requirement to exclude up to $80,000, plus adjustments for inflation since 2004, in foreign earned income from U.S. taxes. In addition, if these taxpayers are provided housing by their employers, then they may also exclude the cost of such housing from their income to the extent that it exceeds 16 percent of the earned income exclusion limit. This housing exclusion is capped at 30 percent of the earned income exclusion limit, with geographical adjustments. If taxpayers do not receive a specific allowance for housing expenses, they may deduct housing expenses up to the amount by which foreign earned income exceeds their foreign earned income exclusion.

3. ***Exclusion of certain allowances for Federal employees abroad.***—In general, all compensation received by U.S. citizens and residents is properly included in their taxable income. It makes no difference whether the compensation is a result of working abroad or whether it is labeled as an allowance for the high cost of living abroad. In contrast to this treatment, U.S. Federal civilian employees and Peace Corps members who work outside the continental United States are allowed to exclude from U.S. taxable income certain special allowances they receive to compensate them for the relatively high costs associated with living overseas. The allowances supplement wage income and cover expenses such as rent, education, and the cost of travel to and from the United States.

4. ***Reduced tax rate on active income of controlled foreign corporations (normal tax method).***—Under the baseline tax system, worldwide income forms the tax base of U.S. corporations. In contrast, U.S. tax law exempts or preferentially taxes certain portions of this income. Prior to the passage of the Tax Cuts and Jobs Act (TCJA; Public Law 115-97) (effective January 1, 2018), active foreign income was generally taxed only upon repatriation. TCJA changed these rules, so that certain active income (called "global intangible low tax income" or "GILTI") is taxed currently, even if it is not distributed. However, U.S. corporations generally receive a 50 percent deduction from U.S. tax on their GILTI (the deduction decreases to 37.5 percent in 2026), resulting in a substantially reduced rate of tax. In addition, some ac-

[4] Gross income does, however, include transfer payments associated with past employment, such as Social Security benefits.

[5] In the case of individuals who hold "passive" equity interests in businesses, the pro-rata shares of sales and expense deductions reportable in a year are limited. A passive business activity is defined generally to be one in which the holder of the interest, usually a partnership interest, does not actively perform managerial or other participatory functions. The taxpayer may generally report no larger deductions for a year than will reduce taxable income from such activities to zero. Deductions in excess of the limitation may be taken in subsequent years, or when the interest is liquidated. In addition, costs of earning income may be limited under the Alternative Minimum Tax.

tive income is excluded from tax, and distributions out of active income are no longer taxed upon repatriation. These reductions and exemptions from U.S. taxation are considered tax expenditures.

5. ***Deduction for foreign-derived intangible income derived from trade or business within the United States.***—Under the baseline tax system, the United States taxes income earned by U.S. corporations from serving foreign markets (e.g., exports and royalties) at the full U.S. rate. After the passage of TCJA, domestic corporations are allowed a deduction equal to 37.5 percent of "foreign-derived intangible income," which is essentially income from serving foreign markets (defined on a formulaic basis). The deduction falls to 21.875 percent in 2026.

6. ***Interest Charge Domestic International Sales Corporations (IC-DISCs).***—Under the baseline tax system, taxpayer earnings are subject to tax using the regular tax rates applied to all taxpayers. In contrast, IC-DISCs allow a portion of income from exports to be taxed at the qualified dividend rate which is no higher than 20 percent (plus a 3.8 percent surtax for high-income taxpayers).

General Science, Space, and Technology

7. ***Expensing of research and experimentation expenditures (normal tax method).***—The baseline tax system allows a deduction for the cost of producing income. It requires taxpayers to capitalize the costs associated with investments over time to better match the streams of income and associated costs. Research and experimentation (R&E) projects can be viewed as investments because, if successful, their benefits accrue for several years. It is often difficult, however, to identify whether a specific R&E project is successful and, if successful, what its expected life will be. Because of this ambiguity, the reference tax law baseline system would allow expensing of R&E expenditures. In contrast, under the normal tax method, the expensing of R&E expenditures is viewed as a tax expenditure. The baseline assumed for the normal tax method is that all R&E expenditures are successful and have an expected life of five years. Current law requires R&E expenditures paid or incurred in taxable years beginning after December 31, 2021, to be capitalized and amortized over 5 years, while allowing R&E expenditures paid or incurred in prior taxable years to be expensed.

8. ***Credit for increasing research activities.***—The baseline tax system would uniformly tax all returns to investments and not allow credits for particular activities, investments, or industries. In contrast, the Tax Code allows an R&E credit of up to 20 percent of qualified research expenditures in excess of a base amount. The base amount of the credit is generally determined by multiplying a "fixed-base percentage" by the average amount of the company's gross receipts for the prior four years. The taxpayer's fixed base percentage generally is the ratio of its research expenses to gross receipts for 1984 through 1988. Taxpayers can elect the alternative simplified credit regime, which equals 14 percent of qualified research expenses that exceed 50 percent of the average qualified research expenses for the three preceding taxable years.

Energy

9. ***Expensing of exploration and development costs, oil and gas.***—Under the baseline tax system, the costs of exploring and developing oil and gas wells would be capitalized and then amortized (or depreciated) over an estimate of the economic life of the property. This ensures that the net income from the well or mine is measured appropriately each year. In contrast to this treatment, current law allows immediate deduction, i.e., expensing, of intangible drilling costs for successful investments in domestic oil and gas wells (such as wages, the cost of using machinery for grading and drilling, and the cost of unsalvageable materials used in constructing wells). Because expensing allows recovery of costs sooner, it is more advantageous to the taxpayer than amortization. Expensing provisions for exploration expenditures apply only to properties for which a deduction for percentage depletion is allowable. For oil and gas wells, integrated oil companies may expense only 70 percent of intangible drilling costs and must amortize the remaining 30 percent over five years. Non-integrated oil companies may expense all such costs.

10. ***Expensing of exploration and development costs, coal.***—This is similar to the above provision but limited to coal. Current law allows immediate deduction of eligible exploration and development costs for domestic coal mines and other natural fuel deposits.

11. ***Excess of percentage over cost depletion, oil and gas.***—The baseline tax system would allow recovery of the costs of developing certain oil and gas properties using cost depletion. Cost depletion is similar in concept to depreciation, in that the costs of developing or acquiring the asset are capitalized and then gradually reduced over an estimate of the asset's economic life, as is appropriate for measuring net income. In contrast, the Tax Code generally allows independent oil and gas producers and royalty owners to take percentage depletion deductions rather than cost depletion on limited quantities of output. Under percentage depletion, taxpayers deduct a percentage of gross income from oil and gas production. In certain cases the deduction is limited to a fraction of the asset's net income. Over the life of an investment, percentage depletion deductions can exceed the cost of the investment. Consequently, percentage depletion may provide more advantageous tax treatment than would cost depletion, which limits deductions to an investment's cost.

12. ***Excess of percentage over cost depletion, coal.***—This is similar to the above provision but limited to coal.

13. ***Exception from passive loss limitation for working interests in oil and gas properties.***—The baseline tax system accepts current law's general rule limiting taxpayers' ability to deduct losses from passive activities against nonpassive income (e.g., wages, interest, and dividends). Passive activities generally are defined as those in which the taxpayer does not materially participate, though there are numerous additional considerations brought to bear on the determination of which activities are passive for a given taxpayer. Losses

are limited in an attempt to limit tax sheltering activities. Passive losses that are unused may be carried forward and applied against future passive income. An exception from the passive loss limitation is provided for a working interest in an oil or gas property that the taxpayer holds directly or through an entity that does not limit the liability of the taxpayer with respect to the interest. Thus, taxpayers can deduct losses from such working interests against nonpassive income without regard to whether they materially participate in the activity.

14. ***Enhanced oil recovery credit.***—A credit is provided equal to 15 percent of the taxpayer's costs for enhanced oil recovery on U.S. projects. The credit is reduced in proportion to the ratio of the reference price of oil for the previous calendar year minus $28 (adjusted for inflation from 1990) to $6.

15. ***Marginal wells credit.***—A credit is provided for crude oil and natural gas produced from a qualified marginal well. A marginal well is one that does not produce more than 1,095 barrel-of-oil equivalents per year, with this limit adjusted proportionately for the number of days the well is in production in a given year. The credit is no more than $3.00 per barrel of qualified crude oil production and $0.50 per thousand cubic feet of qualified natural gas production. The credit for natural gas is reduced in proportion to the amount by which the reference price of natural gas per thousand cubic feet at the wellhead for the previous calendar year exceeds $1.67and is zero for a reference price that exceeds $2.00. The credit for crude oil is reduced in proportion to the amount by which the reference price of oil per barrel for the previous calendar year exceeds $15.00 and is zero for a reference price that exceeds $18.00. All dollar amounts are adjusted for inflation from 2004.

16. ***Amortize all geological and geophysical expenditures over two years.***—The baseline tax system allows taxpayers to deduct the decline in the economic value of an investment over its economic life. However, the Tax Code allows geological and geophysical expenditures incurred in connection with oil and gas exploration in the United States to be amortized over two years for non-integrated oil companies, a span of time that is generally shorter than the economic life of the assets.

17. ***Capital gains treatment of royalties on coal.***—The baseline tax system generally would tax all income under the regular tax rate schedule. It would not allow preferentially low tax rates to apply to certain types or sources of income. Current law allows capital gains realized by individuals to be taxed at a preferentially low rate that is no higher than 20 percent (plus the 3.8 percent surtax). Certain sales of coal under royalty contracts qualify for taxation as capital gains rather than ordinary income.

18. ***Exclusion of interest on energy facility bonds.***—The baseline tax system generally would tax all income under the regular tax rate schedule. It would not allow preferentially low (or zero) tax rates to apply to certain types or sources of income. In contrast, the Tax Code allows interest earned on State and local bonds used to finance construction of certain energy facilities to be exempt from tax. These bonds are generally subject to the State private-activity-bond annual volume cap.

19. ***Qualified energy conservation bonds.***—The baseline tax system would uniformly tax all returns to investments and not allow credits for particular activities, investments, or industries. However, the Tax Code provides for the issuance of energy conservation bonds which entitle the bond holder to a Federal income tax credit in lieu of interest. As of March 2010, issuers of the unused authorization of such bonds could opt to receive direct payment with the yield becoming fully taxable.

20. ***Exclusion of utility conservation subsidies.***—The baseline tax system generally takes a comprehensive view of taxable income that includes a wide variety of (measurable) accretions to wealth. In certain circumstances, public utilities offer rate subsidies to non-business customers who invest in energy conservation measures. These rate subsidies are equivalent to payments from the utility to its customer, and so represent accretions to wealth, income that would be taxable to the customer under the baseline tax system. In contrast, the Tax Code exempts these subsidies from the non-business customer's gross income.

21. ***Credit for holding clean renewable energy bonds.***—The baseline tax system would uniformly tax all returns to investments and not allow credits for particular activities, investments, or industries. In contrast, the Tax Code provides for the issuance of Clean Renewable Energy Bonds that entitle the bond holder to a Federal income tax credit in lieu of interest. As of March 2010, issuers of the unused authorization of such bonds could opt to receive direct payment with the yield becoming fully taxable.

22. ***Energy production credit.***—The baseline tax system would not allow credits for particular activities, investments, or industries. Instead, it generally would seek to tax uniformly all returns from investment-like activities. In contrast, the Tax Code provides a credit for certain electricity produced from wind energy, biomass, geothermal energy, solar energy, small irrigation power, municipal solid waste, or qualified hydropower and sold to an unrelated party. Facilities that began construction in 2017 receive 80 percent of the credit, facilities that began construction in 2018 receive 60 percent of the credit, facilities that began construction in 2019 receive 40 percent of the credit, and facilities that began construction in 2020 or 2021 receive 60 percent of the credit. The full credit amount is available for projects that began construction after 2021, but the full rate is dependent on prevailing wage and apprenticeship requirements. Two additional bonus credits worth 10 percent each are available for projects that meet domestic content requirements and projects located in energy communities, as defined by the Tax Code. Starting in 2025, the credit becomes a technology neutral credit, and it begins to phase out as early as 2034.

23. ***Energy investment credit.***—The baseline tax system would not allow credits for particular activities, investments, or industries. Instead, it generally would seek to tax uniformly all returns from investment-like

activities. However, the Tax Code provides credits for investments in solar and geothermal energy property, qualified fuel cell property, stationary microturbine property, geothermal heat pumps, waste energy recovery property, small wind property, offshore wind, energy storage technology, qualified biogas property, microgrid controllers, and combined heat and power property. The credit is 30 percent for projects that began construction before 2020 and 26 percent for projects that begin construction in 2020–2022. The credit returns to 30 percent for projects that begin construction after 2022 but the full credit rate is dependent on meeting prevailing wage and apprenticeship requirements. Additional bonus credits of up to 10 percent of the investment basis are available for projects that meet domestic content requirements and projects located in energy communities , as defined by the Tax Code. The credit could begin to phase out as early as 2034 depending on annual greenhouse gas emissions from the production of electricity in the United States. Owners of renewable power facilities that qualify for the energy production credit may instead elect to take an energy investment credit at a rate specified by law.

24. ***Advanced nuclear power facilities production credit.***—The baseline tax system would not allow credits or deductions for particular activities, investments, or industries. Instead, it generally would seek to tax uniformly all returns from investment-like activities. In contrast, the Tax Code allows a tax credit equal to 1.8 cents times the number of kilowatt hours of electricity produced at a qualifying advanced nuclear power facility. A taxpayer may claim no more than $125 million per 1,000 megawatts of capacity. The Treasury may allocate up to 6,000 megawatts of credit-eligible capacity. Any unutilized national capacity limitation shall be allocated after December 31, 2020, according to prioritization rules set forth by statute.

25. ***Zero-emission nuclear power production credit.***—The baseline tax system would not allow credits or deductions for particular activities, investments, or industries. Instead, it generally would seek to tax uniformly all returns from investment-like activities. In contrast, the Tax Code allows a tax credit per unit of electricity produced at a nuclear facility placed in service before enactment of the IRA. The credit is based on the gross receipts of the facility, the electricity produced, any other Federal/State/local zero-emissions credits or grants received, and whether the facility adopts certain labor standards.

26. ***Reduced tax rate for nuclear decommissioning funds.***—The baseline tax system would uniformly tax all returns to investments and not allow special rates for particular activities, investments, or industries. In contrast, the Tax Code provides a special 20-percent tax rate for investments made by Nuclear Decommissioning Reserve Funds.

27. ***Alcohol fuel credits.***—The baseline tax system would not allow credits for particular activities, investments, or industries. Instead, it generally would seek to tax uniformly all returns from investment-like activities. In contrast, the Tax Code provides an income tax credit for qualified cellulosic biofuel production which was renamed the Second generation biofuel producer credit. This provision expires on December 31, 2024.

28. ***Biodiesel and small agri-biodiesel producer tax credits.***—The baseline tax system would not allow credits for particular activities, investments, or industries. Instead, it generally would seek to tax uniformly all returns from investment-like activities. However, the Tax Code allows an income tax credit for bi-odiesel and for biodiesel derived from virgin sources. In lieu of the biodiesel credit, the taxpayer can claim a refundable excise tax credit. In addition, small agri-biodiesel producers are eligible for a separate income tax credit for biodiesel production, and a separate credit is available for qualified renewable diesel fuel mixtures. This provision expires on December 31, 2024.

29. ***Clean fuel production credit.***—The baseline tax system would not allow credits for particular activities, investments or industries. Instead, it would generally seek to tax uniformly all returns from investment-like activities. In contrast, the Tax Code allows an income tax credit for the production of qualifying transportation fuel with zero or low greenhouse gas emissions. The amount of the credit is calculated from the base amount, or alternate amount, of the credit and the emissions factor of a transportation fuel, with a special rate for sustainable aviation fuel. Producers are eligible for larger credits as the emission of the fuels they produce approach zero. The credit applies to fuel produced after December 31, 2024 and sold on or before December 31, 2027.

30. ***Clean hydrogen production credit.***—The baseline tax system would not allow credits for particular activities, investments, or industries. Instead, it generally would seek to tax uniformly all returns from investment-like activities. In contrast, the Tax Code allows credits for the production of clean hydrogen. Clean hydrogen is defined in relation to its lifecycle greenhouse gas emissions rate; no credit is allowed for hydrogen with a lifecycle greenhouse gas emissions rate greater than 4 kilograms of carbon dioxide equivalent per kilogram of hydrogen. The credit applies to qualified clean hydrogen produced at a qualified clean hydrogen production facility during the 10-year period beginning on the date such facility was originally placed in service. Qualifying facilities must be placed in service before December 31, 2033.

31. ***Tax credits for clean vehicles.***—The baseline tax system would not allow credits for particular activities, investments, or industries. Instead, it generally would seek to tax uniformly all returns from investment-like activities. In contrast, the Tax Code allows a credit of up to $7,500 for qualifying new plug-in electric vehicles or fuel cell vehicles purchased in 2023.

32. ***Tax credits for refueling property.***—The baseline tax system would not allow credits for particular activities, investments, or industries. Instead, it generally would seek to tax uniformly all returns from investment-like activities. In contrast, the Tax Code allows credits for alternative fuel vehicle refueling property.

33. ***Allowance of deduction for certain energy efficient commercial building property.***—The baseline

tax system would not allow deductions in lieu of normal depreciation allowances for particular investments in particular industries. Instead, it generally would seek to tax uniformly all returns from investment-like activities. In contrast, the Tax Code allows a deduction for certain energy efficient commercial building property. The basis of such property is reduced by the amount of the deduction. Starting in 2021, the maximum deduction amount per square foot will be increased by a cost-of -living adjustment.

34. ***Credit for construction of new energy efficient homes.***—The baseline tax system would not allow credits for particular activities, investments, or industries. Instead, it generally would seek to tax uniformly all returns from investment-like activities. However, the Tax Code allowed contractors a tax credit of $2,000 for the construction of a qualified new energy-efficient home that had an annual level of heating and cooling energy consumption at least 50 percent below the annual consumption under the 2006 International Energy Conservation Code. The credit equaled $1,000 in the case of a new manufactured home that met a 30 percent standard or requirements for EPA's Energy Star homes. This provision expired on December 31, 2017.

35. Credit for energy efficiency improvements to existing homes.—The baseline tax system would not allow credits for particular activities, investments, or industries. However, the Tax Code provided an investment tax credit for expenditures made on insulation, exterior windows, and doors that improved the energy efficiency of homes and met certain standards. The Tax Code also provided a credit for purchases of advanced main air circulating fans, natural gas, propane, or oil furnaces or hot water boilers, and other qualified energy efficient property. This provision expired on December 31, 2017, but legislation enacted in 2020 allowed taxpayers to claim tax credits retroactively for three years.

36. ***Credit for residential energy efficient property.***—The baseline tax system would uniformly tax all returns to investments and not allow credits for particular activities, investments, or industries. However, the Tax Code provides a credit for the purchase of qualified photovoltaic property and solar water heating property, as well as for fuel cell power plants, geothermal heat pumps, small wind property, and qualified battery storage technology used in or placed on a residence. The credit is 30 percent for property placed in service before January 1, 2020, 26 percent for property placed in service in 2020-2021, 30 percent for property placed in service in 2022–2032, 26 percent for property placed in service in 2033, and 22 percent for property placed in service in 2034. The credit expires after December 31, 2034.

37. ***Advanced energy property credit.***—The baseline tax system would not allow credits for particular activities, investments, or industries. However, the Tax Code provides a 30-percent investment credit for property used in a qualified advanced energy manufacturing project. The Treasury may award up to $12.3 billion in tax credits for qualified investments. Of the total $12.3 billion, $4 billion is reserved for projects located in energy communities.

38. ***Advanced manufacturing production credit.***—The baseline tax system would not allow credits for particular activities, investments, or industries. However, the Tax Code provides credits of varying amounts for the production within the United States and sale of specified eligible components, including specified solar energy components, wind energy components, inverters, qualifying battery components, and applicable critical minerals. The production of an eligible component is only eligible for a credit if sold after 2022. For all eligible components other than applicable critical minerals, the credit is phased out from 2030 to 2032, with components other than critical minerals no longer receiving any credit if sold after 2032.

Natural Resources and Environment

39. ***Expensing of exploration and development costs, nonfuel minerals.***—The baseline tax system allows the taxpayer to deduct the depreciation of an asset according to the decline in its economic value over time. However, certain capital outlays associated with exploration and development of nonfuel minerals may be expensed rather than depreciated over the life of the asset.

40. ***Excess of percentage over cost depletion, nonfuel minerals.***—The baseline tax system allows the taxpayer to deduct the decline in the economic value of an investment over time. Under current law, however, most nonfuel mineral extractors may use percentage depletion (whereby the deduction is fixed as a percentage of receipts) rather than cost depletion, with percentage depletion rates ranging from 22 percent for sulfur to 5 percent for sand and gravel. Over the life of an investment, percentage depletion deductions can exceed the cost of the investment. Consequently, percentage depletion may provide more advantageous tax treatment than would cost depletion, which limits deductions to an investment's cost.

41. ***Exclusion of interest on bonds for water, sewage, and hazardous waste facilities.***—The baseline tax system generally would tax all income under the regular tax rate schedule. It would not allow preferentially low (or zero) tax rates to apply to certain types or sources of income. In contrast, the Tax Code allows interest earned on State and local bonds used to finance construction of sewage, water, or hazardous waste facilities to be exempt from tax. These bonds are generally subject to the State private-activity bond annual volume cap.

42. ***Capital gains treatment of certain timber income.***—The baseline tax system generally would tax all income under the regular tax rate schedule. It would not allow preferentially low tax rates to apply to certain types or sources of income. However, under current law certain timber sales can be treated as a capital gain rather than ordinary income and therefore subject to the lower capital-gains tax rate. Current law allows capital gains to be taxed at a preferentially low rate that is no higher than 20 percent (plus the 3.8 percent surtax).

43. ***Expensing of multiperiod timber growing costs.***—The baseline tax system requires the taxpayer to capitalize costs associated with investment property. However, most of the production costs of growing timber may be expensed under current law rather than capitalized and deducted when the timber is sold, thereby accelerating cost recovery.

44. ***Tax incentives for preservation of historic structures.***—The baseline tax system would not allow credits for particular activities, investments, or industries. However, expenditures to preserve and restore certified historic structures qualify for an investment tax credit of 20 percent for certified rehabilitation activities. The taxpayer's recoverable basis must be reduced by the amount of the credit. The credit must be claimed ratably over the five years after the property is placed in service, for property placed in service after December 31, 2017.

45. ***Carbon oxide sequestration credit.***—The baseline tax system would uniformly tax all returns to investments and not allow credits for particular activities, investments, or industries. In contrast, the Tax Code allows a credit for qualified carbon oxide captured at a qualified facility and disposed of in secure geological storage. In addition, the provision allows a credit for qualified carbon oxide that is captured at a qualified facility and used as a tertiary injectant in a qualified enhanced oil or natural gas recovery project. The credit differs according to whether the carbon was captured using equipment which was originally placed in service before February 9, 2018, or thereafter.

46. ***Deduction for endangered species recovery expenditures.***—The baseline tax system would not allow deductions in addition to normal depreciation allowances for particular investments in particular industries. Instead, it generally would seek to tax uniformly all returns from investment-like activities. In contrast, under current law farmers can deduct up to 25 percent of their gross income for expenses incurred as a result of site and habitat improvement activities that will benefit endangered species on their farm land, in accordance with site specific management actions included in species recovery plans approved pursuant to the Endangered Species Act of 1973.

Agriculture

47. ***Expensing of certain capital outlays.***—The baseline tax system requires the taxpayer to capitalize costs associated with investment property. However, farmers may expense certain expenditures for feed and fertilizer, for soil and water conservation measures, and certain other capital improvements under current law.

48. ***Expensing of certain multiperiod production costs.***—The baseline tax system requires the taxpayer to capitalize costs associated with an investment over time. However, the production of livestock and crops with a production period greater than two years is exempt from the uniform cost capitalization rules (e.g., for costs for establishing orchards or structure improvements), thereby accelerating cost recovery.

49. ***Treatment of loans forgiven for solvent farmers.***—Because loan forgiveness increases a debtors net worth the baseline tax system requires debtors to include the amount of loan forgiveness as income or else reduce their recoverable basis in the property related to the loan. If the amount of forgiveness exceeds the basis, the excess forgiveness is taxable if the taxpayer is not insolvent. For bankrupt debtors, the amount of loan forgiveness reduces carryover losses, unused credits, and then basis, with the remainder of the forgiven debt excluded from taxation. Qualified farm debt that is forgiven, however, is excluded from income even when the taxpayer is solvent.

50. ***Capital gains treatment of certain agriculture income.***—The baseline tax system generally would tax all income under the regular tax rate schedule. It would not allow preferentially low tax rates to apply to certain types or sources of income. In contrast, current law allows capital gains to be taxed at a preferentially low rate that is no higher than 20 percent (plus the 3.8 percent surtax). Certain agricultural income, such as unharvested crops, qualify for taxation as capital gains rather than ordinary income, and so benefit from the preferentially low 20 percent maximum tax rate on capital gains (plus the 3.8 percent surtax).

51. ***Income averaging for farmers.***—The baseline tax system generally taxes all earned income each year at the rate determined by the income tax. However, taxpayers may average their taxable income from farming and fishing over the previous three years.

52. ***Deferral of gain on sale of farm refiners.***—The baseline tax system generally subjects capital gains to taxes the year that they are realized. However, the Tax Code allows a taxpayer who sells stock in a farm refiner to a farmers' cooperative to defer recognition of the gain if the proceeds are re-invested in a qualified replacement property.

53. ***Expensing of reforestation expenditures.***—The baseline tax system requires the taxpayer to capitalize costs associated with an investment over time. In contrast, the Tax Code provides for the expensing of the first $10,000 in reforestation expenditures with 7-year amortization of the remaining expenses.

Commerce and Housing

This category includes a number of tax expenditure provisions that also affect economic activity in other functional categories. For example, provisions related to investment, such as accelerated depreciation, could be classified under the energy, natural resources and environment, agriculture, or transportation categories.

54. ***Exemption of credit union income.***—Under the baseline tax system, corporations pay taxes on their profits under the regular tax rate schedule. However, in the Tax Code the earnings of credit unions not distributed to members as interest or dividends are exempt from the income tax.

55. ***Exclusion of life insurance death benefits.***—Under the baseline tax system, individuals and corporations would pay taxes on their income when it is (actually or constructively) received or accrued.

Nevertheless, current law generally excludes from tax amounts received under life insurance contracts if such amounts are paid by reason of the death of the insured.

56. ***Exemption or special alternative tax for small property and casualty insurance companies.***—The baseline tax system would require corporations to pay taxes on their profits under the regular tax rate schedule. It would not allow preferentially low (or zero) tax rates to apply to certain types or sources of income. Under current law, however, stock non-life insurance companies are generally exempt from tax if their gross receipts for the taxable year do not exceed $600,000 and more than 50 percent of such gross receipts consist of premiums. Mutual non-life insurance companies are generally tax-exempt if their annual gross receipts do not exceed $150,000 and more than 35 percent of gross receipts consist of premiums. Also, non-life insurance companies with no more than a specified level of annual net written premiums generally may elect to pay tax only on their taxable investment income provided certain ownership diversification requirements are met. The underwriting income (premiums, less insurance losses and expenses) of electing companies is excluded from tax. The specified premium limit is indexed for inflation; for 2023, the premium limit is $2.45 million.

57. ***Tax exemption of insurance income earned by tax-exempt organizations.***—Under the baseline tax system, corporations pay taxes on their profits under the regular tax rate schedule. The baseline tax system would not allow preferentially low (or zero) tax rates to apply to certain types or sources of income. Generally the income generated by life and property and casualty insurance companies is subject to tax, albeit under special rules. However, income from insurance operations conducted by certain tax-exempt organizations, such as fraternal societies, voluntary employee benefit associations, and others are exempt from tax.

58. ***Exclusion of interest spread of financial institutions.***—The baseline tax system generally would tax all income under the regular tax rate schedule. It would not allow preferentially low (or zero) tax rates to apply to certain types or sources of income. Consumers pay for some deposit-linked services, such as check cashing, by accepting a below-market interest rate on their demand deposits. If they received a market rate of interest on those deposits and paid explicit fees for the associated services, they would pay taxes on the full market rate and (unlike businesses) could not deduct the fees. The Government thus foregoes tax on the difference between the risk-free market interest rate and below-market interest rates on demand deposits, which under competitive conditions should equal the value of deposit services.

59. ***Exclusion of interest on owner-occupied mortgage subsidy bonds.***—The baseline tax system generally would tax all income under the regular tax rate schedule. It would not allow preferentially low (or zero) tax rates to apply to certain types or sources of income. In contrast, the Tax Code allows interest earned on State and local bonds used to finance homes purchased by first-time, low-to-moderate-income buyers to be exempt from tax. These bonds are generally subject to the State private-activity-bond annual volume cap.

60. ***Exclusion of interest on rental housing bonds.***—The baseline tax system generally would tax all income under the regular tax rate schedule. It would not allow preferentially low (or zero) tax rates to apply to certain types or sources of income. In contrast, the Tax Code allows interest earned on State and local government bonds used to finance multifamily rental housing projects to be tax-exempt.

61. ***Deductibility of mortgage interest expense on owner-occupied residences.***—Under the baseline tax system, expenses incurred in earning income would be deductible. However, such expenses would not be deductible when the income or the return on an investment is not taxed. In contrast, the Tax Code allows an exclusion from a taxpayer's taxable income for the value of owner-occupied housing services and also allows the owner-occupant to deduct mortgage interest paid on his or her primary residence and one secondary residence as an itemized non-business deduction. In general, the mortgage interest deduction is limited to interest on debt no greater than the owner's basis in the residence, and is also limited to interest on debt of no more than $1 million. Interest on up to $100,000 of other debt secured by a lien on a principal or second residence is also deductible, irrespective of the purpose of borrowing, provided the total debt does not exceed the fair market value of the residence. As an alternative to the deduction, holders of qualified Mortgage Credit Certificates issued by State or local governmental units or agencies may claim a tax credit equal to a proportion of their interest expense. In the case of taxable years beginning after December 31, 2017, and before January 1, 2026: 1) the $1 million limit is reduced to $750,000 for indebtedness incurred after December 15, 2017; and 2) the deduction for interest on home equity indebtedness is disallowed.

62. ***Deductibility of State and local property tax on owner-occupied homes.***—Under the baseline tax system, expenses incurred in earning income would be deductible. However, such expenses would not be deductible when the income or the return on an investment is not taxed. In contrast, the Tax Code allows an exclusion from a taxpayer's taxable income for the value of owner-occupied housing services and also allows the owner-occupant to deduct property taxes paid on real property. In the case of taxable years beginning after December 31, 2017, and before January 1, 2026: 1) the deduction for foreign real property taxes paid is disallowed; and 2) the deduction for taxes paid in any taxable year, which includes the deduction for property taxes on real property, is limited to $10,000 ($5,000 in the case of a married individual filing a separate return).

63. ***Deferral of income from installment sales.***—The baseline tax system generally would tax all income under the regular tax rate schedule. It would not allow preferentially low (or zero) tax rates, or deferral of tax, to apply to certain types or sources of income. Dealers in real and personal property (i.e., sellers who regularly hold property for sale or resale) cannot defer taxable in-

come from installment sales until the receipt of the loan repayment. Nondealers (i.e., sellers of real property used in their business) are required to pay interest on deferred taxes attributable to their total installment obligations in excess of $5 million. Only properties with sales prices exceeding $150,000 are includable in the total. The payment of a market rate of interest eliminates the benefit of the tax deferral. The tax exemption for nondealers with total installment obligations of less than $5 million is, therefore, a tax expenditure.

64. ***Capital gains exclusion on home sales.***—The baseline tax system would not allow deductions and exemptions for certain types of income. In contrast, the Tax Code allows homeowners to exclude from gross income up to $250,000 ($500,000 in the case of a married couple filing a joint return) of the capital gains from the sale of a principal residence. To qualify, the taxpayer must have owned and used the property as the taxpayer's principal residence for a total of at least two of the five years preceding the date of sale. In addition, the exclusion may not be used more than once every two years.

65. ***Exclusion of net imputed rental income.***—Under the baseline tax system, the taxable income of a taxpayer who is an owner-occupant would include the implicit value of gross rental income on housing services earned on the investment in owner-occupied housing and would allow a deduction for expenses, such as interest, depreciation, property taxes, and other costs, associated with earning such rental income. In contrast, the Tax Code allows an exclusion from taxable income for the implicit gross rental income on housing services, while in certain circumstances allows a deduction for some costs associated with such income, such as for mortgage interest and property taxes.

66. ***Exception from passive loss rules for $25,000 of rental loss.***—The baseline tax system accepts current law's general rule limiting taxpayers' ability to deduct losses from passive activities against nonpassive income (e.g., wages, interest, and dividends). Passive activities generally are defined as those in which the taxpayer does not materially participate, and there are numerous additional considerations brought to bear on the determination of which activities are passive for a given taxpayer. Losses are limited in an attempt to limit tax sheltering activities. Passive losses that are unused may be carried forward and applied against future passive income. In contrast to the general restrictions on passive losses, the Tax Code exempts certain owners of rental real estate activities from "passive income" limitations. The exemption is limited to $25,000 in losses and phases out for taxpayers with income between $100,000 and $150,000.

67. ***Credit for low-income housing investments.***—The baseline tax system would uniformly tax all returns to investments and not allow credits for particular activities, investments, or industries. However, under current law taxpayers who invest in certain low-income housing projects are eligible for a tax credit. The credit rate is set so that the present value of the credit is equal to at least 70 percent of the building's qualified basis for new construction and 30 percent for: 1) housing receiving other Federal benefits (such as tax-exempt bond financing); or 2) substantially rehabilitated existing housing. The credit can exceed these levels in certain statutorily defined and State designated areas where project development costs are higher. The credit is allowed in equal amounts over 10 years and is generally subject to a volume cap.

68. ***Accelerated depreciation on rental housing (normal tax method).***—Under a comprehensive economic income tax, the costs of acquiring a building are capitalized and depreciated over time in accordance with the decline in the property's economic value due to wear and tear or obsolescence. This ensures that the net income from the rental property is measured appropriately each year. Current law allows depreciation that is accelerated relative to economic depreciation. However, the depreciation provisions of the Tax Code are part of the reference tax law, and thus do not give rise to tax expenditures under reference tax law. Under normal tax baseline, in contrast, depreciation allowances reflect estimates of economic depreciation.

69. ***Discharge of mortgage indebtedness.***—Under the baseline tax system, all income would generally be taxed under the regular tax rate schedule. The baseline tax system would not allow preferentially low (or zero) tax rates to apply to certain types or sources of income. In contrast, the Tax Code allows an exclusion from a taxpayer's taxable income for any discharge of indebtedness of up to $750,000 ($375,000 in the case of a married individual filing a separate return) from a qualified principal residence. The provision applies to debt discharged after December 31, 2020, and before January 1, 2026.

70. ***Discharge of business indebtedness.***—Under the baseline tax system, all income would generally be taxed under the regular tax rate schedule. The baseline tax system would not allow preferentially low (or zero) tax rates to apply to certain types or sources of income. In contrast, the Tax Code allows an exclusion from a taxpayer's taxable income for any discharge of qualified real property business indebtedness by taxpayers other than a C corporation. If the canceled debt is not reported as current income, however, the basis of the underlying property must be reduced by the amount canceled.

71. ***Exceptions from imputed interest rules.***—Under the baseline tax system, holders (issuers) of debt instruments are generally required to report interest earned (paid) in the period it accrues, not when received. In addition, the amount of interest accrued is determined by the actual price paid, not by the stated principal and interest stipulated in the instrument. But under current law, any debt associated with the sale of property worth less than $250,000 is exempted from the general interest accounting rules. This general $250,000 exception is not a tax expenditure under reference tax law but is under normal tax baseline. Current law also includes exceptions for certain property worth more than $250,000. These are tax expenditure under reference tax law and normal tax baselines. These exceptions include, sales of personal residences worth more than $250,000, and sales of farms and small businesses worth between $250,000 and $1 million.

72. ***Treatment of qualified dividends.***—The baseline tax system generally would tax all income under the regular tax rate schedule. It would not allow preferentially low tax rates to apply to certain types or sources of income. For individuals, tax rates on regular income vary from 10 percent to 39.6 percent in the budget window (plus a 3.8 percent surtax on high income taxpayers), depending on the taxpayer's income. In contrast, under current law, qualified dividends are taxed at a preferentially low rate that is no higher than 20 percent (plus the 3.8 percent surtax).

73. ***Capital gains (except agriculture, timber, iron ore, and coal).***—The baseline tax system generally would tax all income under the regular tax rate schedule. It would not allow preferentially low tax rates to apply to certain types or sources of income. Under current law, capital gains on assets held for more than one year are taxed at a preferentially low rate that is no higher than 20 percent (plus the 3.8 percent surtax).

74. ***Capital gains exclusion of small corporation stock.***—The baseline tax system would not allow deductions and exemptions or provide preferential treatment of certain sources of income or types of activities. In contrast, the Tax Code provided an exclusion of 50 percent, applied to ordinary rates with a maximum of a 28 percent tax rate, for capital gains from qualified small business stock held by individuals for more than 5 years; 75 percent for stock issued after February 17, 2009, and before September 28, 2010; and 100 percent for stock issued after September 27, 2010. A qualified small business is a corporation whose gross assets do not exceed $50 million as of the date of issuance of the stock.

75. ***Step-up basis of capital gains at death.***—Under the baseline tax system, unrealized capital gains would be taxed when assets are transferred at death. It would not allow for exempting gains upon transfer of the underlying assets to the heirs. In contrast, capital gains on assets held at the owner's death are not subject to capital gains tax under current law. The cost basis of the appreciated assets is adjusted to the market value at the owner's date of death which becomes the basis for the heirs.

76. ***Carryover basis of capital gains on gifts.***—Under the baseline tax system, unrealized capital gains would be taxed when assets are transferred by gift. In contrast, when a gift of appreciated asset is made under current law, the donor's basis in the transferred property (the cost that was incurred when the transferred property was first acquired) carries over to the donee. The carryover of the donor's basis allows a continued deferral of unrealized capital gains.

77. ***Ordinary income treatment of loss from small business corporation stock sale.***—The baseline tax system limits to $3,000 the write-off of losses from capital assets, with carryover of the excess to future years. In contrast, the Tax Code allows up to $100,000 in losses from the sale of small business corporate stock (capitalization less than $1 million) to be treated as ordinary losses and fully deducted.

78. ***Deferral of capital gains from like-kind exchanges.***—The baseline tax system generally would tax all income under the regular tax rate schedule. It would not allow preferentially low (or zero) tax rates, or deferral of tax, to apply to certain types or sources of income. In contrast, current law allows the deferral of accrued gains on assets transferred in qualified like-kind exchanges.

79. ***Depreciation of buildings other than rental housing (normal tax method).***—Under a comprehensive economic income tax, the costs of acquiring a building are capitalized and depreciated over time in accordance with the decline in the property's economic value due to wear and tear or obsolescence. This ensures that the net income from the property is measured appropriately each year. Current law allows depreciation deductions that differ from those under economic depreciation. However, the depreciation provisions of the Tax Code are part of the reference tax law, and thus do not give rise to tax expenditures under reference tax law. Under normal tax baseline, in contrast, depreciation allowances reflect estimates of economic depreciation.

80. ***Accelerated depreciation of machinery and equipment (normal tax method).***—Under a comprehensive economic income tax, the costs of acquiring machinery and equipment are capitalized and depreciated over time in accordance with the decline in the property's economic value due to wear and tear or obsolescence. This ensures that the net income from the property is measured appropriately each year. Current law allows depreciation deductions that are accelerated relative to economic depreciation. In particular, in 2023, 80 percent of the purchase cost of qualified property is eligible to be expensed immediately; this percentage phases out to zero through 2027. Additionally, subject to investment limitations, the Tax Code allows up to $1 million (indexed for inflation) in qualifying investments in tangible property and certain computer software to be expensed rather than depreciated over time. The depreciation provisions of the Tax Code are part of the reference tax law, and thus do not give rise to tax expenditures under reference tax law. Under the normal tax baseline, in contrast, depreciation allowances reflect estimates of economic depreciation.

81. ***Exclusion of interest on small issue bonds.***—The baseline tax system generally would tax all income under the regular tax rate schedule. It would not allow preferentially low (or zero) tax rates to apply to certain types or sources of income. In contrast, the Tax Code allows interest earned on small issue industrial development bonds (IDBs) issued by State and local governments to finance manufacturing facilities to be tax exempt. Depreciable property financed with small issue IDBs must be depreciated, however, using the straight-line method. The annual volume of small issue IDBs is subject to the unified volume cap discussed in the mortgage housing bond section above.

82. ***Special rules for certain film and TV production.***—The baseline tax system generally would tax all income under the regular tax rate schedule. It would not allow deductions and exemptions or preferentially low (or zero) tax rates to apply to certain types or sources of income. In contrast, the Tax Code allowed taxpayers to deduct up to $15 million per production ($20 million

in certain distressed areas) in non-capital expenditures incurred during the year. This provision is scheduled to expire at the end of 2025.

83. Allow 20-percent deduction to certain pass-through income.—The baseline tax system generally would tax all income under the regular tax rate schedule. It would not allow deductions and exemptions or preferentially low (or zero) tax rates to apply to certain types or sources of income. In contrast, for tax years 2018 to 2025, the Tax Code allows for a deduction equal to up to 20 percent of income attributable to domestic pass-through businesses, subject to certain limitations.

84. Advanced manufacturiung investment credit.—The baseline tax system would not allow credits for particular activities, investments, or industries. Instead, it generally would seek to tax uniformly all returns from investment-like activities. However, the Tax Code provides credits for investments in semiconductor manufacturing equipment within the United States. The credit is 25 percent for qualified property placed into service after December 31, 2022. Construction on a qualified facility must begin by December 31, 2025. Owners of facilities that qualify for the advanced manufacturing investment credit may elect to treat investment credits as a payment of tax equal to the amount of the credit.

Transportation

85. ***Tonnage tax.***—The baseline tax system generally would tax all profits and income under the regular tax rate schedule. U.S. shipping companies may choose to be subject to a tonnage tax based on gross shipping weight in lieu of an income tax, in which case profits would not be subject to tax under the regular tax rate schedule.

86. ***Deferral of tax on shipping companies.***—The baseline tax system generally would tax all profits and income under the regular tax rate schedule. It would not allow preferentially low (or zero) tax rates to apply to certain types or sources of income. In contrast, the Tax Code allows certain companies that operate U.S. flag vessels to defer income taxes on that portion of their income used for shipping purposes (e.g., primarily construction, modernization and major repairs to ships, and repayment of loans to finance these investments).

87. ***Exclusion of reimbursed employee parking expenses.***—Under the baseline tax system, all compensation, including dedicated payments and in-kind benefits, would be included in taxable income. Dedicated payments and in-kind benefits represent accretions to wealth that do not differ materially from cash wages. In contrast, the Tax Code allows an exclusion from taxable income for employee parking expenses that are paid for by the employer or that are received by the employee in lieu of wages. In 2023, the maximum amount of the parking exclusion is $300 per month. The tax expenditure estimate does not include any subsidy provided through employer-owned parking facilities. However, beginning in 2018, parking expenses are no longer deductible to employers.

88. ***Exclusion for employer-provided transit passes.***—Under the baseline tax system, all compensation, including dedicated payments and in-kind benefits, would be included in taxable income. Dedicated payments and in-kind benefits represent accretions to wealth that do not differ materially from cash wages. In contrast, the Tax Code allows an exclusion from a taxpayer's taxable income for passes, tokens, fare cards, and vanpool expenses that are paid for by an employer or that are received by the employee in lieu of wages to defray an employee's commuting costs. Due to a parity to parking provision, the maximum amount of the transit exclusion is $300 per month in 2023. However, beginning in 2018, transit expenses are no longer deductible to employers.

89. ***Tax credit for certain expenditures for maintaining railroad tracks.***—The baseline tax system would not allow credits for particular activities, investments, or industries. However, the Tax Code allowed eligible taxpayers to claim a credit equal to the lesser of 50 percent of maintenance expenditures and the product of $3,500 and the number of miles of railroad track owned or leased. This provision applies to maintenance expenditures in taxable years beginning before January 1, 2017.

90. ***Exclusion of interest on bonds for highway projects and rail-truck transfer facilities.***—The baseline tax system generally would tax all income under the regular tax rate schedule. It would not allow preferentially low (or zero) tax rates to apply to certain types or sources of income. In contrast, the Tax Code provides for $15 billion of tax-exempt bond authority to finance qualified highway or surface freight transfer facilities.

Community and Regional Development

91. ***Exclusion of interest for airport, dock, and similar bonds.***—The baseline tax system generally would tax all income under the regular tax rate schedule. It would not allow preferentially low (or zero) tax rates to apply to certain types or sources of income. In contrast, the Tax Code allows interest earned on State and local bonds issued to finance high-speed rail facilities and Government-owned airports, docks, wharves, and sport and convention facilities to be tax-exempt. These bonds are not subject to a volume cap.

92. ***Exemption of certain mutuals' and cooperatives' income.***—Under the baseline tax system, corporations pay taxes on their profits under the regular tax rate schedule. In contrast, the Tax Code provides for the incomes of mutual and cooperative telephone and electric companies to be exempt from tax if at least 85 percent of their receipts are derived from patron service charges.

93. ***Empowerment zones.***—The baseline tax system generally would tax all income under the regular tax rate schedule. It would not allow preferentially low tax rates to apply to certain types or sources of income, tax credits, and write-offs faster than economic depreciation. In contrast, the Tax Code allows qualifying businesses in designated economically depressed areas to receive tax benefits such as an employment credit and special tax-exempt financing. A taxpayer's ability to accrue new tax benefits for empowerment zones expires on December 31, 2025.

94. ***New markets tax credit.***—The baseline tax system would not allow credits for particular activities, investments, or industries. However, the Tax Code allows taxpayers who make qualified equity investments in a community development entity (CDE), which then make qualified investments in low-income communities, to be eligible for a tax credit that is received over 7 years. The total equity investment available for the credit across all CDEs is generally $5 billion for each calendar year 2020 through 2025, the last year for which credit allocations are authorized.

95. ***Credit to holders of Gulf and Midwest Tax Credit Bonds.***—The baseline tax system would not allow credits for particular activities, investments, or industries. Instead, under current law taxpayers that own Gulf and Midwest Tax Credit bonds receive a non-refundable tax credit rather than interest. The credit is included in gross income.

96. ***Recovery Zone Bonds.***—The baseline tax system would not allow credits for particular activities, investments, or industries. In addition, it would tax all income under the regular tax rate schedule. It would not allow preferentially low (or zero) tax rates to apply to certain types or sources of income. In contrast, the Tax Code allowed local governments to issue up $10 billion in taxable Recovery Zone Economic Development Bonds in 2009 and 2010 and receive a direct payment from Treasury equal to 45 percent of interest expenses. In addition, local governments could issue up to $15 billion in tax exempt Recovery Zone Facility Bonds. These bonds financed certain kinds of business development in areas of economic distress.

97. ***Tribal Economic Development Bonds.***—The baseline tax system generally would tax all income under the regular tax rate schedule. It would not allow preferentially low (or zero) tax rates to apply to certain types or sources of income. In contrast, the Tax Code was modified in 2009 to allow Indian tribal governments to issue tax exempt "tribal economic development bonds." There is a national bond limitation of $2 billion on such bonds.

98. ***Opportunity Zones.***—The baseline tax system generally would tax all income under the regular tax rate schedule. It would not allow deferral or exclusion from income for investments made within certain geographic regions. In contrast, the Tax Code allows the temporary deferral of the recognition of capital gain if reinvested prior to December 31, 2026, in a qualifying opportunity fund which in turn invests in qualifying low-income communities designated as opportunity zones. For qualifying investments held at least 5 years, 10 percent of the deferred gain is excluded from income; this exclusion increases to 15 percent for investments held for at least 7 years. In addition, capital gains from the sale or exchange of an investment in a qualified opportunity fund held for at least 10 years are excluded from gross income.

99. ***Disaster Employee Retention Credit.***—The baseline tax system would not allow credits for particular activities, investments, or industries. In contrast, the Tax Code provides employers located in certain presidentially declared disaster areas during the years 2017 through 2020 a 40 percent credit for up to $6,000 in wages paid to each eligible employee while the business was inoperable as a result of the disaster. Only wages paid after the disaster occurred and within 150 days of the last day of the incident period are eligible for the credit. Employers must reduce their deduction for wages paid by the amount of the credit claimed.

Education, Training, Employment, and Social Services

100. ***Exclusion of scholarship and fellowship income (normal tax method).***—Scholarships and fellowships are excluded from taxable income to the extent they pay for tuition and course-related expenses of the grantee. Similarly, tuition reductions for employees of educational institutions and their families are not included in taxable income. From an economic point of view, scholarships and fellowships are either gifts not conditioned on the performance of services, or they are rebates of educational costs. Thus, under the baseline tax system of the reference tax law method, this exclusion is not a tax expenditure because this method does not include either gifts or price reductions in a taxpayer's gross income. The exclusion, however, is considered a tax expenditure under the normal tax method, which includes gift-like transfers of Government funds in gross income. (Many scholarships are derived directly or indirectly from Government funding.)

101. ***Tax credits for post-secondary education expenses.***—The baseline tax system would not allow credits for particular activities, investments, or industries. Under current law in 2023, however, there are two credits for certain post-secondary education expenses. The American Opportunity Tax Credit (AOTC) allows a partially refundable credit of up to $2,500 per eligible student for qualified tuition and related expenses paid. The AOTC may be claimed during each of the first four years of the student's post-secondary education. The Lifetime Learning Credit (LLC) allows a non-refundable credit for 20 percent of an eligible student's qualified tuition and fees, up to a maximum credit of $2,000 per return. The LLC may be claimed during any year of the student's post-secondary education. Only one credit may be claimed per student per year. The combined credits are phased out for taxpayers with modified adjusted gross income (AGI) between $160,000 and $180,000 if married filing jointly ($80,000 and $90,000 for other taxpayers), not indexed. Married individuals filing separate returns cannot claim either credit.

102. ***Deductibility of student loan interest.***—The baseline tax system accepts current law's general rule limiting taxpayers' ability to deduct non-business interest expenses. In contrast, taxpayers may claim an above-the-line deduction of up to $2,500 on interest paid on an education loan. In 2023, the maximum deduction is phased down ratably for taxpayers with modified AGI between $155,000 and $185,000 if married filing jointly ($75,000 and $90,000 for other taxpayers). Married individuals filing separate returns cannot claim the deduction.

103. ***Qualified tuition programs (includes "Education IRAs").***—The baseline tax system generally would tax all income under the regular tax rate schedule. It would not allow preferentially low (or zero) tax rates to apply to certain types or sources of income. Some States have adopted prepaid tuition plans, prepaid room and board plans, and college savings plans, which allow persons to pay in advance or save for college expenses for designated beneficiaries. Under current law, investment income, or the return on prepayments, is not taxed when earned, and is tax-exempt when withdrawn to pay for qualified expenses. Beginning in 2018, the definition of a qualified expense was expanded to include up to $10,000 per child per year of expenses for primary or secondary education, including tuition at religious schools.

104. ***Exclusion of interest on student loan bonds.***—The baseline tax system generally would tax all income under the regular tax rate schedule. It would not allow preferentially low (or zero) tax rates to apply to certain types or sources of income. In contrast, interest earned on State and local bonds issued to finance student loans is tax-exempt under current law. The volume of all such private activity bonds that each State may issue annually is limited.

105. ***Exclusion of interest on bonds for private nonprofit educational facilities.***—The baseline tax system generally would tax all income under the regular tax rate schedule. It would not allow preferentially low (or zero) tax rates to apply to certain types or sources of income. In contrast, under current law interest earned on State and local Government bonds issued to finance the construction of facilities used by private nonprofit educational institutions is not taxed.

106. ***Credit for holders of zone academy bonds.***—The baseline tax system would not allow credits for particular activities, investments, or industries. Under current law, however, financial institutions that own zone academy bonds receive a non-refundable tax credit rather than interest. The credit is included in gross income. Proceeds from zone academy bonds may only be used to renovate, but not construct, qualifying schools and for certain other school purposes. The total amount of zone academy bonds that may be issued was limited to $1.4 billion in 2009 and 2010. As of March 2010, issuers of the unused authorization of such bonds could opt to receive direct payment with the yield becoming fully taxable. An additional $0.4 billion of these bonds with a tax credit was authorized to be issued each year in 2011 through 2016.

107. ***Exclusion of interest on savings bonds redeemed to finance educational expenses.***—The baseline tax system generally would tax all income under the regular tax rate schedule. It would not allow preferentially low (or zero) tax rates to apply to certain types or sources of income. Under current law, however, interest earned on U.S. savings bonds issued after December 31, 1989, is tax-exempt if the bonds are transferred to an educational institution to pay for educational expenses. The tax exemption is phased out for taxpayers with AGI between $137,800 and $167,800 if married filing jointly ($91,850 and $106,850 for other taxpayers) in 2023.

108. ***Parental personal exemption for students age 19 or over.***—Under the baseline tax system, a personal exemption would be allowed for the taxpayer, as well as for the taxpayer's spouse and dependents who do not claim a personal exemption on their own tax returns. These exemptions are repealed for taxable years beginning after December 31, 2017, and before January 1, 2026. However, the definitions regarding eligibility for dependent exemptions for children (and qualifying relatives), which determine eligibility for a number of family-related provisions, remain in place. These provisions include a $500 credit for dependents other than qualifying children (Other Dependent Credit, or ODC). In general, to be considered a dependent child, a child would have to be under age 19. In contrast, the Tax Code allows taxpayers to consider their children aged 19 to 23 as dependents, as long as the children are full-time students and reside with the taxpayer for over half the year (with exceptions for temporary absences from home, such as for school attendance). Absent this provision, children over 18 would need to meet the more stringent rules for qualified relatives in order to qualify the taxpayer for certain benefits, including the ODC.

109. ***Deductibility of charitable contributions (education).***—The baseline tax system would not allow a deduction for personal expenditures. In contrast, the Tax Code provides taxpayers a deduction for contributions to nonprofit educational institutions that are similar to personal expenditures. Moreover, taxpayers who donate capital assets to educational institutions can deduct the asset's current value without being taxed on any appreciation in value. An individual's total charitable contribution generally may not exceed 50 percent (60 percent for tax years 2018 through 2025) of AGI; a corporation's total charitable contributions generally may not exceed 10 percent of pre-tax income.

110. ***Exclusion of employer-provided educational assistance.***—Under the baseline tax system, all compensation, including dedicated payments and in-kind benefits, should be included in taxable income because it represents accretions to wealth that do not materially differ from cash wages. Under current law, however, employer-provided educational assistance is excluded from an employee's gross income, even though the employer's costs for this assistance are a deductible business expense. The maximum exclusion is $5,250 per taxpayer. From March 27, 2020, through December 31, 2025, employer-provided student loan payments are considered eligible educational assistance.

111. ***Special deduction for teacher expenses.***—The baseline tax system would not allow a deduction for personal expenditures. In contrast, the Tax Code allowed educators in both public and private elementary and secondary schools, who worked at least 900 hours during a school year as a teacher, instructor, counselor, principal or aide, to subtract up to $300 of qualified expenses when determining their AGI.

112. ***Discharge of student loan indebtedness.***—Under the baseline tax system, all compensation, including dedicated payments and in-kind benefits,

should be included in taxable income. In contrast, the Tax Code allows certain professionals who perform in underserved areas or specific fields, and as a consequence have their student loans discharged, not to recognize such discharge as income.

113. ***Qualified school construction bonds.***—The baseline tax system would not allow credits for particular activities, investments, or industries. Instead, it generally would seek to tax uniformly all returns from investment-like activities. In contrast, the Tax Code was modified in 2009 to provide a tax credit in lieu of interest to holders of qualified school construction bonds. The national volume limit is $22.4 billion over 2009 and 2010. As of March 2010, issuers of such bonds could opt to receive direct payment with the yield becoming fully taxable.

114. ***Work opportunity tax credit.***—The baseline tax system would not allow credits for particular activities, investments, or industries. Instead, it generally would seek to tax uniformly all returns from investment-like activities. In contrast, the Tax Code provides employers with a tax credit for qualified wages paid to individuals. The credit applies to employees who began work on or before December 31, 2025 and who are certified as members of various targeted groups. The amount of the credit that can be claimed is 25 percent of qualified wages for employment less than 400 hours and 40 percent for employment of 400 hours or more. Generally, the maximum credit per employee is $2,400 and can only be claimed on the first year of wages an individual earns from an employer. However, the credit for long-term welfare recipients can be claimed on second year wages as well and has a $9,000 maximum. Also, certain categories of veterans are eligible for a higher maximum credit of up to $9,600. Employers must reduce their deduction for wages paid by the amount of the credit claimed.

115. ***Employer-provided child care exclusion.***—Under the baseline tax system, all compensation, including dedicated payments and in-kind benefits, should be included in taxable income. In contrast, current law allows up to $5,000 of employer-provided child care to be excluded from an employee's gross income even though the employer's costs for the child care are a deductible business expense. The amount was temporarily increased to $10,500 for 2021.

116. ***Employer-provided child care credit.***—The baseline tax system would not allow credits for particular activities, investments, or industries. In contrast, current law provides a credit equal to 25 percent of qualified expenses for employee child care and 10 percent of qualified expenses for child care resource and referral services. Employer deductions for such expenses are reduced by the amount of the credit. The maximum total credit is limited to $150,000 per taxable year.

117. ***Assistance for adopted foster children.***—Under the baseline tax system, all compensation, including dedicated payments and in-kind benefits, should be included in taxable income. Taxpayers who adopt eligible children from the public foster care system can receive monthly payments for the children's significant and varied needs and a reimbursement of up to $2,000 for nonrecurring adoption expenses; special needs adoptions receive the maximum benefit even if that amount is not spent. These payments are excluded from gross income under current law.

118. ***Adoption credit and exclusion.***—The baseline tax system would not allow credits for particular activities. In contrast, taxpayers can receive a tax credit for qualified adoption expenses under current law. Taxpayers may also exclude qualified adoption expenses provided or reimbursed by an employer from income, subject to the same maximum amounts and phase-out as the credit. The same expenses cannot qualify for tax benefits under both programs; however, a taxpayer may use the benefits of the exclusion and the tax credit for different expenses.

119. ***Exclusion of employee meals and lodging (other than military).***—Under the baseline tax system, all compensation, including dedicated payments and in-kind benefits, should be included in taxable income. Furthermore, all compensation would generally be deductible by the employer. In contrast, under current law employer-provided meals and lodging are excluded from an employee's gross income. Additionally, beginning in 2018, employers are allowed a deduction for only 50 percent of the expenses of employer-provided meals, except that in 2021 and 2022, employers are eligible for a full deduction on restaurant meals provided to employees. Employer-provided lodging is fully deductible by the employer, in general.

120. ***Credit for child and dependent care expenses.***—The baseline tax system would not allow credits for particular activities or targeted at specific groups. In contrast, the Tax Code provides a tax credit to parents who work or attend school and who have child and dependent care expenses. In taxable year 2023, expenditures up to a maximum $3,000 for one dependent and $6,000 for two or more dependents are eligible for a nonrefundable credit. The credit is equal to 35 percent of qualified expenditures for taxpayers with incomes of up to $15,000. The credit is reduced to a minimum of 20 percent by one percentage point for each $2,000 of income in excess of $15,000.

121. ***Credit for disabled access expenditures.***—The baseline tax system would not allow credits for particular activities, investments, or industries. In contrast, the Tax Code provides small businesses (less than $1 million in gross receipts or fewer than 31 full-time employees) a 50 percent credit for expenditures in excess of $250 to remove access barriers for disabled persons. The credit is limited to $5,000.

122. ***Deductibility of charitable contributions, other than education and health.***—The baseline tax system would not allow a deduction for personal expenditures including charitable contributions. In contrast, the Tax Code provides taxpayers a deduction for contributions to charitable, religious, and certain other nonprofit organizations. Taxpayers who donate capital assets to charitable organizations can deduct the assets' current value without being taxed on any appreciation in value. An individual's total charitable contribution generally may not exceed 50 percent (60 percent between 2018

and 2025) of AGI; a corporation's total charitable contributions generally may not exceed 10 percent of pre-tax income.

123. ***Exclusion of certain foster care payments.***—The baseline tax system generally would tax all income under the regular tax rate schedule. It would not allow preferentially low (or zero) tax rates to apply to certain types or sources of income. Foster parents provide a home and care for children who are wards of the State, under contract with the State. Under current law, compensation received for this service is excluded from the gross incomes of foster parents; the expenses they incur are nondeductible.

124. ***Exclusion of parsonage allowances.***—Under the baseline tax system, all compensation, including dedicated payments and in-kind benefits, would be included in taxable income. Dedicated payments and in-kind benefits represent accretions to wealth that do not differ materially from cash wages. In contrast, the Tax Code allows an exclusion from a clergyman's taxable income for the value of the clergyman's housing allowance or the rental value of the clergyman's parsonage.

125. ***Indian employment credit.***—The baseline tax system would not allow credits for particular activities, investments, or industries. Instead, it generally would seek to tax uniformly all returns from investment-like activities. In contrast, the Tax Code provides employers with a tax credit for qualified wages paid to employees who are enrolled members of Indian tribes. The amount of the credit that could be claimed is 20 percent of the excess of qualified wages and health insurance costs paid by the employer in the current tax year over the amount of such wages and costs paid by the employer in 1993. Qualified wages and health insurance costs with respect to any employee for the taxable year could not exceed $20,000. Employees have to live on or near the reservation where they work to be eligible for the credit. Employers must reduce their deduction for wages paid by the amount of the credit claimed. The credit does not apply to taxable years beginning after December 31, 2021.

126. ***Employer-provided paid family and medical leave credit.***—The baseline tax system would not allow credits for particular activities, investments, or industries. In contrast, current law provides a credit equal to 12.5 to 25 percent of wages paid to qualifying employees while on family and medical leave for up to 12 weeks per year. In order to qualify for the credit, an employer must have a written policy in place that provides at least two weeks of paid family and medical leave per year for full-time workers; additionally, employers must pay at least 50 percent of an employee's normal wages while they are on paid leave.

Health

127. ***Exclusion of employer contributions for medical insurance premiums and medical care.***—Under the baseline tax system, all compensation, including dedicated payments and in-kind benefits, should be included in taxable income. In contrast, under current law, employer-paid health insurance premiums and other medical expenses (including long-term care or Health Reimbursement Accounts) are not included in employee gross income even though they are deducted as a business expense by the employee.

128. ***Self-employed medical insurance premiums.***—Under the baseline tax system, all compensation and remuneration, including dedicated payments and in-kind benefits, should be included in taxable income. In contrast, under current law self-employed taxpayers may deduct their family health insurance premiums. Taxpayers without self-employment income are not eligible for this special deduction. The deduction is not available for any month in which the self-employed individual is eligible to participate in an employer-subsidized health plan and the deduction may not exceed the self-employed individual's earned income from self-employment.

129. ***Medical Savings Accounts and Health Savings Accounts.***—Under the baseline tax system, all compensation, including dedicated payments and in-kind benefits, should be included in taxable income. Also, the baseline tax system would not allow a deduction for personal expenditures and generally would tax investment earnings. In contrast, individual contributions to Archer Medical Savings Accounts (Archer MSAs) and Health Savings Accounts (HSAs) are allowed as a deduction in determining AGI whether or not the individual itemizes deductions. Employer contributions to Archer MSAs and HSAs are excluded from income and employment taxes. Archer MSAs and HSAs require that the individual have coverage by a qualifying high deductible health plan. Earnings from the accounts are excluded from taxable income. Distributions from the accounts used for medical expenses are not taxable. The rules for HSAs are generally more flexible than for Archer MSAs and the deductible contribution amounts are greater (in 2023, $3,850 for taxpayers with individual coverage and $7,750 for taxpayers with family coverage). Thus, HSAs have largely replaced MSAs.

130. ***Deductibility of medical expenses.***—The baseline tax system would not allow a deduction for personal expenditures. In contrast, under current law personal expenditures for medical care (including the costs of prescription drugs) exceeding 7.5 percent of the taxpayer's AGI are deductible. For tax years beginning after 2012, only medical expenditures exceeding 10 percent of the taxpayer's AGI are deductible. However, for the years 2013, 2014, 2015 and 2016, if either the taxpayer or the taxpayer's spouse turned 65 before the end of the taxable year, the threshold remained at 7.5 percent of adjusted income. Beginning in 2017, the 10 percent threshold applied to all taxpayers, including those over 65.

131. ***Exclusion of interest on hospital construction bonds.***—The baseline tax system generally would tax all income under the regular tax rate schedule. It would not allow preferentially low (or zero) tax rates to apply to certain types or sources of income. In contrast, under current law interest earned on State and local government debt issued to finance hospital construction is excluded from income subject to tax.

132. ***Refundable Premium Assistance Tax Credit.***—The baseline tax system would not allow credits for particular activities or targeted at specific groups. In contrast, for taxable years ending after 2013, the Tax Code provides a premium assistance credit to any eligible taxpayer for any qualified health insurance purchased through a Health Insurance Exchange. In general, an eligible taxpayer is a taxpayer with annual household income between 100 percent and 400 percent of the federal poverty level for the taxpayer's family size and who does not have access to affordable minimum essential health care coverage. The amount of the credit equals the lesser of: 1) the actual premiums paid by the taxpayer for such coverage; or 2) the difference between the cost of a statutorily-identified benchmark plan offered on the exchange and a required payment by the taxpayer that increases with income. The American Rescue Plan Act of 2021 (ARP; Public Law 117-2) and the IRA temporarily increased the Premium Tax Credit in three ways. For 2021 through 2025, the legislation increased the Premium Tax Credit for currently eligible individuals and families, providing access to free benchmark plans for those earning 100 to 150 percent of the federal poverty level and expanded eligibility to newly include individuals and families with income above 400 percent of the federal poverty level.

133. ***Credit for employee health insurance expenses of small business.***—The baseline tax system would not allow credits for particular activities or targeted at specific groups. In contrast, the Tax Code provides a tax credit to qualified small employers that make a certain level of non-elective contributions towards the purchase of certain health insurance coverage for its employees. To receive a credit, an employer must have fewer than 25 full-time-equivalent employees whose average annual full-time-equivalent wages from the employer are less than $50,000 (indexed for taxable years after 2013). However, to receive a full credit, an employer must have no more than 10 full-time employees, and the average wage paid to these employees must be no more than $25,000 (indexed for taxable years after 2013). A qualifying employer may claim the credit for any taxable year beginning in 2010, 2011, 2012, and 2013 and for up to two years for insurance purchased through a Health Insurance Exchange thereafter. For taxable years beginning in 2010, 2011, 2012, and 2013, the maximum credit is 35 percent of premiums paid by qualified taxable employers and 25 percent of premiums paid by qualified tax-exempt organizations. For taxable years beginning in 2014 and later years, the maximum tax credit increases to 50 percent of premiums paid by qualified taxable employers and 35 percent of premiums paid by qualified tax-exempt organizations.

134. ***Deductibility of charitable contributions (health).***—The baseline tax system would not allow a deduction for personal expenditures including charitable contributions. In contrast, the Tax Code provides individuals and corporations a deduction for contributions to nonprofit health institutions. Tax expenditures resulting from the deductibility of contributions to other charitable institutions are listed under the education, training, employment, and social services function.

135. ***Tax credit for orphan drug research.***—The baseline tax system would not allow credits for particular activities, investments, or industries. In contrast, under current law drug firms can claim a tax credit of 25 percent of the costs for clinical testing required by the Food and Drug Administration for drugs that treat rare physical conditions or rare diseases.

136. ***Special Blue Cross/Blue Shield tax benefits.***—The baseline tax system generally would tax all profits under the regular tax rate schedule using broadly applicable measures of baseline income. It would not allow preferentially low tax rates to apply to certain types or sources of income. In contrast, certain Blue Cross and Blue Shield (BC/BS) health insurance providers and certain other health insurers are provided with special tax benefits, provided that their percentage of total premium revenue expended on reimbursement for clinical services provided to enrollees or for activities that improve health care quality is not less than 85 percent for the taxable year. A qualifying insurer may take as a deduction 100 percent of any net increase in its unearned premium reserves, instead of the 80 percent allowed other insurers. A qualifying insurer is also allowed a special deduction equal to the amount by which 25 percent of its health-claim expenses exceeds its beginning-of-the-year accounting surplus. The deduction is limited to the insurer's taxable income determined without the special deduction.

137. ***Distributions from retirement plans for premiums for health and long-term care insurance.***—Under the baseline tax system, all compensation, including dedicated and deferred payments, should be included in taxable income. In contrast, the Tax Code provides for tax-free distributions of up to $3,000 from governmental retirement plans for premiums for health and long term care premiums of public safety officers.

138. Credit for family and sick leave taken by self-employed individuals.—The baseline tax system would not allow credits for particular activities or targeted as specific groups. Under current law, however, self-employed individuals are allowed a refundable credit equal to certain family or sick leave taken. In general, the sick leave credit is equal to 100 percent of daily self-employment income (equal to self-employment income divided by 260) during a period of qualified sick leave, up to $511 per day for 10 days. The family leave credit is equal to two thirds of daily self-employment income (but no greater than two thirds of $200) during a period of qualified family leave for up to 10 weeks. Under current law, the credit applies to leave taken prior to October 1, 2021.

Income Security

139. ***Child tax credit.***—The baseline tax system would not allow credits for particular activities or targeted at specific groups. Under current law, however, taxpayers with children under age 18 can qualify for a child tax credit. In taxable years 2022 through 2025, taxpayers may claim a $2,000 per child partially refundable child tax credit. In 2023, up to $1,600 per child of unclaimed

credit due to insufficient tax liability may be refundable—taxpayers may claim a refund for 15 percent of earnings in excess of a $2,500 floor, up to the lesser of the amount of unused credit or $1,600 per child. A taxpayer may also claim a nonrefundable credit of $500 for each qualifying child not eligible for the $2,000 credit (those over sixteen and those without SSNs) and for each dependent relative. The total combined child and other dependent credit is phased out for taxpayers at the rate of $50 per $1,000 of modified AGI above $400,000 if married filing jointly ($200,000 for all other filers). For tax years beginning after December 31, 2025, the credit returns to its pre-TCJA value of $1,000. At that time, up to the full value of the credit (subject to a phase-in of 15 percent of earnings in excess of $3,000) will be refundable and the $500 other dependent credit will expire. The credit will once again phase out at the rate of $50 per $1,000 of modified AGI above $110,000 if married filing jointly ($75,000 for single or head of household filers and $55,000 for married taxpayers filing separately).

140. ***Other dependent tax credit.***—The baseline tax system would not allow credits for particular activities or targeted at specific groups. Under current law, however, taxpayers with dependents who don't qualify for the child tax credit may be able to claim a maximum of $500 in credits for each dependent who meets certain conditions.

141. ***Exclusion of railroad retirement (Social Security equivalent) benefits.***—Under the baseline tax system, all compensation, including dedicated and deferred payments, should be included in taxable income. In contrast, the Social Security Equivalent Benefit paid to railroad retirees and the disabled is not generally subject to the income tax unless the recipient's modified gross income reaches a certain threshold under current law. See provision number 162, Social Security benefits for retired and disabled workers and spouses, dependents, and survivors, for a discussion of the threshold.

142. ***Exclusion of workers' compensation benefits.***—Under the baseline tax system, all compensation, including dedicated payments and in-kind benefits, should be included in taxable income. However, workers compensation is not subject to the income tax under current law.

143. ***Exclusion of public assistance benefits (normal tax method).***—Under the reference tax law baseline, gifts and transfers are not treated as income to the recipients. In contrast, the normal tax method considers cash transfers from the Government as part of the recipients' income, and thus, treats the exclusion for public assistance benefits under current law as a tax expenditure.

144. ***Exclusion of special benefits for disabled coal miners.***—Under the baseline tax system, all compensation, including dedicated payments and in-kind benefits, should be included in taxable income. However, disability payments to former coal miners out of the Black Lung Trust Fund, although income to the recipient, are not subject to the income tax.

145. ***Exclusion of military disability pensions.***—Under the baseline tax system, all compensation, including dedicated payments and in-kind benefits, should be included in taxable income. In contrast, most of the military disability pension income received by current disabled military retirees is excluded from their income subject to tax.

146. ***Defined benefit employer plans.***—Under the baseline tax system, all compensation, including deferred and dedicated payments, should be included in taxable income. In addition, investment income would be taxed as earned. In contrast, under current law certain contributions to defined benefit pension plans are excluded from an employee's gross income until the money is withdrawn, even though employers can deduct their contributions. In addition, the tax on the investment income earned by defined benefit pension plans is deferred until the money is withdrawn.

147. ***Defined contribution employer plans.***—Under the baseline tax system, all compensation, including deferred and dedicated payments, should be included in taxable income. In addition, investment income would be taxed as earned. In contrast, under current law individual taxpayers and employers can make tax-preferred contributions to employer-provided 401(k) and similar plans (e.g. 403(b) plans and the Federal Government's Thrift Savings Plan). In 2023, an employee could exclude up to $22,500 of wages from AGI under a qualified arrangement with an employer's 401(k) plan. Employees age 50 or over could exclude up to $30,000 in contributions. The defined contribution plan limit, including both employee and employer contributions, is $66,000 in 2023. The tax on contributions made by both employees and employers and the investment income earned by these plans is deferred until withdrawn.

148. ***Individual Retirement Accounts.***—Under the baseline tax system, all compensation, including deferred and dedicated payments, should be included in taxable income. In addition, investment income would be taxed as earned. In contrast, under current law individual taxpayers can take advantage of traditional and Roth Individual Retirement Accounts to defer or otherwise reduce the tax on the return to their retirement savings. The Individual Retirement Account contribution limit is $6,500 in 2023; taxpayers age 50 or over are allowed to make additional "catch-up" contributions of $1,000. Contributions to a traditional Individual Retirement Account are generally deductible but the deduction is phased out for workers with incomes above certain levels if the workers or their spouses are active participants in an employer-provided retirement plan. Contributions and account earnings are includible in income when withdrawn from traditional Individual Retirement Accounts. Roth Individual Retirement Account contributions are not deductible, but earnings and withdrawals are exempt from taxation. Income limits also apply to Roth Individual Retirement Account contributions.

149. ***Low- and moderate-income savers' credit.***—The baseline tax system would not allow credits for particular activities or targeted at specific groups. In contrast, the Tax Code provides an additional incentive for lower-income taxpayers to save through a nonrefund-

able credit of up to 50 percent on Individual Retirement Account and other retirement contributions of up to $2,000. This credit is in addition to any deduction or exclusion. The credit is completely phased out by $73,000 for joint filers, $54,750 for head of household filers, and $36,500 for other filers in 2023.

150. ***Self-employed plans.***—Under the baseline tax system, all compensation, including deferred and dedicated payments, should be included in taxable income. In addition, investment income would be taxed as earned. In contrast, under current law self-employed individuals can make deductible contributions to their own retirement plans equal to 25 percent of their income, up to a maximum of $66,000 in 2023. Total plan contributions are limited to 25 percent of a firm's total wages. The tax on the investment income earned by self-employed SEP, SIMPLE, and qualified plans is deferred until withdrawn.

151. ***Small employer pension plan startup credit.***—The baseline tax system would not allow credits for particular activities or targeted at specific groups. However, under current law, certain small employers are eligible for a tax credit for the start-up cost of a new plan for the first three years in which the plan is maintained.

152. ***Premiums on group term life insurance.***—Under the baseline tax system, all compensation, including deferred and dedicated payments, should be included in taxable income. In contrast, under current law employer-provided life insurance benefits are excluded from an employee's gross income (to the extent that the employer's share of the total costs does not exceed the cost of $50,000 of such insurance) even though the employer's costs for the insurance are a deductible business expense.

153. ***Premiums on accident and disability insurance.***—Under the baseline tax system, all compensation, including dedicated payments and in-kind benefits, should be included in taxable income. In contrast, under current law employer-provided accident and disability benefits are excluded from an employee's gross income even though the employer's costs for the benefits are a deductible business expense.

154. ***Exclusion of investment income from Supplementary Unemployment Benefit Trusts.***—Under the baseline tax system, all compensation, including dedicated payments and in-kind benefits, should be included in taxable income. In addition, investment income would be taxed as earned. Under current law, employers may establish trusts to pay supplemental unemployment benefits to employees separated from employment. Investment income earned by such trusts is exempt from taxation.

155. ***Exclusion of investment income from Voluntary Employee Benefit Associations trusts.***—Under the baseline tax system, all compensation, including dedicated payments and in-kind benefits, should be included in taxable income. Under current law, employers may establish associations, or VEBAs, to pay employee benefits, which may include health benefit plans, life insurance, and disability insurance, among other employee benefits. Investment income earned by such trusts is exempt from taxation.

156. ***Special Employee Stock Ownership Plan (ESOP) rules.***—Under the baseline tax system, all compensation, including dedicated payments and in-kind benefits, should be included in taxable income. In addition, investment income would be taxed as earned. In contrast, employer-paid contributions (the value of stock issued to the ESOP) are deductible by the employer as part of employee compensation costs. They are not included in the employees' gross income for tax purposes, however, until they are paid out as benefits. In addition, the following special income tax provisions for ESOPs are intended to increase ownership of corporations by their employees: 1) annual employer contributions are subject to less restrictive limitations than other qualified retirement plans; 2) ESOPs may borrow to purchase employer stock, guaranteed by their agreement with the employer that the debt will be serviced by the payment (deductible by firm) of a portion of wages (excludable by the employees) to service the loan; 3) employees who sell appreciated company stock to the ESOP may defer any taxes due until they withdraw benefits; 4) dividends paid to ESOP-held stock are deductible by the employer; and 5) earnings are not taxed as they accrue.

157. ***Additional deduction for the blind.***—Under the baseline tax system, the standard deduction is allowed. An additional standard deduction for a targeted group within a given filing status would not be allowed. In contrast, the Tax Code allows taxpayers who are blind to claim an additional $1,850 standard deduction if single or $1,500 if married in 2023.

158. ***Additional deduction for the elderly.***—Under the baseline tax system, the standard deduction is allowed. An additional standard deduction for a targeted group within a given filing status would not be allowed. In contrast, the Tax Code allows taxpayers who are 65 years or older to claim an additional $1,850 standard deduction if single or $1,500 if married in 2023.

159. ***Deductibility of casualty losses.***—Under the baseline tax system, neither the purchase of property nor insurance premiums to protect the property's value are deductible as costs of earning income. Therefore, reimbursement for insured loss of such property is not included as a part of gross income, and uninsured losses are not deductible. In contrast, the Tax Code provides a deduction for uninsured casualty and theft losses of more than $100 each, to the extent that total losses during the year exceed 10 percent of the taxpayer's AGI. In the case of taxable years beginning after December 31, 2017, and before January 1, 2026, personal casualty losses are deductible only to the extent they are attributable to a Federally declared disaster area.

160. ***Earned income tax credit (EITC).***—The baseline tax system would not allow credits for particular activities or targeted at specific groups. In contrast, the Tax Code provides an EITC to low-income workers at a maximum rate of 45 percent of income. In 2023, for a family with one qualifying child, the credit is 34 percent of the first $11,750 of earned income. The credit is 40 percent of the first $16,510 of income for a family with two qualifying children, and it is 45 percent of the first $16,510 of

income for a family with three or more qualifying children. Low-income workers with no qualifying children are eligible for a 7.65 percent credit on the first $7,840 of earned income. The credit plateaus and then phases out with the greater of AGI or earnings at income levels and rates which depend upon how many qualifying children are eligible and marital status. Earned income tax credits in excess of tax liabilities are refundable to individuals. Beginning in 2018, the parameters of the EITC are indexed by the chained CPI, which results in a smaller inflation adjustment than previously.

161. Recovery rebate credits.—The baseline tax system would not allow credits for particular activities or targeted at specific groups. In contrast, the Coronavirus Aid, Relief, and Economic Security Act (CARES Act; Public Law 116-136) provided rebates of $1,200 ($2,400 for married couples filing jointly) and $500 per child. The total rebate amount begins phasing out at AGI over $75,000 ($150,000 for married couples filing jointly, $112,500 for heads of household). This was followed by the Consolidated Appropriations Act, 2021 (Public Law 116-260) which provided rebates of $600 per eligible taxpayer ($1,200 for married couples filing jointly) plus an additional $600 per child, with phase-out features similar to the CARES Act. The ARP provided another rebate credit of $1,400 ($2,800 for married couples filing jointly) and $1,400 per dependent in 2021. The phase out begins at the same thresholds as the CARES Act, but the full credit is phased out proportionately by $80,000 of AGI ($160,000 for married couples filing jointly, $120,000 for heads of household).

Social Security

162. ***Social Security benefits for retired and disabled workers and spouses, dependents, and survivors.***—The baseline tax system would tax Social Security benefits to the extent that contributions to Social Security were not previously taxed. Thus, the portion of Social Security benefits that is attributable to employer contributions and to earnings on employer and employee contributions (and not attributable to employee contributions which are taxed at the time of contribution) would be subject to tax. In contrast, the Tax Code may not tax all of the Social Security benefits that exceed the beneficiary's contributions from previously taxed income. Actuarially, previously taxed contributions generally do not exceed 15 percent of benefits, even for retirees receiving the highest levels of benefits. Therefore, up to 85 percent of recipients' Social Security and Railroad Social Security Equivalent retirement benefits are included in (phased into) the income tax base if the recipient's provisional income exceeds certain base amounts. (Provisional income is equal to other items included in AGI plus foreign or U.S. possession income, tax-exempt interest, and one half of Social Security and Railroad Social Security Equivalent retirement benefits.) The untaxed portion of the benefits received by taxpayers who are below the income amounts at which 85 percent of the benefits are taxable is counted as a tax expenditure. Benefits paid to disabled workers and to spouses, dependents, and survivors are treated in a similar manner. Railroad Social Security Equivalent benefits are treated like Social Security benefits. See also provision number 141, Exclusion of railroad retirement (Social Security equivalent) benefits.

163. ***Credit for certain employer contributions to Social Security.***—Under the baseline tax system, employer contributions to Social Security represent labor cost and are deductible expenses. Under current law, however, certain employers are allowed a tax credit, instead of a deduction, against taxes paid on tips received from customers in connection with the providing, delivering, or serving of food or beverages for consumption. The tip credit equals the full amount of the employer's share of FICA taxes paid on the portion of tips, when added to the employee's non-tip wages, in excess of $5.15 per hour. The credit is available only with respect to FICA taxes paid on tips.

Veterans Benefits and Services

164. ***Exclusion of veterans death benefits and disability compensation.***—Under the baseline tax system, all compensation, including dedicated payments and in-kind benefits, should be included in taxable income because they represent accretions to wealth that do not materially differ from cash wages. In contrast, all compensation due to death or disability paid by the Veterans Administration is excluded from taxable income under current law.

165. ***Exclusion of veterans pensions.***—Under the baseline tax system, all compensation, including dedicated payments and in-kind benefits, should be included in taxable income because they represent accretions to wealth that do not materially differ from cash wages. Under current law, however, pension payments made by the Veterans Administration are excluded from gross income.

166. ***Exclusion of G.I. Bill benefits.***—Under the baseline tax system, all compensation, including dedicated payments and in-kind benefits, should be included in taxable income because they represent accretions to wealth that do not materially differ from cash wages. Under current law, however, G.I. Bill benefits paid by the Veterans Administration are excluded from gross income.

167. ***Exclusion of interest on veterans housing bonds.***—The baseline tax system generally would tax all income under the regular tax rate schedule. It would not allow preferentially low (or zero) tax rates to apply to certain types or sources of income. In contrast, under current law, the interest earned on general obligation bonds issued by State and local governments to finance housing for veterans is excluded from taxable income.

General Government

168. ***Exclusion of interest on public purpose State and local bonds.***—The baseline tax system generally would tax all income under the regular tax rate schedule. It would not allow preferentially low (or zero) tax rates to apply to certain types or sources of income. In contrast, under current law, the interest earned on State and local government bonds issued to finance public pur-

pose construction (e.g., schools, roads, sewers), equipment acquisition, and other public purposes is tax-exempt. The interest earned on bonds issued by Indian tribal governments for essential governmental purposes is also tax-exempt.

169. ***Build America Bonds.***—The baseline tax system would not allow credits for particular activities or targeted at specific groups. In contrast, the Tax Code in 2009 allowed State and local governments to issue taxable bonds through 2010 and receive a direct payment from Treasury equal to 35 percent of interest expenses. Alternatively, State and local governments could issue taxable bonds and the private lenders would receive the 35 percent credit which is included in taxable income.

170. ***Deductibility of nonbusiness State and local taxes other than on owner-occupied homes.***—Under the baseline tax system, a deduction for personal consumption expenditures would not be allowed. In contrast, the Tax Code allows taxpayers who itemize their deductions to claim a deduction for State and local income taxes (or, at the taxpayer's election, State and local sales taxes) and property taxes, even though these taxes primarily pay for services that, if purchased directly by taxpayers, would not be deductible. (The estimates for this tax expenditure do not include the estimates for the deductibility of State and local property tax on owner-occupied homes, which are presented in provision number 62.) In the case of taxable years beginning after December 31, 2017, and before January 1, 2026: 1) the deduction for foreign real property taxes paid is disallowed; and 2) the deduction for taxes paid in any taxable year, which includes the deduction for property taxes on real property, is limited to $10,000 ($5,000 in the case of a married individual filing a separate return).

Interest

171. ***Deferral of interest on U.S. savings bonds.***—The baseline tax system would uniformly tax all returns to investments and not allow an exemption or deferral for particular activities, investments, or industries. In contrast, taxpayers may defer paying tax on interest earned on U.S. savings bonds until the bonds are redeemed.

APPENDIX

Performance Measures and the Economic Effects of Tax Expenditures

The Government Performance and Results Act of 1993 (GPRA) directs Federal agencies to develop annual and strategic plans for their programs and activities. These plans set out performance objectives to be achieved over a specific time period. Most of these objectives are achieved through direct expenditure programs. Tax expenditures—spending programs implemented through the tax code by reducing tax obligations for certain activities—contribute to achieving these goals in a manner similar to direct expenditure programs.

Tax expenditures by definition work through the tax system and, particularly, the income tax. Thus, they may be relatively advantageous policy approaches when the benefit or incentive is related to income and is intended to be widely available. Because there is an existing public administrative and private compliance structure for the tax system, income-based programs that require little oversight might be efficiently run through the tax system. In addition, some tax expenditures actually simplify the operation of the tax system. Tax expenditures also implicitly subsidize certain activities in a manner similar to direct expenditures. For example, exempting employer-sponsored health insurance from income taxation is equivalent to a direct spending subsidy equal to the forgone tax obligations for this type of compensation. Spending, regulatory or tax-disincentive policies can also modify behavior, but may have different economic effects. A variety of tax expenditure tools can be used, e.g., deductions, credits, exemptions, deferrals, floors, ceilings, phase-ins, phase-outs, and these can be dependent on income, expenses, or demographic characteristics (age, number of family members, etc.). This wide range of policy instruments means that tax expenditures can be flexible and can have very different economic effects.

Tax expenditures also have limitations. In many cases they add to the complexity of the tax system, which raises both administrative and compliance costs. For example, exemptions, deductions, credits, and phase-outs can complicate filing and decision-making. The income tax system may have little or no contact with persons who have no or very low incomes, and does not require information on certain characteristics of individuals used in some spending programs, such as wealth or duration of employment. These features may reduce the effectiveness of tax expenditures for addressing socioeconomic disparities. Many tax expenditures, particularly those that are structured as deductions or exemptions, also deliver higher benefits to taxpayers in higher tax brackets, an outcome that may not be desireable or intentional in some contexts, and which could be avoided if the benefit was structured as an outlay program. Relatedly, tax expenditures generally do not enable the same degree of agency discretion as an outlay program. For example, grant or direct Federal service delivery programs can prioritize activities to be addressed with specific resources in a way that is difficult to emulate with tax expenditures.

Outlay programs have advantages where the direct provision of Government services is particularly warranted, such as equipping and maintaining the Armed Forces, administering the system of justice, building and maintance of public infrastructure, and other provision of clear public goods. Outlay programs may also be specifically designed to meet the needs of low-income families who would not otherwise be subject to income taxes or need to file a tax return. Outlay programs may also receive more year-to-year oversight and fine tuning through the legislative and executive budget process. In addition, many different types of spending programs include direct Government provision; credit programs; and payments to State and local governments, the private sector, or individuals in the form of grants or contracts, which provide flexibility for policy design. On the other hand, certain outlay programs may rely less directly on economic incentives and private-market provision than tax incentives, which could reduce the relative efficiency of spending programs for some goals. Spending programs, particularly on the discretionary side, may respond less rapidly to changing activity levels and economic conditions than tax expenditures.

Regulations may have more direct and immediate effects than outlay and tax-expenditure programs because regulations apply directly and immediately to the regulated party (i.e., the intended actor), generally in the private sector. Regulations can also be fine-tuned more quickly than tax expenditures because they can often be changed as needed by the Executive Branch without legislation. Like tax expenditures, regulations often rely largely on voluntary compliance, rather than detailed inspections and policing. As such, the public administrative costs tend to be modest relative to the private resource costs associated with modifying activities. Historically, regulations have tended to rely on proscriptive measures, as opposed to economic incentives. This reliance can diminish their economic efficiency, although this feature can also promote full compliance where (as in certain safety-related cases) policymakers believe that trade-offs with economic considerations are not of paramount importance. Also, regulations generally do not directly affect Federal outlays or receipts. Thus, like tax expenditures, they may escape the degree of scrutiny that outlay programs receive.

A Framework for Evaluating the Effectiveness of Tax Expenditures

Across all major budgetary categories—from housing and health to space, technology, agriculture, and national defense—tax expenditures make up a significant portion of Federal activity and affect every area of the economy. For these reasons, a comprehensive evaluation framework that examines incentives, direct results, and spillover effects will benefit the budgetary process by informing decisions on tax expenditure policy.

As described above, tax expenditures, like spending and regulatory programs, have a variety of objectives and economic effects. These include encouraging certain types of activities (e.g., saving for retirement or investing in certain sectors); increasing certain types of after-tax income (e.g., favorable tax treatment of Social Security income) and preferencing other types of pre-tax income (e.g. preferential rates on capital gains); and reducing private compliance costs and Government administrative costs (e.g., the exclusion for up to $500,000 of capital gains on home sales). Some of these objectives are well-suited to quantitative measurement and evaluation, while others are less well-suited.

Performance measurement is generally concerned with inputs, outputs, and outcomes. In the case of tax expenditures, the principal input is usually the revenue effect. Outputs are quantitative or qualitative measures of goods and services, or changes in income and investment, directly produced by these inputs. Outcomes, in turn, represent the changes in the economy, society, or environment that are the ultimate goals of programs. Evaluations assess whether programs are meeting intended goals, but may also encompass analyzing whether initiatives are superior to other policy alternatives.

Similar to prior years, the Administration is working towards examining the objectives and effects of the wide range of tax expenditures in the President's Budget, despite challenges related to data availability, measurement, and analysis. Evaluations include an assessment of whether tax expenditures are achieving intended policy results in an efficient manner, with minimal burdens on individual taxpayers, consumers, and firms, and an examination of possible unintended effects and their consequences.

As an illustration of how evaluations can inform budgetary decisions, consider education, and research investment credits.

Education. There are millions of individuals taking advantage of tax credits designed to help pay for educational expenses. There are a number of different credits available as well as other important forms of Federal support for higher education such as subsidized student loans and grants. An evaluation would explore the possible relationships between use of the credits and the use of student loans and grants, seeking to answer, for example, whether the use of credits reduces or increases the likelihood of students applying for loans. Such an evaluation would allow stakeholders to determine the need for programs—whether they involve tax credits, subsidized loans, or grants.

Investment. A series of tax expenditures reduce the cost of investment, both in specific activities such as research and experimentation, extractive industries, and certain financial activities, and more generally throughout the economy, through accelerated depreciation for plant and equipment. These provisions can be evaluated along a number of dimensions. For example, it is useful to consider the strength of the incentives by measuring their effects on the cost of capital (the return which investments must yield to cover their costs) and effective tax rates. The impact of these provisions on the amount of corresponding forms of investment (e.g., research spending, exploration activity, equipment) might also be estimated. In some cases, such as research, there is evidence that this private investment can provide significant positive externalities—that is, economic benefits that are not reflected in the market transactions between private parties. It could be useful to quantify these externalities and compare them with the size of tax expenditures. Measures could also indicate the effects on production from these investments such as numbers or values of patents, energy production and reserves, and industrial production. Issues to be considered include the extent to which the preferences increase production (as opposed to benefiting existing output) and their cost-effectiveness relative to other policies. Analysis could also consider objectives that are more difficult to measure but could be ultimate goals, such as promoting energy security or economic growth. Such an assessment is likely to involve tax analysis as well as consideration of non-tax matters such as market structure, scientific, and other information.

The tax proposals subject to these analyses include items that indirectly affect the estimated value of tax expenditures (such as changes in income tax rates), proposals that make reforms to improve tax compliance and administration, as well as proposals which would change, add, or delete tax expenditures.

Barriers to Evaluation. Developing a framework that is sufficiently comprehensive, accurate, and flexible is a significant challenge. Evaluations are constrained by the availability of appropriate data and challenges in economic modeling:

- Data availability—Data may not exist, or may not exist in an analytically appropriate form, to conduct rigorous evaluations of certain types of expenditures. For example, measuring the effects of tax expenditures designed to achieve tax neutrality for individuals and firms earning income abroad, and foreign firms could require data from foreign governments or firms which are not readily available.
- Analytical constraints—Evaluations of tax expenditures face analytical constraints even when data are available. For example, individuals might have access to several tax expenditures and programs aimed at improving the same outcome. Isolating the effect of a single tax credit is challenging absent a well-specified research design.
- Resources—Tax expenditure analyses are seriously constrained by staffing considerations. Evaluations typically require expert analysts who are often engaged in other areas of work related to the budget.

The Executive Branch is focused on addressing these challenges to lay the foundation for the analysis of tax expenditures comprehensively, alongside evaluations of the effectiveness of direct spending initiatives.

Table 20–1. ESTIMATES OF TOTAL INCOME TAX EXPENDITURES FOR 2023-2033[1]

(In millions of dollars)

		Total from corporations and individuals											
		2023	2024	2025	2026	2027	2028	2029	2030	2031	2032	2033	2024-2033
National Defense													
1	Exclusion of benefits and allowances to armed forces personnel	15,990	16,600	17,250	17,940	16,740	16,990	17,650	18,440	19,310	20,250	21,250	182,420
International affairs:													
2	Exclusion of income earned abroad by U.S. citizens	5,420	5,600	5,730	5,870	6,000	6,140	6,280	6,420	6,570	6,720	6,880	62,210
3	Exclusion of certain allowances for Federal employees abroad	280	300	310	330	350	370	390	410	430	450	480	3,820
4	Reduced tax rate on active income of controlled foreign corporations (normal tax method)	45,190	46,540	47,940	41,940	43,200	44,490	45,830	47,200	48,620	50,080	51,580	467,420
5	Deduction for foreign-derived intangible income derived from trade or business within the United States	15,240	15,690	16,170	9,950	10,250	10,560	10,870	11,200	11,530	11,880	12,240	120,340
6	Interest Charge Domestic International Sales Corporations (IC-DISCs)	1,620	1,690	1,780	2,010	2,200	2,330	2,440	2,560	2,660	2,770	2,900	23,340
General science, space, and technology:													
7	Expensing of research and experimentation expenditures (normal tax method)	-38,660	-28,850	-17,940	-5,610	0	0	0	0	0	0	0	-52,400
8	Credit for increasing research activities	28,220	30,040	31,880	33,800	35,710	37,640	39,640	41,700	43,840	46,060	48,340	388,650
Energy:													
9	Expensing of exploration and development costs, oil and gas	700	70	-50	-80	140	330	350	340	330	300	290	2,020
10	Expensing of exploration and development costs, coal	50	0	0	-10	10	30	30	30	30	30	20	170
11	Excess of percentage over cost depletion, oil and gas	1,530	1,590	1,490	1,470	1,490	1,530	1,560	1,610	1,670	1,740	1,820	15,970
12	Excess of percentage over cost depletion, coal	90	90	90	110	110	120	130	140	140	150	150	1,230
13	Exception from passive loss limitation for working interests in oil and gas properties	10	10	10	10	10	10	10	10	10	10	10	100
14	Enhanced oil recovery credit	0	0	0	0	0	0	0	0	0	0	0	0
15	Marginal wells credit	190	180	270	270	180	80	20	0	0	0	0	1,000
16	Amortize all geological and geophysical expenditures over 2 years	140	150	150	150	150	150	150	140	140	140	140	1,460
17	Capital gains treatment of royalties on coal	50	50	50	50	60	50	50	50	50	50	50	510
18	Exclusion of interest on energy facility bonds	0	0	0	0	10	10	10	10	10	10	0	60
19	Qualified energy conservation bonds [2]	30	30	30	30	30	30	30	30	30	30	30	300
20	Exclusion of utility conservation subsidies	50	50	40	40	40	30	30	30	30	20	20	330
21	Credit for holding clean renewable energy bonds [2]	70	70	70	70	70	70	70	70	70	70	70	700
22	Energy production credit [2]	7,450	7,570	9,530	13,540	19,580	26,180	31,610	36,980	41,090	43,270	47,260	276,610
23	Energy investment credit [2]	25,970	27,510	18,670	13,760	14,710	12,600	8,680	17,190	11,510	11,040	12,350	148,020
24	Advanced nuclear power production credit	30	150	220	240	270	280	280	280	240	90	10	2,060
25	Zero-emission nuclear power production credit [2]	0	0	0	0	0	0	0	170	790	1,580	630	3,170
26	Reduced tax rate for nuclear decommissioning funds	120	120	130	130	140	150	150	160	170	170	180	1,500
27	Alcohol fuel credits [3]	20	20	0	0	0	0	0	0	0	0	0	20
28	Bio-Diesel and small agri-biodiesel producer tax credits [4]	20	20	0	0	0	0	0	0	0	0	0	20
29	Clean fuel production credit [2, 5]	0	0	4,940	5,990	6,490	1,300	330	0	0	0	0	19,050
30	Clean hydrogen production credit [2]	340	540	860	1,330	1,960	2,780	3,830	5,170	6,840	8,910	11,490	43,710
31	Tax credits for clean vehicles [2]	10,560	15,570	23,580	28,930	30,260	26,230	14,340	4,670	-3,080	-11,320	-17,130	112,050
32	Tax credits for refueling property [2]	170	280	460	710	990	1,230	1,510	1,680	1,830	1,950	630	11,270

Table 20–1. ESTIMATES OF TOTAL INCOME TAX EXPENDITURES FOR 2023-2033[1] —Continued

(In millions of dollars)

		Total from corporations and individuals											
		2023	2024	2025	2026	2027	2028	2029	2030	2031	2032	2033	2024-2033
33	Allowance of deduction for certain energy efficient commercial building property	430	520	610	630	630	650	690	710	740	740	710	6,630
34	Credit for construction of new energy efficient homes	280	200	210	230	230	240	240	240	240	240	240	2,310
35	Credit for energy efficiency improvements to existing homes	1,970	1,580	1,500	1,420	1,350	1,280	1,220	1,160	1,100	1,050	700	12,360
36	Credit for residential energy efficient property	7,090	9,250	6,150	4,850	4,000	3,700	4,620	4,260	4,310	4,220	4,180	49,540
37	Advanced energy property credit [2]	260	1,170	1,560	1,010	970	1,090	920	190	150	260	110	7,430
38	Advanced manufacturing production credit [2]	430	790	1,330	1,940	2,620	6,990	9,710	9,290	6,850	2,980	1,840	44,340
Natural resources and environment:													
39	Expensing of exploration and development costs, nonfuel minerals	70	0	0	-10	10	30	40	40	30	30	30	200
40	Excess of percentage over cost depletion, nonfuel minerals	310	330	300	310	310	310	330	340	350	360	380	3,320
41	Exclusion of interest on bonds for water, sewage, and hazardous waste facilities	290	230	240	260	290	290	290	320	310	310	220	2,760
42	Capital gains treatment of certain timber income	150	150	160	180	200	210	220	230	240	250	270	2,110
43	Expensing of multiperiod timber growing costs	260	260	260	280	290	300	320	320	340	360	370	3,100
44	Tax incentives for preservation of historic structures	710	670	650	650	670	700	720	770	820	850	780	7,280
45	Carbon oxide sequestration credit [2]	330	400	510	680	1,500	2,230	2,670	4,840	7,070	7,960	8,290	36,150
46	Deduction for endangered species recovery expenditures	30	40	40	40	60	60	60	70	70	80	90	610
Agriculture:													
47	Expensing of certain capital outlays	120	120	120	140	150	150	150	140	140	140	150	1,400
48	Expensing of certain multiperiod production costs	250	260	270	310	330	330	330	320	320	320	330	3,120
49	Treatment of loans forgiven for solvent farmers	60	60	60	70	70	70	70	70	70	70	70	680
50	Capital gains treatment of certain agriculture income	1,550	1,530	1,590	1,770	1,970	2,070	2,180	2,280	2,400	2,530	2,660	20,980
51	Income averaging for farmers	210	210	220	230	230	230	230	230	230	230	230	2,270
52	Deferral of gain on sale of farm refiners	15	20	20	20	20	20	20	25	25	25	25	220
53	Expensing of reforestation expenditures	60	70	70	80	80	80	80	80	80	90	90	800
Commerce and housing:													
	Financial institutions and insurance:												
54	Exemption of credit union income	2,970	2,940	3,110	3,300	3,460	3,570	3,680	3,820	3,850	3,900	4,170	35,800
55	Exclusion of life insurance death benefits	15,320	16,260	16,670	17,360	18,320	18,610	19,020	19,510	19,980	20,430	20,880	187,040
56	Exemption or special alternative tax for small property and casualty insurance companies	1,400	1,430	1,470	1,510	1,540	1,560	1,590	1,630	1,670	1,710	1,750	15,860
57	Tax exemption of insurance income earned by tax-exempt organizations	370	380	390	390	400	410	420	430	430	440	440	4,130
58	Exclusion of interest spread of financial institutions	11,100	9,010	9,330	9,810	10,200	10,360	10,440	10,610	10,830	11,010	11,140	102,740
	Housing:												
59	Exclusion of interest on owner-occupied mortgage subsidy bonds	880	710	730	790	860	860	890	950	940	910	640	8,280
60	Exclusion of interest on rental housing bonds	1,610	1,300	1,350	1,460	1,580	1,590	1,630	1,750	1,730	1,670	1,160	15,220
61	Deductibility of mortgage interest on owner-occupied homes	31,820	30,770	30,920	67,280	87,740	91,630	95,620	99,780	104,210	108,570	111,950	828,470
62	Deductibility of State and local property tax on owner-occupied homes [6]	6,910	6,410	6,090	34,180	50,080	52,530	54,640	56,890	59,490	62,120	64,830	447,260

Table 20–1. ESTIMATES OF TOTAL INCOME TAX EXPENDITURES FOR 2023-2033[1] —Continued

(In millions of dollars)

		Total from corporations and individuals											
		2023	2024	2025	2026	2027	2028	2029	2030	2031	2032	2033	2024-2033
63	Deferral of income from installment sales	1,750	1,720	1,780	1,860	1,940	2,020	2,100	2,190	2,290	2,380	2,490	20,770
64	Capital gains exclusion on home sales	54,410	58,230	60,400	66,830	71,490	74,300	77,040	79,900	83,100	86,410	89,690	747,390
65	Exclusion of net imputed rental income	147,240	151,950	156,250	174,960	183,050	191,070	199,350	208,160	217,490	226,790	236,720	1,945,790
66	Exception from passive loss rules for $25,000 of rental loss	5,470	5,460	5,600	5,840	5,600	5,270	4,830	4,340	4,030	4,010	4,140	49,120
67	Credit for low-income housing investments	12,800	13,630	14,400	15,130	15,790	16,270	16,700	17,100	17,400	17,670	17,920	149,510
68	Accelerated depreciation on rental housing (normal tax method)	2,440	2,150	2,530	3,240	3,960	4,620	5,300	5,960	6,590	7,200	7,800	49,350
69	Discharge of mortgage indebtedness	220	140	140	50	0	0	0	0	0	0	0	330
	Commerce:												
70	Discharge of business indebtedness	-10	10	40	60	70	60	50	40	20	20	30	400
71	Exceptions from imputed interest rules	60	70	70	80	80	80	80	80	80	90	90	800
72	Treatment of qualified dividends	35,880	38,390	39,990	44,470	49,190	51,470	53,730	56,150	58,710	61,380	64,170	517,650
73	Capital gains (except agriculture, timber, iron ore, and coal)	115,630	114,130	118,590	132,180	146,890	154,710	162,580	170,590	179,150	188,540	198,600	1,565,960
74	Capital gains exclusion of small corporation stock	1,780	1,850	1,930	2,000	2,070	2,150	2,240	2,330	2,430	2,530	2,640	22,170
75	Step-up basis of capital gains at death	49,240	33,560	35,940	38,960	44,060	48,230	52,300	56,600	61,240	66,620	72,070	509,580
76	Carryover basis of capital gains on gifts	4,590	4,130	4,470	5,720	6,890	6,860	6,790	6,890	7,170	7,800	8,830	65,550
77	Ordinary income treatment of loss from small business corporation stock sale	70	80	80	80	80	80	90	90	90	90	100	860
78	Deferral of capital gains from like-kind exchanges	4,020	4,230	5,430	5,569	4,870	5,130	5,380	5,640	5,940	6,240	6,440	54,869
79	Depreciation of buildings other than rental housing (normal tax method)	920	-190	-390	-400	-360	-130	220	740	970	1,300	1,610	3,370
80	Accelerated depreciation of machinery and equipment (normal tax method)	10,430	-3,730	-11,580	-18,420	-25,860	-17,160	-4,110	3,770	8,800	12,180	14,790	-41,320
81	Exclusion of interest on small issue bonds	60	60	60	70	70	70	70	70	70	70	50	660
82	Special rules for certain film and TV production	100	180	240	-380	-520	-250	-120	-50	-20	0	0	-920
83	Allow 20-percent deduction to certain pass-through income	37,240	61,850	65,180	27,000	0	0	0	0	0	0	0	154,030
84	Advanced manufacturing investment credit [2]	190	3,630	3,830	4,080	2,820	2,860	2,610	2,590	1,950	1,350	1,010	26,730
Transportation:													
85	Tonnage tax	100	100	100	100	100	110	110	110	110	110	120	1,070
86	Deferral of tax on shipping companies	10	10	10	10	10	10	10	10	10	10	10	100
87	Exclusion of reimbursed employee parking expenses	1,827	1,890	1,957	2,025	2,116	2,211	2,311	2,415	2,523	2,637	2,756	22,841
88	Exclusion for employer-provided transit passes	369	381	394	408	431	455	479	506	534	563	594	4,745
89	Tax credit for certain expenditures for maintaining railroad tracks	130	80	60	40	30	30	20	10	10	0	0	280
90	Exclusion of interest on bonds for Highway Projects and rail-truck transfer facilities	140	140	130	130	120	110	110	100	100	80	80	1,100
Community and regional development:													
91	Exclusion of interest for airport, dock, and similar bonds	1,050	840	870	950	1,020	1,030	1,060	1,130	1,120	1,080	750	9,850
92	Exemption of certain mutuals' and cooperatives' income	100	100	110	110	110	110	120	120	120	120	130	1,150
93	Empowerment zones	90	90	100	80	60	40	20	20	20	20	10	460
94	New markets tax credit	1,210	1,250	1,310	1,360	1,340	1,230	1,060	870	640	410	160	9,630
95	Credit to holders of Gulf and Midwest Tax Credit Bonds	100	80	80	80	80	70	60	60	50	30	20	610

Table 20–1. ESTIMATES OF TOTAL INCOME TAX EXPENDITURES FOR 2023-2033[1] —Continued

(In millions of dollars)

		Total from corporations and individuals											
		2023	2024	2025	2026	2027	2028	2029	2030	2031	2032	2033	2024-2033
96	Recovery Zone Bonds [2]	90	70	70	70	70	60	60	50	40	30	10	530
97	Tribal Economic Development Bonds	10	10	10	10	10	10	10	10	10	10	10	100
98	Opportunity Zones	2,080	2,160	1,990	-6,400	-12,400	670	880	1,130	1,320	1,550	1,650	-7,450
99	Disaster employee retention credit	50	40	40	20	20	20	10	10	10	10	10	190
Education, training, employment, and social services:													
	Education:												
100	Exclusion of scholarship and fellowship income (normal tax method)	4,430	4,670	4,920	5,440	6,200	6,530	6,850	7,220	7,610	8,010	8,430	65,880
101	Tax credits for post-secondary education expenses [2]	13,940	13,860	13,660	13,390	13,270	13,030	12,790	12,490	12,220	11,910	11,600	128,220
102	Deductibility of student-loan interest	560	940	2,490	2,690	3,110	3,160	3,290	3,320	3,400	3,420	3,450	29,270
103	Qualified tuition programs (includes Education IRA)	3,020	3,350	3,800	4,630	5,570	6,660	8,120	10,090	12,740	16,260	20,940	92,160
104	Exclusion of interest on student-loan bonds	150	130	120	140	150	150	160	170	170	160	110	1,460
105	Exclusion of interest on bonds for private nonprofit educational facilities	2,280	1,850	1,900	2,070	2,230	2,250	2,310	2,480	2,440	2,370	1,650	21,550
106	Credit for holders of zone academy bonds [2]	90	80	60	50	50	40	40	40	30	30	30	450
107	Exclusion of interest on savings bonds redeemed to finance educational expenses	40	40	40	50	50	50	50	50	50	60	60	500
108	Parental personal exemption for students age 19 or over	2,210	3,280	3,200	6,110	7,550	7,480	7,470	7,410	7,300	7,220	7,170	64,190
109	Deductibility of charitable contributions to educational institutions	6,230	6,290	6,300	7,360	10,350	11,050	11,850	12,170	12,580	13,060	13,560	104,570
110	Exclusion of employer-provided educational assistance	1,660	1,770	1,880	1,660	1,570	1,650	1,730	1,820	1,920	2,010	2,100	18,110
111	Special deduction for teacher expenses	160	160	160	170	190	190	210	230	190	200	200	1,900
112	Discharge of student loan indebtedness	100	110	130	150	170	200	240	280	320	380	440	2,420
113	Qualified school construction bonds [2]	490	470	440	410	390	360	330	320	290	260	240	3,510
	Training, employment, and social services:												
114	Work opportunity tax credit	2,070	2,130	2,200	1,400	520	340	260	190	150	110	80	7,380
115	Employer provided child care exclusion	760	840	910	1,180	1,330	1,380	1,440	1,500	1,560	1,620	1,670	13,430
116	Employer-provided child care credit	20	20	20	20	20	20	30	40	40	40	40	290
117	Assistance for adopted foster children	880	940	1,000	1,040	1,100	1,170	1,270	1,340	1,330	1,530	1,620	12,340
118	Adoption credit and exclusion	870	900	920	930	940	950	960	970	980	990	990	9,530
119	Exclusion of employee meals and lodging (other than military)	7,530	6,960	6,900	8,140	8,890	9,190	9,520	9,850	9,190	10,510	10,870	90,020
120	Credit for child and dependent care expenses [2]	3,480	3,690	3,850	3,920	3,950	3,980	4,010	4,040	4,070	4,100	4,120	39,730
121	Credit for disabled access expenditures	10	10	10	10	10	10	10	10	10	10	10	100
122	Deductibility of charitable contributions, other than education and health	47,410	47,940	48,030	56,740	81,110	86,690	92,850	98,230	104,630	111,540	118,910	846,670
123	Exclusion of certain foster care payments	500	530	560	590	640	700	780	870	970	1,100	1,270	8,010
124	Exclusion of parsonage allowances	959	1,009	1,058	1,118	1,177	1,246	1,305	1,375	1,444	1,523	1,602	12,857
125	Indian employment credit	30	30	20	20	20	20	0	0	0	0	0	110
126	Employer-provided paid family and medical leave credit	70	90	90	50	10	0	0	0	0	0	0	240
Health:													
127	Exclusion of employer contributions for medical insurance premiums and medical care [7]	215,860	231,010	246,510	289,890	321,980	340,080	359,210	379,310	400,400	422,430	445,530	3,436,350

Table 20–1. ESTIMATES OF TOTAL INCOME TAX EXPENDITURES FOR 2023-2033[1] —Continued

(In millions of dollars)

	Total from corporations and individuals											
	2023	2024	2025	2026	2027	2028	2029	2030	2031	2032	2033	2024-2033
128 Self-employed medical insurance premiums	8,150	8,520	9,030	11,210	12,990	14,060	15,040	16,290	17,610	18,790	19,770	143,310
129 Medical Savings Accounts / Health Savings Accounts	12,830	13,610	14,180	16,270	17,690	18,260	18,820	19,500	20,190	20,820	21,540	180,880
130 Deductibility of medical expenses	12,260	12,900	13,550	18,620	22,370	24,140	25,910	27,850	30,040	32,460	35,100	242,940
131 Exclusion of interest on hospital construction bonds	3,120	2,530	2,600	2,830	3,050	3,080	3,160	3,390	3,350	3,240	2,260	29,490
132 Refundable Premium Assistance Tax Credit [2]	15,047	14,935	15,413	12,440	10,816	10,684	10,507	10,913	11,914	12,707	13,277	123,606
133 Credit for employee health insurance expenses of small business	10	10	0	0	0	0	0	0	0	0	0	10
134 Deductibility of charitable contributions to health institutions	9,000	9,060	9,050	10,110	13,340	14,250	15,220	16,090	17,080	18,180	19,350	141,730
135 Tax credit for orphan drug research	1,740	1,940	2,160	2,420	2,700	3,020	3,370	3,770	4,210	4,700	5,250	33,540
136 Special Blue Cross/Blue Shield tax benefits	370	380	400	420	450	470	500	530	570	610	650	4,980
137 Distributions from retirement plans for premiums for health and long-term care insurance	470	490	500	590	630	650	660	670	670	680	690	6,230
138 Credit for family and sick leave taken by self-employed individuals [2]	520	0	0	0	0	0	0	0	0	0	0	0
Income security:												
139 Child credit [2]	67,520	63,740	65,370	45,890	15,780	15,390	14,990	14,540	14,050	13,560	13,110	276,420
140 Other Dependent Tax Credit												
141 Exclusion of railroad retirement (Social Security equivalent) benefits	300	280	260	270	270	250	220	200	160	130	90	2,130
142 Exclusion of workers' compensation benefits	8,870	8,870	8,870	8,860	8,860	8,850	8,850	8,850	8,840	8,840	8,840	88,530
143 Exclusion of public assistance benefits (normal tax method)	760	720	720	770	800	830	850	840	890	920	970	8,310
144 Exclusion of special benefits for disabled coal miners	20	20	20	20	10	10	10	10	10	10	10	130
145 Exclusion of military disability pensions	200	210	210	240	260	260	270	280	280	290	300	2,600
Net exclusion of pension contributions and earnings:												
146 Defined benefit employer plans	70,100	68,860	68,880	77,890	77,310	76,940	76,680	77,780	77,950	77,510	76,910	756,710
147 Defined contribution employer plans	133,860	136,290	141,780	170,240	177,930	186,430	195,500	205,940	218,260	229,800	242,050	1,904,220
148 Individual Retirement Accounts	32,690	33,210	34,470	41,470	43,930	46,180	48,460	51,170	54,430	58,190	62,140	473,650
149 Low and moderate income savers credit	1,860	1,990	1,970	2,140	2,100	4,170	4,160	4,090	4,120	4,060	4,020	32,820
150 Self-Employed plans	43,180	43,960	45,730	54,910	57,390	60,130	63,060	66,430	70,400	74,120	78,080	614,210
151 Small employer pension plan startup credit	0	0	320	380	360	310	280	230	180	130	130	2,320
Exclusion of other employee benefits:												
152 Premiums on group term life insurance	3,440	3,500	3,610	4,100	4,360	4,500	4,650	4,810	4,970	5,130	5,300	44,930
153 Premiums on accident and disability insurance	1,720	1,730	1,760	1,970	2,060	2,100	2,140	2,190	2,230	2,280	2,320	20,780
154 Income of trusts to finance supplementary unemployment benefits	40	50	50	50	50	50	50	60	60	60	60	540
155 Income of trusts to finance voluntary employee benefits associations	1,500	1,560	1,630	1,700	1,770	1,850	1,930	2,010	2,100	2,200	2,290	19,040
156 Special Employee Stock Ownership Plan (ESOP) rules	220	220	230	230	240	240	260	270	270	280	290	2,530
157 Additional deduction for the blind	50	50	60	50	50	50	60	60	60	60	70	570
158 Additional deduction for the elderly	7,540	8,070	8,650	7,460	7,810	8,280	8,780	9,290	9,500	9,980	10,480	88,300
159 Deductibility of casualty losses	0	0	0	680	1,040	1,090	1,140	1,190	1,260	1,310	1,360	9,070
160 Earned income tax credit [2]	2,700	3,030	3,180	3,290	5,020	5,220	5,410	5,550	5,760	5,990	6,170	48,620
161 Recovery rebate credits [2]	3,460	990	220	0	0	0	0	0	0	0	0	1,210

Table 20–1. ESTIMATES OF TOTAL INCOME TAX EXPENDITURES FOR 2023-2033[1] —Continued

(In millions of dollars)

	Total from corporations and individuals											
	2023	2024	2025	2026	2027	2028	2029	2030	2031	2032	2033	2024-2033
Social Security:												
Exclusion of social security benefits:												
162 Social Security benefits for retired and disabled workers and spouses, dependents and survivors	30,700	30,810	30,440	34,430	39,930	41,350	42,850	44,380	46,220	48,170	50,150	408,730
163 Credit for certain employer contributions to social security	1,520	1,610	1,700	1,790	1,880	1,970	2,060	2,150	2,240	2,330	2,420	20,150
Veterans benefits and services:												
164 Exclusion of veterans death benefits and disability compensation	11,640	13,120	14,040	15,200	17,380	18,120	18,840	19,600	20,430	21,290	22,160	180,180
165 Exclusion of veterans pensions	220	210	200	210	220	220	210	210	210	200	200	2,090
166 Exclusion of GI bill benefits	1,460	1,510	1,560	1,650	1,850	1,890	1,930	1,970	2,010	2,050	2,090	18,510
167 Exclusion of interest on veterans housing bonds	80	60	70	80	80	80	80	90	80	80	50	750
General purpose fiscal assistance:												
168 Exclusion of interest on public purpose State and local bonds	29,810	24,120	24,880	27,000	29,140	29,450	30,180	32,320	32,000	30,900	21,590	281,580
169 Build America Bonds [2]	0	0	0	0	0	0	0	0	0	0	0	0
170 Deductibility of nonbusiness State and local taxes other than on owner-occupied homes [6]	7,030	6,580	6,090	65,920	91,280	92,130	96,490	101,330	106,750	112,220	117,920	796,710
Interest:												
171 Deferral of interest on U.S. savings bonds	820	810	800	800	790	780	770	760	750	750	740	7,750
Addendum: Aid to State and local governments:												
Deductibility of:												
Property taxes on owner-occupied homes	6,910	6,410	6,090	34,180	50,080	52,530	54,640	56,890	59,490	62,120	64,830	447,260
Nonbusiness State and local taxes other than on owner-occupied homes	7,030	6,580	6,090	65,920	91,280	92,130	96,490	101,330	106,750	112,220	117,920	796,710
Exclusion of interest on State and local bonds for:												
Public purposes	29,810	24,120	24,880	27,000	29,140	29,450	30,180	32,320	32,000	30,900	21,590	281,580
Energy facilities	0	0	0	0	10	10	10	10	10	10	0	60
Water, sewage, and hazardous waste disposal facilities	290	230	240	260	290	290	290	320	310	310	220	2,760
Small-issues	60	60	60	70	70	70	70	70	70	70	50	660
Owner-occupied mortgage subsidies	880	710	730	790	860	860	890	950	940	910	640	8,280
Rental housing	1,610	1,300	1,350	1,460	1,580	1,590	1,630	1,750	1,730	1,670	1,160	15,220
Airports, docks, and similar facilities	1,050	840	870	950	1,020	1,030	1,060	1,130	1,120	1,080	750	9,850
Student loans	150	130	120	140	150	150	160	170	170	160	110	1,460
Private nonprofit educational facilities	2,280	1,850	1,900	2,070	2,230	2,250	2,310	2,480	2,440	2,370	1,650	21,550
Hospital construction	3,120	2,530	2,600	2,830	3,050	3,080	3,160	3,390	3,350	3,240	2,260	29,490
Veterans' housing	80	60	70	80	80	80	80	90	80	80	50	750

[1] All years referenced are fiscal years.

[2] See Table 20-4 for outlay estimates.

[3] The alternative fuel mixture credit results in a reduction in excise tax receipts (in millions of dollars) as follows: 2023 $810; 2024 $750; 2025 $520; and $0 thereafter.

[4] In addition, the biodiesel producer tax credit results in a reduction in excise tax receipts (in millions of dollars) as follows: 2023 $4,170; 2024 $3,690; 2025 $1,950; and $0 thereafter.

[5] In addition, the sustainable aviation fuel tax credit results in a reduction in excise tax receipts (in millions of dollars) as follows: 2023 $0; 2024 $270; 2025 $130; 2026 $80; 2027 $50; and $0 thereafter.

[6] Because of interactions with the $10,000 cap on state and local tax deductions for the years 2018 through 2025, these estimates understate the combined effects of repealing deductions for both property taxes on owner occupied housing and other non-business taxes. The estimate of repealing both is (in millions of dollars): 2023 $21,300; 2024 $20,780; 2025 $19,830; 2026 $100,470; 2027 $137,230; 2028 $139,780; 2029 $145,830; 2030 $152,440; 2031 $159,920; 2032 $167,440; and 2033 $175,180.

[7] In addition, the employer contributions for health have effects on payroll tax receipts (in millions of dollars) as follows: 2023 $127,310; 2024 $138,340; 2025 $148,040; 2026 $156,990; 2027 $166,080; 2028 $175,030; 2029 $184,190; 2030 $193,780; 2031 $203,560; 2032 $213,880; and 2033 $224,760..

Table 20–2. INCOME TAX EXPENDITURES RANKED BY TOTAL 2024–2033 PROJECTED REVENUE EFFECT [1]

(In millions of dollars)

	Provision	2023	2024	2024–33
127	Exclusion of employer contributions for medical insurance premiums and medical care [7]	215,860	231,010	3,436,350
65	Exclusion of net imputed rental income	147,240	151,950	1,945,790
147	Defined contribution employer plans	133,860	136,290	1,904,220
73	Capital gains (except agriculture, timber, iron ore, and coal)	115,630	114,130	1,565,960
122	Deductibility of charitable contributions, other than education and health	47,410	47,940	846,670
61	Deductibility of mortgage interest on owner-occupied homes	31,820	30,770	828,470
170	Deductibility of nonbusiness State and local taxes other than on owner-occupied homes [6]	7,030	6,580	796,710
146	Defined benefit employer plans	70,100	68,860	756,710
64	Capital gains exclusion on home sales	54,410	58,230	747,390
150	Self-Employed plans	43,180	43,960	614,210
72	Treatment of qualified dividends	35,880	38,390	517,650
75	Step-up basis of capital gains at death	49,240	33,560	509,580
148	Individual Retirement Accounts	32,690	33,210	473,650
4	Reduced tax rate on active income of controlled foreign corporations (normal tax method)	45,190	46,540	467,420
62	Deductibility of State and local property tax on owner-occupied homes [6]	6,910	6,410	447,260
162	Social Security benefits for retired and disabled workers and spouses, dependents and survivors	30,700	30,810	408,730
8	Credit for increasing research activities	28,220	30,040	388,650
168	Exclusion of interest on public purpose State and local bonds	29,810	24,120	281,580
22	Energy production credit [2]	7,450	7,570	276,610
139	Child credit [2]	67,520	63,740	276,420
130	Deductibility of medical expenses	12,260	12,900	242,940
55	Exclusion of life insurance death benefits	15,320	16,260	187,040
1	Exclusion of benefits and allowances to armed forces personnel	15,990	16,600	182,420
129	Medical Savings Accounts / Health Savings Accounts	12,830	13,610	180,880
164	Exclusion of veterans death benefits and disability compensation	11,640	13,120	180,180
83	Allow 20-percent deduction to certain pass-through income	37,240	61,850	154,030
67	Credit for low-income housing investments	12,800	13,630	149,510
23	Energy investment credit [2]	25,970	27,510	148,020
128	Self-employed medical insurance premiums	8,150	8,520	143,310
134	Deductibility of charitable contributions to health institutions	9,000	9,060	141,730
101	Tax credits for post-secondary education expenses [2]	13,940	13,860	128,220
132	Refundable Premium Assistance Tax Credit [2]	15,047	14,935	123,606
5	Deduction for foreign-derived intangible income derived from trade or business within the United States	15,240	15,690	120,340
31	Tax credits for clean vehicles [2]	10,560	15,570	112,050
109	Deductibility of charitable contributions to educational institutions	6,230	6,290	104,570
58	Exclusion of interest spread of financial institutions	11,100	9,010	102,740
103	Qualified tuition programs (includes Education IRA)	3,020	3,350	92,160
119	Exclusion of employee meals and lodging (other than military)	7,530	6,960	90,020
142	Exclusion of workers' compensation benefits	8,870	8,870	88,530
158	Additional deduction for the elderly	7,540	8,070	88,300
100	Exclusion of scholarship and fellowship income (normal tax method)	4,430	4,670	65,880
76	Carryover basis of capital gains on gifts	4,590	4,130	65,550
108	Parental personal exemption for students age 19 or over	2,210	3,280	64,190
2	Exclusion of income earned abroad by U.S. citizens	5,420	5,600	62,210
78	Deferral of capital gains from like-kind exchanges	4,020	4,230	54,869
36	Credit for residential energy efficient property	7,090	9,250	49,540
68	Accelerated depreciation on rental housing (normal tax method)	2,440	2,150	49,350
66	Exception from passive loss rules for $25,000 of rental loss	5,470	5,460	49,120
160	Earned income tax credit [2]	2,700	3,030	48,620
152	Premiums on group term life insurance	3,440	3,500	44,930
38	Advanced manufacturing production credit [2]	430	790	44,340
30	Clean hydrogen production credit [2]	340	540	43,710
120	Credit for child and dependent care expenses [2]	3,480	3,690	39,730
45	Carbon oxide sequestration credit [2]	330	400	36,150
54	Exemption of credit union income	2,970	2,940	35,800
135	Tax credit for orphan drug research	1,740	1,940	33,540

Table 20–2. INCOME TAX EXPENDITURES RANKED BY TOTAL 2024–2033 PROJECTED REVENUE EFFECT[1] —Continued

(In millions of dollars)

	Provision	2023	2024	2024–33
149	Low and moderate income savers credit	1,860	1,990	32,820
131	Exclusion of interest on hospital construction bonds	3,120	2,530	29,490
102	Deductibility of student-loan interest	560	940	29,270
6	Interest Charge Domestic International Sales Corporations (IC-DISCs)	1,620	1,690	23,340
87	Exclusion of reimbursed employee parking expenses	1,827	1,890	22,841
74	Capital gains exclusion of small corporation stock	1,780	1,850	22,170
105	Exclusion of interest on bonds for private nonprofit educational facilities	2,280	1,850	21,550
50	Capital gains treatment of certain agriculture income	1,550	1,530	20,980
153	Premiums on accident and disability insurance	1,720	1,730	20,780
63	Deferral of income from installment sales	1,750	1,720	20,770
163	Credit for certain employer contributions to social security	1,520	1,610	20,150
29	Clean fuel production credit [2, 5]	0	0	19,050
155	Income of trusts to finance voluntary employee benefits associations	1,500	1,560	19,040
166	Exclusion of GI bill benefits	1,460	1,510	18,510
110	Exclusion of employer-provided educational assistance	1,660	1,770	18,110
11	Excess of percentage over cost depletion, oil and gas	1,530	1,590	15,970
56	Exemption or special alternative tax for small property and casualty insurance companies	1,400	1,430	15,860
60	Exclusion of interest on rental housing bonds	1,610	1,300	15,220
115	Employer provided child care exclusion	760	840	13,430
124	Exclusion of parsonage allowances	959	1,009	12,857
35	Credit for energy efficiency improvements to existing homes	1,970	1,580	12,360
117	Assistance for adopted foster children	880	940	12,340
32	Tax credits for refueling property [2]	170	280	11,270
91	Exclusion of interest for airport, dock, and similar bonds	1,050	840	9,850
94	New markets tax credit	1,210	1,250	9,630
118	Adoption credit and exclusion	870	900	9,530
159	Deductibility of casualty losses	0	0	9,070
143	Exclusion of public assistance benefits (normal tax method)	760	720	8,310
59	Exclusion of interest on owner-occupied mortgage subsidy bonds	880	710	8,280
123	Exclusion of certain foster care payments	500	530	8,010
171	Deferral of interest on U.S. savings bonds	820	810	7,750
37	Advanced energy property credit [2]	260	1,170	7,430
114	Work opportunity tax credit	2,070	2,130	7,380
44	Tax incentives for preservation of historic structures	710	670	7,280
33	Allowance of deduction for certain energy efficient commercial building property	430	520	6,630
137	Distributions from retirement plans for premiums for health and long-term care insurance	470	490	6,230
136	Special Blue Cross/Blue Shield tax benefits	370	380	4,980
88	Exclusion for employer-provided transit passes	369	381	4,745
57	Tax exemption of insurance income earned by tax-exempt organizations	370	380	4,130
3	Exclusion of certain allowances for Federal employees abroad	280	300	3,820
113	Qualified school construction bonds [2]	490	470	3,510
79	Depreciation of buildings other than rental housing (normal tax method)	920	–190	3,370
40	Excess of percentage over cost depletion, nonfuel minerals	310	330	3,320
25	Zero-emission nuclear power production credit [2]	0	0	3,170
48	Expensing of certain multiperiod production costs	250	260	3,120
43	Expensing of multiperiod timber growing costs	260	260	3,100
41	Exclusion of interest on bonds for water, sewage, and hazardous waste facilities	290	230	2,760
145	Exclusion of military disability pensions	200	210	2,600
156	Special Employee Stock Ownership Plan (ESOP) rules	220	220	2,530
112	Discharge of student loan indebtedness	100	110	2,420
151	Small employer pension plan startup credit	0	0	2,320
34	Credit for construction of new energy efficient homes	280	200	2,310
51	Income averaging for farmers	210	210	2,270
141	Exclusion of railroad retirement (Social Security equivalent) benefits	300	280	2,130
42	Capital gains treatment of certain timber income	150	150	2,110
165	Exclusion of veterans pensions	220	210	2,090
24	Advanced nuclear power production credit	30	150	2,060
9	Expensing of exploration and development costs, oil and gas	700	70	2,020

Table 20–2. INCOME TAX EXPENDITURES RANKED BY TOTAL 2024–2033 PROJECTED REVENUE EFFECT[1] —Continued

(In millions of dollars)

	Provision	2023	2024	2024–33
111	Special deduction for teacher expenses	160	160	1,900
26	Reduced tax rate for nuclear decommissioning funds	120	120	1,500
16	Amortize all geological and geophysical expenditures over 2 years	140	150	1,460
104	Exclusion of interest on student-loan bonds	150	130	1,460
47	Expensing of certain capital outlays	120	120	1,400
12	Excess of percentage over cost depletion, coal	90	90	1,230
161	Recovery rebate credits [2]	3,460	990	1,210
92	Exemption of certain mutuals' and cooperatives' income	100	100	1,150
90	Exclusion of interest on bonds for Highway Projects and rail-truck transfer facilities	140	140	1,100
85	Tonnage tax	100	100	1,070
15	Marginal wells credit	190	180	1,000
77	Ordinary income treatment of loss from small business corporation stock sale	70	80	860
53	Expensing of reforestation expenditures	60	70	800
71	Exceptions from imputed interest rules	60	70	800
167	Exclusion of interest on veterans housing bonds	80	60	750
21	Credit for holding clean renewable energy bonds [2]	70	70	700
49	Treatment of loans forgiven for solvent farmers	60	60	680
81	Exclusion of interest on small issue bonds	60	60	660
46	Deduction for endangered species recovery expenditures	30	40	610
95	Credit to holders of Gulf and Midwest Tax Credit Bonds.	100	80	610
157	Additional deduction for the blind	50	50	570
154	Income of trusts to finance supplementary unemployment benefits	40	50	540
96	Recovery Zone Bonds [2]	90	70	530
17	Capital gains treatment of royalties on coal	50	50	510
107	Exclusion of interest on savings bonds redeemed to finance educational expenses	40	40	500
93	Empowerment zones	90	90	460
106	Credit for holders of zone academy bonds [2]	90	80	450
70	Discharge of business indebtedness	–10	10	400
20	Exclusion of utility conservation subsidies	50	50	330
69	Discharge of mortgage indebtedness	220	140	330
19	Qualified energy conservation bonds [2]	30	30	300
116	Employer-provided child care credit	20	20	290
89	Tax credit for certain expenditures for maintaining railroad tracks	130	80	280
52	Deferral of gain on sale of farm refiners	15	20	220
39	Expensing of exploration and development costs, nonfuel minerals	70	0	200
99	Disaster employee retention credit	50	40	190
10	Expensing of exploration and development costs, coal	50	0	170
144	Exclusion of special benefits for disabled coal miners	20	20	130
125	Indian employment credit	30	30	110
13	Exception from passive loss limitation for working interests in oil and gas properties	10	10	100
86	Deferral of tax on shipping companies	10	10	100
97	Tribal Economic Development Bonds	10	10	100
121	Credit for disabled access expenditures	10	10	100
18	Exclusion of interest on energy facility bonds	0	0	60
27	Alcohol fuel credits [3]	20	20	20
28	Bio-Diesel and small agri-biodiesel producer tax credits [4]	20	20	20
133	Credit for employee health insurance expenses of small business	10	10	10
14	Enhanced oil recovery credit	0	0	0
138	Credit for family and sick leave taken by self-employed individuals [2]	520	0	0
140	Other Dependent Tax Credit	0	0	0
169	Build America Bonds [2]	0	0	0
82	Special rules for certain film and TV production	100	180	–920
98	Opportunity Zones	2,080	2,160	–7,450
80	Accelerated depreciation of machinery and equipment (normal tax method)	10,430	–3,730	–41,320
7	Expensing of research and experimentation expenditures (normal tax method)	–38,660	–28,850	–52,400

Note:See Table 20–1 footnotes for specific table information.

Table 20–3. PRESENT VALUE OF SELECTED TAX EXPENDITURES FOR ACTIVITY IN CALENDAR YEAR 2023

(In millions of dollars)

	Provision	2023 Present Value of Revenue Loss
9	Expensing of exploration and development costs, oil and gas	870
10	Expensing of exploration and development costs, coal	80
39	Expensing of exploration and development costs, nonfuel minerals	80
43	Expensing of multiperiod timber growing costs	220
48	Expensing of certain multiperiod production costs	160
47	Expensing of certain capital outlays - agriculture	70
54	Expensing of reforestation expenditures	50
68	Accelerated depreciation on rental housing	4,380
79	Depreciation of buildings other than rental	2,100
80	Accelerated depreciation of machinery and equipment	27,760
67	Credit for low-income housing investments	12,790
103	Qualified tuition programs	8,690
146	Defined benefit employer plans	82,853
147	Defined contribution employer plans	198,720
148	Exclusion of IRA contributions and earnings	2,530
	Exclusion of Roth earnings and distributions	650
	Exclusion of non-deductible IRA earnings	550
152	Exclusion of contributions and earnings for Self-Employed plans	8,330
167	Exclusion of interest on public purpose State and local bonds	21,720
	Exclusion of interest on non-public purpose bonds [1]	7,640
170	Deferral of interest on U.S. savings bonds	240

[1] Includes all components, other than public purpose, listed under 'Exclusion of interest on State and local bonds' in the Addendum to Table 20–1.

Table 20-4. ESTIMATES OF OUTLAY TAX EXPENDITURES FOR 2023-2033 [1]

(In millions of dollars)

	Total											
	2023	2024	2025	2026	2027	2028	2029	2030	2031	2032	2033	2024-2033
Energy:												
19 Qualified energy conservation bonds [2]	40	30	30	30	30	30	30	30	30	30	30	300
21 Credit for holding clean renewable energy bonds [2]	40	40	40	40	40	40	40	40	40	40	40	400
22 Energy production credit [2]	0	390	400	570	840	1,180	1,520	1,790	2,060	2,360	2,490	13,600
23 Energy investment credit [2]	0	1,600	1,260	790	700	810	650	580	950	590	630	8,560
25 Zero-emission nuclear power production credit [2]	0	0	0	0	0	0	0	20	90	190	90	390
29 Clean fuel production credit [2,4]	0	0	240	330	340	90	0	0	0	0	0	1,000
30 Clean hydrogen production credit [2]	0	310	610	950	1,390	1,960	2,690	3,630	4,780	6,510	8,480	31,310
31 Tax credits for clean vehicles [2]	0	1,150	2,210	3,330	4,640	5,720	7,470	8,610	9,830	11,030	4,690	58,680
32 Tax credits for refueling property [2]	0	0	0	0	10	10	10	10	10	10	0	60
37 Advanced energy property credit [2]	0	30	70	80	50	50	60	40	0	10	10	400
38 Advanced manufacturing production credit [2]	0	5,840	8,420	13,560	19,270	24,510	26,030	27,090	23,390	19,060	11,100	178,270
Natural resources and environment:												
45 Carbon oxide sequestration credit [2]	0	190	350	470	1,100	1,600	1,840	3,490	5,030	5,700	5,900	25,670
84 Advanced manufacturing investment credit [2]	0	1,910	1,970	2,080	1,400	1,340	1,120	1,100	860	720	560	13,060
96 Recovery Zone Bonds [2]	60	60	60	60	60	60	60	50	50	50	50	560
Education:												
101 Tax credits for post-secondary education expenses [2]	2,490	2,560	2,480	2,430	2,390	2,350	2,310	2,270	2,230	2,180	2,130	23,330
106 Credit for holders of zone academy bonds [2]	40	40	40	40	40	40	40	40	40	40	40	400
113 Qualified school construction bonds [2]	560	555	550	550	545	540	540	535	530	560	550	5,455
Training, employment, and social services:												
120 Credit for child and dependent care expenses [2]	50	0	0	0	0	0	0	0	0	0	0	0
Health:												
132 Refundable Premium Assistance Tax Credit [2]	66,670	66,620	68,680	60,590	59,710	62,150	64,730	67,810	75,290	80,200	84,170	689,950
138 Credit for family and sick leave taken by self-employed individuals [2]	130	0	0	0	0	0	0	0	0	0	0	0
Income security:												
139 Child credit [2]	40,840	45,190	44,040	42,790	24,010	23,910	23,890	24,060	24,360	24,740	25,050	302,040
159 Earned income tax credit [2]	59,780	67,180	67,480	67,180	67,030	68,370	69,990	72,000	74,430	76,880	79,390	709,930
160 Recovery rebate credits [2]	2,150	590	130	0	0	0	0	0	0	0	0	720
General purpose fiscal assistance:												
168 Build America Bonds [2]	2170	2150	2120	2010	1980	1960	1940	1910	1890	1870	1850	19,680

[1] All years referenced are fiscal years.

[2] See Table 20-1 for corresponding revenue loss estimates.

21. FEDERAL BORROWING AND DEBT

Debt is the largest legally and contractually binding obligation of the Federal Government. At the end of 2023, the Government owed $26,236 billion of principal to the individuals and institutions who had loaned it the money to fund past deficits. During that year, the Government paid the public approximately $710 billion of interest on this debt.[1] At the same time, the Government also held financial assets, net of financial liabilities other than debt, of $2,508 billion. Therefore, debt held by the public net of financial assets was $23,728 billion.

The $26,236 billion debt held by the public at the end of 2023 represents an increase of $1,982 billion over the level at the end of 2022. This increase is the result of the $1,694 billion deficit in 2023 and other financing transactions (discussed in more detail below) that increased the need to borrow by $288 billion. Debt held by the public as a percent of Gross Domestic Product (GDP) grew from 97.0 percent of at the end of 2022 to 97.3 percent of GDP at the end of 2023. The deficit is estimated to increase to $1,859 billion in 2024 and then to fall to $1,781 billion in 2025. After 2025, the deficit is projected to somewhat decrease and then remain relatively stable at 4-5 percent of GDP. Debt held by the public is projected to grow to $28,156 billion (99.6 percent of GDP) at the end of 2024 and $29,984 billion (102.2 percent of GDP) at the end of 2025. After 2025, debt held by the public as a percent of GDP is projected to continue to gradually increase through 2029, and then remain around 106 percent of GDP. Debt net of financial assets is expected to grow to $25,587 billion (90.6 percent of GDP) at the end of 2024 and $27,370 billion (93.3 percent of GDP) at the end of 2025. After 2025, debt net of financial assets is projected to gradually increase and then to remain fairly stable at around 98 percent of GDP.

Trends in Debt Since World War II

Table 21–1 depicts trends in Federal debt held by the public from World War II to the present and estimates from the present through 2034. (It is supplemented for earlier years by Tables 7.1–7.3 in the Budget's *Historical Tables*, available as supplemental budget material.[2]) Federal debt peaked at 106.1 percent of GDP in 1946, just after the end of the war. From that point until the 1970s, Federal debt as a percentage of GDP decreased almost every year because of relatively small deficits, an expanding economy, and unanticipated inflation. With households borrowing large amounts to buy homes and consumer durables, and with businesses borrowing large amounts to buy plant and equipment, Federal debt also decreased almost every year as a percentage of total credit market debt outstanding. The cumulative effect was impressive. From 1950 to 1975, debt held by the public declined from 78.6 percent of GDP to 24.6 percent, and from 53.3 percent of credit market debt to 17.8 percent. Despite rising interest rates during this period, interest outlays became a smaller share of the budget and were roughly stable as a percentage of GDP.

Federal debt relative to GDP is a function of the Nation's fiscal policy as well as overall economic conditions. During the 1970s, large budget deficits emerged as spending grew faster than receipts and as the economy was disrupted by oil shocks and rising inflation. Federal debt relative to GDP and credit market debt stopped declining for several years in the middle of the decade. The growth of Federal debt accelerated at the beginning of the 1980s, due in large part to a deep recession, and the ratio of Federal debt to GDP grew sharply. It continued to grow throughout the 1980s as large tax cuts, enacted in 1981, and substantial increases in defense spending were only partially offset by reductions in domestic spending. The resulting deficits increased the debt to almost 48 percent of GDP by 1993. The ratio of Federal debt to credit market debt also rose during this period, though to a lesser extent. Interest outlays on debt held by the public, calculated as a percentage of either total Federal outlays or GDP, increased as well.

The growth of Federal debt held by the public was slowing by the mid-1990s. In addition to a growing economy, two major budget agreements were enacted in the 1990s, implementing revenue increases and spending reductions and significantly reducing deficits. The debt declined markedly relative to both GDP and total credit market debt, with the decline accelerating as budget surpluses emerged from 1998 to 2001. Debt fell from 47.9 percent of GDP in 1993 to 31.5 percent of GDP in 2001. Over that same period, debt fell from 26.1 percent of total credit market debt to 17.1 percent. Interest as a share of outlays peaked at 16.5 percent in 1989 and then fell to 8.9 percent by 2002; interest as a percentage of GDP fell by a similar proportion.

The progress in reducing the debt burden stopped and then reversed course beginning in 2002. The attacks of September 11, 2001, a recession, two major wars, and tax cuts all contributed to increasing deficits, causing debt to rise, both in nominal terms and as a percentage of GDP. Following the recession that began in December 2007, the deficit increased rapidly in 2008 and 2009, as the Government intervened in the potential collapse of several major corporations and financial institutions as well as enacting a major stimulus bill. Additional tax cuts enacted in 2017 also contributed to higher deficits. Debt

[1] This is 2023 nominal interest on debt held by the public. For a discussion of real net interest, see the "Long-Term Budget Outlook" chapter of this volume.

[2] The *Historical Tables* are available at *https://whitehouse.gov/omb/historical-tables/*.

Table 21–1. TRENDS IN FEDERAL DEBT HELD BY THE PUBLIC AND INTEREST ON THE DEBT HELD BY THE PUBLIC

(Dollar amounts in billions)

Fiscal Year	Debt held by the public		Debt held by the public as a percent of		Interest on the debt held by the public[3]		Interest on the debt held by the public as a percent of[3]	
	Current dollars	FY 2023 dollars[1]	GDP	Credit market debt[2]	Current dollars	FY 2023 dollars[1]	Total outlays	GDP
1946	241.9	3,034.7	106.1	N/A	4.2	52.4	7.6	1.8
1950	219.0	2,220.6	78.6	53.3	4.8	49.1	11.4	1.7
1955	226.6	2,019.4	55.8	42.1	5.2	46.2	7.6	1.3
1960	236.8	1,870.3	44.3	33.1	7.8	61.7	8.5	1.5
1965	260.8	1,930.2	36.8	26.4	9.6	70.9	8.1	1.4
1970	283.2	1,746.7	27.1	20.3	15.4	94.8	7.9	1.5
1975	394.7	1,793.2	24.6	17.8	25.0	113.6	7.5	1.6
1980	711.9	2,248.8	25.5	18.4	62.8	198.2	10.6	2.2
1985	1,507.3	3,628.8	35.3	22.2	152.9	368.1	16.2	3.6
1990	2,411.6	4,987.9	40.9	22.4	202.4	418.6	16.2	3.4
1995	3,604.4	6,575.4	47.7	26.1	239.2	436.4	15.8	3.2
2000	3,409.8	5,732.8	33.7	18.5	232.8	391.5	13.0	2.3
2005	4,592.2	6,898.6	35.8	16.8	191.4	287.5	7.7	1.5
2010	9,018.9	12,278.1	60.6	24.8	228.2	310.6	6.6	1.5
2015	13,116.7	16,414.1	72.5	29.9	260.6	326.2	7.1	1.4
2016	14,167.6	17,589.0	76.4	30.9	283.8	352.4	7.4	1.5
2017	14,665.4	17,903.9	76.2	30.8	309.9	378.3	7.8	1.6
2018	15,749.6	18,810.2	77.6	31.3	371.4	443.6	9.0	1.8
2019	16,800.7	19,700.7	79.4	31.9	423.3	496.3	9.5	2.0
2020	21,016.7	24,328.0	99.8	35.6	387.4	448.5	5.9	1.8
2021	22,284.0	24,934.6	98.4	35.5	412.8	461.9	6.1	1.8
2022	24,253.4	25,364.5	97.0	36.1	533.6	558.1	8.5	2.1
2023	26,235.6	26,235.6	97.3	37.3	710.1	710.1	11.6	2.6
2024 estimate	28,156.2	27,243.1	99.6	N/A	959.4	934.5	13.8	3.4
2025 estimate	29,983.8	28,577.6	102.2	N/A	1,032.7	984.2	14.2	3.5
2026 estimate	31,639.4	29,540.7	103.6	N/A	1,082.5	1,010.7	14.6	3.5
2027 estimate	33,249.6	30,407.7	104.5	N/A	1,146.3	1,048.4	14.9	3.6
2028 estimate	34,892.1	31,257.2	105.3	N/A	1,212.2	1,085.9	15.0	3.7
2029 estimate	36,441.1	31,976.0	105.6	N/A	1,267.7	1,112.4	15.3	3.7
2030 estimate	38,139.4	32,781.9	106.0	N/A	1,321.6	1,136.0	15.0	3.7
2031 estimate	39,794.5	33,502.9	106.0	N/A	1,386.1	1,166.9	15.2	3.7
2032 estimate	41,502.0	34,223.4	105.9	N/A	1,438.8	1,186.5	15.1	3.7
2033 estimate	43,339.3	35,004.9	106.0	N/A	1,512.2	1,221.4	15.0	3.7
2034 estimate	45,055.7	35,642.4	105.6	N/A	1,574.6	1,245.6	15.3	3.7

N/A = Not available.

[1] Amounts in current dollars deflated by the GDP chain-type price index with fiscal year 2023 equal to 100.

[2] Total credit market debt owed by domestic nonfinancial sectors. Financial sectors are omitted to avoid double counting, since financial intermediaries borrow in the credit market primarily in order to finance lending in the credit market. Source: Federal Reserve Board flow of funds accounts. Projections are not available.

[3] Interest on debt held by the public is estimated as the interest on Treasury debt securities less the "interest received by trust funds" (subfunction 901 less subfunctions 902 and 903). The estimate of interest on debt held by the public does not include the comparatively small amount of interest paid on agency debt or the offsets for interest on Treasury debt received by other Government accounts (revolving funds and special funds).

as a percent of GDP grew from 35.2 percent at the end of 2007 to 79.4 percent in 2019. However, due to a decline in interest rates, despite the rising debt, net interest as a share of GDP dropped from 1.8 percent of GDP in 2007 to as low as 1.4 percent of GDP in 2015, before rising again to 2.0 percent by 2019.

As a result of the COVID-19 pandemic and the Government's actions to address the pandemic and support the economy, debt held by the public increased sharply in 2020, growing from 79.4 percent of GDP at the end of 2019 to 99.8 percent at the end of 2020. In 2021, a $1,567 billion decrease in the Department of the Treasury's operating cash balance offset a significant portion of the $2,775 billion deficit. Although debt held by the public continued to grow in dollar terms in 2021 and 2022, it fell as a percent of GDP, to 98.4 percent in 2021 and to 97.0 percent in 2022. In 2023, debt held by the public grew by $1,982 billion, to 97.3 percent of GDP.

In 2024, the deficit is projected to increase to $1,859 billion. As a result of the $1,859 billion deficit and $61 billion in borrowing due to other financing transactions (discussed in more detail below), debt held by the public is projected to grow to $28,156 billion, or 99.6 percent of GDP. The deficit is projected to fall to $1,781 billion in 2025, and debt held by the public is projected to grow to $29,984 billion, or 102.2 percent of GDP. As a percent of GDP, the deficit is projected to decrease in 2026 and then to remain at around 4-5 percent of GDP. Debt held by the public is expected to continue to grow in dollar terms but to roughly stabilize at around 106 percent of GDP beginning in 2029. Debt net of financial assets is estimated to increase to $25,587 billion, or 90.6 percent of GDP, at the end of 2024 and $27,370 billion, or 93.3 percent of GDP, at the end of 2025. Similar to debt held by the public, debt net of financial assets is projected to reach 98 percent of GDP by the end of 2030 and then remain relatively steady as a percent of GDP.

Debt Held by the Public and Gross Federal Debt

The Federal Government issues debt securities for two main purposes. First, it borrows from the public to provide for the Federal Government's financing needs, including both the deficit and the other transactions requiring financing, most notably disbursements for direct student loans and other Federal credit programs.[3] Second, it issues debt to Federal Government accounts, primarily trust funds, that accumulate surpluses. By law, trust fund surpluses must generally be invested in Federal securities. The gross Federal debt is defined to consist of both the debt held by the public and the debt held by Government accounts. Nearly all the Federal debt has been issued by the Treasury and is sometimes called "public debt," but a small portion has been issued by other Government agencies and is called "agency debt."[4]

Borrowing from the public, whether by the Treasury or by some other Federal agency, is important because it represents the Federal demand on credit markets. Regardless of whether the proceeds are used for tangible or intangible investments or to finance current consumption, the Federal demand on credit markets has to be financed out of the saving of households and businesses, the State and local sector, or the rest of the world. Borrowing from the public can thus affect the size and composition of assets held by the private sector and the amount of saving imported from abroad and increase the amount of future resources required to pay interest to the public on Federal debt. Borrowing from the public is therefore an important consideration in Federal fiscal policy. Borrowing from the public, however, is an incomplete measure of the Federal impact on credit markets. Different types of Federal activities can affect the credit markets in different ways. For example, under its direct loan programs, the Government uses borrowed funds to acquire financial assets that might otherwise require financing in the credit markets directly. (For more information on other ways in which Federal activities impact the credit market, see the discussion at the end of this chapter.) By incorporating the change in direct loan and other financial assets, debt held by the public net of financial assets adds useful insight into the Government's financial condition.

Issuing debt securities to Government accounts performs an essential function in accounting for the operation of these funds. The balances of debt represent the cumulative surpluses of these funds due to the excess of their tax receipts, interest receipts, and other collections over their spending. The interest on the debt that is credited to these funds accounts for the fact that some earmarked taxes and user fees will be spent at a later time than when the funds receive the monies. The debt securities are assets of those funds but are a liability of the general fund to the funds that hold the securities, and are a mechanism for crediting interest to those funds on their recorded balances. These balances generally provide the fund with authority to draw upon the Treasury in later years to make future payments on its behalf to the public. Public policy may result in the Government's running surpluses and accumulating debt in trust funds and other Government accounts in anticipation of future spending.

However, issuing debt to Government accounts does not have any of the current credit market effects of borrowing from the public. It is an internal transaction of the Government, made between two accounts that are both within the Government itself. Issuing debt to a Government account is not a current transaction of the Government with the public; it is not financed by private savings and does not compete with the private sector for available funds in the credit market. While such issuance provides the account with assets—a binding claim against the Treasury— those assets are fully offset by the

[3] For the purposes of the Budget, "debt held by the public" is defined as debt held by investors outside of the Federal Government, both domestic and foreign, including U.S. State and local governments and foreign governments. It also includes debt held by the Federal Reserve.

[4] The term "agency debt" is defined more narrowly in the budget than customarily in the securities market, where it includes not only the debt of the Federal agencies listed in Table 21–4, but also certain Government-guaranteed securities and the debt of the Government-sponsored enterprises listed in the supplemental materials to the "Credit and Insurance" chapter of this volume. (These supplemental materials are available at: *https://whitehouse.gov/omb/analytical-perspectives/*.)

Table 21–2. FEDERAL GOVERNMENT FINANCING AND DEBT

(In billions of dollars)

	Actual 2023	Estimate 2024	2025	2026	2027	2028	2029	2030	2031	2032	2033	2034
Financing:												
Unified budget deficit	1,693.7	1,859.4	1,781.0	1,546.6	1,510.3	1,572.9	1,482.9	1,640.5	1,613.9	1,671.0	1,801.4	1,676.5
Other transactions affecting borrowing from the public:												
Changes in financial assets and liabilities:[1]												
Change in Treasury operating cash balance	20.9	143.1	....	....	....	....	....	....	....	....	....	....
Net disbursements of credit financing accounts:												
Direct loan and Troubled Asset Relief Program (TARP) equity purchase accounts	259.2	-102.3	43.3	103.5	97.3	66.2	62.6	53.9	37.5	32.7	32.0	35.8
Guaranteed loan accounts	37.2	21.5	3.4	6.5	3.5	4.5	4.5	4.7	4.6	4.6	4.5	4.7
Subtotal, net disbursements	296.4	-80.7	46.7	110.0	100.8	70.7	67.1	58.6	42.1	37.2	36.5	40.4
Net purchases of non-Federal securities by the National Railroad Retirement Investment Trust	1.2	-1.1	-0.1	-1.0	-0.9	-0.9	-0.9	-0.8	-0.7	-0.8	-0.6	-0.5
Net change in other financial assets and liabilities[2]	-30.1	....	....	....	....	....	....	....	....	....	....	....
Subtotal, changes in financial assets and liabilities	288.4	61.3	46.6	109.0	99.9	69.8	66.1	57.8	41.3	36.5	35.9	39.9
Seigniorage on coins	....	-0.1	-0.1	-0.1	-0.1	-0.1	-0.1	-0.1	-0.1	-0.1	-0.1	-0.1
Total, other transactions affecting borrowing from the public	288.4	61.2	46.6	109.0	99.8	69.7	66.1	57.8	41.2	36.4	35.9	39.9
Total, requirement to borrow from the public (equals change in debt held by the public)	1,982.2	1,920.6	1,827.6	1,655.6	1,610.2	1,642.6	1,549.0	1,698.3	1,655.2	1,707.4	1,837.3	1,716.4
Changes in Debt Subject to Statutory Limitation:												
Change in debt held by the public	1,982.2	1,920.6	1,827.6	1,655.6	1,610.2	1,642.6	1,549.0	1,698.3	1,655.2	1,707.4	1,837.3	1,716.4
Change in debt held by Government accounts	168.2	198.3	160.9	287.5	137.8	30.7	155.1	49.2	33.1	-16.4	-135.5	-35.4
Less: change in debt not subject to limit and other adjustments	50.8	-0.6	-2.4	-1.8	-1.1	0.5	0.6	0.4	1.0	1.1	1.5	1.5
Total, change in debt subject to statutory limitation	2,201.2	2,118.3	1,986.1	1,941.3	1,746.9	1,673.8	1,704.6	1,747.9	1,689.3	1,692.1	1,703.3	1,682.6
Debt Subject to Statutory Limitation, End of Year:												
Debt issued by Treasury	32,968.4	35,085.7	37,071.4	39,012.2	40,758.2	42,431.1	44,135.1	45,882.8	47,572.0	49,264.0	50,966.9	52,648.9
Less: Treasury debt not subject to limitation (-)[3]	-6.0	-5.0	-4.6	-4.1	-3.2	-2.3	-1.7	-1.6	-1.5	-1.4	-1.0	-0.5
Agency debt subject to limitation	*	*	*	*	*	*	*	*	*	*	*	*
Adjustment for discount and premium[4]	108.0	108.0	108.0	108.0	108.0	108.0	108.0	108.0	108.0	108.0	108.0	108.0
Total, debt subject to statutory limitation[5]	33,070.5	35,188.8	37,174.9	39,116.2	40,863.0	42,536.8	44,241.4	45,989.3	47,678.5	49,370.6	51,073.9	52,756.5
Debt Outstanding, End of Year:												
Gross Federal debt:[6]												
Debt issued by Treasury	32,986.4	35,085.7	37,071.4	39,012.2	40,758.2	42,431.1	44,135.1	45,882.8	47,572.0	49,264.0	50,966.9	52,648.9
Debt issued by other agencies	20.6	22.2	25.0	27.4	29.4	29.8	29.9	29.6	28.6	27.6	26.6	25.5
Total, gross Federal debt	32,989.0	35,107.9	37,096.4	39,039.6	40,787.5	42,460.9	44,164.9	45,912.4	47,600.6	49,291.6	50,993.4	52,674.5
As a percent of GDP	122.3%	124.3%	126.4%	127.8%	128.2%	128.2%	128.0%	127.6%	126.8%	125.8%	124.7%	123.5%
Held by:												
Debt held by Government accounts	6,753.4	6,951.7	7,112.7	7,400.2	7,538.0	7,568.7	7,723.8	7,773.0	7,806.1	7,789.6	7,654.2	7,618.8
Debt held by the public[7]	26,235.6	28,156.2	29,983.8	31,639.4	33,249.6	34,892.1	36,441.1	38,139.4	39,794.5	41,502.0	43,339.3	45,055.7
As a percent of GDP	97.3%	99.6%	102.2%	103.6%	104.5%	105.3%	105.6%	106.0%	106.0%	105.9%	106.0%	105.6%

*$50 million or less.

[1] A decrease in the Treasury operating cash balance (which is an asset) is a means of financing a deficit and therefore has a negative sign. An increase in checks outstanding (which is a liability) is also a means of financing a deficit and therefore also has a negative sign.

[2] Includes checks outstanding, accrued interest payable on Treasury debt, uninvested deposit fund balances, allocations of special drawing rights, and other liability accounts; and, as an offset, cash and monetary assets (other than the Treasury operating cash balance), other asset accounts, and profit on sale of gold.

[3] Consists primarily of debt issued by the Federal Financing Bank.

[4] Consists mainly of unamortized discount (less premium) on public issues of Treasury notes and bonds (other than zero-coupon bonds) and unrealized discount on Government account series securities.

[5] Legislation enacted June 3, 2023 (Public Law 118-5), temporarily suspends the debt limit through January 1, 2025.

[6] Treasury securities held by the public and zero-coupon bonds held by Government accounts are almost all measured at sales price plus amortized discount or less amortized premium. Agency debt securities are almost all measured at face value. Treasury securities in the Government account series are otherwise measured at face value less unrealized discount (if any).

[7] At the end of 2023, the Federal Reserve Banks held $4,952.9 billion of Federal securities and the rest of the public held $21,282.7 billion. Debt held by the Federal Reserve Banks is not estimated for future years.

increased liability of the Treasury to pay the claims, which will ultimately be covered by the collection of revenues or by borrowing. Similarly, the current interest earned by the Government account on its Treasury securities does not need to be financed by other resources.

The debt held by Government accounts may differ from the estimated amount of the account's obligations or responsibilities to make future payments to the public. For example, if the account records the transactions of a social insurance program, the debt that it holds does not necessarily represent the actuarial present value of estimated future benefits (or future benefits less taxes) for the current participants in the program; nor does it necessarily represent the actuarial present value of estimated future benefits (or future benefits less taxes) for the current participants plus the estimated future participants over some stated time period. The future transactions of Federal social insurance and employee retirement programs, which own 88 percent of the debt held by Government accounts, are important in their own right and need to be analyzed separately. This can be done through information published in the actuarial and financial reports for these programs.[5]

The Budget uses a variety of information sources to analyze the condition of Social Security and Medicare, the Government's two largest social insurance programs. The excess of future Social Security and Medicare benefits relative to their dedicated income is very different in concept and much larger in size than the amount of Treasury securities that these programs hold.

For all of these reasons, debt held by the public and debt held by the public net of financial assets are both better gauges of the effect of the budget on the credit markets than gross Federal debt.

Government Deficits or Surpluses and the Change in Debt

Table 21–2 summarizes Federal borrowing and debt from 2023 through 2034.[6] In 2023, the Government borrowed $1,982 billion, increasing the debt held by the public from $24,253 billion at the end of 2022 to $26,236 billion at the end of 2023. The debt held by Government accounts grew by $168 billion, and gross Federal debt increased by $2,150 billion to $32,989 billion.

Debt held by the public.—The Federal Government primarily finances deficits by borrowing from the public, and it primarily uses surpluses to repay debt held by the public.[7] Table 21–2 shows the relationship between the Federal deficit or surplus and the change in debt held by the public. The borrowing or debt repayment depends on the Government's expenditure programs and tax laws, on the economic conditions that influence tax receipts and outlays, and on debt management policy. The sensitivity of the budget to economic conditions is analyzed in the "Economic Assumptions" chapter of this volume.

The total or unified budget consists of two parts: the on-budget portion; and the off-budget Federal entities, which have been excluded from the budget by law. Under present law, the off-budget Federal entities are the two Social Security trust funds (Old-Age and Survivors Insurance and Disability Insurance) and the Postal Service Fund.[8] The on-budget and off-budget surpluses or deficits are added together to determine the Government's financing needs.

Over the long run, it is a good approximation to say that "the deficit is financed by borrowing from the public" or "the surplus is used to repay debt held by the public." However, the Government's need to borrow in any given year has always depended on several other factors besides the unified budget surplus or deficit, such as the change in the Treasury operating cash balance. These other factors—"other transactions affecting borrowing from the public"—can either increase or decrease the Government's need to borrow and can vary considerably in size from year to year. The other transactions affecting borrowing from the public are presented in Table 21–2 (where an increase in the need to borrow is represented by a positive sign, like the deficit).

In 2023 the deficit was $1,694 billion while these other factors increased the need to borrow by $288 billion, or 15 percent of total borrowing from the public. As a result, the Government borrowed $1,982 billion from the public. The other factors are estimated to increase borrowing by $61 billion (3 percent of total borrowing from the public) in 2024, and by $47 billion (3 percent) in 2025. In 2026–2034, these other factors are expected to increase borrowing by annual amounts ranging from $36 billion to $109 billion.

Three specific factors, presented in Table 21–2 and discussed below, have historically been especially important.

Change in Treasury operating cash balance.—In 2023, the operating cash balance increased by $21 billion, to $657 billion. The cash balance is projected to increase by $143 billion, to $800 billion, at the end of 2024. For prudent risk management purposes, Treasury seeks to maintain a cash balance at least equal to projected Government outflows, including maturing securities, over the following week, subject to a $150 billion floor. Changes in the operating cash balance, while occasionally large, are inherently limited over time. Decreases in cash—a means of financing the Government—are limited

[5] Extensive actuarial analyses of the Social Security and Medicare programs are published in the annual reports of the boards of trustees of these funds. The actuarial estimates for Social Security, Medicare, and the major Federal employee retirement programs are summarized in the *Financial Report of the United States Government*, prepared annually by Treasury in coordination with the Office of Management and Budget, and presented in more detail in the financial statements of the agencies administering those programs.

[6] For projections of the debt beyond 2034, see the "Long-Term Budget Outlook" chapter.

[7] Treasury debt held by the public is measured as the sales price plus the amortized discount (or less the amortized premium). At the time of sale, the book value equals the sales price. Subsequently, it equals the sales price plus the amount of the discount that has been amortized up to that time. In equivalent terms, the book value of the debt equals the principal amount due at maturity (par or face value) less the unamortized discount. (For a security sold at a premium, the definition is symmetrical.) For inflation-protected notes and bonds, the book value includes a periodic adjustment for inflation. Agency debt is generally recorded at par.

[8] For further explanation of the off-budget Federal entities, see the "Coverage of the Budget" chapter of this volume.

by the amount of past accumulations, which themselves required financing when they were built up. Increases are limited because it is generally more efficient to repay debt.

Net financing disbursements of the direct loan and guaranteed loan financing accounts.—Under the Federal Credit Reform Act of 1990 (FCRA),[9] the budgetary program account for each credit program records the estimated subsidy costs—the present value of estimated net losses—at the time when the direct or guaranteed loans are disbursed. The individual cash flows to and from the public associated with the loans or guarantees, such as the disbursement and repayment of loans, the default payments on loan guarantees, the collection of interest and fees, and so forth, are recorded in the credit program's non-budgetary financing account. Although the non-budgetary financing account's cash flows to and from the public are not included in the deficit (except for their impact on subsidy costs), they affect Treasury's net borrowing requirements.[10]

In addition to the transactions with the public, the financing accounts include several types of intragovernmental transactions. They receive payment from the credit program accounts for the subsidy costs of new direct loans and loan guarantees and for any upward reestimate of the costs of outstanding direct and guaranteed loans. They also receive interest from Treasury on balances of uninvested funds. The financing accounts pay any negative subsidy collections or downward reestimate of costs to budgetary receipt accounts and pay interest on borrowings from Treasury. The total net collections and gross disbursements of the financing accounts, consisting of transactions with both the public and the budgetary accounts, are called "net financing disbursements." They occur in the same way as the "outlays" of a budgetary account, even though they do not represent budgetary costs, and therefore affect the requirement for borrowing from the public in the same way as the deficit.

The intragovernmental transactions of the credit program, financing, and downward reestimate receipt accounts do not affect Federal borrowing from the public. Although the deficit changes because of the budgetary account's outlay to, or receipt from, a financing account, the net financing disbursement changes in an equal amount with the opposite sign, so the effects are cancelled out. On the other hand, financing account disbursements to the public increase the requirement for borrowing from the public in the same way as an increase in budget outlays that are disbursed to the public in cash. Likewise, receipts from the public collected by the financing account can be used to finance the payment of the Government's obligations, and therefore they reduce the requirement for Federal borrowing from the public in the same way as an increase in budgetary receipts.

Credit net financing disbursements increased borrowing by $296 billion in 2023. Credit financing accounts are projected to reduce borrowing by $81 billion in 2024 and increase borrowing by $47 billion in 2025. From 2026 to 2034, the credit financing accounts are expected to increase borrowing by amounts ranging from $37 billion to $110 billion.

In some years, large net upward or downward reestimates in the cost of outstanding direct and guaranteed loans may cause large swings in the net financing disbursements. In 2024, upward reestimates for Department of Education student loans and Small Business Administration COVID Economic Injury Disaster Loans are partially offset by downward reestimates for Federal Housing Administration (FHA) guarantees, resulting in a net upward reestimate of $89 billion. In 2023, there was a net upward reestimate of $17 billion.

Net purchases of non-Federal securities by the National Railroad Retirement Investment Trust (NRRIT).—This trust fund, which was established by the Railroad Retirement and Survivors' Improvement Act of 2001,[11] invests its assets primarily in private stocks and bonds. The Act required special treatment of the purchase or sale of non-Federal assets by the NRRIT trust fund, treating such purchases as a means of financing rather than as outlays. Therefore, the increased need to borrow from the public to finance NRRIT's purchases of non-Federal assets is part of the "other transactions affecting borrowing from the public" rather than included as an increase in the deficit. While net purchases and redemptions affect borrowing from the public, unrealized gains and losses on NRRIT's portfolio are included in both the "other transactions" and, with the opposite sign, in NRRIT's net outlays in the deficit, for no net impact on borrowing from the public. In 2023, net increases, including purchases and gains, were $1.2 billion. A $1.1 billion net decrease is projected for 2024 and net annual decreases ranging from $0.1 billion to $1.0 billion are projected for 2025 and subsequent years.[12]

Debt held by Government accounts.—The amount of Federal debt issued to Government accounts depends largely on the surpluses of the trust funds, both on-budget and off-budget, which owned 87 percent of the total Federal debt held by Government accounts at the end of 2023. Net investment may differ from the surplus due to changes in the amount of cash assets not currently invested. In 2023, there was a total trust fund surplus of $183 billion,[13] while trust fund investment in Federal securities grew by $191 billion. The remainder of debt issued to Government accounts is owned by a number of special funds and revolving funds. The debt held in major accounts and the annual investments are shown in Table 21–5, available online.

---

[9] Title V of Public Law 93-344.

[10] FCRA (sec. 505(b)) requires that the financing accounts be non-budgetary. They are non-budgetary in concept because they do not measure cost. For additional discussion of credit programs, see the "Credit and Insurance" and "Budget Concepts" chapters of this volume.

[11] Title I of Public Law 107-90.

[12] The budget treatment of this fund is further discussed in the "Budget Concepts" chapter.

[13] For further discussion of trust funds, see the "Trust Funds and Federal Funds" chapter of this volume.

Table 21–3. DEBT HELD BY THE PUBLIC NET OF FINANCIAL ASSETS AND LIABILITIES

(Dollar amounts in billions)

	Actual 2023	Estimate										
		2024	2025	2026	2027	2028	2029	2030	2031	2032	2033	2034
Debt Held by the Public:												
Debt held by the public	26,235.6	28,156.2	29,983.8	31,639.4	33,249.6	34,892.1	36,441.1	38,139.4	39,794.5	41,502.0	43,339.3	45,055.7
As a percent of GDP	97.3%	99.6%	102.2%	103.6%	104.5%	105.3%	105.6%	106.0%	106.0%	105.9%	106.0%	105.6%
Financial Assets Net of Liabilities:												
Treasury operating cash balance	656.9	800.0	800.0	800.0	800.0	800.0	800.0	800.0	800.0	800.0	800.0	800.0
Credit financing account balances:												
Direct loan and TARP equity purchase accounts	1,598.1	1,495.8	1,539.1	1,642.6	1,739.9	1,806.1	1,868.7	1,922.6	1,960.1	1,992.7	2,024.8	2,060.5
Guaranteed loan accounts	82.7	104.2	107.6	114.1	117.6	122.2	126.6	131.4	135.9	140.5	145.0	149.7
Subtotal, credit financing account balances	1,680.8	1,600.0	1,646.7	1,756.7	1,857.6	1,928.3	1,995.3	2,054.0	2,096.0	2,133.2	2,169.8	2,210.2
Government-sponsored enterprise stock [1]	240.4	240.4	240.4	240.4	240.4	240.4	240.4	240.4	240.4	240.4	240.4	240.4
Air carrier worker support warrants and notes [2]	12.4	12.3	10.9	10.3	9.8	9.3	8.9	4.9	0.2	0.2	....	....
Emergency capital investment fund securities	2.5	2.5	2.3	2.2	2.1	2.0	1.9	1.8	1.7	1.6	1.5	1.4
Non-Federal securities held by NRRIT	23.8	22.7	22.7	21.7	20.8	19.8	18.9	18.1	17.4	16.6	16.0	15.6
Other assets net of liabilities	-108.9	-108.9	-108.9	-108.9	-108.9	-108.9	-108.9	-108.9	-108.9	-108.9	-108.9	-108.9
Total, financial assets net of liabilities	2,507.8	2,569.0	2,614.1	2,722.4	2,821.6	2,890.8	2,956.4	3,010.2	3,046.8	3,083.2	3,118.8	3,158.7
Debt Held by the Public Net of Financial Assets and Liabilities:												
Debt held by the public net of financial assets	23,727.8	25,587.2	27,369.7	28,917.0	30,427.9	32,001.3	33,484.7	35,129.2	36,747.8	38,418.8	40,220.5	41,897.0
As a percent of GDP	88.0%	90.6%	93.3%	94.6%	95.6%	96.6%	97.0%	97.6%	97.9%	98.1%	98.4%	98.2%

[1] Treasury's warrants to purchase 79.9 percent of the common stock of the enterprises expire after September 7, 2028. The warrants were valued at $4 billion at the end of 2023.

[2] Portions of the notes and warrants issued under the Air carrier worker support program (Payroll support program) are scheduled to expire in 2025, 2026, 2030, and 2031.

Debt Held by the Public Net of Financial Assets and Liabilities

While debt held by the public is a key measure for examining the role and impact of the Federal Government in the U.S. and international credit markets and for other purposes, it provides incomplete information on the Government's financial condition. The U.S. Government holds significant financial assets, which can be offset against debt held by the public and other financial liabilities to achieve a more complete understanding of the Government's financial condition. The acquisition of those financial assets represents a transaction with the credit markets, broadening those markets in a way that is analogous to the demand on credit markets that borrowing entails. For this reason, debt held by the public is also an incomplete measure of the impact of the Federal Government in the United States and international credit markets.

One transaction that can increase both borrowing and assets is an increase to the Treasury operating cash balance. When the Government borrows to increase the Treasury operating cash balance, that cash balance also represents an asset that is available to the Federal Government. Looking at both sides of this transaction—the borrowing to obtain the cash and the asset of the cash holdings—provides much more complete information about the Government's financial condition than looking at only the borrowing from the public. Another example of a transaction that simultaneously increases borrowing from the public and Federal assets is Government borrowing to issue direct loans to the public. When the direct loan is made, the Government is also acquiring an asset in the form of future payments of principal and interest, net of the Government's expected losses on the loan. Similarly, when NRRIT increases its holdings of non-Federal securities, the borrowing to purchase those securities is offset by the value of the asset holdings.

The acquisition or disposition of Federal financial assets largely explains the difference between the deficit for a particular year and that year's increase in debt held by the public. Debt held by the public net of financial assets is a measure that is conceptually closer to the measurement of Federal deficits or surpluses; cumulative deficits and surpluses over time more closely equal the debt held by the public net of financial assets than they do the debt held by the public.

Table 21–3 presents debt held by the public net of the Government's financial assets and liabilities. Treasury debt is presented in the Budget at book value, with no adjustments for the change in economic value that results from fluctuations in interest rates. The balances of credit financing accounts are based on projections of future cash flows. For direct loan financing accounts, the balance generally represents the net present value of anticipated future inflows such as principal and interest payments from borrowers. For guaranteed loan financing accounts, the balance generally represents the net present value of anticipated future outflows, such as default claim payments net of recoveries, and other collections, such as program fees. NRRIT's holdings of non-Federal securities are marked to market on a monthly basis. Government-sponsored enterprise stock, Air carrier worker support warrants and notes, and Emergency capital investment fund securities are measured at market value.

Due largely to the growth of credit financing account balances, net financial assets increased by $304 billion, to $2,508 billion, in 2023. This $2,508 billion in net financial assets included a cash balance of $657 billion, net credit financing account balances of $1,681 billion, and other assets and liabilities that aggregated to a net asset of $170 billion. At the end of 2023, debt held by the public was $26,236 billion, or 97.3 percent of GDP. Therefore, debt held by the public net of financial assets was $23,728 billion, or 88.0 percent of GDP. As shown in Table 21–3, the value of the Government's net financial assets is projected to grow to $2,569 billion in 2024. The projected 2024 increase is due to the anticipated $143 billion increase in the cash balance, partly offset by the projected $81 billion decrease in net credit financing account balances. While debt held by the public is expected to increase from 97.3 percent to 99.6 percent of GDP during 2024, debt net of financial assets is expected to increase from 88.0 percent to 90.6 percent of GDP.

Debt securities and other financial assets and liabilities do not encompass all the assets and liabilities of the Federal Government. For example, accounts payable occur in the normal course of buying goods and services; Social Security benefits are due and payable as of the end of the month but, according to statute, are paid during the next month; and Federal employee salaries are paid after they have been earned. Like debt securities sold in the credit market, these liabilities have their own distinctive effects on the economy. The Federal Government also has significant holdings of non-financial assets, such as land, mineral deposits, buildings, and equipment. The different types of assets and liabilities are reported annually in the financial statements of Federal agencies and in the *Financial Report of the United States Government*, prepared by the Treasury in coordination with the Office of Management and Budget (OMB).

Treasury Debt

Nearly all Federal debt is issued by the Department of the Treasury. Treasury meets most of the Federal Government's financing needs by issuing marketable securities to the public. These financing needs include both the change in debt held by the public and the refinancing—or rollover—of any outstanding debt that matures during the year. Treasury marketable debt is sold at public auctions on a regular schedule and, because it is very liquid, can be bought and sold on the secondary market at narrow bid-offer spreads. Treasury also sells to the public a relatively small amount of nonmarketable securities, such as savings bonds and State and Local Government Series (SLGS) securities.[14] Treasury nonmarketable debt cannot be bought or sold on the secondary market.

[14] Under the SLGS program, the Treasury offers special low-yield securities to State and local governments and other entities for temporary investment of proceeds of tax-exempt bonds.

Treasury issues marketable securities in a wide range of maturities, and issues both nominal (non-inflation-protected) and inflation-protected securities. Treasury's marketable securities include:

Treasury Bills—Treasury bills have maturities of one year or less from their issue date. In addition to the regular auction calendar of bill issuance, Treasury issues cash management bills on an as-needed basis for various reasons such as to offset the seasonal patterns of the Government's receipts and outlays. In 2020, Treasury began issuing four different maturities of cash management bills on a weekly basis in relation to the financing needed due to the impacts of the COVID-19 pandemic and the Government's response. Treasury phased out three of the four maturities of these weekly cash management bills in 2021. In 2023, Treasury added the 17-week bill—the remaining of these four maturities—to its regular weekly auction calendar.

Treasury Notes—Treasury notes have maturities of more than one year and up to 10 years.

Treasury Bonds—Treasury bonds have maturities of more than 10 years. The longest-maturity securities issued by Treasury are 30-year bonds.

Treasury Inflation-Protected Securities (TIPS)—Treasury inflation-protected—or inflation-indexed—securities are coupon issues for which the par value of the security rises with inflation. The principal value is adjusted daily to reflect inflation as measured by changes in the Consumer Price Index (CPI-U-NSA, with a two-month lag). Although the principal value may be adjusted downward if inflation is negative, at maturity, the securities will be redeemed at the greater of their inflation-adjusted principal or par amount at original issue.

Floating Rate Securities—Floating rate securities have a fixed par value but bear interest rates that fluctuate based on movements in a specified benchmark market interest rate. Treasury's floating rate notes are benchmarked to the Treasury 13-week bill. Currently, Treasury is issuing floating rate securities with a maturity of two years.

Historically, the average maturity of outstanding debt issued by Treasury has been about five years. The average maturity of outstanding debt was 72 months at the end of 2023.

In addition to quarterly announcements about the overall auction calendar, Treasury publicly announces in advance the auction of each security. Individuals can participate directly in Treasury auctions or can purchase securities through brokers, dealers, and other financial institutions. Treasury accepts two types of auction bids: competitive and noncompetitive. In a competitive bid, the bidder specifies the yield. A significant portion of competitive bids are submitted by primary dealers, which are banks and securities brokerages that have been designated to trade in Treasury securities with the Federal Reserve System. In a noncompetitive bid, the bidder agrees to accept the yield determined by the auction.[15] At the close of the auction, Treasury accepts all eligible noncompetitive bids and then accepts competitive bids in

[15] Noncompetitive bids cannot exceed $10 million per bidder.

ascending order beginning with the lowest yield bid until the offering amount is reached. All winning bidders receive the highest accepted yield bid.

Treasury marketable securities are highly liquid and actively traded on the secondary market, which enhances the demand for Treasuries at initial auction. The demand for Treasury securities is reflected in the ratio of bids received to bids accepted in Treasury auctions; the demand for the securities is substantially greater than the level of issuance. Because they are backed by the full faith and credit of the United States Government, Treasury marketable securities are considered to be credit "risk-free." Therefore, the Treasury yield curve is commonly used as a benchmark for a wide variety of purposes in the financial markets.

In May 2023, Treasury announced that in 2024 it would launch a buyback program, under which it will repurchase a small portion of outstanding marketable securities. Treasury is creating the buyback program for cash management and liquidity support purposes. Treasury previously conducted buybacks in 2000–2002, for purposes of managing the Federal debt during a time of budget surplus. Since 2015, Treasury has also conducted very small-scale buybacks once or twice annually to test its systems.

Whereas Treasury issuance of marketable debt is based on the Government's financing needs, Treasury's issuance of nonmarketable debt is based on the public's demand for the specific types of investments. Decreases in outstanding balances of nonmarketable debt, such as occurred in 2023, increase the need for marketable borrowing.[16]

Agency Debt

A few Federal agencies other than Treasury, shown in Table 21–4 (available online), sell or have sold debt securities to the public and, at times, to other Government accounts. At the end of 2023, agency debt was $20.6 billion, less than one-tenth of one percent of total Federal debt held by the public. Agency debt is estimated to grow to $22.2 billion at the end of 2024 and to $25.0 billion at the end of 2025.

The predominant agency borrower is the Tennessee Valley Authority (TVA), which had borrowings of $20.5 billion from the public as of the end of 2023, or over 99 percent of the total debt of all agencies other than Treasury. TVA issues debt primarily to finance capital projects.

TVA has traditionally financed its capital construction by selling bonds and notes to the public. Since 2000, it has also had available two types of alternative financing methods, lease financing obligations and prepayment obligations. Under the lease financing obligations method, TVA signs long-term contracts to lease some facilities and equipment. The lease payments under these contracts ultimately secure the repayment of third-party capital used to finance construction of the facility. TVA retains substantially all of the economic benefits and risks related to ownership of the assets.[17] At the end of 2023, lease financing obligations were $1.0 billion. Table 21–4 presents lease financing obligations separately from TVA bonds and notes to distinguish between the types of borrowing. As of the end of 2019, there are no outstanding obligations for prepayments.[18]

OMB determined that each of the two alternative financing methods is a means of financing the acquisition of assets owned and used by the Government, or of refinancing debt previously incurred to finance such assets. They are equivalent in concept to other forms of borrowing from the public, although under different terms and conditions. The budget therefore records the upfront cash proceeds from these methods as borrowing from the public, not offsetting collections.[19] The budget presentation is consistent with the reporting of these obligations as liabilities on TVA's balance sheet under generally accepted accounting principles.

Although the Federal Housing Administration generally makes direct disbursements to the public for default claims on FHA-insured mortgages, it may also pay claims by issuing debentures. Issuing debentures to pay the Government's bills is equivalent to selling securities to the public and then paying the bills by disbursing the cash borrowed, so the transaction is recorded as being simultaneously an outlay and borrowing. The debentures are therefore classified as agency debt.

A number of years ago, the Federal Government guaranteed the debt used to finance the construction of a building for the Architect of the Capitol and subsequently exercised full control over the design, construction, and operation of the building. This arrangement is equivalent to direct Federal construction financed by Federal borrowing. The construction expenditures and interest were therefore classified as Federal outlays, and the borrowing was classified as Federal agency borrowing from the public. This borrowing is scheduled to mature by the end of 2024.

Several Federal agencies borrow from the Bureau of the Fiscal Service (Fiscal Service) or the Federal Financing

[16] Detail on the marketable and nonmarketable securities issued by Treasury is found in the *Monthly Statement of the Public Debt*, published on a monthly basis by Treasury.

[17] This arrangement is at least as governmental as a "lease-purchase without substantial private risk." For further detail on the current budgetary treatment of lease-purchase without substantial private risk, see OMB Circular No. A–11, Appendix B.

[18] Under the prepayment obligations method, TVA's power distributors prepay a portion of the price of the power they plan to purchase in the future. In return, they obtain a discount on a specific quantity of the future power they buy from TVA. The quantity varies, depending on TVA's estimated cost of borrowing.

[19] This budgetary treatment differs from the treatment in the *Monthly Treasury Statement of Receipts and Outlays of the United States Government* (Monthly Treasury Statement) Table 6 Schedule C, and the *Combined Statement of Receipts, Outlays, and Balances of the United States Government* Schedule 3, both published by the Treasury. These two schedules, which present debt issued by agencies other than Treasury, exclude the TVA alternative financing arrangements. This difference in treatment is one factor causing minor differences between debt figures reported in the Budget and debt figures reported by Treasury. The other factors are: adjustments for the timing of the reporting of Federal debt held by NRRIT; and treatment of the Federal debt held by the Securities Investor Protection Corporation and the Public Company Accounting Oversight Board.

Bank (FFB), both within the Department of the Treasury. Agency borrowing from the FFB or the Fiscal Service is not included in gross Federal debt. It would be double counting to add together: (a) the agency borrowing from the Fiscal Service or FFB; and (b) the Treasury borrowing from the public that is needed to provide the Fiscal Service or FFB with the funds to lend to the agencies.

Debt Held by Government Accounts

Trust funds, and some special funds and public enterprise revolving funds, accumulate cash in excess of current needs in order to meet future obligations. These cash surpluses are generally invested in Treasury securities.

The total investment holdings of trust funds and other Government accounts increased by $168 billion in 2023. Net investment by Government accounts is estimated to be $198 billion in 2024 and $161 billion in 2025, as shown in Table 21–5. The holdings of Federal securities by Government accounts are estimated to grow to $7,113 billion by the end of 2025, or 19 percent of the gross Federal debt. The percentage is estimated to decrease gradually over the next 10 years.

The Government account holdings of Federal securities are concentrated among a few funds: the Social Security Old-Age and Survivors Insurance and Disability Insurance trust funds; the Medicare Hospital Insurance and Supplementary Medical Insurance trust funds; and four Federal employee retirement funds. These Federal employee retirement funds include two trust funds, the Military Retirement Fund and the Civil Service Retirement and Disability Fund (CSRDF), and two special funds, the Department of Defense Medicare-Eligible Retiree Health Care Fund (MERHCF) and the Postal Service Retiree Health Benefits Fund (PSRHBF). At the end of 2024, these Social Security, Medicare, and Federal employee retirement funds are estimated to own 88 percent of the total debt held by Government accounts. During 2023–2025, the Military Retirement Fund has a large surplus and is estimated to invest a total of $500 billion, 95 percent of total net investment by Government accounts. Some Government accounts are projected to have net disinvestment in Federal securities during 2023–2025.

Technical note on measurement.—The Treasury securities held by Government accounts consist almost entirely of the Government account series. Most were issued at par value (face value), and the securities issued at a discount or premium are traditionally recorded at par in the OMB and Treasury reports on Federal debt. However, there are two kinds of exceptions.

First, Treasury issues zero-coupon bonds to a very few Government accounts. Because the purchase price is a small fraction of par value and the amounts are large, the holdings are recorded in Table 21–5 at par value less unamortized discount. The only Government accounts that held zero-coupon bonds during 2023 are the Nuclear Waste Disposal Fund in the Department of Energy, the Military Retirement Fund, and the MERHCF. The unamortized discount on zero-coupon bonds held by these three funds was $22.6 billion at the end of 2023.

Second, Treasury subtracts the unrealized discount on other Government account series securities in calculating "net Federal securities held as investments of Government accounts." Unlike the discount recorded for zero-coupon bonds and debt held by the public, the unrealized discount is the discount at the time of issue and is not amortized over the term of the security. In Table 21–5 it is shown as a separate item at the end of the table and not distributed by account. The amount was $46.8 billion at the end of 2023.

Debt Held by the Federal Reserve

The Federal Reserve acquires marketable Treasury securities as part of its exercise of monetary policy. For purposes of the Budget and reporting by Treasury, the transactions of the Federal Reserve are considered to be non-budgetary, and accordingly the Federal Reserve's holdings of Treasury securities are included as part of debt held by the public.[20] Federal Reserve holdings were $4,953 billion (19 percent of debt held by the public) at the end of 2023. Over the last 10 years, the Federal Reserve holdings have averaged 19 percent of debt held by the public. The historical holdings of the Federal Reserve are presented in Table 7.1 in the Budget's *Historical Tables*. The Budget does not project Federal Reserve holdings for future years.

Limitations on Federal Debt

Definition of debt subject to limit.—Statutory limitations have usually been placed on Federal debt. Until World War I, the Congress ordinarily authorized a specific amount of debt for each separate issue. Beginning with the Second Liberty Bond Act of 1917, however, the nature of the limitation was modified in several steps until it developed into a ceiling on the total amount of most Federal debt outstanding. This last type of limitation has been in effect since 1941. The limit currently applies to most debt issued by the Treasury since September 1917, whether held by the public or by Government accounts; and other debt issued by Federal agencies that, according to explicit statute, is guaranteed as to principal and interest by the U.S. Government.

The third part of Table 21–2 compares total Treasury debt with the amount of Federal debt that is subject to the limit. Nearly all Treasury debt is subject to the debt limit.

A large portion of the Treasury debt not subject to the general statutory limit was issued by the Federal Financing Bank. The FFB is authorized to have outstanding up to $15 billion of publicly issued debt. The FFB has on occasion issued this debt to CSRDF in exchange for equal amounts of regular Treasury securities. The FFB securities have the same interest rates and maturities as the Treasury securities for which they were exchanged. Most recently, the FFB issued: $9 billion to the CSRDF on October 1, 2013, with maturity dates from June 30, 2015, through June 30, 2024; $3 billion of securities to the CSRDF on October 15, 2015, with maturity dates

[20] For further detail on the monetary policy activities of the Federal Reserve and the treatment of the Federal Reserve in the Budget, see the "Coverage of the Budget" chapter.

from June 30, 2026, through June 30, 2029; and $2 billion to the CSRDF on May 25, 2023, with maturity dates ranging from June 30, 2023, through June 30, 2035. The outstanding balance of FFB debt held by CSRDF was $5.5 billion at the end of 2023 and is projected to be $4.5 billion at the end of 2024.

The other Treasury debt not subject to the general limit consists almost entirely of silver certificates and other currencies no longer being issued. It was $477 million at the end of 2023 and is projected to gradually decline over time.

The sole agency debt currently subject to the general limit, $209 thousand at the end of 2023, is certain debentures issued by the Federal Housing Administration.[21]

Some of the other agency debt, however, is subject to its own statutory limit. For example, TVA is limited to $30 billion of bonds and notes outstanding.

The comparison between Treasury debt and debt subject to limit also includes an adjustment for measurement differences in the treatment of discounts and premiums. As explained earlier in this chapter, debt securities may be sold at a discount or premium, and the measurement of debt may take this into account rather than recording the face value of the securities. However, the measurement differs between gross Federal debt (and its components) and the statutory definition of debt subject to limit. An adjustment is needed to derive debt subject to limit (as defined by law) from Treasury debt. The amount of the adjustment was $108 billion at the end of 2023 compared with the total unamortized discount (less premium) of $199 billion on all Treasury securities.

Changes in the debt limit.—The statutory debt limit has been changed many times. Since 1960, the Congress has passed 88 separate acts to raise the limit, revise the definition, extend the duration of a temporary increase, or temporarily suspend the limit.[22]

Between 2013 and 2019, seven laws addressing the debt limit each provided for a temporary suspension followed by an increase in an amount equivalent to the debt that was issued during that suspension period in order to fund commitments requiring payment through the specified end date. The Bipartisan Budget Act of 2019[23] suspended the $21,988 billion debt ceiling from August 2, 2019, through July 31, 2021, and then raised the debt limit on August 1, 2021, by $6,414 billion to $28,401 billion. On October 14, 2021, enacted legislation[24] increased the dollar debt ceiling by $480 billion, to $28,881 billion. On December 16, 2021, enacted legislation[25] further increased the dollar debt ceiling by $2,500 billion, to $31,381 billion. The Government reached this $31,381 billion ceiling in January 2023. The Fiscal Responsibility Act of 2023,[26] enacted June 3, 2023, suspended the debt limit through January 1, 2025.

At many times in the past several decades, including 2019, 2021, and 2023, the Government has reached the statutory debt limit before an increase has been enacted. When this has occurred, it has been necessary for the Treasury to take "extraordinary measures" to meet the Government's obligation to pay its bills and invest its trust funds while remaining below the statutory limit.

One such extraordinary measure is the partial or full suspension of the daily reinvestment of the Thrift Savings Plan (TSP) Government Securities Investment Fund (G-Fund).[27] The Treasury Secretary has statutory authority to suspend investment of the G-Fund in Treasury securities as needed to prevent the debt from exceeding the debt limit. Treasury determines each day the amount of investments that would allow the fund to be invested as fully as possible without exceeding the debt limit. The TSP G-Fund had an outstanding balance of $295 billion at the end of January 2024. The Treasury Secretary is also authorized to suspend investments in the CSRDF and to declare a debt issuance suspension period, which allows the redemption of a limited amount of securities held by the CSRDF. The Postal Accountability and Enhancement Act[28] provides that investments in the PSRHBF shall be made in the same manner as investments in the CSRDF.[29] Therefore, Treasury is able to take similar administrative actions with the PSRHBF. The law requires that when any such actions are taken with the G-Fund, the CSRDF, or the PSRHBF, the Treasury Secretary is required to make the fund whole after the debt limit has been raised by restoring the forgone interest and investing the fund fully. Another measure for staying below the debt limit is disinvestment of the Exchange Stabilization Fund. The outstanding balance in the Exchange Stabilization Fund was $13 billion at the end of January 2024.

As the debt has neared the limit, including in 2019, 2021, and 2023, Treasury has also suspended the issuance of SLGS to reduce unanticipated fluctuations in the level of the debt. At times, Treasury has also adjusted the schedule for auctions of marketable securities.

In addition to these steps, Treasury has previously exchanged Treasury securities held by the CSRDF with borrowing by the FFB, which, as explained above, is not subject to the debt limit. This measure was most recently taken in May 2023.

The debt limit has always been increased prior to the exhaustion of Treasury's limited available administrative actions to continue to finance Government operations when the statutory ceiling has been reached. Failure to enact a debt limit increase before these actions were exhausted would have significant and long-term negative consequences. The Federal Government could be forced to delay or discontinue payments on its broad range of ob-

[21] At the end of 2023, there were also $18 million of FHA debentures not subject to limit.

[22] The Acts and the statutory limits since 1940 are listed in Table 7.3 of the Budget's *Historical Tables.*

[23] Public Law 116-37.

[24] Public Law 117-50.

[25] Public Law 117-73.

[26] Public Law 118-5.

[27] The TSP is a defined contribution pension plan for Federal employees. The G-Fund is one of several components of the TSP.

[28] Title VIII of Public Law 109-435.

[29] Both the CSRDF and the PSRHBF are administered by the Office of Personnel Management.

Table 21–6. FEDERAL FUNDS FINANCING AND CHANGE IN DEBT SUBJECT TO STATUTORY LIMIT

(In billions of dollars)

Description	Actual 2023	Estimate										
		2024	2025	2026	2027	2028	2029	2030	2031	2032	2033	2034
Change in Gross Federal Debt:												
Federal funds deficit	1,877.2	2,102.1	2,053.6	1,771.0	1,587.5	1,560.3	1,595.0	1,640.5	1,590.3	1,609.2	1,607.1	1,571.5
Other transactions affecting borrowing from the public -- Federal funds[1]	287.2	62.3	46.6	109.9	100.8	70.6	67.0	58.6	42.0	37.2	36.4	40.3
Increase (+) or decrease (-) in Federal debt held by Federal funds	17.5	35.2	50.3	62.7	60.2	42.9	42.6	48.8	56.3	45.1	58.6	69.4
Adjustments for trust fund surplus/deficit not invested/ disinvested in Federal securities[2]	8.6	-80.7	-162.0	-0.5	-0.5	-0.5	-0.5	-0.4	-0.4	-0.5	-0.3	-0.2
Change in unrealized discount on Federal debt held by Government accounts	-40.0	....	....	....	....	....	....	....	....	....	....	....
Total financing requirements	2,150.4	2,118.9	1,988.5	1,943.1	1,748.0	1,673.3	1,704.1	1,747.5	1,688.2	1,691.0	1,701.8	1,681.0
Change in Debt Subject to Limit:												
Change in gross Federal debt	2,150.4	2,118.9	1,988.5	1,943.1	1,748.0	1,673.3	1,704.1	1,747.5	1,688.2	1,691.0	1,701.8	1,681.0
Less: increase (+) or decrease (-) in Federal debt not subject to limit	0.8	0.6	2.4	1.8	1.1	-0.5	-0.6	-0.4	-1.0	-1.1	-1.5	-1.5
Less: change in adjustment for discount and premium[3]	-51.6	....	....	....	....	....	....	....	....	....	....	....
Total, change in debt subject to limit	2,201.2	2,118.3	1,986.1	1,941.3	1,746.9	1,673.8	1,704.6	1,747.9	1,689.3	1,692.1	1,703.3	1,682.6
Memorandum:												
Debt subject to statutory limit[4]	33,070.5	35,188.8	37,174.9	39,116.2	40,863.0	42,536.8	44,241.4	45,989.3	47,678.5	49,370.6	51,073.9	52,756.5

[1] Includes Federal fund transactions that correspond to those presented in Table 21–2, but that are for Federal funds alone with respect to the public and trust funds.

[2] Includes trust fund holdings in other cash assets and changes in the investments of the National Railroad Retirement Investment Trust in non-Federal securities.

[3] Consists of unamortized discount (less premium) on public issues of Treasury notes and bonds (other than zero-coupon bonds).

[4] Legislation enacted June 3, 2023 (Public Law 118-5), temporarily suspends the debt limit through January 1, 2025.

ligations, including Social Security and other payments to individuals, Medicaid and other grant payments to States, individual and corporate tax refunds, Federal employee salaries, payments to vendors and contractors, principal and interest payments on Treasury securities, and other obligations. If Treasury were unable to make timely interest payments or redeem securities, investors would cease to view Treasury securities as free of credit risk and Treasury's interest costs would increase. Because interest rates throughout the economy are benchmarked to the Treasury rates, interest rates for State and local governments, businesses, and individuals would also rise. Foreign investors would likely shift out of dollar-denominated assets, driving down the value of the dollar and further increasing interest rates on non-Federal, as well as Treasury, debt.

The debt subject to limit is estimated to increase to $35,189 billion by the end of 2024 and to $37,175 billion by the end of 2025. The Budget anticipates timely congressional action to address the statutory limit as necessary before exhaustion of Treasury's extraordinary measures.

Federal funds financing and the change in debt subject to limit.—The change in debt held by the public, as shown in Table 21–2, and the change in debt held by the public net of financial assets are determined primarily by the total Government deficit or surplus. The debt subject to limit, however, includes not only debt held by the public but also debt held by Government accounts. The change in debt subject to limit is therefore determined both by the factors that determine the total Government deficit or surplus and by the factors that determine the change in debt held by Government accounts. The effect of debt held by Government accounts on the total debt subject to limit can be seen in the second part of Table 21–2. The change in debt held by Government accounts is equal to 9 percent of the estimated total 2024 increase in debt subject to limit.

The Budget is composed of two groups of funds, Federal funds and trust funds. The Federal funds, in the main, are derived from tax receipts and borrowing and are used for the general purposes of the Government. The trust funds, on the other hand, are financed by taxes or other receipts dedicated by law for specified purposes, such as for paying Social Security benefits or making grants to State governments for highway construction.[30]

A Federal funds deficit must generally be financed by borrowing, which can be done either by selling securities to the public or by issuing securities to Government accounts that are not within the Federal funds group. Federal funds borrowing consists almost entirely of Treasury securities that are subject to the statutory debt limit. Very little debt subject to statutory limit has been issued for reasons except to finance the Federal funds deficit. The change in debt subject to limit is therefore determined primarily by the Federal funds deficit, which is equal to the difference between the total Government

[30] For further discussion of the trust funds and Federal funds groups, see the "Trust Funds and Federal Funds" chapter.

deficit or surplus and the trust fund surplus. Trust fund surpluses are almost entirely invested in securities subject to the debt limit, and trust funds hold most of the debt held by Government accounts. The trust fund surplus reduces the total budget deficit or increases the total budget surplus, decreasing the need to borrow from the public or increasing the ability to repay borrowing from the public. When the trust fund surplus is invested in Federal securities, the debt held by Government accounts increases, offsetting the decrease in debt held by the public by an equal amount. Thus, there is no net effect on gross Federal debt.

Table 21–6 derives the change in debt subject to limit. In 2023 the Federal funds deficit was $1,877 billion, and other factors increased financing requirements by $287 billion. In addition, special funds and revolving funds, which are part of the Federal funds group, invested a net of $18 billion in Treasury securities. Adjustments are also made for the difference between the trust fund surplus or deficit and the trust funds' investment or disinvestment in Federal securities (including the changes in NRRIT's investments in non-Federal securities) and for the change in unrealized discount on Federal debt held by Government accounts. As a net result of all these factors, $2,150 billion in financing was required, increasing gross Federal debt by that amount. Since Federal debt not subject to limit grew by $1 billion and the adjustment for discount and premium changed by $52 billion, the debt subject to limit increased by $2,201 billion, while debt held by the public increased by $1,982 billion.

Debt subject to limit is estimated to increase by $2,118 billion in 2024 and by $1,986 billion in 2025. The projected increases in the debt subject to limit are caused by the continued Federal funds deficit, supplemented by the other factors shown in Table 21–6. While debt held by the public increases by $18,820 billion from the end of 2023 through 2034, debt subject to limit increases by $19,686 billion.

Foreign Holdings of Federal Debt

Foreign holdings of Federal debt are presented in Table 21–7. During most of American history, the Federal debt was held almost entirely by individuals and institutions within the United States. In the late 1960s, foreign holdings were just over $10 billion, less than 5 percent of the total Federal debt held by the public. Foreign holdings began to grow significantly in the early 1970s, and then remained about 15–20 percent of total Federal debt until the mid-1990s. During 1995–97, growth in foreign holdings accelerated, reaching 33 percent by the end of 1997. From 2004 to 2019, foreign holdings of Federal debt generally represented around 40 percent or more of outstanding debt. Foreign holdings increased to 48 percent by the end of 2008 and then remained relatively stable through 2015.

After 2015, foreign holdings continued to grow in dollar terms but began to decline as a percent of total Federal debt held by the public. In 2023, foreign holdings were $7,604 billion, 29 percent of total debt held by the public.[31] The dollar increase in foreign holdings was about 18 percent of total Federal borrowing from the public in 2023 and 13 percent over the last five years. Changes in foreign holdings have been almost entirely due to decisions by foreign central banks, corporations, and individuals, rather than the direct marketing of these securities to foreign investors. All of the foreign holdings of Federal debt are denominated in dollars.

In 2023, foreign central banks and other foreign official institutions owned 49 percent of the foreign holdings of Federal debt; private investors owned the rest. At the end of 2023, the nations holding the largest shares of U.S. Federal debt were Japan, which held 14 percent of all foreign holdings, and China, which held 10 percent.

Foreign holdings of Federal debt are around 20–25 percent of the foreign-owned assets in the United States, depending on the method of measuring total assets. The foreign purchases of Federal debt securities do not measure the full impact of the capital inflow from abroad on the market for Federal debt securities. The capital inflow supplies additional funds to the credit market generally, and thus affects the market for Federal debt. For example, the capital inflow includes deposits in U.S. financial intermediaries that themselves buy Federal debt.

Federal, Federally Guaranteed, and Other Federally Assisted Borrowing

The Government's effects on the credit markets arise not only from its own borrowing but also from the direct loans that it makes to the public and the provision of assistance to certain borrowing by the public. The Government guarantees various types of borrowing by individuals, businesses, and other non-Federal entities, thereby providing assistance to private credit markets. The Government is also assisting borrowing by States through the Build America Bonds program, which subsidizes the interest that States pay on such borrowing. In addition, the Government has established private corporations—Government-sponsored enterprises—to provide financial intermediation for specified public purposes; it exempts the interest on most State and local government debt from income tax; it permits mortgage interest to be deducted in calculating taxable income; and it insures the deposits of banks and thrift institutions, which themselves make loans.

Federal credit programs and other forms of assistance are discussed in the "Credit and Insurance" chapter of this volume. Detailed data are presented in tables accompanying that chapter.

[31] The debt calculated by the Bureau of Economic Analysis is different, though similar in size, because of a different method of valuing securities.

Table 21–7. FOREIGN HOLDINGS OF FEDERAL DEBT

(Dollar amounts in billions)

Fiscal Year	Debt held by the public			Change in debt held by the public[2]	
	Total	Foreign[1]	Percentage foreign	Total	Foreign
1965	260.8	12.2	4.7	3.9	0.3
1970	283.2	14.0	4.9	5.1	3.7
1975	394.7	66.0	16.7	51.0	9.1
1980	711.9	126.4	17.8	71.6	1.3
1985	1,507.3	222.9	14.8	200.3	47.3
1990	2,411.6	463.8	19.2	220.8	72.0
1995	3,604.4	820.4	22.8	171.3	138.4
2000	3,409.8	1,038.8	30.5	-222.6	-242.6
2005	4,592.2	1,929.6	42.0	296.7	135.1
2010	9,018.9	4,316.0	47.9	1,474.2	745.4
2011	10,128.2	4,912.1	48.5	1,109.3	596.1
2012	11,281.1	5,476.1	48.5	1,152.9	564.0
2013	11,982.7	5,652.8	47.2	701.6	176.7
2014	12,779.9	6,069.2	47.5	797.2	416.4
2015	13,116.7	6,105.9	46.6	336.8	36.7
2016	14,167.6	6,155.9	43.5	1,050.9	50.0
2017	14,665.4	6,301.9	43.0	497.8	146.0
2018	15,749.6	6,225.9	39.5	1,084.1	-76.0
2019	16,800.7	6,923.5	41.2	1,051.1	697.6
2020	21,016.7	7,069.2	33.6	4,216.0	145.7
2021	22,284.0	7,570.9	34.0	1,267.4	501.7
2022	24,253.4	7,251.5	29.9	1,969.4	-319.4
2023	26,235.6	7,604.1	29.0	1,982.2	352.6

[1] Estimated by Treasury. These estimates exclude agency debt, the holdings of which are believed to be small. The data on foreign holdings are recorded by methods that are not fully comparable with the data on debt held by the public. Projections of foreign holdings are not available.

[2] Change in debt held by the public is defined as equal to the change in debt held by the public from the beginning of the year to the end of the year.

22. CURRENT SERVICES ESTIMATES

Current services, or "baseline" estimates, are designed to provide a benchmark against which Budget proposals can be measured. A baseline is not a prediction of the final outcome of the annual budget process, nor is it a proposed budget. However, it can still be a useful tool in budgeting. It can be used as a benchmark against which to measure the magnitude of the policy changes in the President's Budget or other budget proposals, and it can also be used to warn of future problems if policy is not changed.

Ideally, a current services baseline would provide a projection of estimated receipts, outlays, deficits or surpluses, and budget authority reflecting this year's enacted policies and programs for each year in the future. Defining this baseline is challenging because funding for many programs in operation today expires within the 10-year budget window. Most significantly, funding for discretionary programs is typically provided one year at a time in annual appropriations acts. Mandatory programs are not generally subject to annual appropriations, but many operate under multiyear authorizations that expire within the budget window. The framework used to construct the baseline must address whether and how to project forward the funding for these programs beyond their scheduled expiration dates.

Since the early 1970s, when the first requirements for the calculation of a "current services" baseline were enacted, OMB has constructed the baseline using a variety of concepts and measures. Throughout the 1990s, OMB calculated the baseline using a detailed set of rules in the Balanced Budget and Emergency Deficit Control Act of 1985, as amended (BBEDCA) by the Budget Enforcement Act of 1990 (BEA; Title XIII of Public Law 101-508). Although BBEDCA's baseline rules lapsed for a period when the enforcement provisions of the BEA expired in 2002, budget practitioners continued to adhere to them. The Budget Control Act of 2011 (BCA; Public Law 112-25) formally reinstated the BEA's baseline rules.

The Administration believes certain adjustments to the BBEDCA baseline are needed to better represent the deficit outlook under current policy and to serve as a more appropriate benchmark against which to measure

Table 22–1. CATEGORY TOTALS FOR THE ADJUSTED BASELINE
(In billions of dollars)

	2023	2024	2025	2026	2027	2028	2029	2030	2031	2032	2033	2034
Receipts	4,441	4,964	5,087	5,426	5,765	6,076	6,376	6,661	6,979	7,324	7,684	8,029
Outlays:												
Discretionary:												
Defense	806	852	884	902	923	938	958	972	998	1,022	1,046	1,070
Non-defense	912	965	995	993	1,003	1,009	1,019	1,033	1,054	1,087	1,112	1,136
Subtotal, discretionary	1,718	1,818	1,879	1,894	1,926	1,947	1,977	2,005	2,052	2,109	2,158	2,206
Mandatory:												
Social Security	1,348	1,452	1,543	1,637	1,730	1,824	1,919	2,018	2,118	2,221	2,325	2,432
Medicare	839	839	936	997	1,075	1,219	1,176	1,335	1,423	1,534	1,789	1,766
Medicaid and CHIP	633	584	605	642	682	723	765	809	852	900	955	1,011
Other mandatory	938	1,291	1,019	1,019	1,016	1,019	1,083	1,149	1,172	1,215	1,269	1,276
Subtotal, mandatory	3,758	4,165	4,104	4,294	4,503	4,786	4,943	5,311	5,565	5,870	6,339	6,484
Net interest	658	890	969	1,022	1,088	1,158	1,220	1,278	1,347	1,425	1,500	1,572
Total, outlays	6,135	6,873	6,952	7,211	7,517	7,891	8,140	8,594	8,964	9,404	9,997	10,262
Unified deficit(+)/surplus(–)	1,694	1,909	1,865	1,784	1,752	1,815	1,763	1,933	1,985	2,080	2,313	2,233
(On-budget)	*(1,666)*	*(1,837)*	*(1,753)*	*(1,648)*	*(1,590)*	*(1,637)*	*(1,550)*	*(1,692)*	*(1,712)*	*(1,770)*	*(1,990)*	*(1,872)*
(Off-budget)	*(27)*	*(72)*	*(112)*	*(136)*	*(162)*	*(178)*	*(213)*	*(241)*	*(273)*	*(310)*	*(323)*	*(361)*
Memorandum:												
Adjusted baseline deficit	1,694	1,909	1,865	1,784	1,752	1,815	1,763	1,933	1,985	2,080	2,313	2,233
Effect of 2024 and 2025 negotiated discretionary funding levels and other Fiscal Responsibility Act agreements	....	4	20	30	34	34	35	6	1	27	38	44
Extension of emergency funding	....	....	3	7	10	13	17	17	18	18	19	19
Savings from proposed discretionary program integrity adjustments	....	....	2	4	6	7	8	9	10	11	12	13
Related debt service	....	....	1	2	3	5	7	8	9	11	13	15
BBEDCA baseline deficit	1,694	1,913	1,891	1,827	1,805	1,875	1,830	1,974	2,023	2,147	2,396	2,325

*Less than $500 million.

policy changes. The baseline adjustments are discussed in more detail below. Table 22–1 shows estimates of receipts, outlays, and deficits under the Administration's baseline for 2023 through 2034.[1] The table also shows the Administration's estimates by major component of the budget. The estimates are based on the economic assumptions underlying the Budget, which, as discussed later in this chapter, were developed on the assumption that the Administration's budget proposals will be enacted. The memorandum bank on Table 22–1 provides additional detail about the effects of the adjustments made to the BBEDCA baseline to produce the adjusted baseline.

Conceptual Basis for Estimates

Receipts and outlays are divided into two categories that are important for calculating the baseline: those controlled by authorizing legislation (receipts and direct or mandatory spending) and those controlled through the annual appropriations process (discretionary spending). Different estimating rules apply to each category.

Direct spending and receipts.—Direct spending includes the major entitlement programs, such as Social Security, Medicare, Medicaid, Federal employee retirement, unemployment compensation, and the Supplemental Nutrition Assistance Program (SNAP). It also includes such programs as deposit insurance and farm price and income supports, where the Government is legally obligated to make payments under certain conditions. Taxes and other receipts are like direct spending in that they involve ongoing activities that generally operate under permanent or long-standing authority, and the underlying statutes generally specify the tax rates or benefit levels that must be collected or paid, and who must pay or who is eligible to receive benefits.

The baseline generally—but not always—assumes that receipts and direct spending programs continue in the future as specified by current law. The budgetary effects of anticipated regulatory and administrative actions that are permissible under current law are also reflected in the estimates. BBEDCA requires several exemptions to this general rule. Exceptions in BBEDCA are described below:

- Expiring excise taxes dedicated to a trust fund are assumed to be extended at the rates in effect at the time of expiration. During the projection period of 2024 through 2034, the taxes affected by this exception are:
  - — taxes deposited in the Airport and Airway Trust Fund, which expire on March 8, 2024;
  - — taxes deposited in the Oil Spill Liability Trust Fund, which expire on December 31, 2025;
  - — taxes deposited in the Patient-Centered Outcomes Research Trust Fund, which expire on September 30, 2029;
  - — taxes deposited in the Sport Fish Restoration and Boating Trust Fund, which expire on September 30, 2028;
  - — taxes deposited in the Highway Trust Fund and the Leaking Underground Storage Tank Trust Fund, which expire on September 30, 2028; and
  - — taxes deposited in the Hazardous Substances Superfund, which expire on December 31, 2031.
- Expiring authorizations for direct spending programs that were enacted on or before the date of enactment of the Balanced Budget Act of 1997 are assumed to be extended if their current year outlays exceed $50 million. For example, even though the Environmental Quality Incentives Program, which was authorized prior to the Balanced Budget Act of 1997, continues only through 2031 under current law, the baseline estimates assume continuation of this program through the projection period, because the program's current year outlays exceed the $50 million threshold.[2]

The baseline also includes an adjustment to reflect savings to mandatory entitlement programs due to the activities funded by discretionary program integrity cap adjustments allowed by the Fiscal Responsibility Act (FRA, Public Law 118-5). Given the history of consistent enactment of these adjustments, the Administration believes that this presentation provides a more accurate representation of expected mandatory outlays for these programs.[3]

Discretionary spending.—Discretionary programs differ in one important aspect from direct spending programs: the Congress provides spending authority for almost all discretionary programs one year at a time. The spending authority is normally provided in the form of annual appropriations. Absent appropriations of additional funds in the future, discretionary programs would cease to operate after existing balances were spent. If the baseline were intended strictly to reflect current law, then a baseline would reflect only the expenditure of remaining balances from appropriations laws already enacted. Instead, the BBEDCA baseline provides a mechanical definition to reflect the continuing costs of discretionary programs. Under BBEDCA, the baseline estimates for discretionary programs in the current year are based on that year's enacted appropriations, or on the annualized levels provided by a continuing resolution if final full-year appropriations have not been enacted.[4] For the budget year and beyond, the spending authority in the

[1] The estimates are shown on a unified budget basis; i.e., the off-budget receipts and outlays of the Social Security trust funds and the Postal Service Fund are added to the on-budget receipts and outlays to calculate the unified budget totals.

[2] If enacted after the Balanced Budget Act of 1997 (Public Law 105-33), programs that are expressly temporary in nature expire in the baseline as provided by current law, even if their current year outlays exceed the $50 million threshold.

[3] See the "Budget Process" chapter of this volume for a more thorough discussion of program integrity initiatives.

[4] At the time the budget was prepared, 2024 discretionary appropriations were incomplete and most discretionary programs were operating under continuing appropriations provided in the Continuing Appropriations Act, 2024 (Division A of Public Law 118-15, as amended, "the 2024 CR").

current year is adjusted for inflation, using specified inflation rates.[5] The definition attempts to keep discretionary spending for each program roughly level in real terms.

The Administration believes adjustments to the BBEDCA baseline are needed to make the baseline a more useful benchmark for assessing the deficit outlook and the impact of Budget proposals. These adjustments, described below, are to comply with the the discretionary spending levels agreed to with the FRA for 2024 and 2025, including aligning program integrity funding with the levels authorized in BBEDCA, and to remove the extension and inflation of certain emergency spending in the outyears.

For 2024, the adjustment to reflect the discretionary spending levels agreed to with the FRA reflects the topline appropriations agreement announced by congressional leadership in January 2024, which assumes that appropriations will be enacted in line with the original discretionary "caps" enacted in the FRA and certain savings will be included to achieve those caps. Beyond 2025, the 2025 cap levels are adjusted for inflation through the budget window using the inflation rates required by BBEDCA. The baseline also assumes that "shifted base" funding[6] will continue to be used as a concept in final 2024 appropriations.

In addition, BBEDCA allows for adjustments to the discretionary cap levels for specified programs and funding for other discretionary programs is excluded from the caps by statute. These adjustments and exclusions are described below:

- Emergency requirements.—Funding that was provided for 2024 and designated as emergency funding, other than the "shifted base" funding noted above, has been removed from the baseline beginning in 2025. Removing the extension and inflation of this funding allows the baseline to provide a more meaningful benchmark for discretionary spending than a baseline strictly following the BBEDCA rules.
- Disaster relief and wildfire suppression.—The BBEDCA baseline projects forward the $20.1 billion of continuing disaster relief funding for the Department of Homeland Security and the Small Business Administration in 2024. The BBEDCA baseline also projects the $2.6 billion in continuing funding for wildfire suppression activities at the Departments of Agriculture and the Interior. Both the disaster and wildfire amounts are increased after 2024 by the BBEDCA inflation rates. The amounts of these cap adjustments in the baseline do not exceed the funding ceilings for these adjustments included in BBEDCA.
- Program integrity.—The BBEDCA baseline assumes the cap adjustment levels at the annualized level provided in the 2024 CR, and inflates those amounts after the current year. The adjusted baseline assumes full funding for the enacted cap adjustments levels in the FRA through 2025, and inflates those amounts after 2025. Additionally, as explained above, the adjusted baseline assumes savings from enacting the program integrity cap adjustments at their full levels.
- In addition to the cap adjustments specified in BBEDCA, there is other discretionary funding that is, by statute, not included in base amounts subject to the caps and for which BBEDCA does not allow cap adjustments. This includes 21st Century Cures Act appropriations, certain revenues provided for the Environmental Protection Agency's Superfund program, appropriations for the Harbor Maintenance Trust Fund in the Corps of Engineers, and certain appropriations provided in the Infrastructure Investment and Jobs Act and the Bipartisan Safer Communities Act. These amounts are included in the baseline outside of the discretionary cap totals at enacted or authorized levels and adjusted for inflation where applicable.

BBEDCA § 251A sequestration.—BBEDCA § 251A requires reductions to non-exempt mandatory spending through 2031 for most programs and through the first month of 2033 for Medicare.[7] The BBEDCA baseline includes the effects of the across-the-board reductions ("sequestration") already invoked by the BBEDCA § 251A sequestration orders for 2013 through 2024, the BBEDCA § 251A sequestration order for mandatory spending for 2025 issued with the transmittal of the 2025 Budget, and the extension of sequestration of mandatory spending through 2031 for most programs or through the first month of 2033 for Medicare.[8] Amounts that are sequestered in the baseline but return in the subsequent year as available (pop-up) are shown through 2032.

Economic Assumptions

As discussed above, an important purpose of the baseline is to serve as a benchmark against which policy proposals are measured. By convention, the President's Budget constructs baseline and policy estimates under

[5] The Administration's baseline uses the inflation rates for discretionary spending required by BBEDCA. This requirement results in an overcompensation in the calculation for Federal pay as a result of the calendar-year timing of Federal pay adjustments. Updating the calculation to address this annual timing discrepancy would have only a small effect on the discretionary baseline.

[6] A subset of appropriations in the Consolidated Appropriations Act, 2023 (Public Law 117-328) that were intended to be base appropriations in the 2023 appropriations process were designated by the Congress as emergency requirements for purposes of the 2023 Omnibus agreement. This subset of appropriations, which are continued in the 2024 CR, and additional amounts agreed upon along with enactment of the FRA are commonly refered to as "shifted base" funding. These amounts are extended and inflated in the baseline since they are counted as base funds in the Administration's discretionary presentation.

[7] Since enactment of the BCA, the Congress has extended sequestration of mandatory spending through a series of amendments to section 251A of BBEDCA (2 U.S.C. 901a). Most recently, the National Defense Authorization Act for Fiscal Year 2024 (Public Law 118-31) extended sequestration for Medicare through the first month of 2033.

[8] The effects of the sequestration reductions are reflected in the detailed schedules for the affected budget accounts for all years. See the "Budget Concepts" chapter of this volume for a more thorough discussion of sequestration procedures.

Table 22–2. SUMMARY OF ECONOMIC ASSUMPTIONS
(Fiscal years; in billions of dollars)

	2023	2024	2025	2026	2027	2028	2029	2030	2031	2032	2033	2034
Gross Domestic Product (GDP):												
Levels, in billions of dollars:												
Current dollars	26,977	28,255	29,340	30,553	31,816	33,129	34,511	35,984	37,546	39,176	40,877	42,654
Real, chained (2017) dollars	22,205	22,656	23,021	23,484	23,953	24,432	24,929	25,462	26,022	26,594	27,179	27,777
Percent change, year over year:												
Current dollars	6.6	4.7	3.8	4.1	4.1	4.1	4.2	4.3	4.3	4.3	4.3	4.3
Real, chained (2017) dollars	1.9	2.0	1.6	2.0	2.0	2.0	2.0	2.1	2.2	2.2	2.2	2.2
Inflation measures (percent change, year over year):												
GDP chained price index	4.6	2.7	2.2	2.1	2.1	2.1	2.1	2.1	2.1	2.1	2.1	2.1
Consumer price index (all urban, seasonally adjusted)	5.1	3.1	2.4	2.3	2.3	2.3	2.3	2.3	2.3	2.3	2.3	2.3
Unemployment rate, civilian (percent)	3.6	3.9	4.1	3.9	3.9	3.8	3.8	3.8	3.8	3.8	3.8	3.8
Interest rates (percent):												
91-day Treasury bills	4.8	5.2	4.2	3.5	3.1	3.0	2.9	2.8	2.7	2.7	2.7	2.7
10-year Treasury notes	3.8	4.6	4.1	4.0	3.9	3.8	3.8	3.7	3.7	3.7	3.7	3.7
MEMORANDUM:												
Related program assumptions:												
Automatic benefit increases (percent):												
Social security and veterans pensions	8.7	3.2	2.8	2.3	2.3	2.3	2.3	2.3	2.3	2.3	2.3	2.3
Federal employee retirement	8.7	3.2	2.8	2.3	2.3	2.3	2.3	2.3	2.3	2.3	2.3	2.3
Supplemental Nutrition Assistance Program	12.5	3.6	2.3	2.3	2.3	2.3	2.3	2.3	2.3	2.3	2.3	2.3
Insured unemployment rate	1.2	1.4	1.4	1.4	1.4	1.3	1.3	1.3	1.3	1.3	1.3	1.3

the same set of economic and technical assumptions. These assumptions are developed on the basis that the President's Budget proposals will be enacted.

Of course, the economy and the budget interact. Government tax and spending policies can influence prices, economic growth, consumption, savings, and investment. In turn, changes in economic conditions due to the enactment of proposals affect tax receipts and spending, including for unemployment benefits, entitlement payments that receive automatic cost-of-living adjustments (COLAs), income support programs for low-income individuals, and interest on the Federal debt.

Because of these interactions, it would be reasonable, from an economic perspective, to assume different economic paths for the baseline projection and the President's Budget. However, this would greatly complicate the process of producing the Budget, which normally includes a large number of proposals that could have potential economic feedback effects. Agencies would have to produce two sets of estimates for programs sensitive to economic assumptions even if those programs were not directly affected by any proposal in the Budget. Using different economic assumptions for baseline and policy estimates would also diminish the value of the baseline estimates as a benchmark for measuring proposed policy changes, because it would be difficult to separate the effects of proposed policy changes from the effects of different economic assumptions. Using the same economic assumptions for the baseline and the President's Budget eliminates this potential source of confusion.

The economic assumptions underlying the Budget and the Administration's baseline are summarized in Table 22–2. The economic outlook underlying these assumptions is discussed in greater detail in the "Economic Assumptions" chapter of this volume.

Major Programmatic Assumptions

A number of programmatic assumptions must be made to calculate the baseline estimates. These include assumptions about annual cost-of-living adjustments in the indexed programs and the number of beneficiaries who will receive payments from the major benefit programs. Assumptions about various automatic cost-of-living-adjustments are shown in Table 22–2, and assumptions about baseline caseload projections for the major benefit programs are shown in Table 22–3, available at *https://whitehouse.gov/omb/analytical-perspectives/*. These assumptions affect baseline estimates of direct spending for each of these programs, and they also affect estimates of the discretionary baseline for a limited number of programs. For the administrative expenses for Medicare, Railroad Retirement, and unemployment insurance, the discretionary baseline is increased (or decreased) for changes in the number of beneficiaries in addition to the adjustments for inflation described earlier. It is also necessary to make assumptions about the continuation of expiring programs and provisions. As explained above, in the baseline estimates provided here, expiring excise taxes dedicated to a trust fund are extended at current rates. In general, mandatory programs with spending of at least $50 million in the current year are also assumed to continue, unless the programs are explicitly temporary in nature. Table 22–4, available at *https://whitehouse.gov/omb/analytical-perspectives/*, provides a listing of

Table 22–5. RECEIPTS BY SOURCE IN THE PROJECTION OF ADJUSTED BASELINE
(In billions of dollars)

	2023 Actual	Estimate										
		2024	2025	2026	2027	2028	2029	2030	2031	2032	2033	2034
Individual income taxes	2,176.5	2,509.8	2,639.0	2,914.7	3,145.4	3,325.2	3,496.1	3,658.4	3,848.1	4,055.2	4,265.4	4,486.1
Corporation income taxes	419.6	519.5	467.0	453.1	440.0	454.1	483.0	494.0	512.0	550.2	558.8	570.2
Social insurance and retirement receipts	1,614.5	1,692.5	1,754.2	1,832.5	1,910.2	2,005.2	2,083.5	2,173.1	2,264.1	2,354.4	2,479.2	2,578.4
(On-budget)	*(420.7)*	*(452.3)*	*(469.6)*	*(489.8)*	*(511.5)*	*(535.8)*	*(555.8)*	*(580.7)*	*(605.8)*	*(629.6)*	*(662.7)*	*(691.5)*
(Off-budget)	*(1,193.8)*	*(1,240.2)*	*(1,284.5)*	*(1,342.7)*	*(1,398.7)*	*(1,469.4)*	*(1,527.8)*	*(1,592.4)*	*(1,658.3)*	*(1,724.8)*	*(1,816.5)*	*(1,887.0)*
Excise taxes	75.8	96.7	97.5	99.9	100.0	99.2	100.8	103.2	102.8	103.6	104.6	104.6
Estate and gift taxes	33.7	29.0	31.3	33.2	48.8	51.1	53.5	56.1	60.1	64.7	69.5	74.7
Customs duties	80.3	81.4	60.7	52.5	52.9	54.5	56.6	58.8	61.2	53.4	55.6	57.7
Miscellaneous receipts	40.6	34.7	37.1	40.4	67.9	86.9	102.6	117.4	130.8	142.0	150.5	157.7
Total, receipts	4,440.9	4,963.7	5,086.7	5,426.2	5,765.1	6,076.1	6,376.1	6,660.9	6,979.2	7,323.5	7,683.6	8,029.3
(On-budget)	*(3,247.2)*	*(3,723.5)*	*(3,802.2)*	*(4,083.6)*	*(4,366.4)*	*(4,606.8)*	*(4,848.4)*	*(5,068.5)*	*(5,320.9)*	*(5,598.7)*	*(5,867.1)*	*(6,142.4)*
(Off-budget)	*(1,193.8)*	*(1,240.2)*	*(1,284.5)*	*(1,342.7)*	*(1,398.7)*	*(1,469.4)*	*(1,527.8)*	*(1,592.4)*	*(1,658.3)*	*(1,724.8)*	*(1,816.5)*	*(1,887.0)*

mandatory programs and taxes assumed to continue in the baseline after their expiration.[9] Many other important assumptions must be made in order to calculate the baseline estimates. These include the timing and content of regulations that will be issued over the projection period, the use of administrative discretion under current law, and other assumptions about the way programs operate. Table 22–4 lists many of these assumptions and their effects on the baseline estimates. The list is not intended to be exhaustive; the variety and complexity of Government programs are too great to provide a complete list. Instead, the table shows some of the more important assumptions.

Current Services Receipts, Outlays, and Budget Authority

Receipts.—Table 22–5 shows the Administration's baseline receipts by major source. Table 22–6 shows the scheduled increases in the Social Security taxable earnings base, which affect both payroll tax receipts for the program and the initial benefit levels for certain retirees.

Outlays.—Table 22–7 shows the growth from 2024 to 2025 and average annual growth over the five-year and ten-year periods for certain discretionary and major mandatory programs. Tables 22–8 and 22–9 show the Administration's baseline outlays by function and by agency, respectively. A more detailed presentation of these outlays (by function, category, subfunction, and program) is provided as part of Table 22–12. The last three of these tables are available on the internet at *https://whitehouse.gov/omb/analytical-perspectives/*.

Budget authority.—Tables 22–10 and 22–11 show estimates of budget authority in the Administration's baseline by function and by agency, respectively. A more detailed presentation of this budget authority with program-level estimates is provided as part of Table 22–12. These tables are available on the internet at *https://whitehouse.gov/omb/analytical-perspectives/*.

[9] Unless otherwise described in this chapter, all discretionary programs are assumed to continue, and are therefore not presented in Table 22–4.

Table 22–6. EFFECT ON RECEIPTS OF CHANGES IN THE SOCIAL SECURITY TAXABLE EARNINGS BASE

(In billions of dollars)

Social security (OASDI) taxable earnings base increases:	2025	2026	2027	2028	2029	2030	2031	2032	2033	2034
$168,600 to $176,700 on Jan. 1, 2025	4.8	12.0	13.1	14.3	15.4	16.8	18.2	19.6	21.5	23.2
$176,700 to $184,800 on Jan. 1, 2026	....	4.7	11.9	13.0	14.1	15.3	16.5	17.9	19.6	21.2
$184,800 to $192,000 on Jan. 1, 2027	....	....	4.2	10.6	11.5	12.5	13.5	14.6	16.0	17.4
$192,300 to $199,500 on Jan. 1, 2028	....	....	....	4.4	11.1	12.0	13.0	14.1	15.4	16.7
$199,500 to $207,300 on Jan. 1, 2029	....	....	....	....	4.6	11.5	12.5	13.6	14.9	16.1
$207,300 to $215,400 on Jan. 1, 2030	....	....	....	....	....	4.8	12.0	13.0	14.3	15.4
$215,400 to $223,800 on Jan. 1, 2031	....	....	....	....	....	....	5.0	12.5	13.7	14.8
$223,800 to $232,200 on Jan. 1, 2032	....	....	....	....	....	....	....	5.0	12.7	13.7
$232,200 to $241,500 on Jan. 1, 2033	....	....	....	....	....	....	....	....	5.6	14.1
$241,500 to $250,800 on Jan. 1, 2034	....	....	....	....	....	....	....	....	....	5.6

Table 22–7. CHANGE IN OUTLAY ESTIMATES BY CATEGORY IN THE ADJUSTED BASELINE

(In billions of dollars)

											Change 2024 to 2025		Change 2024 to 2029		Change 2024 to 2034	
	2024	2025	2026	2027	2028	2029	2030	2031	2032	2033	Amount	Percent	Amount	Average annual rate	Amount	Average annual rate
Outlays:																
Discretionary:																
Defense	852	884	902	923	938	958	972	998	1,022	1,046	32	3.7%	105	2.4%	218	2.3%
Non-defense	965	995	993	1,003	1,009	1,019	1,033	1,054	1,087	1,112	30	3.1%	54	1.1%	171	1.6%
Subtotal, discretionary	1,818	1,879	1,894	1,926	1,947	1,977	2,005	2,052	2,109	2,158	62	3.4%	159	1.7%	389	2.0%
Mandatory:																
Farm programs	27	22	21	21	21	21	19	19	20	20	-5	-18.3%	-6	-5.1%	-7	-3.1%
Medicaid	567	587	622	662	701	742	785	833	885	940	19	3.4%	175	5.5%	428	5.8%
Other health	188	174	163	166	172	180	186	180	185	193	-14	-7.7%	-8	-0.9%	13	0.6%
Medicare	839	936	997	1,075	1,219	1,176	1,335	1,423	1,534	1,789	97	11.6%	337	7.0%	927	7.7%
Federal employee retirement and disability	181	194	200	206	219	212	225	232	239	253	13	7.0%	31	3.2%	71	3.4%
Unemployment compensation	52	49	44	43	45	47	52	55	57	59	-4	-6.9%	-5	-2.1%	9	1.6%
Food and nutrition assistance	178	155	161	165	168	171	174	177	181	185	-23	-13.0%	-7	-0.8%	11	0.6%
Other income security programs	247	202	198	185	194	187	195	198	200	209	-45	-18.3%	-61	-5.5%	-40	-1.7%
Social Security	1,452	1,543	1,637	1,730	1,824	1,919	2,018	2,118	2,221	2,325	92	6.3%	468	5.7%	980	5.3%
Veterans programs	203	234	247	262	297	277	315	336	359	405	31	15.4%	74	6.4%	203	7.2%
Other mandatory programs	375	157	158	158	88	177	178	170	172	148	-218	-58.1%	-198	-13.9%	-231	-9.1%
Undistributed offsetting receipts	−145	−149	−155	−168	−163	−166	−171	−175	−182	-186	4	3.1%	-21	2.8%	-45	2.8%
Subtotal, mandatory	4,165	4,104	4,294	4,503	4,786	4,943	5,311	5,565	5,870	6,339	-62	-1.5%	777	3.5%	2,319	4.5%
Net interest	890	969	1,022	1,088	1,158	1,220	1,278	1,347	1,425	1,500	79	8.9%	330	6.5%	682	5.9%
Total, outlays	6,873	6,952	7,211	7,517	7,891	8,140	8,594	8,964	9,404	9,997	79	1.2%	1,267	3.4%	3,390	4.1%

*Less than $500 million.

23. TRUST FUNDS AND FEDERAL FUNDS

As is common for State and local government budgets, the budget for the Federal Government contains information about collections and expenditures for different types of funds. This chapter presents summary information about the transactions of the two major fund groups used by the Federal Government, trust funds and Federal funds. It also presents information about the income and outgo of the major trust funds and certain Federal funds that are financed by dedicated collections in a manner similar to trust funds.

The Federal Funds Group

The Federal funds group includes all financial transactions of the Government that are not required by law to be recorded in trust funds. It accounts for a larger share of the budget than the trust funds group.

The Federal funds group includes the "general fund," which is used for the general purposes of Government rather than being restricted by law to a specific program. The general fund is the largest fund in the Government and it receives all collections not dedicated for some other fund, including virtually all income taxes and many excise taxes. The general fund is used for all programs that are not supported by trust, special, or revolving funds.

The Federal funds group also includes special funds and revolving funds, both of which receive collections that are dedicated by law for specific purposes. Where the law requires that Federal fund collections be dedicated to a particular program, the collections and associated disbursements are recorded in special fund receipt and expenditure accounts.[1] An example is the portion of the Outer Continental Shelf mineral leasing receipts deposited into the Land and Water Conservation Fund. Money in special fund receipt accounts must be appropriated before it can be obligated and spent. The majority of special fund collections are derived from the Government's power to impose taxes or fines, or otherwise compel payment, as in the case of the Crime Victims Fund. In addition, a significant amount of collections credited to special funds is derived from certain types of business-like activity, such as the sale of Government land or other assets or the use of Government property. These collections include receipts from timber sales and royalties from oil and gas extraction.

Revolving funds are used to conduct continuing cycles of business-like activity. Revolving funds receive proceeds from the sale of products or services, and these proceeds finance ongoing activities that continue to provide products or services. Instead of being deposited in receipt accounts, the proceeds are recorded in revolving fund expenditure accounts. The proceeds are generally available for obligation and expenditure without further legislative action. Outlays for programs with revolving funds are reported both gross and net of these proceeds; gross outlays include the expenditures from the proceeds and net program outlays are derived by subtracting the proceeds from gross outlays. Because the proceeds of these sales are recorded as offsets to outlays within expenditure accounts rather than receipt accounts, the proceeds are known as "offsetting collections."[2] There are two classes of revolving funds in the Federal funds group. Public enterprise funds, such as the Postal Service Fund, conduct business-like operations mainly with the public. Intragovernmental funds, such as the Federal Buildings Fund, conduct business-like operations mainly within and between Government agencies.

The Trust Funds Group

The trust funds group consists of funds that are designated by law as trust funds. Like special funds and revolving funds, trust funds receive collections that are dedicated by law for specific purposes. Some of the larger trust funds are used to budget for social insurance programs, such as Social Security, Medicare, and unemployment compensation. Other large trust funds are used to budget for military and Federal civilian employees' retirement benefits, highway and transit construction and maintenance, and airport and airway development and maintenance. There are a few trust revolving funds that are credited with collections earmarked by law to carry out a cycle of business-type operations. There are also a few small trust funds that have been established to carry out the terms of a conditional gift or bequest.

There is no substantive difference between special funds in the Federal funds group and trust funds, or between revolving funds in the Federal funds group and trust revolving funds. Whether a particular fund is designated in law as a trust fund is, in many cases, arbitrary. For example, the National Service Life Insurance Fund is a trust fund, but the Servicemen's Group Life Insurance Fund is a Federal fund, even though both receive dedicated collections from veterans and both provide life insurance payments to veterans' beneficiaries.

The Federal Government uses the term "trust fund" differently than the way in which it is commonly used. In common usage, the term is used to refer to a private fund that has a beneficiary who owns the trust's income and may also own the trust's assets. A custodian or trustee manages the assets on behalf of the beneficiary accord-

[1] There are two types of budget accounts: expenditure (or appropriation) accounts and receipt accounts. Expenditure accounts are used to record outlays and receipt accounts are used to record governmental receipts and offsetting receipts. For further detail on expenditure and receipt accounts, see the "Budget Concepts" chapter of this volume.

[2] See the "Offsetting Collections and Offsetting Receipts" chapter of this volume for more information.

ing to the terms of the trust agreement, as established by a trustor. Neither the trustee nor the beneficiary can change the terms of the trust agreement; only the trustor can change the terms of the agreement. In contrast, the Federal Government owns and manages the assets and the earnings of most Federal trust funds, and can unilaterally change the law to raise or lower future trust fund collections and payments or change the purpose for which the collections are used. Only a few small Federal trust funds are managed pursuant to a trust agreement whereby the Government acts as the trustee; even then, the Government generally owns the funds and has some ability to alter the amount deposited into or paid out of the funds.

Deposit funds, which are funds held by the Government as a custodian on behalf of individuals or a non-Federal entity, are similar to private-sector trust funds. The Government makes no decisions about the amount of money placed in deposit funds or about how the proceeds are spent. For this reason, these funds are not classified as Federal trust funds, but are instead considered to be non-budgetary and excluded from the Federal budget.[3]

The income of a Federal Government trust fund must be used for the purposes specified in law. The income of some trust funds, such as the Employees and Retired Employees Health Benefits Fund, is spent almost as quickly as it is collected. In other cases, such as the military and Federal civilian employees' retirement trust funds, the trust fund income is not spent as quickly as it is collected. Currently, these funds do not use all of their annual income (which includes intragovernmen-

[3] Deposit funds are also discussed in the "Coverage of the Budget" chapter of this volume.

Table 23–1. RECEIPTS, OUTLAYS, AND SURPLUS OR DEFICIT BY FUND GROUP

(In billions of dollars)

	2023 Actual	Estimate					
		2024	2025	2026	2027	2028	2029
Receipts:							
Federal funds cash income:							
From the public	3,548.1	3,663.6	3,973.9	4,322.8	4,566.2	4,848.8	5,020.0
From trust funds	1.9	2.4	2.2	2.1	1.9	1.8	1.7
Total, Federal funds cash income	3,550.0	3,666.0	3,976.2	4,324.9	4,568.1	4,850.6	5,021.7
Trust funds cash income:							
From the public	1,950.1	2,058.7	2,253.0	2,307.0	2,411.6	2,533.0	2,642.2
From Federal funds:							
Interest	169.2	184.2	177.0	196.7	205.7	212.0	220.7
Other	822.4	904.8	966.7	1,021.1	963.2	1,022.5	1,104.8
Total, Trust funds cash income	2,941.6	3,147.6	3,396.7	3,524.8	3,580.5	3,767.5	3,967.8
Offsetting collections from the public and offsetting receipts:							
Federal funds	–797.6	–381.2	–463.2	–463.5	–475.4	–535.2	–472.6
Trust funds	–1,253.1	–1,350.9	–1,424.7	–1,513.4	–1,487.0	–1,573.2	–1,687.0
Total, offsetting collections from the public and offsetting receipts	–2,050.7	–1,732.1	–1,887.9	–1,976.9	–1,962.4	–2,108.4	–2,159.6
Unified budget receipts:							
Federal funds	2,752.4	3,284.8	3,512.9	3,861.4	4,092.7	4,315.4	4,549.2
Trust funds	1,688.5	1,796.8	1,972.0	2,011.4	2,093.5	2,194.2	2,280.7
Total, unified budget receipts	4,440.9	5,081.5	5,484.9	5,872.7	6,186.2	6,509.6	6,829.9
Outlays:							
Federal funds cash outgo	5,427.2	5,768.1	6,029.7	6,095.9	6,155.7	6,410.9	6,616.7
Trust funds cash outgo	2,758.1	2,904.9	3,124.1	3,300.5	3,503.3	3,780.0	3,855.7
Offsetting collections from the public and offsetting receipts:							
Federal funds	–797.6	–381.2	–463.2	–463.5	–475.4	–535.2	–472.6
Trust funds	–1,253.1	–1,350.9	–1,424.7	–1,513.4	–1,487.0	–1,573.2	–1,687.0
Total, offsetting collections from the public and offsetting receipts	–2,050.7	–1,732.1	–1,887.9	–1,976.9	–1,962.4	–2,108.4	–2,159.6
Unified budget outlays:							
Federal funds	4,629.6	5,386.9	5,566.5	5,632.4	5,680.3	5,875.7	6,144.2
Trust funds	1,505.0	1,554.0	1,699.4	1,787.0	2,016.3	2,206.8	2,168.7
Total, unified budget outlays	6,134.7	6,940.9	7,266.0	7,419.4	7,696.6	8,082.5	8,312.8
Surplus or deficit(–):							
Federal funds	–1,877.2	–2,102.1	–2,053.6	–1,771.0	–1,587.5	–1,560.3	–1,595.0
Trust funds	183.5	242.8	272.6	224.3	77.2	–12.5	112.1
Total, unified surplus/deficit(–)	–1,693.7	–1,859.4	–1,781.0	–1,546.6	–1,510.3	–1,572.9	–1,482.9

Note: Receipts include governmental, interfund, and proprietary, and exclude intrafund receipts (which are offset against intrafund payments so that cash income and cash outgo are not overstated).

tal interest income). This surplus of income over outgo adds to the trust fund's balance, which is available for future expenditures. Trust fund balances are generally required by law to be invested in Federal securities issued by the Department of the Treasury.[4] The National Railroad Retirement Investment Trust is a rare example of a Government trust fund authorized to invest balances in equity markets.

A trust fund normally consists of one or more receipt accounts (to record income) and an expenditure account (to record outgo). However, a few trust funds, such as the Veterans Special Life Insurance fund, are established by law as trust revolving funds. Such a fund is similar to a revolving fund in the Federal funds group in that it may consist of a single account to record both income and outgo. Trust revolving funds are used to conduct cycle of business-type operations; offsetting collections are credited to the funds (which are also expenditure accounts) and the funds' outlays are displayed net of the offsetting collections.

Income and Outgo by Fund Group

Table 23–1 shows income, outgo, and the surplus or deficit by fund group and in the aggregate (netted to avoid double-counting) from which the total unified budget receipts, outlays, and surplus or deficit are derived. Income consists mostly of governmental receipts (derived from governmental activity, primarily income, payroll, and excise taxes). Income also includes offsetting receipts, which include proprietary receipts (derived from business-like transactions with the public), interfund collections (derived from payments from a fund in one fund group to a fund in the other fund group), and gifts. Outgo consists of payments made to the public or to a fund in the other fund group.

Two types of transactions are treated specially in the table. First, income and outgo for each fund group exclude all transactions that occur between funds within the same fund group.[5] These intrafund transactions constitute outgo and income for the individual funds that make and collect the payments, but they are offsetting within the fund group as a whole. The totals for each fund group measure only the group's transactions with the public and the other fund group. Second, outgo is calculated net of the collections from Federal sources that are credited to expenditure accounts (which, as noted above, are referred to as offsetting collections); the spending that is financed by those collections is included in outgo and the collections from Federal sources are subsequently subtracted from outgo.[6] As a result, both interfund and intrafund offsetting collections from Federal sources are offset against outgo in Table 23–1 and are not shown separately.

The vast majority of the interfund transactions in the table are payments by the Federal funds to the trust funds. These payments include interest payments from the general fund to the trust funds for interest earned on trust fund balances invested in interest-bearing Treasury securities. The payments also include payments by Federal agencies to Federal employee benefits trust funds and Social Security trust funds on behalf of current employees and general fund transfers to employee retirement trust funds to amortize the unfunded liabilities of these funds. In addition, the payments include general fund transfers to the Supplementary Medical Insurance (SMI) trust fund for the cost of Medicare Parts B (outpatient and physician benefits) and D (prescription drug benefits) that is not covered by premiums or other income from the public. The Budget includes proposals to extend the solvency of the Medicare Hospital Insurance (HI) trust fund indefinitely, by increasing the net investment income tax (NIIT) rate and additional Medicare tax rate for high-income taxpayers, and directing the revenue from the NIIT to the trust fund. The Budget also directs an amount equivalent to the savings from proposed Medicare drug reforms into the HI trust fund.

In addition to investing their balances with the Treasury, some funds in the Federal funds group and most trust funds are authorized to borrow from the general fund of the Treasury.[7] Similar to the treatment of funds invested with the Treasury, borrowed funds are not recorded as receipts of the fund or included in the income of the fund. Rather, the borrowed funds finance outlays by the fund in excess of available receipts. Subsequently, any excess fund receipts are transferred from the fund to the general fund in repayment of the borrowing. The repayment is not recorded as an outlay of the fund or included in fund outgo. This treatment is consistent with the broad principle that borrowing and debt redemption are not budgetary transactions but rather a means of financing deficits or disposing of surpluses.[8]

---

[4] Securities held by trust funds (and by other Government accounts), debt held by the public, and gross Federal debt are discussed in the "Federal Borrowing and Debt" chapter of this volume.

[5] For example, the railroad retirement trust funds pay the equivalent of Social Security benefits to railroad retirees in addition to the regular railroad pension. These benefits are financed by a payment from the Federal Old-Age and Survivors Insurance trust fund to the railroad retirement trust funds. The payment and collection are not included in Table 23–1 so that the total trust fund income and outgo shown in the table reflect transactions with the public and with Federal funds.

[6] Collections from non-Federal sources are shown as income and spending that is financed by those collections is shown as outgo. For example, postage stamp fees are deposited as offsetting collections in the Postal Service Fund. As a result, the Fund's income reported in Table 23–1 includes postage stamp fees and the Fund's outgo is gross disbursements, including disbursements financed by those fees.

[7] For example, the Unemployment Trust Fund is authorized to borrow from the general fund for unemployment benefits; the Bonneville Power Administration Fund, a revolving fund in the Department of Energy, is authorized to borrow from the general fund; and the Black Lung Disability Trust Fund, a trust fund in the Department of Labor, is authorized to receive appropriations of repayable advances from the general fund, which constitute a form of borrowing.

[8] Borrowing and debt repayment are discussed in the "Federal Borrowing and Debt" and "Budget Concepts" chapters.

Table 23–2. COMPARISON OF TOTAL FEDERAL FUND AND TRUST FUND RECEIPTS TO UNIFIED BUDGET RECEIPTS, FISCAL YEAR 2023
(In billions of dollars)

Gross Federal fund and Trust fund cash income:	
Federal funds	3,965.3
Trust funds	3,010.8
Total, gross Federal fund and Trust fund cash income	6,976.1
Deduct: intrabudgetary offsetting collections (from funds within same fund group):	
Federal funds	–366.0
Trust funds	–62.1
Subtotal, intrabudgetary offsetting collections	–428.1
Deduct: intrafund receipts (from funds within same fund group):	
Federal funds	–49.3
Trust funds	–7.1
Subtotal, intrafund receipts	–56.3
Federal fund and Trust fund cash income net of intrabudgetary offsetting collections and intrafund receipts:	
Federal funds	3,550.0
Trust funds	2,941.6
Total, Federal fund and Trust fund cash income net of intrafund receipts	6,491.6
Deduct: offsetting collections from the public:	
Federal funds	–328.6
Trust funds	–25.1
Subtotal, offsetting collections from the public	–353.8
Deduct: other offsetting receipts:	
Federal fund receipts from Trust funds	–1.9
Trust fund receipts from Federal funds:	
Interest in receipt accounts	–169.2
General fund payments to Medicare Parts B and D	–443.9
Employing agencies' payments for pensions, Social Security, and Medicare	–115.0
General fund payments for unfunded liabilities of Federal employees' retirement funds	–171.1
Transfer of taxation of Social Security and RRB benefits to OASDI, HI, and RRB	–86.8
Other receipts from Federal funds	–5.6
Subtotal, Trust fund receipts from Federal funds	–991.5
Proprietary receipts:	
Federal funds	–452.2
Trust funds	–236.5
Subtotal, proprietary receipts	–688.7
Offsetting governmental receipts:	
Federal funds	–14.8
Trust funds	–*
Subtotal, offsetting governmental receipts	–14.8
Subtotal, other offsetting receipts	–1,696.9
Unified budget receipts:	
Federal funds	2,752.4
Trust funds	1,688.5
Total, unified budget receipts	4,440.9
Memoradum:	
Gross receipts:[1]	
Federal funds	3,270.7
Trust funds	2,923.6
Total, gross receipts	6,194.2

* $50 million or less.
[1] Gross income excluding offsetting collections.

Some income in both Federal funds and trust funds consists of offsetting receipts.[9] Offsetting receipts are not considered governmental receipts (such as taxes), but they are instead recorded on the outlay side of the budget.[10] Expenditures resulting from offsetting receipts are recorded as gross outlays and the collections of offsetting receipts are then subtracted from gross outlays to derive net outlays. Net outlays reflect the Government's net transactions with the public.

As shown in Table 23–1, 38 percent of all governmental receipts were deposited in trust funds in 2023 and the remaining 62 percent of governmental receipts were deposited in Federal funds, which, as noted above, include the general fund. As noted above, most outlays between the trust fund and Federal fund groups (interfund outlays) flow from Federal funds to trust funds, rather than from trust funds to Federal funds. As a result, while trust funds accounted for 25 percent of total 2023 outlays, they accounted for 29 percent of 2023 outlays net of interfund transactions.

Because the income for Federal funds and trust funds recorded in Table 23–1 includes offsetting receipts and offsetting collections from the public, offsetting receipts and offsetting collections from the public must be deducted from the two fund groups' combined gross income in order to reconcile to total governmental receipts in the unified budget. Similarly, because the outgo for Federal funds and trust funds in Table 23–1 consists of outlays gross of offsetting receipts and offsetting collections from the public, the amount of the offsetting receipts and offsetting collections from the public must be deducted from the sum of the Federal funds' and the trust funds' gross outgo in order to reconcile to total (net) unified budget outlays. Table 23–2 reconciles, for fiscal year 2023, the gross total of all trust fund and Federal fund receipts with the receipt total of the unified budget.

Income, Outgo, and Balances of Trust Funds

Table 23–3 shows, for the trust funds group as a whole, the funds' balance at the start of each year, income and outgo during the year, and the end-of-year balance. Income and outgo are divided between transactions with the public and transactions with Federal funds. Receipts from Federal funds are divided between interest and other interfund receipts.

The definitions of income and outgo in this table differ from those in Table 23–1 in one important way. Trust fund collections that are offset against outgo (offsetting collections from Federal sources) within expenditure accounts instead of being deposited in separate receipt accounts are classified as income in this table, but not in Table 23–1. This classification is consistent with the definitions of income and outgo for trust funds used elsewhere in the budget. It has the effect of increasing both income and outgo by the amount of the offsetting collections from

[9] Interest on borrowed funds is an example of an intragovernmental offsetting receipt and Medicare Part B's premiums are an example of offsetting receipts from the public.

[10] For further discussion of offsetting receipts, see the "Offsetting Collections and Offsetting Receipts" chapter.

Federal sources. The difference was approximately $62 billion in 2023. Table 23–3, therefore, provides a more complete summary of trust fund income and outgo.

In 2023, the trust funds group ran a surplus of $183 billion. The trust fund group is expected to run a $243 billion surplus in 2024 and a $273 billion surplus in 2025.

The size of the trust fund balances is largely the consequence of the way some trust funds are financed. Some of the larger trust funds (primarily Social Security and the Federal retirement funds) are fully or partially advance funded, with collections on behalf of individual participants received by the funds years earlier than when the associated benefits are paid. For example, under the Federal military and civilian retirement programs, Federal agencies and employees together are required to pay the retirement trust funds an amount equal to accruing retirement benefits. Since many years pass between the time when benefits are accrued and when they are paid, the trust funds accumulate substantial balances over time.[11]

[11] Until the 1980s, most trust funds operated on a pay-as-you-go basis as distinct from a pre-funded basis. Taxes and fees were set at levels sufficient to finance current program expenditures and administrative expenses, and to maintain balances generally equal to one year's worth of expenditures (to provide for unexpected events). As a result, trust fund balances tended to grow at about the same rate as the funds' annual expenditures. In the 1980s, pay-as-you-go financing was replaced by full or partial advance funding for some of the larger trust funds. The Social Security Amendments of 1983 (Public Law 98-21) raised payroll taxes above the levels necessary to finance then-current expenditures. Legislation enacted in the mid-1980s established the requirement for full accrual basis funding of Federal military and civilian retirement benefits.

Due to advance funding and economic growth (both real and nominal), trust fund balances increased from $205 billion in 1982 to $5.9 trillion in 2023. Based on the estimates in the 2025 Budget, which include the effect of the Budget's proposals, the balances are estimated to be $6.8 trillion at the end of 2029. Almost all of these balances are invested in Treasury securities and earn interest.

From the perspective of the trust fund, these balances are assets that represent the value, in today's dollars, of past taxes, fees, and other income from the public and from other Government accounts that the trust fund has received in excess of past spending. Trust fund assets held in Treasury securities are legal claims on the Treasury, similar to Treasury securities issued to the public. Like all other fund assets, these are available to the fund for future benefit payments and other expenditures. From the perspective of the Government as a whole, however, the trust fund balances do not represent net additions to the Government's balance sheet. The trust fund balances are assets of the agencies responsible for administering the trust fund programs and liabilities of the Department of the Treasury. These assets and liabilities cancel each other out in the Government-wide balance sheet. The effects of Treasury debt held by trust funds and other Government accounts are discussed further in the "Federal Borrowing and Debt" chapter of this volume.

Table 23–4, available online, shows estimates of income, outgo, surplus or deficit, and balances for 2023 through 2029 for the major trust funds. With the exception of transactions between trust funds, the data for the

Table 23–3. INCOME, OUTGO, AND BALANCES OF TRUST FUNDS GROUP

(In billions of dollars)

	2023 Actual	Estimate					
		2024	2025	2026	2027	2028	2029
Balance, start of year	5,727.6	5,912.4	6,157.6	6,430.7	6,655.1	6,732.3	6,719.7
Adjustments to balances	0.5	....	....	....	....	....	....
Total balance, start of year	5,728.1	5,912.4	6,157.6	6,430.7	6,655.1	6,732.3	6,719.7
Income:							
Governmental receipts	1,688.5	1,796.8	1,972.0	2,011.4	2,093.5	2,194.2	2,280.7
Offsetting governmental	*	*	*	*	*	*	*
Proprietary	258.4	260.5	278.2	294.0	316.6	337.4	360.2
From Federal funds:							
Interest	174.6	189.0	183.2	201.9	210.8	217.1	225.8
Other	882.2	966.3	1,032.1	1,090.2	1,036.5	1,100.0	1,187.0
Total income during the year	3,003.7	3,212.6	3,465.6	3,597.4	3,657.4	3,848.8	4,053.7
Outgo (–)	–2,820.2	–2,969.9	–3,193.0	–3,373.1	–3,580.2	–3,861.3	–3,941.6
Change in fund balance:							
Surplus or deficit(–):							
Excluding interest	8.9	53.7	89.4	22.5	–133.6	–229.6	–113.7
Interest	174.6	189.0	183.2	201.9	210.8	217.1	225.8
Subtotal, surplus or deficit (–)	183.5	242.8	272.6	224.3	77.2	–12.5	112.1
Borrowing, transfers, lapses, & other adjustments	0.9	2.4	0.6	....	....	....	....
Total change in fund balance	184.4	245.2	273.1	224.3	77.2	–12.5	112.1
Balance, end of year	5,912.4	6,157.6	6,430.7	6,655.1	6,732.3	6,719.7	6,831.8

* $50 million or less.

Note: In contrast to Table 23–1, income also includes income that is offset within expenditure accounts as offsetting collections from Federal sources, instead of being deposited in receipt accounts.

individual trust funds are conceptually the same as the data in Table 23–3 for the trust funds group. As explained previously, transactions between trust funds are shown as outgo of the fund that makes the payment and as income of the fund that collects it in the data for an individual trust fund, but the collections are offset against outgo in the data for the trust fund group as a whole.

As noted above, trust funds are funded by a combination of payments from the public and payments from Federal funds, including payments directly from the general fund and payments from agency appropriations. Similarly, the fund outgo amounts in Table 23–4 represent both outflows to the public—such as for the provision of benefit payments or the purchase of goods or services—and outflows to other Government accounts—such as for reimbursement for services provided by other agencies or payment of interest on borrowing from Treasury. The outgo amounts reflect the Budget's assumption that all obligations of the trust funds are met.

Because trust funds and Federal special and revolving funds conduct transactions both with the public and with other Government accounts, the surplus or deficit of an individual fund may differ from the fund's impact on the surplus or deficit of the Federal Government. Transactions with the public affect both the surplus or deficit of an individual fund and the Federal Government surplus or deficit. Transactions with other Government accounts affect the surplus or deficit of the particular fund. However, because that same transaction is offset in another Government account, there is no net impact on the total Federal Government surplus or deficit.

A brief description of the major trust funds is given below; additional information for these and other trust funds can be found in the Status of Funds tables in the Budget *Appendix*.

- Social Security Trust Funds: The Social Security trust funds consist of the Old Age and Survivors Insurance (OASI) trust fund and the Disability Insurance (DI) trust fund. The trust funds are funded by payroll taxes from employers and employees, interest earnings on trust fund balances, Federal agency payments as employers, and a portion of the income taxes paid on Social Security benefits.

- Medicare Trust Funds: Like the Social Security trust funds, the Medicare HI trust fund is funded by payroll taxes from employers and employees, Federal agency payments as employers, and a portion of the income taxes paid on Social Security benefits. The HI trust fund also receives transfers from the general fund of the Treasury for certain HI benefits and premiums from certain voluntary participants. The other Medicare trust fund, SMI, finances Part B (outpatient and physician benefits) and Part D (prescription drug benefits). SMI receives premium payments from covered individuals, transfers from States toward Part D benefits, excise taxes on manufacturers and importers of brand-name prescription drugs, and transfers from the general fund of the Treasury for the portion of Part B and Part D costs not covered by premiums or transfers from States. In addition, like other trust funds, these two trust funds receive interest earnings on their trust fund balances.

- Highway Trust Fund: The fund finances Federal highway and transit infrastructure projects, as well as highway and vehicle safety activities. The Highway Trust Fund is financed by Federal motor fuel taxes and associated fees, and, in recent years, by general fund transfers, as those taxes and fees have been inadequate to support current levels of spending.

- Unemployment Trust Fund: The Unemployment Trust Fund is funded by Federal and State taxes on employers, payments from Federal agencies, taxes on certain employees, and interest earnings on trust fund balances. Unemployment insurance is administered largely by the States, following Federal guidelines. The Unemployment Trust Fund is composed of individual accounts for each State and several Federal accounts, including accounts related to the separate unemployment insurance program for railroad employees.

- Civilian and military retirement trust funds: The Civil Service Retirement and Disability Fund is funded by employee and agency payments, general fund transfers for the unfunded portion of retirement costs, and interest earnings on trust fund balances. The Military Retirement Fund likewise is funded by payments from the Department of Defense, general fund transfers for unfunded retirement costs, and interest earnings on trust fund balances.

Table 23–5, available online, shows income, outgo, and balances of two Federal funds that are designated as special funds. These funds are similar to trust funds in that they are financed by dedicated receipts, the excess of income over outgo is invested in Treasury securities, the interest earnings add to fund balances, and the balances remain available to cover future expenditures. The table is illustrative of the Federal funds group, which includes many revolving funds and special funds

24. COMPARISON OF ACTUAL TO ESTIMATED TOTALS

The Budget is required by statute to compare budget year estimates of receipts and outlays with the subsequent actual receipts and outlays for that year. This chapter meets that requirement by comparing the actual receipts, outlays, and deficit for 2023 with the current services estimates shown in the 2023 Budget, published in March 2022.[1] It also presents a more detailed comparison for mandatory and related programs, and reconciles the actual receipts, outlays, and deficit totals shown here with the figures for 2023 previously published by the Department of the Treasury (Treasury).

Receipts

Actual receipts for 2023 were $4,441 billion, $68 billion less than the $4,509 billion current services estimate in the 2023 Budget. As shown in Table 24-1, this increase was the net effect of legislative changes, economic conditions that differed from what had been expected, and technical factors that resulted in different tax liabilities and collection patterns than had been assumed.

Policy differences. Legislated tax changes enacted after the March 2022 estimates were finalized increased 2023 receipts by a net $12 billion relative to the 2023 Budget current services estimate.

The Ending Importation of Russian Oil Act (Public Law 117-109) prohibited the importation of energy products from Russia that are classified under chapter 27 of the Harmonized Tariff Schedule. This Act was signed into law on April 8, 2022, and decreased 2023 receipts by $2 million.

The Suspending Normal Trade Relations with Russia and Belarus Act (Public Law 117-110) authorized the President to proclaim increases in the rates of duty applicable to products of Russia or Belarus; this authority terminated on January 1, 2024. This Act was signed into law on April 8, 2022, and increased 2023 receipts by an estimated $150 million.

Public Law 117-167, commonly referred to as the CHIPS and Science Act of 2022, established a 25 percent investment tax credit for investments in semiconductor manufacturing. The Act was signed into law on August 9, 2022, and reduced 2023 receipts by an estimated $2 billion.

Public Law 117-169, commonly referred to as the Inflation Reduction Act of 2022, imposed a 15 percent minimum alternative tax beginning tax years after 2022 on corporations with a three-year average income of more than $1 billion, determined on the basis of the corporation's adjusted financial statement income (i.e., book income). It imposed a one percent excise tax of the fair market value of any repurchased stock during the taxable year by a publicly traded U.S. corporation. It also appropriated funding for Internal Revenue Service enforcement activities, operations support, business systems modernization, and taxpayer services, available through 2031, which is expected to reduce the tax gap by improving taxpayer compliance. The law imposed an excise tax on the sale by the manufacturer, producer, or importer of any selected drug who fails to enter into a drug pricing agreement. Finally, it included various green energy tax

[1] The current services concept is discussed in the "Current Services Estimates" chapter of this volume. For mandatory programs and receipts, the March 2022 current services estimate was based on laws then in place, adjusted for certain expiring provisions. For discretionary programs, the current services estimate was based on the levels provided by the continuing resolution for 2022 (Public Law 117-43, division A, as amended by Public Law 117-70, division A; Public Law 117-86, division A; and Public Law 117-95), adjusted for inflation and for transportation obligation limitations at the levels of contract authority enacted in Public Law 117-58. The current services estimate for discretionary programs also included several additional laws which provided appropriations to certain accounts in 2022 (Public Law 117-43, division B; Public Law 117-43, division C; Public Law 117-58, division J, except for provisions designated as emergency funding; Public Law 117-70, division B), adjusted for inflation. The current services estimates also reflected the effects of mandatory sequestration as required by the Balanced Budget and Deficit Control Act (BBEDCA) section 251A. For a detailed explanation of the 2023 estimate, see the "Current Services Estimates" chapter of the 2023 *Analytical Perspectives* volume of the President's Budget.

Table 24–1. COMPARISON OF ACTUAL 2023 RECEIPTS WITH THE INITIAL CURRENT SERVICES ESTIMATES

(In billions of dollars)

	Estimate (March 2022)	Changes			Total Changes	Actual
		Legislative	Economic	Technical		
Individual income taxes	2,305	–8	23	–144	–129	2,176
Corporation income taxes	412	19	15	–26	8	420
Social insurance and retirement receipts	1,511	....	–24	127	104	1,614
Excise taxes	90	*	–4	–11	–15	76
Estate and gift taxes	25	....	3	6	9	34
Customs duties	54	*	3	24	26	80
Miscellaneous receipts	112	....	–94	23	–71	41
Total receipts	4,509	12	–78	–2	–68	4,441

* $500 million or less

credits and incentives for businesses and individuals, including: a production tax credit for electricity generated from renewable energy sources; a new tax credit for qualifying zero-emission nuclear power produced by facilities placed in service prior to enactment; the extension of the residential clean energy efficient credit for qualified energy efficiency improvements; an advanced manufacturing production credit for projects beginning in 2023; new clean electricity production and investment credits; and tax credits related to electric vehicles, including credits for the purchase of clean and plug-in vehicles. The Act was signed into law on August 16, 2022, and increased 2023 receipts by an estimated $14 billion.

The Consolidated Appropriations Act, 2023 (Public Law 117-328) included the SECURE 2.0 Act of 2022, which made numerous changes to retirement law. It required that employee-sponsored retirement plans automatically enroll all eligible employees with a contribution rate in the first year of at least three percent up to a maximum of 10 percent, with certain exceptions for new and small businesses. It improved access to retirement accounts for part-time workers who have completed 500 hours of service for two consecutive years. It increased the three-year small business startup credit from 50 to 100 percent for employers with up to 50 employees. It replaced the nonrefundable credit for qualified individuals making contributions to individual retirement accounts with a "Saver's Match" Federal contribution of up to $2,000 per year for individuals with incomes up to $71,000. It increased the age to begin mandatory distributions from retirement plans, and increased the catch-up limits beginning in 2025 for individuals ages 60 to 63. It provided for a pension-linked emergency savings account of up to $2,500, in addition to permitting employees to withdraw up to $1,000 per year for personal or family emergencies without penalty, as well as withdraw funds penalty free for those that are terminally ill, are victims of domestic abuse, or are affected by a Stafford Act disaster. The Act also treated student loan payments as elective deferrals for purposes of retirement plan matching. Finally, it limited the deduction for charitable conservation easements, subject to a three-year holding period test. The Act was signed into law on December 29, 2022, and decreased 2023 receipts by $399 million.

Economic differences. Differences between the economic assumptions upon which the current services estimates were based and actual economic performance decreased 2023 receipts by a net $78 billion relative to the March 2022 current services estimate. Higher interest rates than initially projected reduced deposits of earnings by the Federal Reserve System by $94 billion below the March 2022 estimate. Social insurance and retirement receipts decreased by $24 billion relative to the March 2022 estimate due to revisions in wage and salary projections. The economic recovery after the COVID-19 crisis meant that wage, salary, and sole proprietor income was higher in 2023 than initially projected, which along with other economic changes drove an increase in individual income tax of $23 billion above the March 2022 estimate. Different economic factors than those assumed in March 2022 had a smaller effect on other sources of receipts, increasing collections by a net $17 billion.

Technical factors. Technical factors decreased receipts by a net $2 billion relative to the March 2022 current services estimate. These factors had the greatest effect on individual income tax receipts, decreasing collections by $144 billion, largely offset by an increase in social insurance and retirement receipts of $127 billion. The models used to prepare the March 2022 estimates of individual income taxes were based on historical economic data and then-current tax and collections data that were all subsequently revised and account for the net decrease in this source of receipts attributable to technical factors. The increase in social insurance and retirement receipts was largely due to wage certification data that reallocated receipts to social insurance receipts from individual income tax receipts to adjust the initial estimated transfers to the social insurance trust funds.

Outlays

Outlays for 2023 were $6,135 billion, $450 billion more than the $5,685 billion current services estimate in the 2023 Budget. Table 24–2 distributes the $450 billion net increase in outlays among discretionary and mandatory

Table 24–2. COMPARISON OF ACTUAL 2023 OUTLAYS WITH THE INITIAL CURRENT SERVICES ESTIMATES
(In billions of dollars)

	Estimate (March 2022)	Changes			Total Changes	Actual
		Policy	Economic	Technical		
Discretionary:						
Defense	766	78	....	–38	40	806
Nondefense	873	71	....	–33	38	912
Subtotal, discretionary	1,639	149	....	–70	79	1,718
Mandatory:						
Social Security	1,313	....	40	–5	35	1,348
Other programs	2,337	–34	98	10	73	2,410
Subtotal, mandatory	3,650	–34	138	4	108	3,758
Net interest	396	2	244	17	263	658
Total outlays	5,685	116	382	–48	450	6,135

Table 24–3. COMPARISON OF THE ACTUAL 2023 DEFICIT WITH THE INITIAL CURRENT SERVICES ESTIMATE

(In billions of dollars)

	Estimate (March 2022)	Changes			Total Changes	Actual
		Policy	Economic	Technical		
Receipts	4,509	12	-78	-2	-68	4,441
Outlays	5,685	116	382	-48	450	6,135
Deficit	1,176	105	460	-46	518	1,694

Note: Deficit changes are outlays minus receipts. For these changes, a positive number indicates an increase in the deficit.

programs and net interest.[2] The table also shows rough estimates according to three reasons for the changes: policy; economic conditions; and technical estimating differences, a residual.

Policy differences. Policy changes are the result of legislative actions that change spending levels, primarily through higher or lower appropriations or changes in authorizing legislation, which may themselves be in response to changed economic conditions. For 2023, policy changes increased outlays by $116 billion relative to the initial current services estimates. Policy changes increased discretionary outlays by $149 billion, largely due to the Consolidated Appropriations Act, 2023 and several emergency supplemental appropriations. Policy changes decreased mandatory outlays by a net $34 billion. Debt service costs associated with all policy changes increased outlays by $2 billion.

Economic and technical factors. Economic and technical estimating factors resulted in a net increase in outlays of $333 billion. Technical changes result from changes in such factors as the number of beneficiaries for entitlement programs, crop conditions, or other factors not associated with policy changes or economic conditions. Defense and non-defense discretionary spending decreased relative to the current services estimate largely due to slower-than-estimated spending of both new and prior-year authority. In addition to the increases in discretionary outlays due to legislation, as discussed above, technical factors led to $70 billion in decreased spending. Outlays for mandatory programs increased $143 billion due to economic and technical factors, mostly driven by a net increase in outlays of $138 billion as a result of differences between actual economic conditions versus those forecast in March 2022.

Outlays for Social Security were $35 billion higher than anticipated in the 2023 Budget mainly due to a higher than projected cost-of-living adjustment, which was partially offset by a lower than estimated number of beneficiaries. Overall, mandatory human resources programs including health programs and higher education programs were $3 billion higher than anticipated. The remaining changes were spread throughout government programs and raised outlays by $111 billion, largely driven by a $96 billion increase for deposit insurance resulting from actions by the Federal Deposit Insurance Corporation to respond to bank failures in 2023. Outlays for net interest were approximately $261 billion higher due to economic and technical factors, primarily due to higher interest rates than originally assumed.

Deficit

The preceding two sections discussed the differences between the initial current services estimates and the actual Federal Government receipts and outlays for 2023. This section combines these effects to show the net deficit impact of these differences.

As shown in Table 24–3, the 2023 current services deficit was initially estimated to be $1,176 billion. The actual deficit was $1,694 billion, which was a $518 billion increase from the initial estimate. Receipts were $68 billion lower and outlays were $450 billion higher than the initial estimate. The table shows the distribution of the changes according to the categories in the preceding two sections. The net effect of policy changes for receipts and outlays increased the deficit by $105 billion. Economic conditions that differed from the initial assumptions in March 2022 increased the deficit by $460 billion. Technical factors decreased the deficit by an estimated $46 billion.

Comparison of the Actual and Estimated Outlays for Mandatory and Related Programs for 2023

This section compares the original 2023 outlay estimates for mandatory and related programs in the current services estimates of the 2023 Budget with the actual outlays. Major examples of these programs include Social Security and Medicare benefits, Medicaid and unemployment compensation payments, and deposit insurance for banks and thrift institutions. This category also includes net interest outlays and undistributed offsetting receipts.

A number of factors may cause differences between the amounts estimated in the Budget and the actual mandatory outlays. For example, legislation may change benefit rates or coverage, the actual number of beneficiaries may differ from the number estimated, or economic conditions (such as inflation or interest rates) may differ from what was assumed in making the original estimates.

Table 24–4 shows the differences between the actual outlays for these programs in 2023 and the current services estimates included in the 2023 Budget. Actual outlays for mandatory spending and net interest in 2023 were $4,417 billion, which was $371 billion more than the current services estimate of $4,046 billion in May 2022.

As Table 24–4 shows, actual outlays for mandatory human resources programs were $3,964 billion, $3 billion

[2] Discretionary programs are controlled by annual appropriations, while mandatory programs are generally controlled by authorizing legislation. Mandatory programs are primarily formula benefit or entitlement programs with permanent spending authority that depends on eligibility criteria, benefit levels, and other factors.

Table 24–4. COMPARISON OF ACTUAL AND ESTIMATED OUTLAYS FOR MANDATORY AND RELATED PROGRAMS UNDER CURRENT LAW

(In billions of dollars)

	2023		
	Estimate	Actual	Change
Mandatory outlays:			
Human resources programs:			
Education, training, employment, and social services:			
Higher Education	23	–181	–205
Other	85	55	–30
Total, education, training, employment, and social services	109	–126	–235
Health:			
Medicaid	536	616	80
Other	135	173	37
Total, health	671	789	117
Medicare	847	839	–8
Income security:			
Retirement and disability	202	229	28
Unemployment compensation	48	30	–18
Food and nutrition assistance	140	165	25
Other	197	250	53
Total, income security	587	674	87
Social security	1,313	1,348	35
Veterans benefits and services:			
Income security for veterans	144	151	7
Other	20	19	–1
Total, veterans benefits and services	164	170	6
Total, mandatory human resources programs	3,691	3,694	3
Other functions:			
Agriculture	20	26	6
International	–1	–14	–13
Mortgage credit	–7	–16	–10
Deposit insurance	–5	91	96
Other advancement of commerce	16	14	–2
Other functions	62	96	35
Total, other functions	85	196	111
Undistributed offsetting receipts:			
Employer share, employee retirement	–120	–125	–5
Rents and royalties on the outer continental shelf	–6	–7	–1
Other undistributed offsetting receipts	–*	....	*
Total, undistributed offsetting receipts	–126	–132	–6
Total, mandatory	3,650	3,758	108
Net interest:			
Interest on Treasury debt securities (gross)	577	879	302
Interest received by trust funds	–132	–169	–38
Other interest	–50	–52	–2
Total, net interest	396	658	263
Total, outlays for mandatory and net interest	4,046	4,417	371

* $500 million or less

higher than originally estimated. This increase was the net effect of legislative action, differences between actual and assumed economic conditions, differences between the anticipated and actual number of beneficiaries, and other technical differences.

Outlays in higher education programs were $205 billion lower than estimates primarily due to the modification resulting from the Supreme Court overturning student debt relief, which was partially offset by modifications resulting from administrative actions on student loans, including the regulation creating the SAVE income-driven repayment plan and the final extension of the student loan payment pause. Health program outlays were $117 billion higher than estimates, driven mainly by a $80 billion increase in Medicaid outlays. The increase in Medicaid outlays were a result of ongoing costs associated with the legislative response to the COVID-19 pandemic, as well as differences in assumed economic conditions and number of beneficiaries, and other technical shifts. In addition, income security, veterans benefits and services programs, and other functions accounted for an increase of outlays of $205 billion, including a $96 billion increase for deposit insurance largely driven by actions by the Federal Deposit Insurance Corporation to respond to bank failures in 2023. Outlays for net interest were $658 billion, or $263 billion higher than the original estimate. As shown on Table 24–4, interest payments on Treasury debt securities increased by $302 billion. Interest earnings of trust funds increased by $38 billion, decreasing net outlays, while net outlays for other interest further decreased net outlays by $2 billion.

Reconciliation of Differences with Amounts Published by the Treasury for 2022

Table 24-5 provides a reconciliation of the receipts, outlays, and deficit totals for 2023 published by the Treasury in the September 2023 Monthly Treasury Statement (MTS) and those published in the 2025 Budget. The Treasury made adjustments to the estimates for the Combined Statement of Receipts, Outlays, and Balances that increased outlays by $93 million. Additional adjustments for the 2025 Budget increased receipts by $1,662 million and increased outlays by $147 million. Some of these adjustments were for financial transactions that are not reported to the Treasury but are included in the Budget, including those for the Affordable Housing Program, the Electric Reliability Organization, the Federal Financial Institutions Examination Council Appraisal Subcommittee, Federal Retirement Thrift Investment Board Program Expenses, the National Oilheat Research Alliance, the Public Company Accounting Oversight Board, the Puerto Rico Oversight Board, the Securities Investor Protection Corporation, fees and payments related to the Standard Setting Body, and the United Mine Workers of America benefit funds. There was also an adjustment for the National Railroad Retirement Investment Trust (NRRIT), which relates to a conceptual difference in reporting. NRRIT reports to the Treasury with a one-month lag so that the fiscal year total provided in the Treasury Combined Statement covers September 2022 through August 2023. The Budget has been adjusted to reflect NRRIT transactions that occurred during the actual fiscal year, which begins October 1.

Table 24–5. RECONCILIATION OF FINAL AMOUNTS FOR 2023
(In millions of dollars)

	Receipts	Outlays	Deficit
Totals published by Treasury (September MTS)	4,439,284	6,134,432	1,695,148
Miscellaneous Treasury adjustments	1	93	92
Totals published by Treasury in Combined Statement	4,439,285	6,134,525	1,695,240
Affordable Housing Program	698	698	....
Electric Reliability Organization	101	101	....
Federal Financial Institutions Examination Council Appraisal Subcommittee	17	17	....
Federal Retirement Thrift Investment Board Program Expenses	....	–53	–53
National Oilheat Research Alliance	8	6	–2
National Railroad Retirement Investment Trust	....	–800	–800
Public Company Accounting Oversight Board	332	324	–8
Puerto Rico Oversight Board	60	60	....
Securities Investor Protection Corporation	393	61	–332
Standard Setting Body	44	44	....
United Mine Workers of America benefit funds	11	–310	–321
Other	–2	–1	1
Total adjustments, net	1,662	147	–1,515
Totals in the Budget	4,440,947	6,134,672	1,693,725
MEMORANDUM:			
Total change since year-end statement	1,663	240	–1,423